FONTANA DICTIONARY OF AFRICA SINCE 1960

JOHN GRACE was born in London, and travelled, lived and worked in a number of African countries. After being awarded an MA from Victoria University, B.C., Canada, he returned to Sierra Leone to study the history of slavery. His thesis earned him a doctorate from Aberdeen University and was published in 1975 under the title of *Domestic Slavery in West Africa*. While teaching at the Jos Campus of Ibadan University he did research on local tin-mining. He continued to write articles and to contribute to reference books, and was an extremely popular Senior Lecturer at The Henley College, Henley-on-Thames, until he died, on 14 December 1990.

JOHN LAFFIN, an international authority on the Middle East, the Arab world and Islam, is the author of 110 books. Many of them concern war and international affairs. Much travelled in North Africa over a period of nearly fifty years, Dr Laffin has interviewed several national leaders, including King Farouk of Egypt, King Idris of Libya, Presidents Nasser and Sadat of Egypt, Bourguiba of Tunisia and Colonel Gaddafi of Libya. Dr Laffin, who is Australian-born, lives in Wales with his wife, Hazelle, his constant travelling companion.

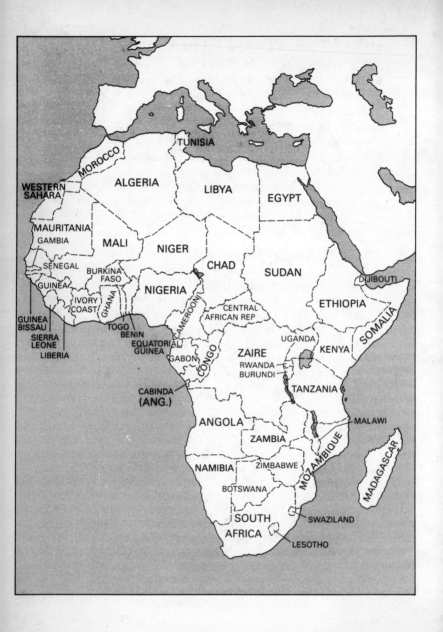

FONTANA

DICTIONARY OF

AFRICA

SINCE 1960

JOHN GRACE & JOHN LAFFIN

FontanaPress
An Imprint of HarperCollinsPublishers

A FONTANA PRESS ORIGINAL

First published in 1991 by Fontana Press,
an imprint of HarperCollins Publishers,
77–85 Fulham Palace Road,
Hammersmith, London W6 8JB

9 8 7 6 5 4 3 2 1

Printed and bound in Great Britain by
HarperCollins Manufacturing, Glasgow

Authors' Introduction

The fifty-four countries of Africa hold immense interest for millions of readers beyond the great continent's borders. In selecting entries for inclusion in a dictionary of manageable size, we have chosen those which add to the knowledge of readers outside Africa. Of course, the dictionary should be useful to African readers as well, but they should not expect to find in it the name of every person considered important in every country. A truly comprehensive work would require many fat volumes. The purpose of this book is to provide the political, historical, economic, literary and, to some extent, general background to events since 1960. To put such events in context it has often been necessary to provide a thread of understanding which reaches back to earlier years.

The period since 1960 has been universally dramatic in Africa. Turbulence and upheaval have engulfed the continent. Few states have avoided wars and insurrections, and assassinations have been commonplace. Taken as a whole, Africa since 1960 has produced leaders who range from the brutally grotesque, such as Emperor Bokassa of the Central African Empire and President Amin of Uganda, to impressive statesmen like President Nasser of Egypt, President Nyerere of Tanzania and (despite the unhappiness of his last years) President Nkrumah of Ghana.

Africa is a continent of extremes; its nations are struggling to overcome the problems they have inherited as well as those they have made for themselves. The colonial legacy has made it difficult for African states to find political stability. Their state borders often bear little relation to ethnic composition, separating people of the same ethnic origins or combining those of different races and religions. New states have not found it easy to establish forms of economic, social and political organization to replace those disrupted by imperial powers. Equally, many states have intervened, uninvited, in the affairs of their neighbours. For example, South Africa's attacks on its neighbours in Southern Africa have disrupted progress in a number of countries, especially Angola and Mozambique.

Particularly striking at the time of independence was the speed with which most governments abandoned multi-party democracy in favour of the one-party state; some of them became nothing less than brutal tyrannies. More recently, following the changes in Eastern Europe and increasing domestic pressure, a number of states have realized the need to allow more freedom of choice. By 1990 Algeria, Angola, Benin, The Congo, Gabon, İvory Coast, Mozambique, Somalia, Zaire and Zambia were among those either beginning to dismantle the one-party system or seriously considering the prospect of dismantling it. Nonetheless, other governments, like those of Cameroon, Equatorial Guinea and Kenya, have firmly resisted demands for the establishment of multi-party democracies.

Africa's population is increasing rapidly, while its old fashioned subsistence farmers are in most cases unable to meet the rising demand for food. The young men have left the country for the excitements of urban life. Most African states have been unable to fulfil the aspirations of their town dwellers – let alone those in remote rural areas. The continent is woefully short of technical, managerial and administrative skills, educational provision and efficient transport and communications. With the exception of states blessed with oil, gas and rich mineral deposits, African states have had to rely on cash crops to support themselves in the international economy. While the cost of Western manufactures and services has remained high, the prices paid for commodities like coffee, cocoa, cotton and sugar have been unstable. In many cases African states have been devastated by sudden dramatic falls in the value of their most important cash crops – or by natural disasters like droughts and floods. Some of the problems have been made in Africa itself, but the rest of the world does not always make it easy for Africa to solve its own problems.

*

In general, John Grace has been responsible for the entries relevant to black Africa, John Laffin for those concerning Arab Africa and other north African states. Both authors acknowledge with gratitude the practical help and moral support of their wives, Megan Grace and Hazelle Laffin.

Suggested Further Reading

It is not easy to keep up with events in contemporary Africa, where so much is changing so rapidly. Bias and distortion from within and without Africa make it difficult to get an accurate picture of events.

Generally quality newspapers and periodicals are the best sources of up to date information, even though they can contradict each other and sometimes contradict themselves from one day to the next.

Very few books deal with the whole of Africa; Africa south of the Sahara is usually considered separately from North Africa. Useful sources which have been updated (some more regularly than others) include the following:

Africa Handbook — Penguin, London

African Historical Dictionaries — a series on individual African countries, Scarecrow Press, Folkestone

African Political Facts Since 1945 — Macmillan, London

Africa South of the Sahara — Europa Publications, London

A Year Book of the Commonwealth — Foreign and Commonwealth Office, London

Barclays Bank Economic Intelligence Unit 'Country Reports'

Cambridge Encyclopaedia of the Middle East and North Africa

Encyclopaedia Britannica and yearbooks

Keesing's Contemporary Archives

New African Yearbook — IC Publications, London

The Annual Register — Longman, Harlow

The International Year Book and Statesmen's Who's Who — IPC Business Press, East Grinstead

The Middle East and North Africa — Europa Publications, London

The Statesman's Year Book — Macmillan, London

Whitaker's *Almanack*

World Statistics in Brief: UN Statistical Pocketbook — UN Publications

There have been a number of useful books published during the 1980s, including the following:

D. Adey *et al*, *Companion to South African English Literature* (Ad. Donker, Johannesburg 1986)

R.B. Betts, *Christians in the Arab East* (SPCK, London 1980)

P. Calvocoressi, *Independent Africa and the World* (Longman, New York, 1985)

R. Dumont, *False Start in Africa* (Earthscan Press, London and Washington 1988) – first published in French in 1962

S. Gastrow, *Who's Who in South African Politics*, Number Two (Ravan Press, Johannesburg 1987)

R. Graham, *The Da Capo Guide to Contemporary African Music (Da Capo Press, New York 1988)*

I. LL. Griffiths, *An Atlas of African Affairs* (Methuen, London 1984)

A.T. Grove, *The Changing Geography of Africa* (Oxford University Press 1989)

B. Harden, *Africa: Dispatches from a Fragile Continent* (W.W. Norton, New York and HarperCollins, London 1991)

A. Horne, *A Savage War of Peace: Algeria 1954–62* (Macmillan, London 1980)

R. Lawless and A. Findlay (eds.), *North Africa: Contemporary Politics and Economic Development* (London 1984)

G. Moore and U. Beier (eds.), *The Penguin Book of Modern African Poetry* (Penguin, Middlesex 1984)

G. Morrison, *The Southern Sudan and Eritrea* (Minority Rights Group, London 1983)

R. Nyrop, Morocco, *A Country Study* (The American University, Morocco 1981)

R. Omond, *The Apartheid Handbook* (Penguin, Middlesex 1985)

R. Owen, *The Middle East in the World Economy* (London 1981)

D.M. Smith, *Apartheid in South Africa* (Cambridge University Press 1987)

A. Sparks, *The Mind of South Africa* (Heinemann 1990)

L. Timberlake, *Africa in Crisis* (Earthscan Press, London and Washington 1985)

P.J. Vatikiotis, *The History of Egypt* (Faber, London 1985)

J. Waterbury, *The Egypt of Nasser and Sadat* (Princeton University Press, 1983)

P. Williams & B. Hackland, *The Dictionary of Contemporary Politics of Southern Africa* (Macmillan, London 1989)

J. Wright, *Libya: A Modern History* (London 1982)

H. Zell, C. Bundy and V. Coulon, *A New Reader's Guide to African Literature* (Revised edition 1983 – Heinemann, London)

Chronology of Africa since 1960

All names featured in this chronology possess full entries in the dictionary itself.

01 Jan.	1960	Cameroon became independent
21 Mar.	1960	Sharpeville massacre
27 Apr.	1960	Togo became independent
20 Jun.	1960	Mali became independent
26 Jun.	1960	Madagascar became independent
30 Jun.	1960	Zaire became independent
01 Jul.	1960	Somalia became independent
05 Aug.	1960	Upper Volta became independent
11 Aug.	1960	Chad became independent
11 Aug.	1960	Ivory Coast became independent
15 Aug.	1960	The Congo became independent
17 Aug.	1960	Gabon became independent
20 Aug.	1960	Senegal became independent
01 Oct.	1960	Nigeria became independent
28 Nov.	1960	Mauritania became independent
04 Feb.	1961	Rising against Portugal in Luanda
15 Mar.	1961	Rising against Portuguese in northern Angola
27 Apr.	1961	Sierra Leone became independent
31 May	1961	South Africa left Commonwealth
31 May	1961	South Africa became a republic
09 Dec.	1961	Tanganyika became independent
25 Jun.	1962	Formation of Frelimo
01 Jul.	1962	Algeria became independent
01 Jul.	1962	Burundi became independent

01 Jul.	1962	Rwanda became independent
09 Oct.	1962	Uganda became independent
09 Dec.	1962	Tanganyika became a republic
13 Jan.	1963	President Olympio of Togo assassinated
18 Mar.	1963	Guinea–Bissau liberation war launched
25 May	1963	Organization of African Unity charter signed
15 Aug.	1963	President Youlou of The Congo overthrown
01 Oct.	1963	Nigeria became a republic
09 Oct.	1963	Uganda became a republic
23 Oct.	1963	Col Soglo assumed power in Dahomey
09 Dec.	1963	Zanzibar became independent
12 Dec.	1963	Kenya became independent
17 Dec.	1963	Soglo overthrown in Dahomey
31 Dec.	1963	Dissolution of the Central African Federation
27 Apr.	1964	Tanganyika and Zanzibar merged as Tanzania
06 Jul.	1964	Malawi became independent
24 Oct.	1964	Zambia became independent
18 Feb.	1965	The Gambia became independent
08 Jun.	1965	State of emergency declared in Morocco
16 Jun.	1965	Beginning of Chad civil war
19 Jun.	1965	Boumedienne overthrew Ben Bella in Algeria
11 Nov.	1965	UDI in Southern Rhodesia
21 Nov.	1965	Mobutu seized power in Zaire
01 Jan.	1966	Bokassa ousted Dacko in Central African Republic
15 Jan.	1966	Balewa overthrown in Nigeria's first military coup
24 Feb.	1966	Nkrumah overthrown in Ghana's first military coup
28 Apr.	1966	Zimbabwean independence war launched
24 May	1966	Nigerian federation replaced by unitary state
29 Jul.	1966	Aguiyi-Ironsi overthrown in Nigerian coup

30 Sep. 1966	Botswana became independent
04 Oct. 1966	Lesotho became independent
13 Jan. 1967	Eyadema ousted Grunitzsky in Togo
05 Feb. 1967	Arusha Declaration
30 May 1967	Biafran secession from Nigeria and civil war
08 Sep. 1967	Uganda's new constitution abolished old kingdoms
06 Sep. 1968	Swaziland became independent
12 Oct. 1968	Equatorial Guinea became independent
19 Nov. 1968	Keita overthrown by Moussa Traore in Mali
01 Sep. 1969	Gaddafi overthrew King Idris of Libya
01 Oct. 1969	Ghana returned to civilian rule
01 Nov. 1969	Barre became ruler of Somalia
13 Dec. 1969	British withdrawal from Libya
12 Jan. 1970	End of Nigerian civil war
23 Jul. 1970	Nimeiri became ruler of Sudan
28 Sep. 1970	Death of President Nasser of Egypt
25 Jan. 1971	In Uganda Amin seized power from Obote
13 Jan. 1972	Busia overthrown in Ghanaian coup
05 Jul. 1973	Kayibanda overthrown in Rwandan coup
10 Sep. 1974	Guinea–Bissau became independent
12 Sep. 1974	Emperor Haile Selassie of Ethiopia deposed
13 Apr. 1975	Felix Malloum seized power in Chad
28 May 1975	ECOWAS treaty signed
11 Jun. 1975	Ratsiraka elected President of Madagascar
25 Jun. 1975	Mozambique became independent
05 Jul. 1975	Cape Verde Islands became independent
06 Jul. 1975	Comoro Islands declared independence
29 Aug. 1975	Gowon overthrown in Nigerian coup
01 Oct. 1975	Murtala Muhammed promised Nigerian civilian rule
11 Nov. 1975	Angola became independent

04 Feb. 1976	Nigeria divided into nineteen states
13 Feb. 1976	Murtala Muhammed assassinated in Nigeria
14 Feb. 1976	Lt-Gen Obasanjo became Nigerian head of state
29 Jun. 1976	The Seychelles became independent
05 Feb. 1977	Chama Cha Mapinduzi founded in Tanzania
17 Mar. 1977	Gaddafi declared Libya the Great Libyan Jamahiriyya
05 Jun. 1977	Coup in the Seychelles; Mancham overthrown
16 Jun. 1977	Djibouti became independent
12 Sep. 1977	Steve Biko died in custody in South Africa
22 Aug. 1978	Death of Jomo Kenyatta
17 Sep. 1978	Sadat signed Camp David Accords
29 Sep. 1978	UNSC Resolution 435 for Namibian independence
07 Feb. 1979	Chadli elected President of Algeria
18 May 1979	Ould Heydalla became President of Mauritania
23 Mar. 1979	Start of Moshi Conference
13 Apr. 1979	Amin driven out of Uganda
04 Jun. 1979	Flight-Lt Rawlings seized power in Ghana
20 Jun. 1979	Lule ousted in Uganda
24 Sep. 1979	Ghana returned to civilian rule
01 Oct. 1979	Nigeria returned to civilian rule
12 Apr. 1980	Master Sergeant Doe seized power in Liberia
18 Apr. 1980	Zimbabwe became independent
10 May 1980	Binaisa ousted in Uganda
14 Nov. 1980	Vieira seized power in Guinea-Bissau
15 Dec. 1980	Obote sworn in as President of Uganda
06 Oct. 1981	President Sadat of Egypt assassinated
31 Dec. 1981	Flight-Lt Rawlings seized power in Ghana
18 May 1982	Ojukwu of 'Biafra' pardoned in Nigeria
06 Nov. 1982	Biya became President of Cameroon
04 Aug. 1983	Sankara seized power in Burkina Faso

20 Aug. 1983	United Democratic Front launched in South Africa
02 Nov. 1983	South African whites approved new constitution
31 Dec. 1983	Buhari seized power in Nigeria
06 Apr. 1985	Nimeiri overthrown in Sudan
27 Jul. 1985	Obote overthrown in Uganda
27 Aug. 1985	In Nigeria Babangida ousted Buhari
20 Jan. 1986	Lekhanya seized power in Lesotho
04 Aug. 1986	Failure of Commonwealth summit on South Africa
19 Oct. 1986	President Machel of Mozambique died in plane crash
15 Oct. 1987	Compaore seized power in Burkina Faso
07 Nov. 1987	Bourguiba deposed by Ben Ali in Tunisia
22 Dec. 1988	Angolan/South African peace accord ratified
01 Apr. 1989	Namibia began transition to independence
30 Jun. 1989	Al-Bashir seized power in Sudan
01 Nov. 1989	Elections for Namibian Constituent Assembly
26 Nov. 1989	President Abdallah of Comoros assassinated
11 Feb. 1990	Mandela freed in South Africa
21 Mar. 1990	Namibia became independent
03 Sep. 1990	Civil war broke out in Rwanda
11 Sep. 1990	President Doe of Liberia murdered
06 Jan. 1991	Deby seized power in Chad
29 Jan. 1991	Barré deposed by United Somali Congress
20 Feb. 1991	Monteiro elected President of Cape Verde

Cross References

Within the dictionary itself a cross-reference is set in small capitals and indicated by an asterisk.

ANC – *see* African National Congress

ASU – *see* Arab Socialist Union

Baganda – *see* Buganda

Bantustans – *see* Homelands

British Somaliland – *see* Somalia

Broederbond – *see* Afrikaner Broederbond

Brotherhood – *see* Muslim Brotherhood

Bureau of State Security – *see* BOSS

Bushmen – *see* San

Cassinga Massacre – *see* Kassinga Massacre

CEAO – *see* Communauté Economique de l'Afrique de l'Ouest

CILSS – *see* Comité Permanent Inter-State de Lutte Contre la Secheresse dans la Sahel

CCM – *see* Chama Cha Mapinduzi

Conferência das Organizações Nacionalistas das Colonias Portuguesas – *see* CONCP

Côte d'Ivoire – *see* Ivory Coast

CPP – *see* Convention People's Party

Day of the Vow – *see* Day of the Covenant

de Andrade – *see* Pinto de Andrade

Democratic Turnhalle Alliance – *see* DTA

Department of National Security – *see* BOSS

Dhimmi – *see* Coptic Christians

Dhlamini – *see* Dlamini

Dutch Reformed Church – *see* Nederduitse
    Gereformeerde Kerk

EPLF & EPF – *see* Eritrea

Economic Community of West African States – *see*
    ECOWAS

Federal Capital Territory of Nigeria – *see* Abuja

FIS – *see* Islamic Salvation Front

FLN – *see* Front de Libération Nationale

Forças Populares de Libertação de Moçambique – *see*
    FPLM

French Somaliland – *see* Somalia

Frente de Libertaçao de Moçambique – *see* FRELIMO

Front for the Liberation of Mozambique – *see* FRELIMO

Front de la Libération Nationale Tchadien – *see*
    FROLINAT

Fufu – *see* cassava

Fundamentalism – *see* Islamic Fundamentalism

Ganda – *see* Buganda

Gari – *see* cassava

Gold Coast – *see* Ghana

Great Rift Valley – *see* East African Rift Valley

Holden, Roberto – *see* Roberto, Holden

Holy War – *see* Jihad

Horeau, Gerard – *see* Hoarau, Gerard

Hottentots – *see* Khoi

IMF – *see* International Monetary Fund

International Bank for Reconstruction and Development
    – *see* International Monetary Fund

Ironsi – *see* Aguiyi-Ironsi

Jamaat el Islamiya – *see* Gamaat al Islamiya

Jamahiriyya – *see* Libya

KADU – *see* Kenya African Democratic Union

KANU – *see* Kenya African National Union

Katanga – *see* Shaba

Khoisan – *see* Khoi and San

Kiswahili – *see* Swahili

Komati Accord – *see* Nkomati Accord

Koran – *see* Islam

Krio – *see* Creole

League of Arab States – *see* Arab League

Mali Federation – *see* Mali and Senegal separately

Mass Democratic Movement – *see* United Democratic Front

MESAN – *see* Mouvement d'Evolution Sociale de l'Afrique Noire

MNR – *see* Renamo

Moçambique – *see* Mozambique

Mouvement national Congolais – *see* MNC

Mouvement populaire de la révolution – *see* MPR

Mouvement révolutionnaire national pour le développement – *see* MRND

Movimento Popular de Libertaçao de Angola – *see* MPLA

Mozambique National Resistance – *see* Renamo

MPC – *see* Multi-Party Conference

Muganda – *see* Buganda

Muldergate – *see* Mulder, Connie

Muslim Brothers – *see* Republican Brothers

National Convention of Nigerian Citizens – *see* NCNC

National Council of Nigeria and the Cameroons – *see* NCNC

National Party of Nigeria – *see* NPN

Nigerian Civil War – *see* Biafra

Nigerian National Democratic Party – *see* NNDP

South West Africa People's Organization of Namibia –
  see SWAPO

SPPF – *see* Seychelles People's Progressive Front

SPUP – *see* Seychelles People's United Party

Tanganyika African National Union – *see* TANU

TAZARA – *see* TANZAM

UDF – *see* United Democratic Front

União Nacional Para a Independêngia Total de Angola –
  see UNITA

União Populações de Angola – *see* UPA

Unilateral Declaration of Independence – *see* UDI

Union pour le Progres National – *see* UPRONA

United Democratic Alliance – *see* Basotho Democratic
  Alliance

United National Independence Party – *see* UNIP

United Nations *see* UN

United Party of Nigeria – *see* UPN

Upper Volta – *see* Burkina Faso

Western Contact Group – *see* Contact Group

World Bank – *see* International Monetary Fund

A

Abbas, Ferhat (1899–1989), one of the most influential of Algerian politicians in the period prior to independence from France. Born in Constantine, Abbas was educated at the local lycée and Algiers University, where he trained as a pharmacist and became President of the Algerian Muslims Student Union. Becoming involved in municipal politics, he founded and edited the weekly journal *L'Entente*, 1933–9. He was a signatory to the Manifeste du Peuple Algérien, a nationalistic proclamation, issued on 12 February 1943. As the Second World War ended, in 1945 Abbas founded the Union Démocratique du Manifeste Algérien. His increasing status led to his being elected as a deputy to the French National Assembly, 1946, but he resigned in protest at French colonial policies the following year. In 1954, he founded and was first editor of *La République Algérienne*. The following year he joined the principal resistance organization, ★FRONT DE LIBÉRATION NATIONALE (FLN) and, while working for this organization, was based in Switzerland, 1956–7. He was President of the provisional government in exile, 1958–61. When Algeria won its independence in 1962 Abbas, as elder statesman, might have expected to become president. However, his old colleague, Ahmed ★BEN BELLA, had him expelled from the FLN. He went into exile and did not again take part in politics. In Algeria, Abbas, liberal and moderate, has never been given credit enough for his contribution to securing the nation's independence.

Abboud, Ferik Ibrahim (b. 1900), Sudanese army officer who led the coup against the government and became Prime Minister of Sudan (1958–64). Commissioned in the Egyptian Army (1918–25), Abboud served with the British Army in the North African campaign during the Second World War. He was Commander-in-Chief of the Sudan Army at the time of his coup. His regime was overthrown by a civilian coup in 1964 and he did not re-enter politics.

Abuja, federal capital of Nigeria since October 1982. In 1975 the military government announced that the federal capital would be moved from Lagos on the coast to Abuja in the centre of Nigeria, about 800 km north-east of Lagos. Lagos was overcrowded and congested; the northerners who controlled the government felt it was too far south. Despite heavy costs and serious difficulties in developing this remote area, the capital did become operational in 1982.

Acheampong, General Ignatius Kutu (1931–79), Ghanaian soldier and leader. He enlisted in the colonial army (1953), earned his commission (1959) and served with distinction in the United Nations Belgian Congo Peacekeeping Force (1959; 1962–3).

Back in Ghana he became a brigade commander.

He led the 1972 army coup which overthrew *BUSIA and made himself head of state – as Chairman of the National Redemption Council and of the Supreme Military Council, and also Minister of Defence and Sport. General Acheampong suspended the 1969 constitution, banned political activity, detained over a thousand people and set up powerful military tribunals. He promised to redeem Ghana and initially gained great popularity by repudiating some of Ghana's foreign debts. He preached self-reliance and launched Operation Feed Yourself (1972). Ghana failed to achieve self-reliance while corruption, smuggling, inflation and shortages continued. Economic hardship led to outbreaks of discontent which he suppressed; harsh measures were taken against strikers and the trade union movement.

Acheampong proposed a 'Union Government' in which power would be shared by civilian politicians and the armed forces; this led to violent student demonstrations (Jan. 1977) and the closure of Ghana's universities. Nevertheless, the 'Union Government' was approved in a rigged referendum (Mar. 1978). The general was so unpopular that he was ousted by his military colleagues and replaced by General *AKUFFO (Jul. 1978). He was charged with sabotaging the economy and cashiered by Akuffo (1979). In June 1979 he was executed after a short trial by the Armed Forces Revolutionary Council which had seized power under the leadership of Flt.-Lt. *RAWLINGS.

Achebe, Chinua (b. 1930), Nigerian author whose early novels brought him international acclaim. After graduating from Ibadan (1953), he worked in Nigerian broadcasting (1954–66). In 1967 he began his academic career in Nigeria and was twice a visiting professor in the United States. During the civil war (1967–70) Achebe went abroad seeking support for *BIAFRA. He was successively Director of African Studies at the Enugu campus of the University of Nigeria and a visiting Professor in the United States for the second time (1971–6) before settling in Nigeria as Professor of English at the Nsukka campus (1976–86). When the ban on political activity was lifted he joined the *PEOPLE'S REDEMPTION PARTY and became its Deputy National President (1983). Since 1986 Achebe has been Pro-Chancellor of the Anambra State University of Technology in Enugu. In 1990 it was reported that his legs were paralysed after a road accident.

Achebe's literary reputation was established with the publication of his first four novels. *Things Fall Apart* (1958) sold over two million copies in thirty languages; it was followed by *No Longer at Ease* (1960), *Arrow of God* (1964) and *A Man of the People* (1966). In these books he argued that African culture, history and religion are worthy of the respect of European colonialists and expressed his disenchantment with the corruption and brutality endemic in many African states since independence. Achebe has also written poetry, essays and short stories. His most recent novel, *Anthills of the Savannah*, was published in 1987 to great acclaim.

Action Group (AG), Nigerian political party formed in secret in 1950 and publicly launched in 1951. Led by Chief *AWOLOWO (1951–66) it had strong support from the Yoruba of the west. As independence approached it campaigned for strong regional governments and argued that the Western Region's earnings from cocoa should be used mainly for its own benefit and not to subsidize other parts of Nigeria.

The AG won the 1952 regional elections and formed the Western Region government. In 1959 Awolowo went into federal politics and was replaced as premier of the Western Region by Chief *AKINTOLA. After the pre-independence federal elections (1959) the AG became the official opposition to the federal coalition of northerners and easterners (*NPC – Northern People's Congress and the *NCNC – National Council of Nigeria and the Cameroons). The Action Group and the west were excluded from any share of power at the national level.

By 1962 frustration at being excluded from federal power and personal animosities led to a disastrous split in the party. Akintola led the minority faction which wanted to join a government of national unity; Awolowo and the majority strongly opposed this. When Awolowo tried to oust Akintola from the premiership there was turmoil in the Western Region and fighting in the regional House of Assembly. The federal government proclaimed a state of emergency and took over the government of the west. It tried and imprisoned Awolowo and some of his supporters for treasonable felony.

Akintola formed his own party and returned as premier at the end of the state of emergency (Jan. 1963). After blatant corruption and rigging of results by Akintola, the Action Group lost the October 1965 regional elections, and its supporters took to the streets and protested violently. The inability of the federal government to restore law and order in the west was partly responsible for the decision of the military to overthrow the civilian government in the January 1966 coup. The military government banned the Action Group and all other political parties.

Active Revolt (Revolta Activa), leftist political faction in Angola. A number of intellectuals, including the poet Mário *PINTO DE ANDRADE and his brother Joaquim, opposed Agostinho *NETO's leadership. They broke with the *MPLA to form a more radical revolutionary group, Revolta Activa (May 1974). The shortlived threat to the authority of the MPLA was suppressed by 1976.

Adekunle, Brigadier Benjamin Maja Adesanya (b. 1937), Nigerian soldier who was nicknamed the Black Scorpion because of his successes against the *BIAFRAN forces during the civil war (1967–70). He was retired from the army in 1975. When the ban on political activity was lifted (1978) he supported the *NPP (Nigerian People's Party) before shifting his allegiance to the *NPN (National Party of Nigeria).

Administrator-General, official appointed by South Africa to govern Namibia. The first holder of the post, Justice Marthinus Steyn (1977–9) was appointed after the *CONTACT GROUP rejected the internal settlement favoured by South Africa. He was instructed to prepare for national elections to an assembly which would draw up a constitution for an independent Namibia. Steyn and his successors rejected the United Nations plan for independence, trying to exclude *SWAPO from the political process and to install a government amenable to South African direction. The last Administrator-General was Louis Pienaar, appointed in 1985. He co-operated with the United Nations as it supervised the transition to independence (1989–90).

Adoula, Cyrille, Zairean politician whom President *KASAVUBU appointed to head a government of national unity in Zaire (then the Congo) in August 1961. Except for *TSHOMBE's party, all major political groups initially supported his efforts to reunite the country. With United Nations help the secession of Katanga (now *SHABA) was crushed by early 1963, but when there was renewed conflict in the country President Kasavubu sacked Adoula (1964). After *MOBUTU's second coup (Nov. 1965) Adoula remained politically active until disgraced by Mobutu in the late 1960s.

African National Congress (ANC – South Africa), multi-racial opposition movement operating in exile and in South Africa. Founded as the South African Native National Congress (1912), for many years it opposed white supremacy and gained wide support for its passive resistance campaign against *APARTHEID in the 1950s. In a protracted treason trial (1956–61) several ANC leaders were tried and finally acquitted. After the events of *SHARPEVILLE and the banning of the ANC in 1960 it was forced underground and a new more violent phase of the struggle began. Nelson *MANDELA formed and led the military wing, *UMKONTO WE SIZWE, in a campaign of sabotage and limited guerrilla warfare until he and his associates were arrested and convicted (1964) at the *RIVONIA Trial. The ANC reorganized itself in exile under the leadership of Oliver *TAMBO.

With support from the Soviet bloc and some radical African and Arab states the ANC has intensified its fight to overthrow apartheid. It welcomes all races in its struggle to establish a non-racial democratic South African state, according to the principles of the *FREEDOM CHARTER. It has headquarters in Zambia and sanctuaries and guerrilla bases in countries near South Africa. It has continued operations in South Africa's black townships; after the *SOWETO troubles (1976–7) many young people left South Africa to join the ANC. Until 1990 the government's main response to the ANC was to try to crush it with official bans, the imprisonment or assassination of its leaders, tight security measures, raids on ANC bases and sanctuaries outside South Africa and by diplomatic and economic pressure on neighbouring states who were helping the ANC. The *NKOMATI ACCORD (1984) is an example of the success of South African pressure; Mozambique had to agree to limit ANC activity in the country. ANC bases in Angola have been jeopardized by the accord on Namibian independence (1988–9) and the withdrawal of Cuban troops from Angola.

Despite all obstacles, the ANC played a leading role in the protests in South African townships during the 1980s, especially after it was strengthened by the formation of the *UNITED DEMOCRATIC FRONT (1983), which included hundreds of bodies sympathetic to the ANC. Despite challenges from more militant movements, the ANC is the leading opponent of apartheid; it has sympathy and support from many parts of the world and is seen as the true representative of the South African people.

Since taking office in 1989 President *DE KLERK has been willing to negotiate. Early in 1990 he lifted the ban on the ANC and released Nelson Mandela, its best-known leader. In May 1990 there were preliminary talks between the ANC and the government to prepare the way for constitutional talks in 1991. During 1990 there was still considerable tension between the ANC and the government, fuelled by the government's measures to control unrest in the townships and by the failure to make progress on the release of about three thousand political prisoners and the return of about thirty thousand political exiles. Bloody clashes between ANC and *INKATHA factions in the townships have further compromised the chances of a peaceful constitutional settlement in South Africa and the efforts of the ANC to establish itself as the sole legitimate body representing the interests of the South African people.

African National Congress (ANC–Southern Rhodesia), first formed in Southern Rhodesia (now Zimbabwe) in 1934 by Africans protesting against racial discrimination. In 1957 the original ANC joined other groups to form a new ANC under the leadership of Joshua *NKOMO to campaign for African rights. In 1959 the government banned the ANC and arrested most of its leaders. It was succeeded by the more militant *NDP (National Democratic Party) in 1960.

African National Congress (ANC – Zambia), Zambian political party founded and led by Harry *NKUMBULA (1951), it was based on the Northern Rhodesia African National Congress (founded in 1948). In the early 1950s the party led unsuccessful campaigns against racial discrimination and the *CENTRAL AFRICAN FEDERATION. The leadership's willingness to take part in the federal elections caused a split in the party (1958). Led by Kenneth *KAUNDA the younger radicals left the party to form the Zambia African National Congress, later *UNIP (United National Independence Party). Before independence (1962–4) the ANC was UNIP's junior partner in a coalition government. It became the main opposition party after independence, but was dissolved when Zambia became a one-party state (Dec. 1972).

African National Council, founded in 1971 in Rhodesia (now Zimbabwe) by Bishop *MUZOREWA, the first African political party allowed to operate effectively in the country after nationalist parties were finally banned (1964). The council rallied African opinion against the proposed Anglo-Rhodesian settlement of 1971 and played an important part in persuading the *PEARCE COMMISSION and the British government to reject the plan in 1972. In December 1974 it joined with other nationalist groups to form the United African National Council. In 1978 it agreed to co-operate with the *SMITH regime in forming a transitional government leading to independence under majority rule and won most seats in the elections which followed (Apr. 1979). Bishop Muzorewa became prime minister of Zimbabwe-Rhodesia. This government was not recognized either by the international community or by the nationalists who continued to fight for independence until Britain resumed control in December 1979. In the pre-independence elections

early in 1980 the council won only three seats in parliament. In the 1985 elections it won 2.3 per cent of the votes and no seats.

Afrifa, Lt.-Gen. Okatakyie Akawasi Amankwaa (1936–79), Ghanaian soldier and leader. Commissioned in 1960, he served in the United Nations Belgian Congo Peacekeeping Force (1960) and had reached the rank of major by 1965. From 1966 to 1969 he was the member of the National Liberation Council (NLC) in charge of finance and emerged as one of the most powerful members of the military government. He displaced General *ANKRAH as Chairman of the NLC and served as head of state while Ghana was returning to civilian rule (Apr.–Sep. 1969).

He was associated with *BUSIA's government (1969–72) first as chairman of the Presidential Commission and then as a member of the Council of State. General Afrifa was arrested and detained (1972–3) by *ACHEAMPONG's military government. He became politically active again in 1978–9 as preparations were made for a return to civilian rule. In June 1979 he was executed by the Armed Forces Revolutionary Council which had seized power under the leadership of Flt.-Lt. *RAWLINGS.

Afrikaner Broederbond (Afrikaner union of brothers), secret and powerful South African society with twelve thousand members who must be white, male, Afrikaans and Protestant. Since its formation in 1918 to promote Afrikaner unity and culture this elite body has exercised strong political, social and economic influence. Its members hold or have held most of the key positions in white South Africa, including all heads of government up to President *DE KLERK and most cabinet ministers since the *NATIONAL PARTY's victory in the 1948 election. For its first sixty years the organization strongly supported Afrikaner supremacy, but by the 1980s its attitude had changed. Early in the 1980s it supported President P.W. *BOTHA's modest reforms; later in the 1980s it concluded that a black president with limited powers was acceptable, and generally supported President *DE KLERK's attempts to initiate reform. These ideas led to the defection of some conservatives to a new body called the *AFRIKANER VOLKSWAG. In the late 1980s Professor J.P. de Lange led the Broederbond.

Afrikaner Volkswag (Afrikaner People's Guard), a shadowy coalition of right-wing white South African groups launched in 1984 by Carel Boshoff, a former leader of the *AFRIKANER BROEDERBOND. Boshoff leads the Afrikaner Volkswag which is pledged to the cause of white supremacy and supported by the *AFRIKANER WEERSTANDSBEWEGING. Members of the Volkswag feel that the government's constitutional reforms in the early 1980s betrayed the Afrikaner cause and there are fears that they may lead a white backlash against what they regard as the liberalism of President *DE KLERK.

Afrikaner Weerstandsbeweging (AWB) (Afrikaner Resistance Movement), an extreme right-wing South African organization of South African whites founded in 1973 and led by Mr Eugene *TERREBLANCHE. It regards the *NATIONAL PARTY government's modifications of *APARTHEID as dangerously left-wing and dreams of a racially pure white Afrikaner state from which all Jews would be expelled and where non-whites would only be allowed as temporary labour. Its red, white and black banners, its rallies, chants, and uniformed 'bodyguards' are strongly reminiscent of Nazi Germany. The movement's rapidly growing membership includes many policemen and at least four *CONSERVATIVE PARTY members of parliament. Although the AWB is prepared to use violence the authorities have taken only limited action against it. Mr Terreblanche and other leaders were briefly detained after the discovery of an illegal arms cache in 1982. In March 1988 some policemen were sacked after the AWB was investigated by internal security forces. In 1989 and 1990 it condemned the policies of President *DE KLERK as a betrayal of South African whites; in May 1990 it threatened to form commando groups to protect white rule.

Afro-Shirazi Party, radical party formed in *ZANZIBAR (1957), it included Africans and Arabs who claimed that their ancestors had come from Shiraz in Persia. It won five out of the six contested seats in the 1957 elections but lost the elections before independence

(1963). After the revolution early in 1964 it absorbed *UMMA and took power in Zanzibar. After a power struggle Abeid *KARUME became party leader and President of Zanzibar (1964–72). In 1977 the party merged with *TANU to form Tanzania's only legal political party – *CHAMA CHA MAPINDUZI.

Aggett, Dr Neil (1953–82), one of the first white victims of South African police brutality. He was working for a multi-racial trade union when the Security Police arrested and detained him under the *TERRORISM ACT (27 Nov. 1981). He was tortured and found hanged in his cell (5 Feb. 1982). His death caused widespread protests and his funeral was attended by fifteen thousand people.

Aguiyi-Ironsi, Maj.-Gen. Johnson Thomas Umunankwe (1924–66), Nigerian soldier who seized power in 1966. Ironsi enlisted in the Nigerian Regiment (1942) and had reached the rank of Lieutenant-Colonel when Nigeria became independent. By 1961 he was a Brigadier serving in the United Nations peacekeeping force in the Congo. Back in Nigeria he became a Major-General and General Officer Commanding the Nigerian Army (1965). When the military overthrew the civilian government in Nigeria's first military coup (Jan. 1966) Ironsi took office as Head of the Federal Military Government and Supreme Commander of the Armed Forces. Ironsi and his close associates were Ibo; other groups in Nigeria, especially the northerners, feared Ibo domination of the country. There were anti-Ibo riots in the north and even more tension after Ironsi abolished the federal structure and declared that Nigeria was a unitary state (May 1966). Ironsi was assassinated in Nigeria's second military coup (Jul. 1966).

Ahidjo, Ahmadou (1924–89), first President of Cameroon. Born in Garoua, northern Cameroon, Ahidjo had only a rudimentary education but was a professional politician from an early age. He was a member of the territorial assembly, 1947–58, and Vice-Premier and Minister of Interior, 1957–8. On 19 February 1958 he became Prime Minister of 'Autonomous French Cameroon'. When Cameroon was declared independent in 1960, Ahidjo was elected President by eighty-nine votes to ten. As a policymaker, Ahidjo was invariably cautious; nevertheless he began many projects with the general objective of diversifying Cameroon's economy. He succeeded in this objective. In 1970 and again in 1975 he was re-elected president, on the latter occasion with 99 per cent of the votes. On 5 April 1980 he stood for a fifth five-year term of office, this time as the only candidate, and was duly declared elected.

On 4 November, only seven months into his term, Ahidjo unexpectedly announced his resignation, apparently because of fatigue and ill health. He had been president of his country for twenty-two years. Ahidjo retired to France but retained his presidency of the *UNION NATIONALE

CAMEROUNAISE (UNC) party. In this capacity, a year later, he scathingly attacked his successor, Paul Biya, for 'maladministration.' As the instigator of a bloody coup attempt in April 1984, Ahidjo tried to regain power. After the coup's failure, Ahidjo was sentenced to death in his absence and thus forced to remain in exile in France. He is remembered in Cameroon and West Africa with grudging respect but without affection. People were too afraid of him, his secret police and his prison camps to like him. Nevertheless, Cameroon was economically buoyant and an African success story when he left it.

Ahtisaari, Martti (b. 1937), Finnish diplomat who served as the United Nations Commissioner for Namibia (1977–81) and has been the Secretary-General's special representative for Namibia since 1978. With the assistance of *UNTAG he is responsible for the peaceful implementation of *UN SECURITY COUNCIL RESOLUTION 435 (1978) (which laid down a timetable for Namibian independence). The transition period of one year began badly. The numbers of UNTAG were reduced to save money and in April 1989 the peaceful transition to independence was threatened when *SWAPO guerrillas moved into Namibia from their Angolan bases and clashed with South African forces. Ahtisaari managed to settle this crisis and secured the co-operation of both SWAPO and South Africa in the smooth transition to independence in March 1990.

Aids in Africa One million Africans, most of them in Central Africa, will die of Aids before the end of the century, according to the Panos Institute, the authoritative research body. Whereas in the United States and Europe the most vulnerable groups are homosexuals and intravenous drug users, in Arica the most common means of transmitting the HIV virus is through heterosexual activity. In some countries both the ruling and professional classes are being badly hit. The 'African condition' – the name given to the complex of traditions, taboos, poverty, political upheavals and economic instability – makes it difficult to assess the incidence of Aids and to curb its spread. With some exceptions Aids is an entirely urban phenomenon. Surveys show that up to 8 per cent of the adult population of Kinshasa, capital of Zaire, are Aids carriers. Aids will have a profound impact on Africa's agricultural and industrial output. It cannot afford to lose its skilled manpower which, through lack of educational facilities, is already scarce. According to research by the World Health Organization (WHO), Africa accounts for a relatively insignificant 8 per cent of the world's known Aids cases. But figures mask the true extent of the epidemic, which centres on the eastern and central African countries of Zaire, Burundi, Rwanda, Tanzania, Kenya, Uganda and Zambia.

Researchers suspect that because early death is common in Africa and drugs scarce, many people suffering from Aids do not bother to go to hospital. A large number of other cases either remain undiagnosed or are attributed to other killers, such as tuberculosis or pneumonia. Some doctors estimate that the number of Aids cases in Kampala, Uganda, is doubling every six months. In Burundi about half the predominantly Tutsi army are thought to be Aids carriers. If Aids becomes epidemic in the countryside it will kill the farm-workers and could trigger widespread famine. Kenya, which does not want to risk damage to its tourist trade, has refused to allow welfare organizations to implement educational campaigns against Aids. In contrast, Rwanda has one of the best education programmes in the Third World. President Juvenal *HABYARIMANA made Aids a legitimate subject for discussion by declaring it a national menace. The Red Cross was then able to distribute fifty thousand booklets on Aids facts. Disseminating information in Rwanda is far easier than in Zaire, a vast and multi-lingual nation where the communications infrastructure is in chaos and illiteracy is high.

Akintola, Chief Samuel Ladoke (1910–66), controversial Nigerian politician. After being admitted to the Bar in London (1949), he returned to Nigeria and joined *AWOLOWO's *ACTION GROUP (1951) which represented the interests and concerns of the Yoruba people and the Western Region. During the 1950s he was active in regional and national politics as deputy leader of the Action Group from 1955 and as a member of the national coalition government (1957–9).

When Awolowo bid unsuccessfully for power at the federal level (1959), Akintola succeeded him as premier of the Western Region. The two men quarrelled and Chief Awolowo persuaded the Action Group to sack Akintola (1962). The party split into two factions which fought in the streets and even in the Western Region House of Assembly. The federal government suspended the regional government and declared a state of emergency in the west (1962). Akintola returned as premier when the state of emergency ended (Jan. 1963), but made little attempt to bring order and prosperity to the region.

Akintola organized his supporters in the *NNDP (Nigerian National Democratic Party) in 1964 and contested the Western Regional elections (Oct. 1965). He was expected to lose, but announced his victory after blatant corruption and electoral fraud. Three months of bloodshed and turmoil followed, and the federal government seemed helpless. The disorder in the Western Region was largely responsible for the decision of the military to stage the coup in which Akintola and other Nigerian political leaders were assassinated (Jan. 1966).

Akuffo, Lt.-Gen. Fred W.K. (1937–79), Ghanaian soldier and leader. After working in the Civil Service (1955–7), he joined the army and served in the United Nations Belgian Congo Peacekeeping Force. He was a member of the Supreme Military Council (1975–9) and Chief of Defence Staff (1976–8). In July 1978 he replaced General *ACHEAMPONG as Chairman of the Supreme Military Council and head of state. He proposed a national government for Ghana for four years from July 1979 and at the beginning of 1979 lifted the ban on political parties – but not the ban on 105 politicians. In June 1979 he was executed after a short trial by the Armed Forces Revolutionary Council with had seized power under the leadership of Flt.-Lt. *RAWLINGS.

Al Azhar, university and mosque in Cairo which is the font of Islamic learning for the entire Muslim world. For more than a thousand years the opinions of Al Azhar scholars have had the most profound effect on Islamic thought and institutions everywhere. Its instruction and guidance on matters of jurisprudence are the essence of *ISLAM itself. While the university retains much of its influence and prestige abroad, many Islamic authorities in Egypt warn that Al Azhar is in serious decline. They complain that as an institution it has become like a government agency, with all the defects of the Egyptian bureaucracy.

The beginnings of Al Azhar's decline coincide with two developments, both of which came about as a result of Egypt's 1952 revolution. One was the creation of the Ministry of Religious Affairs in 1953,

which removed from Al Azhar's control huge amounts of money and the attendant prestige and patronage. The other development was the dismantling, also during the 1950s, of the Al Azhar-sponsored kutab primary school system. This had provided every generation of Egyptians with the basics of Islamic education. Also responsible for Al Azhar's loss of influence was the consolidation, in 1956, of all family and personal legal matters within the civil court system. The imposition of a non-Koranic school curriculum robbed Al Azhar of its importance. Under *NASSER, a new social contract was implanted in Egypt, one between government and people. The state, not organized religion, would assume responsibility for people's welfare. The disappearance of the kutab schools not only deprived Al Azhar of the gratitude of poor and middle class parents whose children would not otherwise have had an education; it also deprived Al Azhar of a constantly growing pool of young people, versed in the *Koran* and the basics of Islam, as students of Al Azhar and its several related colleges and institutes. Some Egyptians argue that the dismantling of Egypt's traditional school system is responsible for the restlessness among Islamic youth and even for the growth of violent underground Muslim groups.

aldeamentos, villages established in Angola by the Portuguese authorities during the independence war (1961–74). Officially, peasants were moved to these villages from areas

The Democratic and Popular Republic of Algeria

THE COUNTRY	THE PEOPLE	THE STATE
2,381,741 sq. km.	25 million	Multi-party presidential republic
Major Cities	*Ethnic Groups*	*Head of State*
Algiers (capital)	Arabs	President Chadli
Tebessa	Berbers	Benjedid
Constantine	Some Europeans	
Annaba		*Ruling Bodies*
Oran	*Languages*	President
Tlemcen	Arabic (official)	Cabinet of 23
	Berber dialects 25%	
Economy	French is common in	*Ruling Party*
Oil and natural gas	the cities	National Liberation Front
Wine, olives, fruit, dates		(FLN)
Forestry	*Religion*	
Tourism	99% of the populace	
	are Muslims of the	
Principal Exports	Sunni or Malekite rites	
Oil and gas		
Currency		
Algerian dinar of 100		
centimes		

of guerrilla activity for their own safety, but the resettlement was an effective way of depriving guerrillas of support from sympathetic rural areas.

Algeria The Republic of Algeria is situated on the Mediterranean with 1150 km of coastline between Libya to the east and Morocco to the west. South of the fertile coastal strip, which is between one and two hundred miles wide, is a vast area of mountains and desert and beyond that wasteland lie Mauritania, Mali and Niger.

The original inhabitants – and still a major part of the population – were *BERBERS. Much

invaded, Algeria was ruled successively by the Phoenicians, Carthaginians, Romans, Vandals and Arabs. French occupation began in 1830 and was considered complete by 1902. Scholars recognize that Algeria had no national identity before the French occupation, though ardent nationalists would dispute this. Algeria's national identity was formed in reaction to the French. No other country was so heavily colonized by Europeans and probably none has been so profoundly transformed by its experience with foreigners. Almost from the beginning, the French saw Algeria as part of France and every government of France encouraged its citizens to settle there. At the end of the Second World War, in 1945, more than one million French settlers, or colons, lived in Algeria and collectively they owned more than forty per cent of the cultivated land.

Beginning in 1945, various political movements were founded by Algerian intellectuals who sought to improve local rights without destroying the French administrative framework. All these groups were enveloped and absorbed, or destroyed, by the *FRONT LIBÉRATION NATIONALE (FLN) which began a war against the French in November 1954. (See ALGERIAN CIVIL WAR.) The murderous war had reached an intractable state when President Charles de Gaulle returned to power in France in 1958. The French used Algerian Sahara in 1960 to test France's first nuclear weapons, but, despite Algeria's strategic value, in 1961 de Gaulle's government began negotiations with the FLN to bring about independence. That same year, Algerian oil exports began, with France as the chief market. Terrorists of the French Organization de l'Armée Sécrète (OAS) fought treasonably and savagely to hold Algeria but the army as a whole remained loyal to de Gaulle.

Algeria became independent on 5 July 1962. Many Algerians had lost their lives in the struggle, which also had the effect of bringing about the downfall of the Fourth French Republic. The war had been one of the bloodiest and most destructive anti-colonial struggles ever. An estimated one million Algerians – one in every ten – lost their lives; another two million were displaced during the conflict, largely because of the French security policy of moving people into 'regroupment villages'. By 1961 about a third of the rural population had been relocated. Within months of independence being granted to Algeria, 800,000 Europeans had fled the country. At the same time, because of Arab hatred 150,000 Algerian Jews were driven out. This exodus deprived the country of most of its administrators, entrepreneurs, technicians, physicians, teachers and skilled workers. Factories and shops were closed and farms abandoned, leaving 70 per cent of the population unemployed.

The war had one positive outcome; it created an overwhelming sense of national solidarity and ensured that the post-war nation builders had revolutionary legitimacy and the goodwill of their own people and of revolutionary regimes abroad.

Ahmed *BEN BELLA was the first president. He purged the FLN of its conservatives, nationalized French property and linked Algeria with 'Afro-Asian' solidarity. Colonel Houari *BOUMEDIENNE took power in 1965 on a platform of national independence, socialism and rapid economic growth. In the first ten years of his rule he sacrificed social welfare and democracy to the achievement of long-term economic goals. In 1976 a national debate took place on a National Charter. As a result, Boumedienne gave greater priority to improving the living conditions of the people. The FLN, which had become moribund, was revived.

When Boumedienne died in 1978 a special FLN congress named Colonel Chadli *BENJEDID as sole presidential candidate and he was duly elected in February 1979, committed to liberalization and the raising of living standards. The government's efforts did not satisfy popular expectations. In 1980 there were serious riots in Tizi-Ouzou, capital of the Berber *KABYLE region. The *BERBERS were hostile to the central authority's Arabization programme.

During the period 1985–8, Algeria's political reputation in North Africa, within the Arab world and in the wider Islamic world became more significant. Its relationship with Morocco remained strained because Algeria supported the claims of the people of South-West Sahara for independence from Morocco and directly aided the *POLISARIO resistance movement. Algerian diplomacy has played a skilful and crucial role in resolving crises caused by terrorism, as during the negotiations for the release of US hostages in Iran in 1981.

As 1987 drew to a close the National Popular Assembly adopted legislation which dismantled much of the centralized socialist edifice within which the Algerian economy had lived for a quarter of a century. The most important of six new laws due to come in force from the end of December 1988, removed public companies from direct control by the responsible government ministries, though firm control was kept of 'strategic' industries, such as hydrocarbons. Banks were no longer under restraint and could compete for business. Individual companies would have total control over their own resources and budget. State firms had approval to manage their day-to-day planning. The government made it clear that if reforms looked like working, from 1989 and beyond, it would not hesitate to proceed further with liberalization.

The reforms came too late. On 5 October 1988, rioting started in Algiers and spread along the Mediterranean coast, where most of the country's people live. The trouble reached Oran in the west and as far as Annaba in the east. In less than a week about a thousand demonstrators, nearly all young people, were killed, most of them machine-gunned down on the boulevards of Algiers. The extraordinary events, the most violent in Algeria since the end of the Algerian Civil War, were caused by an array of problems: a drastic loss of revenue from oil production; a large population of young unemployed people; an official austerity programme derived from a proud insistence on promptly repaying foreign loans; the increasing influence of Muslim fundamentalists. A previously unknown organization, the Popular Movement for the Renewal of Algeria (MPRA), claimed to have organized the uprisings, but most likely

14

they were largely spontaneous. The President promised reforms but they did not seem adequate to prevent further serious unrest.

Algeria contains the potentially explosive amalgam of two very different races – the minority Berber Kabyles and the Arabs. Before, and even during, the War of Liberation they were often at each other's throats. However, the main threat to political stability and economic viability comes from over-population. The Government is trying to convince women that the traditional desire for ten or twelve children condemns them to lifelong drudgery and the country to ruination. Even Algeria's wealth, derived from oil and gas, cannot support the 3.2 per cent population growth, one of the highest in the world. In 1989 the total of 24 million was forecast to rise to 37 million by the year 2000. Nonetheless, Algerian religious authorities are more progressive about contraception than those in many Mediterranean countries; they announced as early as the 1960s that contraception is not unlawful in Islam.

However, as a result of the nation's first democratic elections in the summer of 1989 much of the new liberalism may be swept away. This is because the elections – held only at local and district level – brought to political prominence the *ISLAMIC SALVATION FRONT. Its fundamentalist Islamic policies, were they to be imposed at national level, would probably reverse the reforms produced by the very democratic processes which gave life to the Islamic Salvation Front itself.

Rich mineral resources are the mainstay of Algeria's foreign trade. Oil exports annually contribute about 90 per cent of total exports. Natural gas is set to replace oil as Algeria's main export by 1996. On the agricultural side, the 'Green Dam', a land reclamation project, includes one of the biggest forestry schemes ever undertaken. Results are already impressive with whole mountain chains covered with saplings. The project is designed to arrest the steady encroachment of the *SAHARA and make the high plateau between the fertile coastal strip and the desert more productive. It is government policy to open up the Sahara for the exploration of oil and for tourists.

Algerian Civil War The war was the inevitable result of the demand for independence which swept across the European nations' empires after the Second World War. In Algeria, the first clash between the French army and the Algerian nationalists occurred on 8 May 1954, when 88 French and more than 1000 Algerians were killed. Soon after, the *FRONT DE LIBÉRATION NATIONALE (FLN), under Houari *BOUMEDIENNE, began organized warfare. Its guerrilla units ambushed French army units, raided bases and blew up installations. In turn, the French ruthlessly hunted down and destroyed Algerian rebels. Fighting took place in every city and in many parts of the mountainous interior.

Because the FLN used Tunisian bases, French relations with Tunisia became strained. The war drew into Algeria more than 160,000 French soldiers, about one half of the entire French army.

On 1 June 1958 President de Gaulle, desperate for peace, offered self-determination by referendum but this was opposed by the *pieds-noirs* – Algerians of French descent. They feared that, in the event of a victory by the FLN, they would be victimized. Rioting and terrorism was provoked by the *ORGANISA-TION DE L'ARMÉE SÉCRÈTE (OAS). Early in 1960 the French Rightists in Algeria rose against de Gaulle and his move towards independence but the uprising was suppressed by loyal French troops.

French military casualties were: 892 officers and 16,764 men killed, 64,985 wounded and 1000 missing. French civilian casualties exceeded 10,000, with another 500 'disappeared'. The Algerians estimated their war dead at one million, or one in ten of the population. Impartial research shows that the real figure could not have been much less than this enormous total. However, hundreds of thousands of Algerian Muslims died during the savage inter-factional fighting that took place concurrently with the war against the French, and in the struggle for supremacy at the end of the war. These disturbing figures have been glossed over by successive governments. Nobody has ever attempted to assess the number of wounded.

Allam, Muhammad (b. 1949), Egyptian painter, writer and book-maker. Allam uses his books, none of which have a title, to make political comments. The books require that the reader participate on the artist-writer's terms, demanding that he suspend belief and be prepared for magic. Some of the script is in mirror-language and can only be read when seen in reflection. Insults, especially, are written backwards. In his most recent novel, letters and numbers become interchangeable. The crucial unit is three; most of the sentences have three words; the story involves a quest for three things; the book has 333 pages. Allam is a cult figure and literary and political circles believe that his influence is growing.

All People's Congress (APC), political party founded in Sierra Leone by Siaka *STEVENS (1957), it became the official opposition to the *SIERRA LEONE PEOPLE'S PARTY (SLPP). In March 1967 the APC narrowly won the elections, but was unable to take office because the ruling SLPP refused to step down and the military intervened. In 1968 it was able to form a government under the leadership of Stevens. The APC won subsequent elections in 1973 and 1977, but both were marked by violence and irregularities. The 1978 constitution made Sierra Leone a one-party state, with the APC as the only officially recognized political party. The APC delegates elect the President of Sierra Leone; since 1985 its officials have had the power to nominate the candidates for the

House of Representatives. The current Secretary-General of the APC is President *MOMOH.

Alves, Nito, Angolan nationalist who rose through the ranks to the Central Committee of the *MPLA by 1974. He was an eloquent speaker who became independent Angola's first Minister of the Interior (1975), but was sacked by President *NETO for factionalism (1976). In 1977 he staged an unsuccessful coup in which the Minister of Finance and other leaders of the MPLA were murdered.

Alvor Agreement, reached at Alvor in Portugal (Jan. 1975) by Portugal and leading Angolan nationalist movements. The Alvor agreement established a cease-fire, set 11 November 1975 as the date for independence and created a transitional government of Angola representative of Portugal and the nationalists (*MPLA, *FNLA, *UNITA). Hostility between the three nationalist organizations made the agreement unworkable. Increasing violence developed into civil war and Portugal terminated the transitional government in August 1975.

Amin Dada, Idi Oumee (b. 1924), ex-President of Uganda. Born into the Kakwa tribe in West Nile province, Amin had little formal education. He began his successful military career in 1943 and served in Burma during the Second World War and in Kenya during the *MAU MAU emergency (1952–6). He was an officer when Uganda won independence (1962). In 1966 he led the forces which stormed the *BUGANDAN palace and became commander of Uganda's armed forces (1966–70). Shortly after being sacked as Chief of Staff, Amin overthrew President *OBOTE (Jan. 1971).

As President of Uganda Amin made himself a dictator by removing political and civil rights, abolishing the constitution and making himself Life-President. To ensure the loyalty of the army and the special police he massacred thousands of them from the Acholi and Langi tribes which he mistrusted, and recruited heavily from the West Nile Province. The armed forces were given extraordinary powers to arrest, detain and try civilians. Eventually the army was empowered to do anything it saw fit to maintain public order. The result was the collapse of law and order by the late 1970s; a wave of uncontrolled brutality and terror claimed the lives of 300,000 Ugandans from all walks of life, including the Chief Justice (1976) and the Anglican Archbishop (1977).

Amin's economic policies were disastrous. In a fertile land thousands starved and once prosperous farmers were barely able to survive as subsistence farmers. The nationalization of foreign businesses and the expulsion of forty thousand Asian residents added to the economic catastrophe. While Amin became more and more capricious the infrastructrue collapsed; public utilities and transport broke down.

Amin looked far afield for help. The Soviet Union gave military assistance. As a follower of Islam

Amin gained technical and military aid, money and friendship from Libya and Saudi Arabia. He demonstrated his hostility to Israel by supporting the Palestinian hijacking of a French plane with Jewish passengers to Entebbe (1976). An elderly Jewish woman was taken away by Ugandans and murdered during this incident.

At the same time Ugandan relations with neighbouring states went from bad to worse. Amin claimed large areas of Kenya and Sudan and bitterly criticized President *NYERERE of Tanzania for supporting exiled Ugandan dissidents. Amin's invasion of Tanzania (Oct. 1978) was followed by the invasion of Uganda by Tanzanian forces and Ugandan dissidents who overthrew Amin by April 1979. Amin escaped to exile in Libya and Saudi Arabia, but some of his soldiers escaped to neighbouring Sudan and Zaire and continued to fight. In 1985 when the military government of Uganda organized these men to fight for it there were rumours that Amin would return to Uganda. Early in 1989 he flew to Zaire with a false passport and planned to return to Uganda, but was sent back to Saudi Arabia by the authorities in Zaire.

Anglo-American Corporation, powerful South African business concern which controls much of South African mining and has considerable international interests. The leading members of the corporation generally favour a liberal approach to South Africa's political problems. Its former chairman,

Harry Oppenheimer, was the Progressive Party's most important financial backer; its current chairman, Gavin Relly, joined the South African businessmen who went to Lusaka in 1986 to talk to *AFRICAN NATIONAL CONGRESS leaders.

Angola, the People's Republic of Angola is a vast and sparsely populated country in the south-western sector of Africa; its people belong to about one hundred different tribal or ethnic groups. Although Angola is in the tropics, most of the country occupies a plateau over one thousand metres high and enjoys a temperate climate. The coastal plains are hot; to the south they form part of the Namib desert. North of Angola is the oil-rich enclave of *CABINDA, separated from the rest of the country by Zaire's corridor to the Atlantic Ocean.

In addition to oil Angola has other sources of wealth. It has rich diamond deposits as well as copper, manganese, phosphates, salt and iron ore. It has been, and could be again, a major producer of coffee, cotton, maize, rice, sugar and *SISAL.

Portuguese explorers reached the Angolan coast late in the fifteenth century and founded the colony of Luanda (1575). During the nineteenth and early twentieth centuries Portugal conquered and settled Angola. After years of bitter fighting Portugal could claim in 1922 that the 'pacification' of Angola was complete.

Before independence Portugal took the profits from Angola's

The People's Republic of Angola

THE COUNTRY	THE PEOPLE	THE STATE
1,246,700 sq. km.	9,243,000	Single-party republic
Major Cities	*Ethnic Groups*	*Head of State*
Luanda (capital)	Ovimbundu	President dos Santos
Lobito	Mbundu	
Huambo	Kongo	*Ruling Bodies*
Lubango	Lunda-Chokwe	Council of Ministers
	Nganguela	National People's
Economy		Assembly
Farming	*Languages*	
Mining	Portuguese (official)	*Official Party*
	Kilongo	MPLA-PT
Principal Exports	Umbundu	
Oil & Petroleum	Kimbundu	
Coffee	Kioko	
Diamonds		
	Religion	
Currency	Christian	
Kwanza (Kz) of 100 lwei	Traditional	

natural resources. The colonial authorities forced local people to work on coffee, sisal and maize plantations; only the very small number of *ASSIMILADOS were exempt from forced labour. The extraction of diamonds and after 1956 the exploitation of petroleum provided Portugal with rich revenues. The lucrative *BENGUELA railway carried minerals from Zaire and Zambia to the Angolan port of Lobito. Encouraged by the Portuguese authorities and lured by the prospect of the wealth to be gained from the coffee boom, many settlers came to Angola after the Second World War; at independence the white settler population was about 330,000.

Post-war Angola also saw the development of a cultural and nationalist movement by those who had met other African nationalists while studying abroad. Salazar's repressive dictatorship and Angolan resentment at the colonial system of forced labour fuelled the fires of Angolan nationalism and led to the formation of resistance movements which initiated the long struggle for independence in 1961. The *MPLA (Popular Movement for the Liberation of Angola) was founded in Luanda (1956). It welcomed all races, including whites and *MESTIÇOS (of mixed African and European ancestry). The *FNLA (National Front for the Liberation of Angola) was formed as a coalition of tribally based groups (1962). Southerners quit the FNLA in protest against its domination by northerners (1964); they formed *UNITA (National Union for the Total Independence of Angola) (1966) – a movement strongly supported by the Ovimbundu.

The war of liberation began with the MPLA rising in Luanda (Feb. 1961) and the northern peasant rebellion led by Holden *ROBERTO (Mar. 1961). In the north Portuguese landowners and their families were savagely killed. The authorities retaliated brutally; a British missionary society estimated that in 1961 alone twenty thousand Angolans were killed for sympathizing with the nationalists.

Some nationalists escaped into exile and reorganized the three main nationalist groups. Under the command of Agostinho *NETO the MPLA embarked on a full-scale armed struggle for an independent, non-racial and democratic people's republic, but the FNLA and UNITA were regionally based. By the late 1960s intense efforts gave the nationalists control of large parts of Angola. Portugal's heavy casualties and weariness with the colonial wars were partly responsible for the collapse of the Salazar dictatorship (1974). Portugal's new leaders were quick to negotiate the *ALVOR AGREEMENT which scheduled independence for 11 November 1975; until then Portugal and the three main nationalist movements (MPLA, FNLA, UNITA) were to form a transitional government.

From the beginning the transitional government was torn apart by nationalist feuds and interference from foreign countries. Zaire helped

the FNLA in the north and South Africa sent troops into the south. The United States helped FNLA and UNITA while the Soviet bloc backed the MPLA. Civil War had broken out when Portugal abandoned the transitional government (Aug. 1975). On 11 November 1975 the MPLA proclaimed the People's Republic of Angola; at the same time FNLA and UNITA proclaimed their governments, and later formed an anti-MPLA alliance. Only after the first Cuban troops arrived (Nov. 1975) did the MPLA make substantial progress against its enemies. By March 1976 South Africa had withdrawn its troops and UNITA and FNLA guerrillas had retreated into the bush. Following Nigeria, countries outside the Soviet bloc (but not the United States) recognized the People's Republic of Angola.

The legacy of Portuguese colonialism, the long and bitter war of independence (1961–74), the continuing civil war and foreign destabilization of Angola have devastated Angola and its economy. After the FNLA was crushed the main protagonists in the continuing struggle were the Angolan government and the UNITA rebels. Angola has spent up to two thirds of its annual budget and half of its foreign currency earnings on the military. It has sought foreign help; by 1988 an estimated fifty thousand Cuban troops were fighting for the MPLA government. UNITA was able to intensify its efforts with financial and military aid from South Africa and the United States, which delivered Stinger missiles in 1986.

After their withdrawal in 1976 South African forces repeatedly invaded southern Angola and made frequent air-strikes – ostensibly against *SWAPO bases in Angola. South Africa's motives were clear. It wanted to remove a Marxist government from its borders and to stop Angola helping SWAPO in its fight for Namibian independence.

Attempts to settle the conflict, including the *LUSAKA AGREEMENT (Feb. 1984), failed because South Africa insisted that peace with Angola had to be part of a regional plan which would include a Namibian settlement and the end of Angolan aid to the *AFRICAN NATIONAL CONGRESS. Since then progress has been made. In 1988 South Africa again withdrew its forces from Angola and Chester Crocker, the United States' mediator, persuaded Angola, Cuba and South Africa to sign an agreement (Dec. 1988). Cuba will withdraw its troops from Angola by July 1991 and South Africa has left Namibia according to the terms of *UNITED NATIONS SECURITY COUNCIL RESOLUTION 435. It has been informally agreed that South Africa will stop supporting UNITA and Angola will close ANC bases. An agreement in Zaire (Jun. 1989) aroused hopes that the Angolan government and UNITA would make peace, but the cease-fire broke down. Early in 1990 the government was making major advances against UNITA, which has asked for another cease-fire. There are hopes that the civil war will soon be over.

If the war does end soon, it will take many years for Angola to recover from the disruption caused by the fighting. Agriculture and communications have suffered greatly. Angola was able to feed itself; now it imports large quantities of food. UNITA has blocked and partly destroyed the *BENGUELA Railway, once a rich source of revenue. The disruption of diamond mining by UNITA and by smugglers has cut revenues and reduced foreign earnings.

Falling oil prices have added to the problems. Angola cannot afford to invest in its economy and infrastructure; it is burdened by foreign debt, high inflation and shortages of vital goods. Its people are desperately poor. After the departure of so many Portuguese settlers at independence there was a catastrophic shortage of administrative and technical skills. Industry has suffered from nationalization and inefficient state management. Angola needs to organize economic activity more efficiently, develop the skills of its people, crush the black market and raise living standards.

The government has also had to transform a revolutionary movement into an orderly party of efficient government. President Neto faced factional rivalries while establishing the MPLA as a Marxist-Leninist party. After defeating the leftist challenge mounted by the *ACTIVE REVOLT, he was faced with the *ALVES coup attempt in which prominent MPLA leaders were murdered (1977). At the

21

ANGOLA

first party congress (Dec. 1977) the MPLA was reorganized as a Workers' Party – the MPLA-PT. In a move to rid the party of dissidents President Neto sacked his prime minister, Lopo do Nascimento, and reshuffled the government in late 1978.

After Neto's death (Sep. 1979) José *DOS SANTOS became president. To establish his authority he also had to purge the government and the party of elements unhappy at his pragmatism and his willingness to look for friends outside the Soviet bloc. In 1980 he strengthened his position by replacing the Council for Revolution with an elected People's Assembly. President dos Santos is regarded as a moderate, who is fighting corruption and inefficiency and working to achieve security and a decent standard of living for the people of Angola. He will have chance of success only when the civil war and foreign intervention cease. The agreement between Angola, Cuba and South Africa (Dec. 1988) has offered the best hope for peace so far.

During 1990 the MPLA government and UNITA held peace talks, but made little progress. The government offered negotiations on a multi-party constitution, but UNITA would not agree to a cease-fire without certain guarantees. Despite UNITA's reluctance to co-operate, the government announced it would introduce a multi-party system in March 1991. The fighting has continued, and by late 1990 up to two million people

22

in the war area were threatened with starvation. In November 1990 a United Nations food convoy began taking food to the most adversely affected areas. Crucially, in December 1990, the Soviet Union and USA told UNITA and the MPLA that they would no longer aid the war effort. A cease-fire is in sight.

Ankrah, General Joseph Arthur (b. 1915), Ghanaian soldier and leader, who was commissioned in 1947. He served in the United Nations Belgian Congo Peacekeeping Force (1960–1) before returning to serve President *NKRUMAH as Deputy Chief of Defence Staff (1961–5). Suspicious of the army's loyalty, Nkrumah established his personal presidential guard which was independent of the army and in 1965 dismissed General Ankrah. In February 1966 the army and the police seized power and set up the National Liberation Council (NLC) of four army officers and four police officers to run Ghana. Ankrah, who had not taken part in the coup, served as Chairman of the NLC and head of state from 1966 to 1969.

Ankrah and the NLC ruled Ghana during years of mounting economic crisis, but Ankrah's pledge to honour Ghana's foreign debts earned him western support and approval. The NLC was weakened by factional rivalries and personal jealousies which led to Ankrah's resignation (Apr. 1969), as the NLC was preparing for the return of Ghana to civilian rule.

Ansar Movement The economically powerful Islamic religious sect and brotherhood which was influential in Sudan in the 1952–70 period. The Ansars, who as fundamentalists advocated a national return to the tenets of *ISLAM, had their base on Aba Island in the *NILE River. Their leader in the 1960s was Sadiq al-Mahdi. The officers who came to power in the *NIMEIRI coup of May 1969 stated that the 'struggle against religious fanaticism is a social and economic necessity' and blamed the Ansars for the nation's ills. Though well armed, the Ansars suffered a decisive defeat on Aba Island in June 1970 and between fifteen and twenty thousand of them were massacred. Sadiq al-Mahdi was exiled, but returned in 1977 and in 1985 became Prime Minister. The Umma Party, a conservative party, was based on the Ansar Religious Brotherhood and the Mahdi family. In effect, the Umma Party *is* the Ansar movement.

Anti-Apartheid Movement, international movement based in London and founded (1959) after Chief Albert *LUTHULI appealed for an international boycott of South Africa. It has mobilized world opinion against *APARTHEID and helped persuade prominent firms to quit South Africa. It supports the oil and arms sanctions and the expulsion of South Africa from international bodies. Apartheid lives on, but the South African authorities have reacted to international pressure by limited relaxations of apartheid, notably in sport, and by discouraging the use of the word 'apartheid'.

Aouita, Said, Moroccan athlete and Olympic champion. Born in Casablanca in 1961, Aouita is one of a handful of athletes to transcend what were considered the boundaries of their sport. Unassailable over 5000 metres, of which he is the world and Olympic champion, he won both the 800 metres and 1500 metres at the Seoul Olympics in 1988. He was the first person to break the thirteen-minute barrier for 5000 metres and the first man for forty-five years to hold both the 1500 and 5000 metres world records simultaneously. In addition, he is one of only four men to break three minutes thirty seconds for the 1500 metres.

Aouzou Strip, a large area of land in northern Chad which has been the subject of dispute between Chad and Libya. This strip, 1040 km long by 80 km wide, contains valuable iron ore and uranium deposits but Libya occupied it in 1975 on legal grounds. The LIbya-Chad boundary had been agreed to by France and Libya in 1919. However, an agreement between France and Italy in 1935 – Italy had colonized Libya – would have given Libya and not Chad, the Aouzou Strip. The treaty had not been ratified when World War Two broke out in 1939 and it was never implemented. Libya's occupation of this remote, sparsely populated desert territory is likely to become permanent. The dispute went almost unnoticed until Libyan forces advanced deeper into Chad in 1983 and became embroiled in the Chad civil war.

apartheid, Afrikaans word meaning separateness, but which the South African authorities prefer to call separate development. Idealistic supporters see apartheid as a blueprint for a future in which different groups can maintain their own racial and cultural identities in separate southern African states living in harmony with each other. Its opponents and some supporters see it as a blueprint for the continuation of white supremacy in South Arica.

After the *NATIONAL PARTY won power in 1948 apartheid became official policy and the concept behind a wide ranging programme of political, economic, social and cultural separation. The *MIXED MARRIAGES ACT and the *IMMORALITY ACT were repealed (1985) and there has been some relaxation of apartheid in sport and public amenities; the Separate Amenities Act was scrapped in 1990. Yet apartheid will continue as long as the *BANTU EDUCATION ACT, the *GROUP AREAS ACT, *PASS LAWS, population registration and the *HOMELANDS remain. Non-whites have suffered great hardship from apartheid, often losing their jobs and their homes and being removed to the homelands which are too small and too poor to give them a decent life. The homelands appear to have been organized as pools of cheap labour for neighbouring white-run industries to exploit.

Economic pressures within South Africa, domestic and international protests and international sanctions, persuaded President P.W. *BOTHA to discourage the use of the word 'apartheid', to modify the system and even to argue that it is as dead as a dodo. The *CONSERVATIVE PARTY, the official opposition, disagrees; after its successes in local elections in the Transvaal (1988) it reimposed strict apartheid in a number of municipalities. The government has accepted that apartheid is the focus of massive international opposition to South Africa and therefore the major source of South Africa's international difficulties. In April 1990 President *DE KLERK made a speech promising to amend or repeal the remaining pillars of apartheid. He specifically referred to the Group Areas Act, the Land Act, the Separate Amenities Act and the Population Registration Act.

Arab League In 1945, the British government, still a powerful voice in the Arab world, encouraged seven nations to form the Arab League. They were Lebanon, Egypt, Syria, Iraq, Transjordan, Saudi Arabia and Yemen. Later, these founder members were joined by Algeria, Libya, Tunisia, Mauritania, Morocco, Somalia, Kuwait, Oman, Qatar, Bahrain, Sudan and United Arab Emirates. When Yemen divided into North Yemen and South Yemen both countries joined afresh. The *PALESTINE LIBERATION ORGANIZATION (PLO) was admitted as a member and the last to join was Djibouti, in 1977.

In 1945 the League's principal stated aims were to strengthen ties among the participant states and to produce closer co-operation economically, culturally and in communications. By 1947, the League was preoccupied with termination of the British mandate over Palestine and an end to Jewish emigration to Palestine, the western part of which became Israel in 1948. From that time the League became so obsessed with support for the PLO and the destruction of Israel that it neglected its work in other fields. In 1953 the members signed the Arab League Collective Security Pact but it had little significance and was never invoked. In 1978 the League committed itself to a donation of $250 million a year to the PLO but few states have paid their contributions.

For many years the League's headquarters were in Cairo but when Egypt, through President *NASSER, signed a peace treaty with Israel in 1979 they were moved to Tunis in protest against the treaty. Egypt's membership was suspended. The expulsion of Egypt seriously hurt the League. Egypt, besides being by far the leading Arab country, had been the organization's principal sponsor and founder. The relocation of the General Secretariat to Tunis disrupted operations. Egypt refused to co-operate and many vital documents remained in Cairo. The League also lost many of its most valued employees. Egypt was readmitted to the League in 1989.

The League operates through a Supreme Council and the General Secretariat and speaks through its Secretary-General, Chedli Klibi. The organization arranges Arab summit conferences. Some of these conferences forge a consensus, others bring Arab divisions into sharp focus and set back the cause of unity. On balance, though, Arab League summits have contributed positively to the elaboration of a common strategy.

Numerous specialized autonomous agencies are associated with the League. They include the Tunis-based Arab League Educational, Cultural and Scientific Organization (ALESCO), the Baghdad-based Arab Labour Organization and the Amman-based Arab Organization for Standardization and Metrology. Other specialized agencies include an Arab Postal Union, and an Arab States Broadcasting Union, both Tunis-based.

In addition, *ad hoc* committees are frequently set up to restore good relations between members who are in dispute. Numerous bitter divisions in the Arab world result in the League's having little political strength but it has served its purpose as an information exchange and debating forum. In 1986 it launched its own communications satellite, Arabsat.

In 1987 the League became concerned that political enmities and hatreds within the Arab world were giving Arabs a bad reputation for lack of tolerance and an inability to settle their differences peacefully. It began a 'campaign of cordiality' to bring leaders together, if possible outside their own countries so that they could meet without confrontation. This happened in October 1989 when the League tried to find a way of ending the long-running war in Lebanon. It brought together, in Saudi-Arabia, all the parties involved in the war but failed to find a solution acceptable to the Christians of Lebanon.

However, in August 1990, any unity within the Arab League was destroyed when Saddam Hussein, the president of Iraq, invaded and annexed Kuwait. The Arab states then divided into three groups – anti-Iraq, pro-Iraq and neutralist. Of the African Arab stated, Egypt, Morocco, Somalia and Algeria joined the anti-Hussein alliance. Libya was at first pro–Iraq but then turned against it. Tunisia and Mauritania attempted a balancing act. Sudan's regime favoured Saddam Hussein but is dependent on Saudi Arabian finance so it tried to remain friendly with both sides. The damage done to Arab unity during this violent dispute led to the resignation of the secretary-general and it could well bring about the end of the Arab League.

Arab Socialist Union (ASU), Libyan movement founded in 1971 was the country's sole legitimate political party. Colonel *GADDAFI and his revolutionary colleagues intended it to radicalize Libyan society by channelling everybody's political energies into this one party. The ASU achieved this aim but it became redundant when 'popular' committees began to appear as a device to radicalize Libyan life still further. In 1975, the ASU was transformed into Libya's General People's Congress, which produced

a new national constitution. Since no political parties were now considered necessary, the ASU passed into oblivion.

Arusha Declaration (1967), expression of President *NYERERE's socialist ideals and a development plan which is incorporated into the Tanzanian constitution. The declaration has three main sections. One deals with human rights, another with the active role of the state in the economic life of the nation, the third is concerned with the policy of self-reliance and calls for hard work and dedication by the people and the leaders. There have been successes in the development of health care and education, but generally the authorities have been unable to carry out the ideals of the declaration. Party leaders were supposed to renounce private incomes; they did not. Despite technical and financial aid the *UJAMAA have not been in the forefront of rural development; they have proved expensive and inefficient. Tanzanians continue to forsake their farms for urban life. State control of the means of production has meant excessive bureaucracy, corruption and declining production. By the early 1980s it was clear that the socialism of the declaration had to be modified. Tanzania's severe economic problems compelled it to reduce state intervention in the economy and to adopt a more liberal attitude towards private enterprise.

assimilados, Portuguese word used to describe the Africans in the colonies of Angola, Mozambique

26

and Portuguese Guinea, whom the authorities considered civilized. By abandoning their traditional way of life, by speaking Portuguese fluently and by holding a suitable job these people were supposed to have assimilated the Portuguese way of life. They enjoyed the same political and civic rights as the 'whites' in the colonies. Less than one per cent of the Africans in Portugal's empire qualified as *assimilados*.

Authorized Person, hereditary office in Swaziland, usually held by one of the royal *DLAMINI clan. The holder speaks for tribal elders and can on occasion exercise significant power. In August 1983 the traditionalists used the power of the authorized person to oust Queen Regent *DZELIWE.

Awolowo, Chief Obafemi (1909–87), Nigerian politician, he was a journalist before being called to the Bar in London (1946). Back in Nigeria he practised law and became an influential leader in the campaign for independence. He argued that independent Nigeria should be a federation in which each ethnic group was free to have its own institutions. From 1951 he was the highly effective leader of the *ACTION GROUP, which represented the interests and concerns of the Yoruba people and the Western Region. He was elected to the Western Region House of Assembly (1951) and served as regional premier from 1954 to 1959, when he unsuccessfully contested the pre-independence federal elections.

As leader of the opposition to the federal government Chief Awolowo was frustrated at the way in which he and his party were excluded from any share of national power. He turned his attention back to the west and in 1962 quarrelled with *AKINTOLA, his successor as premier of the Western Region. After he persuaded the Action Group executive to sack Akintola, there was violence between the supporters of the two men in the Western Region House of Assembly. The federal government intervened and declared a state of emergency in the region.

In September 1962 Awolowo was arrested and charged with treasonable felony. After a dubious trial Awolowo was found guilty and sentenced to ten years in prison. He was pardoned and released by *GOWON (Aug. 1966) and served Gowon's military government as Federal Commissioner for Finance (1967–71). In 1971 he returned to his legal practice.

As the military stepped down he returned to politics and founded the *UPN (Unity Party of Nigeria) in 1978. In 1979 the party did well in the west and came second nationally. With 4.9 million votes Awolowo came second in the presidential race to *SHAGARI, who had 5.7 million votes. In 1981 he made an alliance with his old political rival, *AZIKIWE. They might have defeated Shagari in the 1983 election if they had not both insisted on standing for the presidency and split the anti-Shagari vote. Awolowo was second again – with nearly 8 million votes. After the coup at the end of 1983 he retired from politics.

AWOONOR

Awoonor, Kofi (b. 1935), Ghanaian poet and playwright who became his country's ambassador to Brazil in 1983. He worked for the Ghanaian Ministry of Information (1964–7) and followed an academic career in Ghana and the United States. His writing has been greatly influenced by African oral tradition. His play. *Night of My Blood* (1971), mourns the loss of Africa's identity. The poems in *Ride Me, Memory* (1973) give a vivid picture of his experiences in the United States. In 1975 he was arrested and imprisoned by the military government for harbouring a fugitive; the poems in *The House by the Sea* (1978) reflect the bitterness of his year in prison. In 1984 he published *The Ghana Revolution* and a collection of folk tales – *Fire in the Valley*.

Azania, Graeco–Persian word dating from the first century AD. Then it referred to the coast of East Africa and meant land of the blacks. In the 1960s the *PAN-AFRICANIST CONGRESS chose it as their name for South Africa and this name is generally used by supporters of black liberation.

Azanian People's Organization (AZAPO), a black South African liberation movement founded in 1978. Rejecting white values and help from sympathetic whites in the struggle against *APARTHEID, it supports the idea of *BLACK CONSCIOUSNESS. As a revolutionary black movement it has been actively involved in protests in South Africa and it has clashed with the more moderate *AFRICAN NATIONAL CONGRESS (ANC).

AZAPO joined like-minded groups in the *NATIONAL FORUM in 1983. It disagrees with the decision of the ANC to enter into a dialogue with the South African government in 1990.

Azikiwe, Chief Nnamdi (b. 1904), veteran Nigerian political leader popularly known as Zik. He was born in northern Nigeria, but his parents were Ibo from the east. After studying and lecturing in the United States (1921–34) and editing a newspaper in Accra (1935–8), he returned to Nigeria and started a daily newspaper – *The West African Pilot*. In 1944 he was joint founder of the *NCNC (National Council of Nigeria and the Cameroons), which mainly represented the interests and concerns of the Ibo and the Eastern Region. After a general strike in 1945 Zik's newspapers were banned by the government and he alleged there was a plot to assassinate him.

As constitutional arrangements were discussed Azikiwe argued for more rapid progress to independence. He favoured one central government or a strong federal government which would share the revenues from the different regions equally throughout the country. Following his election success (1952), he became Premier of the Eastern Region (1954–9). He was President of the Senate (1960), the first Governor-General of independent Nigeria (1960–3) and the first President of the Republic (1963–6).

During the civil war (1967–70) he supported *BIAFRA, and then spent most of the 1970s quietly in Onitsha.

Back in politics as the *NPP (Nigerian People's Party) candidate, he came third in the 1979 presidential election. Azikiwe and his party briefly co-operated with President Shagari's government until this understanding was terminated in July 1981. Azikiwe and the NPP then made an electoral alliance with the leading opposition party – *AWOLOWO's Unity Party of Nigeria (*UPN). There were hopes that the two old rivals would work together to defeat Shagari, but neither would step down for the other in the 1983 presidential elections. Both stood, enabling Shagari to win; Azikiwe came third again. He formally retired from politics in 1986.

B

Babangida, Maj.-Gen. Ibrahim
Gbadamosi (b. 1941), military
ruler and President of Nigeria since
August 1985. A Muslim from central
Nigeria, he was commissioned in the
Nigerian Army (1963) and as a battalion commander played an important part in the Biafran civil war
(1967–70). He was also credited with
disarming the leader of the abortive
coup of February 1976 and helping
*OBASANJO to regain control from
the conspirators.

In 1983 he became a major-general
and after the coup at the end of the
year he became Chief of Staff under
General *BUHARI (1984). Buhari's
authoritarianism and his unpopular
austerity measures did nothing to
solve the country's economic problems, but prompted Babangida to
oust Buhari in a bloodless coup
and to take office as President
and Commander-in-Chief of the
Nigerian Armed Forces (Aug. 1985).

In office Babangida has carefully
avoided being too closely identified
with factionalism and he has not been
too concerned with the trappings of
power. He can be ruthless and his
pragmatism may ensure his survival
in power until Nigeria returns to
civilian rule in 1992. His two most
pressing concerns are the economy
and arrangements for a return to
civilian rule. He hopes that his
structural adjustment programme
will lead to economic recovery
by imposing austerity, making the
public sector more efficient, cutting inflation and promoting self-
sufficiency. His austerity measures
and a declining standard of living for
most Nigerians have caused unrest –
in May 1989 there were a hundred
deaths in riots against his economic
policies.

In carrying out his promise to
return Nigeria to civilian rule in 1992
Babangida has run into problems.
The local government elections in
1987 were chaotic. The constituent
assembly has made limited progress
and Babangida caused consternation
by scrapping existing political parties and setting up two of his own
(Oct. 1989). These are to be the
only parties contesting the elections
in the run up to civilian rule. One he
described as a little to the left and the
other a little to the right of centre. On
the last day of 1989 he reshuffled his
cabinet, dismissing the most influential Christian from his two posts and
replacing him by Muslims. This led
to protests by Christians against the
policy of giving top jobs to Muslims
and forced him to postpone his official visit to the United States. It
is very difficult to predict whether
Babangida will go down in history as
the national leader who put Nigeria
on the path to recovery or as yet
another leader who disappointed the
hopes of his countrymen.

Babu, Abdul Rahman, exiled radical Tanzanian politician from *ZAN-
ZIBAR, founder of *UMMA (1963). As

a member of Tanzania's government from 1964 he was critical of President *NYERERE's slow progress on the path to socialism. He was suspected of involvement in the assassination of Abeid *KARUME (1972) and detained until President Nyerere declared an amnesty (1978). In exile he continued to urge the adoption of socialism in Tanzania.

Bagaza, Col. Jean-Baptiste (b. 1946), former President of Burundi who gave his country a measure of political stability for eleven years. One of the dominant Tutsi people, Bagaza was educated in Belgium before joining the Burundi army. He was deputy Chief of Staff when he seized power from President *MICOMBERO in a bloodless coup (Nov. 1976). During Bagaza's years of power (1976–87) the Tutsi military elite continued to rule Burundi, although he did make some attempt to reconcile the Hutu majority with his regime. Bagaza became increasingly authoritarian and quarrelled with the Catholic Church. His regime was criticized by Amnesty International and other bodies for its abuse of human rights. He made no progress in dealing with Burundi's worsening economic problems; it was probably discontent in the army that prompted the coup which ousted him (Sep. 1987) and sent him into exile in Belgium.

bairro, Portuguese word meaning neighbourhood. The *bairro* is the basic unit of political and social organization in independent Angola. *Bairro* committees organize local schools, health, food co-operatives, and disseminate information and political education.

Bakara, Djibo (b. 1922), Niger politician who founded the Parti Progressiste Nigérien, the Niger section of the *RASSEMBLEMENT DÉMOCRATIQUE AFRICAIN (RDA). He then split with the RDA and left his own PPN to form yet another organization, the Union Démocratique Nigerienne (UDN) in 1951. It was a radical group, close to the French Communist Party. In the referendum of that year, Bakara opposed President de Gaulle's proposal that Niger become part of the French Community. The proposal was affirmed by the referendum and Bakara, politically isolated and with his life threatened, went into exile.

Balewa, Alhaji Sir Abubakar Tafawa (1912–66), politician who led Nigeria to independence. A Muslim from the northeast he qualified as a teacher (1933) and studied education at London University (1945–6). Back in Nigeria he was an education officer, but soon began his political career as a member of the Central Legislative Council (1947–52). In 1951 Balewa joined Sir Ahmadu *BELLO in transforming the *NPC (Northern People's Congress) into a political party under Bello's leadership. Balewa became deputy leader and served as Minister of Works in the central government (1952–4) and as Federal Minister of Transport (1954–7).

After further constitutional changes Balewa, the leader of the NPC in the Federal House of Representatives,

31

took office as Nigeria's first prime minister (1957). He was at the head of a coalition government which he hoped would ensure a smooth transition to independence. After the NPC's success in the 1959 pre-independence elections he formed a coalition with the *NCNC (National Council of Nigeria and the Cameroons) and led Nigeria to independence (Oct. 1960).

As prime minister of an important African state Balewa enjoyed considerable international prestige and was respected as a moderate and pragmatic leader by Britain and other western countries. In Nigeria his attempts to build a stable and prosperous country were thwarted by religious, economic, social and ethnic rivalries. While a corrupt few became rich and powerful, the low-paid workers and the unemployed suffered. In desperation they went on strike in 1963 and 1964.

The constitutional powers of the regions hampered the federal government and there were particular problems in the Western Region where the federal opposition party, the *ACTION GROUP, was in power. Balewa's attempts to exploit the factional divisions in the Action Group backfired and provoked conflicts with his coalition partner – the NCNC. Balewa's position was further weakened because he was deputy leader of the NPC and had to defer to the party leader, Sir Ahmadu Bello.

The political crisis intensified after the 1963 census showed an unexpectedly high population count in the Muslim north. Fearing Muslim domination, the NCNC withdrew from the coalition with the NPC. Revelations of malpractice in 1964 federal elections further discredited Balewa's government. The final blow to the government came from the Western Region where the blatantly corrupt and rigged regional elections (Oct. 1965) were followed by months of turmoil and violence. Balewa's government was unable to restore law and order; so the army intervened (Jan. 1966) and staged a military coup during which Balewa was assassinated.

Bamangwato (the Ngwato people), a Tswana-speaking *BANTU people, the largest of Botswana's eight ethnic groups. They make up one-third of the country's population. Chief Khama III did much to establish their power in the nineteenth century and Sir Seretse *KHAMA, the first president of independent Botswana, was Khama III's descendant and hereditary chief of the Bamangwato.

Banana, The Reverend Canaan Sodindo (b. 1936), a teacher and a minister who became first President of Zimbabwe (1980–7). A founder member of the *AFRICAN NATIONAL COUNCIL (1971), he was a prominent campaigner against the proposed internal settlement of 1971. After some time in the United States (1973–5) he returned to Zimbabwe where he was arrested and imprisoned. After his release (1976) he was allowed to attend a conference in Geneva, where he announced he was joining *ZANU. Back in Zimbabwe he was arrested and detained for eighteen months (1978–9). He held the ceremonial post of President of Zimbabwe until his resignation when the constitutional changes of 1987 brought in an executive presidency.

Banda, Dr Hastings Kamuzu (b. 1906) (his date of birth may have been as early as 1898 but his age seems to be a state secret). President of Malawi since 1966, he is revered by his people despite the authoritarian and sometimes brutal nature of his regime. The Malawi media refer to him by the godlike title of Ngwazi – an African designation meaning saviour and conqueror. He is an elder of the Church of Scotland and he has imposed many of his puritanical ideas on Malawi. Men are not allowed to grow their hair long and women's skirts must be below the knee. Films, books and magazines are strictly censored.

A farmer's son, Banda went to mission school before working as a clerk on a South African gold mine. He then spent twelve years qualifying and practising as a doctor in the United States. While he practised in London during the 1940s and early 1950s his home was a meeting place for radical African nationalists and intellectuals. He then worked in Ghana (1954–58) until Henry *CHIPEMBERE and other young Malawian nationalists persuaded him to return home to lead the *NYASALAND AFRICAN CONGRESS in its struggle against the *CENTRAL AFRICAN FEDERATION.

Banda's relentless campaign for secession from the Federation had massive support in the country. The authorities declared a state of emergency (1959), banned the Nyasaland African Congress and imprisoned Banda and other nationalist leaders. Banda's supporters founded the *MALAWI CONGRESS PARTY (MCP) in 1959 and continued their campaign. Realizing the depth of hostility to the federation, Britain secured Banda's release (1960) and the end of the state of emergency. Banda then led the MCP to victory in the 1961 elections and self government in 1962. After the dissolution of the federation at the end of 1963 he led Malawi to independence (1964) and served as independent Malawi's first prime minister (1964–6). When Malawi became a republic (1966) Banda took office as Executive President – and as Life–President since 1971. Banda has strengthened his power by holding most of the important ministries as well as being Life-President of the Malawi Congress Party – the only legal party since 1966.

Since independence Banda's conservative policies have surprised and infuriated his neighbours. He has rejected African socialism in favour of private enterprise and relied on expatriate skills instead of encouraging rapid Africanization. He has adopted a pro-Western stance and established diplomatic relations with South Africa, even exchanging official visits (1970–71). With technical and financial help from South Africa he has built a new capital at Lilongwe and has developed Malawi's agriculture to achieve self-sufficiency in food and foreign currency earnings from tobacco, tea and sugar exports.

During the 1980s Banda made some attempt to improve relations with his neighbours; he joined the *SOUTHERN AFRICAN DEVELOPMENT CO-ORDINATION CONFERENCE and established diplomatic relations with Tanzania, Zambia and Zimbabwe. Good relations with Malawi's neighbours have been soured by his refusal to attend Zimbabwe's independence celebrations, by the kidnapping of Orton and Vera *CHIRWA and their son from Zambian soil (1981) and by the aid Malawi has given to *RENAMO (Mozambican rebels).

Banda has exercised strong personal control over Malawi and acted ruthlessly both against his radical opponents and his potential successors. He crushed invasions by his former colleagues Henry Chipembere (1965) and Yatuto Chisiza (1967). In 1977 he hanged Albert *NQUMAYO, Secretary-General of the MCP, for treason. During the 1970s he attacked or drove into exile the thousands of Jehovah's Witnesses who refused to join the MCP. One possible successor, Gwanda Chakuamba, was jailed for twenty-two years (1981) and another, Dick *MATENJE, died in a mysterious car crash (1983). Orton and Vera Chirwa have been imprisoned for life.

Most Malawians seem to find Banda's violation of human rights less significant than his devotion to their cause and his vital role in leading them to independence. Despite his great age he has kept such a firm grip on power that there is no heir apparent. Malawi's future after Banda's death is uncertain.

banning order, method of silencing opponents used by the authorities in South Africa and Namibia. Introduced in the *SUPPRESSION OF COMMUNISM ACT (1950) and later incorporated into the *INTERNAL SECURITY ACT (1982), a banning order is a form of house arrest which severely restricts the freedom of the banned person. Conditions vary, but a banned person may not be allowed to change residence, to attend meetings, to join associations, nor to visit educational institutions, newspaper offices, publishers, airports and harbours. They cannot be quoted and may have to obey curfews and report to the police regularly. The South African authorities say an appeal can be made against a banning order, but nobody has appealed successfully.

Bantu means people, it refers to the predominant group of languages in southern and central Africa and to the five hundred or more negroid peoples who speak Bantu and have certain cultural similarities. In South Africa the term is officially used to refer to black people. There the Bantu are divided into four major groups; about 60 per cent are Nguni (including Zulu, Ndebele, Swazi, Xhosa), 32 per cent Sotho, 5 per cent Tsonga and 2 per cent Venda. In pursuance of *APARTHEID South Africa has established ten different Bantu *HOMELANDS; in theory these will all achieve real independence.

Bantu Education Act (1953), a pillar of South Africa's *APARTHEID legislation, it set up a separate educational system for blacks under strict government control. The author of the act, Dr *VERWOERD, made it clear that blacks should not be educated up to the level of whites. In the late 1970s, in the wake of the *SOWETO uprising, the system was improved and the Bantu Education Department became the Department of Education and Training, but Bantu education is still inferior to the education of other races; in South Africa blacks have the highest pupil-teacher ratio and the lowest expenditure per pupil.

Barré, Muhammad Siad (b. *c.* 1919), ex-President of Somalia. Born in northern Somalia – he is probably several years older than his stated birthdate – Barré was educated at village schools and then at a military academy in Italy, when that country controlled Italian Somaliland. Between 1941 and 1950 he was a police officer, first under the Italians and then under the British. In 1960 he joined the Somali army as a colonel and within a few years was a major-general. On 21 October 1969 he led a bloodless coup which deposed the ineffectual President Abdelrashid Ali Shermarke. He ordered the ministers of the Supreme Revolutionary Council to adopt the designation *Jalle*, meaning Comrade. His Somali Socialist Revolutionary Party (SSRP) was to be the only legal party.

Barré at first favoured the Soviet bloc but switched allegiance to the West because it promised more aid than the Russians did. He did not appoint a prime minister and became increasingly authoritarian, dealing ruthlessly with any opposition to his rule. His frequent foreign tours showed that he felt politically secure at home. On 23 May 1986 he was badly injured when his presidential car smashed into a bus near Mogadishu. He suffered serious fractures to the head and chest and was flown to Jeddah, Saudi Arabia, for specialist treatment. It was then thought that a coup would overthrow him but none of his opponents dared make the attempt. In September 1986, the SSRP confirmed his appointment as president for a further seven years. Barré owed his survival, as always, to his ruthlessness and to his skill in manipulating his associates and opponents. Despite his political skills, in January 1991, after weeks of clan warfare, he was deposed and forced to flee, after twenty-one years' rule.

Basotho, Sesotho speaking *BANTU people living in Southern Africa. The 1.5 million people of Lesotho are almost all Basotho and many more Basotho live in the Republic of South Africa.

Basotho Congress Party (BCP), Lesotho's first modern political party, founded as the Basutoland African Congress by Ntsu *MOKHEHLE (1952). Initially aligned to the *AFRICAN NATIONAL CONGRESS in South Africa, it switched support to the *PAN-AFRICANIST CONGRESS. In the 1960 elections the party, then called the Basutoland Congress Party, won most of the seats in the National Council. The BCP's radical socialism alarmed the British authorities, the Catholic Church and South Africa who supported the other major political party, the *BASOTHO NATIONAL PARTY (BNP). Under the leadership of Chief *JONATHAN the BNP narrowly won the pre-independence elections (1965). With twenty-five of the sixty parliamentary seats the BCP went into opposition.

When it was clear that the BCP was winning the next election in 1970 Chief Jonathan staged a coup, declaring the election null and void and arresting BCP leaders. After an attempted coup (1974) the government hunted down BCP leaders. The party was involved in violent outbreaks in 1979. In 1981 it formed the *LESOTHO LIBERATION ARMY and with some help from South Africa launched the armed struggle against Chief Jonathan. When the military seized power (Jan. 1986) the BCP and other political parties were banned, but Mokhehle returned to Lesotho for talks with the Military Council in May 1988.

Basotho Democratic Alliance (BDA), Lesotho political party founded in 1984 to contest the 1985 elections which Chief *JONATHAN cancelled shortly before they were due. The BDA's first leader was Charles Molapo who had broken with Chief Jonathan in protest against diplomatic links with the communist world. The BDA also wanted to ban communism in Lesotho and to improve relations with South Africa. Chief Jonathan alleged that South Africa was plotting with the BDA to overthrow his government. In 1985 there was a leadership struggle which ended when Phoka Chaolane replaced Molapo as party leader. When the military seized power (Jan. 1986) the BDA and other political parties were banned.

Basotho National Party (BNP), Lesotho political party founded as the Basutoland National Party by Chief *JONATHAN (1959). As a conservative anti-communist party it had strong support from village chiefs and headmen but won only a few seats in the 1960 election. The British authorities, the Catholic Church and South Africa favoured the BNP which narrowly won the pre-independence election in 1965 and formed the government which led Lesotho to independence (1966).

The BNP government soon became unpopular and was losing the 1970 election when Chief Jonathan staged his coup by declaring the election null and void and suspending the constitution. Late in the 1970s plans to make the party Lesotho's only political party caused strong opposition. When the military seized power in Lesotho (Jan. 1986) the BNP and other political parties were banned.

Basters (Afrikaans word meaning bastards), a Namibian community of about twenty-five thousand people of mixed ancestry who live in the dry central Rehoboth area. They are mainly descended from Afrikaners and Malayan and Javanese slaves. Under South African rule the Basters were given a measure of self government. Concerned about their future in independent Namibia they have threatened to form their own separate state.

Basutoland (or Basutoland Protectorate), name for Lesotho when it was under British influence and protection from 1868 until independence in 1966. See *LESOTHO.

Basutoland Freedom Party, Lesotho political party (1961–3), founded by B. M. Khaketla who had been deputy president of the *BASOTHO CONGRESS PARTY (BCP). Members of the new party had been angered by the BCP's hostility to traditional rulers and Christianity. In 1963 the party merged with the *MAREMA-TLOU PARTY to form the *MAREMA-TLOU FREEDOM PARTY.

Bechuanaland (or Bechuanaland Protectorate), name given to Botswana when it was under British influence and protection in the nineteenth and twentieth centuries. On achieving independence (1966) the country became the Republic of Botswana. See BOTSWANA.

Bedouin, used as a synonym for 'Arab' in early societies in North Africa. The word also had a corollary meaning as 'raider'. Bedouin comes from the word 'Bedawiyin', meaning people who lived in the open country and deserts. In modern times the nomadic bedouin are the free men of the Arab world and they are difficult subjects to rule.

Because of their mobility and frequent raiding and skirmishing, the central government of each Arab country has, since 1945, decided that it is better to let the nomads go their own way with a minimum of governmental interference. Bedouin inhabit every Arab country in Africa, most notably Egypt, Tunisia, Algeria, Libya and Morocco. They are estimated to number five million.

Belgian Congo, name given to Zaire when it was a Belgian colony (1908–60). From 1876 King Leopold II of Belgium and his agents took control of large areas in the Congo basin. At the Berlin Conference (1884–5) King Leopold's claims to rule the 'Congo Free State' were formally recognised by the European powers. From 1885 to 1908 Leopold made a great fortune from the territory. International protests at the brutality of Leopold's regime persuaded him to hand over the territory to the Belgian government (1908). It was known as the Belgian Congo from 1908 until it achieved independence in 1960 as the Congo Republic (Kinshasa). In 1971 it was renamed Zaire by President *MOBUTU. See ZAIRE.

Bello, Alhaji Sir Ahmadu (1910–66), Sardauna of Sokoto, political leader and traditional ruler from Northern Nigeria. He was a Muslim and a grandson of Usman Dan Fodio, founder of the Fulani-Hausa Empire in the nineteenth century. He was appointed to represent Sokoto in the Northern House of Assembly (1949). He played a leading role in the remodelling of the *NPC (Northern

People's Congress) and became its leader (1951). When Nigeria became a federation (1954) Bello decided to stay in the north as Premier of the Northern Region (1954–66) while his deputy, Sir Abubakar Tafawa *BALEWA, led the NPC in the federal parliament and served as federal prime minister before and after independence (1957–66).

After independence politicians from the Eastern and Western Regions believed that Bello dominated the whole of Nigeria from his northern power base. They believed that the federal prime minister, Balewa, deferred to him as party leader and consulted him on many major federal issues. Bello was able to use his power to further the interests of the traditional rulers, the north and Islam at the expense of the rest of the country. When the army seized power (Jan. 1966) Bello was assassinated.

Ben Bella, Ahmed (b. 1918), one of the most significant figures in Algerian politics. Ben Bella was born at Marnia, near Oran. After an education in Oran he joined the French Army and during the 1940 campaign in France was awarded the Croix de Guerre. After the fall of France he was demobilized and sent home, but he rejoined a Moroccan regiment of the Free French Army and fought throughout the Italian campaign of 1943–4. He won the coveted Médaille Militaire, which was presented to him personally by General de Gaulle.

In 1945, now out of the army, Ben Bella joined the Mouvement pour le Triomphe des Libertés Démocratiques (MTLD) and by 1948 was leader of its military wing, the Organisation Spécial (OS). A dynamic leader, he built up OS until it comprised 4500 members before his capture by security forces in 1950. He was in prison until 1952 before escaping to become an organiser of the *FRONT DE LIBÉRATION NATIONALE (FLN). He helped to lead the 1954 uprising against the French, soon to become a full-blown war of independence. Two years later he was again captured and languished in a French prison until 1962. As Algeria became independent the interfactional struggle for power was intense but Ben Bella triumphed. He became the first President of the new Algeria, largely through the support of Houari *BOUMEDIENNE and the army.

Though charismatic and imaginative, Ben Bella was too individualistic to put together a coherent policy, though he clearly enough articulated his socialist leanings. His impulsiveness led him to interfere in the business of his ministers. In particular, he alienated his former friend Boumedienne, the Minister of Defence, who deposed him in a military coup in June 1965. Able and courageous, Ben Bella might well have continued in power beyond 1965 but he was essentially a loner, politically and psychologically.

Ben Bella was under house arrest for fifteen years. In 1979 he went into exile in Switzerland from where he continually tried to bring about an uprising in Algeria in the hope

BENIN

that it could lead to his return as President. In May 1984, he founded in Switzerland the Mouvement pour la Démocratie en Algérie and a year later he joined another original FLN member, Hocine Ait Ahmed, on a platform to advocate the establishment of a pluralist democratic regime.

He had to wait until June 1990 for the first democratic elections, when the new political freedoms – and a guarantee that he would not be arrested – enabled him to return to Algeria. Warmly welcomed in the country he had helped to free from colonialism, Ben Bella still wants to become president, but to many Algerians he is very much a figure now consigned to history.

Benguela Railway, Angolan railway line of great economic, strategic and political importance in Southern and Central Africa. The line runs 1350 kilometres through central Angola from the Atlantic port of Lobito to Luau on the border of Zaire. At Luau the line joins Zaire's railway network, which connects with the Zambian *COPPERBELT. Portugal built the line and earned lucrative revenues from the transport of copper and other minerals from Zaire and Zambia to the coast.

The line was closed in 1975 by the Angolan civil war; since then *UNITA has continually attacked the railway and allowed only very limited and spasmodic traffic in the 1980s. UNITA has offered to allow the line to reopen if it does not carry military equipment and

personnel, but the Angolan government was not then prepared to talk with UNITA. This closure suits South Africa which has backed UNITA and which wants to force Zaire and Zambia to send their exports through South Africa. The Angolan government wants to restore the line with its concomitant income. Zaire and Zambia want to use the Benguela Railway which is cheaper and quicker than the South African route. The *SOUTHERN AFRICAN DEVELOPMENT CO-ORDINATION CONFERENCE wants the railway to run efficiently to lessen the dependence of its members on South Africa.

Benin, with a narrow coastal base on the Bight of Benin, stretching 720 km into West Africa, to the Niger River. Benin falls naturally into three regions: a coastal belt, where the capital, Cotonou, is situated; the fertile central plateau; and a mountain range in the north. The country shares its borders with Togo, Burkina Faso, Niger and Nigeria. The people are of three major ethnic groups – the Yoruba, the Fon and Aja tribes, and the Bariba-Somba tribes. The country has the highest proportion in Africa of devotees of traditional religions – nearly 70 per cent. Christians and Muslims are almost evenly divided among the other 30 per cent.

Until 1894 the country was known as Abomey. In that year the colonizing French renamed it Dahomey. In 1946 the French declared Dahomey to be a French overseas territory, which gave it

39

The People's Republic of Benin

THE COUNTRY	THE PEOPLE	THE STATE
112,622 sq. km.	4.225 million	Multi-party presidential republic
Major Cities	*Ethnic Groups*	*Head of State*
Porto Novo (official capital)	Fon	Lt. Col. Mathieu Kérékou
Cotonou (administrative & economic capital)	Yoruba Bariba Somba	*Ruling Body* National Political
Grand Popo		Bureau of Parti de la
Ouidah	*Languages*	Révolution
Abomey	French (official)	Populaire du Benin
	Fon	(PRPB)
Economy	Yoruba	
Cotton, palm produce,	Bariba	*Official Party*
groundnuts, cocoa,	Dendi	Parti de la Révolution
coffee		Populaire du Benin
Sugar factories	*Religion*	
Cement works	Mainly traditional	
Tourism is potentially the	Christianity 17%	
largest source of foreign	Islam 15%	
currency.		
Principal Exports		
Coffee, cotton		
Currency		
CFA franc of 100		
centimes		

the right to send representatives to the French assemblies and to elect a local administrative council. Several political parties came into being, the most important being the Parti Progressiste Dahoméen (PPD) which favoured remaining in the French community. In common with most colonies in French black Africa, Dahomey gained independence in 1960, with Hubert Maga as its first president. Maga quarrelled with the vice-president, Apithy, and with Ahomadegbe, another tribal leader. This discord so damaged the new state's chances of stability that, in 1963, Colonel Christophe Soglo, the army commander, overthrew the government. For two years he preserved the fiction that he was not a dictator, merely an overseer, before forming the Comité de Rénovation Nationale (CRN) and taking supreme power. His administration endured only two years before Soglo was himself the victim of a coup. Colonel Alphonse Alley became president with Major Maurice Kouandète as prime minister. Alley, Kouandète and their ruling military committee soon asked Dr Émile Zinsou to form a civilian government. Zinsou lasted less than a year before Kouandète seized power in 1969 and announced that national unrest must end. His plan was that the three tribal leaders who had been so important in 1960 – Maga, Apithy and Ahomadegbe – should hold the presidency for two years each. The system fell apart within two years. On 22 October 1972, Major Mathieu *KÉRÉKOU seized power, created the National Council of the Revolution and promised sweeping economic, social and political reforms. While Kérékou at this time was virtually apolitical he was quickly influenced by the young intellectuals who supported him. It was their triumph, in November 1974, when Kérékou declared Dahomey to be a socialist state on Marxist–Leninist principles. Less than a year later, on 30 November 1975, Kérékou changed Dahomey, 'a misbegotten French name', into the Popular Republic of Benin.

Plots, assassinations and strikes followed but Kérékou held firm, created a Popular Militia, crushed political opposition and sought support from communist countries. He was wise enough to maintain links with France, which continued to be Benin's main trading partner. This did not prevent France, together with Morocco and Gabon, from

paying a force of eighty mercenaries to overthrow Kérékou. The attempt, in January 1977, failed and in frustration Gabon drove out the ten thousand Beninois who had been living in Libreville. One of Kérékou's responses was to bring in 'revolutionary dictatorship', with the Parti de la Révolution Populaire du Bénin (PRPB), holding all power. Kérékou's form of dictatorship was benign and for the first time the people had constitutional rights, including equality for all tribes.

On 6 February 1980, the 336 members of the Revolutionary National Assembly elected Kérékou, now a colonel, as first President of Benin. Three years later he promoted himself to Brigadier-General, a rank he regarded as more befitting for a president. In July 1984 he was re-elected as he continued with the process of moving his own nominees into positions of authority. He strove for good relations with his neighbours but tensions erupted from time to time. In May 1985, Nigeria expelled 'alien' Beninois in order to ease its own unemployment problems. Nevertheless, Benin's links with other West African states have become stronger since 1980 and relations with France have improved. By mid-1988 Benin's co-operation with the Soviet Union and with Libya had strengthened. Presidents Kérékou and *GADDAFI signed an agreement which was to make Benin the centre of Libyan efforts to destabilize a number of pro-Western countries in the region, including Nigeria, Senegal, Niger and Gambia. For his

41

co-operation, Kérékou was promised almost $85 million by Gaddafi. The pro–Libyan foreign minister, Martin Azomino Dohou, regained control over Benin's foreign policy, which he had earlier lost in the wake of Kérékou's overtures to the West. Relations between Benin and the US deteriorated sharply in consequence.

The need to rescue Benin from its long economic stagnation has forced Kérékou's government to allow Nigeria and Niger to use Benin's ports and transport network. As a result, Cotonou is a rapidly developing commercial centre which earns much foreign currency. France is helping to improve the port of Cotonou and the railway system. Encouraged by the prospect of self-sufficiency in staple foods, the government began a 'national production campaign' in 1982. Oil, limestone and iron-ore deposits are on the verge of serious development, with Nigerian participation and international capital.

Benin is said to have more tourist sights per square kilometre than any other African country. Its two national parks are among the best in West Africa. The lake villages of Ganvie and So-Awa and the great old palaces of King Ghezo and King Glele in Abomey province are particular attractions now accessible to visitors.

Ben Jalloun, Tahar (b. 1944), the leading Maghrebi French-speaking novelist. Born in Fez, Morocco, Ben Jalloun first came to prominence in 1977 with *The Great Solitude*, a study of the sexual situation of immigrant workers in France. He went on to produce other works and in 1985 had a major success with *The Sand Child*, the story of an Arab girl raised as a boy by a father determined to have a male heir. *The Sand Child* sold 200,000 copies in France and was translated into fifteen languages. Ben Jalloun wrote *The Sacred Night* to satisfy readers who had wanted to know the sand child's fate when she grew up. In 1988, this novel brought Ben Jalloun the *Prix Goncourt*, France's most prestigious literary award. The Paris newspaper, *Le Monde*, commented, 'The Moroccan novelist brings a whiff of youth into French writing by reviving the ancient tradition of Arab story-telling. With him the language of Racine and Balzac is put at the service of the oriental story.' To others, Ben Jalloun's role is sociological as well as literary. To them he is the voice of those who have no voice.

Benjedid, Chadli (b. 1929), Algerian head of state from 1979. Born in Algiers, Benjedid was educated in Arab and French-speaking schools and was active in politics from an early age. A member of the Mouvement pour le Triomphe des Libertés Démocratiques (MTLD), founded by the revolutionary, Hadd Messali, he joined the war of liberation against the French in 1955 and became a battalion commander of the *FRONT DE LIBÉRATION NATIONALE (FLN) forces. Captured by the French in 1961, he remained in prison until the war ended a year later. Appointed to command a military region in independent Algeria in 1963, he became involved in the army plot, led by Houri *BOUMEDIENNE, to depose Ahmed *BEN BELLA. On becoming president, Boumedienne appointed Benjedid a member of the ruling Revolutionary Council. By 1978, having risen through the army's ranks, he had become Co-ordinator of the Armed Forces, virtually equivalent to chief-of-staff.

On Boumedienne's death, in 1979, Benjedid succeeded to the presidency. He posthumously rehabilitated many of the old guard, many of whom had been his friends, liquidated by Boumedienne. Benjedid made some economic and social reforms and though they were limited they aroused the anger of Islamic fundamentalists. A mild-mannered man, Benjedid seemed to many people to be more professorial than soldierly, yet he used the army to crush street riots in October 1988. His reputation for liberalism suffered as a result. Some of his most bitter opponents criticize Benjedid for 'abandoning' the *POLISARIO guerrillas in the *WESTERN SAHARA in favour of a settlement with King *HASSAN of Morocco. Regarded as a moderate among Arab leaders, Benjedid has had generally good relations with both the Western world and the Soviet bloc.

Berbers, the original inhabitants of what is now Morocco and Algeria. Even in 1989, Morocco was still 40 per cent Berber and Algeria 25 per cent Berber. Because the Berbers have no written language of their own they use the Arabic script, but they do have a distinctive spoken language. Differences between Berbers and Arabs are complex. While Arabs generally dominate the coastal plains and lowlands, the Berber strongholds are in the Rif, Middle Atlas, Kabylia and Aures Mountains. Berbers speak at least three distinct dialects and have little of cultural or political cohesion. Their communal allegiance is to a tribe or region rather than to any 'Berber nation'. They have no clear central authority and no authoritarian political structure, yet they participate fully in national life and do not threaten Morocco or Algeria with the kind of communal conflict that has occurred elsewhere in Africa.

Beti, Mongo (b. 1932), a novelist born as Alexandre Biyidi in French-ruled Cameroun. From school in Yaoundé, Beti went to France (1951) where he graduated and taught for about twenty years. He is a controversial writer who has bitterly criticized not only colonial rule, but also the governments of independent Africa – in particular the *AHIDJO government in Cameroon, which he last visited in 1959 and where many of his novels have been banned. His study of Cameroon after independence, *Main basse sur le Caméroun* (1972), was banned in France for many years. Beti's best known novel *Le Pauvre Christ de Bomba* (1956) created a furore in Paris by satirizing French colonial administration and Catholic missions in Africa. Since 1978 Beti has been the publisher of a radical journal in France – *Peuples Noirs, Peuples Africains*.

Biafra, name given to the Eastern Region of Nigeria when Lt.-Col. *OJUKWU proclaimed its secession from the Federal Republic of Nigeria (May 1967), three days after *GOWON proposed dividing Nigeria into twelve states. This would have broken up the regions and given control of rich oil deposits to non-Ibo minorities in the Eastern Region. Tension between the Eastern Region and the federal government had mounted since northern military officers had seized power in July 1966. Many Ibo had been murdered in the north and many more had returned home to the Eastern Region from all parts of Nigeria. The federal government was determined to end what it saw as a rebellion and two and a half years of civil war followed (1967–70).

The 'Biafrans' fought determinedly and desperately; they had able leaders and many feared genocide. They successfully campaigned for international support. Hoping to split one of Africa's most powerful nations, South Africa, Rhodesia and Portugal gave their support – so did France. Gabon, the Ivory Coast, Tanzania and Zambia recognized the 'Biafran' regime. Despite many protests in Britain, the British government supported the federal government.

The superior resources and determination of the federal government won the day. Gradually it tightened its grip on the region and starved it into submission. There were an estimated 100,000 military casualties, but up to two million died of starvation and disease. When the 'Biafrans' surrendered (Jan. 1970), Gowon treated them leniently and adopted a policy of national reconciliation.

Biko, Steve (1946–77), black South African nationalist and a founder of *BLACK CONSCIOUSNESS. Politically active since his days as a university student, Biko was arrested and detained on a number of occasions. He was arrested for the last time in August 1977 and died in prison of brain injuries in September 1977. His death caused a worldwide outcry and he has been regarded as a martyr for his cause. *Cry Freedom*, a major film has been made about Biko and popular songs have been written and become anthems. Despite international concern the South African government has still not made the circumstances of his death public.

Binaisa, Godfrey Lukwongwa (b. 1920), ex-President of Uganda. He studied at *MAKERERE University before being called to the Bar in London. While practising law in Uganda (1956–62) he joined the Uganda National Congress and then the *UGANDA PEOPLE'S CONGRESS. Binaisa served as Attorney-General (1962–7) in President *OBOTE's government, but resigned in protest when Obote imposed a new constitution without consulting the electorate. He returned to private practice in Uganda and, after *AMIN's coup (1971), in New York.

After Amin fell (Apr. 1979) Binaisa returned to Uganda and during the preparations for the 1980 elections succeeded Professor *LULE as President of Uganda (Jun. 1979). President Binaisa had little success in his campaign against the tribal factionalism which was tearing his country apart and he was unable to cope with mounting violence and rocketing inflation. He was deposed by the armed forces (May 1980) and was a virtual prisoner until President Obote ordered his release shortly after winning the December 1980 election.

Black Consciousness, a political creed first clearly expressed by *BIKO and his associates in the late 1960s. It maintains that only blacks can win the struggle against *APART-HEID and it rejects co-operation with sympathetic whites because whites are a major part of the problem. 'Black man, you are on your own' most clearly summarizes the movement's attitude. In the *SOWETO uprising (1976–7) Black Consciousness exerted great influence, which led to the banning of key Black Consciousness organizations (Oct. 1977). Since then new organizations, notably *AZANIAN PEOPLE'S ORGANIZATION, have been formed. Various Black Consciousness bodies came together in the *NATIONAL FORUM (1983).

Black Sash, liberal South African organization whose members wear black sashes while they stand in silence to mourn and to protest against violations of human rights by the South African government. It began as the Women's Defence of the Constitution League (1955), formed to campaign against the removal of *COLOURED voters from the common voters' roll. The Press nicknamed it the Black Sash Movement. Initially its members were white women, but it is now open to women of all races resident in South Africa. Since 1986 Mary Burton has been the movement's president. Black Sash protests have greatly embarrassed the South African authorities by focusing national and international attention on their disregard for social, civil and political rights.

black spots, South African term used to describe parts of the proclaimed white areas where blacks live. Because it is against the laws of *APARTHEID for a black to live in a white area the black spots are disposed of by forcibly removing black residents – whatever claims to residence the black people might have.

Boer, word of Dutch origin meaning farmer and used to describe the Afrikaners – white South Africans descended from early Dutch, French Protestant and German arrivals in South Africa. They speak Afrikaans which resembles modern Flemish and eighteenth-century Dutch. Most Boers belong to one of the strict Calvinist churches in South Africa.

Boesak, Revd Dr Allan (b. 1946), *COLOURED South African clergyman, a courageous and outspoken critic who has gained international recognition for his attacks on *APARTHEID and the South African government. As President of the World Alliance of Churches he persuaded it to declare that apartheid was a sin and to suspend from

45

its membership the *NEDERDUITSE GEREFORMEERDE KERK (Dutch Reformed Church) in 1982. His own Calvinist church has declared apartheid a heresy. A founder and patron of the *UNITED DEMOCRATIC FRONT, Dr Boesak was arrested during the state of emergency imposed in 1985. Early in 1988 he joined Archbishop *TUTU and other church leaders in protesting against the banning of bodies critical of the government. In July 1990, after revelations of an extra-marital affair, Boesak resigned his ministry and announced he would make himself available for a career in politics.

Bokassa, Jean Bedel (b. 1921), former head of state of Central African Republic (CAR). After education in Christian mission schools, Bokassa joined the French army in 1939, became a sergeant and was commissioned lieutenant in 1956. He was still only a lieutenant when appointed chief-of-staff in 1962, a meteoric advance which he owed to his close family relationship with David *DACKO, first president of CAR. In 1962 he led the coup which deposed Dacko and declared himself president. He retained this title until 1976, when he declared a 'revolution' and boasted that he was modelling CAR on Libya. Within weeks he went much further than *GADDAFI and announced that he was to be the 'emperor'. The expensive coronation on 4 December 1977, and all that went with it – including a palace – might have seemed comical except that the Bokassa regime was now notorious for waste, corruption and cruelty.

In January 1979 Bokassa handed down an Imperial Order for schoolchildren to buy uniforms from Bokassa's own clothing factory. Facing massive unrest that month, Bokassa used Zairean troops to quell disturbances in which about 350 people died. He had taken the precaution of withdrawing all ammunition from his own army, other than the 'Imperial Guard'. Becoming increasingly megalomaniacal, Bokassa ordered the Guard to take action against supposed ringleaders of protest movements. The soldiers arrested 700 teenagers in Bangui. On 17–19 April 1979 about 120 of these young people were beaten and tortured to death, with Bokassa personally butchering some of the victims. When France withdrew monetary support, Bokassa flew to Libya to beg for Gaddafi's support. In his absence, David Dacko led a coup and Bokassa fled first to France and then to Ivory Coast. In 1986 he was taken back to Bangui to be tried for many crimes including massacre. He was sentenced to life imprisonment.

Bongo, Albert-Bernard (Omar) (b. 1935), President of Gabon since 1967. He was a civil servant and served in the air force before joining the Ministry of Foreign Affairs (1960). After gaining President *M'BA's confidence and holding various ministerial posts he became vice-president (Mar. 1967) and succeeded to the presidency when M'Ba died (Nov. 1967). Soon after coming to power he made Gabon a one party state and founded its only legal party, the *PDG. President Bongo has maintained political stability for over twenty years, despite coup plots and protests against his government. Harsh austerity measures, particularly those imposed in 1986, have made him unpopular. His opponents have accused him of corruption and condemned his authoritarian rule. In May 1990 his authority was challenged by demonstrations in Port Gentil and Libreville. France sent in the Foreign Legion to protect her nationals, but is apparently unwilling to use force to keep Bongo in power.

Bophuthatswana, a South African *HOMELAND, set aside for the Tswana people, it was declared 'independent' in December 1977, a status not recognised outside South Africa. It covers 44,000 sq. km. in seven scattered landlocked enclaves surrounded by South Africa and Botswana. In the 1980 census its resident population was 1.3 million, with a further 1.2 million citizens living in South Africa. In 1986 it was agreed with South Africa that those living and working permanently in South Africa would be entitled to South African citizenship. Bophuthatswana's economy is based on agriculture, mining and tourism – in addition to help from South Africa. It has rich platinum deposits to exploit, and the entertainments provided at Sun City have brought in lucrative revenues.

The Homeland has been governed by President Lucas Mangope since

its 'independence'. The government has been accused of corruption and brutality. It has been challenged by strikes and unrest. In February 1988 President Mangope was detained by dissident army officers until South African security forces rescued him; he had to call in South African forces again in March 1990 to quell protesters calling for his resignation and reintegration into a reformed South Africa. In November 1990 Chief Mangope accused members of the *AFRICAN NATIONAL CONGRESS of plotting against him and arrested over thirty of its leaders in Bophuthatswana.

BOSS, South African security service responsible for 'dirty tricks', clandestine operations and violence against opponents of the government in South Africa and other countries. It was renamed the Department of National Security (1981) and is now called the National Intelligence Service.

Botha, Pieter Willem (b. 1916), South African Prime Minister (1978–84) and Executive President (1984–9). As a young man he was a fierce advocate of the Afrikaner cause and a member of the pro-Nazi Ossewabrandwag (literally ox-wagon guard). As a *NATIONAL PARTY MP from 1948 and as *VERWOERD's Minister of Community Development and Coloured Affairs (1961–6) he was an extremist supporter of *APARTHEID who made the purity and supremacy of the Afrikaner his great aim. As Minister of Defence in *VORSTER's government (1966–78) and during his own government (1978–80) he earned a reputation for his toughness and for not hesitating to mount armed incursions against South Africa's neighbours. He ran the armed forces efficiently and made them into an up to date and formidable fighting machine.

When he became prime minister he surprised many with his apparent moderation and his warning that white South Africans must 'adapt or die'. His insistence on reforms to broaden support for the government and to lessen the danger of revolution infuriated right-wing elements in the National Party who broke away to form the *CONSERVATIVE PARTY (1982). He repealed the *IMMORALITY ACT and the *MIXED MARRIAGES ACT and allowed black trade unions and racially mixed political parties. In 1984 his constitutional reforms gave a limited share of political power to *COLOUREDS and *INDIANS in their separate houses of parliament and the chance of places in the cabinet, but the blacks had no part in this limited experiment in power-sharing.

From 1985 any faint illusions that President Botha might make real reforms in South Africa were dispelled. Under the state of emergency imposed in July 1985 his government arrested and detained thousands; the army and the police attacked and killed black South Africans. President Botha responded to the worsening situation with draconian measures, including bans on virtually all black-led opposition groups early in 1988. After a stroke

(Jan. 1989) Botha was replaced as leader of the National Party by F.W. *DE KLERK, but refused to resign the presidency. There were bitter arguments between the two men until Botha finally resigned the presidency in Aug. 1989. Botha has been critical of the attempts of his successor, President de Klerk, to lessen tension and to make reforms. In May 1990 it was announced that he was leaving the National Party.

Botha, Roelof Frederik ('Pik'), (b. 1932), South African Minister of Foreign Affairs and Minister of Information. After graduating in law 'Pik' Botha worked as a diplomat and became South African representative at the United Nations. In 1970 he became a *NATIONAL PARTY MP and served on a number of parliamentary committees before his appointment as ambassador to the United States and representative at the United Nations (1975–7). His strong defence of South African interests made him very popular among South African whites and he was called back to South Africa to become Foreign Minister. He became known as a *VERLIGTE (one of the more enlightened members of the government) and strongly supported the attempts of President P.W. *BOTHA to make reforms. A particularly successful year for his foreign policy was 1984; it was the year of the *NKOMATI ACCORD, President P.W. *BOTHA's European tour, and progress towards an agreement for Namibia and Angola. In 1986 'Pik' Botha created a storm in South Africa by saying that

The Republic of Botswana

THE COUNTRY	THE PEOPLE	THE STATE
582,000 sq. km.	1,256,000	Multi-party republic
Major Cities	*Ethnic Groups*	*Head of State*
Gaborone (capital)	Batswana	President Quett Masire
Selebi-Pikwe	San	
Francistown		*Ruling Bodies*
	Languages	Presidential cabinet
Economy	Setswana	House of Chiefs
Subsistence farming	English	National Assembly
Ranching		
Diamond mining	*Religion*	*Party in Power*
Copper mining	Traditional beliefs	Botswana Democratic
	Christian	Party
Principal Exports		
Diamonds		*Political Opposition*
Copper		Botswana National Front
Meat		Botswana People's Party
Currency		
Pula (P) of 100 thebe		

South Africa could have a black President in the future; he had to withdraw this statement. After President Botha resigned (Aug. 1989) 'Pik' continued as Minister of Foreign Affairs in President *DE KLERK's cabinet.

Botswana, a member of the Commonwealth, was the *BECHUANALAND Protectorate before independence. The Republic of Botswana is a vast and sparsely populated land-locked country in Southern Africa; it is bordered by Namibia to the west, the *CAPRIVI Strip to the north, Zimbabwe to the north-east and South Africa to the south and south-east. Botswana is crossed by the Tropic of Capricorn, but is reasonably temperate because much of the country is a plateau averaging 900 metres above sea-level. It is generally arid, especially in the south and west where the few remaining *SAN people live as nomads in the *KALAHARI Desert. The north-west is dominated by the Okavango River and the Okavango Swamp. About eighty per cent of the population lives in the east, the only area with a moderate rainfall and land suitable for ranching and growing crops – despite frequent droughts.

Little is known of Botswana's history before the arrival of the Tswana, *BANTU peoples. By the early nineteenth century Tswana tribal groups were established in the country and enjoying the benefits of successful economies based on ranching and the cultivation of grain. They also had complicated and sophisticated political structures. The most successful Tswana leader in the nineteenth century was Khama III, chief of the *BAMANGWATO from 1872. He united his people, built a strong army, repelled invaders and skilfully negotiated with the European arrivals in his territory. Khama III was a committed Christian who won the protection of the British government (1885) against his *BOER neighbours. After the British protectorate was formally established (1891) Bechuanaland was administered from Mafeking in South Africa (1895–1960). Many in Britain and South Africa expected Bechuanaland and the other two *HIGH COMMISSION territories to join the Union of South Africa (formed in 1910); but strong opposition from Bechuanaland and the election of a South African government committed to *APARTHEID (1948) persuaded Britain not to implement this plan.

There was little conflict between Bechuanaland and Britain until the crisis of 1948 caused by the marriage of Seretse *KHAMA, hereditary chief of the Bamangwato, to Ruth Williams, an Englishwoman. The couple were exiled (1950–56) and only allowed back home when Seretse renounced his chieftainship. He then entered politics as an ordinary citizen and founded the *BECHUANALAND DEMOCRATIC PARTY (1962). Seretse emerged as a cautious and conservative politician, more acceptable to Britain than his

radical rivals because he was prepared to guarantee the rights of white landowners in Bechuanaland, to accept foreign investment and to deal cautiously with his neighbours under white rule – Rhodesia and South Africa. As a descendant of Khama III, Seretse also enjoyed substantial rural and traditional support in Bechuanaland. The pre-independence general election (1965) gave his party a sweeping victory; in 1966 Sir Seretse Khama became the first President of the independent Republic of Botswana.

Since independence Botswana has been a multi-party democracy. In addition to the ruling *BOTSWANA DEMOCRATIC PARTY, there are the *BOTSWANA NATIONAL FRONT and the *BOTSWANA PEOPLE'S PARTY. The National Assembly consists of thirty-four elected members and six others. The leader of the majority party in the National Assembly is the executive president. There is also a House of Chiefs representing traditional rulers. Opposition parties have enjoyed little electoral success and since independence the *BOTSWANA DEMOCRATIC PARTY has had substantial majorities in the National Assembly. In the fifth general election since independence (Oct. 1989) the Botswana Democratic Party won by a landslide. After Sir Seretse's death (1980) Quett *MASIRE (Vice President and Sir Seretse's trusted colleague since 1962) became Botswana's second President. Generally President Masire has continued the cautious domestic policies of his predecessor.

At independence Botswana was one of Africa's poorest states, with only ten university graduates and 1700 secondary school pupils. Its fragile agricultural economy was further weakened by devastating droughts in 1965–6 and 1982–4. In 1985 it grew 20,000 tonnes of grain, only 10 per cent of its food consumption, but by 1985 mining had made Botswana Africa's fifth richest state in terms of GDP per capita. Diamond pipes have been exploited since 1971 to make it the world's third largest producer (15 million carats in 1987). Copper and nickel have been mined at Selebi–Pikwe since 1974. Some of this wealth has been used for rural development, especially ranching, but agricultural production is low and peasants are still abandoning farms for the mines and the towns.

High unemployment and a heavy dependence on remittances from migrant workers in South Africa cause serious economic and social problems. Political opposition groups are concerned by the government's heavy reliance on foreign investment and they oppose the extensive use of expatriate staff on the grounds that this limits opportunities for Botswanans to acquire technical and managerial skills.

Some of Botswana's problems have arisen from its proximity to white-ruled states. In the 1970s Zimbabwean nationalists fighting white minority rule in Rhodesia found sanctuary in Botswana. Botswana had to cope not only with the influx of refugees but also armed incursions from Rhodesia. Botswana's communications network and its trading links with Rhodesia suffered from the sanctions against white-ruled Rhodesia; traffic on Botswana's railway linking South Africa to Rhodesia was considerably disrupted. After Zimbabwean independence (1980) political dissidents took refuge in Botswana and relations between Botswana and Zimbabwe were strained; but by early 1989 there was some progress in the voluntary repatriation of refugees to Zimbabwe.

Since independence its close geographic and economic links with South Africa have caused problems for Botswana. Botswana has attempted to reduce its economic dependence on South Africa by replacing the South African rand with its own currency, the pula (1976), but it is still linked with South Africa in a customs union. It is active in the *SOUTHERN AFRICAN DEVELOPMENT CO-ORDINATION CONFERENCE (SADCC) which aims to reduce its members' dependence on South Africa. The presence of the *AFRICAN NATIONAL CONGRESS (ANC) in Botswana has caused security problems. Alleging that Botswana is providing bases for terrorists, South Africa has mounted a number of attacks not only against the ANC but also against refugees in Botswana. Despite considerable pressure from South Africa, President Masire has refused to conclude a security pact with South Africa, which would among other things

51

entail the expulsion of the ANC from Botswana.

Despite poor agricultural prospects Botswana has made substantial progress since independence. Much of its mining revenue has been invested in development plans for the future. Despite its difficult strategic position and the problems of its neighbours, Botswana has been a peaceful and stable multi-party democracy with little racial and tribal tension. It has been a haven of peace in the troubled region of Southern Africa, and it can look forward to the future with a degree of confidence.

Botswana Democratic Party, Botswana's ruling party, founded as the Bechuanaland Democratic Party (1962) by Seretse *KHAMA, Quett *MASIRE and others to campaign for independence. As a moderate and non-racial party it won the support of both the traditional rulers and the British authorities as independence approached. After victory in the election during the run-up to independence, its leader, Sir Seretse Khama, became Prime Minister (1965) and first president of the Republic of Botswana (1966). At independence the party changed its name, replacing Bechuanaland with Botswana. At every general election the party has won substantial majorities in the National Assembly. Most recently it won the fifth general election since independence by a landslide (Oct. 1989). When Sir Seretse died (1980) the party chose Quett Masire as leader and he became Botswana's second president.

Botswana National Front, militant nationalist and socialist party in opposition to the ruling *BOTSWANA DEMOCRATIC PARTY. Since its formation by Dr Kenneth Koma in 1965 the party has enjoyed some success in town council elections, but has made little impact in rural Botswana. It has not fared well in general elections; after modest gains in the 1984 election it had five MPs in the National Assembly. Its representation was increased when two MPs defected to it from the Botswana Democratic Party.

Botswana People's Party (BPP), radical opposition political party in Botswana, originally the Bechuanaland People's Party (founded by Kgaleman Motetse in 1960). The party, which had close links to the *AFRICAN NATIONAL CONGRESS in South Africa, made radical demands which upset the traditionalists and the whites in Botswana; it wanted immediate independence, Africanization of the administration and the abolition of the powers of the chiefs. The BPP was torn apart by personal rivalries and differences over policies. Since winning only three seats in the 1965 general election it has had further setbacks.

Boumedienne, Houari (1925–78), Algerian nationalist leader and president of the republic. Born near Bône, he was educated in Tunis and Cairo and served in the French army. In 1955 Boumedienne joined the *FRONT DE LIBÉRATION NATIONALE (FLN) in the war of independence. His rise was rapid: FLN commander in Wilaya sector (1955–7; chief-of-staff FLN 1960–2; chief-of-staff Algerian Army 1962–5; Minister of Defence 1962; First Vice-Premier 1963–5. Having led the coup which overthrew *BEN BELLA, he became president. In the first decade of his rule, Boumedienne sacrificed democracy and social welfare in favour of long-term economic goals. 'The State must be wealthy before the people can be given privileges,' he said. In 1976 the public began to demand a 'National Charter' and in the ensuing debate the government was strongly criticized. An intelligent politician, Boumedienne was impressed by the popular view and announced that living conditions would be given a higher priority. Just as important, he proposed to revive the moribund FLN, the old freedom-fighters organization, as a way of putting pressure on the government. Boumedienne did not live to see his reforms enacted, dying of a rare blood disease in December 1978. See *ALGERIAN CIVIL WAR

Bourguiba, Habib Ben Ali (b. 1903), Tunisian politician, first president of the independent Tunisia and architect of its fortunes. Born and educated in Tunis, he became a member of the Destour Party, a socialist organization, in 1921. His socialist ideals became even stronger during his university years in France, 1924–30. In 1934 he broke away from his old party to form the *Party Socialiste Destourièn* (PSD) or Neo-Destour Party. The PSD was dedicated to moderate socialism and Bourguiba planned to establish it among trade unionists, peasants, women and young people. The French twice imprisoned him for nationalist activities, in 1934–6 and 1938–43. Even when they did not have the outspoken Bourguiba in prison, the French harried him relentlessly. He lived outside Tunisia (1946–9), and then returned to Tunisia in order to establish himself as a political leader. The French still feared him and in 1952 they imprisoned him again, for a time in solitary confinement. Released in 1954, he was still unbroken and returned to his work of preparing his people for independence.

When it was granted, in 1957, Bourguiba became its first president. For two years he was concurrently president, minister of foreign affairs and of defence. From 1959 he was virtually a dictator, though a generally benevolent one. With increasing seniority and experience he became one of Africa's most influential leaders. His stature enabled him to keep Tunisia largely aloof from the other Arab states' preoccupation with hostility towards Israel. He regarded this as 'self-destructive and economically wasteful'. His own major problem in the 1980s was the growth of Islamic fundamentalism, which threatened his government. He was also threatened by his own passing years. In his mid-80s he had become rather inflexible and also incapable of handling the nation's many pressing problems. On 7 November 1987 Bourguiba was gently deposed by General Zine El Abidine Ben Ali. Bourguiba will be remembered as a strong politician who established modern Tunisia and in the process became a world statesman.

Breytenbach, Breyten (b. 1939), white South African poet, painter and opponent of *APARTHEID. After dropping out of university he settled in Paris and married a Vietnamese (who would be classified as non-white in South Africa). For most of his career he has written in Afrikaans. His poetry and prose include memoirs of youth and prison experiences, political allegory and sweeping condemnations of apartheid and the South African regime. During a visit to South Africa (1973) he warned his fellow Afrikaners that their racist society was doomed. In 1975 he travelled to South Africa under an alias. He was discovered, arrested and tried. He pleaded guilty and was sentenced to nine years in prison. Another trial (1977) ended in his acquittal on all but one nominal charge. After official French protests he was released from prison (Dec. 1982) and he returned to live in Paris, announcing that he would no longer write in Afrikaans.

Brink, André (b. 1935), South African writer of novels and non-fiction in both English and Afrikaans. In 1961 he began teaching literature and drama at Rhodes University, where he became Professor of Afrikaans and Dutch Literature. Despite his hatred of *APARTHEID Brink has decided to stay in South Africa. He writes about the brutality of the South African system and the suffering of its victims. *Looking on Darkness* (1974) was banned in South Africa; *A Dry White Season* won the Martin Luther King Memorial Prize in 1980.

Buganda, originally part of the Bunyoro Kingdom it was the most powerful feudal kingdom in Uganda by the nineteenth century. It was ruled by the Kabaka (King) and royal council. When Uganda became independent in 1962, Buganda, which had enjoyed special rights under British rule, was given semi-federal status. Kabaka Yekka, the royalist Bugandan party, formed a coalition with the government of Prime Minister *OBOTE (1962), and the 36th Kabaka of Buganda, *MUTESA II, became the first President of the Republic of Buganda (1963–6). In 1966 Obote imposed a unitary constitution on Uganda, suspended Buganda's special status and sent in the army to storm the royal palace. In 1967 the kingdom of Buganda was abolished and replaced by four administrative districts. Mutesa II went into exile and died in Britain. His son and heir, Prince Ronald, has returned to Uganda. The people are called the Baganda, an individual is a Muganda. The adjectival word is Ganda.

Buhari, Major-General Muhammadu (b. 1942), former military ruler of Nigeria (1983–5). A Muslim from the north, he joined the army in 1962 and served in the United Nations forces in the Congo. After holding various command and staff positions, Buhari became a Military State Governor (1975) and Federal Commissioner for Petroleum and Energy (1976); when Nigeria returned to civilian rule in 1979 he went back to the barracks.

Disgusted at the corruption and inefficiency of President *SHAGARI's government, the military seized power on the last day of 1983. Buhari became Head of State and Commander-in-Chief of the Armed Forces. He identified himself with the policies of the late Murtala *MUHAMMED and pledged to fight corruption and to reform the economy.

Buhari's arbitrary and ill-considered economic measures led to bitter opposition and did nothing to improve the country's fortunes. His authoritarian methods made him unpopular; in February 1985 he dealt with a strike of doctors and hospital workers by arresting leading activists and banning leading medical professional associations. There were also long delays in trying members of the previous regime for corruption. Discontent increased and in August 1985 he was ousted by *BABANGIDA and placed under arrest. He was freed in December 1988.

Burkina Faso (formerly Upper Volta), a land-locked state of West Africa, with semi-desert in its northern areas and wooded savannah in the south. It has six neighbours: clockwise, they are Niger, Benin, Togo, Ghana, Ivory Coast and Mali. More than 60 per cent of its people follow traditional religious beliefs and 30 per cent are Muslim; the remainder are Christian. The Mossi tribe is the most numerous, making up 50 per cent of the population,

but the Fulani people are equally important.

The Upper Volta region was huge when the French claimed it at the end of the nineteenth century. In 1932 they partitioned large areas to Mali, the Ivory Coast and Niger, all of which were under French control. The most significant local politician after 1945 was Maurice *YAMEOGO. In 1958 he was leader of the combined Union Démocratique Voltaique (UDV) and Rassemblement Démocratique Africain (RDA). When independence was proclaimed, on 5 August 1960, Yameogo became president and Upper Volta, as a member of the 'Council of the Entente' – together with Ivory Coast, Dahomey, Niger and Togo, from 1966 – could reasonably have expected a stable future. Yameogo was a disappointment as a leader and his dictatorial regime led to an uprising in January 1966. Yameogo was deposed and imprisoned and Colonel Sangoule *LAMIZANA took power. He was unable to satisfy the aspirations of the unions and peasants, largely because of matters beyond his control, such as famine and drought. Lamizana held on to power and helped to produce a new constitution in 1977. Reforms did not go far enough and on 25 November 1980 Colonel Saye Zerbo led a coup which removed Lamizana without bloodshed.

Zerbo created the Comité Militaire de Redressement pour le progrès national (MRPN), most of whose thirty-one members were young officers. In addition, he appointed a

Burkina Faso (formerly Upper Volta)

THE COUNTRY	THE PEOPLE	THE STATE
274,500 sq. km.	8.3 million	Presidential republic
Major Cities	*Ethnic Groups*	*Head of State*
Ouagadougou (capital)	Mossi (50%)	President Blaise
Bobo-Dioulasso	Fulani	Compaore
Tambao	Gourmantché	
	Bobo	*Ruling Body*
Economy	Lobi	'Popular Front' with
More than 2 million	Senoufou	a majority of civilian
Burkinabes work in Ivory	Bissa	members
Coast; their remittances		
are the mainstay of the	*Languages*	*Official Party*
economy.	French (official)	National Committee of
Subsistence farming:	More (spoken by the	the Revolution
sorghum, millet, rice,	Mossi)	
maize, groundnuts.	Dioula and	
Processing of agricultural	Gourmantché	
products.		
	Religion	
Principal Exports	Traditional	
Cheap labour, cattle,	Islam	
seasonal vegetables		
Currency		
CFA franc of 100		
centimes		

new cabinet which had a majority of civilian members. The government felt impelled to control the unions by introducing heavy penalties for strikes. Despite his obvious good intentions, Zerbo lasted less than two years as president. On 7 November 1982 non-commissioned officers rose in an armed coup and after two days of fighting overthrew Zerbo. The rebels appointed Major Jean-Baptiste Ouedraogo as chairman of a 'Peoples' Salvation Council'. Unidentified leaders announced over national radio that the coup's objective was to 'obtain justice for the people against the high treason, corruption, bankruptcy and degraded morals of the regime'.

In January 1983 the Council, rather than Ouedraogo, appointed Captain Thomas *SANKARA as prime minister. Sankara, only thirty-four, was a popular officer who had been Secretary for Information in the Zerbo administration. With Sankara elevated to high office, Ouedraogo feared for his own position and in May arrested Sankara. This foolish act provoked some army units into a show of force in Sankara's support and Ouedraogo released him. Sankara waited only until August 1983 when in a brief but violent coup he overthrew Ouedraogo.

With himself as chairman, Sankara set up the National Committee of the Revolution (CNR). It consisted of three left-wing groupings, which appeared to work harmoniously. The CNR implemented wide-ranging measures, including depriving the traditional chiefs of their oppressive privileges, and instituting rigorous anti-corruption legislation. Committees for the Defence of the Revolution were set up at neighbourhood level to serve as a focus for community activity. Sankara, who admitted to being a 'Marxist populist', was deeply influenced by his friend, Flt.-Lt. Jerry *RAWLINGS of *GHANA. Rawlings paid several state visits to Upper Volta, which Sankara renamed Burkina Faso in August 1984. According to Sankara, the words mean 'the land of incorruptible men'.

As part of his campaign to reform the new state Sankara brought before 'popular revolutionary tribunals' many men accused of 'attempting to destroy the state through corruption'. The only prominent member of earlier regimes to escape punishment was Sangoule Lamizana. Colonel Zerbo was sentenced to fifteen years in prison and ordered to repay 61 million CFA francs of state money allegedly embezzled. A former prime minister, Gerard Ouedraogo, was given ten years in prison. Many other 'state criminals' also went to gaol. Most were released, by presidential decree, within two years.

While Sankara seriously considered a merger of Burkina Faso with Ghana, his relationships with Ivory Coast and Mali were less harmonious. On 25 December 1985 he was misguided enough to send troops into Mali over a border dispute. They occupied some villages but were driven out by Malian units. Peace between the two countries was restored by a delegation sent to the disputed area by a group of West-African countries.

Impatient for reforms and feeling that he was being obstructed, Sankara dismissed the cabinet on 18 August 1985 and appointed his best friend, the Justice Minister Captain Blaise Compaore, and two other officers as 'state-co-ordinators' with wide administrative powers. On 15 October 1987 Compaore, led a coup in which Sankara was killed. Compaore and two senior officials formed a new government, which called itself the Popular Front. They explained that they had seized power because Sankara had become autocratic and his 'whimsical and immature political style' was leading the country into political and economic chaos. In fact, Sankara's regime was much more stable than Compaore's turned out to be. Burkinabes resented the Sankara killing enormously. Killing is alien to their culture and the murder of a best friend is regarded as a heinous crime.

In December 1988 President Yoweri *MUSEVENI of *UGANDA questioned Compaore's credentials as leader of a revolutionary government and called for an international investigation into the circumstances of Sankara's death. Under Compaore, Burkina Faso's relations with all its neighbours and most of west and central Africa became strained.

Burkina Faso's economy depends on the Ivory Coast, where two million Burkinabe work. Owing to limited national resources, infertile soil and high population density in relation to other *SAHEL countries, Burkina Faso is one of the poorest countries in the world. The average income is only £75 a year. Amid such abject poverty President Compaore's purchase of a £7 million luxury jet caused resentment even among his supporters. Inadequate communications, a product of the country's landlocked position, hamper economic development. Its narrow production and export base leads to heavy dependence on importing goods, food and foreign aid, mostly from France.

Agriculture, accounting for 40 per cent of GNP, is almost entirely at subsistence level with sorghum and millet the chief staples although cash crops, notably cotton, are grown. The development programme for 1981–90 – total expenditure 810 billion CFA francs – allocated a third of funds to rural development. Mineral reserves of zinc, manganese, silver and gold have been identified but only gold is being exploited in commercial quantities. The manufacturing sector in the mid-1980s accounted for only 12 per cent of GDP. Infrastructural development, allocated 25 per cent of 1981–90 expenditure, is concentrated on railways, roads and electricity generation: the construction of a massive 15 MW hydroelectric station on the Kompienga river was completed in 1988. No amount of improvement to the infrastructure can compensate for the lack of long-term stable government. With six coups in thirty years Burkina Faso has wounds from which it will take many years to recover.

Burundi, the Republic of Burundi is a small and densely populated country in east central Africa. This mountainous and land-locked state is bordered by Tanzania to the east and south, Lake Tanganyika and Zaire to the south and west and Rwanda to the north. The western border of Burundi is the western floor of the *EAST AFRICAN RIFT VALLEY. Eastwards the land rises sharply to plateaux from 1400 to 1800 metres above sea-level; they cover most of the country, which has a pleasant climate except for the hot and humid low-lying areas.

The Twa pigmies, who now amount to only 1 per cent of the population were early inhabitants; they were hunters and gatherers. A thousand years ago *BANTU peasant farmers, the Hutu, settled in the area. They now comprise 84 per cent of the population. In the seventeenth century the cattle-owning Tutsi began moving into the country from the

The Republic of Burundi

THE COUNTRY	THE PEOPLE	THE STATE
27,834 sq. km.	4,978,000	Military/single-party republic
Major Cities	*Ethnic Groups*	*Head of State*
Bujumbura (capital)	Hutu (80%+)	President Buyoya
	Tutsi (15%)	
Economy		*Ruling Body*
Subsistence farming	*Languages*	Military Committee for
Coffee	Kirundi (official)	National Salvation
	French (official)	
Principal Export	Swahili	*Official Party*
Coffee		UPRONA
	Religion	
Currency	Traditional beliefs	
Burundi franc of 100	Catholicism	
centimes		

north and soon came to dominate the Hutu; now about 15 per cent of the population is Tutsi.

Burundi's economy depends heavily on agriculture, with over 90 per cent of the working population in subsistence agriculture, growing *CASSAVA, sweet potatoes and bananas. Coffee is the most important cash crop; it accounted for 90 per cent of export revenues in 1986, despite the problems caused by erratic world prices. Tea is the second most lucrative cash crop. Attempts have been made to develop cotton, rice and sugar plantations and to promote fishing and the export of leather. Apart from the processing of agricultural products, industrial development is limited. Burundi's valuable mineral deposits include tin, tungsten, gold, nickel and vanadium; but transport difficulties have hindered their exploitation. Few of the roads are tarred and it is a long and difficult journey by lake and rail from Bujumbura, the capital, to Dar es Salaam (the nearest port) 1440 kilometres away. In 1987 it was announced that a railway would be built from Uganda through Rwanda and Burundi to Tanzania, but for much of the 1980s Burundi's trade with the outside world has been disrupted by troubles in Uganda.

With a per capita GNP of only $230 in 1985 Burundi is one of the poorest countries in the world. It has suffered from inflation (13 per cent in 1989), trade deficits and a high level of foreign debt ($745 million in 1988). In rural areas there have been food shortages and malnutrition. In 1986 Burundi agreed a structural adjustment programme with the IMF and the World Bank. In exchange for international credit Burundi devalued its franc, increased taxes and reduced expenditure by disbanding some costly state enterprises. There was a further devaluation in 1988. It is not clear how much progress has been made in economic reform, but the ethnic violence in August 1988 was a severe setback to hopes of prosperity and stability.

Little is known of the early history of Burundi. The Twa pygmy hunters and gatherers were displaced by two main waves of immigrants, the Hutu and the Tutsi. When Europeans arrived in the nineteenth century the Tutsi feudal kingdom of Burundi dominated the country. Late in the nineteenth century Burundi and Rwanda, then called *RUANDA-URUNDI, were annexed to German East Africa. Belgium seized the territory (1916) and it became a Belgian mandate after the First World War. From 1925 it was administered with the *BELGIAN CONGO and the German system of indirect rule through the Tutsi princes was continued. Education was left to Catholic missionaries.

As independence approached Tutsi and Hutu leaders formed *UPRONA (Union pour le progrès national) in 1958. Internal self-government (Jan. 1962) and independence (Jul. 1962) were achieved peacefully under the Tutsi monarchy, but UPRONA was unable to control ethnic tension between the Tutsi and the Hutu. Until he was deposed by his son (*NTARE V) in July 1966, Mwami (King) *MWAMBUTSA IV tried to ensure a fair balance of ethnic interests in successive governments.

Ntare V appointed *MICOMBERO as prime minister (Jul. 1966), but in November 1966 Micombero overthrew the monarchy and proclaimed a republic with himself as president. From 1966 to 1976 Micombero's military government tightened Tutsi domination of Burundi, sometimes provoking ethnic violence. It made UPRONA the sole legal political party and purged Hutu from key posts in UPRONA, the army, the police and the administration. In October 1971 Micombero established the Conseil suprême de la République, a military junta of twenty-seven members. In April 1972 the Hutu rebelled and killed up to ten thousand Tutsi. The government retaliated by executing Ntare V and by slaughtering many Hutu, especially the educated; estimates of the dead vary from 80,000 to 250,000.

In 1973 Micombero appointed a Presidential Bureau of seven to rule the country; he was both President and Prime Minister. In 1974 a new constitution vested power in UPRONA, with Micombero as Secretary General of the party. In November 1976 Col. *BAGAZA overthrew Micombero and became President. Bagaza made some moves towards national reconciliation, but Tutsi domination continued now with another Tutsi group. In 1980 the UPRONA Central Committee, headed by Bagaza, replaced the military junta. In 1981 a new constitution provided for the election of the National Assembly from UPRONA candidates. In August 1984 Bagaza was the sole candidate in the presidential election; he won 99.63 per cent of the votes. By 1985 Bagaza was at loggerheads with the Catholic Church whom he accused of inciting the Hutu. Priests were arrested, tried, imprisoned or expelled. There was mounting international criticism of the regime's abuse of human rights.

Bagaza strengthened the army and developed links with the Soviet bloc, China and Libya, even receiving an official visit from Col. *GADAFFI in 1985. In September 1987 Major *BUYOYA, another Tutsi officer, overthrew Bagaza and made himself president, suspending UPRONA, the 1981 constitution and the National Assembly. Buyoya and the thirty-one army officers in the Military Committee for National Salvation have tried to improve Burundi's image. They settled some disputes with the Catholic Church and appointed a few Hutu to senior government posts, but in August 1988 a fresh outbreak of genocide shocked the world. After a bridge was destroyed, the army massacred over twenty thousand men, women and children; tens of thousands fled to neighbouring countries.

The political and economic future of Burundi is uncertain. The domination of the Hutu majority by the Tutsi minority has evoked comparisons with the *APARTHEID system in South Africa. There has been a long history of bitterness between the two ethnic groups, before and after independence. The massacres of 1988, bad weather and falling world prices for coffee have damaged the country's economy; but despite the poverty of the country the peasant farmers generally manage to feed themselves and their families from their small holdings of land.

Busia, Dr Kofi Abrefa (1913–78), a distinguished Ghanaian sociologist and political leader, the author of books on education, the church and politics in Africa. He was an early associate of *NKRUMAH and a member of the National Assembly (1951–9). He broke with Nkrumah and in 1957 became leader of the United Party, the parliamentary opposition. In the early 1960s Busia was forced into an exile which lasted until Nkrumah was overthrown. As the military returned Ghana to civilian rule, Busia became a major political force. His Progress Party, representative of middle-class and business interests, won the August 1969 elections and Busia took office as prime minister of a government of self-styled technocrats.

Initially Busia was popular; Ghanaians believed they were making a new start. Their hopes were soon disappointed. Busia was unable to deal with the economic problems he had inherited. The economic decline continued and unemployment mounted. The austerity measures of 1971 were ineffective. Busia's expulsion of aliens, mainly Nigerians, and his other measures to encourage Ghanaian capitalism disrupted industry and commerce and increased unemployment. His dismissal of civil servants to save money and his attempts to smash trade union opposition further contributed to his unpopularity. In January 1972 the military overthrew Busia. He went into exile in England where he died.

Buthelezi, Chief Mangosuthu Gatsha (b. 1928), leading black South African politician, Chief Minister of *KWAZULU since 1976. A descendant of Zulu warrior kings, he has been hereditary chief of the Buthelezi clan since 1953. He studied at *FORT HARE UNIVERSITY COLLEGE (1948–50) and graduated despite his expulsion after a student protest. He worked as a clerk, as Chief Executive Officer for the KwaZulu territorial authority (1970–2), and as Chief Executive Councillor of the KwaZulu Legislative Assembly (1972–6) before becoming Chief Minister.

Chief Buthelezi exerts considerable power as the leader of the seven million Zulus who form South Africa's largest racial or ethnic group. He leads *INKATHA which is the country's largest political group with over a million fiercely loyal members. The political and administrative structures of KwaZulu provide him with an important power base. Buthelezi wants a non-tribal, non-racial and democratic South Africa, as does the *AFRICAN NATIONAL CONGRESS. Yet, for years there has been bitter fighting between his supporters and ANC supporters, mainly in Natal. What distinguishes him from other African leaders is his

opposition to sanctions and the use of violence to overthrow the government. He believes that investment from abroad would increase pressures for change.

Chief Buthelezi has been criticized for collaboration with *APARTHEID, but he is prepared to oppose the government. He argued for the release of Nelson *MANDELA; he thwarted plans to grant 'independence' to KwaZulu and he campaigned against President P.W. *BOTHA's constitutional proposals in 1983. He is a moving force behind the *INDABA, a forum for discussion which was formed in 1986 and proposed a joint non-racial government for KwaZulu and Natal. White liberals see him as a future partner in government, but black radicals reject him. In 1990 there was increasing tension between Buthelezi and Nelson Mandela. Buthelezi met Mandela in January 1991 to discuss a settlement which would end the bloody factional infighting between Inkatha and the African National Congress.

Buyoya, Major Pierre, President of Burundi since he seized power from Colonel *BAGAZA (Sep. 1987). Buyoya is a Tutsi and he was a friend of Bagaza. In power he seemed more liberal than his predecessor and appointed Hutu to ministerial posts, but his reputation has been damaged by the outbreaks of ethnic violence which began in August 1988.

Cabinda, part of the Angolan state, this northern coastal enclave is separated from the rest of Angola by Zairean territory to its east and south; north of it is the People's Republic of the Congo. Its valuable oil deposits were discovered during the 1960s and earn vital foreign currency for Angola. Cabinda also produces coffee, phosphates, potassium, cocoa and timber. Since 1974 the Front for the Liberation of the Enclave of Cabinda has been opposing Angolan rule, but has been ineffective despite some help from Zaire, France and Gabon.

Cabral, Amílcar (1924–73), born in Bafutu, in Portuguese Guinea, to Cape Verde parents, Cabral was educated in Bissau and then at Lisbon University as an agronomist and hydraulic engineer. In both these professions, he was employed by the government in Portuguese Guinea and Angola. Always politically minded, Cabral founded the revolutionary party, *PARTIDO AFRICANO DE INDEPENDÊNÇIA DA GUINÉ E CABO VERDE (PAIGC), in Portuguese Guinea in 1956. He quickly showed himself to be one of Africa's most dynamic new leaders and was constantly hunted by the Portuguese security forces. Establishing his base at Conakry, in independent Guinea, Cabral directed the guerrilla war against the Portuguese. Killers in the pay of the Portuguese assassinated him early in 1973,

the year in which the PAIGC unilaterally proclaimed independence for Guinea-Bissau. Cabral had been almost wholly responsible for the success.

Cabral, Luiz (b. 1931), Guinean nationalist leader. Brother of Amílcar *CABRAL, Luiz became a trade union organizer (1953–60). A member of the *PAIGC, he fled the country in 1960 and became a leader of the struggle for independence. Appointed President of the Republic of Guinea-Bissau in 1973, he was overthrown in a coup in 1980.

Cameroon, with a short coastline on the Gulf of Guinea, covers a full eleven degrees of longitude from just north of the equator to deep central Africa. This gives the country great vegetational diversity, from the equatorial rain forest in the south to the barren *SAHEL region in the north. Religion is also geographically divided: the population is mainly Muslim in the north and Christian in the south.

After the end of the First World War in 1918 the League of Nations placed the former German colony under British and French mandate, in the west and east respectively. This arrangement was confirmed by the UN after the Second World War. In 1948, a small group of nationalists founded the Union des Populations de Cameroun (UPC) and demanded unification and immediate independence. Demonstrations

The Republic of Cameroon

THE COUNTRY	THE PEOPLE	THE STATE
475,442 sq. km.	11.1 million	Single-party presidential republic
Major Cities	*Ethnic Groups*	*Head of State*
Yaoundé (capital)	Negroes	President Paul Biya
Douala	Berbers	
		Ruling Body
Economy	*Languages*	President and cabinet of
Mainly agricultural	French (official)	15
(coffee, cocoa, cotton)	Local languages	
Oil, forestry, bauxite		*Official Party*
smelting.	*Religion*	Rassemblement
	Christianity	démocratique du peuple
Principal Exports	Islam	camerounais
Coffee and cocoa	Animism	
Currency		
CFA franc of 100		
centimes		

organized by the UPC in 1952 were harshly suppressed by the French military and the UPC was forced underground. Nevertheless, in May 1957, a new legislative assembly met for the first time. The French High Commissioner installed A. M. Mbida as Prime Minister to lead the country to independence. Rivalry among the various parties, followed by military repression, kept Cameroon unstable. When East Cameroon became independent on 1 January 1960, rebellion was raging in the west and in Bassa tribal country. The French General Briand, with five thousand troops and a squadron of fighter bombers, spent eight months in suppressing what was known as the 'Bamileke Uprising'. The French were ruthless and killed

so many rebels that ever since there has been a campaign to conceal the exact number. During a relatively peaceful period, Ahmadou *AHIDJO was elected president on 5 May 1960. From exile, two of the UPC's original founders, Félix Moumie and Ernest Ouandie, continued to cause difficulties. Then, on 3 November 1960, a French agent assassinated Moumie in Geneva. However, the rebellion in Cameroon continued until Ernest Ouandie was arrested during a clandestine visit to the country. He was executed by firing squad, for treason and subversion, on 15 January 1961. That year, on 1 October, East and West Cameroon were reunified by referendum. It was now a federal state with three assemblies and three governing bodies. It seemed that at last the more than two hundred ethnic groups had reached some kind of accord and on 20 May 1972 the country become the United Republic of Cameroon. On 5 April 1975, Ahmadou Ahidjo was re-elected president. He installed Paul Biya as the country's first prime minister. Ahidjo sought total unity and in September 1966 the six political parties merged into a single party, the *UNION NATIONALE CAMEROUNAISE (UNC). The three trade unions were later forced to merge into a single trade union.

Ahidjo resigned in 1982, handing over to Biya. Formerly close friends, the two men fell out and Ahidjo retired to France. He was found guilty and sentenced to death *in absentia* for 'plotting against the security of the state, corruption and insulting President Biya'. The greater part of the National Guard, mostly northerners recruited by Ahidjo, rose on 6 April 1984 and tried to overthrow the government. After two days' heavy fighting the coup was put down and forty-six guardsmen were tried and executed. Biya, who had tried to democratize the government, now swung violently towards authoritarianism, purging the government and later the party of anybody even remotely suspected of having supported the coup attempt. More than 1200 people were questioned and 491 brought to trial. Of these, 51 were condemned to death. The public still hoped for more democratic government, including opposition parties, but Biya continued to allow only one party to exist. His 'concession' was that its name would be changed to the Rassemblement Démocratique du Peuple Camerounais (RDPC) with the new motto, 'Unity, Truth and Democracy'. In March 1986, the President permitted a free election for cell leaders and committee presidents at the lowest level but at the same time heavily crushed riots in the English-speaking areas of Cameroon. On 26 August 1986 Cameroon, which had been one of twenty-nine African countries to break with Israel after the 1973 Middle East War, restored relations. During a two-day visit by the Israeli Prime Minister, Shimon Peres, the two countries agreed to co-operate in many fields.

Co-operation was put to the test immediately when a volcanic lake in the north-west belched masses of toxic gas, killing two thousand people while they slept and seriously poisoning another twenty thousand. A team of doctors travelling with the Israeli Prime Minister was sent to the stricken area and aid was sent at once by the UN, France, Britain and the USA.

While Cameroon's relationship with other African countries is stable enough, internally it stumbles from one minor political crisis to another. The basic cause of unrest remains the lack of genuine democratic government. On visits to Cameroon in 1989 and 1990, French ministers and officials urged the president to permit opposition parties to form, and to hold free elections, but with no result. Foreign diplomats in

Yaoundé believe that no reforms will take place until the departure of Biya from the president's office.

Cameroon, although its economy is essentially agrarian, owes much of its recent prosperity to the rapid expansion of the oil industry since the late 1970s. This has contributed to high real economic growth rates, which averaged an annual eleven per cent annually during 1979–82. Oil revenues underpin the agricultural sector which remains vitally important and ensures a high degree of self-sufficiency in foodstuffs. Conversely, government intervention in the manufacturing sector has been less successful. consequently policy has been changed to emphasize the privatization of public concerns and easing of bureaucratic constraints. Lower water levels have reduced hydroelectric power; this contraction has been detrimental to energy-intensive heavy industry, particularly aluminium smelting. Long-term economic strategy is embodied in the 1986–91 Development Plan, which calls for total investment of CFA francs 7830 billion. The target for average real growth is almost 7 per cent per annum with the key priorities, besides agriculture, being rural electrification, urban renewal, transport and communications.

Oil output in 1978 was 13,000 barrels per day; in 1986 it was 202,000 and by 1989 production levels had peaked at 210,000. Without significant new discoveries the country's estimated 750 million barrels will be exhausted by AD 2000. Cameroon is not a member of OPEC and pursues its own pricing and production policies. Less than 5 per cent of the land is under cultivation but agriculture and forestry provide employment for the majority of the population, contribute a quarter of the GDP and make a significant contribution to foreign exchange earnings. Cocoa, coffee and timber are the major export commodities; cotton, rubber, palm oil and bananas are important cash crops. Great emphasis is placed on development of the agro-industrial sector. Projects include maize, soya and sorghum processing and pineapple canning. Cameroon possesses 20 million hectares of forested land but only 8 million are exploited.

The European Community is Cameroon's most important market, accounting for almost 80 per cent of exports and 70 per cent of imports in 1986. Within the Community, France, the Netherlands and West Germany are pre-eminent, with the USA being the principal non-European trading partner.

Camp David Accords, an agreement reached by Egypt and Israel in an attempt to resolve the Arab-Israeli conflict. On 9 November 1977, President *SADAT of Egypt announced before the People's Assembly (parliament) that he was prepared to go to Israel to try to bring about peace in the Middle East. In one of the most dramatic events seen in the region since the establishment of Israel in 1948, Sadat addressed the Knesset (Israel's parliament) on 21 November. After negotiations between Israeli and Egyptian

CAPE VERDE ISLANDS

officials, with the brokerage of US President Jimmy Carter, Sadat and Prime Minister Menachem Begin of Israel signed the Camp David Accords, on 17 September 1978. The accords consisted of two agreements, one covering the return of Sinai to Egyptian ownership, the other proposing a solution to the problem of the West Bank. The accords were formalized in a treaty signed in Washington in 26 March 1979. The *ARAB LEAGUE denounced the Camp David Accords as a 'betrayal of the Arab and Islamic worlds'. Arab states cut diplomatic ties with Egypt, the Arab League's head office was moved from Cairo to Tunis, and Egypt was denied all Arab aid. However, the accords held firm and no further conflict between Israel and Egypt has occurred.

Cape Verde Islands, more commonly known simply as Cape Verde, the ten main islands of the group lie in the Atlantic four hundred miles off Senegal. Colonized by the Portuguese in the mid-fifteenth century they became a base for slave-trading operations. The end of slavery and later, the effects of repeated droughts brought the islands to the verge of economic destruction. Meanwhile, miscegenation between the early white settlers and their slaves resulted in a distinct Cape Verdian nationality.

In 1951 the Portuguese government changed Cape Verde's status from colony to overseas province. The Cape Verdean intellectual Amílcar *CABRAL founded, in 1956, the *PARTIDO AFRICANO DA INDEPENDÊNCIA DA GUINÉ E CABO VERDE (PAIGC), which survived despite Portuguese oppression. A war of liberation broke out in 1963 and was relatively low-key until the downfall of Portugal's dictator, Salazar, in April 1974. Then war intensified and tens of thousands of men and women participated. The Portuguese negotiated with the PAIGC to create a transitional government until independence was declared on 5 July 1975. Under the new constitution, the PAIGC, later renamed PAICV (Partido Africano da Independência da Cabo Verde, became the sole legal party. The National Council of 32 members effectively ran the country, while the National People's Assembly of 83 members met a few days each year. On 14 November 1980 Cape Verde's hopes for unity with Guinea Bissau on the African mainland came to an end when Joao Vieira took power and arrested President Luiz *CABRAL, brother of Amílcar. The coup was directed against the mainly Cape Verdean leadership.

In 1989 the population of the islands was about 320,000, but even more have left to find work: 300,000 live in the United States, 50,000 in Holland, Portugal and other parts of Europe. Their remittances make up 30 per cent of the country's GNP; another 60 per cent is provided by foreign aid donors. Exports of goods, mainly fish, earn $2.5 million. Cape Verde, in its poverty, puts some of its neighbours, richer in resources, to shame. World Bank statistics show that the islands' GNP

Republic of Cape Verde

THE COUNTRY 4,003 sq. km.	THE PEOPLE 328,000	THE STATE Multi-party presidential republic
Major Cities Praia (capital) 9 of the 15 islands are inhabited	*Ethnic Groups* Majority of population is of mixed Portuguese- African descent	*Head of State* President Mascarenhas Monteiro
Economy Subsistence agriculture and pastoral farming much affected by drought.	*Languages* Portuguese (official)	*Ruling Body* Cabinet; President appoints prime minister
	Religion Roman Catholic 99%	*Ruling Parties* Partido Africano da Independência da Cabo Verde
Principal Exports Invisibles only: airport fees; workers' remittances		Movement for Democracy
Currency Cape Verde escudo of 100 centavos		

grew at 5.5 per cent a year on average between 1973 and 1988. The islanders have persuaded some donors to make long-term promises of food and money. They have also won some general balance-of-payments support, in addition to aid tied to specific projects. Their requirements are not huge: at their conference with aid donors in December 1988 they asked for $90 million a year for five years and got it.

Drought has brought more problems to Cape Verde than to any Sahelian country. Many harvests and herds were lost in 1969–89. The islands' precarious economy caused the PAIGV to formulate a pragmatic foreign policy, such as allowing South African Airways landing rights at the international airport on the island of Sal. Cape Verde's president, Aristides Pereira, favours economic sanctions against South Africa, but only when applied with prudence. 'We are for solidarity,' he said, 'but not for suicidal solidarity.' When the US suspended air services between America and South Africa in 1987 the islands' income was cut by $3.5 million a year, leaving only $1.5 million in airport fees. Since workers' remittances were also declining by 1989 and the government's export-promotion policies can have no sudden effect, the 1990s are expected to be difficult. In January 1991 the Cape Verdeans welcomed multi-party democracy and in February Monteiro of Movement for Democracy, became President.

Caprivi Strip, long and narrow strip of land linking north-east Namibia to Zambia and Zimbabwe and sharing a border with Angola and Botswana. It was ceded to Germany late in the nineteenth century to give the German colony of *SOUTH WEST AFRICA access to the Zambezi River. From the 1960s South Africa built up a strong military presence in the strip, the front line of the conflict between South Africa and black-ruled states. It is now part of independent Namibia.

Casablanca bloc (1958–63), an early attempt by radical and socialist African states to co-operate. In 1958 Ghana and Guinea (later joined by Mali) drafted proposals for a union of African states. In 1961 these three states, Morocco, Libya and the provisional Algerian government met at Casablanca to draw up plans for an African military command and an African Common Market. The Casablanca bloc was superseded by the *ORGANIZATION OF AFRICAN UNITY in 1963.

Central African Federation (1953–63), set up by the British government to link Southern Rhodesia, Northern Rhodesia and Nyasaland (now Zimbabwe, Zambia and Malawi) together. The Federation was meant to promote economic development and be an example of multi-racial partnership, but it was created at the insistence of the white communities of Southern Rhodesia and the *COPPERBELT. The African majority was barely consulted; it protested vigorously against the plan which would mainly benefit the whites of the self-governing colony of Southern Rhodesia. The two Federal Prime Ministers were Godfrey Huggins (1953–6) and Roy *WELENSKY (1956–63).

The Federation never came near to achieving its stated aim of multi-racial co-operation. The blacks were suspicious of white aims and mounted massive campaigns of resistance against this constitutional experiment which mainly benefited the whites. Despite stern measures the protests of the black nationalists continued and grew stronger. Successes by nationalist leaders in territorial elections (*BANDA in Nyasaland in 1961 and *KAUNDA in Northern Rhodesia in 1962) sealed the fate of the Federation which Britain formally terminated at the end of 1963.

Central African Republic, appropriately named since it is indeed in almost the exact geographic centre of the continent. Covering an area of 623,000 sq. km., it is basically a plateau, with mountain ranges in the north-east and south-east. Its vegetation ranges from that of a semi-desert in parts of the north to tropical rainforest in the south-west. It is bordered by Chad, Sudan, Zaire, Congo and Cameroon and with all of them it has tribal links. The country's area was once divided into kingdoms, most of

Central African Republic

THE COUNTRY	THE PEOPLE	THE STATE
622,984 sq. km.	2.95 million	Single-party presidential republic
Major Cities	*Ethnic Groups*	*Head of State*
Bangui (capital)	Banda and Baya tribes	General
Bakouma	are dominant	Andre Kolingba
Berberati	Zande	
Bossangoa	Baka	*Ruling Body*
		Cabinet of presidential appointees
Economy	*Languages*	
Disorganized but	French (official)	
recovering with IMF	Arabic in north	*Official Party*
help. Still largely	Swahili in east	Rassemblement
subsistence-based	Some Hausa and Sango	Democratique
and resistant to central		Centraficain
control.	*Religion*	
	Roman Catholic *c.* 40%	
Principal Exports	Islam *c.* 35%	
Diamonds, cotton,	Traditional	
coffee, timber		
Currency		
CFA franc of 100		
centimes		

which disappeared in the eighteenth and nineteenth centuries as a result of the infamous slave trade.

Central Africa was a great and desirable reservoir for slavers, partly because its people were outstandingly skilled craftsmen. For many centuries they had been making weapons and implements, ornaments and musical instruments. The people of what was to become Central African Republic or CAR were also well-built and intelligent. The Arab slave markets of Egypt were selling 20,000 Central African natives a year by 1800. About as

many were driven westwards to the coast for shipment to the West Indies and Brazil.

As the slave trade was slowly overcome, the Africans who had survived it by fleeing into the forests reassembled in the empty lands. The Baya tribe claimed the west, the Azande the east and the Banda the centre. They did not remain long at peace. In the 1880s the empire-building French and Belgians exploited various regions.

Almost without exception, the European administrators, traders and settlers were no lesser slavers

CENTRAL AFRICAN (CAR)

than their professional predecessors. Conditions were worst of all in the new colony of Oubangui-Chari, where thousands of Africans perished under French maltreatment. Some of the tribes resisted, especially the Baya people, and the French fought outright wars against them. Having conquered them, the French established coffee and cotton plantations and developed diamond-mining. The region was then known as French Equatorial Africa. During the Second World War, this colony sided with de Gaulle's Free French and Britain.

Barthélemy Boganda, one of the first Africans to receive an education at French mission schools, established in 1949 the Mouvement d'Evolution Sociale de l'Afrique Noire (MESAN), in opposition to the French. This courageous and far-sighted man demanded basic political and economic rights for the Africans and openly accused the French of racism. Despite attempts on his life and many moves to discredit him, Boganda persisted in his campaign and in 1956, 1957 and 1958 MESAN won much support in the limited elections which the French permitted.

Boganda's 1958 successes were too much for the French. On March 1959 he died in a plane crash which is believed to have been 'arranged' by his French enemies and their local accomplices. David *DACKO, a close associate of Boganda, became MESAN's leader and under his leadership it deteriorated into a French-controlled agency.

Another Boganda associate, Abel Goumba, broke with Dacko to form the Mouvement d'Evolution de l'Afrique Centrale (MEDAC). For the French, MEDAC was too much like the old progressive MESAN and in 1960 they banned it and arrested its leaders. Meanwhile, they permitted Dacko to declare independence for the new Central African Republic on 13 August, though he was nothing more than a puppet. In 1962 the French brought into being a national CAR army with Lieutenant Jean-Bedel *BOKASSA as chief-of-staff.

Because of French incompetence and Dacko's corruption, the CAR's economy was soon in ruins, despite Israeli efforts to revive the diamond trade. The army turned against Dacko and in December 1965 a general strike was called. The French met this crisis by telling Dacko to hand over the presidency to Jean Izambo but on 1 January 1966 Bokassa, having won rapid promotion to colonel, forced Dacko and Izambo to move aside and seized power. He changed the title of the country to the Central African Empire.

Within a year Bokassa had managed to turn the entire populace against him by his dictatorial, erratic and incompetent administration. Grossly corrupt, he made himself immensely wealthy and protected his power by executing or imprisoning his more vocal opponents. Despite Bokassa's revolting cruelty, France continued to support him, largely because French interests held the uranium concession. Only

71

CENTRAL AFRICAN (CAR)

when Bokassa ordered a massacre of children did the French move to bring him down. This was not easily accomplished, even when riots occurred in 1979. Bokassa ordered his brutal 'Imperial Guard' to arrest suspected ringleaders, 120 of whom, all teenagers, were tortured to death in April 1979. The protest movement gathered strength and various exile groups were formed, while France cut all aid to CAR.

Bokassa flew to Libya to seek *GADDAFI's help and simultaneously, on 20 September 1979, the French flew Dacko to Bangui to replace Bokassa as president. Dacko did not bring CAR the freedoms which the people had hoped for. For instance, he banned all strikes and proscribed the one trade union. Six Bokassa supporters were tried and executed for their complicity in the massacres, but Bokassa himself had found asylum in the Ivory Coast.

On 1 September 1981, the armed forces' chief-of-staff, General André Kolingba, overthrew Dacko, survived two attempted coups and promised a return to civilian rule by 1985. As always, the French made sure of close involvement in CAR affairs; they appointed Colonel Mansion as Kolingba's chief adviser. In the turbulent 1980s, CAR lurched from one crisis to another, some of them created by Bokassa, who made many attempts to return home and seize power again. He so acutely embarrassed his Ivory Coast hosts that they deported him to France.

Kolingba's promise of civilian government by 1985 came to

nothing. On 14 February 1985 François Gueret, the last civilian politician in the government, was arrested and falsely charged with plotting against the regime. Hopes for a more democratic form of government rose again in September 1985 when Kolingba appointed eight civilians to ministerial posts and abolished the national military committee which had dominated the nation's political life. On 7 May 1986 Kolingba announced the setting up of the Rassemblement Démocratique Centrafricain as the official ruling party. Far from bringing in democratic reforms, Kolingba was establishing a one-party state.

Not one of CAR's presidents has improved the country's economy, which is still dominated by Europeans. Foreign exchange comes from the export of diamonds, coffee, timber and coffee, with France buying more than half the total. Facing ruin in 1981, Kolingba appealed for help to the IMF, whose experts introduced an austerity programme in an effort to organize CAR's chaotic economy, to reduce the foreign debt, and to establish manufacturing enterprises. By 1986 the IMF was able to announce that CAR should have a 'more viable' economy by 1990; in that year, the IMF declared that the results were 'encouraging'.

However, until CAR's agriculture is on a proper footing no substantial reform is possible. The great mass of peasants refuse to co-operate with government bodies or with private co-operatives. To evade taxes and

72

get better prices, the peasants sell their cash crops and other produce straight to town markets. Large quantities of food are smuggled into Congo and Zaire, with the result that the increasingly large urban populations of CAR, especially in Bangui, are sometimes short of food.

Neither the IMF nor the CAR administrators have been able to improve the transport system. The country is dependent on river and rail transport through the Congo, where it is inefficient. Petrol reaches CAR intermittently, a further cause of transport disruption.

CAR is an unfortunate country. Having survived foreign exploiters, it was then betrayed by its own leaders. Only a genuinely democratic government will be able to bring stability and prosperity to CAR. There was little sign of either in 1990.

Ceuta, the oldest European settlement on the African continent. Ceuta became a Spanish enclave in what is now Morocco in 1580. A free port since 1963, Ceuta covers less than ten square miles and is only twelve miles across the straits from Gibraltar. Spain maintains twelve thousand troops in Ceuta and *MELILLA, another enclave in Morocco. Morocco claims the enclaves and gives the name Sebta to Ceuta. The Spanish government insists that the enclaves were Spanish long before modern Morocco took shape, but the Spanish residents of Ceuta fear 'creeping Moroccanization', rather as Gibraltarians are afraid of 'going

Spanish'. A third of Ceuta's population of 75,000 are Muslims, the rest are Christians of Spanish descent. Many Moroccans cross the border daily to work in Ceuta's tourist industry. Both enclaves become potential flashpoints in times of crisis. In 1975, at the time of King *HASSAN's *GREEN MARCH into Spanish Sahara, Spain feared invasion and sent troops and warships to Ceuta and Melilla. Morocco's claims to Ceuta became more vehement in 1986 but with one war already in *WESTERN SAHARA, King Hassan was unlikely to start another.

Chad, the vast country of Chad, covering more than one million square miles, lies deep in the centre of North Africa. Much of the country is desert and semi-desert and only in the south is it fertile. Clockwise, it is bordered by Libya, Sudan, Central African Republic, Cameroon, Nigeria and Niger. While not an Islamic republic, Chad has a population which is 50 per cent Muslim. Only 5 per cent is Christian, while the remainder of the people follow traditional beliefs.

As a nation Chad was most powerful under Muslim leaders in the sixteenth and seventeenth centuries. During the nineteenth century the entire economy was based on the slave trade. The slaves were captured in the south and driven north to the markets of the Mediterranean and Arabia. When French imperialists arrived in the 1880s and stopped the trade in people the southern tribes welcomed them as deliverers but the *SENUSSI empire, which had

The Republic of Chad

THE COUNTRY 1,284,000 sq. km.	THE PEOPLE 5.06 million	THE STATE Presidential Republic
Major Cities Ndjamena (capital) Doba Bongor Am Timan	*Ethnic Groups* Arabs and Tuareg in the north Sara tribespeople in the south	*Head of State* President Idriss Deby *Ruling Body* Council of State or 'Commissioners'
Economy Pastoral farming, cotton, dates	*Languages* French (official) Arabic is common in the north Many African tongues	*Official Party* Chad National Party
Principal Export Cotton		
Currency CFA franc of 100 centimes	*Religion* Islam 45% Christianity 5% Traditional beliefs 40%	

grown southwards from Libya and had become involved in slavery, was hostile. One kingdom within Chad held out against France until 1911 and only in 1916 did France proclaim Chad to be a colony. Even then it was 1920 before the army subjugated eastern Chad. The northern provinces of Borkou, Ennedi and Tibesti were never wholly pacified, not even by Foreign Legion forces backed by air power.

The French kept their large territory under control by limiting its economic and educational development. However, in 1946 Gabriel Lisette formed a radical national party, the Parti Progressiste Tchadien (PPT) which won the 1957 elections. As a foreigner – he was West Indian by birth – and therefore distrusted, Lisette

was forced to surrender his leadership of Chad's first autonomous government to his friend François *TOMBALBAYE, who became president of an independent Chad in 1960. The Chad National Liberation Front, *FROLINAT, came into being in 1966 to combat the corruption of PPT administrators. With strife threatening to destroy Chad, in 1968 Tombalbaye appealed for French military help against Frolinat rebels. He persuaded Libya to stop supporting Frolinat by allowing Colonel *GADDAFI to occupy the *AOUZOU strip in northern Chad.

Tombalbaye instituted his own bizarre concept of a 'cultural revolution', which alienated practically all groups, including the military. During a coup in 1975, President

Tombalbaye was killed and General Felix *MALLOUM became head of the new military government. Malloum turned into a repressive dictator, Frolinat grew stronger as a result and by early 1978 it controlled Borkou, Ennedi and Tibesti provinces. Under French pressure, a former Frolinat chief, Hissène Habré, became Prime Minister and was soon embroiled in a power struggle with Malloum. Meanwhile, Frolinat was beset by a divisive internal conflict – Goukouni Oueddei leading his faction against that of Acyl Ahmat, who had Libyan support. Following a civil war in 1979, Malloum was forced into exile, Oueddei became President and Hissène Habré Defence Minister.

Civil war raged anew as Habré's supporters fought those of Oueddei. Most of the population of Ndjamena, the capital, fled into neighbouring Cameroon. Oueddei and his Libyan allies forced Habré from the country but he continued his fight from Sudan. Under United Nations' urging, an African peace-keeping force entered Chad in 1981 but its presence did not stop the war with his Armed Forces of the North (FAN), which Habré won. Oueddei sought refuge in Libya, which provided him with an army to capture Faya Largeau in June 1983. France and Libya signed a non-intervention agreement in September 1984 but Gaddafi, even while signing, was sending more troops into Chad.

As Gaddafi consolidated the Libyan presence in Chad with six military bases, the *ORGANIZATION OF AFRICAN UNITY (OAU) tried vainly to end the war. Fighting continued throughout 1986 and became less a war between Chadian factions than one between Chad and Libya. The continual conflict prevented any improvement in Chad's economy.

In 1987 Libya again attacked Chad but the Chad army, under Hassan Djammous, knocked out about one tenth of the enemy forces. On 13 September, a cease-fire negotiated by the OAU came into effect but nobody expected Gaddafi to respect it fully and Libyan aircraft continued to carry out daily flights over Chad. Elements of Libya's 'Islamic Legion' were several times repulsed when they tried to enter Chad. In November, the victorious Hassan Djammous strengthened the already firm ties between France and Chad by visiting Paris.

Gaddafi consolidated his grip on the Aouzou Strip, digging fortifications and bringing in more tanks and anti-aircraft batteries, but on 25 May 1988 he stated that he was prepared to recognize Hissène Habré's government and restore normal relations. This seemed to suggest that Libya was ready to disentangle itself from the Chad civil war but no interested party could trust Gaddafi's offer and some observers suspected that he was simply planning a trade for Libyan prisoners of war held in Chad, which indeed he was. He then had his troops engage in what he called 'symbolic warfare' to show that he would take the offensive at any time, but for the time being the war was at an end.

Chad's wars cost her twenty years of economic development. In 1989 the country was among the ten poorest nations and survived only with international aid. The World Bank announced in 1989 that Chad needed $400 million just to repair roads. Outside Ndjamena, there were only twenty-five miles of paved highway in a country the size of France and Spain combined. The World Bank director in Chad, Horst Scheffold, said that until 2000 Chad would need general aid even to reach the low level of other *SAHEL countries.

Chad's five million inhabitants have a per capita annual income of only $78 and Chad relies on cotton for eighty-five per cent of its hard currency earnings. However, during the 1980s the cotton market was in depression. Land-locked Chad has always had difficulties in getting its cotton to the world market. Money from *Band Aid* concerts organized by the Irish pop singer Bob Geldof went to help build a new bridge across the Lagone river, two hundred miles south of Ndjamena. The bridge improves the route from the cotton-growing regions of southern Chad across neighbouring Cameroon to the Atlantic port of Douala.

The state-controlled Coton-Tchad, the main cotton company, nearly went bankrupt when it ran up debts of $134 million between 1984 and 1986. Eleven of the twenty-three cotton mills were closed permanently and seven others stopped work temporarily. This disaster led to Western aid donors imposing a restructuring of the company. In 1985 an armed rebellion by dissidents called *codos*, short for commandos, led to a complete collapse of the economy in the animist and Christian south. Habré's northern-based army crushed the uprising and the last warlords of the cotton region rallied to Habré.

Apart from the effects of war, Chad's fragile economy is often badly hit by drought. The country has poor communications and remains bereft of adequate funds for development. Oil has been found in the Kanem district and could transform the economy, but the foreign capital needed is unlikely to be found until genuine peace has been restored by treaty and international guarantee. The uranium reserves in the Aouzou strip are more likely to be exploited by Libya than by Chad.

Land-locked Chad is not all barren. In the south it has one of Africa's largest game reserves, Zakouma National Park, and Lake Chad is the eleventh largest lake in the world. Since hunting is forbidden, Chad is considered a paradise for the naturalist, though its potential cannot be realized until all war ceases. At the end of 1990 calamity befell Chad. Habré had begun to accept assistance from Saddam Hussein of Iraq. As a result, he fell out with France, Chad's main backer, who thus let Idriss Deby, Habré's former ally, bid for power in Chad unhindered. As Deby's rebels surged into Ndjamena, the national army panicked and fled, as did Habré. Deby had accepted weapons from Gaddafi, but he is not regarded as his satrap; he pledged to establish good relations with Chad's neighbours and released hundreds of Libyan prisoners of war. With a more neutral government in Ndjamena, Gaddafi has furthered his ambition to extend Libyan influence south of the Sahara.

Chahine, Youssef (sometimes spelled Shahin) (b. 1924), leading Arab film producer. An Egyptian Christian born in Alexandria, Chahine made his first film in 1946 and ever since then has devoted his energies to writing, directing and producing controversial films with, as he puts it, 'a message of truth'. His work has been criticized as appealing only to intellectuals. He says that intellectuals are the people who best understand his films, but many others pay to see his productions. Among his best known films are *Bonaparte*, which deals with Napoleon's campaign in Egypt 1800–1, and *The Sparrow*, which shows President *NASSER's ignominious defeat by Israel in 1967 – the Six Day War. Chahine is an ambassador for Arab culture, expressed through cinema, and the leading campaigner against film piracy in the Arab world.

Chama Cha Mapinduzi (CCM), the Party of the Revolution, Tanzania's only legal political party, formed in 1977 by the merger of *TANU and the *AFRO-SHIRAZI PARTY. A democratic socialist party, it follows the principles of the *ARUSHA DECLARATION. The CCM's considerable powers include making the policy which the government carries out and the approval or rejection of all candidates for election to the National Assembly. Since 1982 an eighteen member Central Committee has run the party and President *NYERERE has been chairman of the party since the beginning. During the late 1980s there were differences between the socialist stalwarts and the more pragmatic members of the party and the government. It is thought that ex-President Nyerere decided not to step down as chairman in 1987 because he wanted to continue arguing the socialist case.

Chidzero, Bernard (b. 1927), Zimbabwean politician, Minister of Finance, Economic Planning and Development since 1981. He worked for the United Nations and became Deputy Secretary-General of UNCTAD. In 1980 he was elected a *ZANU (PF) Senator and appointed to the cabinet the following year. Chidzero has also served as Chairman of an International Monetary Fund committee and as President of UNCTAD VII.

Chimurenga, in Zimbabwe it means 'war of liberation'. On Chimurenga Day, 28 April, two chimurenga are celebrated. The first was the unsuccessful struggle of the Mashona and Ndebele peoples from 1893 to 1897 against the white settlers. The second was the successful struggle by nationalist forces against the white minority government in Rhodesia. It began with the Battle of Chinjoyi (Sinoia) between *ZANLA and government forces (28 April 1966) and ended when the Rhodesian government signed the *LANCASTER HOUSE AGREEMENT (Dec. 1979), accepting majority rule. An estimated 14,000 guerrillas and 1000 government troops were killed during the second chimurenga.

Chipembere, Henry Blasius Masauko (1930–75) radical Malawian politician who played a leading part in the campaign for independence and died in exile. After graduating from *FORT HARE UNIVERSITY COLLEGE he became a district officer in Nyasaland (now Malawi) and won election to the Legislative Council in 1956. As a member of the *NYASALAND AFRICAN CONGRESS he organized the militant campaign for self-government and universal suffrage and urged Hastings *BANDA to lead the campaign for Malawi independence.

After his release from prison (1961) Chipembere became Minister of Local Government (1962–4) and Minister of Education after independence (Jul. 1964). In September 1964 Banda dismissed six of his cabinet who were demanding more radical policies, including speedier Africanization. Chipembere resigned in protest and organized a rebellion which Banda crushed. Chipembere escaped to exile first in Tanzania (1964) and then in the United States (1965) where he died.

Chirwa, Orton Edgar Ching'oli (b. 1919), radical Malawian politician who played a leading part in the campaign for independence and is now imprisoned for life in Malawi. After qualifying as a lawyer in London, he was a founder of the *MALAWI CONGRESS PARTY (1959) and acting president until *BANDA's release from prison (1960). He was

closely associated with Banda in the successful campaign for independence and served in the cabinet as Minister of Justice before and after independence (1962–4). Shortly after independence Chirwa and five other cabinet ministers were sacked for protesting against Banda's refusal to speed up Africanization and to adopt more radical policies (Sep. 1964). With Henry *CHIPEMBERE he escaped to exile in Tanzania (Oct. 1964) and lived in Dar-es-Salaam where he practised law and founded the *MALAWI FREEDOM MOVEMENT (1977) a Malawi opposition exile group.

Late in 1981, Chirwa, his wife Vera and their son Fumbani were seized in Zambia and taken across the border to Malawi where they were tried and convicted of treason; husband and wife were both sentenced to death (May 1983). After protests from the international community and their adoption as Amnesty International Prisoners of Conscience their sentences were commuted to life imprisonment.

Chissano, Joaquim Alberto (b. 1939), President of Mozambique since 1986 and a founder member of *FRELIMO while still at university in Portugal. He played an important role in the struggle for independence as secretary to Eduardo *MONDLANE, *FRELIMO's leader, (1966–9), and as Frelimo's representative in Tanzania (1969–74), earning the rank of major-general. He was Prime Minister during the transition from colonial rule to independence (1974–5). After independence Chissano served as Foreign Minister

(1975–86) and as a member of the Politburo was involved in Mozambique's major political decisions. He was elected to succeed President Samora *MACHEL in November 1986.

He has professed Marxist-Leninist ideas, but he is also a pragmatist who is prepared to be liberal on economic issues and to look to capitalist countries for aid to solve his country's severe economic problems. Early in 1987 he took the advice of the IMF and introduced austerity measures, including a 40 per cent currency devaluation and a cut in government spending. At the fifth Frelimo Congress (Jul. 1989) delegates approved Chissano's programme to drop the party's commitment to Marxism-Leninism and to open up membership to religious believers, property owners and others previously regarded as class enemies. The delegates also backed his proposals to negotiate an end to the civil war with *RENAMO, an initiative which did not succeed.

Chitepo, Herbert Wiltshire Tfumaindini (1923–75), Zimbabwean nationalist leader now buried in *HEROES' ACRE. The first black barrister in Zimbabwe (then Southern Rhodesia), he joined the *NDP (1960) and *ZAPU (1961). While he was Director of Public Prosecutions in Tanzania he joined *ZANU and became its National Chairman (1963). In 1965 he went to Lusaka to play a major role in planning and recruiting for the struggle against white minority rule in Zimbabwe. He was Chairman of *ZANU's Zimbabwe Revolutionary Council when he was assassinated in Lusaka, presumably by agents of the Rhodesian government.

Chiume, Kanyama, Malawian politician who played an important part in the campaign for independence, but quarrelled with Hastings *BANDA. He was Minister for Education and Social Development (1962–3) and then Minister for Foreign Affairs (1963–4). In September 1964 he was one of the six ministers sacked by Banda for criticizing his refusal to adopt radical policies – including speedy Africanization. Chiume fled to Zambia and later founded the Congress for a Second Republic – a moderate exile opposition group in Tanzania.

Ciskei, a South African *HOMELAND, the second to be set aside for the Xhosa people, it was declared 'independent' in December 1981, a status not recognized outside South Africa. It is a small, poverty-stricken, overcrowded territory covering 8500 sq. km. At 'independence' its resident population was 660,000, with a further 1,400,000 citizens in South Africa. In 1986 it was agreed with South Africa that those living and working permanently in South Africa would be entitled to South African citizenship. Its economy depends on agriculture and remittances from migrant labour in South Africa.

Ciskei was ruled by President Lennox Sebe who made himself President-for-Life in 1983. His regime was troubled and corrupt. Sebe used violence and terror to quell unrest. In 1986 a bitter Sebe family feud further destabilized the government and involved Ciskei in a quarrel with *TRANSKEI, which had opposed the creation of a second Xhosa Homeland from the beginning. In March 1990 Sebe was overthrown in a military coup. The new leader, Brigadier Josh Gqozo, wants Ciskei to be reintegrated into a reformed South Africa.

Clark, John Pepper (b. 1935), Nigerian poet, playwright and academic. Clark worked as a journalist before starting to teach at the University of Lagos (1966), where he is now Professor of English. In his work Clark strongly asserts the positive values of African tradition and culture. He berated the United States for its values and way of life In *America, Their America* (1964).

Clegg, Johnny, South African musician and member of a multi-racial band. He became internationally known after a very successful European tour in 1987. His first single was a tribute to the heroes of the struggle against *APARTHEID.

Coetzee, John Michael (b. 1940), South African novelist and academic who writes in Afrikaans and English. He studied and taught in the United States before starting to lecture at the University of Cape Town (1972), where he has been Professor of General Literature since 1984. Much of his work is set in rural Afrikaans society and is concerned with the horrors of violence and oppression as practised both by individuals and by society. His novel, *The Life and Times of Michael K* (1983) won the Booker Prize in Britain. Among his other works are *In the Heart of the Country* (1977), *Foe* (1983), *Dusklands* (1986) and *Age of Iron* (1990).

Coloureds, official South African term to describe those of mixed race, descended from *BANTU, European, Indian, Malay and *HOTTENTOT ancestors. Most had their origins in the Cape Province. They suffer from racial discrimination and usually identify with black South Africans. President P.W. *BOTHA's tricameral constitution gave them a limited share of power in their chamber of parliament – the *HOUSE OF REPRESENTATIVES.

Comité Permanent Inter-états de Lutte contre la Sécheresse dans le Sahel, or CILSS (Permanent interstate committee on drought control in the Sahel). The serious problems brought about by drought in the *SAHEL brought together eleven states in an attempt to improve conditions: Burkina Faso, Cape Verde, Chad, Gambia, Guinea-Bissau, Guinea, Mali, Mauritania, Niger, Nigeria and Senegal. Formed in 1973, CILSS works with the United Nations Sudan-Sahelian office in tackling drought problems. CILSS's office is in Ouagadougou, Burkina Faso, and it holds regular conferences of heads of state. In 1976 CILSS set up the Club du Sahel (Club of the Sahel) to co-ordinate long-range policies and strategies between CILSS members and foreign donors.

Commonwealth, the: former colonies of the British Empire are now members of the Commonwealth. Except for Mauritius which has a Governor-General, the African members of the Commonwealth are independent republics. In the Commonwealth, members from all over the world meet and co-operate in pursuit of their common interests. On a number of occasions pressure from the members has had tangible results. The conference of 1979 helped persuade the British government to support elections in Zimbabwe and the achievement of independence in 1980. In 1960 South Africa had no option but to withdraw from the Commonwealth after its members expressed their abhorrence of *APARTHEID, whilst in 1985, despite British opposition, the Commonwealth agreed to set up the *EMINENT PERSONS GROUP which went to South Africa to assess the situation and concluded that tough economic sanctions were the only way of averting a bloodbath in South Africa.

Communauté Economique de l'Afrique de l'Ouest, or CEAO (Economic Community of West Africa). A grouping of West African states which promotes trade and rationalizes customs regulations. It spends part of its revenue on the development of its members' economies. CEAO's members are Burkina Faso, Ivory Coast, Mali, Mauritania, Niger and Senegal, with Benin and Togo as observers. Within the community raw materials move freely, but manufacturers from the more developed states are subject to a 'regional co-operation tax'. Member states finance a community development fund according to their share of trade within CEAO. In practice,

Ivory Coast and Senegal contribute almost the entire fund. CEAO has a general secretariat in Ouagadougou, Burkina Faso.

Comoro Islands, forming an archipelago between East Africa and Madagascar, the Comoros consist of four main islands – Grand Comore, Anjouan, Moheli and Mayotte. In area, the islands, of volcanic origin, cover only 2236 sq. km. However, they have attracted many races of people. In the early Christian centuries, Malayan and Polynesian people are believed to have settled there, to be followed in the fifth century by Arabs and Africans. The Arabs made the islands into a slave-trading centre and from the seventh century on Islam dominated.

A French expedition landed on Mayotte in 1841 and its leader induced the sultan to sell the island to France, for a mere 1000 piastres. Gradually, the rulers of the other islands sold their territories and in 1912 the French proclaimed the group a colony, Les Comores. However, they put Les Comores under the authority of the successive governor-generals of neighbouring Madagascar, all of whom neglected the islands and kept their people in total subjection. No political party or newspaper was permitted, while the local nobility was allowed to exploit the natives, who continued with their subsistence farming.

After many minor revolts and much civil disobedience, all ruthlessly suppressed by the French security forces, the islands became nominally autonomous in 1961,

The Federal Islamic Republic of the Comoros

THE COUNTRY	THE PEOPLE	THE STATE
2,236 sq. km.	440,000	Single-party presidential republic
Major Cities Moroni (capital) Mutsamudu Mamutzu	*Ethnic Groups* Africans Arabs French settlers	*Head of State* Muhammad Taki
Economy Subsistence farming 50% of the budget is spent on imported food. Tourism developing	*Languages* French and Arabic, both 'official' Kishwahili is the most common	*Ruling Body* Revolutionary Council of State *Official Party* United National Front
Principal Exports Copra, coffee, cocoa cloves, vanilla	*Religion* Shafi Muslim 99%	*Special Note* The island of Mayotte, while a *de facto* part of the Comoros, is ruled separately by the French.
Currency Comoro franc of 100 centimes		

though a French high commissioner had ultimate control. Nevertheless, political parties became legal and numerous parties were formed. In 1972 the islands' richest man, Ahmed Abdallah Abderemane, of the Union Démocratique des Comoros (UDC), was elected president. His election broke the tradition of native princes holding the greatest power under the French.

Abdallah became leader of the Council of Government, whose new chamber of deputies sought independence. In 1973 French delaying tactics brought about a treaty which stipulated a five-year delay before independence. They also planned a referendum, to be held island by island. A referendum in 1974 produced a 94 per cent vote in favour of independence but the French officials declared that in Mayotte 64 per cent had voted against independence. On this suspect vote the French proposed other tactics to delay freedom for the Comoros.

Ahmed Abdallah unilaterally declared independence on 6 July 1975. The *OAU admitted the Comoros to membership a mere twelve days later, with Abdallah as Head of State. A new group of parties, the United National Front (FNU), opposed Abdallah and on 3 August the FNU leader, Ali Soilih, deposed him. An extraordinary situation now arose. While the UN admitted the Comoros to membership, France continued with its preparations for a referendum on Mayotte. In December, France recognized Grand Comore, Anjouan and Moheli as independent. A year later, the government in Paris declared Mayotte to be a French 'territorial community'. In anger, the other three islands expelled all their French citizens.

President Ali Soilih survived four coup attempts but fell in May 1978, when a white mercenary, Bob Denard, seized power. Under the most suspicious circumstances, Ali Soilih was shot dead while 'attempting to escape' from custody only two weeks after being deposed. On Denard's invitation, Abdallah returned to the Comoros to become President of the Directorate. On 1 October 1978 the islands officially became the Federal Islamic Republic of the Comoros, but this step did not induce the people of Mayotte to join.

Abdallah turned the Comoros into a fundamentalist Islamic state. This meant, for instance, that women were obliged to wear the veil and most aspects of the Islamic law were reimposed after having been relaxed by Ali Soilih. Arab oil states were gratified by Abdallah's Islamic decrees, while the French were pleased that he returned foreign estates to their former owners, the French colonists.

Denard took the Muslim name of Said Mustapha M'Hadjou and, with a group of mercenaries, stayed in the Comoros to ensure the security of Abdallah's rule. The mercenaries'

influence and authority became so pervasive that the OAU, in protest, expelled the Comoro delegation from a foreign ministers' conference in Khartoum. Tanzania, the Seychelles and Madagascar also denounced the power of the white mercenaries. Good relations were not restored until 1982, but the mercenaries remained.

A plot to overthrow Abdallah was uncovered in 1983 and on 8 March 1985 mutineers of the Presidential Guard tried to seize power during President Abdallah's absence in France. Bob Denard and his mercenaries brutally quelled the attempted coup and several hundred people were arrested. According to Amnesty International, some mutineers were tortured to death. Others were sentenced to forced labour for life but were released under a presidential amnesty.

In November 1989, Abdallah ordered Denard and his mercenaries out of the Comoros. In the argument which followed, on 19 November, Denard and another mercenary assassinated Abdallah and in an attempted cover-up claimed that he had been killed by a rebel rocket fired through his bedroom window.

Denard then made it difficult for Said Djohar, who had assumed control as interim president, to exercise authority. France sent warships and troops to remove Denard from the Comoros, by force if necessary. No fighting took place and Denard surrendered to the French army, which flew him out of the islands.

Muhammad Taki, who had fled to France in 1984 to escape Abdallah's tyranny, returned to become the new president and promised to introduce a Western-style democracy.

The Comoros remain backward and poor and the great majority of the population of 400,000 live by subsistence farming. At least sixty per cent of the land, including the most fertile areas, is owned by French companies, which trade in coffee, cocoa, copra, cloves and vanilla. Traditional ruling families own much of the rest of the land. The tourist industry is undeveloped but will perhaps one day greatly assist the general economy.

The high unemployment rate has driven many Comorians to emigrate to Madagascar, Kenya, Tanzania and Reunion. The Comoros have a major illiteracy problem and social services generally are poor. In 1990, under a UN scheme, foreign French-speaking and Arabic-speaking teachers were sent to the Comoros while the Arab League promised finance for improved social services for 1991.

CONCP (Conferência das Organizações Nacionalistas das Colonias Portuguesas), founded in 1961, in the struggle for independence a common front of African nationalists which opposed Portuguese colonial rule, including *FRELIMO, *MPLA and *PAIGC. The co-operation of these socialist independence movements in CONCP helped to promote common aims through joint diplomatic activity and public relations. Its members also shared military experience and intelligence.

Congo, the People's Republic of the Congo is situated on the West African coast and lies across the Equator. It is bordered by Cameroon and the Central African Republic to the north, by the Zaire River on its long eastern border, by Zaire and the *CABINDA enclave to the south, by the Atlantic Ocean in the south-west and by Gabon in the west and north-west. Pointe Noire is a major port serving equatorial Africa. The Congo has a variety of natural features, including coastal swamps, tropical forests, plateaus, mountains and arable valleys. The climate is generally hot and humid.

The original inhabitants were probably pygmies, who were displaced by *BANTU immigrants. The main ethnic groups today are the Vili, the Kongo, the Téké, the M'Bochi and the Sanga.

Compared to most African countries the Congo is highly industrialized and urbanized. Only a third of the population depends on agriculture, in decline since independence and accounting for only six per cent of the GDP. Despite the efforts of the authorities, the Congo is not self-sufficient in cassava, its staple food. Other subsistence crops are maize, plantains, yams and sweet potatoes. Sugar, tobacco, cocoa, coffee, groundnuts and palm oil are exported, but contribute little to foreign earnings. The country has large forests and timber was the principal export until 1973 when it was overtaken by oil, which currently accounts for about 90 per cent of

The People's Republic of the Congo

THE COUNTRY	THE PEOPLE	THE STATE
342,000 sq. km.	1,913,000	Single-party republic
Major Cities	*Ethnic Groups*	*Head of State*
Brazzaville (capital)	Vili	President Sassou-
Pointe-Noire	Kongo	Nguesso
	Teke	
Economy	M'Bochi	*Ruling Bodies*
Petroleum	Sanga	Council of Ministers
Manufacturing		National People's
Agriculture	*Languages*	Assembly
	French (official)	
Principal Exports	Kongo	*Official Party*
Oil & Petroleum	Teke	Parti congolais du travail
Timber		
	Religion	
Currency	Traditional beliefs	
CFA franc of 100	Christian	
centimes		

foreign earnings. By the mid-1980s the economy was suffering from low oil prices and there were worries about the future as the more easily recoverable reserves were being used up.

Yet, the Congo had favourable trade balances during the 1980s, mainly because of its oil exports but also because of trade surpluses with fellow members of *UDEAC. Generally economic growth has been satisfactory and a substantial manufacturing sector, including food and timber processing, and textile factories, has been established. Despite the inefficiency of the state bodies which manage large industrial enterprises, the Congo has attracted substantial foreign aid for development from both the West and communist states.

Before the Congo was taken over by France late in the nineteenth century, Europeans had come to the country as slave traders in the sixteenth century, and later in search of rubber and palm products. In 1908 the Congo (then called the Middle Congo) became a constituent territory in French Equatorial Africa. In 1946 the Middle Congo was given its own territorial assembly; this gave its leaders the chance to gain political experience. After the 1958 referendum the Middle Congo became the Congo Republic, an autonomous member of the French Community. France supported the full independence of the Congo in August 1960, under the leadership of President Fulbert *YOULOU. President Youlou changed the constitution to give himself extensive presidential powers (Mar. 1961),

85

but he lost support because of his unpopular pro-Western policies and his support of the *KATANGA secession. Government corruption, his attempts to subdue trade unions and his plans for a one-party state provoked the rebellion which toppled him (Aug. 1963).

During the presidency of Alphonse Massamba-Débat (1963–8) the country moved to the left with the establishment of a Marxist-Leninist party, the Mouvement national de la révolution (MNR) as the sole legal party (1964). In January 1966 the MNR was declared to be the 'supreme organ of the nation'. The MNR was undisciplined and soon its youth wing was making itself into a semi-independent paramilitary force and challenging the leadership. The MNR's radicalism also alarmed and antagonized the army. With support from left- and right-wing groups, Major *NGOUABI seized power; he dissolved the MNR (Aug. 1968) and forced Massamba-Débat out of the presidency (Sep. 1968). Once in power he moved to the left and adopted socialist policies. In December 1969 he replaced the MNR with the *PARTI CONGOLAIS DU TRAVAIL (PCT), another Marxist-Leninist party with supreme power, but more tightly controlled from the centre than its predecessor. In January 1970 the country was renamed the People's Republic of the Congo.

President Ngouabi was unable to achieve stability; he was challenged by student demonstrations, protests and attempted coups which involved leading members of the government. In 1973 a new constitution was approved by a referendum; this provided for the election of a national people's assembly from a list of PCT candidates. Although he had considerable popular support Ngouabi was unable to crush the rebellion led by Ange Diawara, who had been his vice-president, and equally unable to control the army. After several attempts on his life, he was assassinated in March 1977; the country was then led by Yhombi-Opango (1978–9) and a military committee of the PCT.

Yhombi-Opango found it difficult to maintain his authority and was soon at odds with the left wing of the PCT. He was replaced as head of state by Col. Denis *SASSOU-NGUESSO, who had supported Ngouabi. The military committee was dissolved and power was handed back to the Central Committee of the PCT.

President Sassou-Nguesso has survived for over a decade and brought a measure of stability to the Congo, by keeping a careful balance between socialist orthodoxy and pro-Western pragmatism. Despite declarations of loyalty to Ngouabi's ideals of socialism, he has liberalized economic policy and adopted an increasingly pro-Western foreign policy. He has improved relations with his more conservative neighbours, Cameroon, Gabon and Zaire. Tribal rivalries and austere budgets set to strengthen the economy have led to tension. There have been demonstrations, including serious riots in the capital, Brazzaville (Nov. 1985). The president has tried to reconcile various factions and to broaden his support, but his government is still threatened by the plotting of coups. In July 1990 the central committee of the Parti congolais du travail announced that reforms would be made in 1991; these are expected to include widening party membership, abandoning Marxism – Leninism as the official ideology and allowing other political parties to form.

Conscription In South Africa, young white men are called up for military service. Some of the campaigners against conscription have been imprisoned for refusing military service. South African attempts to introduce conscription for all young males in Namibia (1980–5) were effectively abandoned, although South Africa maintained it still had the right to conscript.

Conservative Alliance of Zimbabwe, political party founded in 1985 to represent the interests of the white minority in Zimbabwe, in succession to the *RHODESIAN FRONT (1962–81) and the Republican Front (1981–5). In the 1985 elections it won fifteen out of the twenty seats reserved for whites. Ian *SMITH led the party until 1987 when he had to resign after making comments detrimental to Zimbabwe. Mark Partridge succeeded him. The party lost its parliamentary representation in 1987 when the reserved seats for whites were abolished, but it had already been weakened by splits and the defection of some of its members to *ZANU (PF). During the campaign for the March 1990 election it announced its support for Edgar *TEKERE's *ZIMBABWE UNITY MOVEMENT.

Conservative Party, extreme right-wing South African political party, which has been the official parliamentary opposition since 1987. It was founded in 1982 after Dr *TREURNICHT and seventeen other MPs quit the *NATIONAL PARTY to fight President P.W. *BOTHA's constitutional proposals to give *COLOUREDS and *INDIANS a limited share of political power. The party will not compromise on the principle of *APARTHEID; it is determined to keep large areas of South Africa under white rule and to relegate the other races to separate *HOMELANDS. Under Treurnicht's leadership the party has steadily gained support from the white electorate and in the 1989 election for the *HOUSE OF ASSEMBLY increased its representation to thirty-nine MPs. Some members, including four MPs, are known to have links with the neo-Nazi *AFRIKANER WEERSTANDSBEWEGING. After gaining control of a number of local authorities in the Transvaal in 1988 the Conservative Party tried to reimpose rigid apartheid; public amenities like parks, swimming pools and libraries were reserved for whites only. The non-whites retaliated with a boycott that drove several whites out of business.

During 1990 the party bitterly opposed the government's negotiations with the *AFRICAN NATIONAL CONGRESS and the plans for constitutional talks in 1991. It accuses President *DE KLERK of betraying the white people of South Africa and argues that if there was an election on the issue of reform the white electorate would reject the government in favour of the Conservative Party.

Contact Group, five western powers (Canada, France, United Kingdom, United States, West Germany) with economic and strategic interests in Namibia, who set themselves up in 1977 as mediators between South Africa and *SWAPO (the Namibian nationalists). Both sides accepted their proposals in principle (1978) but they were rejected by South Africa shortly before being adopted by the United Nations as *UN RESOLUTION 435. As South Africa continued its delaying tactics and as President Reagan of the United States preferred direct negotiations with South Africa through his envoy Chester Crocker, the Contact Group was rendered ineffective from 1982 onwards.

Convention People's Party (CPP), Ghanaian political party (1949–66), it was founded by *NKRUMAH and other radicals who broke away from the United Gold Coast Convention. The CPP campaigned for immediate self-government; its programme of democratic socialism stressed denunciation of imperialism, organization of the masses, political education and a Ghanaian nationalist press. The CPP won the elections of 1951, 1954 and 1956; it formed

the government of the colony under British rule (1951–7) and led Ghana to independence in 1957.

After independence real power in Ghana was transferred to Nkrumah and the officials of the CPP. When Ghana became a single-party socialist state in 1964 the CPP was the only legal party. In the 1965 elections all candidates were CPP nominees, but in the event, not a single vote was cast, and the government simply declared all its own candidates duly elected. In addition to being an instrument of state power, the CPP became associated with corruption and intrigue during the 1960s. When the military seized power in 1966 the CPP was banned.

Copperbelt, region of Zambia on the border with Zaire. The Copperbelt's rich deposits of copper and cobalt have been mined since the 1920s and have made Zambia a leading exporter of copper. Declining copper prices since 1975 have seriously damaged Zambia's economic development. By the early twenty-first century the copper reserves will be nearly exhausted and Zambia urgently needs to succeed in its efforts to diversify its economy. Kitwe and Ndola are the biggest Copperbelt towns. In December 1986 rising food prices caused riots in the Copperbelt, the worst since Zambia became independent.

Coptic Christians, the largest of the Christian groups in North Africa, the Copts – officially the Coptic Orthodox Church – are found almost exclusively in the Nile Valley. Some estimate that there are as many as eight million Copts but the Egyptian government claims only five million. Copts have long regarded themselves as the true Egyptians – the direct descendants of the Pharaonic race – but neither the Egyptian state nor their Muslim compatriots give them this status.

During the 1940s, when Arabs demonstrated violently against Jewish settlement in Palestine, Christian minorities came under attack as well. Copts were often victims of political abuse and physical assault and some tried to resolve their difficulties by saying, 'I am Christian by religion but Muslim by nationality.' The tactic was not generally successful. One of the few leading Egyptians to accept Copts as equals was the author Taha ★HUSSEIN, who argued that, as a state responsibility, Coptic Christianity should be taught in state schools. His suggestion was treated as a heresy.

Since the rise of ★ISLAMIC FUNDAMENTALISM in the 1950s, the Copts have lost certain property and professional rights and have been relegated, as in earlier centuries, to *dhimmi* or second-class citizen status. In 1981, President ★SADAT placed the Coptic Pope, Shenouda III, under restraint and ordered him not to leave Wadi Natrun monastery in the desert. He had annoyed the Sadat administration by urging the Copts to 'breed rapidly' so that they could catch up with the Muslims and he had protested against his people's oppression. President ★MUBARAK released Pope Shenouda in January 1985.

The Coptic Catholic Church is different from the Coptic Orthodox Chuch. The Coptic Catholics trace their origins back to a confrontation between St Francis of Assisi and the Ayyubid Sultan Al-Kamil in 1219, but the church has officially been in existence only since 1895. The patriarch, Michael Cardinal Sidarus, governs a community of about 100,000 converts from the parent church. Most of them live in Cairo, Alexandria, Minya and Assuit.

COREMO (Comite Revolucionário de Moçambique), founded in 1965. It was an attempt, encouraged by Zambia, to resolve factional differences among Mozambican nationalists. ★FRELIMO withdrew when the others refused to accept its supremacy and COREMO collapsed.

COSATU (The Congress of South African Trade Unions), formed in December 1985 to unite progressive South African trade unions. The affiliated trade unions cover a wide variety of industry and services; COSATU initially had close to six hundred thousand members. Membership is predominantly black, although it is open to all races. About a third of the members belong to the National Union of Miners. COSATU campaigns not only on shop floor issues but also on wider political issues, arguing that it is naive to try to separate economics and industry from politics. From the beginning it has worked closely with the ★UNITED DEMOCRATIC FRONT and since restrictions on ★AFRICAN NATIONAL CONGRESS (ANC) activities were lifted early

COVENANT

in 1990 it has also worked closely with the ANC in the campaign to establish a non-racial, democratic South African state. COSATU is also associated with the South African Communist Party. The General Secretary of COSATU is currently Jay Naidoo.

Covenant, Day of the, an official South African public holiday celebrated on 16 December. This day has a special significance for the Afrikaners because it commemorates the victory of the *voortrekkers* (pioneers) over the Zulu at the battle of Blood River in 1838, a victory the *voortrekkers* had sworn to celebrate annually if God granted it.

Creoles (or Krio), people in Sierra Leone descended from the freed slaves who settled in and around Freetown from 1787 until about 1880. They number about 2 per cent of the population of Sierra Leone. The first freed slaves were settled there by British philanthropists; after Sierra Leone became a colony (1808) the British government settled people who had been rescued from slave-trading ships by the Royal Navy. During the nineteenth century the Creoles were given good educational opportunities by mission schools and had West Africa's oldest university at Fourah Bay. Many became Anglicized and some qualified as doctors and lawyers; others held high posts in the colonial administration.

From the beginning of the twentieth century the British authorities looked less favourably on the Creoles, a reflection perhaps

90

of twentieth-century racism. When Sierra Leone became independent the Creole community lost any political power they might have had to the majority from the interior. The Creoles have developed their own distinctive culture and speak a language called Krio which is largely derived from English, but has the status of a separate language.

Crossroads, black shanty town near Cape Town in South Africa, it is inhabited by those who have found neither housing nor permits to work in the city. The authorities have repeatedly tried to demolish Crossroads and send its inhabitants to the *HOMELANDS. In February 1985 eighteen inhabitants died fighting eviction. In 1986 sixty-nine died during factional violence in Crossroads between the radical 'comrades' and the conservative 'fathers' who are apparently helped by the government. Crossroads has become a symbol of resistance to the South African government which is now prepared to allow some people to live there under strict conditions.

Cunene River Hydroelectric Scheme, ambitious project to harness the Cunene River on the border of Angola and Namibia for power and irrigation. It was first planned by Portugal and South Africa in the 1920s, and work began after South Africa took direct charge of Namibia (1969). Independent Angola has been unwilling to buy power while South Africa was in control but this will presumably change now that Namibia is independent.

Dacko, David (b. 1930), first President of the Central African Republic. Born in Bouchia and educated at Brazzaville, Dacko was leader of the teachers' union when elected to the territorial assembly in 1957. That same year he was appointed Minister of Agriculture and the following year Minister of Administrative Affairs. For the period 1958–9 he was Minister of the Interior. Throughout the 1950s he was a close associate of Barthélemy Boganda in the Mouvement d'Évolution Sociale de l'Afrique Noire (MESAN). When the much respected Boganda died in a mysterious air crash in 1959, Dacko became leader and at once threw out his more progressive associates. MESAN became nothing more than a self-interested group of men with French connections.

When Central African Republic won its independence in 1960, Dacko became president. He banned all opposition parties and gradually he ran his country into bankruptcy. Facing Central African Republic's first general strike, in 1965, Dacko was preparing to hand over to a French-appointed candidate when Jean-Bedel *BOKASSA, a close relative of Dacko, deposed him and seized power. Dacko spent the next ten years in prison. In September 1979, during Bokassa's absence in Libya, Dacko, with French connivance, took over the government and again became president. He held power for just two years before being deposed by General André Kolinga. He then went into exile in France.

Daddah, Moktar Ould (b. 1924), first President of Mauritania. Daddah had the great advantage of being born into a *zawya* or 'great tent' of the Berber Oulad Birri tribe. He became one of the tribe's principal leaders and was educated in Paris as a lawyer and an interpreter. Elected to the territorial assembly in 1957, he was quickly appointed vice-president of the executive council. Two years later, in 1959, he became prime minister and held this position until Mauritania was declared an Islamic Republic in 1961, when he became its first president. In December he brought together representatives from all parties and by sheer force of personality persuaded them to set up a single movement, the Parti du Peuple Mauritanian (PPM). A shrewd manipulator who disliked opposition, Daddah made PPM a state institution in 1964. He used the army to put down strikes and in 1974 nationalized MIFERMA, the giant foreign-owned mining consortium. Since 1957 Daddah had been vigorously urging that the Spanish territory of *WESTERN SAHARA should be absorbed into Mauritania but in 1974–5 he endorsed Morocco's plans to partition Western Sahara. This was a breathtaking policy reversal typical of Daddah. His move brought about *détente* with Morocco but it also plunged poverty-stricken Mauritania into a war against *POLISARIO. Most Mauritanians hated him for this, especially when Polisario guerrillas humiliated the small national army by travelling six hundred miles to lob shells into Nouakchott, the capital. The army, having lost confidence in Daddah, deposed him on 10 July 1978.

Danquah, Dr Joseph Kwame Kyereti Boakye (1895–1965), leading Ghanaian lawyer and politician. After being called to the Bar (1926) he practised law in Ghana (then the Gold Coast colony) and founded the *Times of West Africa* (1931). He subsequently founded the United Gold Coast Convention (1947), a moderate political party campaigning for self-government, and was detained by the British authorities after the 1948 disturbances.

His policies were too cautious for *NKRUMAH who formed the more radical *CONVENTION PEOPLE'S PARTY (1949) and led Ghana to independence (1957). Alarmed by Nkrumah's radicalism Danquah joined other opponents of the government in the United Party (1957) and unsuccessfully stood against Nkrumah in the 1960 presidential election. He was arrested in 1961 and detained for eighteen months; two years after being freed he was detained once more, and died in captivity in 1965.

de Blank, The Rt. Revd Joost (1908–68), Anglican Archbishop of Cape Town (1957–63), he was one of the first senior white churchmen in South Africa to speak out against the racial policies of the government. He infuriated the government by strongly condemning *APARTHEID and insisting that all Anglican Church services should be open to all races. He told other churches to break with the *NEDERDUITSE GEREFORMEERDE KERK (Dutch Reformed Church) until it renounced apartheid. He resigned after a heart attack.

de Klerk, Frederik Willem (b. 1936), President of South Africa since 1989. A member of a leading Afrikaner political family, he was in the youth section of the *NATIONAL PARTY. While practising law (1961–72) he played an active part locally in the National Party. In 1972, just after he had been appointed Professor of Administrative Law at Potchefstroom University, he won a seat in parliament in a by-election. In 1975 he became Information Officer of the Transvaal National Party and in 1978 joined the cabinet as Minister of Posts and Telecommunications. He then held a variety of posts, in charge of Social Welfare and Pensions, Sport and Recreation, Mining and Energy, Internal Affairs, Home Affairs and National Education. He became leader of the National Party in the Transvaal in 1982.

In February 1989 he succeeded P.W. *BOTHA as leader of the National Party and in August of that year succeeded him as President of South Africa. Since coming to power President de Klerk has stunned his countrymen and the rest of the world by his attempts to break the stalemate in South Africa. In a few months he released prominent political prisoners, removed restrictions on the *AFRICAN NATIONAL CONGRESS (ANC) and many other banned bodies, and promised to end *APARTHEID. In May 1990 he had talks with an ANC delegation led by Nelson *MANDELA. He hopes that these talks will pave the way for a constitutional settlement acceptable to all South Africans, but there are enormous obstacles to be overcome. First, de Klerk will not accept simple majority rule; he believes there must be guarantees for the white minority. Equally, the ANC is not likely to make concessions on the principles of 'one man, one vote' and simple majority rule. Nor will de Klerk accept the redistribution of wealth from wealthy whites to poor blacks; but it is difficult to see how political stability can be achieved without the transfer of considerable resources to the poorest in the country. Third, many Afrikaners regard him as a traitor to his people; there may yet be a vicious backlash against his attempts to make reforms.

Democratic Party (DP), left of centre South African political party, which opposes *APARTHEID. It is the first party with substantial white support that favours universal suffrage. The DP was formed in April 1989 by merging three parties, the *PROGRESSIVE FEDERAL PARTY, the National Democratic Movement and the Independent Party; it began with twenty MPs. The party has two leaders – Zach de Beer and Denis Worrall. In the September 1989 election it won thirty-three seats, and is the third largest party in the white *HOUSE OF ASSEMBLY after the *NATIONAL PARTY and the *CONSERVATIVE PARTY.

Democratic Party. moderate Ugandan political party founded in 1956 with the encouragement of Catholic priests which mainly represents southerners and Catholics. The Democratic Party won a parliamentary majority in Uganda's first national elections (1961) because it did so well in *BUGANDA where most people boycotted the election; the small minority that did register there supported the Democratic Party. The party formed the government (1962) before independence, but lost the elections for independent Uganda's first legislature in 1962 and became the official opposition to *OBOTE's government.

The party was banned by Obote in the late 1960s and only resumed open political activity after the fall of President *AMIN (Apr. 1979). Led by Paul *SSEMOGERERE it contested the December 1980 elections, and with some justification claimed victory, but the rather dubious results gave it only fifty-one of the hundred and twenty-six seats in the legislature. Once again the official opposition to President Obote, the Democratic Party fiercely attacked the government's poor record on human and political rights. In 1986 members of the party joined the

93

new military government led by President *MUSEVENI; in February 1988 Mr Ssemogerere became one of Uganda's three Deputy Prime Ministers.

Dergue, the, Ethiopian ruling committee since 1973. Senior army officers had attempted a coup to overthrow Emperor *HAILE SELASSIE in 1960. The next initiative was taken by ordinary soldiers and non-commissioned officers. They were quickly joined by junior officers, most of whom had the same background as the intelligentsia. Collectively, these officers and NCOs forced out the military hierarchy and took control of the armed forces. A Co-ordinating Committee of the Armed Forces assumed command. It was quickly called *Dergue*, the Amharic word for committee. The Dergue's unidentified membership of about 130 ranged in rank from private to major. Gradually the Dergue provided the leadership for an attack against the imperial regime. Step by step, it broke down the old feudal system and on 12 September 1974 deposed Emperor Haile Selassie. The Dergue then changed itself into the Provisional Military Administrative Council but the label of 'the Dergue' remains in popular use. The Dergue, having appointed itself 'the guide of the Ethiopian Revolution', decreed reforms which have changed the entire structure of Ethiopian society. For instance, local committees were empowered to overrule parents' decisions about their children's future. Political 'instructors' were given the power to dictate farming patterns to individual farmers and co-operatives.

Dia, Mamadou (b. 1910), Senegalese politician and onetime President of Senegal. After a basic education in mission schools, Dia attended a Paris university, after which he became a teacher and journalist. Always involved in politics, in 1946 Dia was appointed a councillor for Senegal in the French Assembly and held this position until 1952, when he became a grand councillor for French West Africa and a deputy in the French National Assembly. In 1958, he became the President of the Autonomous Republic of Senegal, a position he held until 1960. For the period 1959–60 he was also Vice-President of the Mali Federation, an ill-advised and brief union of Mali and Senegal. When the federation broke up in 1960 Dia became Prime Minister of the newly independent Senegal under President Léopold *SENGHOR. Following his attempt to overthrow Senghor in 1963 Dia was imprisoned until 1974. Even after he was released he was deprived of political rights for a further two years. Bitter and disillusioned, he disappeared from public life.

DIAMANG (Companhia de Diamantes de Angola), Angolan diamond company founded in 1917 by South African (including *ANGLO-AMERICAN) and Belgian interests. After independence the Angolan government took a majority shareholding (77 per cent) in the company which continued to monopolize the extraction and sale of diamonds. In 1986 DIAMANG was reorganized into smaller companies with the same shareholders. In the mid-1970s transport delays, the loss of technical experts, widespread smuggling and the activities of *UNITA caused a sharp drop in diamond exports; but during the 1980s there was a recovery.

Dikko, Umaru (b. 1936), controversial Nigerian politician from Northern Nigeria. He was a commissioner in North Central State during military rule (1967–75). During *SHAGARI's presidency (1979–83) he was the second most powerful man in Nigeria as Minister of Transport and the Chairman of the Presidential Task Force controlling the import of rice and other essential commodities. In 1983 he was in charge of the successful but corrupt election campaign of the *NPN (National Party of Nigeria) – the party led by President Shagari.

Dikko became immensely rich, with an estimated fortune of £1 billion. The military government which seized power at the end of 1983 alleged he had made his fortune corruptly, that he had hoarded rice to force its price up and that he had misappropriated money donated to the NPN 1983 election fund. When the military seized power Dikko fled the country and reached Britain early in 1984. The Nigerian government applied in vain for Dikko's extradition. In July 1984 he was kidnapped and drugged by three Israelis and a Nigerian, and placed in a crate to be flown back to Nigeria. He was rescued by the police at Stansted Airport. Since then he has applied in vain for political asylum. In 1989 Dikko's right of residence in Britain was withdrawn and he has appealed against deportation.

Diop, Birago (1906–89), Senegalese poet, story-teller and diplomat, Birago Diop was one of the best-known voices to emerge from Francophone West Africa. Born in Dakar, Diop was left fatherless at the age of two months and grew up in a close-knit extended family. Educated at the Lycée Faidherbe in St Louis, the old capital of Senegal, Diop distinguished himself in the sciences and literature. After graduating as a veterinary surgeon in Toulouse in 1933, he went to Paris for further study. Here he met the founders of the *NÉGRITUDE movement – a collective asserting black African identity – who included Léopold *SENGHOR, who was to become first president of the Senegalese Republic. Diop served as a veterinary surgeon in Sudan, Upper Volta (later Burkino Faso), Ivory Coast and Mauritania. In 1960, Senghor appointed Diop ambassador to Tunisia. He retired from this post to Dakar in 1965. His stories have appeared in three separate collections, *Les contes d'Amadou Koumba* (1947), *Les nouveau contes d'Amadou Koumba* (1958), and *Contes et Lavanes* (1963). Some of these stories have been translated into English. Diop's importance lies in his introduction of Senegalese literature to the West.

Diop, David (1927–60), an important and influential West African poet. Diop was born in France;

95

his father was from Senegal and his mother from Cameroon. After an education in France and West Africa, Diop taught in Senegal during the 1950s and wrote his most successful poetry. His poetry expressed his anti-colonialism and his opposition to France's policy of assimilation. He wrote of his deep love of Africa and, inspired by *SENGHOR, embraced the philosophy of *NÉGRITUDE. His major collection of poetry was *Coups de pilon* (Poundings, 1957); in this volume he bitterly blamed Europe for the suffering it had inflicted on Africa and called for a revolution to bring Africa a glorious future. In the year Senegal gained independence (1960), Diop died in an aeroplane crash.

Diori, Hamani (b. 1916), first President of Niger. Educated in Dahomey, (now Benin) Diori was initially a language teacher for the French colonial administration, 1938–46. He was a founder member of the Niger branch of *RASSEMBLEMENT DÉMOCRATIQUE AFRICAIN (RDA) in 1946 and he represented Niger in the French National Assembly, 1946–51 and 1956–7. In that year he founded the Niger Progressive Party (PPN), which was affiliated to the African Democratic Rally. Diori, as able as he was ambitious, became Head of Niger Government Council in 1958 and in that year his party won the referendum which decided that Niger would join the French Community. Niger proclaimed its independence on 3 August 1960

and Diori became the first president. He gained further prestige in 1973 when he was elected chairman of the West African Economic Community. The great drought of 1973 caused serious economic and social problems and Lt.-Gen. Seyni Kountche seized power. Deposed from the presidency, Hamani Diori was imprisoned and not released until 1984. His ten years in prison were all the more tragic because he had spent his life as a moderate and had encouraged moderation in others. He took no further part in public life.

District Six, area near central Cape Town where a thriving community of up to fifty thousand *COLOUREDS lived for many generations. Using its powers under the *GROUP AREAS ACT, the South African government declared in 1963 that the area must be reserved for white occupation only. Despite considerable opposition the inhabitants were all finally evicted by 1983; the district was flattened by bulldozers and redeveloped as a suburb for whites.

Djibouti, only a small part of East Africa, but much larger than the speck it makes on a map suggests – over 20,000 square kilometres. The Gulf of Tadjoura reaches deeply into the country, which is enclosed by Ethiopian territory to the north, west and south and Somalia land to the south-east. The population of 405,000 consists of Afars, Issas, Arabs and Somalis, all of whom are Sunni Muslim, with some Europeans,

The Republic of Djibouti

THE COUNTRY 21,783 sq. km.	THE PEOPLE 430,000	THE STATE Single-party republic
Major Cities Djibouti (capital) Arta Dikhil	*Ethnic Groups* Issars 60% Afars	*Head of State* Hassan Gouled Aptidon
Economy Almost entirely dependent on transit trade to Ethiopia, French military spending and, to a much lesser extent, tourism	*Languages* French and Arabic (official) Afar and Somali spoken locally Some English	*Ruling Body* National Assembly *Official Party* Rassemblement Populaire pour le Progrès
Principal Exports None	*Religion* Islam Small Christian minority	
Currency Djibouti franc of 100 centimes		

mostly French. Another 25,000 people are refugees from Somalia and Ethiopia.

The French established themselves as colonial masters in 1861 and called the territory the French Somali Coast, though it was generally known as French Somaliland. The colonizers built a railway to Addis Ababa, and Djibouti became the main transhipment port for Ethiopian trade. France's main purpose in being in Djibouti was to counter the presence of its old enemy, Britain, in Aden, across the Straits of Bab-el-Mandeb. For the latter part of the Second World War Djibouti was linked to the Free French and General de Gaulle,

against the pro-Nazi Vichy government. In 1957 French Somaliland was given a degree of autonomy with the establishment of a territorial assembly of thirty-two members elected by direct popular vote. The French governor presided over a council of ministers, which was responsible to the Assembly. In a referendum, in 1958, a majority of people voted to remain with France, but some Somalis and many members of the Issa tribe wanted independence. In 1966 President de Gaulle visited Djibouti and faced a hostile reception from nationalists demanding independence.

In an attempt to please both major tribes, the French changed the name of the country, in 1966, to the French Territory of the Afars and Issas. The following year, they cunningly prepared for a referendum by expelling large numbers of Somalis and arresting others. In this way they gained a sixty per cent vote in favour of unity with France. The UN, aware of the manipulation, appealed to France to grant the territory independence. France responded by increasing its military presence to support its local puppet, Ali Aref. Opposition revived in the 1970s and Hassan Gouled's African Popular Union (mostly Somalis) linked with Ahmed Dini's League for the Future and for Order (mostly Afars). Together they became the African People's League for Independence (LPAI). With the elections rigged against it year after year, the LPAI demanded independence. The party gained wide foreign support but the French, through Ali Aref, resisted with arrests and expulsions.

Resentment against Ali Aref became so great that the French finally abandoned him and in July 1976 he resigned. Even then, the French insisted on a government which would remain an ally of France. On independence, Hassan Gouled was elected Head of State and Ahmed Dini became Prime Minister, with a forty-seat chamber of deputies. The old Afar-Issa animosity soon showed itself and Afars were forced out of governmental offices. Facing massive problems, including high unemployment and political differences with Ethiopia and Somalia, the president sought

reconciliation with leading Afars by offering them senior posts in the civil service, armed forces and security services.

Following the formation of a new government in September 1978, Hassan Gouled tried to unify the north and south of Djibouti and created a party, the Rassemblement Populaire pour la Progrès (RPPP) to replace LPAI. French military and financial support was essential. The army kept a garrison of five thousand in Djibouti and provided 350 million francs annually. In June 1981, Djibouti held its first presidential elections since independence. President Gouled, as the only candidate, was re-elected. Djibouti's sovereignty now depends more on the volatile politics of the *HORN OF AFRICA than on the French military presence. Its prosperity depends on stability as well as on development of the tourist potential of the capital, the only important centre. The mixture of African, European and Middle Eastern cultures makes the territory interesting.

Djibouti had been the world's fifth largest container port but its trade fell away when the Suez Canal was closed, between 1967 and 1975, because of Egyptian-Israeli military activities and wrecked ships in the Canal. After the Canal reopened, Jeddah displaced Djibouti as a ship maintenance and supply port. The Israeli shipping line Zim paid large sums to use the port but after joining the Arab League in 1977 Djibouti reluctantly closed the port to Zim. Saudi

Arabia, Kuwait, Oman and Bahrain provided financial assistance to help the new League member. President Gouled attracted to Djibouti the headquarters of the Intergovernment Authority for Drought and Development (IGADD), whose other members are Ethiopia, Kenya, Somalia, Sudan and Uganda. IGADD hopes to develop Djibouti's neglected river basins. To please Djibouti, which has only 0.4 per cent of the six countries' combined population, it was agreed that French should be the official language, alongside English.

Dlamini, the dominant Swaziland clan which includes King *MSWATI III, the many members of the royal family and commoners. The royal family which created the Swazi nation in the nineteenth century traces its ancestry to Dlamini I who led his followers to settle in what is now Swaziland during the sixteenth century. Members of the clan have great power and influence in Swaziland.

Dlamini, Prince Bhekimpi, a member of the royal family who was Prime Minister of Swaziland (1983–6). A leading conservative and traditionalist, he played an important part in the royal family's feuds. With support from the *LIQOQO he replaced Prince Mabandla *DLAMINI as prime minister (Mar. 1983) and ousted Queen Regent *DZELIWE (Aug. 1983). He welcomed the *NKOMATI ACCORD between South Africa and Mozambique (1984) and favoured the proposed deal with

South Africa which would have given Swaziland more territory and a corridor to the Indian Ocean in exchange for Swazi co-operation. Prince Bhekimpi was sacked by King *MSWATI III (1986), arrested (1987) and found guilty of treason (1988). He is now in prison.

Dlamini, Prince Mabandla, a member of the royal family who was Prime Minister of Swaziland (1979–83). He was managing a sugar estate when King *SOBHUZA II unexpectedly made him prime minister. Prince Mabandla was a reformer who alarmed the traditionalists of the *LIQOQO with his attacks on corruption and his plans to modernize Swaziland. He enraged the Liqoqo by opposing the proposed land deal with South Africa which would have given Swaziland more territory and a corridor to the Indian Ocean in exchange for Swazi co-operation. The Liqoqo forced Queen Regent *DZELIWE to sack Prince Mabandla (1983); he then went into exile.

Dlamini, Prince Mfanasibili (b. 1939), a member of the Swazi royal family who led the traditionalist faction in the struggle for power. He was a powerful member of the *IMBOKODVO NATIONAL MOVEMENT, a leading member of the *LIQOQO and a senior cabinet minister. After surviving an investigation for corruption he played an important part in the sacking of Prince Mabandla *DLAMINI from the premiership and the ousting of Queen Regent *DZELIWE (1983). He was arrested in 1985 and sentenced to seven years in prison (1986) for attempting to undermine the monarchy.

Dlamini, Sotcha Ernest, Prime Minister of Swaziland since October 1986, he was the personal choice of King *MSWATI III and the first commoner to be made prime minister. In 1974 he was suddenly dismissed by the *LIQOQO from his post as assistant police commissioner. He was head of security on a sugar estate at the time of his appointment as prime minister. He has strongly condemned South African attacks on *AFRICAN NATIONAL CONGRESS exiles in Swaziland and supports the king against the traditionalist faction.

Dodoma, proposed capital of Tanzania since 1973. Because Dar es Salaam was growing so rapidly the authorities designated Dodoma as the country's capital. Its main advantage is its central location at the junction of the railway and the Great North Road, but its inadequate water supply and the heavy expense of administrative relocation at a time of economic difficulties have persuaded the government to postpone plans to move the capital from Dar es Salaam to Dodoma.

Doe, Gen Samuel Kanyon (1950–90), leader of Liberia since he seized power in April 1980. He joined the Liberian Army as a private in 1969 and was promoted to Master Sergeant in 1979. Doe opposed the government of President *TOLBERT as corrupt and elitist and the disorder of 1979–80 prompted him to join other NCOs in overthrowing the government.

Doe became chairman of the new ruling body, the People's Redemption Council (1980–5). His first actions were to order the public execution of senior officials from the old regime and to double civil service and army pay. Under Liberia's new constitution he won the 1985 elections and was sworn in as President of Liberia at the beginning of 1986.

Although President Doe expressed radical ideas and argued for justice and equality, he made little progress in achieving these aims during his decade of power in Liberia. He was challenged by nine coup plots (or alleged coup plots). A major rebellion against his government began in the Nimba province late in 1989 and was threatening Monrovia, the capital, by May 1990. He made no progress in strengthening Liberia's economy. The mismanagement of the economy, the diversion of aid funds and the debt arrears alienated the United States and other donors.

Late in 1989 Doe's regime was challenged by the *NATIONAL PATRIOTIC FRONT OF LIBERIA under the command of Charles *TAYLOR. In September 1990 Doe was wounded, captured and killed by a rebel faction led by Prince *JOHNSON.

Dos Santos, José Eduardo (b. 1942), President of Angola since September 1979. After joining the *MPLA youth wing (1961) Dos Santos spent seven years in the Soviet Union (1963–70), first training as a petroleum engineer and then studying military telecommunications. He rejoined the fight against Portugal (1970–74) and became a member of MPLA's Central Committee and Politburo (1974). At independence he became Angola's first Foreign Minister (1975–8). He lost the Foreign Ministry in a reshuffle (1978), but remained as Minister of National Planning (1977–9). He was Deputy Prime Minister (1978–9) and acting Head of State when President *NETO died in Moscow (Sep. 1979).

As Angola's second President Dos Santos has proved himself a moderate and a pragmatist who has repeatedly purged the party and the government of its more radical members, including many veterans of the independence war. In 1984 he sacked the pro-Soviet Foreign Minister and took over foreign affairs himself. Dos Santos has campaigned against corruption and inefficiency and has replaced doctrinaire Marxism with a more flexible approach to Angola's economic problems – but with limited success by the late 1980s. He has continued the fight against UNITA and its South African backers, but his success in reaching an agreement with South Africa (Dec. 1988) was a breakthrough which may lead to peace. In June 1989 President Dos Santos agreed to a ceasefire and a peace plan drawn up in Zaire; fighting resumed but in 1990 there have been attempts to negotiate. If the civil war does end he will have a much better chance of bringing stability and prosperity to Angola.

dos Santos, Marcelino (b. 1931), Mozambican poet, nationalist and one of * FRELIMO's most influential ideologists. He studied in Paris and Lisbon and was a founder member of Frelimo. A revolutionary socialist who looked to the communist world for support, he played an important part in the military and ideological campaign against Portuguese rule in Mozambique. He was elected Secretary for External Relations at Frelimo's inaugural meeting (1962) and then became the movement's Secretary for External Affairs (1969–75) and Vice-President (1970–8). After the assassination of Eduardo *MONDLANE he joined Samora *MACHEL and Uria *SIMANGO in Frelimo's ruling triumvirate.

At independence he was Minister for Development and Economic Planning (1975–8) and Minister for Planning (1978–80). When President Machel instituted economic reforms and began looking to the capitalist world for aid he removed dos Santos from his ministerial post, but made him Frelimo's Secretary for Economic Affairs (1980). When President Machel died (1986) dos Santos was a leading contender for the succession. As Secretary of the Permanent Commission of the People's Assembly he was second in rank to the President, but he was passed over in favour of Joaquim *CHISSANO. According to some reports he refused to put himself forward for the presidency.

DTA (Democratic Turnhalle Alliance), South African-backed political organisation in Namibia. South Africa organized the meeting of representatives of eleven ethnic groups at the *TURNHALLE CONSTITUTIONAL CONFERENCE (1975–7) to work out an internal settlement for Namibian independence. In November 1977 these groups combined to form the DTA, a multi-ethnic body committed to a complicated constitution based on local, ethnic and central government and led by the conservative white politician, Dirk Mudge. The DTA gained support from some traditional authorities, but *SWAPO was not prepared to co-operate with the South African plan and boycotted the elections in December 1978. The DTA won forty-one of the fifty seats in the Constituent Assembly and Mudge became Chairman of the Council of Ministers, effectively prime minister.

The DTA government had many problems. Although it was seen as a South African puppet, right-wing whites were hostile. It tried and failed to persuade South Africa to grant autonomy. Some of its members wanted to change it into a single ethnic party. The eleven ethnic administrations were extravagant and corrupt. Finally after the DTA lost the support of the Ovambo group Mudge resigned (Jan. 1983) and Namibia returned to direct rule by South Africa. In the 1989 elections during the transition to independence the DTA was the main opponent of SWAPO; it won twenty-one of the seventy-two seats in the Constituent Assembly and 28.6 per cent of the vote.

Duncan, Patrick (1918–67), son of Sir Patrick Duncan who had been Governor-General of South Africa. One of the first prominent white opponents of *APARTHEID he devoted himself from 1952 to the fight against racial laws. Initially he hoped that passive resistance would destroy apartheid, but later advocated violence. He escaped to Basutoland (1962) and was stripped of his South African citizenship (1964).

Dzeliwe, Queen Regent of Swaziland (1982–3) with the title of Indlovukazi (The Great She-Elephant). She was the senior wife chosen by King Sobhuza II to be regent after his death until his successor reached the age of twenty-one and assumed the throne. Princess Dzeliwe clashed with the traditionalists of the *LIQOQO and was forced to dismiss the prime minister, Prince Mabandla *DLAMINI (Mar. 1983). She refused to transfer power to the *AUTHORIZED PERSON and was ousted at the orders of the Liqoqo (Aug. 1983).

East African Community, regional association of Kenya, Tanzania and Uganda set up in 1967 by the Treaty of East African Co-operation. Its aim was to promote trade among its members and to harmonize common services in air travel, harbours and rail links. In 1963 the leaders of Kenya, Tanzania and Uganda had made a declaration of intent to form an East African federation; some observers thought the Community would lead to such a federation. Initially there was progress, but there were soon serious divisions over import duties and the resentment of the other two members at Kenya's disproportionate share of the community's trade.

There were growing differences between Tanzanian socialism and Kenyan capitalism, culminating in the closure of the borders between the two countries. In addition President *NYERERE refused to sit at the same table as President *AMIN who had seized power in Uganda in 1971. Without direction from the heads of state the Community agencies were mismanaged; in particular there were revelations of great inefficiency in East African Airways. The Community collapsed in 1977 and there were long negotiations about the disposal of its assets and liabilities among the three countries. By late 1983 relations between Kenya and Tanzania had improved sufficiently for them to reopen their borders and to resume trade and tourism with each other. By 1984 the three countries had agreed on the distribution of the Community's assets and liabilities.

East African Rift Valley or Great Rift Valley, the African section of the world's most extended rift, which begins in south west Asia and extends southwards from the Red Sea through Ethiopia, Kenya and Tanzania. The average drop from the plateaux to the valley is from six to nine hundred metres, but in some parts the drop is close to one thousand metres. There are vast lakes covering the floor of the rift; the floor of Lake Tanganyika is Africa's lowest point at 358 metres below sea level. The formation of the rift was accompanied by volcanic activity and the formation of such mountains as Mount *KILIMANJARO (Africa's highest peak) and Mount Kenya.

ECOWAS (Economic Community of West African States), founded in 1975 by the Treaty of Lagos to promote trade, co-operation and self-reliance in West Africa, it has sixteen members. Heads of state and government meet annually and the Council of Ministers meets twice a year. There is a permanent executive secretariat in Lagos and there are four specialized commissions dealing with trade, industry, communications and social and cultural affairs. Various programmes have

The Arab Republic of Egypt

THE COUNTRY
1,001,449 sq. km.

Major Cities
Cairo (capital)
Alexandria
Asyut
Aswan
Ismailia
Mersa Matruh
Port Said

Economy
Oil, natural gas
Suez canal fees
Tourism
Cotton
Rice

Principal Exports
Oil, cotton, rice

Currency
Egyptian pound of 100
piastres

THE PEOPLE
57 million (increasing
by 1 million every 9
months)

Ethnic Groups
Predominantly Arab
Some Nubians

Languages
Arabic (official)
French and English are
widely spoken

Religion
Islam dominant
Christianity represented,
notably the Coptic
Church, which has up
to 8 million followers

THE STATE
Presidential republic

Head of State
President Husni Mubarak

Ruling Body
Cabinet
President

Official Party
National Democratic
Party

---

been adopted to eliminate trade tariffs between members, and to develop industry, energy, agriculture and transport. In August 1990 ECOWAS sent a peace-keeping force to Liberia in the hopes of imposing a cease-fire in the civil war, but less than half the members contributed men to the force.

Egypt, set in the north-east corner of Africa, facing the Mediterranean and with the Red Sea on its flank, in one of the world's most strategic positions. A crossroads throughout

its eight thousand years of recorded inhabitation, it has had a chequered history. It covers an area of over a million square kilometres, the greater part being flat, barren desert. The population, most of it Muslim, is the largest of any African nation other than Nigeria.

The modern history of Egypt really begins with the Anglo-Egyptian Treaty of 1936, which was to end the British occupation of the country. It gave Britain the right, however, to station troops in the *SUEZ CANAL ZONE. Because of the onset of world war in 1939 the planned British evacuation did not take place and hundreds of thousands of other troops arrived in Egypt for the campaigns in North Africa. The British were still influential in Egypt after the war. In 1948 Egypt, ruled by King Farouk, attacked the new state of Israel and was soundly defeated. This humiliation contributed to the growth of the *FREE OFFICERS MOVEMENT led by General Muhammad *NAGUIB and Colonel Gamal Abdel *NASSER. Meanwhile, guerrilla activity against the British forces in the Canal Zone intensified throughout 1951 and early 1952. On 25 January 1952, British troops destroyed the police barracks in Ismailia, killing fifty Egyptian policemen. During the consequent riots in Cairo British and other foreigners were killed. On 23 July that year the Free Officers Movement deposed the corrupt and inefficient King Farouk and his government. General Naguib became chairman of the Revolutionary Command Council (RCC) and commander of the armed forces. Soon after the British forces withdrew in 1954, Colonel Nasser ousted Naguib and became Egypt's leader. He banned political parties as part of his first aim which was to consolidate his hold on the country but he became increasingly embroiled in international issues. After the *SUEZ CRISIS and the Egyptian victory, Nasser's prestige was enormous.

Between 1958 and 1961 Egypt became known as the United Arab Republic in an unsuccessful union with Syria. Nasser inaugurated radical nationalization and gave the Soviet Union its first important economic influence in Egypt by accepting Russian finance for the Aswan High Dam after a Western withdrawal. The *SIX DAY WAR of June 1967 ended disastrously for Egypt. Nasser died in September 1970 and was succeeded by Anwar *SADAT who, in 1972, expelled Soviet military personnel. In October 1973 he masterminded the attack on the Israeli military occupation of the Sinai, an operation known as 'The Victory' or 'The Great Crossing'. Following this inconclusive war Sadat, in 1977, made peace with Israel under the *CAMP DAVID ACCORD. Assassinated in 19 October 1981, by Islamic fundamentalists from among his own soldiers, Sadat was succeeded by Hosni *MUBARAK.

Since 1984 Egypt has adopted an 'Open Door' economic policy, offering generous incentives to foreign investors and banks. With an international debt of $17 billion (1987) Egypt depends on an annual US grant of $3.1 billion. The principal reason for the nation's continuous economic crisis is the rapid population growth. Egypt's land area is ninety per cent desert but the country is heavily dependent on its agriculture. This is only possible on the banks of the *NILE and in the Nile delta. Half the population is involved in the growing of food and cotton. The main crops for export are cotton and rice; other products

105

are fruit, vegetables, wheat, barley, maize, millet and sugar. Attempts to reclaim land have not been successful and Egypt relies heavily on food imports. The expansion of industry – iron and steel, fertilizers, cement and paper – is not enough to reduce Egypt's social problems and unemployment.

There is a continual drift of people from the countryside to the towns. With a population believed to number twelve million, Cairo is the largest city in Africa; many of the poor live on rooftops or in cemeteries where they have neither water, power nor sewerage. New transport systems, such as the Metro, may help to relieve the city's extreme traffic congestion.

Over-population is the greatest danger to the nation's stability. In January 1986 the National Family Planning Council estimated that at the current rate of increase the population would grow from 50 to 75 million within 15 years. The increase was said to be 1 million every 9 months, with babies being born at the rate of one every 24 seconds. Religion prohibits sterilization and the law bans abortion; religious leaders give contraception only qualified approval. President Mubarak is the first Egyptian president to confront the problem. 'The people plague', he is said to have told a friend, 'is the worst one Egypt has ever faced and disaster is inevitable.'

*ISLAMIC FUNDAMENTALISM, which opposes any form of population control, is rife in Egypt and has many followers

among university students. The *MUSLIM BROTHERHOOD is also active and has consistently tried to cause the downfall of the Mubarak government, which the Brotherhood considers too liberal and 'dangerously democratic'. Islamic extremists brought about, in 1985, the repeal of an Act which gave women more rights. Egypt is the largest Arab nation by population and the most important by prestige but the *ARAB LEAGUE suspended it from membership following the Egypt-Israel peace treaty. The treaty was seen as contrary to the teachings of the Koran and a betrayal of Arab unity. Since the *CAMP DAVID ACCORD fewer Arab tourists visit Egypt but more than a million other tourists annually go to this ancient nation with its unique attractions.

Between 1981 and 1988 Egypt moved a long way from the totalitarian regime of Nasser and the authoritarian rule of Sadat. Under Mubarak, Egyptian society exhibited a curious mixture of freedom and control. Freedom of speech was remarkable, even by Western standards, and the courts were increasingly an independent source of power. However, the Mubarak liberalism allowed Islamic parties to assert themselves to the point of terrorism. Nasserites shot American and Israeli diplomats and fundamentalists tried to kill former cabinet ministers. Such excesses led the authorities to make wholesale arrests in 1989. At the end of that year Egyptian gaols held nine thousand detainees of 'various political allegiances', according to a Bar Association report.

Economic considerations continue to exert a strong influence on political matters, and policy continues to focus on expanding the market economy. While the economy is still heavily regulated by the state, steps are being taken to increase foreign and domestic investment in the private sector. Consequently, the government's firm stand in controlling the Islamic investment companies is more a fight against the excesses of the parallel market than an attack on private enterprise. President Mubarak believes that it is no longer feasible to impose onerous burdens on the population as a consequence of the reform programme. He has consequently adopted a strategy of gradual change rather than the rapid implementation of structural alterations. In 1988–9, high priority was given to increasing output in specific industrial sectors. Production from the food processing sectors, for instance, increased by 7.7 per cent, textiles by 5.7 per cent and production in the chemical and metal-working industries by 7.8 per cent and 6.7 per cent respectively. Egypt is self-sufficient in oil and natural gas and has an exportable surplus of crude oil, which, directly or indirectly, provides the bulk of hard currency earnings. Egypt, which is not a member of the Organization of Oil Exporting Countries (OPEC), normally produces an average of 870,000 barrels of crude daily. The country's annual share of global output is about 1.5 per cent.

In 1990 no prognosis about Egypt's future could be hopeful, despite the nation's welcome re-admission to the Arab League. The problems posed by over-population and Islamic fundamentalism are likely to prove too great for Mubarak's government to master.

The pressure of population – an increase of one million every nine months – affects agriculture, oil, revenues and employment and colours everything to do with politics. The land is highly productive and can be cropped throughout the year, but the exploding population constantly cuts exports and has rendered Egypt a net importer of wheat, sugar and other basic foodstuffs; 75 per cent of wheat consumed is imported and 50 per cent of sugar. In oil, Egypt has a capacity of a million barrels a day but by AD 2003 Egypt will be a net importer of oil. The government has a long-standing policy of subsidizing basic foods. The entire earnings from the Suez Canal, £3 billion, are spent in this way. But removal of subsidies could cause riots as serious as those of 1977 when President Sadat tried to raise the price of bread. About 85 per cent of the work force is employed by the government but each year another 500,000 workers come onto the labour market. Egypt's main economic and political pressures will come, for many

107

years, from trying to employ these new workers without allowing the public sector to veer even further out of control.

President Mubarak and those of his ministers who are progressive and enlightened know that some of the Egyptians' frustrations and tensions are the result of the policies of Nasser and Sadat. During 1990, Finance Minister Mustapha Said criticized both presidents. 'Nasser made promises, Sadat fed expectations,' he said. 'They obliged us to provide our people with more than the present state of development can allow.'

Ekwensi, Cyprian (b. 1921), prolific Nigerian writer of novels, short stories and children's fiction. He has had a varied career in forestry, pharmacy, teaching, broadcasting and journalism. During the civil war (1967–70) Ekwensi was a *BIAFRAN spokesman. His short stories and novels like *People of the City* (1954) are satirical, witty descriptions of low life in urban Africa. He is equally capable of writing a powerful novel like *Divided We Stand* (1980), set against the background of the civil war. He shows his love and understanding of rural Africa in children's stories and in his collections of folk tales – on which he concentrated most of his efforts during the 1980s – and in his novel about nomadic Fulani herdsmen – *Burning Grass* (1962).

Elders of the Nation, traditional body in Swaziland. Its members are heads of important clans and its spokesman is the *AUTHORIZED

PERSON. Under certain circumstances they can have the power to override the monarch's decisions.

Emecheta, Buchi (Florence Onye) (b. 1944), Nigerian novelist who came to London with her husband (1962) and stayed on with their five children after the marriage ended. Her earlier novels on the exploitation of Nigerian women in Nigeria and in England were based on personal experience of the difficulties such women faced in the struggle to free themselves from the restrictions of both traditional and modern life. Emecheta has extended the range of her work with historical fiction in *Destination Biafra* (1982) and political fantasy in *The Rape of Shavi* (1984). Her most recent book, *Gwendolen*, was published in 1990.

Eminent Persons Group, seven eminent citizens of Commonwealth countries appointed under the terms of the Nassau Accord (Oct. 1985). The Nassau Accord was made by Commonwealth heads of government in response to the challenge of *APARTHEID. The Eminent Persons Group was sent to South Africa to promote change by opening up a dialogue which would lead to the establishment of a non-racial democracy in South Africa. Malcolm Fraser (former Prime Minister of Australia) and General Olusegun *OBASANJO (former military ruler of Nigeria) were the group's joint chairmen; the other members were Lord Barber of Wentridge from Britain, Dame Nita Barrow from Barbados,

John *MALECELA from Tanzania, Sardar Swaran Singh from India and The Most Reverend Edward Scott from Canada.

The full group made two visits to South Africa (Mar. & May 1986); its members were able to travel freely and to interview a wide range of South Africans from government ministers to leaders of banned organizations and township residents and even Nelson *MANDELA in prison. Their second visit was marred by President *BOTHA's speech condemning outside interference and by South African raids on *AFRICAN NATIONAL CONGRESS exiles in the capitals of Botswana, Zambia and Zimbabwe (19 May 1986). The group concluded that there had been no progress in the dismantling of apartheid and in creating democracy in South Africa; it recommended economic sanctions as the last chance to save South Africa from a bloodbath.

Enahoro, Chief Anthony Eronsele (b. 1923), politician from western Nigeria. A founding member of the *ACTION GROUP, he was a close associate of Chief *AWOLOWO and Minister of Home Affairs in the Western Regional government (1954–9). He then went on to be opposition spokesman on foreign affairs in the federal assembly from 1959 until his arrest in 1962 during the Action Group crisis. Enahoro managed to escape to Britain, but after a bitter row in Britain he was extradited to Nigeria (1963) and sentenced to seven years in prison for treasonable felony. In 1966 he

was freed by *GOWON and he served as a Federal Commissioner from 1967 until the coup of 1975. He went into business, but became politically active again in 1978 as Nigeria was returning to civilian rule.

EPLA (Exército Popular de Libertação de Angola), military wing of the *MPLA, one of the three nationalist movements in the Angolan independence war (1961–74). Founded in 1961 shortly after Portugal had crushed the Luanda rising, EPLA began its operations with guerrilla actions launched from bases in neighbouring countries and the Angolan bush. Initially its operations were on a small scale, but with training and other military help from friends – notably the Soviet bloc – EPLA gained ground against the Portuguese and commanded large areas of Angola by 1974. Its soldiers were sometimes undisciplined but they were able not only to win victories but also the hearts and minds of peasants in areas they controlled. As Portugal's military effort collapsed in August 1974, EPLA was replaced by *FAPLA (Forças Armadas Populares para a Libertação de Angola) which is now Angola's national army.

Equatorial Guinea, small in size for an African country, has an Atlantic coastline and lies between Cameroon to the north and Gabon to the south. Its mainland segment was Rio Muni before independence and the chief of its several islands was Fernando Po, now Bioko

The Republic of Equatorial Guinea

THE COUNTRY	THE PEOPLE	THE STATE
28,051 sq. km.	400,000	Single-party presidential republic
Major Cities Bata (capital) Malabo (on Bioko Island) Mongomo Micomeseng	*Ethnic Groups* Pamues (or Fang) on mainland	*Head of State* President Teodoro Obiang Nguema Mbasogo
Economy Cocoa and coffee, bananas, palm oil, timber, fish	*Languages* Spanish (official) Several tribal languages	*Ruling Body* Cabinet
Principal Exports Cocoa and coffee	*Religion* Roman Catholic with traditional beliefs	*Official Party* Partido Unico Nacional de Trabajadores
Currency CFA franc of 100 centimes		

Island. Largely mountainous and jungle-covered, Equatorial Guinea has a population of only 385,000, the majority of whom is Christian. The others hold traditional beliefs.

The modern history of the territory began in the 1950s when nationalists founded two parties in exile to agitate for independence. In 1962, they requested that the UN bring about liberation from Spain. The following year Spain granted limited self-government and in 1964 instituted autonomous government. The Spanish also appointed their own local nominee, Ondo Edu, as president. Fernando Po resisted the idea of autonomy because Rio

Muni politicians would inevitably dominate Fernando Po. Nevertheless, by 1967 the movement for total independence was irresistible and in October 1968 Rio Muni – Fernando Po became Equatorial Guinea with Nguema *MACIAS as first president. The first ten years were simultaneously a period of terrible political repression and gross economic decline.

When Lieutenant-Colonel Teodoro Nguema Mbasogo took power in August 1979, Spain and the EC sent economic aid. As Mbasogo limped towards democracy he survived a coup in April 1981, an event which led to his being given a bodyguard of 1000 Moroccan troops and 400 Spanish police. Mbasogo officially became president on 12 October 1982 but the first parliamentary elections were not held until August 1983. Opposition to Mbasogo's increasingly autocratic rule mounted and in July 1986 the government foiled an assassination plot – or claimed to have done so. About thirty people were arrested and after a brief trial thirteen of them were shot. Further assassination attempts seem likely in the years ahead. It is equally likely that, given Mbasogo's protection and his willingness to eliminate possible rivals, they would fail.

Equatorial Guinea depends on coffee, cocoa and timber for its economy but the production of all three collapsed after independence. The Macias regime left President Mbasogo enormous financial problems, some of which he partly resolved by entering the franc zone and joining the French-speaking former colonies' monetary organization, the Central African Customs and Economic Union. He also ended the Soviet fishing monopoly which had brought Equatorial Guinea no income and signed better agreements with Spain and Nigeria. Spanish, French and Italian companies pay for timber concessions. However, Equatorial Guinea could not exist without loans from the International Monetary Fund.

Eritrea, with a coastline on the Red Sea, north of Ethiopia, and an Italian colony until captured by the British in 1941, during the Second World War. On 11 September 1952, according to a United Nations resolution, Eritrea was federated with Ethiopia. Ten years later Ethiopia 'incorporated' Eritrea, in effect annexing it. In 1964 various groups affiliated to the Eritrean Liberation Front (ELF) began to fight for independence. A military coup in Ethiopia overthrew the monarchy and Colonel *MENGISTU became virtual dictator. He continued the war against the ELF but by 1977 the forty thousand ELF fighters were winning the war against eighty thousand Ethiopian troops. The tide of war turned when the Soviet Union began to back Ethiopia. With Russian military planning and massive logistical superiority, the army forced the guerrillas from all the Eritrean towns, though they continued to hold the rural areas. In the 1980s, Soviet support for Ethiopia declined and the guerrillas of the Eritrean People's Liberation Front (EPLF), which had supplanted the ELF, returned to the offensive. The EPLF achieved spectacular victories, such as Tessenei, Marsa Teklal and Barentu in 1984, Nakfa, Maidama and Areza in 1987 and Afabet and Halhal in 1988. In November 1989 an EPLF offensive reached to within seventy miles of Addis Ababa, and in January 1990 the rebels captured the port of Massawa. This was a devastating defeat for the Ethiopian forces and it tilted the outcome of the long war decisively in the EPLF's favour. In April 1990, the EPLF overran garrison towns on the southern front. There seemed to be

111

The People's Democratic Republic of Ethiopia

THE COUNTRY
1,221,900 sq. km.

Major Cities
Addis Ababa (capital)
Asmara
Axum

Economy
Coffee
Subsistence farming
Industry accounts for
12% of the GDP.

Principal Export
Coffee

Currency
Ethiopian Birr of 100
cents

THE PEOPLE
37.7 million

Ethnic Groups
Oromo groups are the
most populous.
Adhere
Nuer
Anuak
Geleb
Amharas
Tigreans

Languages
Amharic (official)
English (official second
language)
French, Italian
and Arabic widely
understood
Over 100 languages
spoken

Religion
Christianity (Ethiopian
Orthodox Church)
Islam
Animist and local beliefs
20%

THE STATE
Presidential republic

Head of State
President Lt. Col.
Mengistu Haile Mariam

Ruling Body
The Provisional Military
Administrative Council
(PMAC) of Socialist
Ethiopia, or Dergue

Official Party
The Workers' Party of
Ethiopia

no doubt that Eritrea's two million people would eventually win their independence but fighting continued at the end of 1990.

Ethiopia, covering an area of nearly three-quarters of a million miles, situated in north-east Africa. Ethiopia has borders with Djibouti, Somalia, Kenya and Sudan. On the whole, it is an inhospitable country with great mountain ranges, immense plateaus and deserts. Yet it supports, though sometimes with

difficulty, thirty-eight million people. The majority are Christians of the ★COPTIC faith but there is a large Muslim minority.

Ethiopia is one of the oldest states in the world and towards the end of the nineteenth century the Ethiopian empire was still expanding. Its rulers took over the vast ★OGADEN region and then blocked the advance of European colonization at the battle of Adowa, 1896. Annexation of southern lands from what are now the states of Uganda, Zaire and Somalia continued well into the twentieth century.

The imperial regime's feudal system was based on religious, ethnic and class divisions. The dominant northern groups imposed Christianity and the Amharic language on all others, including the Muslims, who were a majority in the south. Liberation movements began in the 1960s. Following the disastrous droughts of 1972–4 peasants rose against their landlords while students, workers and intellectuals campaigned against the inefficient government and rapacious employers. Mutinies took place in the army, which was also fighting the *ERITREAN LIBERATION MOVEMENT. Emperor *HAILE SELASSIE was deposed in September 1974 by the *DERGUE, which proclaimed 'Ethiopia Tikdem'. This is a political theory 'which provides for a nationwide socialist reconstruction and ensures freedom among the masses'.

The Dergue, led by Colonel Haile Mariam Mengistu, nationalized virtually everything. It separated church and state and introduced radical reforms in education, agriculture and social welfare. Liberation fronts in *ERITREA began a guerrilla war and Somalia claimed *OGADEN. In 1977 the Dergue called in Soviet and Cuban support to crush the uprising. The Russians and Cubans failed to do so and conflicts continue in several provinces, notably *TIGRE and *OGADEN. Colonel Mengistu

has maintained power by frequent purges; his more prominent enemies have been executed. Political organizations want a return to civilian government and their pressure brought about the administration's approval of the Workers' Party for Ethiopia in 1984.

In March 1975 land was nationalized and peasant associations were formed to work in collaboration with government representatives and foreign development agencies such as Oxfam. Between 1974 and 1978, war, recurrent drought and famine, locust plagues and displacement of millions of people reduced agricultural production by thirty per cent. In this crisis the administration launched a 'national revolutionary economic development campaign' and it slowly improved conditions. Greater earnings from coffee increased Ethiopia's national wealth and higher industrial output lessened the need for foreign imports. The 1984–5 drought and famine killed more than a million people and the government began an enforced resettlement programme.

In the first resettlement programme of 1986, 600,000 people were moved from drought-stricken regions in the north and central highlands to more fertile land in the south and east. Relocation took place at the height of the famine and interrupted relief efforts. Families were split up and sites were poorly prepared to receive settlers. Thousands died because of the harsh, untimely manner in which the programme was carried out. In 1988 a second

113

resettlement drive began, this time to move 1.5 million people at the rate of 60,000 families a year. According to a report by the UN Development Programme and UN Food and Agriculture Organization (FAO), attempts at organized, enforced resettlement could move only a fraction of the numbers needed to make much demographic impact. The FAO estimated that up to seven million people need to be moved over a long term. Spontaneous migration alone can result in more substantial numbers moving.

Relief officials worry that the new settlements are not growing a wide enough variety of food to meet protein requirements. Foreign diplomatic, financial and relief officials say that settlement farms are inefficient because they are farmed collectively. The impact the programme is having on the environment in the newly settled areas is of great concern. Little or no land-use planning has been completed for the sites. The same peasant patterns of land use that led to the devastation of the highlands are being repeated in settlement areas. Some reforestation efforts had begun in 1989 but many more were needed.

Tourism could provide Ethiopia with great wealth as the country has much to offer foreign visitors in cultural variety, scenic beauty and historic sites. However the revolutionary upheaval and armed conflicts have hindered the tourist development plans begun in 1979 and large tracts of Ethiopia are too dangerous for visitors.

In the long term, the greatest threat to Ethiopia's stability and prosperity comes from its high birth-rate. Population growth in the 1980s produced an average 1.3 million new mouths to feed each year. However, the amount of locally grown grain available to each person has fallen by 22 per cent since 1980. Ethiopians are listed by the World Bank as having an average income of a mere $110 a year. Forecasts by the World Bank, the International Monetary Fund and the UN's Food and Agriculture Organization assert that the birth-rate will outstrip all efforts to give Ethiopians a better standard of living.

Eyadèma, Gnassingbe (first name formerly Etienne, (b. 1937), Togo's head of state. Born in northern Togo, Eyadèma served in the French army from 1953. When independence from France was proclaimed in April 1960, Eyadèma transferred to the new Togolese army. In 1963, when Nicolas ★GRUNITZKY became president, Eyadèma was commissioned as a lieutenant. Only two years later he was a general and chief-of-staff. High rank appealed to him and on 13 January 1967 he overthrew Grunitzky in a coup and became head of state himself. He was instrumental in creating, in 1969, the Rassemblement du Peuple Togolais (RTP) and proclaimed it the only legal party. Eyadèma then dissolved all but two trade unions, which he personally controlled, and brutally repressed union activists. He now had what he wanted – no political opposition. In January 1972, after the first RPT congress, he called for a presidential election. It was announced that 99 per cent of the votes cast were in favour of Eyadèma, the only candidate. Hundreds of political prisoners were by then in prison. After several attempts on his life, President Eyadèma established his home within a military barracks. He rarely emerges from it, but did so to greet Pope John Paul II in August 1985.

Falashas, a tribe of black Ethiopian Jews virtually unknown until March 1985. The Falashas were part of a great wave of Ethiopian refugees who fled to eastern Sudan to avoid the Ethiopian famine of 1985. In March, seven hundred Falashas were secretly airlifted from a refugee camp to a sanctuary in Israel. The American Central Intelligence Agency (CIA) played a major part in the operation and Sudan's president, *NIMIERI, was bitterly attacked by the Islamic world for having permitted it to happen. It is unlikely that a row would have occurred had the Falashas been taken anywhere but Israel.

FAPLA (Forças Armadas Populares para a Libertação de Angola), replaced *EPLA (Exército Popular de Libertação de Angola) in August 1974 as the military wing of the *MPLA. It is Angola's national army; the President of the People's Republic of Angola is its commander-in-chief. All Angolan men and women between eighteen and thirty-five are liable to two years' military service followed by a term in the military reserve. FAPLA has about 100,000 members, 50,000 to 70,000 of them regular soldiers and the others in the reserve.

While Portuguese forces were withdrawing in 1974 FAPLA fought rival guerrilla armies to establish MPLA control of Angola. With substantial military aid from the Soviet bloc and up to 50,000 Cuban troops FAPLA has fought a long and bitter civil war since independence. By 1976 it had effectively defeated *FNLA and driven *UNITA into the bush, but FAPLA has not been able to win a final victory over a UNITA assisted by South African forces and military aid from the USA. The arrival of Soviet fighter aircraft (1985) has helped FAPLA win some successes against UNITA. In December 1988 (see ANGOLA) Cuba and Angola agreed to the withdrawal of Cuban troops and South Africa agreed to end direct military help to UNITA. By March 1990 FAPLA had taken the key UNITA town of Mavinga and was making major advances in the war.

Farah, Nuruddin (b. 1946), leading Somalian novelist. Exiled from Somalia since 1974, Farah has written all six of his published novels in English. He began writing in 1965, seven years before Somalia acquired an official written language. His writing attacks dictatorship, corruption and injustice, so it is not popular with the Somali regime. However, his *Sweet and Sour Milk* won the English Speaking Union Literary Award. His female characters have been highly praised: their dilemmas are seen in the context of *ISLAM, which has traditionally kept women subjugated.

Fathy, Hassan (b. 1900), Egypt's most famous architect. He waged a lifelong struggle to convince planners that Egypt needs traditional designs to solve its rural housing problem. Among his achievements was the rescue of the Nubian tradition of mud-vaulted houses, which was on the verge of extinction – properly built, these houses will last many years. Referring to the 3000-year-old mud-brick granaries of Luxor, Fathy remarked drily in his book *Architecture for the Poor* that 'mud seemed to be a fairly durable substance'. His aim was always to escape from the expensive system of dependence on contractors.

Fifth Brigade, Zimbabwean army unit set up by President *MUGABE after independence and trained by North Korean advisers. Early in 1983 the brigade was sent to Matabeleland where it did much to restore order (1983–4), but it was accused of committing atrocities against innocent civilians.

Filali, Abdellatif (b. 1928), Moroccan politician and diplomat. Educated in France, Filali held a succession of ambassadorial posts between 1958 and 1980; his last post abroad was as ambassador to Great Britain. In 1982 he was appointed Minister of Information and in 1985 he became Minister of Foreign Affairs, Co-operation and Information.

First, Ruth (d. 1982), wife of Joe *SLOVO, she was a radical white South African political activist and a prominent member of the *AFRICAN NATIONAL CONGRESS and the South African Communist Party. Having failed to convict her of treason (1956) the South African authorities persecuted her until she went into exile in 1964. In Mozambique she was engaged in research on the Mozambican revolution and was head of a centre for African Studies when she was assassinated by a parcel bomb. She wrote *The Barrel of a Gun: Political Power in Africa and the Coup d'Etat* (1972).

flechas, paramilitary force established by *PIDE to help in the fight against *FRELIMO in Mozambique. The flechas committed a number of atrocities, mainly against the peasants who had provided Frelimo with refuge or food.

FLN (Front de Libération Nationale), revolutionary political party which led Algeria to independence from France. The movement received its name on 10 October 1954 and on that day fixed a date, 1 November, for the outbreak of revolt throughout Algeria. The FLN's first leaders were Hocine Ait Ahmed, Ahmed *BEN BELLA, Mostefa Ben Boulaid, Muhammad Boudiaf, Mourad Didouche, Muhammad Khider, Larbi Ben M'hidi, Rabah Bitat, and Belkacem Krim. The FLN issued a charter which stated its goal of national independence and its internal and external objectives. Throughout the war of more than seven years it did not deviate from the principles expressed in the proclamation. After the war, the FLN dedicated itself to socialism, non-alignment and pan-Arabism and was the only part in Algeria with legal status. The party has often been fiercely divided over economic and ideological policies but it remains one of the most influential and successful parties in twentieth-century African politics. A five-yearly party congress elects the 160-member FLN Central Committee and the general secretary, who is automatically the FLN nominee for the presidency of the republic. From 1987, the FLN went into decline, following allegations – later proved to be true – of economic mismanagement and corruption. The leadership had always been strict, even dictatorial, but in 1990, with a world-wide trend towards liberalism in the traditional parties, the leaders were accused of being tyrannical. Reforms were promised but in the face of growing fundamentalism inspired by the *ISLAMIC SALVATION FRONT they may be slow in coming.

FNLA (Frente Nacional de Libertação de Angola), Angolan nationalist movement founded and led by Holden *ROBERTO (1962), one of the three significant movements in the successful war of independence (1961–74). FNLA was formed by combining *UPA with a smaller northern ethnic group. It was mainly supported by rural people, especially the Bakongo of northern Angola, and it made little effort to widen its appeal to the Angolan people as a whole. Backed by Zaire, the USA and Belgium the FNLA formed a revolutionary government in exile in Leopoldville (later named Kinshasa) in 1962. In

protest against northern domination and tribalism Jonas *SAVIMBI left the FNLA (1964) and then established *UNITA which mainly represents the Ovimbundu and other southerners.

Operating from bases in Zaire during the war of independence the FNLA attacked Portuguese forces in northern Angola. Following the *ALVOR AGREEMENT (Jan. 1975) the FNLA was one of the three nationalist movements in the short-lived transitional government, but it was already in conflict with the *MPLA. By March 1975 it was using western mercenaries in open warfare against the MPLA in northern Angola. On 11 November 1975 the three nationalist movements each separately proclaimed the independence of Angola and set up their governments, but soon after the FNLA and UNITA united their so-called governments. By early 1976 FNLA had lost the civil war against the MPLA government and was no longer a significant force in Angola.

Fort Hare University, the place where many distinguished black South Africans have studied. It began life as the Fort Hare University College (1916), to give Africans post-primary education and to prepare some for admission to university. In 1923 it was incorporated as an institute of higher education, preparing students for University of South Africa degrees. In 1951 Fort Hare was linked to Rhodes University; this assured the students that they would be measured by white academic standards. After the South

African government separated university education on racial lines, the University College was transferred to the control of the Minister of Bantu Education (1960) and it was developed to cater specifically to the needs of Xhosa speaking students. In 1970 it was given autonomy as the University of Fort Hare.

FPLM (Forças Populares de Libertação de Moçambique), Mozambique's army which is entrusted with the defence and reconstruction of the country. It includes regular soldiers and a people's militia. Since 1978 men and women have been expected to serve for two years in the armed forces. The FPLM has been engaged in a bitter struggle against the *RENAMO rebels – with some success since it was reorganized in 1986.

Freedom Charter, adopted at the 'Congress of the People' near Johannesburg (Jun. 1955), a statement of economic, social and political freedoms and rights for all South Africans. The congress was sponsored by four important liberation movements (*AFRICAN NATIONAL CONGRESS (ANC), South African Indian Congress, South African Coloured Peoples Organization, Congress of Democrats) and attended by nearly three thousand opponents of *APARTHEID. The Freedom Charter was adopted by the four sponsoring organizations as their manifesto for a liberated non-racial democratic South Africa. It includes statements of equal rights for everybody irrespective of race, colour and sex, equality before the law, government by the people, respect for each national group, ownership of land and natural wealth by the people, human rights, education and housing for all and international friendship.

Frelimo (Frente de Libertação de Moçambique), Mozambique's only official political party, led by the President of Mozambique, it was founded in Dar es Salaam on 25 June 1962 by various exiled groups and radical intellectuals. Its first president was Eduardo *MONDLANE (1962–9). Frelimo was a fusion of nationalist groups opposed to Portuguese colonial rule of Mozambique. Two years after its formation Frelimo fired the first shots in the war of independence (1964). With help from Algeria, Egypt, Israel, Zaire and the Soviet bloc Frelimo was increasingly successful in the armed struggle, but it was damaged by internal divisions and splits. Much of the argument centred on whether Frelimo should commit itself to the cause of international socialism or not. Some members left to join the less radical organization, *COREMO.

When Mondlane was assassinated (1969) the Vice-President, Revd Uria *SIMANGO, claimed the leadership, but had to share power in a triumvirate with Marcelino *DOS SANTOS and Samora *MACHEL. Simango angrily quit Frelimo and the way was clear for Machel to become leader and to make Frelimo a Marxist-Leninist party aligned to international socialism (1970).

With additional support from radical Arab states, the *ORGANIZATION FOR AFRICAN UNITY and Tanzania Frelimo built up a seasoned army of 20,000 men and controlled one third of Mozambique by 1974. In August 1974 Frelimo negotiated an agreement with Portugal at a meeting in Lusaka; this provided for a transitional government and independence in June 1975.

At independence (1975) Frelimo became the ruling party; it introduced a socialist programme which included nationalizing industry, land and social services. At its third congress in 1977 Frelimo proclaimed itself a Marxist-Leninist Vanguard Party, formally committing Mozambique to scientific socialism and announcing the formation of mass organizations to establish closer links between the party and the people. By the late 1980s its membership was only about two per cent of the population. Religious believers, property owners and other class enemies were excluded from membership.

By the time of the fourth congress (1983) economic and social problems had persuaded the Frelimo leadership to make reforms in the movement and to moderate socialism by accepting the role of the private sector in Mozambique's economy. At the fifth congress (Jul. 1989) the delegates accepted proposals from President *CHISSANO which moved the party further away from socialism. The commitment to Marxist-Leninism was dropped and membership was opened to all, including the

previously despised class enemies. Foreign policy was to be based on national interests rather than international socialism and further moves were made towards a free-market economy. In November 1990 the Mozambican parliament approved a new constitution which will end Frelimo's monopoly of political power and allow the formation of rival parties.

FROLINAT (Front de la Libération Nationale Tchadien), the Chad government's main opponent in the civil war. FROLINAT was formed as a guerrilla movement on 22 June 1966 at Nyala in Sudan. Weak in numbers at first, the movement spread through Chad's east and centre and following an uprising in Tibesti, in the far north, it became much stronger. FROLINAT's first leader was Ibrahim Abatcha, but when he was killed during the fighting Abba Siddick took command. Damaged by internal divisions, FROLINAT lost support in 1972 but revived when Colonel *GADDAFI, Libya's leader, backed it. Following victories in 1977 and 1978, FROLINAT controlled many provinces and agreed a cease-fire with the government on 27 March 1978 when it became one of four factions in a government of national union. FROLINAT lost much of its relevance with the formation of new parties and its members drifted into these parties.

Front Line States, term used by South Africa's neighbours to describe themselves, as they are in the front line of the struggle against *APARTHEID and colonialism. The term was also used in the struggle against white minority rule in Rhodesia – until it became independent Zimbabwe (1980). The Front Line States meet to co-ordinate their policies and have set up the *SOUTHERN AFRICAN DEVELOPMENT CO-ORDINATION CONFERENCE in an attempt to lessen their dependence on South Africa. The countries which have borders with South Africa are Angola, Botswana, Lesotho, Mozambique, Namibia, Swaziland, Zambia and Zimbabwe; Malawi and Tanzania are also regarded as Front Line States.

Fugard, Athol (b. 1932), South African playwright, novelist, short story writer, actor and theatrical director. He has directed the Serpent Players in Port Elizabeth since 1969 and was a founder of the Space Experimental Theatre in Cape Town (1972). A prolific writer, much of his work is concerned with the effect of political and social repression on individuals. Among his best known plays are *The Blood Knot, Boesman and Lena* and *Sizwe Bansi is Dead*.

G

Gabon, the Gabonese Republic in West Africa lies across the Equator. It is bordered by the Atlantic Ocean on the west, Equatorial Guinea and Cameroon to the north and the Congo to the east and south. Both the coastal plains and the inland plateaux (about five hundred metres above sea-level) have a hot and humid tropical climate. Much of the country is covered by forests of valuable tropical hardwoods. Port Gentil is the country's major port, handling oil exports.

The people of Gabon are mainly descended from *BANTU immigrants who displaced the earlier pygmy peoples. It is not clear when the Bantu came to the country, but some were established there four centuries ago. The largest ethnic groups are the Fang in the north (30 per cent), the Eshira in the southwest (25 per cent) and Adonma in the southeast (17 per cent).

Although over half the population depends on subsistence farming, Gabon has the highest per capita income in sub-Saharan Africa because of its exports of oil, minerals and timber. Despite official concern and ambitious five-year plans the authorities have had little success in encouraging agricultural development. The attractions of urban life have left the rural areas short of labour. The main subsistence crops are cassava and plantains. The main cash crops are grown on plantations; they include coffee, cocoa, sugar cane and palm oil, crops which contribute little to export earnings.

The main source of Gabon's economic growth has been the exploitation of her rich deposits of oil, which accounted for up to 85 per cent of export earnings in the 1970s and 1980s and peaked in 1977. Since then lower production levels and declining world prices, especially the fall in 1986, have caused serious problems. President *BONGO applied to the World Bank and the IMF for aid and imposed unpopular austerity programmes. Gabon's two refineries at Port Gentil had to merge in 1984 when European demand for petroleum fell and there was competition from new refineries in Cameroon and Congo.

In addition to oil and gas, Gabon has valuable deposits of uranium and manganese, but exports have suffered from falling world demand. Timber exports also suffered, but these recovered during the later 1980s. In 1985 the current account went into deficit and deteriorated even further in 1986. With substantial aid from France and international agencies Gabon has made some progress since in improving its balance of trade.

Little is known of Gabon's early history. The Portuguese explored the coastline in the fifteenth century, but showed little interest

The Gabonese Republic

THE COUNTRY
267,667 sq. km.

Major Cities
Libreville (capital)
Port Gentil
Franceville

Economy
Petroleum industry
Mining
Agriculture

Principal Exports
Petroleum products
Manganese
Timber
Uranium

Currency
CFA franc of 100
centimes

THE PEOPLE
1,206,000

Ethnic Groups
Fang
Eshira
Adonma

Languages
French (official)
Fang
Mpongwe

Religion
Christian
Traditional beliefs

THE STATE
Multi-party republic

Head of State
President Bongo

Ruling Bodies
Council of Ministers
National Assembly

Official Party
Parti démocratique
gabonais
(In 1990 opposition
parties allowed to
register)

in the country. In the nineteenth century European traders came to trade in ivory, slaves and tropical hardwoods and the French founded Libreville as a settlement for freed slaves (1849). Gabon was annexed by France by the 1880s as part of the French Congo. From 1910 it was a separate colony, one of the four territories of French Equatorial Africa. In 1946 it became an overseas territory of France. Leon *M'BA and the Bloc Démocratique Gabonais (BDG) won the 1957 elections and M'Ba became Prime Minister when full self-government within the French Community was achieved (1958).

Gabon gained full independence in August 1960 and M'Ba was elected President of the Republic. He formed a government in coalition with his old rival, Jean-Hilaire Aubame. After quarrelling with Aubame, M'Ba dissolved the national assembly (Jan. 1964) and announced that there would be elections the next month. Shortly before the elections were due the military seized power (Feb. 1964) and installed Aubame at the head of a provisional government. France sent soldiers to restore M'Ba, who held elections in April and won a comfortable majority in the national assembly. President M'Ba became increasingly authoritarian and as opposition members defected to the BDG Gabon became virtually a one party state.

M'Ba died in 1967 and was succeeded by his vice-president, *BONGO. The new president made Gabon a one-party state and created the Parti Démocratique Gabonais (*PDG) as the only legal party; its function is to guard national unity. With French support President Bongo has ruled for over twenty years. Since the early 1980s he has been challenged by the Mouvement de Redressement National (*MORENA), an opposition movement attacking presidential corruption and campaigning for the restoration of a multi party democracy. Economic and social difficulties and President Bongo's austerity programmes have caused discontent, which he has dealt with by tough security measures. By 1990 he was forced to bow to pressure and begin reforms, including the registration of opposition parties and the scheduling of elections for August 1990. The riots in Port Gentil and Libreville in May 1990 were apparently a challenge to the reform process. France sent in the Foreign Legion to protect its nationals, presumably not to maintain President Bongo in power. The elections which took place in September 1990 were chaotic. Although a quarter of the constituency results were declared void, President Bongo claimed victory and rejected demands for fresh elections.

Gaddafi, Colonel Muammar (b. 1938), one of the most controversial national leaders of the twentieth century. A *BEDOUIN, Gaddafi was born at Sirta, Libya, and is of the Sunni Muslim sect. During the rule of King *IDRIS he was expelled from school for illegal political activities and joined the army which, in 1965, sent him to study at Benghazi Military Academy. He was then commissioned. He was a signals captain when he seized power in a bloodless military coup in 1969. Profoundly influenced by the example and policies of President *NASSER of Egypt, Gaddafi had himself promoted colonel and quickly established himself as 'the custodian of Arabism', to use his phrase. He saw himself not only as Nasser's successor but as the new Mahdi, or 'Expected One', divinely sent to lead the Islamic world.

From the beginning of his regime he was constantly in dispute with other Arab leaders, who resented his interference in their affairs. He organized an unsuccessful coup against President *NIMEIRI (1975), seized Chad territory (1976), financed an attempted assassination of President Sadat (1976), and fought a brief war against Egypt, a former ally, (1977). He supported the tyrant Idi *AMIN of Uganda and in 1979 he was implicated in the assassination of Sadat. In the Chad Civil War he backed the Arab northerners as a way of occupying the *AOUZOU STRIP. Throughout his twenty years in power, he has aided militant causes everywhere and is a major supporter of the Palestine Liberation

Organization. Financially, and with weapons and explosives, he backs all terrorist groups which he considers are fighting the 'imperialism' which he detests. A notable beneficiary of Gaddafi largesse is the Irish Republican Army (IRA).

Gaddafi's subversive activities have reached as far as Thailand, New Caledonia and Australia, from where his 'cultural bureau' was expelled in 1986. Feeling threatened by coups which might be organized by dissident Libyans living abroad, Gaddafi has sent assassins to kill his opponents in London, Cairo, Paris, Brussels and elsewhere. He propounds a 'Third Universal Theory' in opposition to communism and capitalism. Parliamentary democracies he denounces as 'the most tyrannical dictatorships the world has known'. His Third Theory involves handing over political and economic power to the people. In March 1977, in an attempt to establish ancient Greek fundamentals of democracy combined with extreme Islamic principles, Gaddafi declared Libya's title changed to Socialist People's Libyan Arab Jamahiriyya (state of the masses). At his incitement, workers took over businesses, students replaced diplomats at Libyan embassies abroad and non-professionals moved in to run government departments in Tripoli. The result was administrative and economic chaos.

By 1989, Gaddafi had survived at least eight attempted coups. He executed plotters as part of the traditional Islamic punishments which he introduced for wrongdoers. His strength lies in his conviction that he has a Muhammad-like destiny to lead Islam. To this end he has spent vast amounts of money in black Africa in vigorous attempts to convert Christians to Islam, attempts which have been hugely successful, especially in Nigeria and Rwanda. In 1979 he imposed a 'jihad tax' on Libyans. This fund-raising is symbolic as Gaddafi has immense national wealth from oil, gas and uranium. He has used this money in attempts to form alliances with certain Arab states, as with Syria in 1980 and Morocco in 1984. Between 1979 and 1988 he was an ally of Ayatollah Khomeini of Iran. Other oil wealth is spent in attacks on the Arab monarchies, which Gaddafi declares are anti-Islamic. In 1974 he backed attempts to overthrow King *HASSAN II of Morocco and he financed the uprising, which was bloodily quelled, in the Great Mosque of Mecca in 1979. It had been calculated to bring down the Saudi royal house. In 1980 President Carter of the US described Gaddafi as 'one of the greatest destabilizing influences in Africa'. In that year it was discovered that Gaddafi is the backer, with money and uranium, of the Islamic bomb being developed by Pakistan.

President Reagan of the US called Gaddafi 'the leading international terrorist and criminal'. In 1986 one of his officials at the Libyan People's Bureau in London shot dead a British policewoman. This led to Britain's breaking off diplomatic relations with Libya. Constantly seeking to improve his status and prestige, in September 1989 Gaddafi signed a treaty of friendship with President *MUBARAK of Egypt. Privately, most Arab Africans and Islamic leaders deride Gaddafi, but he is so dangerous that they cannot ignore him.

Gamaat al Islamiya, leading Islamic fundamentalist organization in Egypt. The religious zealots of Gamaat al Islamiya have for years controlled the students' associations and some professional organizations. Their early and abiding objective on Egyptian campuses was to forbid the free association of men and women. Any disagreement with their dogma brings swift punishment, from severe beatings to murder. When the Dean of Cairo Medical College sought to prevent women students from wearing the *niqab* – the full veil – on the grounds that it was incompatible with the practice of medicine, he was beaten by Gamaat Al Islamiya activists, who threatened to cut off his hands and tongue. The movement is a very real danger to the arts because it seeks to prevent music, theatre and singing. According to Gamaat's statements, 'Singing is prohibited because it distracts worshippers from God. Women particularly should not sing because as a whole women are shameful.' The only musical instrument Gamaat sanctions is the tambourine, because it was in use at the time of the Prophet Muhammad. Theatre is prohibited because of the association it brings

between men and women. The future for the Egyptian cultural scene is bleak and the zealots' activities will not cease with art and culture. In 1989–90, Gamaat became even more outspoken and violent, partly to keep pace with newer even more extreme groups, such as Takfir wal Hijra (Repentance and Holy Flight). Some parliamentarians are said to be secret members of Gamaat.

The Gambia, a member of the Commonwealth, the Republic of the Gambia on the West African coast is one of the continent's smallest states. It extends eastwards into the interior for 470 km on either side of the River Gambia and its width varies from 24 to 50 km. Except for the Atlantic on the west it is completely surrounded by Senegal, a country with which it still has much in common despite different experiences of colonial rule. Senegal, now a Francophone state, was a French colony; the Gambia, now an Anglophone state, was a British colony. The major Gambian ethnic groups, the Mandingo, Fula and Wolof, also live in Senegal.

The Gambia has a hot and humid climate and much of the land around the estuary consists of salt swamp; it lacks significant mineral reserves. The economy depends largely on rice and millet crops for subsistence. Groundnuts account for about 90 per cent of export earnings; fishing and tourism are also foreign currency earners. Considering the size of the country and the lack of development in the colonial period, it is surprising that the country's economy has fared reasonably well since independence.

The Republic of the Gambia

THE COUNTRY 11,295 sq. km.	THE PEOPLE 720,000	THE STATE Multi-party republic
Major City Banjul (capital)	*Ethnic Groups* Mandingo Fula	*Head of State* President Jawara
Economy Agriculture	Wolof	*Ruling Bodies* Cabinet
Principal Exports Groundnuts	*Languages* English (official) Mandingo	House of Representatives
Tourism	Fula Wolof	*Party in Power* People's Progressive Party
Currency Dalassi of 100 butut	*Religion* Islam Christian	*Leading Opposition Party* National Convention Party

Portuguese explorers came to the estuary in the fifteenth century, and some English and French merchants were settled there by the seventeenth century to trade in ivory and slaves. By the end of the eighteenth century Britain had displaced the French. From 1807 to 1843 and 1866 to 1888 the Gambia was governed from Sierra Leone. It had a separate administration between these two periods.

After the Second World War responsible government was gradually extended to the colony, which achieved full internal self-government in October 1963 and full independence in the Commonwealth in February 1965. The country became independent as a constitutional monarchy under the leadership of Dawda *JAWARA and the People's Progressive Party (PPP). In April 1970 it became a multi-party republic with Jawara as its first president.

The PPP has convincingly won all the general elections and the only major challenge to the government of President Jawara was the attempted coup of 1981, when rebel soldiers occupied key positions. Jawara called in the Senegalese forces to crush the rebels and in gratitude agreed to closer links between the two countries. In 1982 they came together to form *SENEGAMBIA, a confederation with an assembly and a council of ministers representing both countries. The Gambia saw Senegambia as an expression of the special relationship between the two countries, but Senegal saw it as a first step towards a federation or even union of the two countries. This major difference between the two countries and the Gambia's fear of Senegalese domination led to a deterioration of relations and the dissolution of Senegambia in September 1989.

Gbagho, Laurent (b. 1944), Ivory Coast opposition politician and founder of the Ivorian Popular Front. A former history teacher with degrees from French universities, Gbagho spent the years 1981–7 in exile as a 'trouble-maker'. On his return, in September 1988, he founded the Ivorian Popular Front, the first officially condoned opposition group. Gbagho said that a major political lesson of modern Africa was 'the absence of checks and balances'. He is seen as a possible future president of Ivory Coast.

Ghana, formerly the Gold Coast, the Republic of Ghana is a member of the Commonwealth; it was the first African colony to win its independence (1957). Situated in West Africa, north of the Equator, Ghana is bordered by Burkina Faso on the north, Togo on the east, the Atlantic Ocean on the south and the Ivory Coast on the west. In the hot and humid coastal region there are lagoons, swamps, low-lying plains and the Volta River delta. Inland, the forest zone which covers about a third of the country is the most productive part of Ghana. The hotter and drier northern region is neglected and economically backward. Much of Ghana is dominated by the Volta River, formed by the confluence of the Black and the White Volta and their tributaries. Lake Volta which was formed when the Akosombo Dam was completed (1966) is Africa's largest man-made lake and a major source of hydroelectric power.

Agriculture is vital to Ghana, which is self-sufficient in cassava and maize, two of its staple foods; during the 1980s Ghana has lessened its dependence on imports of its other staple food – rice. Ghana was the world's leading cocoa producer, but falling world prices, drought and the drift of young workers from the farms to the cities reduced cocoa production from 560,000 tonnes in 1965 to 150,000 tonnes in 1981. Between 1983 and 1989 cocoa production doubled, thanks both to the *RAWLINGS' government economic recovery programme and to good weather. Exports of cocoa, which is mostly grown in the forest zone, now account for about two thirds of Ghana's foreign earnings. Other export crops include pineapples, coffee, palm kernels, shea nuts, copra, limes, cotton and tobacco. Ghana's extensive forests are producing increasing timber exports.

Gold is the most lucrative mineral and accounts for about 15 per cent of foreign earnings. Bauxite, diamonds and manganese are also exported. Despite poor transport and a shortage of foreign currency for machinery and spare parts, manufacturing has recovered from its low point in the early 1980s when it was working at a quarter of its capacity. Drought lowered water levels in Lake Volta and led to power shortages in the early 1980s, but heavier rains and a new plant (1986) have improved supplies. An austerity programme,

The Republic of Ghana

THE COUNTRY
238,540 sq. km.

Major Cities
Accra (capital)
Kumasi
Cape Coast
Takoradi

Economy
Farming
Mining

Principal Exports
Cocoa
Gold
Manganese
Diamonds
Bauxite

Currency
Cedi of 100 pesewas

THE PEOPLE
13,599,000

Ethnic Groups
Akan
Ga
Ewe
Guan
Moshi-Dagomba

Languages
English (official)
Twi, Fante, Ga, Ewe,
Dagbeni, Hausa, Nzima

Religion
Christian
Islam
Traditional beliefs

THE STATE
Military state

Head of State
Flt.-Lt. Rawlings

Ruling Bodies
Provisional National
Defence Council
Committee of Secretaries

Political Parties
All banned

including successive devaluations of the official currency (the cedi) down to two per cent of its 1982 value by 1988, led to limited financial and economic advances by 1990. Inflation and budget deficits have fallen while the balance of trade has improved and the Gross Domestic Product per capita has risen. To achieve these successes Ghanaians have endured unemployment, high fuel prices and a high sales tax. With stable world commodity prices and good harvests in the 1990s, there are hopes that the recovery will continue. Ghana could be a model for other Third World countries with financial and economic problems.

The people of Ghana are divided into over seventy ethnic groups, each with their own language or dialect. Most of these are small; the largest are the Akan (44 per cent), Mole-Dagomda (16 per cent), Ewe (13 per cent) and the Ga-Adangbe (8 per cent). Despite ethnic differences Ghanaians are both patriotic and loyal to their traditional cultures, perhaps because high educational standards and the use of English as an official language have weakened ethnic rivalries.

Little is known about the history of Ghana before the Portuguese travellers arrived in search of ivory, gold and spices in the fifteenth century.

GHANA

The original Ghana was a powerful monarchy flourishing from the fourth to the thirteenth century hundreds of miles northwest of modern Ghana. From the thirteenth to the sixteenth century the ancestors of today's Ghanaians arrived in waves of immigration from the north.

From the middle of the sixteenth to the middle of the nineteenth century various European powers established trading posts on the coast and traded in gold and slaves. Britain persuaded the Danes (1850) and the Dutch (1871) to give up their trading posts. After defeating the Ashanti of the forest region Britain made the coastal area a British colony (the Gold Coast) and proclaimed a protectorate over parts of the hinterland. In 1901 the coastal areas, the Ashanti forest region and the Northern Territories were all put under colonial rule. From 1922 until independence part of Togo was administered as part of the Gold Coast.

The educated African middle classes who had been promoted to positions of responsibility in the nineteenth century found that they were relegated to subordinate posts in the twentieth century; they protested and campaigned with some success for a measure of self-government. The Burns Constitution (1946) gave Africans a majority in the Legislative Council. In 1947 *DANQUAH became the first leader of the United Gold Coast Convention (UGCC), an essentially middle class body campaigning for self-government in the shortest possible time. After the detention of UGCC leaders in 1948,

*NKRUMAH and other radical nationalists rejected the gradualism of the UGCC. They formed the *CONVENTION PEOPLE'S PARTY (CPP) in 1949 and demanded immediate self-government. Nkrumah was arrested and imprisoned (1950–51) during a wave of industrial unrest and political protest, but was released and invited to form a government when the CPP won the 1951 election. Nkrumah became Prime Minister in 1952 and after winning the 1954 and 1956 elections he pressed for independence. In March 1957 the Gold Coast merged with British Togoland to become the independent state of Ghana – Nkrumah was its leader for the first nine years (1957–66).

Initially Nkrumah was warmly supported by his own people and the Western world, but his political and economic measures soon alienated his supporters. The Preventive Detention Act (1958) provided for up to five years' detention without trial. The Industrial Relations Act (1958) made all workers pay a monthly levy to the Trades Union Congress which was run by the CPP. The 1960 republican constitution gave President Nkrumah great powers. In 1964 Ghana became a single party socialist state and in 1965 elections the central committee nominated a single list of parliamentary candidates.

As the political atmosphere became increasingly oppressive Ghana moved closer to the Soviet bloc. The CPP crushed all opposition and degenerated into a greedy clique which controlled and exploited the country's social and economic institutions. Nkrumah lost touch with his people, preferring to preach his own doctrine of African socialism ('Nkrumahism') and to surround himself with CPP sycophants. The falling price of cocoa and Nkrumah's economic policies caused grave problems. He spent heavily on prestige-projects and entrusted the economy to corrupt and inefficient bureaucrats. Denunciations of western creditors as imperialists and Ghana's warm relations with the Soviet bloc led to a credit squeeze and further economic problems. In February 1966 the army and the police seized power while Nkrumah was abroad. The National Liberation Council (NLC) under the chairmanship of General *ANKRAH promised the end of repression, an economic recovery and a return to civilian rule.

During three and a half years in power the NLC had little economic success; inflation and foreign debts continued to soar. It did manage to stay together despite internal rivalries, lifted the ban on party politics (May 1969) and organized elections for a new national assembly (Aug. 1969), won by Dr Kofi *BUSIA with an overwhelming majority. Busia took office as prime minister in October 1969 in a climate of optimism which soon faded. The economic crisis worsened as cocoa prices continued falling and the government failed to develop coherent policies. An unsuccessful austerity programme combined with political ineptitude made the Busia government even more unpopular. Lt.-Col. *ACHEAMPONG led Ghana's second military coup (Feb. 1972); he banned party politics and set up a National Redemption Council (NRC) of military and police to run the country. The NRC emphasized a policy of self-reliance, cutting imports, directing funds into Operation Feed Yourself and repudiating some foreign debts; the 1973 trade surplus provided some evidence of success. Another pressing problem for the NRC was the tension between Ghana and Togo over the Ewe people who complained of ill treatment and threatened to secede from Ghana and join Togo. Acheampong negotiated with the Togo authorities and the Ewe settled down for a while, but in 1977 Togo's support for the Ewe in the Togo Liberation Movement in Ghana caused fresh tension between the two countries.

Acheampong tightened his control of Ghana when he reconstituted the military government as the Supreme Military Council (Oct. 1975). The economic crisis continued as Acheampong battled in vain against raging inflation, strikes, political discontent and mounting demands for a return to civilian rule. In July 1977 he promised an elected government by July 1979 and started preparing for the so-called Union Government in which the military and civilians would share power. In July 1978 Acheampong was deposed in a bloodless military coup and replaced by Lt.-Gen. *AKUFFO.

Akuffo also grappled unsuccessfully with Ghana's economic problems while sticking to his timetable for the return to civilian rule. Political parties were legalized from the beginning of 1979 and elections were scheduled for June 1979. A few days before the elections were due, junior officers and NCOs, led by Flt.-Lt. *RAWLINGS seized power and set up the Armed Forces Revolutionary Council (AFRC) which pledged to purify Ghana. It executed Acheampong, Akuffo and others, and took fierce action against those suspected of profiteering, hoarding and corruption. Rawlings made it clear that Ghana would soon return to civilian rule. The elections were held; the People's National Party (PNP) won and in September 1979 the PNP leader, Dr *LIMANN, was sworn in as president.

President Limann faced many difficulties. His austerity measures provoked strikes and protests, the economy continued to deteriorate, corruption scandals and factional disputes discredited the PNP, and he failed to maintain good relations with Rawlings and the army. As Limann's government collapsed Rawlings seized power for the second time on New Year's Eve, 1981.

Rawlings took over as chairman of the Provisional National Defence Council (PNDC). This time he gave no indication that he intended returning Ghana to civilian rule until 1987 when he announced there would be district council elections as the first step to grassroots democracy. Even after these elections in

1988 and 1989 real power still rests with the Committees for the Defence of the Revolution, set up to carry out PNDC policies at the local level, and there have been no indications that national elections will be held. Despite some successes in strengthening the economy, Ghana's political prospects remained uncertain during the 1980s. There were numerous plots to overthrow Rawlings. University students went on strike and the universities were closed, political opponents detained and the press tightly controlled.

The future of Ghana depends on its economic recovery. If the health of the economy continues to improve during the 1990s Rawlings may gradually restore the country to civilian rule.

Gordimer, Nadine (b. 1923), South African novelist and short story writer. She is a liberal who focuses on the dilemmas facing white liberals in South Africa; their weakness and ineffectiveness in a society governed by *APARTHEID is a recurring theme in her works. Her novels include *The Conservationist* (1974), *Lying Days* (1978), *Soldier's Embrace* (1980), *Something Out There* (1984), *Sport of Nature* (1987) and *My Son's Story* (1990).

Gouled, Hassan (b. 1939), first president of Djibouti. Of indigenous Somali extraction, Gouled was moderate in his views from the beginning of his interest in Djibouti politics in the 1960s. He condemned terrorist activities against the French in Djibouti because he realised that without France Djibouti would be defenceless and bankrupt. He and his LPAI party gained the majority vote in Djibouti's elections in May 1977 and Gouled became head of state. In June 1979 he showed statesmanlike qualities in appealing to the people to 'try to exercise self-discipline'. He wanted the civil service to develop a sense of duty and the public to help him in bringing down prices. He has tried to bring about peace between Ethiopia and Somalia by bringing the two sides together for talks in Djibouti and in Addis Abbaba. A strong leader despite his pragmatic and moderate policies, Gouled has not hesitated to dismiss ministers for inefficiency and corruption and, more frequently, for perceived disloyalty. In June 1985 he dismissed the Minister of Defence, Habib Muhammad Loita, for 'actions contrary to cabinet commitments'. In May 1986 he dismissed a vice-president of the party for 'activities incompatible with party objectives'. In the late 1980s Gouled sought to increase his prestige by making state visits to Islamic countries and former French West African states. The Gulf Crisis of August 1990, caused by Iraq's invasion of Kuwait, brought Gouled an unexpected benefit. For the French, Djibouti had suddenly become more important and they quickly reinforced their military presence there. Gouled could not have been more delighted, because his own status became greater.

Gowon, General Yakubu (b. 1934), military ruler of Nigeria (1966–75). A Muslim born in Plateau State, he joined the army in 1954 and served in the United Nations Congo peacekeeping force twice (1960–61; 1963). After rising through the ranks, in 1966 he became Chief of Staff and a member of *AGUIYI–IRONSI's military government. The northern officers who led the July 1966 coup chose him to head the Federal Military Government and to command the Nigerian Army.

As head of state he sought reconciliation and released political prisoners, including Chief *AWOLOWO; but the Ibo in the Eastern Region would not accept his authority and announced the secession of *BIAFRA. In the bitter civil war which followed (1967–70) Gowon fought with determination to hold Nigeria together; at the end of the war his offer of reconciliation and rehabilitation to the defeated 'Biafrans' was applauded in Nigeria and by the international community. Despite his remarkable success in healing the wounds of war, Gowon was unable to solve the country's economic problems. Under his regime shortages, inflation and corruption increased and there was negligible progress in developing Nigeria's economy and infrastructure.

In 1970, General Gowon announced the timetable for a return to civilian rule by 1976, but the results of the 1973 census which recorded a remarkable increase in the population of the Muslim north caused great tension. In 1974 Gowon caused consternation by indefinitely postponing the return to civilian rule.

In July 1975 Gowon was overthrown in a bloodless coup while at an *ORGANIZATION OF AFRICAN UNITY meeting in Kampala; he had sent his family to safety beforehand. He promised to support the new government of Murtala *MUHAMMED and went to study Political Science at the University of Warwick. It was alleged that the plotters of the abortive February 1976 coup planned to instal Gowon in power again; subsequently the Nigerian military government dismissed Gowon from the army and declared him a wanted person. President *SHAGARI pardoned him (1981) and Gowon was warmly received when he visited Nigeria (1983), before settling in Togo (1984). He was awarded a Ph.D. in 1984.

'Greater Morocco', a notional entity, born of the assertion that the authority of the pre-colonial Moroccan sultans extended far into the Algerian Sahara and south to the Senegal River. The concept was first elaborated by Moroccan publicists in 1956 as a way of 'proving' that Mauritania should be part of Morocco. Little evidence exists to support the theory. It was not until 1969–70 that King *HASSAN II of Morocco recognized Mauritania as an independent state. He delayed acceptance of Algeria's frontiers until they were agreed in the Treaty of Ifrane, 15th January 1969. Hassan regards his pragmatic moves in relation to Mauritania and Algeria as concessional and has never renounced his Greater Moroccan ambitions.

Great Zimbabwe, an impressive Iron Age site in modern Zimbabwe. The word Zimbabwe is derived from the Shona phrase for houses of stone. Most of it was built from the thirteenth to the fifteenth centuries when it was the capital of a great trading empire. At its peak the site had about fifteen thousand inhabitants. The Great Enclosure is surrounded by a dry stone wall without cement or mortar. The perimeter wall is 250 metres long and 11 metres high. Inside the enclosure is a 10 metre high conical tower, the purpose of which is unknown. A representation of the Zimbabwe bird from this site forms part of the national flag. Archaeological evidence shows that Great Zimbabwe was built by the Shona people.

Green March On 14 November 1974 King *HASSAN II of Morocco and the Spanish Government signed the Madrid Agreement, handing *WESTERN SAHARA over to Morocco and Mauritania at the end of January 1976. This victory, preceded by a campaign in Morocco to cultivate a *JIHAD, culminated in an epic 'Green March' by 350,000 Moroccans towards Western Sahara in November 1975. The march was organized by the military. While the civilian march entered Western Sahara near the coast, inland, Moroccan troops, with air-cover, launched a blitzkrieg resisted by five thousand *POLISARIO volunteers. It gave Hassan's regime real popularity. The event was called the Green March because of the many thousands of green flags carried – the symbol of Islam.

Group Areas Act (1950), one of the first acts introduced by the *NATIONAL PARTY government of South Africa after its election victory in 1948. The act is one of the pillars of *APARTHEID and it aims to reduce contacts between different races in South Africa by reserving certain areas for different racial groups. By the act the authorities are empowered to proclaim both 'controlled' areas where only members of the designated race can live and work and 'specified' areas where only members of the designated race can live.

The act is complex and has been frequently amended, but it clearly favours the white minority who have been allocated most of the group areas and are rarely forced to move. The *COLOUREDS and the *INDIANS have their areas, but none are reserved for the blacks who are expected to regard their *HOMELANDS as their real home. The forced removal of non-whites has caused much hardship and attracted adverse publicity. During the late 1980s President P.W. *BOTHA's plans to reform the act caused a storm of right-wing opposition, and it looks as though the Group Areas Act will live on – perhaps modified by the development of 'grey' areas where anybody can live. In April 1990 President *DE KLERK announced that the Act would be amended in 1991 to eliminate discrimination.

Grunitzky, Nicolas (b. 1913), Togolese politician and one-time President of Togo. Born in central Togo, Grunitzky was educated as an engineer in France. Always active in politics, he returned to Togo in 1937 and became a Togolese deputy to the French National Assembly in 1951, a position he held until 1956. In that year he formed the Parti Togolais du Progrès (PTP). France reconstituted the country the Autonomous Republic of Togo and chose Grunitzky as Prime Minister, even though his PTP was a less representative party than the rival Comité de l'Unité Togolais (CUT) of Sylvanus *OLYMPIO. In UN-supervised elections, April 1958, PTP won only three seats out of forty-six and Grunitzky went into exile in Dahomey. He returned in 1963 to succeed the murdered Olympio as President. In addition, he took over the functions of Prime Minister and Minister of Foreign Affairs. In January 1967 Grunitzky was overthrown by an army coup and went into exile in France, from where he has never returned.

Guinea, West African state with an Atlantic coastline of 320 kilometres. Virtually the whole territory is productive, from the coastal plain to the hills and plateaux. Its people are tribal, the Susu being coastal dwellers, while the Malinke are settled in the north and centre. The Tenda tribe occupies the east and the Kissi people inhabit the southern forests. Guinea has no fewer than seven neighbours. Clockwise, they are Mali, Ivory Coast, Liberia, Sierra

135

The Republic of Guinea

THE COUNTRY
245,857 sq. km.

Major Cities
Conakry (capital)
Mali
Kerouane

Economy
Subsistence agriculture;
rice, maize, yams,
bananas, coffee,
groundnuts, tobacco.
Mining.

Principal Exports
Bauxite, coffee, tobacco

Currency
Guinean franc (since
January 1986)

THE PEOPLE
6.98 million

Ethnic Groups
Susu, Tenda, Kissi,
Malinke, Fulu

Languages
French (official)
Malinke, Fula, Susu

Religion
Muslim 60%
Traditional beliefs 39%
Christian 1%

THE STATE
Presidential republic

Head of State
Colonel Lansana
Conté

Ruling Body
Military Committee for
National Recovery

Official Party
Nominally, Guinea
Democratic Party

Leone, Guinea-Bissau, Gambia and
Senegal.

The French knew Guinea as 'Rivers of the south', but when they colonized the territory in 1891 they named it Guinea and declared it part of French West Africa. It became a French Overseas Territory in 1946 but already nationalist forces were campaigning for autonomy. The main organization was the Parti Démocratique de Guinée (PDG), founded by Ahmed Sekou *TOURÉ. After a series of electoral victories, PDG won the territorial elections of March 1957 and Touré became vice-president of Guinea's governing council. Passionately 'progressive', he abolished the traditional chiefdoms.

On 28 September 1958 Guinea voted overwhelmingly for complete independence from France, and was the first country to break away from the French empire. Independence became formal on 2 October 1958. The French were angry with the 'betrayal' and withdrew their support. Touré's attempts to merge with Ghana and Mali failed but his attempts to suppress any incipient opposition were all too successful. Because of purges and the failing economy, a quarter of Guinea's population left the country during the 1960s.

Guineans opposed to Touré, backed by Portuguese troops, attempted an invasion at Conakry on 22 November 1970 but it was blocked and Touré began a campaign of oppression against real and imagined dissidents. After the PDG conference of 1973 he announced that there would be no further annual conferences, a ban which remained in force until 1978. In the meantime, Touré was so politically insecure that for five years, 1970–5, he did not leave the country. However, in the period 1976–8 he travelled widely in Africa and the Middle East.

In 1978 Touré reconvened the PDG conference, mainly to pass a resolution making PDG the state party and to give the country the title of Democratic and Popular Republic of Guinea. Following improved relations with Guinea, Giscard d'Estaing visited the country in 1978 and French aid projects followed. They had no effect in reducing the level of terror inflicted by Touré. Each attempt to depose him led to severance of diplomatic relations with countries Touré considered responsible, notably Ivory Coast and Senegal. At the depths of Touré's reign of terror more than half a million Guineans were exiles, including the most prominent academics, journalists, military officers and religious leaders.

Touré died on 26 March 1984 and on 3 April Colonel Lansana Conté took power in a coup. Conté promised a democratic regime and at once freed more than one thousand political prisoners. His far-reaching economic and administrative reforms transformed the economy and made Guinea more appealing to the West. Gradually, the International Monetary Fund, the World Bank and foreign governments, notably France's, gained more confidence in Guinea's future. Guinea is the world's second largest producer of bauxite but under Touré the industry had become depressed. It is now much more competitive. The government's three-year plan, 1987–90, concentrated on mineral resources, energy, and agricultural exports. Guinea is in the midst of a 'green revolution', which should help to bring its people out of the poverty inflicted upon them by Touré and his followers. As an indication of the level of corruption, it may be mentioned that President Conté's new administrators found that the former regime had employed 88,000 'ghost' civil servants and was drawing their salaries.

Guinea-Bissau, tiny by African standards, this tropical country comprises a mainland and numerous coastal islands. Largely a land of rainforests, rivers and swamps, Guinea-Bissau rises gradually from the coastal plains to mountains in the east. It supports a population of nearly one million, most of them tribal people. The largest tribe by far – 32 per cent – is the Balante. Guinea-Bissau's two neighbours are Senegal to the north and Guinea to the east and south.

The Portuguese claimed Guinea-Bissau as a colony in 1879 but they did not manage to subjugate its people fully for seventy years. They controlled it only briefly

GUINEA-BISSAU

The Republic of Guinea-Bissau

THE COUNTRY
36,125 sq. km.

Major Cities
Bissau (capital)
Sao Domingos
Bolamo
Bubaque

Economy
Subsistence agriculture,
rice, vegetables, cotton,
sugarcane, palm oil,
bauxite, timber, fisheries

Principal Exports
Cotton, fish, timber,
groundnuts

Currency
Guinea peso of 100
centavos

THE PEOPLE
950,000

Ethnic Groups
Balante
Fula
Mandinka

Languages
Portuguese (official)
Atlantico, Mande and
other tribal languages

Religion
Traditional beliefs 64%
Muslim 35%
Christian 1%

THE STATE
Presidential republic

Head of State
President Joao Bernado
Vieira

Ruling Body
Revolutionary Council of
nine

Official Party
Partido Africano da
Independência da Guiné
e Cabo Verde
The Cape Verde part of
the title is redundant.

---

before the post-1945 African independence movement brought into being the *PARTIDO AFRICANO DA INDEPENDÊNÇIA DA GUINÉ E CABO VERDE, (PAIGC). Under Amilcar *CABRAL and Aristides *PEREIRA, the PAIGC fought an outstandingly successful guerrilla war. This began in 1961 and after twelve years PAIGC controlled most of the countryside. It did not hold the capital, Bissau, but nevertheless in 1973 it held elections in the liberated areas and on 23 September proclaimed independence. In April 1974 the Portuguese dictator, Salazar, was overthrown and the new government withdrew from Guinea-Bissau on 10 September 1974.

That the PAIGC was able to master the appalling problems left by the long war and by gross Portuguese maladministration was almost entirely due to its immense prestige as a result of the anti-colonial war victory. Moving towards unification with Cape Verde, the PAIGC leaders of Guinea-Bissau set up the Supreme Council of the Struggle and, within this group, the Executive Council of the Struggle. The people were organized into national movements, one of which is for women and another for young people. During the liberation war, PAIGC had been helped by the Soviet Union, China and Cuba but with the coming of peace it turned towards the West for economic aid.

During the late 1970s, certain prominent people opposed the mixed race leadership of Guinea-Bissau – that is, Africans and Cape Verdians – and criticized the military leaders, most of whom lived in Praia, Cape Verde. On 14 November 1980, Joao Bernardo Vieira deposed President Luiz *CABRAL and proceeded to run the country through a nine-man Revolutionary Council, all of them African mainlanders. The idea of unifying Guinea-Bissau and Cape Verde collapsed and relations between the two were strained for three years. Vieira strengthened his position by purging suspected opponents, abolishing the post of prime minister and setting up a small cabinet loyal to himself. Nevertheless, between 1980 and 1985 four coup attempts took place. Six of the plotters arrested after the November 1985 conspiracy died in prison. One leader was shot 'while attempting to escape', and others died of mysterious illnesses. Another six were later executed after trials for treason. Vieira has been praised for his stable regime but stability has been bought at a considerable cost in human rights.

Guinea-Bissau's economy would collapse without foreign aid but it could have a reasonably prosperous future if agriculture is adequately diversified. Sugarcane, cotton and tobacco are current development priorities, while groundnuts remain the most important export crop. Following settlement of fishing disputes with Guinea and Senegal, Guinea-Bissau's fisheries have developed to the point where they account for more than a third of total exports. Petroleum is regarded as the great hope of the future. The historic irony concerning Guinea-Bissau is that Portugal, which had virtually destroyed the country, is now its main trading partner. When the Portuguese withdrew, in 1974, nearly fifty per cent of infants were dying in their first year and average life expectancy was thirty-five years. Infant mortality has been greatly reduced and the life expectancy for those born in the 1990s is sixty-five. In these terms, the PAIGC's policies have been successful.

H

Habyarimana, President Juvénal (b. 1937), a general who has been President of Rwanda since he seized power in 1973. A Hutu from the north, he was educated in Zaire before serving as Chief of Staff (1963–5), and later as Minister for the National Guard and Chief of Staff of Police (1965–73). In addition to holding the office of President he has been Minister of National Defence since 1973 and Prime Minister since 1974. He is also President of the *MRND, Rwanda's only political party which he founded in 1975. His constitutional changes have given the country a civilian government and elections, but the voters have no choice in the presidential elections and only a limited choice in legislative elections. His programme of 'rigour and austerity' which was introduced in 1984 has had little success in solving Rwanda's economic problems.

The President has kept the country tightly under his control and has had some success in giving it political stability. This stability was threatened in October 1990 by the invasion of the Rwandan Patriotic Front from Uganda. Its soldiers were mainly Tutsi exiles and deserters from the Rwandan Army. Within a month the leaders of the invading force had been killed and the men had retreated either to Uganda or to the hills.

Haile Selassie I (1892–1975), emperor of Ethiopia, formerly Abyssinia, and one of the best known African leaders of the twentieth century. Haile Selassie was born into the royal family and was a cousin of Emperor Memelik II. He was appointed governor of Herar Province in 1910 and between 1916 and 1928 he was regent and head of government. When he became emperor in 1930 he managed to master the ruling aristocracy and began the process of modernizing a feudal country. Even so, the workers were kept at poverty level. In 1936 Mussolini's Italian army invaded Ethiopia and Haile Selassie fled. In a famous episode, the diminutive and dignified Haile Selassie appeared before the League of Nations in Geneva to plead for international assistance. He received none and stayed in exile until the Italians, defeated by the British in *ERITREA in 1941, restored him to his kingdom. He became a leading figure in the *ORGANIZATION OF AFRICAN UNITY (OAU), which had its headquarters in Addis Ababa. Haile Selassie survived a coup attempt in 1960 but on 12 September 1974 he was deposed by the *DERGUE. He died the following year while in detention. Since Haile Selassie's death, Rastafarians throughout the world have held him in mythic reverence, as they see him as one of them.

Harambee, frequently used political slogan in Kenya. It means pulling together and also implies individual effort. President *KENYATTA favoured the word because it stressed initiative rather than the ideology of African socialism.

Hassan II (b. 1924), King of Morocco since 1961 and a leading figure on the North African political scene. Born in Rabat, the elder son of King Muhammad V, Hassan showed much political acumen from an early age and from 1945 was official adviser to his father. As the Second World War ended, the Moroccans demanded independence from France, whose government exiled King Muhammad and Prince Hassan in 1953. As unrest mounted, the French returned father and son to Morocco and succeeded in appeasing the Moroccan public. Morocco became independent in 1956 and the king appointed Hassan to be Commander-in-Chief of the army. The following year he was officially designated heir to the throne and in 1960 he became Prime Minister and Minister of Defence. Only a year later, at the age of thirty-one, he succeeded to the throne on the death of his father. During 1972 he was chairman of the *ORGANIZATION OF AFRICAN UNITY (OAU). He survived popular unrest in 1965 and the early 1970s, and coups in 1971 and 1972 as well as a *GADDAFI-backed plot to assassinate him in 1980. Hassan has kept his throne because of his shrewd political skill in mollifying and reconciling army generals, Islamic fundamentalist leaders and ardent republicans. His popular, aggressive nationalist policies keep him on a middle path between the traditional Right and the radical Left.

Hassan Wall, one of the most remarkable innovations in modern warfare. The Hassan Wall was built by Morocco between 1980 and 1982 to prevent the *POLISARIO freedom fighters from penetrating into Morocco and to restrict them to the desert. It is several conjoined structures, two thousand miles in length, and longer than the Great Wall of China. It consists of a wall of sand twelve feet high, protected by barbed wire and interspersed with fortifications and minefields. The Wall seals off 15 per cent of the Western Sahara and blockades some 60 per cent of the territory. The Hassan Wall or Line is, in effect, an alarm tripwire. Its radars and ground sensors can detect an approaching Polisario patrol up to thirty miles away. Behind the wall are quick-response units poised to strike at intruders. The wall was planned with American help and supplied with American surveillance equipment. It is manned by 150,000 Moroccan troops and costs an estimated $1 billion a year to maintain.

Head, Bessie (1938–86), South African novelist, the daughter of a Zulu stablehand and a white woman from a rich family. Her mother was committed to a mental hospital and Bessie was brought up in an orphanage. She worked as a teacher and journalist and was increasingly involved in politics after her marriage to Harold Head. After the marriage ended she and her son moved to

141

Bechuanaland (1964) where she was glad to be free of the restrictions and burdens of South African racism. Her three novels draw on her personal experience and her concern for the fate of outcasts. *Where Rainclouds Gather* (1969) is about a political refugee in a rural setting; *Maru* (1971) deals with prejudice against the *SAN (Bushmen). After a nervous breakdown in 1971 she wrote *A Question of Power* (1974) about a woman's breakdown and her struggle back to sanity. She also wrote short stories and an historical work – *A Bewitched Crossroad: an African Saga* (1984).

Hendrickse, Revd Allan (b. 1927), *COLOURED South African politician who leads the *LABOUR PARTY. A Congregationalist minister, he served on the Coloured People's Representative Council until 1979 when it was dissolved because it was not amenable to the will of the government. Although the great majority of Coloureds boycotted the 1984 election, he decided to campaign and Labour won seventy-six of the eighty seats in the *HOUSE OF REPRESENTATIVES. Hendrickse joined the cabinet as minister with special responsibility for Coloured Affairs.

He soon had doubts about his decision to co-operate with the government and relations with President *BOTHA rapidly deteriorated. Early in 1987 he publicly defied *APARTHEID by swimming on a beach for whites only and was forced to make an embarrassing apology. After another row he resigned from the cabinet (Aug. 1987). He has

criticized the government's failure to repeal the *GROUP AREAS ACT and has threatened to use the right of veto enjoyed by the House of Representatives unless reforms are made.

Heroes' Acre, monument and memorial garden built in 1980 to commemorate the Zimbabweans who died in the struggle for independence. Leading Zimbabweans who have been designated national heroes are buried here.

Herstigte Nasionale Party (HNP), extreme right-wing South African party founded by Albert *HERZOG in 1969. Herzog and three other MPs left the *NATIONAL PARTY in protest against the relaxation of *APARTHEID. Jaap Marais became party leader in 1977. The party did have significant support from the white community, but this declined from 14 per cent of the electorate in 1981 to 3 per cent in 1987. It decided not to contest the 1989 election, which benefited the *CONSERVATIVE PARTY, the other party to the right of the government. Like the Conservative Party the HNP believes in the supremacy and purity of the white Afrikaner race in South Africa. The differences between the two parties are more personal than doctrinal, although of the two the HNP is the most uncompromising supporter of white supremacy, and, to many, is a spectre of the more extreme right-wing regime which awaits the failure of the National Party.

Herzog, Dr Albert (1899–1982), extreme right-wing South African politician, founder of the *HERSTIGTE

NASIONALE PARTY (1969). The son of a former prime minister, he was elected to parliament in 1948 and held various ministerial posts in *NATIONAL PARTY governments until he left the party in 1968 in protest against the relaxation of *APARTHEID. He lost his seat in 1970. His support for the *AFRIKANER WEERSTANDSBEWEGING embarrassed the party and led to his resignation as party leader (1977).

High Commission Territories, these were the three Southern African states of Basutoland, Bechuanaland and Swaziland which obtained British protection against the *BOERS who had designs on their territories. The High Commissioner, who represented Britain in Southern Africa, supervised their governments. When the Union of South Africa was established (1910) there was provision for the incorporation of the High Commission Territories into the union. Britain respected the wishes of the people in the three territories not to join South Africa. With the election of a South African government committed to *APARTHEID (1948) the incorporation of the High Commission Territories into South Africa was out of the question. Independence was achieved by Bechuanaland (now Botswana) and Basutoland (now Lesotho) in 1966; Swaziland became independent in 1968.

Highlife, a form of music which originated in 1920 in Ghana and Sierra Leone; it subsequently spread to other parts of West Africa. Highlife began as a combination of indigenous melodies with more western styles like sea shanties, church hymns and regimental songs.

Hoarau, Gerard (1951–85), political exile from the Seychelles, he was President of the Seychelles National Movement (the reconstituted *MOUVEMENT POUR LA RÉSISTANCE) when he was assassinated in London. Hoarau worked for President *MANCHAM in the department of foreign affairs until the 1977 coup; then for a short time he worked as chief immigration officer in President *RENÉ's government. He was soon disillusioned with the new regime and founded an opposition group, the Mouvement pour la Résistance. Following the discovery of a plot against the government (Nov. 1979) Hoarau was arrested and imprisoned until August 1980. He was also involved in the abortive coup of November 1981 and was forced into exile – first in South Africa and then London. Some commentators believe President René ordered his assassination.

Holy Spirit Movement, fanatical rebel movement in Uganda which has fought President *MUSEVENI's government since 1986. Its leader, Alice *LAKWENA, recruited thousands of followers by a mixture of witchcraft and terror. It resorts to a casual mixture of severe disciplinarian brutality and superstition – followers anoint themselves with 'bulletproof' oil and believe they are invincible. Despite setbacks late

143

in 1987 the movement has fought on. In April 1990 it was reported that forty of its members were killed in battle against government forces.

Homelands for the *BANTU (or Bantustans) were established in South Africa by the Bantu Self-Government Act (1959) – one of the pillars of *APARTHEID. The Act provided for the creation of eight territorial authorities for the eight Bantu nations in South Africa. Later it was decided that ten Bantu nations merited separate territorial authorities. In theory the ten are to progress from self-government to independence. Linked to the white nation economically and in a loose confederation, they are supposed to become politically independent. In 1970 the Bantu Homelands Citizenship Act deprived Bantu of their South African citizenship and made them, even those born in the so-called white areas, citizens of their homeland. This was relaxed in 1986 to allow those living and working permanently in South Africa to claim South African citizenship.

Between 1976 and 1981 'independence' was granted to the *TRANSKEI, *BOPHUTHATSWANA, *VENDA and *CISKEI, a status not recognized outside South Africa. The six other homelands with a measure of self-government are Gazankulu, KwaNdebele, KwaNgwane, KwaZulu, Lebowa and Qwaqwa. Independence for KwaNgwane was expected in 1986, but had to be postponed after months of violence there. The most powerful

homeland leader, Chief *BUTHELEZI of KwaZulu, has rejected independence and called for majority rule. South Africa also tried to set up Namibian homelands, as recommended by the *ODENDAAL COMMISSION.

The homelands are neither politically nor economically viable, even with considerable support from South Africa. Most of them are broken up into separate blocks of land; KwaZulu has ten blocks of land separated from each other by 'white' areas. There are six separate blocks of territory in Bophuthatswana, one of them is nearly 200 miles away from its closest neighbouring block. Situated in the poorer parts of South Africa, the homelands serve as cheap sources of labour for white-run industries on their borders. They have been used as dumping grounds for blacks who are no longer needed in the white cities; they are overcrowded and lack the comforts of 'white' South Africa. The total area of the homelands is 15 per cent of South Africa, hopelessly inadequate for the Bantu who comprise 73 per cent of the population. By the late 1980s 37 per cent of the South African population, or over half the Bantu, were in the homelands. Even if the supporters of apartheid were sincere, it is difficult to see how the homelands could develop into stable and prosperous independent states.

The homelands have been sources of embarrassment to South Africa. Their governments have been violent and corrupt. Chief Sebe of

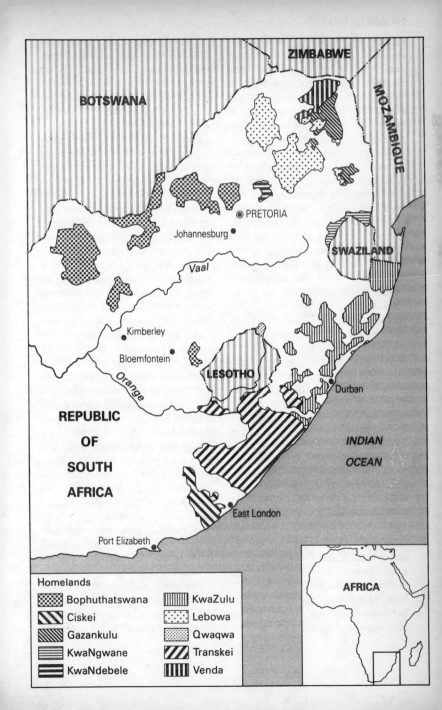

ZIMBABWE

BOTSWANA

MOZAMBIQUE

⊙ PRETORIA

Johannesburg

SWAZILAND

Vaal

Kimberley

Bloemfontein

LESOTHO

Orange

Durban

REPUBLIC

OF

SOUTH

AFRICA

INDIAN

OCEAN

East London

Port Elizabeth

Homelands

Bophuthatswana
Ciskei
Gazankulu
KwaNgwane
KwaNdebele

KwaZulu
Lebowa
Qwaqwa
Transkei
Venda

AFRICA

Ciskei proclaimed himself President for Life. In 1987 there was such tension between Ciskei and Transkei that they almost went to war with each other. In December 1987 General Holomisa seized power in a coup in the Transkei. By 1989 he had aligned himself with the anti-apartheid movement and was arguing for the reintegration of Transkei in South Africa. Following the release of Nelson *MANDELA (Feb. 1990) it looked as though the homelands system was breaking down. In March 1990 the overthrow of Sebe in the Ciskei was followed by rioting and unrest and there were violent protests against the government of President Mangope in Bophutatswana. In April 1990 the military seized power in Venda. The leader of the coup, Colonel Ramushwana, said he would demand reintegration with South Africa and the restoration of citizenship to the people of Venda. When constitutional talks are held in South Africa in 1991 the homelands may well be reintegrated in South Africa or they may become the bases for federal states.

Horn of Africa, geographically, nothing more than a vast promontory projecting from the east coast of Africa into the Indian Ocean, and politically part of Somalia. However, since 1960 it has assumed international political and strategic importance. This is because it commands the oil tanker routes from the Gulf of Aden and the Persian (or Arabian) Gulf, which link the great Middle East oilfields with the markets of Europe and the West. When rivals, the United States and the Soviet Union perceived that whoever held the Horn could dominate oil tanker traffic. Both superpowers and their respective blocks put pressure on Somalia for political alignments in their favour. At first, the Soviets heavily supplied Somalia with arms but in 1977 switched support to Somalia's enemy, Ethiopia. In August 1978 Somalia and the United States, after long, intricate negotiations, signed an agreement which allowed US forces to use the military facilities at the port of Berbera. The arrangement was worth $50 million to Somalia. US ships and aircraft could now control the sea routes along the east African coast. From time to time President Siad *BARRÉ criticized the level of support he received from the US. In 1983 he called for normalization of relations with the Soviet Union, despite its 'involvement and interference' in the internal disputes of the Horn of Africa. However, Somalia did not sever relations with the US and superpower strategic rivalry over the Horn remained until the collapse of the Soviet Union as a great military power in 1989. The Gulf Crisis of August 1990, caused by the Iraqi invasion of Kuwait, made the Horn even more important strategically for the United States and it further developed the port of Berbera.

Houphouët-Boigny, Felix (b. 1900), President of Ivory Coast. Son of a Baoulé tribal chief, Houphouët-Boigny was educated in Bingerville and Senegal and qualified as a doctor in 1925. He earned his living in this profession and as a planter until 1940. In 1944 he became president of the Syndicat Agricole Africain and a year later he founded the Parti Démocratique de la Côte d'Ivoire. He gained further prominence as a deputy to the French National Assembly, 1946–59. He was simultaneously, 1956–9, mayor of Abidjan, a minister of the French colonial government of Ivory Coast and President of the Grand Council of French West Africa. He became prime minister of Ivory Coast in 1959 and from 1960 he was its president. For many years the international press praised Houphouët-Boigny for his economic and social achievements, but towards the end of the 1970s he was blamed for gross social inequalities and political unrest. The president responded with a series of 'days of dialogue' during which disgruntled people could approach him with their grievances. Houphouët-Boigny survived several attempted coups, notably in April 1980, and in 1985 he restored relations with Israel, following the breach of 1973. He built the largest and most expensive cathedral in the world, which in 1990 was consecrated by the Pope. In October 1990, at the age of ninety, Houphouët-Boigny won a landslide victory in the country's first contested presidential election and began his seventh five-year term of office. His endurance is the result of genuine political skill, support from France as the former colonial power, and his system of

rewards, appointments and favours, by which he repays loyalty. See *RASSEMBLEMENT DÉMOCRATIQUE AFRICAIN.

House of Assembly, the most powerful of the three houses in the South African legislature, it represents the white voters. South Africa's tricameral parliament was part of President P.W. *BOTHA's power-sharing constitution (1983), which came into effect in 1984 after its approval by the white electorate. 178 members are elected and 20 are nominated according to the strength of the parties in the election. In the September 1989 election the *NATIONAL PARTY won 93 seats, the *CONSERVATIVE PARTY 39 and the *DEMOCRATIC PARTY 33 seats.

House of Delegates, like the *HOUSE OF ASSEMBLY, one of the three houses in the South African legislature, this represents the Indian voters. 40 members are elected, 2 are appointed by the State President and 3 are chosen by members. Most of South Africa's Indian community feel this chamber wields little real power; in elections only about one fifth of the community bother to vote.

House of Representatives, like the *HOUSE OF ASSEMBLY one of the three houses in South African legislature, it represents the *COLOURED voters. 80 members are elected, 2 appointed by the State President and 3 chosen by members. Most of South Africa's Coloured community feel this chamber wields little real power; in the September 1989 election only about a fifth of the community turned out to vote, giving the *LABOUR PARTY an overwhelming majority.

Hussein, Abdirizak Hadji (b. 1924), former prime minister of Somalia. The son of a poor trader, Hussein was educated at a Koranic school and at *AL-AZHAR UNIVERSITY in Cairo, from where he graduated in 1953. He had joined the Somali Youth League in 1944 and in 1956 he became its president, and as such was an influential politician. In 1958 he founded the Greater Somalia League to defy the Ethiopians, who at that time administered 'Ethiopian Somaliland'. The following year, 1959, Hussein became a member of parliament and after Somalia became independent, in July 1960, he held various ministries until 1964. In that year he became prime minister, a post he filled with reasonable skill until 1967. When Siad *BARRÉ seized power in 1969 Hussein was imprisoned to prevent his becoming a focal point for rebellion. He stayed in gaol until 1973 and in 1974 Barré, now convinced of his loyalty, appointed him Somali permanent representative at the UN.

Hussein, Taha (1889–1973), one of the greatest figures in contemporary Arab literature. Born in Maghagha, a village in Upper Egypt, Hussein came from a very poor family and went blind at the age of three. His rise to eminence has been described as 'a triumph of the will, a patient victory of spiritual light over darkness'. He attended *AL-AZHAR UNIVERSITY but found that many of his teachers were living in the past so, at the same time, he pursued more modern studies at Cairo University. On graduating in 1914 he went to France where he studied French, Greek and Latin and in 1918 earned a doctorate from the Sorbonne. In 1931 he became Dean of the Faculty of Arts at Cairo University and in 1942 he founded the University of Alexandria, of which he became Rector. Made Minister of Education in 1950, he created Al Shama University. His ideas had far-reaching effects on the Egyptian educational system. An original thinker and innovator, he created a modern, flexible way of writing, free from outmoded stylistic conventions. In his critical writings, Hussein fought against fixed ideas, particularly in the field of pre-Islamic literature, and demolished many idols. This brought him the hostility of fundamentalist Muslims. His novels, full of compassion for the humble people of fields and villages, have influenced several generations of readers and have been translated into a dozen languages. Two volumes of his autobiography have been translated into English as *An Egyptian Childhood* and *The Stream of Days*. Two days before his death, on 28 October 1973, Hussein was awarded the United Nations Human Rights Prize.

I

Idris I (1890–1982), the only king of modern Libya. Idris succeeded to the leadership of the *SENUSSI tribe in 1916 and as such was one of the most powerful rulers in North Africa. In 1949 Britain, the occupying power in succession to the defeated Italians, recognized Idris as Amir of Cyrenaica, which makes up a large part of Libya. At the country's independence in 1950 Idris became king. He built himself a palace at Tobruk and adopted all the trappings of kingship but his rule was not enlightened and took no account of the popular demand for better living conditions. Deposed by *GADDAFI in 1969, Idris fled to Egypt. A Libyan court sentenced him to death *in absentia* for 'crimes against the Libyan people'. He died in Cairo at the age of ninety-two.

Idris, Yusuf (b. 1922), Egyptian writer and intellectual. Idris sees himself as an originator of the trend in Arabic literature whose roots are deep in folklore, in people's memory and their collective consciousness. Literary editor of the national daily *Al-Ahram*, since 1973, Idris published three important books in 1984–5: *The Thinking of Poverty and the Poverty of Thinking*; *The Importance of Being Intellectual* and *Playing Solo*. His best known work in English is *The Sinners*. Islamic fundamentalists accuse Idris of being an atheist because of his belief in science. He has predicted that eventually all intellectuals will have to leave Egypt because the fundamentalists oppose fiction, cinema, theatre, music and dance. Idris divides Arab literature into two categories. One, dating from the known beginnings of Arabic writing to the end of the Second World War, represents a pan-Arab, classical literature. The second, from the 1950s onwards, finds the local identity of the Arab people beginning to emerge, creating national literature. Idris' message is this: 'the human being is discovered through his mistakes rather than through his perfection. It is exactly the reverse of what all religion say – that the human being was perfect and then he committed sins.'

Imbokodvo National Movement, royalist Swazi political movement, founded at the instigation of King Sobhuza II (1964) to oppose the influence of radicals in Swaziland. This traditionalist and conservative party was formed with the help of South African advisers and the support of whites in Swaziland. It has remained a powerful force opposed to reform, much bolstered by this white backing. The electoral system favoured Imbokodvo which won all the seats in the 1964 and 1967 elections. After Imbokodvo lost three seats to the radical *NGWANE NATIONAL LIBERATORY CONGRESS in the 1972 elections the king suspended the constitution (1973) and banned all political parties, but allowed Imbokodvo to continue its non-political activities. Imbokodvo means grindstone.

Immorality Amendment Act (1957), a South African law which forbade any 'unlawful carnal intercourse' or 'immoral and indecent act' between a white and a person of another race. Those convicted could face up to seven years' imprisonment with hard labour and the male could also be sentenced to ten lashes. Well over ten thousand people were convicted under the act and police investigations into possible infringements often led to sordid intrusions into people's private lives. Despite right-wing opposition President P.W. *BOTHA repealed the act in 1985 as part of his plans to modify some of the excesses of *APARTHEID.

Indaba, the Zulu word for meeting or discussion, a South African conference set up in April 1986 to consider the options for the future of Natal Province. Representatives of different racial and political groups drew up a plan for a multi-racial government in Natal. This was strongly supported by *INKATHA (led by Chief *BUTHELEZI) and some white liberals, but has been rejected by the *NATIONAL PARTY government and leading black organizations like the *AFRICAN NATIONAL CONGRESS and *AZAPO.

Indians, in South Africa the racial classification of those descended from immigrants from the Indian subcontinent. Their ancestors were brought over to work on the sugar cane fields and the railways late in the nineteenth century and early in the twentieth century. There are about

a million Indians in South Africa, about three per cent of the population. Under P.W. *BOTHA's power-sharing constitution they were given a chamber in parliament, the *HOUSE OF DELEGATES. Most Indians regard power sharing as a sham and many support the multi-racial groups who are working for the establishment of a non-racial democratic South African state. Some of the community's leaders have been prominent in the leadership of the *AFRICAN NATIONAL CONGRESS.

indigena, Portuguese word meaning native, it described the legal status of most Africans in Portuguese colonies until it was abolished in 1961. As distinct from the small percentage who gained rights of citizenship (*ASSIMILADOS) indigenas were subject to forced labour and did not enjoy the rights of Portuguese citizens.

Inkatha ye Nkululeko ye Sizwe, a mainly Zulu political and cultural organization formed by Chief *BUTHELEZI (1975), with its roots in Inkatha ka Zula, a cultural and social body founded in 1928. Its one and a half million members dominate the administration of the KwaZulu *HOMELAND and give Buthelezi a strong power base. To get a good job in KwaZulu people have to be members of Inkatha. Inkatha's support of capitalism and its opposition to sanctions against South Africa have alienated the more radical black groups, who believe that the authorities favour Inkatha above other black political groups. In July 1990 Inkatha relaunched itself as a multi-racial political party which intends to contest elections.

There have been increasingly bloody clashes between Inkatha supporters and those of the *AFRICAN NATIONAL CONGRESS and *UNITED DEMOCRATIC FRONT since the middle of the 1980s. An estimated four thousand were killed in battles in Natal townships in the five years up to late 1990. By the middle of 1990 these battles had spread to townships in Transvaal and the Orange Free State. Since his release early in 1990 Nelson *MANDELA has tried to settle these conflicts which could end the chances of achieving a constitutional settlement in South Africa and even lead to civil war between the Zulus and other black groups. To avert this, in January 1991, Buthelezi and Mandela finally met for talks.

International Monetary Fund (IMF) and the International Bank for Reconstruction and Development (more commonly known as the World Bank) are both organizations affiliated with the United Nations. The IMF was founded at the United Nations Monetary and Financial Conference (Bretton Woods, 1944) to secure international monetary co-operation and to stabilize exchange rates. The World Bank was founded in 1946, also as a result of the Bretton Woods conference; it makes loans for economic development and offers technical assistance.

On a number of occasions these two bodies have intervened to help African states overcome economic crises. They supply credit and technical assistance if the governments of the states are prepared to meet their conditions, usually devaluation and other measures of austerity to balance budgets, to reduce balance of payments deficits and to cut foreign debts. Some states have made progress with their economic rehabilitation under these conditions. Gabon since the late 1970s and Ghana during the 1980s are cited as successes thanks to intervention and aid from the IMF and the World Bank. Others African governments, like Zambia's, have found the political price of austerity too heavy to pay; President *KAUNDA's attempts to impose austerity led to riots in 1986 and in 1990.

Islam, since 1960 more important politically and socially in Africa than it has been for a century. Linguistically, the word Islam means submission (to the will of God) and the world knows Islam as the religious belief of Muslims. In fact, it is more than a religion. Law, politics, economy and culture are equally involved. As a complete way of life, Islam regulates property, marriage, divorce, family, punishment and justice, obligations, diet, sexual relationships, finance, race relations, war, and peace treaties. Islam became resurgent following the retreat of the colonial powers from Africa after 1945. It became revolutionary, with 'Khomeini's Revolution' (or the Iranian Revolution), which began in 1979.

New converts continue to be made by roaming missionaries and merchants in black Africa. In the *MAGHREB, the revival of intense religious belief has led to the

151

creation of hundreds of new organizations, ranging from offshoots of the *MUSLIM BROTHERHOOD, the Ikhwan, to even more militant groups of sheikhs and students, such as the *ISLAMIC SALVATION FRONT in Algeria.

The new Islam must be seen in the historic context of Islam. In demonstrating that it is not just a relic of the past, it is reacting to the economic and political oppression suffered under the colonialist imperialism of the nineteenth and early twentieth centuries. When the great powers withdrew from Arab North Africa (and from the Middle East) in the 1950s and 1960s, they left a void which Islam filled.

Aspects of Western democracy, consumerism and culture were imported and often clashed with Islamic tradition. Many Muslims preferred their own customs and were then branded backward and reactionary. Faith and ritual remain a vital part of expression for a people beset by radical change and social upheaval. The Islam of Africa, in the late twentieth century, has yet to find its balance between reaction to 'the decadent West' (Khomeini's view) and collaboration with 'the liberal progressive West' (President *MUBARAK's view).

Islam is growing in black Africa partly because it offers a form of religious and social security which is unknown in the West. By following the instructions of the Koran, Islam's holy book, Muslims are assured of a certainty in life which does not exist in the West. The Koran, in

association with the Hadith, the reported utterances of the Prophet Muhammad, is a guidebook of unparalleled authority.

The vast majority of Muslims in both Arab Africa and black Africa are of the mainstream Sunni sect or what might be considered orthodox Islam. Sunnis aver that the 'Righteous Caliphs' who followed Muhammad as leaders of Islam constituted the rightful succession to the Prophet. Shiite Muslims claim that Muhammad should have been succeeded by Ali, his son-in-law, and Ali's line. Shiite Muslims, who are much more militant than most Sunnis, are the predominant sect in non-Arab Iran.

Islamic Fundamentalism, the relentless Islamic drive towards a return to the strict tenets or fundamentals of Islam. Fundamentalist is a Western term; Islamic radicals regard themselves as Islamists. They repeatedly state their opposition to Arab monarchs, such as King *HASSAN II of Morocco and to 'traitors', such as Presidents *SADAT and MUBARAK, and to others. Since 1980 and the coming to power of Ayatollah Khomeini in Iran, Islamic fundamentalism has been a potent force in Egypt, Tunisia, Algeria, Sudan and Morocco, and, for that matter, in most of the Islamic world.

At its most extreme, fundamentalism substitutes dogmatism and violence for negotiation and compromise, and aims at instituting a theocracy. A preacher of fundamentalism in Africa is President *GADDAFI of Libya, though his brand of fundamentalism is built on his own ambition to dominate other nations. The assassination of President Sadat in 1981 was carried out by fundamentalist fanatics. They were a party of soldiers, led by Khalid al-Istambuli, belonging to a group calling itself *JIHAD, after the Arabic word for holy war.

Such violent men and episodes have tended to obscure another aspect of fundamentalism, the peaceful demand that all Muslims strictly follow the tenets and practices of their religion, in all its complexity. This is no more extreme than the demands of Christian, Jewish and Hindu groups that the fundamentals of their respective religions be obeyed. Unfortunately, the publicity given to Islamic fundamentalism has obscured such traditional Islamic values as wisdom and learning. Tolerance and hospitality, which are preached among Muslims, have regrettably not been demonstrated by some fundamentalists, to the detriment of Muslims as a whole. The most prominent Islamic fundamentalist organization in North Africa is the Hezb Islamiyya al-Tahrir or Islamic Liberation Party, generally known as 'the Tahrir'. The Tunisian government dismantled a secret cell found in the army in 1986; similar cells have been found in the Egyptian army.

A powerful figure in fundamentalism is Dr Issam al-Irian, an Egyptian who in 1972 was one of the first fundamentalists elected to Cairo University's student leadership. The youngest member of Egypt's parliament, al-Irian said in May 1988: 'In twenty years all peoples of the world will return to Allah. The systems which govern the world today, such as democracy and communism, are going to be discredited. We must move people to an alternative system. Islam is that system. Nobody can doubt the Islamic code of justice. It is the law of Allah.'

Unfortunately, extreme Islamists want a return to the strictures of the sharia or Islamic law. They want women stoned to death when caught in adultery, hand-lopping imposed for theft, women kept in subservience to men and people of other religions reduced to dhimmi status as second-class citizens. The only Arab African state which has used stoning and hand-lopping as punishments is Sudan. While fundamentalism is undoubtedly a potent force in Arab North Africa, it is likely to run its course and be replaced by a liberal pragmatism.

Islamic Salvation Front, Algerian political party known by its French initials FIS, legalized in September 1989. It at once became the biggest challenge to the ruling *NATIONAL LIBERATION FRONT (FLN). Led by the fundamentalist Muslims Abbassi Madani and Sheikh Ali Belhadj, and emboldened by Algeria's new liberal political climate, the FIS demanded a return to strict Islamic values. FIS rallies drew large crowds across Algeria in 1989 and 1990, with the result that the movement did very well in regional and city elections in August 1990. The strength of the FIS is most apparent in the crowded

The Republic of the Ivory Coast

THE COUNTRY
322,463 sq. km.

Major Cities
Abidjan (capital)
Assine
Bouafle
Dimboroko

Economy
'State capitalist' and
'open-door'.
Heavily dependent on
coffee, of which Ivory
Coast is the world's
largest producer

Principal Exports
Coffee, cocoa, timber,
palm-oil, coconuts,
sugar, bananas.

Currency
CFA franc of 100
centimes

THE PEOPLE
11.5 million

Ethnic Groups
60 different tribes in six
main groups
Immigrants from
neighbouring countries
50,000 French

Languages
French (official)
Baoule, Dioula, Bete

Religion
Traditional beliefs 65%
Islam 23%
Christian 12%

THE STATE
Presidential republic

Head of State
President Félix
Houphouët-Boigny

Ruling Body
Political Bureau

Official Party
Parti Démocratique de la
Côte d'Ivoire

inner city slums such as Bab Al Oued in Algiers and it enjoys wide support among the urban poor. The FIS has projected a powerful image of youth in a country where three-quarters of the population are under thirty. 'Allah's Policemen' of the FIS set up their own vigilante force which illegally arrests people it regards as having committed crimes against Islam, such as the wearing of 'immodest' dress. It is likely to become one of the strongest movements in North Africa by the end of the twentieth century.

Ivory Coast (Côte d'Ivoire), situated on the northern coast of the Gulf of Guinea, covers 322,463 sq. km. and falls into two natural divisions, with equatorial rain forests covering the south and savannah the north. It is bordered by Mali, Burkina Faso, Ghana, Liberia and Guinea, a multiplicity of neighbours which in part explains Ivory Coast's ethnic medley; there are sixty-six different tribes. Unlike many West African countries, Ivory Coast has only a brief known history and even the exploring and colonizing Europeans, so much in evidence elsewhere, were late reaching the area. In the 1840s the French induced coastal tribes to sign treaties which, in effect, gave them a monopoly of trade. From this beginning, France won agreement from the other Powers in the 1880s that it could claim Ivory Coast as a possession and in 1893 it became a French colony.

Many tribes in the interior resisted French control and fighting continued for twenty-five years. While the guerrilla war went on, the French administrators used the divide and rule principle by appointing native leaders as paramount chiefs of defined areas. In return for this prestige and authority – which, under a French governor, was always limited – the chiefs were obliged to collect taxes and supply labour for the palm-oil, cocoa and timber plantations. The system of labour was a form of slavery.

Following the Second World War, indigenous political groups emerged, all of them led by men from among the small number of educated, prosperous families. The most significant leader was Félix *HOUPHOUËT-BOIGNY, a doctor of medicine and a planter, who in 1944 established the Syndicate Agricole Africain (SAA). All the other members were planters and their only objective then was to agitate for opportunities equal to those of French planters in recruitment of labour. In 1945 the SAA became truly political as the Parti Démocratique de la Côte d'Ivoire (PDCI). After another year Houphouët-Boigny linked PDCI with many other French West

African parties in the all-embracing *RASSEMBLEMENT DÉMOCRATIQUE AFRICAIN (RDA). PDCI became more radical and revolutionary and in 1948–9 violence erupted in Abidjan. French troops killed 52 demonstrators and arrested 3400 others.

However, the trend towards independence and nationalism was irreversible. PDCI became even more powerful by crushing all other embryo political parties. A new territorial assembly sent Houphouët-Boigny and a colleague to Paris as members of the French Assembly. Houphouët-Boigny's overriding aim now was to keep Ivory Coast out of any new West African federation because he knew that such a union would make demands on Ivory Coast's wealth. On 7 August 1960 he unilaterally declared independence, pre-empting the independence which France then granted to all the other colonies. Simultaneously, this shrewd politician induced Dahomey, Upper Volta (later Burkina Faso) and Niger to join Ivory Coast in the Conseil de l'Entente. This prevented Senegal, Ivory Coast's main rival, from organizing a single federated West African state with itself as leader.

Houphouët-Boigny and PDCI remained unopposed in Ivory Coast for decades. The party created the Political Bureau as its executive wing and it became omnipotent. Whenever any opposition from outside PDCI became apparent the PDCI overcame it, by absorption wherever possible but my suppression when

155

necessary. In this way Houphouët-Boigny avoided or evaded the crises which have afflicted so many African countries. Certainly, in 1963 a plot to overthrow him was uncovered, in 1968 students demonstrated in Abidjan and in 1973 a revolt against the government took place in the Beté district, but Houphouët-Boigny was never endangered.

However, unrest over inflation was so serious in 1978 that the president instituted what he called journées de dialogue (days of dialogue) during which leaders of various groups could put their problems to him. In April 1980, when the president was attending an OAU summit in Lagos, a police lieutenant was arrested for allegedly plotting a coup. It was timed to take place on 10 May, the date of Pope John Paul's arrival in Abidjan. Many people were implicated in the plot and arrested. In the same year, Houphouët-Boigny brought in administrative reforms, one of which was abolition of the post of secretary-general of the PDCI. This had the effect of removing Phillips Yacé from public life. As Secretary-General of the party and virtual vice-president, Yacé had been regarded as Houphouët-Boigny's heir. The president, however, feared that he might seize power.

In March 1981, Ivory Coast police arrested many Ghanaians during an anti-smuggling operation and forty-six of them died hideously in an over-crowded cell. Crowds stormed the Ivory Coast embassy in Accra and war seemed imminent before Ivory Coast apologized and agreed to pay compensation.

Social unrest in the 1980s was sometimes serious and it involved, at various times, students, teachers, doctors, transport workers and civil servants. They were upset about rising costs, loss of grants and privileges, and corruption in state corporations. Nevertheless, on 27 October 1987 Houphouët-Boigny won a sixth five-year mandate as president. Since there was no vice-president, it was arranged that the president of the National Assembly would succeed the ageing Houphouët-Boigny on his death and hold office until elections could be held.

The most serious problems of the regime occurred in February and March 1990 with a multiplicity of strikes and street protests. People were protesting against heavy tax increases and the president's extravagances. For instance, he had built in his home village of Yamoussoukro a huge Roman Catholic basilica, the largest church in the world. The protests took a distinct political turn, with calls for the president's resignation and the introduction of multi-party democracy. Houphouët-Boigny announced that this form of democracy could not take place until national unity had been achieved but his hand was forced and on 1 May the Political Bureau announced that four opposition parties were from that day legalized. This was a big concession by the ruling elite. Almost immediately the parties began negotiations to form a common party front against the PDCI.

Opposition to Houphouët-Boigny has always concentrated on the economy. His unique brand of paternalistic authoritarianism produced a higher average income than anywhere in Africa other than South Africa but it also brought Ivory Coast the biggest debt burden, in *per capita* terms, in Africa. This was a legacy of the heavy borrowing during the cocoa boom of the late 1970s and early 1980s. It took the collapse of this market to force Ivorians to question the wisdom of an economic policy based on the export of such a vulnerable coup.

Houphouët-Boigny once admitted being more interested in the 'creation and multiplication' of wealth rather than its distribution. He described this economic philosophy as 'state capitalism'. His tentative moves, in the mid 1980s, to transfer some state corporations to private ownership showed that state capitalism had not been efficient. World Bank and IMF support became more evident at the same time. These organizations encouraged the development of more small and medium sized businesses. By improving management they also made Ivory Coast's industry more competitive.

During his domination of Ivory Coast politics, Houphouët-Boigny has held to a distinctly individualistic foreign policy. He maintained his resistance to any form of union with African countries unless he could control them. In 1985 he sent his foreign minister on a tour of ten neighbouring nations, to talk about co-operation rather than common policies. On 18 December 1985 he showed considerable courage and independence when Ivory Coast restored diplomatic relations with Israel. They had been broken off in 1973 but even during the long period of diplomatic dislocation, Ivory Coast had maintained many economic ties with Israel. Soon after this move, the president re-established diplomatic links with several Communist countries, including the Soviet Union itself. There was every sign in 1990, that Houphouët-Boigny, as he neared his own nineties, was still seeking to make Ivory Coast a dominant African power in every field except the military one. At the end of the year he won a landslide victory in the national elections, which, according to international observers, were conducted with 'reasonable fairness'.

J

Jawara, Sir Dawda Kairaba (b. 1924), President of The Gambia since 1970. He qualified as a veterinary officer and worked in the colonial civil service until 1960 when he entered politics as leader of the People's Progressive Party (PPP). After electoral successes he became Minister of Education (1960–1) and Premier (1962–5). After Gambian independence Jawara was Prime Minister (1965–70) and the country's first president from 1970. He was Vice-President of the Confederation of *SENEGAMBIA (1982–9).

President Jawara is one of the more moderate African leaders. He has allowed opposition political parties to organize, and in every election the people have shown their confidence in him and the PPP. He has given the country a stability only once seriously threatened by the attempted military coup in 1981.

Jihad, Arabic word meaning, literally, 'a great striving', but more traditionally and popularly it indicates holy war in the name of Islam. *Jihad* is a duty of Muslims in general, even for those living in non-Muslim countries, and by Koranic edict is directed against 'unbelievers' whether Christian, Jewish or pagan. Constant and everlasting *jihad* is generally dormant except in times of crisis. Since 1945, with the rise of nationalism, crises have been frequent. As a result, *jihad* has been officially proclaimed by political or religious leaders on several

occasions. For instance, the Arab states declared *jihad* against Israel in the wars of 1948–9 and 1973 and Algeria called for *jihad* in its war of independence against the French, 1954–62.

Since 1969, President *GADDAFI has intermittently proclaimed *jihad* against 'the imperialistic West'. In 1979 Ayatollah Khomeini of Iran embarked on *jihad* against the United States, and in 1980 Iraq declared it against Iran. In that year too, Saudi Arabia threatened *jihad* against Israel in the dispute over Jerusalem and against any nation which did not move its embassy from Jerusalem. Since 1945 *jihad* has undergone a fundamental development; it now refers to holy war by any means – through economic pressure, terrorism, and propaganda even more than by conventional war. Conversion of Africans and other races to Islam is considered a form of *jihad*. One of its eternal attractions is that men killed in *jihad* are believed to go straight to paradise.

The World Islamic Call Society, which is based in Tripoli, Libya, is one of the principal publicists for *jihad*. Backed by Colonel Gaddafi, the Society publishes, in Arabic, English and French, *Risalat Al Jihad*, a major document of intent and planning. An editorial in the 1986 edition stated: 'The causes for *jihad* by fighting existed from the beginning of Islam and are valid today. Islam, the religion of truth and the call of truth, is in need of a force which will struggle to protect it. A Muslim must be a mujahid [freedom fighter] at all times. Go forth, light-armed and heavy-armed, and strive with all your wealth and lives in the way of Allah.'

Johnson, Prince, a Liberian rebel leader. He was one of Charles *TAYLOR's supporters in the *NATIONAL PATRIOTIC FRONT of Liberia when it invaded Liberia late in 1989, but in March 1990 he quarrelled with Taylor and formed a breakaway rebel movement. Johnson's rebel group reached the centre of Monrovia before Taylor's group, and in September 1990 Johnson captured and killed President *DOE. Late in 1990 Johnson led one of the three forces fighting in the Liberian civil war; the others being Taylor's army and the remnants of Doe's forces.

Jonathan, Chief Leabua (1914–87), prime minister of Lesotho (1965–86), he was descended from the founder of the *BASOTHO nation – Moshoeshoe I. Before entering politics Chief Jonathan was educated at mission schools and worked as a clerk in South Africa and as a legal assistant in Lesotho (then the Besutoland Protectorate). Encouraged by the Catholic Church, in 1959 he founded the *BASOTHO NATIONAL PARTY (BNP). Its conservative and anti-communist policies were supported by village chiefs and headmen, but it did badly in the 1960 elections.

In 1964 Chief Jonathan joined the delegation which persuaded Britain to cede self-government to Lesotho. With support from South Africa and the Catholic Church Chief Jonathan narrowly won the pre-independence elections (1965) and formed the government which led Lesotho to independence (1966). As prime minister Chief Jonathan's anxiety not to offend South Africa made him unpopular. He also offended traditionalists by his treatment of *MOSHOESHOE II, Lesotho's young king. After a bitter power struggle he forced the king to give up all his political power.

The first election after independence (Jan. 1970) was a turning point. When he realized that the opposition *BASOTHO CONGRESS PARTY was winning Chief Jonathan staged a coup in which he suspended the constitution, ruled by decree and arrested opposition leaders. Chief Jonathan became more authoritarian and repressive, but was unable to stop the growth of political and guerrilla opposition to his government.

In the late 1970s Chief Jonathan turned against his South African backers; he infuriated them by opening diplomatic relations with communist states, by condemning *APARTHEID and by giving sanctuary to *AFRICAN NATIONAL CONGRESS exiles from South Africa. He angered the *LESOTHO PARAMILITARY FORCE by refusing to raise its pay and by importing North Koreans to train the BNP Youth League. South Africa exploited the discontent in Lesotho; it gave sanctuary to the *LESOTHO LIBERATION ARMY and allowed it to attack

Lesotho from South Africa. The final blow came at the beginning of 1986 when South Africa imposed a total blockade on Lesotho. Chief Jonathan's government collapsed and the military under Major-General *LEKHANYA seized power (20 Jan. 1986). Chief Jonathan was under house arrest until his death.

Jumbe, Aboud (b.1920), moderate Tanzanian political leader, a teacher from *ZANZIBAR who joined the *AFRO-SHIRAZI PARTY (1960) and was a member of the Zanzibar legislature (1961–84). He held ministerial posts in the Tanzanian government (1964–72) until he succeeded Abeid *KARUME as President of Zanzibar and Vice-President of Tanzania (1972–84). A moderate and respected leader, he made reforms in Zanzibar and was willing to co-operate with mainland Tanzania and to share the revenues from the exports of cloves. He was forced out of office because he was thought to be in sympathy with Zanzibari opponents of the Tanzanian union.

K

Kabyles, the *BERBER people of the Kabylia region of Algeria. The Berbers of Kabylia, together with those of the Aures mountains, number about three million and are the oldest inhabitants of Algeria. The two groups are linguistically and socially different from each other. Kabyles do not feel themselves to be Arabs in the ethnic sense. Kabyle women walk outside without the veil but do not otherwise have many privileges. Algeria's fight for independence began in the Aures mountains and during the war the villages and farms were destroyed by the French. The area, and the Kabyles themselves, have recovered their prosperity.

Kalahari Desert, vast arid area covering parts of Botswana and Namibia in Southern Africa. It is bordered by the Zambezi River in the north, Transvaal and Zimbabwe in the east, the Orange River in the south, and the Namibian highlands in the west. It covers 260,000 sq. km. and has a surprising variety of wildlife despite its lack of surface water. The *SAN people and the Herero have found refuge from their enemies in the desert.

Kano, Alhaji Muhammed Aminu (1920–83), politician from northern Nigeria who attended pre-independence constitutional talks. He was a member of the Federal House of Representatives (1959–65) and served as Deputy Chief Government Whip (1959–64). In Gowon's military government Kano was Federal Commissioner for Communications (1967–71) and for Health (1971–5). In 1978 he founded and led the *PEOPLE'S REDEMPTION PARTY, one of the five parties contesting the 1979 elections. Kano came fourth in the 1979 presidential election with 1.7 million votes.

Kapepwe, Simon (1922–80), a Bemba who was a leading nationalist campaigner against colonial rule and a leading politician in independent Zambia. He worked as a teacher and was active in the *AFRICAN NATIONAL CONGRESS until 1958 when he joined *KAUNDA and other radicals to form the Zambian African National Congress (later *UNIP). He held high office in UNIP. A member of parliament from 1962 to 1971, Kapepwe was Minister of Home Affairs (1964) and Foreign Affairs (1964–7) before becoming Vice-President of Zambia (1967–70). He was then Minister of Local Government (1970–1). In 1971 he accused President Kaunda of treating the Bemba unfairly and resigned from UNIP to form his own political party, the United Progressive Party. This party was banned and Kapepwe was arrested and detained (1972–3). He was reconciled with Kaunda in 1978 at a time of severe economic crisis. He rejoined UNIP and was a respected spokesman for the Bemba until his death.

Kapuuo, Chief Clemens (c.1923–78), Namibian political leader and traditional Herero ruler who was President of the *DTA; he might have played an important part in a South African-sponsored government of Namibia. After his assassination in 1978 the South African authorities assumed emergency powers and detained a number of *SWAPO leaders.

karakul, a sort of lamb reared by white ranchers in Namibia for its high fashion fur which has been a major foreign currency earner. During the 1980s drought and changing fashions have led to a slump in the industry.

Kariba Dam, vast man-made lake on the Zambezi River between Zambia and Zimbabwe. It was built during the days of the *CENTRAL AFRICAN FEDERATION, after a massive operation to rescue the wildlife of the valley. The Kariba hydroelectric schemes supply most of the needs of Zambia and Zimbabwe. Zambia also exports Kariba electricity to Zaire.

Kariuki, Josiah Mwangi (1929–75), outspoken and radical Kenyan politician whose murder sparked off unrest. After being detained during the *MAU MAU emergency he became *KENYATTA's private secretary (1961). After independence Kariuki was the spokesman for a group of radicals who denounced corruption and the way in which Kenyatta's inner circle of Kikuyu friends monopolized power. Calling himself 'the people's friend', he

attacked the growing gap between rich and poor in Kenya.

Although his outspokenness cost him the support of the *KENYA AFRICAN NATIONAL UNION, Kariuki won his seat with an increased majority in the 1974 election. He was taken away by security officers and shortly afterwards found murdered. Following student protests President Kenyatta set up a parliamentary inquiry into the circumstances of Kariuki's death. Although some important officials were implicated no charges were laid.

Karume, Abeid (c.1904–72), controversial and radical political leader in *ZANZIBAR and Tanzania. After a power struggle he emerged as leader of the *AFRO-SHIRAZI PARTY (1964) and became President of Zanzibar. He negotiated union with Tanganyika to form Tanzania and became Vice-President of Tanzania (1964–72), but was in many ways unwilling to co-operate with mainland Tanzania. He was particularly unwilling to share Zanzibar's revenues from the export of cloves with the rest of the country. In Zanzibar he was a ruthless despot who crushed a number of plots against his government. His attempts to ensure racial harmony by forced inter-racial marriages caused great bitterness. Karume established relations with communist countries, but alienated many of his Soviet bloc backers. He was assassinated in 1972 and replaced by the more moderate Aboud *JUMBE.

Kasavubu, Joseph (d.1969), first President of the Congo (now

Zaire) (1960–5). In the middle 1950s he founded and led ABAKO, a Bakongo cultural and political group, and demanded immediate independence from Belgium. A few days after becoming President (Jun. 1960) he and Prime Minister *LUMUMBA were faced with an army mutiny and the secession of Katanga (now *SHABA). Kasavubu's dismissal of Lumumba (1960) led to constitutional deadlock and *MOBUTO's first coup (Sep. 1960). After the suspension of the constitution and a period of confusion Kasavubu appointed *ADOULA as head of a government of national unity (1961), but replaced him with *TSHOMBE (1964). Although Tshombe won over seventy per cent of the parliamentary seats in the 1965 elections, President Kasavubu refused to call on him to form a government. A second constitutional impasse followed and Mobutu staged his second coup (Nov. 1965). Kasavubu quit politics and returned home, where he died in 1969.

Kassinga massacre (4 May 1978), South African attack on Namibians in a *SWAPO camp in Angola. It is believed that up to a thousand men, women and children were killed and that over one hundred women were abducted. The massacre led to a breakdown in negotiations between SWAPO and the *CONTACT GROUP; it is remembered annually as a symbol of the sufferings of Namibians in their struggle for independence.

Kaunda, Kenneth David (b. 1924), President of Zambia since 1964, one of Africa's most enduring leaders, he is a respected elder statesman in the Commonwealth and in the Third World. The son of a missionary, he is a deeply religious man who lives sparingly, neither drinking nor smoking. He won sympathy and respect when he revealed that his son had died of *AIDS.

Born in Northern Rhodesia (now Zambia), he was a founder member of the *AFRICAN NATIONAL CONGRESS II (1951) and fought against racial discrimination and the *CENTRAL AFRICAN FEDERATION. When the party leadership agreed to co-operate in federal elections (1958) Kaunda left the party and founded the Zambian African National Congress (which became *UNIP in 1960) to campaign for independence. In 1959 UNIP was banned and Kaunda was imprisoned. After his release he led a massive campaign of civil disobedience which forced Britain to introduce the 1962 constitution giving Africans a majority in the legislature. Kaunda became a minister in the coalition government (1962–4).

After UNIP's success in the January 1964 elections he became prime minister (Jan–Oct. 1964) and first President of independent Zambia (Oct. 1964). As head of state Kaunda has firmly established his authority by constitutional changes, including making UNIP the sole legal party (Dec. 1972). As president of UNIP he is the sole presidential candidate at elections and he has shown little toleration for opposition.

In regional and international affairs Kaunda has strongly opposed

*APARTHEID and white minority rule in southern Africa. He has supported black nationalist groups, including *ZAPU in its fight against Ian *SMITH's government in Rhodesia, *SWAPO in its fight for Namibian independence and the struggle of the South African *AFRICAN NATIONAL CONGRESS. An effective campaigner for international sanctions against South Africa, he has also been prepared to talk to South African leaders and to act as a mediator – notably over Rhodesia in 1975 and when he persuaded Angola and South Africa to accept the *LUSAKA AGREEMENT in 1984.

President Kaunda has given Zambia political stability, but he has yet to solve his country's severe economic problems which have grown worse with the decline in copper prices since 1975. Generally President Kaunda has been a humane and tolerant ruler, but there is some concern that he is becoming more authoritarian as he struggles to deal with his country's economic problems and growing social discontent. In 1990 President Kaunda agreed that there would be a referendum in 1991 on whether to restore a multi-party system or not.

Kawawa, Rashidi Mfaume (b. 1929), Tanzanian trade-unionist and politician. A strong socialist, at one time he was President *NYERERE's closest colleague. When Nyerere resigned as Prime Minister (Jan. 1962) Kawawa took over as prime minister while Tanganyika became a republic. When Nyerere became President of the Republic of Tanzania (Dec. 1962) Kawawa became Vice-President (1962–77) and Prime Minister again (1972–7). In the 1977 cabinet reshuffle he was made Minister of Defence (1977–80) and has been Minister without Portfolio since 1980. He has been Secretary General of *CHAMA CHA MAPINDUZI since 1982. Kawawa was a strong candidate to succeed to the Presidency (1985) but lost to the more pragmatic Ali *MWINYI.

Kayibanda, Grégoire (1924–76), the first President of Rwanda (1962–73). A Hutu from central Rwanda, he worked first as a journalist. Before independence he was a leading spokesman of the Hutu who were campaigning for reforms and against Tutsi domination. He founded and led the Hutu Social Movement (1957) and the Hutu Democratic Republican Movement (1959), which was renamed *PARMEHUTU. After campaigning successfully for the abolition of the monarchy and winning communal and national elections, he led Rwanda to independence (1962). As President of Rwanda he was plagued by ethnic violence between the dominant Hutu majority and the Tutsi minority. His regime became increasingly authoritarian and he angered the Hutu from the north by giving too many top posts in the administration and Parmehutu to Hutu from central Rwanda. He was overthrown by northern military officers in a bloodless coup (1973) and sentenced to life imprisonment. He died in prison in 1976.

Keita, Modibo (1915–77), Malian politician and one-time president of the state. Born in Dakar, Keita was educated in that city until he went to university in France. In 1946 he helped to found the Rassemblement Démocratique Africain at Bamako and in 1948 he was elected to the territorial assembly. Already a popular figure, Keita was appointed a deputy for Mali in the French National Assembly in 1956. He favoured a federal system for West Africa but this was vehemently opposed by Dahomey (later Benin), Upper Volta (later Burkina Faso) and Ivory Coast. Mali decided to join with Senegal in the Mali Federation, with Keita as prime minister and Léopold *SENGHOR as president. When the federation collapsed two years later Keita declared Mali to be totally independent. As president of the new Mali Republic, Keita worked for socialism and against French imperialism. He remained personally popular but his authoritarian regime of austerity was resented. In a political crisis, Keita dissolved the national assembly early in 1968. On 19 November 1968 a military coup led by Lt. Moussa *TRAORÉ deposed Keita, who was imprisoned. The following year an attempt to reinstate Keita failed and a score of plotters were executed. Keita died in prison in 1977, and many Malians lamented his passing. The circumstances of his death have never been explained.

Kelueljang, Sirr Anai, the most outstanding journalist and author from southern Sudan. Born in 1940, Kelueljang became a journalist at an early age and an activist for the southern Christian cause against the oppression of the ruling Arabs. His *The Myth of Freedom and Other Poems*, first published by the Department of Culture and Information in Juba, southern Sudan, was banned by the Khartoum government. It was published in English, in London, in 1985. Despite constant harassment and detention by successive Sudanese governments since 1969, Kelueljang has refused to go into exile. He is regarded by the Christian negroes of Sudan as 'the voice of the South'.

Kenya, a member of the Commonwealth, the Republic of Kenya straddles the Equator. It is bordered by Sudan and Ethiopia to the north, Somalia and the Indian Ocean to the east, Tanzania to the south and Lake Victoria and Uganda to the west. Physically Kenya is a land of contrasts. Much of the north and north-east is semi-desert – an arid plain less than 600 metres above sea-level. The south-east is also arid except for the coastal strip and the Taita Hills which rise to over 2000 metres. Except for its mountains and Lake Turkana, the north-west is low and arid. Eighty-five per cent of the population and most economic activity is concentrated in the southwest; this includes the fertile highlands, Mount Kenya at 5200 metres and the Aberdare Range. The region is divided by the *EAST AFRICAN RIFT VALLEY sixty-five kilometres wide and nearly a thousand metres below the plateau on either side. The climate is hot and humid on the coast and hot in other low-lying

The Republic of Kenya

THE COUNTRY	THE PEOPLE	THE STATE
582,644 sq. km.	22,097,000	Single-party republic
Major Cities	*Ethnic Groups*	*Head of State*
Nairobi (capital)	Kikuyu	President Moi
Mombasa	Luhya	
Nakuru	Luo	*Ruling Bodies*
Kisumu	Kamba	Presidential Cabinet
	Kalenjin	National Assembly
Economy	Masai	
Farming		*Official Party*
	Languages	KANU
Principal Exports	English (official)	
Coffee	Swahili (official)	
Tea		
Petroleum	*Religion*	
Fruit & Vegetables	Christian	
	Islam	
Currency	Traditional beliefs	
Kenya shilling		

areas. The plateau and the highlands enjoy a temperate climate.

The economy depends heavily on agriculture which is concentrated in high rainfall areas in the highlands and near the coast and Lake Victoria. About eighty per cent of the workers make their living from the land. Before independence the best farming land was owned by white settlers in the highlands. Since independence, programmes of land reform and Africanization have transferred most land to Kenyan ownership. There are about 1.5 million smallholders and about 3000 large farms. Over half the production is for subsistence. Maize is the principal food crop; in years of drought maize has had to be imported to meet Kenya's needs. Potatoes, pulses, cassava, sweet potatoes, wheat, rice, sorghum and millet are also cultivated. Livestock and dairy production are for export and domestic consumption.

The main cash crop is coffee which is grown on large farms and on smallholdings. Production and marketing are controlled by an official board. Tea production has rapidly expanded since 1970 to become the second or third most lucrative earner of foreign exchange. Other cash crops include sisal, sugar, cotton, tobacco, fruit and vegetables. Tourism has become a thriving industry; in some years it has overtaken tea as the second most important earner of foreign exchange.

Kenya has a healthy industrial sector which has been based on import substitution, but in the 1980s the government put more emphasis on manufacturing and processing for export. Exports of refined petroleum products from the Mombasa oil refinery have been a major source of foreign exchange. Industry also includes a large food processing sector, textiles and clothing, vehicle assembly, cement and a whole variety of other consumer goods. Kenya has few mineral resources to exploit except for soda ash, fluorspar and rubies.

Kenya has a comprehensive transport system by road, rail, water and air. Mombasa has been developed as a major container port. During the 1980s with help from abroad the government invested heavily to improve communications and transport, and to increase production of electricity.

For the first decade after independence in 1963 Kenya enjoyed the benefits of a positive balance of payments and an expanding economy. It did well out of the *EAST AFRICAN COMMUNITY (founded in 1967) because its economy was stronger than those of its partners. Tension in East Africa and the collapse of the East African Community by 1977 seriously disrupted the regional trade which had been so profitable for Kenya. Droughts, variations in commodity prices and Kenya's failure to diversify its economy have caused increasing problems since the mid-1970s. It has had to borrow to finance balance of payments deficits and to impose austerity to obtain credit abroad.

The rapid population increase and mass migration from rural to urban areas have caused further problems. There is high unemployment in the big cities, which are surrounded by vast slums. The rural areas are underdeveloped. During the 1980s the government has emphasized the role of private investment in economic recovery, but economic prospects depend more on coffee earnings, maize surpluses and lower bills for oil imports. High coffee prices brightened Kenya's prospects in the 1980s, but prices fell sharply at the end of the decade. To achieve prosperity in the future Kenya needs to relieve the pressure on land, feed its growing population, find jobs for the landless and diversify its economy.

Kenya has long been a meeting place for population movements; its people come from four major linguistic groups – *BANTU, Nilotic, Nilo-Hamitic and Cushitic. The main ethnic groups are Kikuyu (over 20 per cent), Luhya (15 per cent), and Luo (13 per cent). *SWAHILI is the official language, but English, Kikuyu and Luo are widely spoken. About half the population is Christian; about 40 per cent follow traditional religions. There are Muslims on the coast whose presence reflects the Arab and Persian influence.

Before the arrival of Europeans in the nineteenth century the highlands of Kenya were inhabited by small pastoral and agricultural communities. The coast had been open to Arab and Persian traders for centuries and was under the authority of the Sultan of Zanzibar. Arab traders travelled to the interior in search of ivory and slaves.

In 1888 the British East Africa Company obtained a royal charter and began acquiring territory. In 1895 construction of the railway linking Mombasa to Uganda started; to protect it Britain declared a protectorate over Kenya in the same year. In 1905 Kenya was made a colony. Indian labourers were brought out to work on the railway; the first European settlers arrived in 1897 and from early in the twentieth century they were given grants of land appropriated from the local people. The administration favoured the white settlers who prospered, producing coffee, wool and wheat from their large and fertile estates.

In the 1920s local people began protesting against various restrictions imposed on them and the loss of their land. The Kikuyu Central Association sent Jomo *KENYATTA to England in 1929 to campaign for Kikuyu rights. In 1944 educated Africans from different ethnic groups combined to form the Kenya African Union and to press for political reforms. They were largely ignored.

From about 1947 a guerrilla movement, known to the outside world as the *MAU MAU, developed to fight for the expulsion of the white settlers and the restoration of land. By 1952 there was a full-scale insurrection and the authorities declared a state of emergency, arresting and imprisoning Kenyatta and other nationalist leaders. During the emergency Britain began to accept the

need to make concessions; Africans were given their first elected representatives on the Legislative Council in 1957. In 1960 the *KENYA AFRICAN NATIONAL UNION (KANU) was formed; its chosen leader Kenyatta was still in prison. After constitutional talks (1960) KANU won the 1961 elections, but refused to take office until Kenyatta was released from prison (Aug. 1961). It formed a coalition with the minority *KENYA AFRICAN DEMOCRATIC UNION (KADU), which had formed the government briefly in 1961. There was a constitutional settlement which made Kenya a unitary state, as KANU wanted.

Independence came in December 1963 – with Kenyatta as Prime Minister. A month after independence Kenyatta called in British forces to quell an army mutiny. This was followed by greater co-operation with Britain. Also in 1964 the government announced the beginning of land reform to take over estates owned by whites and redistribute the land to peasant farmers. Many peasants were given land before the scheme was abandoned in 1966. In 1964 Kenya became a republic and KANU absorbed KADU to become the only political party in parliament.

Under President Kenyatta (1964–78) Kenya prospered, but the conservative and capitalist policies of the government alienated the radicals. *ODINGA left KANU to form the Kenya People's Union to campaign for democratic socialism (1966). This party was banned and Odinga was arrested (1969). In 1969 there were serious disturbances after the assassination of a leading cabinet minister, Tom *MBOYA. In the 1970s as Kenyatta aged he seemed more authoritarian and the government was apparently being run by a clique of his intimates. There were allegations of corruption by ministers and members of Kenyatta's family. Radicals like Odinga and *KARIUKI condemned the widening gap between rich and poor in Kenya. Kariuki's murder (1975) sparked off violent protests.

When Kenyatta died (1978) the succession passed smoothly to President *MOI, formerly vice-president. Moi aroused hopes of a more liberal regime by releasing political detainees, relaxing press censorship and investigating corruption. These hopes were disappointed when he would not allow Odinga and some of his supporters to stand for parliament (1979) and when Kenya was made a one-party state (1982). After critics of the government were arrested members of the air force attempted a coup (Aug. 1982), which was only suppressed with difficulty. Further arrests and detentions followed.

At the beginning of the 1980s a radical underground resistance movement emerged; *MWAKENYA seeks to overthrow the government and establish a radical socialist state. Many suspected supporters have been detained and imprisoned; some have been tortured. Moi has also had a number of clashes with members of his government. Charles *NJONJO was suddenly

dismissed and disgraced (1983–4), Vice-President *KIBAKI was suddenly demoted to the Ministry of Health (1988), Vice-President Karanja was abruptly sacked (1989), and in February 1990 Robert Ouko, the Foreign Minister, was murdered. Protestors have accused the government of covering up the true circumstances of this murder. In July 1988 the judiciary lost its independence when the President of Kenya was given the power to dismiss judges at will.

During 1990 there were a number of protests and demonstrations calling for the restoration of multiparty democracy. In the middle of 1990 there were riots in at least six towns, apparently prompted by Mwakenya's call for an armed insurrection against the government. The government has cracked down on the opposition and has shown no signs of agreeing to major reforms, although it has indicated that there may be some limited reforms. Despite the authoritarianism of President Moi, Kenya has fared better than most other African states; its people still enjoy some democratic rights and they have at least been spared the horrors of famine and civil war.

In foreign affairs Kenya drew closer to the United States and other western powers during the 1980s. It has also improved its relations with Somalia, Tanzania and Uganda. President Moi has also sought co-operation with Ethiopia and Sudan and attempted to mediate in their civil wars. Relations with

Libya deteriorated and were broken off in 1987.

Kenya African Democratic Union (KADU), Kenyan political party founded by Ronald Ngala (1960), it was supported by coastal and pastoral people who were concerned at the Kikuyu and Luo domination of the *KENYA AFRICAN NATIONAL UNION (KANU). After forming a minority government briefly in 1961, KADU joined a coalition with KANU (1961–3). As independence approached the minority ethnic groups in KADU argued for a federal system of government, but KANU's wish for a centralized system prevailed when Kenya became independent (Dec. 1963). KADU went into opposition at independence. When the new republican constitution abolished regional government late in 1964 KADU merged with KANU.

Kenya African National Union (KANU), Kenyan political party founded to campaign for independence (1960), when *KENYATTA, its first leader, was in prison 'for managing the *MAU MAU'. KANU had strong support from the Kikuyu and Luo peoples. KANU won the 1961 election but refused to take office while Kenyatta was in prison. After Kenyatta's release (Aug. 1961) KANU formed a government in coalition with the *KENYA AFRICAN DEMOCRATIC UNION (KADU) (1961–3) and led Kenya to independence (Dec. 1963). KANU's campaign for a centralized constitution prevailed over KADU's campaign for a federal system.

As the republican constitution came into effect (Dec. 1964) KADU was absorbed by KANU, which became Kenya's only parliamentary party. In the 1960s and 1970s KANU strongly resisted attempts by radicals like *ODINGA and *KARIUKI to form opposition parties. In June 1982 it became Kenya's only legal party; its president is automatically chosen as President of Kenya. The party has been criticized for its domination of the country, for its corruption and for its conservatism. Although President *MOI is not a Kikuyu, some ethnic groups in Kenya believe that KANU is a vehicle for Kikuyu domination of the country.

Kenyatta, Jomo (*c*.1894–1978), a Kenyan who was one of Africa's best known leaders before and after independence. Of Kikuyu origins, he was born (as Kamau Ngengi) in the Kenyan highlands. After a mission education he worked as a clerk in Nairobi's Public Works Department and from 1922 became politically active in the East African Association. As General Secretary of the Kikuyu Central Association he campaigned for the restoration of the highlands to the Kikuyu people. Sent to England by the Kikuyu Central Association, he spent years in Europe (1929–46), campaigning for his people and opposing the efforts of white settlers to secure internal self-government in Kenya. He made contacts with other African nationalist leaders and was a founder member of the Pan-African Federation in 1945. During the 1930s he studied anthropology and wrote

Facing Mount Kenya (1938) – a study of traditional Kikuyu life.

Kenyatta returned to Kenya (1946) and as President of the Kenya African Union (from 1947) gained popular support and proved his ability as an organizer. He was arrested (1952) and on flimsy evidence sentenced to seven years in prison for 'managing the *MAU MAU'. While he was still in prison the founders of the *KENYA AFRICAN NATIONAL UNION (KANU) chose him as their president (1960). KANU won the 1961 election but refused to take office until the release of Kenyatta in August 1961. After the London Conference (1962) Kenya progressed steadily to independence (Dec. 1963) under Kenyatta's leadership. Kenyatta was independent Kenya's first prime minister (1963–4) and president (1964–78).

Kenyatta faced many problems after independence. The need to call in British help to suppress the army mutiny of January 1964 exposed the weakness of his position. A rapid population increase and mass migration from rural to urban areas led to high unemployment, and bred many grave social problems. There were factional and political divisions within KANU. Kenyatta was blamed for corruption and the concentration of wealth and power in Kikuyu hands. Radicals like *ODINGA and *KARIUKI believed that Kenyatta's acceptance of western entrepreneurial capitalism and his emphasis on rewarding personal effort led to the exploitation of poorer

Kenyans. His willingness to allow the United States to use bases in Kenya under certain circumstances was unpopular. The formation of the *EAST AFRICAN COMMUNITY (1967) benefited the Kenyan economy, but by 1977 tensions with Tanzania and Uganda led to the end of this attempt at regional co-operation.

Despite the problems Kenyatta was revered as the grand old man (Mzee) and the father of independence. His support for the non-aligned movement and his vigorous campaigns against colonialism and *APARTHEID were popular in Kenya and enabled him to play an important part in international affairs. He established a system of government which has continued under President *MOI, the man he chose to succeed him. By the time of his death he had made Kenya one of the most stable and prosperous states in Africa.

Kérékou, Mathieu (b.1933), Benin soldier, politician and national president. Born in northern Dahomey (later Benin), Kérékou was educated in French army schools and served in the army. When Dahomey became independent, on 1 August 1960, Kérékou was commissioned into the new national army and only five years later he was a major. He took part in the military coup of 1967 and was Vice-President of the Military Revolutionary Council 1967–8. He led the coup of 26 October 1972, which ended the system of 'rotational presidencies'. Kérékou proved himself a strong president as he strove to modernize his backward

171

country and release its rural areas from the clutch of witchdoctors. He travelled to Rumania, North Korea and China seeking aid and forced the French to be more realistic in the prices they paid for Benin's products. Until 1980, Kérékou was president by virtue of having seized power. On 6 February, as a colonel, he was formally elected president, being the only candidate. In 1984, as a brigadier, he was again elected, a process repeated in 1988. Never afraid to dismiss ministers, Kérékou has given Benin greater stability than most African countries have experienced since 1960.

Khama, Sir Seretse (1921–60), hereditary chief of the *BAMANGWATO, Prime Minister of Bechuanaland (1965–6) and first executive President of the Republic of Botswana (1966–80). Born at Serowe he succeeded his father, Chief Sekgoma II, to the chiefdom of the Bamangwato (1925), under the regency of his uncle, Tshekedi Khama. After attending school and *FORT HARE UNIVERSITY COLLEGE in South Africa he read law at Oxford. In England he fell in love with Ruth Williams, a confidential secretary and a keen church worker. They married in 1948.

Seretse's marriage to a white woman enraged the British authorities and the white governments of South Africa and Rhodesia. Tshekedi Khama challenged his nephew's right to the chiefdom of the Bamangwato, but when Seretse asked a full tribal gathering for support for himself and his wife about six thousand of the crowd acclaimed

him as leader and only forty opposed him. Nevertheless Britain believed that the marriage had caused a political crisis in Bechuanaland and forced the young couple to go into exile in England (1950–6). They were only allowed back in Bechuanaland when he renounced his chiefdom.

Back in Bechuanaland he entered politics, founding the *BECHUANALAND DEMOCRATIC PARTY (1962) and campaigning for independence. After winning the pre-independence elections he became Prime Minister (1965–6) and President (1966–80). As leader Sir Seretse established a non-racial multi-party democratic state and defended the right of other political parties to oppose his government. He guaranteed the freehold rights of white farmers. Sir Seretse rejected socialism in favour of a free-market economy which would encourage foreign investment. As leader of a *FRONT LINE STATE he shared the burdens of the struggle against his neighbours under white minority rule, doing his best to help the thousands of refugees from Ian *SMITH's regime in Rhodesia and allowing the *AFRICAN NATIONAL CONGRESS into Botswana. Despite years of ill health Sir Seretse established Botswana as a stable and peaceful democracy. When he came to power Botswana was one of Africa's ten poorest countries, when he died it was one of Africa's ten richest countries.

Khoi (or Hottentots), like the *SAN, early inhabitants of Southern Africa. They were settled in the Cape when the first European settlers arrived in the seventeenth century. The Khoi were attacked both by the Europeans and the *BANTU arrivals from the north. They were finally wiped out by smallpox and other diseases brought in by the Europeans – diseases to which they had no natural resistance. There are no Khoi left and the race only survives in the ancestry of the *COLOURED people in South Africa. The Khoi and the San are sometimes called the Khoisan.

Kibaki, Mwai (b. 1931), leading Kenyan politician of Kikuyu origins, educated at *MAKERERE UNIVERSITY COLLEGE and the London School of Economics. He was an administrative officer in the *KENYA AFRICAN NATIONAL UNION (KANU) (1960–2) before entering parliament (1963). As the holder of various financial and economic portfolios (1963–78), he played an important role in shaping Kenya's economy and became one of President *KENYATTA's most powerful advisers.

President *MOI's smooth succession to the presidency (1978) depended heavily on Kibaki's support. Kibaki was rewarded with the Vice-Presidency (1978–88) and the Ministries of Home Affairs and Finance. After the 1988 elections Moi dropped Kibaki from the Vice-Presidency and demoted him to the Ministry of Health.

Kimba, Evariste (d. 1966), Zairean politician who served as a minister in the First Republic of the Congo (1960–5). He was appointed prime minister by President *KASAVUBU

(1965), even though *TSHOMBE had won a substantial majority in the 1965 parliamentary elections. Kimba was removed from office by President *MOBUTU's second coup (Nov. 1965) and later executed on charges of plotting against Mobutu's government.

Koevoet (Afrikaans word for crowbar), mainly black paramilitary force of up to three thousand men established by South Africa in Namibia (1979) and led by white South African officers. It was renamed the South West African Police Counter Insurgency Unit and placed under the control of the Namibian police in 1985. Koevoet had considerable success against *SWAPO guerrillas but also acquired a reputation for rape, torture and murder.

Krige, Uys (1910–87), South African writer of poetry, plays and short stories. He wrote all his poems in Afrikaans, but some plays and short stories were in English. Although he rejected the political attitudes of his fellow Afrikaners he wrote about them and the other peoples of South Africa with compassion and humour. His well known play *The Two Lamps* (1964) is about the conflict between father and son and the power of Calvinism.

Kuti, Fela Anikulapo (b. 1938), very popular, politically active and controversial Nigerian musician who sings, composes and plays a number of instruments. Despite intimidation he has spoken out for the rights of the Nigerian people, attacking corruption and military oppression. In 1979 he launched the radical Movement of

173

the People. From 1984 to 1986 he was in prison on a currency smuggling charge; his supporters believed he had been framed.

kwacha, means the dawn. It was a slogan much used by the *NYASALAND AFRICAN CONGRESS in the struggle for independence during the 1950s. It is now the name of Malawi's currency.

Kwela (or pennywhistle) music originated in South African townships near Johannesburg in the 1940s. This lively music was often played by children on the streets and attracted crowds who danced to this rhythmic combination of western jazz and popular African rhythms.

174

L

Labour Party, South African political party of the *COLOUREDS, led by Allan *HENDRICKSE. It was formed in 1969 to campaign for election to a consultative body, the Coloured People's Representative Council. The Labour Party co-operated with the tricameral constitution introduced in 1984, although real power remained firmly in white hands. It fought the 1984 election, which over 80 per cent of the Coloured electorate boycotted, and won seventy-six of the eighty seats in the *HOUSE OF REPRESENTATIVES. The Labour Party was soon disillusioned with the lack of progress in ending *APARTHEID and has been reluctant to co-operate with the South African government.

La Guma, Alex (1925–85), radical South African writer and political activist of *COLOURED ancestry. A member of the South African Communist Party, he was accused of treason (1956); the charge was finally dropped in 1961. He was detained after the events at *SHARPEVILLE (1960) and imprisoned again for organizing a political strike (1961). He was subject to a *BANNING ORDER and placed under house arrest from 1962 until he and his wife went into voluntary exile in 1966. After many years in London (1966–79) he went to Cuba and was the *AFRICAN NATIONAL CONGRESS representative there when he died.

La Guma wrote vivid short stories about political and criminal lawbreakers as well as four novels, all banned in South Africa. *And a Threefold Cord* (1964) is about ghetto life and the struggle against a repressive regime. *The Stone Country* (1967) was inspired by his experiences as a political prisoner; the book is dedicated to political prisoners in South Africa. *In the Fog of the Seasons' End* (1972) continued the theme of political despair. His last novel, *Time of the Butcherbird* (1979), is about the forcible removal and resettlement of non-white communities under the *GROUP AREAS ACT.

Lakwena, Alice (b. 1960), Ugandan leader of the *HOLY SPIRIT MOVEMENT which rose in rebellion against the government of President *MUSEVENI (1986). In Acholi Lakwena means Messiah. A spirit medium and herbalist, she claimed magical powers to protect her followers. After setbacks late in 1987 Alice Lakwena fled to Kenya where she was imprisoned for four months for crossing the border illegally. Her followers are still fighting the government.

Lamizana, Sangoule (b. 1916), onetime Upper Volta (later Burkina Faso) head of state. Born into the Samo tribe, Lamizana joined the French army in 1936 and served with it during the Second World War and, in the 1950s, in Indo-China.

After Upper Volta became independent in 1960, Lamizana transferred to the new national army and in 1961 became its chief-of-staff. In January 1966, Lamizana, as a lieutenant-colonel, took over the government after a popular uprising brought down President Maurice *YAMEOGO. Neither a brilliant politician nor a notably able administrator, Lamizana nevertheless retained his military government and struggled through crises caused by droughts, political feuding, strikes and inflation. Promoted to the rank of general, Lamizana was elected president in 1978 in a fair and open contest. Colonel Saye Zerbo, also of the Samo tribe, ousted Lamizana in a coup on 25 November 1980. Happy to give up power, Lamizana retired to his tribal village.

Lancaster House Agreement, agreement on the independence of Zimbabwe. It was made in London in December 1979 after the Lancaster House talks chaired by the British Foreign Secretary and attended by representatives of the white minority, Bishop *MUZOREWA's government and nationalist leaders. It was agreed that Rhodesia-Zimbabwe would renounce *UDI and become a British colony again. Twenty seats in parliament would be reserved for whites for seven years and parts of the constitution would be entrenched for ten years after independence. Then, under the supervision of Lord Soames, there was a ceasefire, free elections, the formation of a government and independence.

Lára, Lucio, Angolan nationalist intellectual and Marxist theoretician, a founding member of the *MPLA in 1956. He played an important role in the independence war (1961–74) both as an able organizer and a powerful spokesman for the MPLA. Lára was elected to the Politbureau and Central Committee (1974) and served as Secretary-General of the MPLA until he was dropped from the Politbureau at the Second Congress (Dec. 1985). Since his demotion Lára has been Deputy Defence Minister and First Secretary of the National People's Assembly, and he is still a leading political theoretician.

Lekhanya, Major-General Justin Metsing (b.1938), military ruler of Lesotho since January 1986, Chairman of the Military Council, Minister for Defence, Internal Security, Public Services, Youth and Women's Affairs, Food Management Units and the Cabinet Office. He was head of the *LESOTHO PARAMILITARY FORCE in January 1986 when South Africa blockaded Lesotho. When Chief *JONATHAN's government collapsed under South African pressure Lekhanya seized power – possibly with South African backing.

Relations with South Africa improved dramatically after the coup. The blockade was lifted; Lesotho severed relations with communist states, returned *AFRICAN NATIONAL CONGRESS exiles to South Africa, signed a security pact with South Africa and agreed to the Highlands Water Project – a vast scheme which will provide

The Kingdom of Lesotho

THE COUNTRY	THE PEOPLE	THE STATE
30,355 sq. km.	1,629,000	Monarchy under military rule
Major City	*Ethnic Group*	*Head of State*
Maseru (capital)	Basotho	King Letsie III
Economy	*Languages*	*Head of Government*
Farming	English (official)	Maj-Gen Lekhanya
Tourism	Sesotho (official)	
		Ruling Bodies
Principal Exports	*Religion*	Military Council
Wool & mohair	Christian	Council of Ministers
	Traditional beliefs	
Currency		*Political Parties*
Loti of 100 lisente		All banned
South African Rand		

South Africa with water from Lesotho. Lekhanya restored some of the executive powers of King *MOSHOESHOE II – to be exercised on the advice of the Military Council. After Lekhanya shot a student in December 1988, tension rose in Lesotho, although the chief magistrate ruled this was a case of justifiable homicide in defence of a woman being attacked. In February 1990 three of the Military Council were led away at gunpoint and in March 1990 it was announced that King Moshoeshoe II was going into exile. Although Lekhanya has promised a constitution there were no signs of a return to civilian rule by 1990. In November 1990 Lekhanya announced that King Moshoeshoe II would be deposed and that a new king would be chosen.

Lesotho, a member of the Commonwealth, formerly the *BASUTOLAND PROTECTORATE and a *HIGH COMMISSION TERRITORY. Lesotho is a small and mountainous landlocked kingdom surrounded by South Africa. The so-called lowlands in the western third are between 1500 and 1800 metres above sea-level; wheat and maize are grown in the lowlands which are the only parts of Lesotho suitable for intensive cultivation. There are highlands between 2200 and 2800 metres above sea level and in the east and south Drakensberg mountain peaks are over 3200 metres high.

Lesotho's spectacular scenery and pleasant climate could attract tourists, but much of the country is only accessible by light aircraft or by difficult land journey along poor roads or tracks. There are few tarred roads and only one mile of railway which links Maseru, the capital, to the South African rail system. The nearest ports are South African;

Durban is 625 km. and East London 640 km. away. Lesotho's geographical position and its lack of development have made it vulnerable to economic, political and military domination by South Africa, even though as a member of the *SOUTHERN AFRICAN DEVELOPMENT CO-ORDINATION CONFERENCE Lesotho aims to lessen its dependence on South Africa.

During the first half of the nineteenth century King Moshoeshoe I established a powerful kingdom over the Basotho, *BANTU who had moved into the country and mingled with the *SAN – the original inhabitants. The Basotho had a unified and stable state with some democratic consultation in the local and national assemblies (pitso), but they could not resist the incursions of their *BOER and Zulu neighbours. Moshoeshoe I had to cede fertile areas to the Boers (1868), but did secure British protection at the same time.

After Moshoeshoe died (1870) Basutoland was annexed to the Cape Colony (1871–83), but became a protectorate again and a High Commission Territory (1883–1966). Under the British system of indirect rule, economic development was neglected while the traditional rulers enjoyed their power. Basutoland joined a customs union with the Union of South Africa (1910) and was expected to join South Africa eventually. Strong opposition from traditional rulers and the election of a South African government committed to *APARTHEID (1948) put paid to this plan.

The move towards independence began in 1952 with the formation of the *BASOTHO CONGRESS PARTY (BCP) which won most of the elected seats in the Basutoland National Council (1960). A constitution for independence was drafted, and after narrowly winning the 1965 elections to the National Assembly with thirty-one of the sixty seats Chief Leabua *JONATHAN and his *BASOTHO NATIONAL PARTY (BNP) formed the government. In 1966 Chief Jonathan became the first prime minister of independent Lesotho with King *MOSHOESHOE II as head of state.

Chief Jonathan was soon involved in a bitter power struggle with the young king who in 1967 had to give up political power and confine himself to a ceremonial role. Chief Jonathan's power was still not secure. His co-operation with South Africa was unpopular and he alienated powerful traditional rulers. When he realized his BNP was losing to the opposition BCP he stopped the 1970 elections, suspended the constitution, ruled by decree, banned opposition political parties, put the king under house arrest and exiled him for nearly a year. Despite official repression, opposition to Chief Jonathan grew. In 1974 the *LESOTHO LIBERATION ARMY, the military wing of the BCP, launched its first attacks. Late in the 1970s Chief Jonathan sought popularity and support from the outside world when he turned against South Africa; he condemned events in *SOWETO (1976), gave sanctuary to members of the

South African *AFRICAN NATIONAL CONGRESS (ANC), refused to recognize the so-called independence of the *TRANSKEI and established diplomatic relations with Cuba (1979).

South Africa put pressure on Lesotho, imposing border restrictions which severely disrupted supplies to Lesotho. It probably armed the Lesotho Liberation Army and certainly gave it sanctuary and allowed raids on Lesotho from South Africa. As relations deteriorated further the South African Defence Force attacked the ANC in Maseru. In December 1982 thirty ANC refugees and twelve Lesotho citizens were killed; three years later another nine were killed in a South African raid. When Chief Jonathan still refused to return ANC members to South Africa and would not break off diplomatic relations with Cuba, South Africa imposed a total blockade at the beginning of 1986. No goods and no people could cross the border.

As the situation worsened Major-General *LEKHANYA seized power in a bloodless coup (20 Jan. 1986). He banned political activity, set up a military government and restored the legislative and executive powers of the monarch, which were to be exercised only on the advice of the Military Council – which he appointed. Lekhanya broke off relations with Cuba and South Africa lifted its blockade. Relations improved even more when he returned ANC refugees to South Africa and agreed to a security pact in which each agreed to stop its territory from being used for acts of terrorism against the other. Late in 1986 it was confirmed that the two countries had agreed on the Highlands Water Project which will take over twenty-five years to complete. South Africa is to supply most of the billion or more pounds needed for this vast complex of roads, dams, tunnels and pumps. Lesotho will benefit from ample hydroelectric power and will earn revenue by selling water to South Africa.

The Highlands Water Project may eventually help Lesotho, but economic prospects are generally poor. Agriculture is not developing fast enough to feed the rapidly growing population and soil erosion is a serious problem. There is little industry and Lesotho's economic and financial health depends on South Africa. Over half its gross domestic product comes from the earnings of migrant workers in South African mines; much government revenue comes from the customs union with South Africa. Lesotho's only known major mineral resource is a diamond pipe which will be nearly exhausted by the end of the century. With South African help the economy will survive, but, as Chief Jonathan discovered, South Africa expects political compliance in exchange for help. Lekhanya promised a new constitution, but by early 1990 there were no signs of progress towards the restoration of civilian rule. In December 1988 Lekhanya shot a student. Although the chief magistrate ruled that this was justifiable homicide in defence of a woman being attacked,

179

Lekhanya's standing has been weakend and tension has grown. In February 1990 three members of the Military Council were taken away at gunpoint; in March 1990 King Moshoeshoe II went into exile. In November 1990 the government announced the deposition of the King and swore in his son as King Letsie III. This has strengthened both Lekhanya's hold on the country and South African influence.

Lesotho Liberation Army, military wing of the *BASOTHO CONGRESS PARTY, formed in 1981 for the armed struggle against Chief *JONATHAN's government. With some help from South Africa the force launched a campaign of bombing, sabotage, assassination and raids from its bases in South Africa. It was apparently used by South Africa to retaliate against Chief Jonathan's support for the *AFRICAN NATIONAL CONGRESS. After the military coup (Jan. 1986), the force ended its activities.

Lesotho Paramilitary Force, Lesotho's army comprising about 1500 full-time men and a part-time militia of about 4000. During the 1980s the force turned against the prime minister, Chief *JONATHAN. It mutinied over pay and objected to the North Koreans who were brought in to give military training to the *BASOTHO NATIONAL PARTY YOUTH LEAGUE. In January 1986 the head of the force, Major-General *LEKHANYA, seized power in a military coup.

Libandla, traditional council of the Swazi nation, including chiefs, princes and other community leaders who represent the views of the

people and advise the monarch. It played an important part in choosing a successor to King *SOBHUZA II. About fifteen members of the Libandla formed an inner group known as the *LIQOQO, which was dissolved in 1986.

Liberia, the Republic of Liberia was the first independent republic in Africa; it and Ethiopia are the only African states which have not been directly colonized. Situated on the West African coast, it is bordered by Guinea on the north, the Ivory Coast on the east, the Atlantic Ocean to the south and Sierra Leone to the west. Lying north of the Equator, it has a warm and humid climate. There is a narrow coastal plain with many marshes, lagoons and river estuaries which make it difficult to travel between the coastal towns. Inland the central region of plateaux and narrow valleys is from 180 to 360 metres above sea-level. Further north on the border of Guinea are the highlands which reach an altitude of 1750 metres.

The Liberian economy is still primarily agricultural. Although over two thirds of the population work as subsistence farmers producing rice and cassava, Liberia does not produce enough rice to feed its population and has to rely on American imports – often in the form of aid. Palm oil, yams, sweet potatoes, groundnuts and other fruits and vegetables are grown in the country.

The most important export crops are rubber, coffee and cocoa. The rubber industry has been controlled by Firestone and other

The Republic of Liberia

THE COUNTRY	THE PEOPLE	THE STATE
111,369 sq. km.	2,327,000	Multi-party republic
Major City	*Ethnic Groups*	*Head of State*
Monrovia (capital)	Kpelle	None
	Bassa	
Economy	Gio	*Ruling Bodies*
Farming	Kru	Presidential Cabinet
Mining	Vai	National Assembly
	Descendants of settlers	
Principal Exports		*Party in Power*
Iron ore	*Languages*	National Democratic
Rubber	English (official)	Party of Liberia
Coffee	Mande	
Timber		*Political Opposition*
Cocoa	*Religion*	Liberian Action Party
	Christian	Liberia Unification Party
Currency	Islam	Unity party
Liberian dollar (L $) of	Traditional beliefs	
100 cents		

foreign companies, but since the fall in world prices these companies have closed some plantations and disposed of some of their interests. Although Liberia is still Africa's leading rubber producer, its declining exports accounted for only 18 per cent of the value of Liberian exports in 1985.

Timber exports have also declined, but there have been reforestation schemes which may lead to greater exports in the future. Mining is the main source of foreign currency. Iron ore accounts for over half of export earnings; despite smuggling, diamonds and gold are also valuable sources of foreign exchange. Taking advantage of the flag of convenience foreign shipowners have registered in

Liberia, which in 1986 had the world's largest merchant shipping fleet with a registered tonnage of over fifty million.

Despite investment by large international concerns, Liberian industry is limited. Much of it is foreign-owned; the retail and wholesale trades are dominated by Lebanese. Few Liberians are trained as technicians and managers. Industry is concentrated near the capital, Monrovia. The domestic market is small because the subsistence farmers in the hinterland buy very little. Like many other African states Liberia has had adverse trade balances and problems in balancing its budgets. Despite substantial financial help from the United States, in 1989 Liberia was heavily in arrears with

181

payments on its foreign debt of $1.7 billion.

Over ninety per cent of the Liberian population belongs to sixteen ethnic groups, many in the hinterland have been hardly touched by the twentieth century. The political, social and economic life of the country has been dominated by an elite descended from American and West Indian settlers and from those rescued from slave traders during the nineteenth century.

Little is known of the history of Liberia before the nineteenth century. Between 1822 and 1892 the American Colonization Society and other bodies settled over sixteen thousand freed slaves from the United States on the coast; the Royal Navy and the US navy settled about six thousand people rescued from slave ships. Many died, but enough survived to dominate the country and to exploit the indigenous people with a system of forced labour. Liberia became an independent republic in 1847. The *TRUE WHIG PARTY (founded in 1868) was in power continuously from 1878 until its overthrow in the military coup of 1980.

In 1926 the American company, Firestone, moved into Liberia on a large scale and Liberia was nicknamed the Firestone Republic; the United States dominated the Liberian economy. Soon after his inauguration in 1944 President *TUBMAN broke Firestone's monopoly and encouraged other foreign investors – but with limited success. Tubman also made

little progress in reducing the great gulf between the coastal elite of Afro-American origin and the people of the hinterland. During Tubman's long presidency (1944–71) the exploitation of valuable iron ore deposits and United States aid brought prosperity, which benefited only a small section of the population and led to growth without development. Tubman also made Liberia a leading member of the *MONROVIA bloc – the non-socialist African states opposed to the socialist *CASABLANCA BLOC.

President *TOLBERT (1971–80) continued Tubman's policies of maintaining friendly relations with the United States and seeking a prominent role in African affairs. As Liberia suffered from rising petroleum prices and falling demand for its iron ore and rubber in the 1970s President Tolbert tried to make Liberia more efficient and more productive. Despite his efforts the country was still plagued by economic mismanagement and corruption, and the wide gap between the wealthy coastal elite and the rest of the population remained.

Liberia's long years of political stability ended in 1979 when Tolbert raised rice prices to encourage production. The *PROGRESSIVE ALLIANCE of Liberia, an unofficial opposition group, organized massive protests which President Tolbert suppressed harshly. This prompted the military coup in which Master Sergeant *DOE and the People's Redemption Council seized power (Apr. 1980). Tolbert was killed in the coup and thirteen of his senior officials were publicly executed.

From 1980 until 1986 Liberia was under military rule. Doe spoke of building a new society based on justice and human dignity, but soon many Liberians found that the lifestyle and the arrogance of the new leaders reminded them of the Tubman and Tolbert eras. Other African states were initially unwilling to recognize the Doe government, although when Doe stopped the executions diplomatic contacts with other countries were restored. In 1981 Doe announced Liberia would return to civilian rule; a new constitution which bears some resemblance to the pre-1980 constitution was drawn up.

Doe formed the *NATIONAL DEMOCRATIC PARTY OF LIBERIA in 1984 to contest presidential and parliamentary elections. During the campaign leading up to the multi-party elections in October 1985 he arrested four opposition leaders on suspicion of plotting a coup and generally harassed the opposition. He won the presidency and large majorities in both houses of parliament. Doe was sworn in as President of Liberia early in 1986.

Liberia has been politically unstable for the last decade; there were nine coup attempts (or alleged coup attempts) during the 1980s. In October 1988 ten opposition leaders were sentenced to long terms in prison for plotting against the government. On Christmas Eve, 1989, Charles

*TAYLOR and his *NATIONAL PATRIOTIC FRONT OF LIBERIA started a major rebellion in the Nimba province in the north-east. At least thirty thousand refugees fled to the Ivory Coast and thousands died. By September 1990 rebel forces controlled nearly all Monrovia and President Doe was killed. The civil war continued and by late 1990 three groups were fighting in Monrovia: Taylor's main rebel group, another rebel group led by Prince *JOHNSON and the remnants of Doe's supporters. There was also a force from *ECOWAS in Monrovia vainly trying to restore peace to the shattered city.

Liberia Grand Coalition (LGC), a coalition of Liberian opposition groups formed in 1986 under the leadership of Gabriel Kpolleh. The groups in the coalition have some legal status, but the government does not recognize the coalition itself. In the October 1985 elections the groups which later formed the coalition won four seats in the Liberian Senate and thirteen in the House of Representatives. The government has harassed the coalition. Kpolleh and twelve others were charged with treason (Jun. 1988), and Kpolleh and nine others were sentenced to ten years imprisonment (Oct. 1988).

Libya, possesses a coastline on the southern Mediterranean, and an area covering well over one million square miles, 94.6 per cent of which is classified as wasteland. Of the remainder only 1.4 per cent is arable. Libya has six contiguous neighbours, Egypt, Sudan, Chad,

Libya

THE COUNTRY	THE PEOPLE	THE STATE
1,759,540 sq. km.	3.690 million	Socialist People's Libyan Arab Jamahiryya (state of the masses)
Major Cities	*Ethnic Groups*	*Head of State*
Tripoli (capital)	Arab	Colonel Muammar
Benghazi	Bedouin	Gaddafi is *de facto*
Zawia	Senussi	President
Homs	Negroes in the south	
Derna		*Ruling Body*
Tobruk	*Languages*	Government elected
	Arabic (official)	by General People's
Economy	English is widely spoken	Congress, whose
Oil		members are elected by
Natural Gas	*Religion*	popular committees
	Sunni Islam	
Principal Exports		
As above		
Currency		
Dinar of 1,000 Dirhams		

Niger, Algeria and all are on desert frontiers. In 1989 the country had fewer than three million Libyan inhabitants, but with a birthrate of 3.9 per cent the number could increase to more than six million by the year 2000. Most Libyans are Sunni Muslims.

After centuries of Ottoman and occasionally tribal rule, Libya fell, in 1911, to an Italian invasion which drove out the Turks. The Italians neglected Libya until the 1930s when peasants were brought in from Sicily and southern Italy to begin a system of extensive farm settlements, especially in the regions of Tripolitania and Cyrenaica. Thousands of Libyans were dispossessed of their land.

During the Second World War Libya became a battleground for British Commonwealth troops fighting the Germans and Italians. At the end of the war Britain was administering western and eastern Libya and France the south. Under the United Nations, Libya was granted independence on 24 December 1951 with *IDRIS, the leader of the *SENUSSI sect, as king. In that year Libya was one of the poorest societies in the world, with a largely rural population.

In its early years the impoverished kingdom was dependent on British and American economic and military agreements, but by the mid-1960s Libya was one of the world's largest suppliers of oil. In September 1969 a military coup deposed King Idris and his government. Colonel Muammar *GADDAFI and a twelve-man Revolutionary Command Council (RCC) established the Libyan Arab Republic. The RCC sought closer ties with Arab countries, particularly Egypt. A 'Federation of Arab Republics' was agreed with Syria and Egypt but it came to nothing. The Nasserist and Arab nationalist nature of Gaddafi's regime was emphasized when a single party, the *ARAB SOCIALIST UNION, was created in 1971 as a means of radicalizing Libyan society. The traditional power of the old rural and urban elites was drastically cut.

In March 1977 Gaddafi declared Libya to be a Jamahiriyya ('state of the masses'), an attempt to establish Hellenistic fundamentals of democracy combined with extreme Islamic principles. The jamahiriyya obliged all Libyans to take part in popular congresses which were supposed to govern all aspects of Libyan political life.

Gaddafi imposed a remarkable system of administration in 1979. The basic unit was the 'popular committee', elected in villages, towns, government departments, private companies, ports, hospitals, airports and so on. Each committee selected its own members to sit in the General People's Congress. This was considered the ruling body and it certainly discussed most matters of importance. However, all major decisions were made by Gaddafi,

who left Congress members in no doubt about the recommendations he expected from them.

In 1981 Gaddafi brought in a new economic system as part of his master-plan to make Libya a people's state. It included the abolition of private shops and factories, since Gaddafi considered merchants to be 'rapacious capitalists and parasites'. They produced nothing and enriched themselves at the expense of the masses. He replaced shops with people's supermarkets. Through bulk-buying and elimination of middlemen goods would be cheaper, Gaddafi said. His theory did not work in practice. Poor organization, distribution bottlenecks and bureaucratic interference led to chaos in all buy-and-sell mechanisms. Most basic goods became virtually unobtainable and all shopping was done on the black market. In the big towns most cafés closed.

In addition, the zeal of the revolutionary committees which Gaddafi had set up became oppressive. As spies of the regime, committee members terrorized the communities in which they operated. They arbitrarily arrested and gaoled thousands of citizens. Within months, Gaddafi's new system brought Libyan towns to their knees. Streets were deserted and buildings were neglected.

In 1985–6 Libya and Morocco became treaty allies but the union collapsed. Early in 1987 Gaddafi announced that Tripoli (population 750,000) would no longer be the administrative capital. An oasis, 140 miles south of Sirte, was supposed to become the new capital but few Libyans believed that this would happen. By April 1988 Gaddafi was forced to confess that his revolutionary system had not worked. Overnight, private shops and workshops were encouraged to reopen, the revolutionary committees were stripped of most of their powers, freedom to travel abroad was guaranteed and barriers to trade and tourism with Libya's Arab neighbours were eliminated. These changes brought Gaddafi great renewed popularity.

Libya's more general development plans – three between 1973 and 1989 – were more successful than the attempts to change socio-economic life. Industry has expanded and improvements have been made in housing, roads, electricity and water supplies, health and social services. Because of the increasing need for skilled manpower many Egyptians, Tunisians, Algerians, Palestinians, Pakistanis and Turks are employed. The foreign work force reached 900,000 by 1986. In that year, because of radically less income from oil, many of these workers were sent home.

The greatest development project in Libya, and one of the greatest in the world, is the Great Man-Made River (GMR), a scheme to pipe 5.7 cubic metres of water a day from natural reservoirs beneath the southern/ deserts for use along the coast. The GMR is essential since most of the population centres and main agricultural areas are short of water because

of over-pumping. The project's first phase was completed in 1990 and the second is scheduled for completion in the mid-1990s. The total cost of the GMR will be $25 billion.

Once listed by the World Bank as one of the poorest countries in the world with the fewest economic possibilities, Libya has the highest per capita income in Africa ($8800 in 1989) and foreign exchange deposits of more than six billion dollars. This wealth is the result of the country's oil production of two million barrels a day. In 1973 Libya had only one domestic refinery and it had no overseas capacity. By the end of 1988 it had five refineries with a combined capacity of 370,000 barrels a day. While boosting its domestic refining capacity, Libya has gained assured refining and sales outlets in Europe, the biggest market for its oil. Libya has much to offer tourists, including the magnificent Roman ruins at Leptia Magna and Sabratha. However, tourism is difficult because of Gaddafi's hostility towards the West. All travel agents were nationalized in 1977.

Libya's main problem area has long been in the field of foreign relations. Gaddafi has provided bases and training for terrorists from several nations. His involvement in anti-US terrorism in 1985–6 led to the *UNITED STATES RAID on Tripoli and Benghazi in May 1986. From the mid-1970s, Libya was involved in IRA terrorism by supplying the organization with arms, explosives and funds. Gaddafi sent £15M worth of supplies to the IRA in the *Eksund*, which was seized by French customs in October 1987. This episode led to the exposure of the Libyan terrorist connection not only in Northern Ireland and Britain but in Europe as a whole. For many years the Palestine Liberation Organization had training bases in Libya, as did the notorious terrorist Abu Nidal.

Internal dissent in Libya has been much more widespread than that publicized in the West but it has always been short-lived. Gaddafi maintains a very large security apparatus with many students among its members. It is they who have uncovered conspiracies against Gaddafi. By 1990 at least fourteen coups or supposed coups had been discovered and the ringleaders executed. There has never been any evidence of a popular uprising.

With the advent of President Mikhail Gorbachev's *perestroika*, Libya became a backwater for the Soviet Union, and the supply of Russian-made military equipment virtually ceased in 1989. This reduced Libya's prestige among Arab and African states.

Limann, Dr Hilla (b. 1934), former President of Ghana (1979–81). He was active in local politics at an early age and then pursued his academic interests with distinction, gaining two degrees from London University and a doctorate in political science and constitutional law from the University of Paris. After serving on the constitutional committee preparing the return to civilian rule in 1969 he held various diplomatic posts.

He returned to Ghana in 1979 to lead the People's National Party (PNP) in the elections returning Ghana to civilian rule for the second time. The PNP included former members of the *CONVENTION PEOPLE'S PARTY and gained support by associating itself with the greatness of *NKRUMAH while dissociating itself from Nkrumah's socialism. The return to civilian rule in 1979 was disrupted when *RAWLINGS seized power (Jun. 1979), but Limann and the PNP won the elections, Rawlings stepped down and Limann took office as President of Ghana (Sep. 1979).

Limann was unable to solve Ghana's economic problems. The economy continued to deteriorate, corruption flourished and the PNP was torn apart by factional rivalries. There was tension between Limann and Rawlings who was still popular and influential. As Limann's government collapsed Rawlings seized power again on the last day of 1981. Limann was detained (1982–3), but has been released and cleared of all criminal charges.

Liqoqo, traditional body of about fifteen princes and chiefs in Swaziland. King *SOBHUZA II had provided for the Liqoqo to have power as the executive branch of the *LIBANDLA during the regency after his death (1982–6). The Liqoqo effectively controlled the choice of Prince Makhosetive (King *MSWATI III) as Sobhuza's heir. During the regency it was a powerful champion of the traditionalist cause and in 1983 procured the dismissal of the reforming prime minister, Prince Mabandla *DLAMINI, and of Queen Regent *DZELIWE. The Liqoqo favoured the proposed land deal with South Africa which would give Swaziland more territory and a corridor to the Indian Ocean in exchange for Swazi co-operation with South Africa. Its power alarmed other groups, but it was weakened by the failure of the land deal and by accusations of corruption. Queen Regent *NTOMBI sacked two of its most powerful members and reduced its powers (1985). King Mswati III saw it as a challenge to his authority and an obstacle to progress; he dissolved the Liqoqo (May 1986), shortly after his coronation.

Lule, Professor Yusufu K. (1912–85), President of Uganda briefly in 1979. After studying at *FORT HARE COLLEGE, Bristol and Edinburgh Universities, he taught at *MAKERERE COLLEGE before joining the colonial government as Minister of Education and Community Development (1955–60). Before and after independence Professor Lule was Chairman of the Uganda Public Service Commission (1960–3). He was Principal of Makerere University (1963–70) until he left Uganda after disagreements with President *OBOTE.

In London he was Assistant Secretary-General of the Commonwealth (1970–2) and in Ghana Secretary-General of the Association of African Universities (1972–7). He then retired to London until his return to Ugandan

politics as leader of the anti-*AMIN *UGANDA NATIONAL LIBERATION FRONT (Mar. 1979). He was a compromise candidate acceptable to both the supporters and the opponents of Obote. After Amin's fall (Apr. 1979) Lule became President of Uganda, but he and his inexperienced ministers made little progress in tackling the country's appalling problems. After excluding Obote supporters from his government, President Lule was ousted (Jun. 1979) – after little more than two months in power. In exile in London he became leader of the National Resistance Movement, the political arm of the National Resistance Army which launched its fight against President Obote early in 1981.

Lumpa Church, charismatic church founded by Alice Lenshina (1954). Not prepared to accept outside interference in its affairs, the Lumpa Church rebelled against the Zambian government in 1964. President *KAUNDA used armed force to suppress the rebellion. There were about seven hundred casualties.

Lumumba, Patrice (1925–61), first Prime Minister of the Congo (now Zaire). He was a trade union activist and worked in the *BELGIAN CONGO civil service until he was dismissed and imprisoned for embezzlement (1956). As founder (1958) of the *MNC (Mouvement National Congolais) – the country's first nationwide political party – he became a leading figure in the campaign for independence and was imprisoned for anti-Belgian agitation (1959). He was released to attend the Brussels Round Table Conference on independence, where he argued for a unitary rather than a federal constitution to overcome tribal and regional differences.

After the success of the MNC at the pre-independence elections (May 1960), he led the Congo to independence (Jun. 1960). A few days later he was challenged by an army mutiny and the secession of Katanga (now *SHABA) under *TSHOMBE. Alarmed by Lumumba's radicalism and his appeal to the Soviet Union for help to subdue Katanga, President *KASAVUBU dismissed him (Sep. 1960). Lumumba was murdered in Katanga while in Tshombe's custody. The university for foreigners in Moscow is named the Patrice Lumumba University in his honour.

Lusaka Agreement (Feb. 1984), a significant agreement between Angola and South Africa. Despite its failure it prepared the way for further negotiations and the agreement of December 1988 which offers fresh hope for peace in Southern Africa (see entry on Angola). At Lusaka both sides signed a cease-fire and South Africa undertook to withdraw its forces from Angola within a month, under the supervision of a joint Angolan-South African monitoring commission. The agreement did not work well; South Africa took over a year to withdraw, and a month after the withdrawal South African troops were captured on secret operations in *CABINDA (May 1985). In July 1985 the South Africans were still fighting *FAPLA forty kilometres inside Angola. Besides

the formal cease-fire there were unwritten agreements at Lusaka which meant progress towards peace in Angola and Namibia. Angola was prepared to accept the South African demand that the withdrawal of Cuban troops from Angola should be linked to Namibian independence and South Africa was prepared to accept *UN RESOLUTION 435 for the independence of Namibia – which finally happened in March 1990.

Luthuli (or Lutuli), Chief Albert (c.1898–1967), a black South African whose opposition to *APARTHEID attracted worldwide attention. His refusal to advocate violence, his dignity, his religious conviction and his faith in the righteousness of his people's cause earned him international respect. He was a teacher, a religious leader and a Zulu chief (1936–52). Chief Luthuli joined the *AFRICAN NATIONAL CONGRESS (ANC) in 1945. As President-General of the ANC from 1952 he was a very effective leader of a passive resistance campaign against unjust racial laws.

In 1952 the South African government stripped him of his chieftainship for his refusal to leave the ANC. They tried to silence him with detention (1956–7) and tried in vain to prove charges of treason and conspiracy. Despite official intimidation and violence he refused to be silenced and became a world figure who was awarded the Nobel Peace Prize (1960). His autobiography, *Let My People Go* (1962), was banned in South Africa but sold widely abroad. He died when he was hit by a train, under suspicious circumstances.

Luwero Triangle, area north of Kampala in Uganda. Its people strongly supported the National Resistance Movement in the fight against *OBOTE in the early 1980s. Obote's reprisals led to the massacre of an estimated third of the area's population of 750,000 and another third became refugees. President *MUSEVENI has gradually restored order and security there.

M

Machel, Samora Moises (1933–86), first President of Mozambique (1975–86). Educated by Catholics, he was a medical orderly in Maputo (then Lourenço Marques) until his life was changed by his meeting with Eduardo *MONDLANE (first President of *FRELIMO). He joined Frelimo, went to Algeria for military training (1963–4) and took command of the training camp in Tanzania. At the start of the ten-year struggle against Portuguese colonial rule Machel led 250 men into Mozambique (1964) and soon proved himself as an able commander. He became Frelimo's secretary for defence (1966), commander-in-chief (1968) and one of the ruling triumvirate (1969). As sole leader from 1970 he established his authority over the different factions and committed Frelimo to the cause of international socialism. With help from African and Soviet bloc states he built up an army of 20,000 experienced soldiers and by 1974 had won control of a third of Mozambique.

After the Portuguese dictatorship fell (1974) Machel, a guerrilla leader in the mould of Fidel Castro and Che Guevara, became President of Mozambique (Jun. 1975). A nationalist and a Marxist, he believed that as leader of a one-party state he could free his people from poverty and ignorance, but he had to face many difficulties. Ninety per cent of the population was illiterate, ten years of war had devastated the country and the abrupt departure of the Portuguese had left Mozambique woefully short of skilled and well educated people. Initially Machel tackled the problems as a Marxist-Leninist. He denounced the Catholic Church, capitalism and multinational companies; he took land, buildings, industries and businesses under state control.

Marxism-Leninism created more problems for Mozambique than it solved; so Machel began to change direction in 1980. To counter inefficiency, corruption and shortages he relaxed state control of the economy and allowed a measure of private enterprise. He weakened his commitment to Marxism and the Soviet bloc and to encourage faster development he began to look to capitalist countries for financial and technical aid.

Other difficulties beyond Machel's direct control caused grave problems. There were droughts, floods and famine. The nationalist struggle for independence in neighbouring Zimbabwe (then Rhodesia) led to the closure of the border between the two countries (1976) and caused great economic hardship. The efforts of the *RENAMO rebels caused (and still cause) much suffering and disruption of industry and agriculture. He demonstrated his pragmatism by negotiating the *NKOMATI ACCORD with South Africa (1984), but South Africa failed to keep its side of the bargain and continued its efforts to destabilize Machel's government. South African sources were talking about the imminent collapse of Machel's government when he died in a rather puzzling aeroplane crash in South Africa close to the border of Mozambique.

Machungo, Màrio da Graca, an economist, Prime Minister of Mozambique since 1986. During the independence war (1964–74) he was an undercover *FRELIMO agent in Maputo (then Lourenço Marques). Machungo was appointed Prime Minister to free President *MACHEL of his routine administrative burdens so that he could concentrate on military operations against *RENAMO. Machungo has continued as Prime Minister in President *CHISSANO's government.

Macias, Nguema Francisco (1922–79), first president of Equatorial Guinea. Macias was educated in mission schools before becoming a colonial civil servant in 1944. Always involved in local politics, he became president as a result of elections which were to be the last democratic event for ten years. Macias ordered all but one Spanish flag in the country to be pulled down and intimidated Spanish citizens. Then he turned on political opponents and had them tortured to death. He banned political parties but created his own party, the only one permitted to exist. He had himself declared life-president in 1972 and to strengthen his position he eliminated hundreds of politicians prominent in the pre-independence era. He frequently denounced supposed plots and conspiracies – by the Roman Catholic Church and the Spanish government among others – and executed still more people. He ordered members of his youth party, Juventud en Marcha con Marcias, to beat up members of the Nigerian diplomatic mission. Tension steadily mounted until July 1979 when some army officers planned a coup. Hearing of it, Marcias had all the conspirators executed. Less than a month later a successful coup removed him from office. He was tried for multiple murder and treason and executed on 29 September 1979. His rule had been one of the most cruel and maniacal in African history.

Madagascar Stretching 1500 km. from north to south, and covering an area of 587,041 sq. km. the great island of Madagascar lies off the coast of Mozambique. Larger than many mainland African countries, Madagascar has immense agricultural and mineral resources and most of the prerequisites necessary for prosperity.

Arabs, Malayans and Polynesians settled on the island in earlier centuries and European colonists did not arrive until the late nineteenth century. The French invaded Madagascar in 1895 and embarked on a typically French programme of exploitation. Many peasants were treated as little better than slaves in the various plantations and mines. While the French administrators succeeded in creating an intellectual elite, they could not eradicate the

The Democratic Republic of Madagascar

THE COUNTRY	THE PEOPLE	THE STATE
587,041 sq. km.	11.4 million	Presidential republic
Major Cities Antananarivo (capital) Toamasina, Belo, Taolanaro	*Ethnic Groups* 20 tribes, of which Sakalava are most widespread	*Head of State* Didier Ratsiraka *Ruling Body* Supreme
Economy Rice is the staple Coffee and vanilla are main crops on the east coast, cotton, sugar and beans on the west Some light industry	*Languages* Malagasy French *Religion* Christian 60% Islam 30% Traditional beliefs	Revolutionary Council (CSR) *Official Party* National Front for Defence of the Revolution
Principal Exports Coffee, vanilla, cloves, other spices		
Currency Malagasy franc of 100 centimes		

islanders' resentment of the colonial presence. The first major insurrection occurred in 1947–8, when the French army killed many thousands of people who had risen to demand political and economic rights.

Nevertheless, in 1960 France offered independence and the Malagasy Republic came into being with Philibert Tsirinana as its first president. Virtually a French puppet, Tsirinana permitted the French to remain dominant in banking, trade and marketing and in effect his government acted as broker for the French in Africa. French military and naval forces remained in Madagascar to guarantee the island's 'security'

and in May 1971 they helped the president to put down an uprising.

A year later unrest had become so widespread that the military, under General Gabriel Ramanatsoa, took control. Radical changes took place. The French were ordered to close their military bases, aid and trade agreements with France were revised to give Madagascar greater benefits, and Madagascar cut all links with South Africa, Israel and Taiwan. China, the Soviet Union and radical African nations, such as Kenya, became the most favoured partners. None of this brought internal peace and on 25 January 1975 Ramanatsoa dissolved parliament. His successor,

Colonel Richard Ratsimandrava, survived only two weeks before being assassinated on 11 February. The consequent crisis ended only when the Military Directorate voted into presidential power a junior naval officer, Lt.-Commander Didier Ratsirika.

Ratsirika appointed a Supreme Revolutionary Council (CSR) to exercise executive power and to aim for a totally socialist republic by AD 2000. A National Assembly of 137 elected members came into being in 1977. It is a peculiar institution, since all members must belong to the National Front for the Defence of the Revolution (FNDR), even if they represent opposition parties. The Assembly is a discussion and 'evaluation' chamber, with no power of veto over the CSR.

Also in 1977, Ratsirika brought in a system of what he termed 'progressive electoral responsibility'. This begins with the *fokontany*, the village political unit to which every elector must belong by law. The *fokontany* elects an executive committee which selects a president to sit on the *firaisam* or district council. In turn, it elects members of the *faritany* or regional council. This system is considered a form of socialist democracy.

In January 1978 a newly instituted Supreme Court was given the authority to decide constitutional matters and a policy of 'gradual revolution' was announced. In other ways the government was not so enlightened. For instance,

by giving priority to the development of coastal areas it aroused the hostility of inland regions.

In foreign affairs, Ratsirika showed great skill in developing ties with African states, with the West and with the old pre-1989 Soviet bloc. Officially, Madagascar is non-aligned but it supports all diplomatic action against South Africa. Throughout his presidency, Ratsirika has campaigned tirelessly to further Madagascar's claim to various small islands off the coast. Neither France nor other African states support the claim.

In common with other African presidents, Ratsirika has 'discovered' plots against him when he needs to strengthen his authority. In February 1980 it was 'Operation Mafy Ady' (or Hard Blow) and 'D6X80'. The first was intended to overthrow the government; the second planned his assassination. A year later he could not forestall riots over employment and the educational system.

In January 1982 Ratsirika announced the uncovering of another coup plot, reportedly masterminded by a sorcerer, a priest and some army officers. In November the following year, following yet another reported coup, thirty people were imprisoned.

Meanwhile, Monja Jaona, leader of the Madagascar National Independence Party (MONIMA) had been arrested, in 1980, as a serious opponent of the regime. Freed two years later, Jaona challenged Ratsirika in the presidential elections of November 1982. He received one million votes to Ratsirika's four million and complained that he could have won had the ballot not been rigged. When he called for a general strike he was dismissed from the CSR and arrested.

The most serious trouble in Madagascar's modern history were the Kung Fu riots – actually a small war – which began in December 1984. The 20,000 members of the King Fu sect practised the Chinese form of karate made popular by the late Bruce Lee. The sect was also political and religious and it opposed Ratsirika's policies. The leader of the cult and many of his followers were killed in a battle on 2 August 1985 when army commandos stormed their fortress headquarters.

The major event of 1986 was a plane crash in which the Minister of Defence, Rear-Admiral Guy Sabon, and other senior members of the defence establishment were killed. Following the crash, which could only be described as 'mysterious', Ratsirika's brother-in-law, Major-General Christopher Raveloson Mahasampo, was appointed Defence Minister.

The armed forces total less than 12,000 but the leaders have remarkable status and authority. Elitist and well trained, the military's primary function is to support the president and deter possible rivals from mounting a coup attempt. A much larger popular 'army' exists but it is not a military force in the accepted sense. Its task is to carry out projects connected with development and construction, such as roads, irrigation and land reclamation.

In line with Ratsirika's ultimate objective of a socialist economy, the state has taken control of much of the economy since 1975. Finance and banking are nationalized and the greater part of import and export trading is state-managed. Worker participation is mandatory on the boards of state-owned companies.

For many years, centralization of the economy and the inefficiency of state industries caused major problems. In 1980 Ratsirika asked France to cancel its debts and appealed to the IMF for help. As a result, the IMF has been in a position to insist on more liberalized trade, the end of rice subsidies and greater investment in agriculture. Some of the president's grandiose schemes were ended after IMF pressure. More realistically, the government is committed to a 'rice war programme' to make the country self-sufficient. The army and village task-forces are bringing large new areas under cultivation.

At the same time, the production of edible oils, cotton, coffee, sisal, bananas, vanilla and sugar is increasing. Even so, about 80 per cent of the Malagasy people are peasant farmers, existing at subsistence level. The government would like to redistribute the population, which is heavily concentrated along the river valleys and in the highlands.

Following IMF intervention, the 'Paris Club' meeting of official creditors rescheduled Madagascar's debts, which were originally due for repayment in 1986 and 1987. The new arrangement gives the country until 1997. Japan also agreed to reschedule its loan to Madagascar. The various creditors have urged the government to exploit its reserves of bauxite, coal, chromite, iron, graphite, mica and other minerals. Oil has been discovered in at least four separate fields but no major projection is expected until the mid-1990s. By then minerals generally should be helping to balance Madagascar's budget.

The country faces enormous problems, including a high birth rate. The Roman Catholic and Islamic leaders constantly urge their followers to have large families for their respective 'true faith'. The nation's future depends largely on the continuing stability of the Ratsirika administration. Despite the president's increasingly autocratic style, he has succeeded in giving the country hope for the future. Some of his appointments have been shrewd. For instance, in 1985 he gave the departments of industry and agriculture to ministers with technocratic backgrounds. Also, he created ministries of Population, Social Conditions, Youth and Sport and gave great status to the Ministry of Information.

Despite the many improvements to the standard of living, Madagascar's national life is punctuated with riots, generally over food shortages, rising prices and unemployment. Coups were attempted against President Ratsirika in July 1989 and May 1990.

The Maghreb, term for that part of north-west Africa covered by Tunisia, Libya, Algeria, Morocco and Mauritania. It includes two major geographical regions: the mountains and plateaux of the Atlas Mountains in the north and the Sahara deserts in the south. From about 1945 the word Maghreb took on a political dimension to encompass the countries comprising it. Despite the common French colonial heritage shared by four of them for more than a century, and Libya's experience first as an Italian colony and then as a British protectorate, the countries have been unable to create lasting political, economic, social or even racial links. Numerous bilateral and multilateral agreements have collapsed. The nationalists of Morocco, Algeria and Tunisia spoke of Maghreb unity during their independence struggles. In April 1958, at a meeting in Tangier, the three most important parties declared a 'United Maghreb' but it never came into being. The division between radicals (Algeria and Libya) and moderates (Tunisia and Morocco) accounts for much of the tension. In political terms, Mauritania is a newcomer and finds itself somewhere between the two groups. Border disputes have been numerous, notably between Morocco and Algeria, Morocco and Mauritania and between Tunisia and Libya. The four senior countries have meddled in the internal affairs of the others; Libya has been the most subversive.

Power rivalry, now almost traditional, between the leading states,

Algeria and Morocco, is not conducive to Maghreb unity. Dispute over the *WESTERN SAHARA has intensified enmity; Algeria and Libya support *POLISARIO while Morocco persists in its attempts to annex the territory. Earlier, Mauritania had tried to take over Western Sahara. A sudden unexpected union between Libya and Morocco agreed in 1984 was dead by 1985. However, in May 1988 Algeria and Morocco restored diplomatic relations after a twelve-year break. Algeria's major short-term motive was its desire to ensure the success of the Arab summit meeting held in June to discuss the Palestinian uprising in Israel's occupied territories. In the longer term, President *BENJEDID of Algeria wanted to further the cause of regional economic integration. There is much scope for the Algerian purchase of Moroccan consumer goods and for Algerian sales of gas to Morocco.

In November 1989, the five Maghreb states formed their own community, the Union du Maghreb Arabe (UMA). They took this step because the European Community (EC) had urged them to develop a credible working community. The UMA modelled itself on the EC in the hope of being able, as a block, to gain better access to EC markets. The key to the strength of the union is the dominant Algiers-Rabat axis but given the differences between Algeria's socialist government and Morocco's King Hassan any 'common policy' is unpredictable. Equally, there is a major difference of emphasis on regional goals between Libya, on the one hand, and Tunisia and Algeria on the other. However, Colonel *GADDAFI was co-operative at meetings in 1990. He views the EC-UMA process as a preliminary to restoring, at some time, ties with Britain.

The Maghreb's population is predicted to double in the next thirty years, but the average GNP of its member countries is only a tenth of that in the EC. Maghreb politicians say that without trade access to the EC the economy of the Maghreb cannot improve sufficiently to provide employment.

Mahfouz, Naguib (b. 1911), Egypt's leading novelist and revered in the Arab world as 'the scribe of the Nile'. Mahfouz was born in Gamalia, Cairo, and after an education in Koranic schools he studied philosophy at Cairo University. Since there were no professional openings in philosophy, in 1939 Mahfouz became a civil servant. That year his first novel, *A Game of Fates*, was published. His early works were historical novels modelled on those of Scott and Dumas, using an ancient Egyptian background in which to set themes of contemporary relevance. Greatly influenced by socialist thought, Mahfouz soon abandoned the historical setting, in 1945 replacing it with contemporary Cairo, which he portrays with relentless realism. *New Cairo* is a realistic dramatization of life in the city, while *Kernak* is a damning review of Egypt under President Nasser. For years, Nasser accused Mahfouz of attacking him, to which the novelist always replied that he was merely producing literature.

He made his name with *Big Trilogy*, completed in 1957. Critics compared its portrait of the city of Cairo with Charles Dickens' London and Emile Zola's Paris. The partly autobiographical narrative follows an Egyptian family from 1917 to 1944 through a series of historic, cultural and political upheavals. Under the Arab title *Al-thulathiya*, the trilogy is the best of all Arab epic-novel writing. *The Children of Our Quarter*, 1959, was denounced in the mosques as godless and profane, largely because a contemporary prophet in the novel was modelled on Muhammad. Mahfouz's later works plunge into the absurd, the abstruse and the symbolic, reflecting the hopelessness he felt after his nation's 1967 defeat by Israel. His work depicts insoluble dilemmas, with all his characters living in suffering and fear. Mahfouz believes that politics have been used to mislead the people and some of his books – *Mirrors*, (1972); *Heart of the Night*, (1975) – have become political documents.

Mahfouz became the undisputed master of a new school of literature with his invention of 'Nilotic' language, or the third language, a modern mixture of classical Arabic and colloquial Egyptian. His Egyptianism has earned him the wrath of Arab nationalists, who reject his 'delinquent' characters as unrepresentative. However, for most Egyptians Mahfouz enjoys a prestige which a fellow Cairo playwright, Ali Salim, described as 'approaching pharaohism'.

In 1989 Mahfouz was awarded the Nobel Prize for Literature, the first Arab to achieve this distinction. The Swedish Academy of Letters stated that Mahfouz had won the award for 'works rich in nuance, now clear-sightedly realistic, now evocatively ambiguous'. Mahfouz said, 'I dedicate this victory to the Egyptian people who are the real winners of the prize. It was they and my love for them that inspired me with the characters who make up the novels.' Soon after the announcement of the award, Islamic fundamentalists called for Mahfouz's execution. They alleged that his novel *Children of Gebelawi* put him on the same level of apostasy as Salman Rushdie, author of *The Satanic Verses*. *Children of Gebelawi* is a story based on the lives of the prophets as told in the Bible and the Koran. It first appeared in 1959 in serial form in al-Ahram, but has been banned in Egypt for many years because of its portrayal of God in human form. Because Mahfouz supported President Sadat's peace initiative with Israel in 1977 most Arab nations banned all his work. Nearly all his 33 novels and 13 short story collections illustrate a high level of preoccupation with social injustice and oppression in Egyptian society, yet he has never been affiliated with any political party.

Makeba, Miriam (b. 1932), South African singer who has come to represent the spirit of exiled black South Africans. Since she left South Africa

MALAWI

The Republic of Malawi

THE COUNTRY
118,484 sq. km.

Major Cities
Lilongwe (capital)
Blantyre
Limbe
Zomba

Economy
Farming

Principal Exports
Tobacco
Tea
Sugar
Groundnuts

Currency
Kwacha (K) of 100
tambala

THE PEOPLE
7,629,000

Ethnic Groups
Chewa
Yao
Chipoka
Tonga
Tumbuka
Ngonde

Languages
English (official)
Chichewa (official)

Religion
Christian
Islam
Traditional beliefs

THE STATE
Single-party republic

Head of State
President Banda

Ruling Bodies
Presidential Cabinet
National Assembly

Official Party
Malawi Congress Party

for the United States (1959) she has symbolized the repressed people of her country. Harry Belafonte worked to promote her career and she has not only sung in many parts of the world, but has also addressed the United Nations. For some years she lived in Guinea. Miriam Makeba has had a difficult personal life; she has been married five times – once to the black American activist, Stokeley Carmichael. Hugh *MASEKELA was another of her husbands.

Makerere University in Uganda is one of Africa's oldest educational institutions. Many distinguished Africans have studied there. It began as a technical school (1921) before becoming Makerere University College of the University of

East Africa (1963) and Uganda's national university (1970). Student demonstrations there were brutally crushed by President *AMIN in 1976. Currently the university has about seven thousand students.

Malan, Group Captain Adolph Gysbert 'Sailor' (1910–63), a white Afrikaans South African war hero who led protests against the removal of *COLOUREDS from the common voters' rolls. He founded the Torch Commando whose sixty thousand members later campaigned unsuccessfully against the republican constitution for South Africa (1960–1).

Malawi, formerly the Nyasaland Protectorate, the Republic of Malawi is a land-locked state occupying the

199

southern end of the Great Rift Valley. It is bordered by Tanzania on the north and east, Mozambique on the south-east, south and south-west and by Zambia on the west. Over one fifth of this long and narrow country is covered by Lake Malawi, which lies nearly 500 metres above sea level. On either side of the lake are plateaux from 760 to 1370 m. high; there are higher ranges up to 2440 m. in the north and 3050 m. in the south. Generally the climate is temperate. Malawi is one of Africa's most densely populated states – with six major *BANTU groups (Chewa, Yao, Chipoka, Tonga, Tumbuka and Ngonde).

There are large deposits of bauxite to be exploited, but otherwise Malawi lacks important mineral resources. It does, however, possess favourable conditions for agriculture: the soil is fertile and over half the land is suitable for cultivation. Ample supplies of water could be harnessed for irrigation and hydro-electric schemes. Over ninety per cent of the population work in agriculture either on smallholdings or on the estates which produce crops for exports – tobacco and tea are lucrative foreign currency earners. Coffee, cotton, groundnuts, rice and sugar are also exported. During the 1970s most commentators agreed that independent Malawi had one of Africa's most successful agricultural economies, which fed the rapidly growing population and accounted for ninety-five per cent of foreign earnings. By the 1980s it had become apparent that President

Banda's agricultural miracle ignored the problems of the poorest farmers who have only about an acre of land to support themselves and their families and who suffer high rates of infant mortality and malnutrition. In the mid-1980s Malawians had one of the lowest per capita incomes in the world.

There has been industrial development since independence, but this has had little effect on much of the population. Foreign investment in co-operation with the government-owned Malawi Development Corporation has been encouraged. New industrial products include refined sugar, flour, paper, textiles, clothing, footwear, cement, bricks, agricultural tools and locally assembled vehicles. Tourism is being boosted with the construction of hotels and the improvement of communications. The roads are being upgraded and air traffic is encouraged. Malawi's railway system is confined to the south of the country and is linked to the Mozambique ports of Beira and Nacala. There are plans for rail links with Zambia.

Little is known about Malawi's early history. Work by archaeologists has shown that northern Malawi was inhabited in the Stone Age and that the first Bantu arrived from the north about 2000 years ago. In the fifteenth and sixteenth centuries there was another wave of Bantu immigrants, referred to as the Marave or Malawi by Portuguese travellers early in the seventeenth century. In the nineteenth century the Ngoni and Yao invaded from the south and east; they captured local people and sold them to Arab and Portuguese slave traders.

Exploration by David Livingstone, and missionary activity from the middle of the nineteenth century on aroused Britain's interest in the area and in 1891 Britain declared the Nyasaland Protectorate (Britain's name for Malawi). As colonial rule was imposed settlers were encouraged to set up coffee plantations in the highlands and the Africans had to work on the plantations to earn money to pay taxes to the colonial authorities. The loss of land and economic grievances fuelled the short lived Chilembwe rising in 1915.

It was only after the Second World War that popular resentment expressed itself as a powerful nationalist movement. Two major factors were responsible for this. The colonial administration imposed strict regulations to compel peasant farmers to produce cash crops and Britain joined Nyasaland to Northern and Southern Rhodesia in the *CENTRAL AFRICAN FEDERATION (1953). The *NYASALAND AFRICAN CONGRESS (NAC), which began as a reformist movement in 1944, became the foremost nationalist body in the mid 1950s under the leadership of Henry *CHIPEMBERE and Kanyama *CHIUME. The NAC championed the peasants' cause and won substantial support in the rural areas. It led the protests against the federation which furthered the interests of white settlers.

In 1958 Chipembere and Chiume invited Dr *BANDA to return to lead the NAC in its struggle to break up the federation and to win independence. The authorities declared a state of emergency during which they banned the NAC (1959) and imprisoned Banda and other nationalist leaders (1959–60). The nationalists reorganized themselves as the *MALAWI CONGRESS PARTY (MCP) and continued their protests until Britain gave way. Banda was released in April 1960 and invited to talks in London. After the MCP's triumph in the 1961 elections, Malawi won self-government (Jan. 1963). The Central African Federation was dissolved at the end of 1963 and Malawi became independent under the leadership of Banda (Jul. 1964). It became a republic in July 1966.

Since independence Malawi has been dominated by Banda who is Life-President of Malawi and of the Malawi Congress Party, the only political party. He is also the Minister of External Affairs, Works and Supplies, Justice, and Agriculture. Banda has brought his country prosperity and stability and most Malawians revere him as the father of his people. Under Banda Malawi has rejected African socialism and encouraged private enterprise and investment from the west. Malawi's conservative policies have angered urban radicals, but there has been little effective opposition inside Malawi. Frequent cabinet reshuffles and the sudden disgrace of leading contenders for the succession have served to maintain Banda's authority over Malawi. Dick *MATENJE who was seen as a likely successor to Banda died under mysterious circumstances in 1983. Revolts by Chipembere and Yatuta Chisiza were crushed in 1964 and 1966. Orton and Vera *CHIRWA are imprisoned for life. The three best known opposition groups in exile have had little effect. In 1981 Orton Chirwa, who led the *MALAWI FREEDOM MOVEMENT, was kidnapped in Zambia; in 1983 Dr Attati Mpakati, leader of the Socialist League of Malawi, was assassinated in Zimbabwe. The country seems likely to remain under the rule of President Banda until he dies or is clearly incapacitated.

Malawi has infuriated its neighbours by establishing diplomatic relations with South Africa and receiving South African finance for the building of the new capital city at Lilongwe with its international airport. It gave no support to the nationalists who were fighting white rule in neighbouring Mozambique and Zimbabwe, and only recently have relations with these countries started to improve. During the 1980s southern Malawi suffered from the effects of the *RENAMO rebellion against the Mozambique government. Initially Malawians welcomed the guerrillas but Renamo activities have caused disruption in southern Malawi, including the severing of rail links to Mozambique's ports. Relations with Mozambique improved in 1986 when Malawi promised to stop supporting Renamo. Another serious problem has been the arrival of about 650,000 refugees from the

Mozambican troubles: with international aid Malawi is just about coping with the influx. Malawi's improving relations with its neighbours were further demonstrated in 1985 when it established diplomatic relations with Tanzania and Zambia for the first time.

In many ways Banda is Malawi and it is difficult to imagine the country without him. A possible successor is John *TEMBO who has been prominent in Malawian politics since before independence. He is certainly experienced and is thought to be able, but nobody can predict what will happen when Banda goes. Banda's Malawi had many problems during the late 1980s. The rapidly increasing population is struggling to feed itself. The balance of payments is deeply in the red and there is a critical shortage of foreign exchange. Inflation has risen and Malawi's economy has been disrupted by the activities of Renamo and the influx of refugees from Mozambique. Whoever follows Banda will be faced with massive problems and he (or she) will not be able to rely on the devotion and respect of the Malawian people which has supported President Banda.

Malawi Congress Party (MCP), since the establishment of the Republic (1966) Malawi's only legal political party. The Life-President of Malawi, Dr *BANDA, is also its Life-President. The party was founded in 1959 shortly after the imposition of the state of emergency and the banning of the *NYASALAND AFRICAN CONGRESS. Orton *CHIRWA acted as party president while Banda, its first leader, was detained (1959–60).

After his release from detention Banda led the party to triumph in Malawi's first universal suffrage elections in 1961. In subsequent elections (1964, 1971, 1976) all MCP candidates were personally chosen by Banda and returned unopposed. In 1964, Banda's domination of the party was challenged by radicals who were subsequently forced out of the party and into rebellion and exile. In 1974 all adult Malawians were ordered to join the party and the party hierarchy was given a higher rank than members of the government. In the 1978 and 1983 elections the MPC district committees were empowered to choose the three candidates in each constituency, subject to the approval of President Banda.

Malawi Freedom Movement (MAFREMO), left-wing Malawian group of exiles based in Tanzania and founded in 1977 by Orton *CHIRWA. MAFREMO's members are mostly Malawian refugees, but it also claims support in Malawi for its campaign to overthrow President *BANDA's government and to establish a socialist state. It has some support from the authorities in Mozambique, Tanzania and Zimbabwe. After its founder and first president, Orton *CHIRWA, was kidnapped from Zambia (1981), Edward *YAPWANTHA became the leader of the movement (1983).

Malecela, John William Samuel (b.1934), Tanzanian diplomat and politician, Prime Minister since November 1990; he entered the diplomatic service after studying at the Universities of Bombay and Cambridge. Malecela was Tanzania's Permanent Representative at the United Nations (1964–8) before holding a ministerial post in the *EAST AFRICAN COMMUNITY (1968–72). After serving as Minister of Foreign Affairs (1972–5) he held various other ministerial posts until his defeat in the National Assembly elections late in 1985. Malecela then joined the Commonwealth *EMINENT PERSONS GROUP (1985–6) which reported on progress towards ending *APARTHEID in South Africa and made recommendations to the Commonwealth over sanctions.

Mali, land-locked in West Africa, and one of the largest of West African countries, with an area of nearly three quarters of a million miles. Four fifths of Mali is desert or arid land and most of its population lives in the savannah of the south. Mali's seven contiguous neighbours are, clockwise, Algeria, Niger, Burkina Faso, Ivory Coast, Guinea, Senegal and Mauritania.

Before the discovery of the Americas, the ancient empire of Mali – which covered much of West Africa – was the centre of the world's gold trade. Throughout the thirteenth and fourteenth centuries, it controlled the southern trans-Saharan trade routes and Arab traders used its gold to finance the spread of Islam throughout the Middle East. Mali was a fine example of a stable kingdom, practising its traditional religion and living with its neighbours in relative peace. Then, like much of

The Republic of Mali

THE COUNTRY	THE PEOPLE	THE STATE
1,240,000 sq. km.	8.1 million	Single-party republic
Major Cities	*Ethnic Groups*	*Head of State*
Bamako (capital)	Bambara	General Moussa Traoré
Djenne	Dogon	
Mopti	Songhai	*Ruling Body*
Timbuktu	Malinke	Central Executive Bureau
Gao	Senoufo	
		Official Party
Economy	*Languages*	Union démocratique du
Main export crops are	French (official)	peuple Malien
cotton and groundnuts.	Bambara is most widely	
Subsistence farming rice,	spoken	
millet, sorghum.	Senoufo Sarakolle	
Extensive river fishing.	Tuareg	
Remittances from	Arabic	
Malians abroad		
	Religion	
Principal Exports	Islam 75%	
Cotton, groundnuts	Christianity	
	Traditional beliefs	
Currency		
Mali franc of 100		
centimes		

Africa, it took three massive blows from which it has never recovered. The first onslaught was the forced conversion to Islam. The second was the transatlantic slave trade and the third, European colonization, complete with imperial armies, missionaries and schools.

The French, who called the country Soudan, began to colonize it in the 1880s, though their conquest was not complete until 1916. Because the number of French administrators was small, France depended on the support of the 800 tribal chiefs. In 1946 the

nationalists began their campaign for independence with the establishment of the *RASSEMBLEMENT DÉMOCRATIQUE AFRICAIN. The first advance came in 1958 when the French granted autonomy within the French Community and sought to appease nationalist sentiment by renaming the country *République Soudainaise*. Reverting to the name of Mali, it became independent on 22 September 1960. During the regime of the first president, Modibo *KEITA, Mali came closer to bankruptcy and it remained poor after Lieutenant Moussa *TRAORÉ overthrew Keita and became head of state in 1968.

With so much desert or semi-desert, and with little exploitation of natural resources, Mali is the second poorest country in the *SAHEL region. About 10 per cent of the population lives a nomadic existence and 70 per cent of the labour force is engaged in agriculture and fishing, mostly at subsistence level. The main food crops are millet, sorghum and rice. The principal cash crop is cotton, which in an average year accounts for 40 per cent of foreign earnings. Mali's national budget of $200 million is smaller than that of the United States Library of Congress.

Economic activity is mainly confined to the area irrigated by the Niger River. Vulnerability to recurrent drought and declining external terms of trade led inevitably to large current account deficits. When the government showed itself willing to take corrective measures by embarking on a policy of economic liberalization and privatization, it received considerable amounts of aid from international organizations and donor countries. In November 1985 a seventeen-month loan of 22.9 million Senegal francs was agreed and the World Bank pledged US$55 million.

By 1986, the government appeared to have control of the economy, partly by following traditions left over from French colonial days and partly through its adoption of Socialist models. However, there were weaknesses. In an effort to encourage students to extend their education the government had guaranteed all university graduates a job in the civil service. As a result, by 1986 government agencies and nationalized firms employed more than 60 per cent of the nation's salaried workers. At the same time, the government was providing retirement benefits and credit guarantees to any civil servants who retired early to start their own businesses. Socially, this policy was laudable but the money was not available. In 1986 the government acknowledged that the state-controlled economy was not functioning efficiently.

This was very evident, since Mali was spending about $20 million a year more than it was raising in taxes and revenues. Often, it could not afford to pay civil servants' salaries, which consumed about 80 per cent of the budget. Foreign governments and the EEC urged Mali to pare down its bloated bureaucracy, control government spending and abolish or privatize some of its fifty-five state-owned companies. The IMF and World Bank insisted on privatization of state enterprises as a pre-condition for lending Mali $200 million to help repay its $1.7 billion foreign debt. Mali could not afford to ignore its Western donors. With a per capita income of $180 it was one of the world's three poorest countries.

By 1989, Mali seemed to have a more assured future, with the adoption of a national anti-desertification strategy, campaigns for tree-planting, land use management and prevention of brush-fires. The Chinese are developing a 'green-belt' plan to halt the advance of the Sahara desert. Irrigation schemes to be completed before 1998 should bring water to 67,000 acres of land. The World Bank, France and the Netherlands have boosted production in Mali's inefficient rice fields. Despite all foreign aid and all national effort, Mali's future is bleak because of the rapid increase in the birth-rate. With a population that is doubling itself every twenty-five years, Mali has lost the ability to feed itself.

Malloum, Brigadier-General Felix (b.1932), soldier and former President of Chad. After attending military schools in Brazzaville and France, he served in the French Army in Indo-China and Algeria. When Chad became independent (1960) he joined the Chad National Army and rose rapidly to become Commander-in-Chief of the Armed Forces by 1972. Malloum was detained by President *TOMBALBAYE in 1973 and released in 1975 by the leaders of the coup which had toppled Tombalbaye. Malloum became president of a supreme military council and head of the provisional government (1975–8). Under French pressure he agreed to form a government of national unity with Habré in 1978. Malloum was president and Habré was prime minister. There was considerable tension between the two leaders and their supporters. As the situation continued to deteriorate, Malloum was persuaded to resign and go into exile (1979).

Mammeri, Mouloud (b.1917), one of the greatest French-speaking Maghrebi writers. An Algerian, Mammeri's reputation is based on his first three novels, *La Colline Oubliée* (1952) which describes traditional Berber life in Kabylie; *Le Sommeil du Juste* (1955) – later published in English as *The Sleep of the Just*; and *L'Opium et le Baton* (1965). In 1983 he published *La Traversée*, his first novel to deal with an independent Algeria. Like many *KABYLES, Mammeri believed that the freedom for which they fought so hard would be shared equally by all Algerians, that the new Algeria would accommodate *BERBER culture and that there would be two languages in the new Algeria – Arabic and Berber. However, the question of the Berbers now having a cultural identity of their own is taboo in Algeria and this makes Mammeri bitter.

Mancham, Sir James Richard Marie (b.1939), former President of the Seychelles. He was called to the Bar in London (1961) and entered politics in the Seychelles, serving on the Legislative Council (1961) and founding the *SEYCHELLES DEMOCRATIC PARTY (SDP) in 1964. He was also a member of the Government Council (1967–70) and the Legislative Assembly (1970–5). After winning the 1970 election he became Chief Minister (1970–7). At first Mancham opposed independence and favoured an association with the United Kingdom which would have given the Seychelles a status like that of the Isle of Man. When Britain refused to accept association (1973), Mancham campaigned for independence.

Mancham's victory in the 1974 election was followed by a constitutional conference and his appointment as Prime Minister of a coalition government (1975–6). He led the Seychelles to independence as a republic in the Commonwealth and became President (1976). As President (1976–7) he favoured the West and capitalist values. His extravagant lifestyle, neglect of agriculture and industry and promotion of the Seychelles as a tourist centre and an international tax haven aroused much opposition. In 1977 he was ousted by Prime Minister *RENÉ. Now in exile in London, he writes, and acts as an international trade consultant. The *MOUVEMENT POUR LA RÉSISTANCE which attempted a coup (Nov. 1981) planned to reinstate Mancham, but it is not clear how deeply he was involved in the plot. When Mancham, who had been awarded an honorary knighthood at independence, took out British citizenship (1984) and became Sir James the Mouvement Pour la Résistance repudiated him.

Mandela, Nelson (b. 1918), widely known and respected black South African leader in the struggle against *APARTHEID. He is a member of a chiefly family and a lawyer. In 1944 he joined *SISULU, *TAMBO and others to form the youth wing of the *AFRICAN NATIONAL CONGRESS (ANC). As a member of the ANC executive during the 1950s he organized strikes and other non-violent protests against apartheid.

After the events of *SHARPEVILLE the ANC was banned and forced to operate clandestinely. Mandela went to Algeria for military training and took command of the ANC's military wing, *UMKONTO WE SIZWE, which began a campaign of sabotage and limited guerrilla action. Mandela's ability to evade capture until August 1962 earned him the nickname of the 'The Black Pimpernel'.

At the *RIVONIA TRIAL Mandela greatly impressed world opinion with a speech in which he declared his belief in a democratic and free society, an ideal for which he was prepared to die. At the end of the trial in 1964 he was sentenced to life imprisonment plus five years. He was imprisoned under harsh conditions on *ROBBEN ISLAND until his transfer to Pollsmoor Prison in 1982. After being treated for tuberculosis in 1988 he was housed in a warden's bungalow. Despite South African censorship Mandela was not forgotten. His wife, Winnie *MANDELA, did much to keep the fate of her husband in the public eye, nationally and internationally. During the long years of imprisonment the Mandela legend grew.

Many South Africans thought he was the man who would save them, and as pressure grew for his release in the late 1980s South African state officials and politicians began negotiating with him in prison. Although he refused to renounce violence the government released him in February 1990. For the first time in twenty-seven years his face was seen by the outside world. Since his release he has impressed many with his dignity and vigour. He has been made Deputy-President of the ANC; the President, Oliver *TAMBO, is seriously ill after a stroke. He has tried without success so far to resolve the conflict between the supporters of *INKATHA and the ANC. At the beginning of May 1990 he began negotiations with the South African government. If there is to be a democratic and non-racial South African state in the near future Mandela is the man most likely to become its leader.

Mandela, Winnie (b. 1934), a trained medical social worker who married Nelson *MANDELA in 1958. She was an active member of the *AFRICAN NATIONAL CONGRESS when it was banned in 1960. Despite repeated arrests, prison sentences and seventeen months of solitary confinement (1969–70), she continued to defy the South African authorities. She campaigned for the release of her husband and kept his memory alive during his long imprisonment. In 1977 she was banished from her *SOWETO home and confined to the small town of Brandfort, which she left after it was firebombed in 1985. She refused to obey the official order to return to Brandfort.

Although some of her supporters were unruly and violent and although some of her speeches, notably about necklace killings, were unwise, Winnie Mandela did much to boost the morale of black South Africans and to draw the attention of the world to their plight. After her

husband's release in February 1990 she retreated from the limelight, only to re-emerge in the scandal about the behaviour of her bodyguards – the so-called Mandela United Football Club. In September 1990 she was charged with assault and kidnap after the leader of her bodyguards was sentenced to death for the murder of a boy.

Mano River Union, agreed by Liberia and Sierra Leone in 1973 to establish an economic and customs union between the two countries. Guinea joined the union in 1980. In 1977 members adopted a common external tariff. The union has a training institute and an industrial development unit, and it has considered road links and a common hydro-electric scheme. One outcome of the union was the completion of a road linking Freetown and Monrovia.

Marema-Tlou Freedom Party, royalist political party in Lesotho, formed when the Marema-Tlou Party, led by Chief Matete, and the *BASUTOLAND FREEDOM PARTY merged (1963). Under the leadership of Seth Makotoko the party campaigned for independence and won four seats in the pre-independence election (1965). When the military seized power (Jan. 1986) it and all the other political parties were banned.

Margai, Sir Albert (1910–80), Prime Minister of Sierra Leone (1964–7). He qualified as a lawyer (1947) and entered politics as a founder of the *SIERRA LEONE PEOPLE'S PARTY (SLPP) and an elected member of the Legislative Council (1951). During the 1950s he held various ministerial posts until he quarrelled with Milton *MARGAI (his half-brother and leader of the SLPP). After a reconciliation he rejoined the SLPP (1960) and became Minister of Finance (1962).

In 1964 he succeeded Milton as Prime Minister and leader of the SLPP, but soon lost support and caused a crisis in 1966 with constitutional proposals which would probably have made Sierra Leone a one-party state. He narrowly lost the March 1967 election, but refused to step down when the Governor-General invited the opposition leader, Siaka *STEVENS, to form a government. The military seized power and Albert went into exile in London.

Margai, Sir Milton Augustus Striery (1895–1964), first Prime Minister of Sierra Leone. He was the first man from the Sierra Leone Protectorate to qualify as a doctor (1926). He worked for the Sierra Leone medical service (1928–50) and became politically active and influential after the Second World War as leader of the *SIERRA LEONE PEOPLE'S PARTY (SLPP). After success in the 1951 elections he held various ministerial posts and became Chief Minister (1954) and Prime Minister (1956). In 1961 he led Sierra Leone to independence in the Commonwealth. He was an honest and respected political leader who had the support of his own Mende people and the *CREOLES of Freetown. He encouraged economic expansion and educational development at a time when Sierra Leone was profiting from the expansion of diamond and iron ore exports. He died in office and was succeeded by his half-brother, Albert *MARGAI.

Masekela, Hugh (b.1939), South African musician, a trumpeter who has become internationally famous. During the 1950s he played in township bands. After the events of *SHARPEVILLE (1960) he went into exile and studied music in the United States. He was married to Miriam *MAKEBA.

Masire, Quett K. J. (b.1925), President of Botswana since 1980. As Sir Seretse *KHAMA's close associate and as a founder of the (then Bechuanaland) *BOTSWANA DEMOCRATIC PARTY (1962) Masire played a leading part in negotiations for independence. He served in the Bechuanaland Legislative Council (1962–6) and then in the National Assembly (1966–80). As Vice-President and Minister for Finance and Development (1966–80) his hard work and successful economic policies earned respect, but as a member of a minority tribal group he was politically vulnerable. He lost his seat in 1969, but returned to the National Assembly as an appointed member.

As Sir Seretse's health declined Masire took on many presidential duties. When Sir Seretse died the National Assembly chose Masire to succeed him in 1980. President Masire has followed the cautious and moderate policies of his predecessor and Botswana's wealth has continued to grow. Relations with South Africa have been strained by the help Botswana has given to the *AFRICAN NATIONAL CON-GRESS and South African forces have mounted raids on Botswana. President Masire has refused to sign a security pact with South Africa and strongly supports the *SOUTH-ERN AFRICAN DEVELOPMENT CO-ORDINATION CONFERENCE in its efforts to lessen the dependence of its members on South Africa. He has also had some success in improving relations with Zimbabwe, which had been strained by the presence of Zimbabwean dissidents in Bot-swana.

Matenje, Dick Tennyson (1929–83), Malawian politician who worked in education before entering parliament (1971) and holding various ministerial posts from 1972. In 1983 he was Secretary of the *MALAWI CONGRESS PARTY and Minister without Port-folio. He was apparently engaged in a struggle with John *TEMBO to estab-lish himself as President *BANDA's heir when he and three others disap-peared. Their death in a mysterious car crash was reported in May 1983, but there were rumours that they were shot while trying to leave the country.

Mau Mau, name given by the colonial authorities to the Kenyan guerrilla movement organized by the Kikuyu from 1947, they called themselves the Land and Freedom Army. With a long tradition of militancy and proud nationalism the Kikuyu were fighting for the return of their lands which had been taken by white settlers. The campaign comprised not only a savage attack on Europeans but also a civil war among the Kikuyu. The Europeans

suffered from the violence, but far less than those Kikuyu who refused to join the Mau Mau. About thir-teen thousand Kenyans and about a hundred Europeans died during the emergency.

The campaign which began in 1947 was a full scale insurrection by 1952 when the authorities declared a state of emergency, arresting and imprisoning *KENYATTA and other Kikuyu leaders on charges relating to the Mau Mau. Eighty thousand Kikuyu were detained in special camps for 're-education'. By 1956 British troop reinforcements had quelled much of the violence. The emergency had made Britain and some settlers aware of the need to make reforms. In 1957 Africans were directly elected to the Legislative Council. In 1961 the *KENYA AFRI-CAN NATIONAL UNION (KANU) won the elections and refused to take office until Kenyatta, their leader, was released from prison in August 1961. After the end of the emergency Kenya moved swiftly to independence (Dec. 1963).

Mauritania With a four hundred mile Atlantic coastline on the north-west of Africa, Mauritania is 600,000 miles of sandy waste and rocky plat-eaus. It has little water and only the southern strip receives enough rain to grow crops and sustain stock. The vast territory has five contigu-ous neighbours which are, clock-wise, Algeria, Mali, Senegal, West-ern Sahara and Morocco. Except for the Senegal River, which divides Mauritania from Senegal, all other borders are 'imaginary'.

The Islamic Republic of Mauritania

THE COUNTRY
1,030,700 sq. km.

Major Cities
Nouakchott (capital)
Nouadhibou

Economy
Iron ore provides 75% of Mauritania's foreign earnings.
Livestock raising and small plot agriculture.

Principal Export
Iron ore

Currency
Ougviya of 5 Khoums

THE PEOPLE
1.75 million

Ethnic Groups
Moors (or Maures) divided into the Bidan or 'white' Moors (55%) and Harattin 'black' Moors, descended from slaves.
Negroes (Toucouleurs, Sarakoles, Wolofs)
Peulh or Fulani, who are light-skinned nomads.

Languages
Arabic and French (official)
The Moors speak a Berber-Arabic dialect, Hassiniyya
The Negroes of the Senegal valley have their own languages

Religion
Malekite Muslims

THE STATE
Military dictatorship

Head of State
President and Prime Minister Colonel Sid'Ahmed Taya

Ruling Body
Military Committee of National Salvation and Safety

Centuries ago Mauritania was covered by jungle and grassland but the desert has advanced southwards, undermining animal life. At the same time, *BERBERS moved south from North Africa, driving the indigenous black population before them. These people managed to retain their own language and way of life but Moorish emirs held all political authority and economic control. In the late nineteenth century the French negotiated treaties with the emirs and then started the process of colonization. The territory of Mauritania was created in 1904 but was not fully part of the French West African empire until 1933 when the resilient Regueibat tribes were conquered. From 1920 the colony was administered from Saint-Louis, Senegal.

When the 'winds of change' swept Africa in the 1950s and 1960s the French were content to free Mauritania, which now gave them little profit. Morocco claimed Mauritania as a province but quickly abandoned this idea and the country achieved independence on 28 November 1960 as the Islamic

Republic of Mauritania. The capital, Nouakchott, was created on barren dunes 200 km. north of the Senegal River. The first ruler was Moktar Ould *DADDAH, leader of the only political party, the Mauritanian People's Party (MPP).

Throughout its early years most Arab nations refused to recognize Mauritania as a sovereign nation and Morocco did not recognize it until 1969. In 1975 Daddah took Mauritania into the *ARAB LEAGUE. In 1974 he nationalized the iron ore company. With Spanish sponsorship, in 1975, Mauritania and Morocco agreed to divide the former Spanish Sahara between them. The Saharan *POLISARIO Front Movement of the former colony claimed self-determination and made many attacks on Mauritania.

Ould Daddah invited Moroccan troops and French military advisers into Mauritania. His regime's incompetence and corruption prompted a coup led by Colonel Mustapha Ould Salek. Salek agreed a cease-fire with Polisario but could do nothing to bring about internal peace. He was replaced by Lt.-Col. Ahmed Ould Boucief, who was killed in an aircrash in May 1979. The regime's strong man, Lt.-Col. Muhammad Heydalla, assumed power, concluded a peace treaty with Polisario and agreed to hand over Mauritania's part of Spanish Sahara to Polisario. Morocco occupied the area and prevented the transfer from taking place. To resolve the internal north–south conflict, Heydalla announced a complex linguistic programme, playing down the importance of Arabic and recognizing the importance of the Negro languages. Colonel Ould *TAYA replaced Heydalla in a bloodless coup late in 1984. His administration has been widely praised for respecting human rights.

For iron ore to continue as the nation's basic foreign exchange earner the $500 million Arab-financed plan to exploit the deposits at Kedia d'Idjil must be successful. Nearly all Mauritania's 500,000 work-force are subsistence farmers, with millet, sorghum, rice, maize and dates the main crops. There are many nomads who herd cattle, camels and goats. The *SAHEL drought of the early 1970s was ruinous; cattle herds were halved and food production was down by 40 per cent. Mauritania has some of the world's richest fishing waters but it cannot defend them against exploitation by foreign fishing ships. Nevertheless fish exports equal iron ore as a revenue earner. Tourism may provide foreign currency but the industry is in its infancy.

A three-year 'structural adjustment programme', 1985–8, was successful and in November 1986 foreign donors pledged new project investment and balance of payments supports as well as substantial food aid.

Three-quarters of the Mauritanian people are Arab-Berber Moors and they fall into two distinct groups. The larger one comprises the Bidan or 'white' Moors, the other the Harattin or 'black' Moors, who are descended from slaves. Actually, all are the same colour; the division is along social lines, the Harattin being the 'inferior' group. About twenty per cent of the population is Negro. Nearly all Mauritanians are members of Islam's Malekite sect.

The disastrous Sahel drought wrought a great change in Mauritanian life. Before the drought about seventy-five per cent of all Mauritanians had been nomads. Fleeing from the privations brought on by the drought, most nomads moved to the urban centres, where they still live in great shanty towns. Few if any went back to a nomadic life when normal rainfall returned.

Mauritius, Small island lying 2000 km. off Africa's south-east coast. Beyond Madagascar and well into the Indian Ocean, it lies south of the monsoon belt but is nevertheless subject to oceanic storms. An island of coastal plains and a large central plateau, it supports a population of 1.1 million.

Britain captured Mauritius from France in 1810 and freed the slaves working on the sugar plantations. Indentured workers were then brought in from India. Political activity was non-existent until 1910 and even then it was nothing more serious than protests against the poor labour conditions. In 1936, with the establishment of the Labour Party, the island entered the modern age but no demand for independence was made until 1950.

The driving force behind the independence movement was Dr. Seewoosagur Ramgoolam, who

became prime minister on independence in 1968. Opposition to his rule mounted and culminated in the formation of the Mouvement Militant Mauricien (MMM) a left-wing party. In the 1976 general election it became the largest single party, forcing Ramgoolam, who by now had been knighted, to govern by coalition. His style was autocratic and idiosyncratic and in the 1982 elections the MMM won all sixty directly elected seats in parliament. The new prime minister, Aneerood Jugnauth, held MMM together for only a year, when dissidents broke away. Jugnauth, like Ramgoolam before him, was forced to govern by coalition but was comfortably in control in 1990.

Mauritius has never been revolutionary and the various elements of its racially mixed population live in amity. The so-called *population générale* is the basis of the population. In addition, there are people of European, Indian, Chinese, African and Arab descent. The Indians run the government, the Europeans big business and the Chinese the shops.

In the 1970s the island was dependent on a classically vulnerable commodity – sugar – whose price was being dragged down by world over-production. Instead of borrowing, the Mauritians set up an export-processing zone with generous tax incentives. Foreign investment came from South Africa, among other nations. By the early 1980s manufactured exports – such as cheap clothes, cut diamonds and

213

Mauritius

THE COUNTRY	THE PEOPLE	THE STATE
2,040 sq. km.	1.2 million	Constitutional monarchy
Major Cities	*Ethnic Groups*	*Head of State*
Port Louis (capital)	Indian	HM Queen Elizabeth II
Curepipe	Creole	(Sir Veerasamy Ringadoo
Mahébourg	Chinese	is the Governor-General)
Quatre Bornes	European	
Souillac		*Ruling Bodies*
	Languages	Council of Ministers
Economy	English (official)	Legislative Assembly
Sugar	French	
Tourism	Creole	*Party in Power*
Offshore enterprises	Bhojpuri	Coalition
		Aneerood Jugnauth is
Principal Exports	*Religion*	Prime Minister
Sugar	Hinduism	
Textiles	Islam	
	Christian	
Currency		
Mauritius rupee (Rs) of		
100 cents		

gum boots – were worth more than twice those of sugar. Between 1986 and 1990 the economy grew at the satisfactory rate of 5.7 per cent per annum.

Other African countries, envious of the island's prosperity, restricted Mauritian exports of clothing in 1989. To attract new capital for diversifying its industry, Mauritius set up a stock exchange. To encourage banking, it relaxed exchange controls and planned to abolish them by 1992. The objective was to draw in money frightened away from South Africa by the threat of further sanctions.

In October 1989, the Mauritian foreign minister made a fierce attack on South Africa in the United Nations, calling for severe sanctions. The Jugnauth administration was therefore embarrassed in January 1990 when it emerged that his government has made a secret trade agreement with South Africa. Jugnauth stated that he was unlikely to change course and that he intended to maintain the island's growth rate. His government has been consistently pragmatic. When South African Airways was banned from landing in Mauritius in October 1987, Air Mauritius filled the gap. It now flies to Sydney and Perth and serves South African passengers.

Sugar cane still covers 90 per cent of the cultivable land and employs

25 per cent of the work force. Agricultural diversification is in progress, especially with tea. Tourism, which is year-round, is the largest foreign exchange earner, with 165,000 tourists in 1989. The infrastructure necessary to attract and maintain tourism has required the creation of many jobs.

In the 1960s Mauritius had one of the largest birth-rates in the world and ruin from over-population was confidently predicted by several international demographic experts. The government introduced a birth-control campaign which has been remarkably successful and the birth-rate is no longer a problem.

In 1990, Mauritius had probably the fastest growing economy in Africa and the island was being compared to Hong Kong in its economic potential.

M'Ba, Leon (1902–67), the first President of Gabon (1961–7). Considered a troublemaker by the French authorities he was exiled from Gabon for thirteen years (1933–46). Back in Gabon he became a prominent politician as Mayor of Libreville, a member of the territorial assembly and the founder of the Bloc Démocratique Gabonais (BDG) in 1953. After winning the 1957 elections he became Prime Minister of Gabon (1958) and led the country to independence (1960). In 1961 he was elected president. Once in power M'Ba maintained close links with France. When he was deposed in a military coup (1964) French forces intervened to reinstate him as president. He died after a long illness and was succeeded by his deputy, vice-president ★BONGO.

Mbalax, percussion-based music which originated in Senegal. This popular form of music combines traditional with modern forms.

Mbeki, Govan Archibald Mvuyelwa (b.1910), leading black South African nationalist and campaigner against ★APARTHEID. He joined the ★AFRICAN NATIONAL CONGRESS (ANC) while he was studying at ★FORT HARE UNIVERSITY (1935). After graduating he taught until being dismissed for political activities. Then he combined his political career with various jobs in business and journalism. A close associate of Nelson ★MANDELA, Mbeki became National Chairman of the ANC (1956) and was detained during the ★SHARPEVILLE emergency (1960). Shortly afterwards he joined the South African Community Party (1961) only to be detained in solitary confinement (1961–2) and then put under house arrest.

Govan Mbeki went underground and jointed ★UMKONTO WE SIZWE's high command, but was arrested in 1963 and sentenced to life imprisonment for sabotage at the ★RIVONIA TRIAL (1964). Before his release late in 1987 he spent twenty-three years on ★ROBBEN ISLAND; it is thought the authorities released him to prepare the way for the release of Nelson Mandela. In prison he was awarded an honorary doctorate by the University of Amsterdam for his book, *South Africa: The Peasants' Revolt*. Shortly after his release he was placed under a ★BANNING ORDER. His son,

Thabo *MBEKI, is one of the most important and influential members of the ANC.

Mbeki, Thabo Mvuyelwa (b.1942), son of Govan *MBEKI. Thabo Mbeki is a leading representative of black South Africans in their campaign against *APARTHEID. As a schoolboy and a student he was an active member of the ANC in South Africa until 1962 when he left the country on the instructions of the ANC. After being arrested in Southern Rhodesia (now Zimbabwe) he was granted political asylum in Tanganyika (now Tanzania), before studying at the University of Sussex. In 1966 he was awarded an MA in Economics. For the next ten years he served the ANC in various parts of the world and joined its National Executive (1975). After just over a year as ANC representative in Nigeria (1976–8) he returned to headquarters in Lusaka to become the President's Political Secretary and in 1985 Director for Information.

He was one of the ANC leaders who met Afrikaner dissidents in Senegal in 1987, and is currently Director of International Affairs. In May 1990 he was part of the ANC delegation led by Nelson *MANDELA which had preliminary talks with President *DE KLERK and his team. An articulate and effective spokesman, Thabo Mbeki is regarded as a leading representative of the rising generation of ANC leaders – with an important role to play in South Africa in the future.

216

Mboya, Thomas Joseph (1930–69), a powerful and effective Kenyan political leader who was assassinated in Nairobi. He qualified as a sanitary inspector and became active in the trade union movement, serving as General Secretary of the Kenya Federation of Labour (1953–62). A leading nationalist politician, he became Secretary-General of the *KENYA AFRICAN NATIONAL UNION (1960). As Minister of Justice (1963–4) and Minister of Economic Planning and Development (1964–9) he was the most prominent Luo in a government dominated by Kikuyu. His assassination sparked off racial riots between Luo and Kikuyu and threatened the stability of President *KENYATTA's government.

Melilla, a Spanish enclave on the coast of Morocco. Like the enclave of *CEUTA, Melilla has been a Spanish possession and garrison city for more than four hundred years. Melilla has a Muslim population of 30,000, half of them illegal immigrants. When the Spanish administration tightened immigration rules in 1987 there was a noisy and unprecedented Muslim demonstration of protest. In 1988 Melilla's 'moors', as the local Christians disparagingly call their Moroccan neighbours, won several seats on the town council. 'At first they'll change our fiestas,' a Spanish councillor told European journalists, 'and then they will throw us out.' Whether or not this happens depends on the final outcome of talks between Spain and Britain on the future of Gibraltar. Should they reach an agreement in Spain's favour, the inhabitants of Melilla and Ceuta fear that King *HASSAN of Morocco will immediately demand Spain's last overseas possessions.

Mengistu, Colonel Haile Mariam (b.1937), Ethiopian soldier and head of state. Mengistu was educated at primary school and went straight from there to a military academy. Posted to a succession of infantry regiments, he was an obscure major when he became a member of the Armed Forces Co-ordinating Committee (the *DERGUE) which overthrew Emperor *HAILE SELASSIE in 1974. Mengistu was then found to have innate political skills. Ruthlessly eliminating his main rivals and critics, he became leader of the Executive Committee of the Dergue in February 1977. He was also chairman of the so-called Council of Ministers and, even more significantly, he was commander of the armed forces. Though only a lieutenant-colonel, as commander-in-chief he outranked all the generals. Only one man could stand in the way of Mengistu's rise to power, his second-in-command and friend Colonel Atnafu Abate. Mengistu had him executed in November 1977 for supposed 'collusion with a foreign power'. Mengistu was now declared Head of State and in effect was a dictator from the day he was sworn in.

Mengistu signed several agreements with the Soviet Union for economic and military assistance, thus ending earlier contacts with the Americans. With Soviet help, in April 1978 he stepped up the intensity of Ethiopia's campaign against the rebels of *ERITREA, *OGADEN and *TIGRE. Becoming friendly with Fidel Castro, Mengistu negotiated Cuban help for Ethiopia. Constantly seeking to strengthen his dictatorial control over every aspect of Ethiopian life, in September 1984 Mengistu founded the Workers' Party of Ethiopia (WPE) with himself as secretary-general. WPE's central committee had 200 members but Mengistu and his 'gang of four' held all power.

Under Mengistu's increasingly harsh rule, many Ethiopians fled the country. One of these men, the head of Ethiopia's Relief and Rehabilitation Commission, said on arrival in the United States that Mengistu had 'trampled underfoot all human values'. The most senior defector was the Ethiopian Foreign Minister, who denounced Mengistu's 'short-sighted and rigidly doctrinaire Marxist policies'. From 1987, Mengistu routinely executed army generals whom he considered to have failed in operations against the Eritrean and Tigrean guerrillas. He did this in the name of the People's Democratic Republic of Ethiopia, which was proclaimed on 12 September 1986.

Mengistu survived seven known assassination attempts between 1983 and January 1990. All observers in Addis Ababa predicted that this 'man without a friend' would be killed in an army coup but that this fate could be indefinitely delayed because of his policy of executing or imprisoning anybody he suspected of being an enemy.

mestiço, Portuguese word used to describe citizens and subjects of mixed African and Portuguese ancestry in Portugal's African colonies. Mestiços formed a high proportion of the *ASSIMILADO community. Many played a leading part in the struggles for independence from Portugal.

Micombero, Lieutenant-General Michel (1940–83), exiled President of Burundi. One of the dominant Tutsi minority, he studied at the Brussels Military Academy before returning to Burundi (1962). He impressed Mwami (King) *MWAMBUTSA IV, who made him Minister of Defence (1965). In July 1966 Mwambutsa IV was deposed and replaced by his son Mwami (King) *NTARE V. The new king made Micombero, who had helped him take the throne, prime minister; but the two men soon quarrelled. Micombero deposed Ntare V (Nov. 1966) and made himself President of the Republic of Burundi for ten troubled years (1966–76). His military government strengthened the Tutsi stranglehold on the country and purged Hutu from key posts in the army, the police and the administration. In 1972, a few months after Micombero formed a military junta to rule the country, the Hutu rebelled; the government responded with genocide. Estimates of the Hutu victims range from 80,000 to 250,000. In 1973–4 President

Micombero tried to strengthen his position by introducing constitutional change and making himself Prime Minister and Secretary-General of *UPRONA, the only legal political party. Overthrown (Nov. 1976) by Colonel Bagaza, he went to Somalia where he died.

Mixed Marriages Act (1949), one of the first *APARTHEID measures introduced by the *NATIONAL PARTY government of South Africa after its election victory in 1948; its full title is the Prohibition of Mixed Marriages Act. The act aimed to maintain 'the purity of the white race' by making marriages between whites and members of any other racial group illegal. It attracted much unfavourable publicity for South Africa and was repealed in 1985 when President P. W. *BOTHA was trying to give *APARTHEID a more humane image. The Conservative Party and other right-wingers in South Africa strongly opposed the repeal of the act. Mixed marriages are still discouraged in South Africa and the laws of apartheid make life very difficult for couples who do marry across the racial divide.

MNC (Mouvement National Congolais), radical nationalist movement in the *BELGIAN CONGO, founded and led by Patrice *LUMUMBA (1958–61). The only nationalist party which could claim nationwide support, the MNC was active in the agitation against Belgian rule (1958–9) which preceded independence. The MNC strongly favoured a unitary state to curb the tribal divisions in the country and the constitution which was drawn up asserted the unitary principle while allowing the provinces considerable powers.

After winning the pre-independence elections (May 1960) the MNC government under Prime Minister Lumumba led the country to independence (Jun. 1960). Two to three months later a dispute between President *KASAVUBU and Prime Minister Lumumba led to a constitutional stalemate; *MOBUTU staged a coup (Sep. 1960) and suspended all political activity. After Lumumba's murder (Jan. 1961), Antoine Gizenga tried and failed to establish an MNC government in the north-east (1961–2), claiming to be the only legitimate government in the country and gaining support from some African states. In the north in 1964 the MNC leader (Christopher Gbenye) was proclaimed President of the People's Republic of the Congo, but this government was soon crushed by the central government. The MNC is now an illegal opposition party operating in exile.

Mobutu Sese Seko, Marshal (b. 1930), President of Zaire since 1965, born Joseph-Desiré Mobutu in Gbadolite in Zaire (then the *BELGIAN CONGO), he served as a Sergeant-Major in the Accountancy Department (1949–56). He worked as a journalist and was one of the *MNC supporters who attended the pre-independence Round Table Conference in Brussels (1959–60). Lumumba chose him as Secretary of State for National Defence and

Chief of Staff. After the constitutional deadlock between President *KASAVUBU and Prime Minister *LUMUMBA, he staged his first army coup (Sep. 1960) and suspended all political activity for three months. When political activity resumed he serverd as Commander-in-Chief of the Congolese forces (1961–5) and distinguished himself in crushing the rebellions of 1964–5.

When there was a second constitutional deadlock Mobutu seized power again (Nov. 1965) and made himself head of state of the Second Republic with full executive powers. As ruler of Zaire, Mobutu has concentrated executive, legislative and administrative power in his hands. He founded the *MPR (Mouvement populaire de la révolution) in 1966 and made it the sole legal party (1967) and an instrument of his political power. In 1971 he proclaimed his doctrine of authenticity (renamed Mobutism in 1974); the Congo was renamed Zaire in 1971 and people were urged to adopt African-style names and culture.

Mobutu has been widely criticized for his ruthless suppression of opposition and for his lavish lifestyle. Critics say that he has made himself one of the richest men in the world, with a fortune of £3.2 billion. In 1988 Mobutu himself estimated his fortune at £33 million. It has been estimated that more is spent on the presidency than on schools, hospitals, roads and social services combined. Mobutu has spent millions of pounds turning his home village of Gbadolite into a modern

219

city with a magnificent presidential palace and an airport with a runway large enough to accommodate the Concorde he often leases from Air France. Despite his corruption and his abuse of human rights, Mobutu has powerful friends in the west who see him as a force for stability in central Africa, citing his role as mediator in 1989 in the Angolan civil war – even though the mediation failed to end the war. The United States has apparently been putting pressure on Mobutu to make reforms. After riots and protests, in May 1990 he announced a plan for a one-year transition to multi-party democracy.

Moi, Daniel Toroitich Arap (b.1924), President of Kenya since 1978. A member of the Kalenjin, he was educated by missionaries and worked as a teacher for twelve years (1945–57). He won a seat on the Legislative Council (1957) an attended constitutional talks in London (1960). Moi became assistant treasurer of the *KENYA AFRICAN NATIONAL UNION (KANU) in 1960, but resented Kikuyu and Luo domination of KANO and left to join the *KENYA AFRICAN DEMOCRATIC UNION (KADU) in 1961 – a body more representative of the ethnic minorities. As a member of KADU he served in the coalition government before independence as Minister of Education (1961–2) and Minister for Local Government (1962–3).

After independence KADU became the official opposition (1963–4). When KANU absorbed KADU, Moi joined President

*KENYATTA's government as Minister for Home Affairs (1964–7); he later became vice-president (1967–78) and one of Kenyatta's most trusted advisers. As Kenyatta aged, Moi had to fight off a number of Kikuyu attempts to debar him from the presidential succession. In the event his succession to the presidency in 1978 went smoothly; partly as a result of the support of *KIBAKI, who was to be Moi's vice-president (1978–88).

When Moi became President his release of political detainees, his relaxation of press controls and his campaign against corruption were well received, but he has made many enemies since. Radical opponents accuse him of failing to follow through his drive against corruption. They accuse him of an overly strong bias towards capitalism and the west. Despite paying lip-service to African socialism Moi believes that the private sector should lead economic growth and development; he has sold off public assets – starting with the Kenya Commercial Bank.

In 1982 President Moi made Kenya officially a one-party state and detained critics of this move. These actions were cited by the members of the air force who attempted a coup (1982). They particularly objected to the use of preventive detention to silence critics of the government. President Moi has acted firmly against *MWAKENYA, a shadowy radical group which has called for his overthrow. The mere possession of Mwakenya pamphlets has been punished with years of detention.

By 1987 Amnesty International was drawing attention to Moi's poor record of human rights, including detention without trial and the use of torture to make people confess to membership of Mwakenya. In July 1988 parliament gave him the power to dismiss judges at will – effectively ending the independence of the judiciary. He released the last political detainees in June 1989, but Amnesty was still concerned about more than sixty political prisoners convicted after unfair trials.

Moi has also dealt firmly with possible challengers to his power. In 1983 he suspended Charles *NJONJO, one of his most powerful ministers, from the cabinet and ordered an inquiry (1983–4) which found Njonjo guilty of plotting to overthrow the government. He pardoned Njonjo on the twenty-first anniversary of independence (Dec. 1984). For the March 1988 elections Moi introduced the controversial system of voting by queuing behind the chosen candidate – late in 1990 he indicated that this unpopular system would probably be scrapped. Candidates who won 70 per cent of the vote were elected; if no candidate won 70 per cent there was a secret ballot. Obviously this system of public voting led to intimidation. After the election President Moi demoted *KIBAKI from the Vice-Presidency (1988), and replaced him with Karanja, a political novice who was sacked in 1989 and replaced by Saitoti who had little political support of his own. Early in 1990 Robert Ouko, the Foreign Minister, was murdered; protestors have alleged that Moi's government was involved in this murder. In the middle of 1990 there were widespread riots, inspired by *MWAKENYA's call for armed insurrection against the government. President Moi has cracked down on protestors and refused to accede to the demands for a multi-party democracy, although he indicated there might be limited reforms.

Moi has also taken on the role of peacemaker in Sudan and Ethiopia. He has supported the efforts of Sudan's leaders to end the civil war in south Sudan. His officials have had talks with Eritrean rebels and he has had talks with *MENGISTU Haile Mariam, the Ethiopian leader. Despite the doubts about Moi's record on human rights and his refusal to tolerate opposition, Kenya under Moi remains one of the most prosperous and stable states in Africa.

Mokhehle, Ntsu (b.1918), veteran Lesotho politician, a radical socialist who admired *NKRUMAH. Influenced by the *AFRICAN NATIONAL CONGRESS (ANC), in 1952 he founded Lesotho's first modern political party – the Basutoland African Congress which was renamed the *BASOTHO CONGRESS PARTY (BCP). After doing well in the 1960 elections Mokhehle could not prevent factional strife in the party. In 1962 he broke with the ANC and sided with the *PAN-AFRICANIST CONGRESS.

After narrowly losing the pre-independence elections (1965) Mokhehle became leader of the opposition. He was close to victory

221

in the 1970 election when Chief *JONATHAN staged a coup and cancelled the election. Mokhehle was arrested and detained by Chief Jonathan (1970–1). When he was blamed for armed violence (1974) Mokhehle fled into exile in Zambia. In 1981 he formed the *LESOTHO LIBERATION ARMY to fight Chief Jonathan's government and was given some support by South Africa. The BCP and other parties were banned when the military seized power, but in 1988 Mokhehle flew to Maseru for negotiations. There was newspaper speculation that South Africa arranged this visit.

Momoh, Maj.-Gen. Joseph Saidu (b. 1937), President of Sierra Leone since January 1986 and Secretary-General of the *ALL PEOPLE'S CONGRESS (APC). After working as a civil servant (1955–8), he joined the West African Frontier Force (1958) and was rapidly promoted after independence to Captain (1965) and Major (1966). After the 1968 military coup which led to the restoration of civilian government he was detained for seven months, but then returned to the army and resumed his rapid rise to the top. He was made a Colonel (1970) and a Brigadier (1973).

President *STEVENS nominated Momoh for parliament (1974) and made him a cabinet minister (1978). He was made a major-general in 1983. When Stevens retired (Oct. 1985) Momoh was sole candidate for the succession and became President-Elect until his inauguration (Jan. 1986). Initially President Momoh was popular; there were high hopes that he would tackle corruption and economic inefficiency and bring Sierra Leone stability and prosperity. In over four years of power he has achieved little. There have been attempted coups, notably the March 1987 coup for which sixteen defendants were sentenced to death (Oct. 1987). Little progress has been made against corruption and economic mismanagement. President Momoh's attempts to impose financial discipline have provoked riots and general violence. Late in 1987 President Momoh declared an economic state of emergency to curb the activities of smugglers and hoarders, but by the end of the 1980s he was clearly unwilling and unable to implement the austerity demanded by the IMF to put Sierra Leone on the road to economic recovery.

Mondlane, Dr Eduardo (1920–69), leading Mozambican nationalist, founder of *FRELIMO. As a student in Mozambique he ran foul of the Portuguese authorities. In Portugal from 1950 he made friends with Agostinho *NETO, Amilcar *CABRAL and other African nationalists from Portuguese colonies. In the United States Mondlane continued his studies, lectured, and worked for the United Nations (1957–61). After a brief visit to Mozambique he returned to Africa and devoted himself to the struggle for his country's independence.

Mondlane played an important part in the formation of Frelimo (1962) and became its first President (1962–9). He launched the war of independence (1964). With international help Frelimo was making gains in the war by early 1969 when Mondlane was assassinated by a bomb at his home in Tanzania. Many sources blame *PIDE, the Portuguese secret police, for his murder; but others argued that he was killed by fellow nationalists angered at Mondlane's refusal to align Frelimo with revolutionary socialism.

Monrovia bloc (1961–3), an early attempt at co-operation by non-socialist African states. Partly to counter the activities of the *CASABLANCA BLOC, representatives of nineteen African states met at Monrovia in May 1961 and at Lagos in January 1962. Tunisia attended only the Monrovia conference and Zaire only the Lagos conference. The bloc set up a secretariat, provided for financial co-operation and drafted a charter. The Monrovia block was superseded by the *ORGANIZATION OF AFRICAN UNITY in 1963.

Morena (Mouvement de redressement national), Gabonese opposition movement which is now based in Paris. It was founded in 1981 to campaign for a multi-party democracy in Gabon and has accused President *BONGO of corruption and extravagance. Although MORENA is committed to peaceful protests its members have been arrested, detained and tortured. In 1982 several of its leaders were sentenced to twenty years hard labour for crimes against state security. In 1985 MORENA formed a government in exile in Paris, but quarrels in the leadership have weakened its effectiveness.

Morocco, situated on the northwest corner of the African continent, is unique among African countries, since it faces both the Mediterranean and the Atlantic. In its 260,000 square miles it has fertile coastal plains, rugged mountains and high plateaux, and in the interior, large tracts of Saharan desert. Of all the Arab countries of Africa, Morocco has the highest rainfall and thus possesses well-developed river systems that support irrigation in the drier areas.

The intensity and complexity of Morocco's political, racial and cultural background is rarely rivalled anywhere in the world. The early Phoenicians, Romans, Byzantines, Vandals, Muslim Arabs, Spaniards, English and Portuguese were lastly followed by the French. *BERBERS of various tribes – Almohads, Almoravids, Alouites, Riffs – fought for internal supremacy and some of them reached out, in war and in trade, to Sicily and Spain. The ruler who laid the foundations of modern Morocco was the Alouite Moulay Ismael (1672–1727) who pacified the warring tribes, ejected the Portuguese and English, reduced Spanish possessions to the enclaves of *CEUTA and *MELILLA and, in Algeria, blocked the Ottoman Empire from spreading west into Morocco.

In the nineteenth century European traders, explorers and settlers came to Morocco in waves. Spain acquired a protectorate over much of the north while France occupied the

The Kingdom of Morocco

THE COUNTRY
447,000 sq. km.

Major Cities
Rabat (capital)
Casablanca
Meknes
Fez
Tangier
Agadir
Marrakesh

Economy
Phosphates and
derivatives (42%)
Citrus fruits (7%)
Tourism (2.5m visitors in
1986 and rising)

Principal Export
Phosphates

Currency
Dirham of 100 centimes

THE PEOPLE
24.3 million

Ethnic Groups
Moors (Moroccans)
Berbers

Languages
Arabic (official)
French widely used
Large Berber-speaking
minority
English and Spanish are
still spoken

Religion
Predominantly Islam
Christianity
Judaism

THE STATE
Executive monarchy

Head of State
King Hassan II

Ruling Body
Ministerial administration,
appointed by the king.

Legislative Assembly
Elected, 306 seats,
dominated by
centre-right.

---

centre and south. The Moors, influenced by their Islamic faith, reacted to the dismemberment of their country by creating nationalist movements. Neither nationalism nor the spiritual revival which accompanied it made any progress under the oppressive pro-German Vichy regime which ruled Morocco during the earlier part of the Second World War. The Anglo-American landings in 1942 and the end of Vichy domination brought repressed nationalism into the open with renewed vigour.

The focus of the revival was Muhammad V of the Alouite dynasty. Exiled by France and then recalled in the face of great unrest, he took the country to independence in 1956. On his death in 1961, *HASSAN II came to the throne. Hassan has had to contend with diverse political, religious, economic and external influences. Opposing him initially were a radical left and a radical right. The Left's Ben Barka seriously challenged him in the early 1960s until assassinated in Paris in 1965. In June 1971 Hassan survived a palace revolt and in 1972 a coup led by army officers. To win popularity the king introduced nationalist policies which culminated in the take-over of the northern half of the former Spanish colony of *WESTERN SAHARA in 1976.

This annexation gave Hassan internal prestige but *POLISARIO reacted to the Moroccan seizure with guerrilla warfare. The unceasing war has led to strained relations with *ALGERIA, which supports Polisario. The expense of the conflict and the enormous amounts of money spent on the development of that part of Western Sahara formerly under Spanish sway puts great pressure on a weak economy. Agricultural production and employment opportunities have failed to keep pace with the rising population. Morocco has two-thirds of the world's deposits of phosphates, even without the reserves in the annexed Western Sahara. It is also the largest exporter of the mineral, which accounts for 42 per cent of merchandise export revenues. Industrial development is concentrated in light industry: Morocco is almost self-sufficient in textiles, cans much of its own fruit and has car assembly plants. Commercial links with the European Community are particularly strong, with the EC taking 60% of the country's exports and providing around 50% of its imports.

Income from tourism is vital in countering the constantly large trade-deficit. Large-scale tourist developments should boost still further the already buoyant industry. The main centres are Agadir, Casablanca, Fez, Marrakesh, Meknes, Rabat and Tangier; the Mediterranean area has an excellent road network. The spine of the country is the High Atlas mountain range. Between this barrier and the Atlantic are the fertile plains which nurture Morocco's urban heartland.

The constitution confers wide powers on the king who appoints the prime minister and cabinet and has the right to dismiss the legislative assembly. Elections to the 306-member legislature take place every six years, two-thirds being chosen by direct elections and the remainder through a system of elections by community leaders. The assembly is dominated by centre-right parties although there is considerable minority representation of socialist groups. In 1984 King Hassan II and Colonel *GADDAFI signed a Libya–Morocco treaty of friendship. This was based on Morocco's political and diplomatic support for Libya in return for Libya cutting off military aid to Polisario. The accord lasted less than two years; Hassan abrogated it in 1986.

Despite Morocco's fertile soil, varied climate and great mineral resources, the vast majority of the population lives in poverty. This is partly because the big estates owned by rich landowners have not been broken up. Most of the peasants have only subsistence holdings; the main crops are wheat, barley, maize, citrus fruits and olives. Morocco's drive to attract substantial foreign investment and project finance for the Five-Year Plan 1988–82 was not successful. The funds were needed to help Morocco attain self-sufficiency in food by expanding

225

dam-building and irrigation, and to finance new public-sector projects. The Moroccan application, in July 1988, to join the European Community was an effort to put public pressure on the EC to grant greater concessions for trading activities in Western Europe. Morocco sought more compensatory financial aid following the loss of trade after the adhesion of Spain and Portugal – two of Morocco's traditional export rivals – to the EC. With a population of more than twenty-four million in 1990, Morocco is a substantial consumer and food market – the second largest in the Arab world after Egypt.

The nation's location gives it great strategic importance. The US has military airfield landing rights in the country. The king's pragmatism and relatively independent policy regarding Israel was evidenced by his welcome of the Israeli Prime Minister in 1986. Morocco's current stability is threatened by *ISLAMIC FUNDAMENTALISM which is constantly inflamed by mullahs and agitators from Iran, Libya and Saudi Arabia. The fundamentalists claim that monarchies should not exist in Islam but foreign observers can see that Morocco could fall into anarchy if the king were to be assassinated. Despite his connivance in human rights abuses – Amnesty International accuses Morocco of false imprisonment and torture – King Hassan II has a steadying hand on Morocco's innate turbulence.

Moshi Conference, meeting at Moshi in Tanzania of Ugandan

exiles (Mar. 1979). Despite their differences the exiles were united in their determination to oust President *AMIN. They formed the *UGANDA NATIONAL LIBERATION FRONT which fought alongside the Tanzanian army to overthrow Amin. Professor *LULE was chosen as their leader; he was a compromise candidate acceptable to both the supporters and the opponents of *OBOTE. They drew up a timetable for the restoration of democracy to their homeland.

Moshoeshoe II (b. 1938), King of Lesotho, descendant of Moshoeshoe I who founded the *BASOTHO nation. He was christened Constantine Bereng Seeiso and educated in Britain. After his father died (1940) his stepmother became regent. She was reluctant to give up the regency, but the young king finally assumed power as Paramount Chief Moshoeshoe II in 1960.

At independence (1966) he became King of Lesotho, but soon clashed with Chief *JONATHAN – the Prime Minister of Lesotho. After a bitter struggle the king had to renounce political power and accept a purely ceremonial role at the beginning of 1967. He clashed with Chief Jonathan again over the January 1970 coup and went into exile for nearly a year. After seizing power (Jan. 1986) Major-General *LEKHANYA restored some of the monarch's powers, but these could only be exercised on the advice of the Military Council. In February 1990 the king was stripped of his powers, and in March 1990 he went into exile in Britain. In November 1990 the military government announced the deposition of the king and swore in his son, Letsie III as his successor.

Mouvement pour la Résistance, right-wing group of exiles opposed to President *RENÉ of the Seychelles. With the backing of South African mercenaries, Arab financiers and dispossessed Seychellois planters, it came close to success in its plans to overthrow René and to reinstate ex-President *MANCHAM in the abortive coup of November 1981. In 1984 it repudiated Mancham, who had taken out British citizenship, and reorganized itself as the Seychelles National Movement, which planned to concentrate more on clandestine activities. Its leader, Gerard *HOARAU, was assassinated in London in 1985 – possibly at the orders of President René.

Moyo, Jason Ziyapaya (1927–77), Zimbabwean nationalist leader, assassinated and now buried in *HEROES' ACRE. He was an active trade unionist, a prominent member of the *AFRICAN NATIONAL CONGRESS and the leader of *ZAPU while Joshua *NKOMO was in detention (1963–74). He strongly advocated reconciliation between the two main nationalist groups – ZAPU and *ZANU.

Mozambique, The People's Republic of, is situated south of the Equator on the east coast of Africa. It is bordered by South Africa and Swaziland on the south, Zimbabwe, Malawi and Zambia on the west, Tanzania on the north and the Indian Ocean on the east. Much of the country is covered by a broad coastal plain rising to a moderately high plateau, but there are mountainous regions in western Mozambique. The country has many rivers, including the Zambezi on which the Cabora Bassa dam and hydroelectric scheme is situated. Mozambique is strategically very important in providing access to the sea for land-locked members of the *SOUTHERN AFRICAN DEVELOPMENT CO-ORDINATION CONFERENCE, who are keen to use Mozambican ports and lessen their dependence on South African transport links. There are rail links from Botswana to Beira, Malawi to Beira and Nacala, Swaziland to Maputo, Zambia to Beira and from Zimbabwe to Beira and Maputo. There is also a railway to South Africa.

Mozambique's inhabitants come from a variety of different *BANTU groups. The most numerous are the Makua-Lomwe at about 40 per cent of the population; other groups include the Thonga, Chopi, Tonga, Shona, Nyanja, Chewa, Makonde and the Swahili speakers on the coast. Mozambique has deposits of coal, iron and rare metals. Except for coal these still have to be exploited on a large scale. About 90 per cent of the population works on the land, and the country relies on fishing and agriculture for its foreign currency earnings. Among its principal exports are seafood, cashew nuts, tea, cotton and sugar. Cassava,

The People's Republic of Mozambique

THE COUNTRY	THE PEOPLE	THE STATE
799,830 sq. km.	14,591,000	Single-party republic
Major Cities	*Ethnic Groups*	*Head of State*
Maputo (capital)	Makua	President Chissano
Nampula	Yao	
Beira	Makonde	*Ruling Bodies*
Quelimane	Nyanja	Council of Ministers
	Chewa	People's Assembly
Economy		
Farming	*Languages*	*Official Party*
Fishing	Portuguese (official)	Frelimo
	Makua-Lomwe	
Principal Exports		
Seafood	*Religion*	
Cashew nuts	Traditional beliefs	
Sugar	Christian	
Petroleum	Islam	
Citrus		
Currency		
Metical (MT) of 100		
centavos		

maize, rice, potatoes and fruit are also grown.

Before the systematic imposition of colonial rule early in the twentieth century Mozambique was under varying degrees of Portuguese influence for 500 years. Its people and its resources were exploited for the benefit of Portugal. The peasants were forced to grow cash crops either on their own smallholdings or on plantations owned by Europeans. The vast majority of the population was subjected to forced labour and denied the rights of citizenship, which were granted to less than one per cent – the *ASSIMILADOS. In 1951 Mozambique became an overseas province of Portugal with the right to send deputies to Lisbon, but only assimilados could vote.

The first landmark in the struggle for independence was Eduardo *MONDLANE's success in persuading various nationalist groups to combine to form *FRELIMO (1962), the first effective opposition to Portuguese rule. Helped by radical African and Arab states and by the Soviet bloc Frelimo launched the ten year war of independence (1964–74) with Samora *MACHEL's invasion of Mozambique from Tanzania with a force of 250 men. Frelimo was making gains in the war by 1969, when Mondlane was assassinated. Machel,

Frelimo's new leader, and Marcelino *DOS SANTOS were increasingly successful and had gained control of a third of Mozambique by 1974, despite the presence of 60,000 Portuguese troops in the country. After the overthrow of the Salazar dictatorship in Portugal itself (1974) the new Portuguese leaders negotiated the independence of Mozambique despite protests from white settlers.

On 25 June 1975 Mozambique became an independent republic led by Frelimo and President Machel. It became a one-party state with the People's Assembly as its supreme body. The serious problems Mozambique has faced since independence have derived both from factors beyond its control and from an excessively rigid application of socialist dogma. At independence most Portuguese left hurriedly; Mozambique was woefully short of educated and skilled people. Ninety per cent of the population was illiterate and there were hardly any administrators, officials, managers, technicians, artisans or shopkeepers. President Machel was determined to overcome these difficulties and rescue his people from poverty and ignorance by creating a modern industrial and socialist state after the East European model. The government had some success in improving social services with the building of rural schools and health centres, but its attempts to control the country's economy led to disaster. It took over shops and businesses and set up large collective farms and

factories which were plagued by a lack of capital, and by corruption and inefficiency. The failure of the socialist economy led to declining output, shortages, a loss of foreign currency earnings and an adverse balance of trade. In 1988 total economic output was about a quarter of what it had been in Mozambique before independence.

The blame for the economic collapse cannot be solely attributed to the government. The fall in world sugar prices and the reduction of earnings by Mozambicans in South Africa caused problems; as did the imposition of sanctions against the white minority Rhodesian regime (1976). The closure of the border with Rhodesia disrupted the Mozambican economy and deprived its railways and ports of lucrative earnings from Rhodesian traffic. Exceptionally severe droughts compounded the misery and starvation.

South African attempts to destabilize Mozambique caused further suffering. South Africa has mounted raids deep into Mozambique to attack exiled supporters of the *AFRICAN NATIONAL CONGRESS and it has supported the activities of the *RENAMO rebels who have plunged the country into civil war for fifteen years. Renamo has sabotaged vital transport links and other utilities, terrorized large areas, destroyed agriculture, brought the threat of starvation to over three million Mozambicans and driven up to a million refugees into neighbouring countries.

229

MOZAMBIQUE

Faced with these problems the government of Mozambique relaxed its doctrinaire socialism and adopted more pragmatic policies in the early 1980s. Action was taken against corruption, state controls over the economy were slackened, trade unions were allowed and food rationing was instituted. Mozambique distanced itself from the Soviet bloc and began to look to the west for capital and technical and military aid.

Mozambique tried to lessen its dependence on South Africa by joining other southern African states in the Southern African Development Co-ordination Conference (1980). South Africa then increased its economic and military pressure on Mozambique. President Machel accepted the need to negotiate the *NKOMATI ACCORD, a non-aggression pact with South Africa, in 1984 and agreed to supply South Africa with power from Cabora Bassa. South Africa continued to put pressure on Mozambique. It did not honour its Nkomati Accord pledge to stop helping Renamo and in 1986 tightened the economic screws by ending the recruitment of Mozambican miners. At the time of President Machel's death (Oct. 1986) South African sources were talking of the imminent collapse of Mozambique.

President *CHISSANO has continued to adopt a more pragmatic and liberal approach and to look to the capitalist west for aid. In 1987 Chissano implemented austerity measures recommended by the IMF; these included a 40 per cent devaluation of the currency and a cut in government spending. At the fifth Frelimo Congress in July 1989 the party officially dropped Marxist-Leninist principles and moved further towards a free-market economy. Foreign policy is now officially based on national interests rather than on those of the international working classes. Mozambique has continued to negotiate with South Africa over security and Cabora Bassa, and has had some success in persuading Pretoria to distance itself from Renamo. President Chissano has indicated his desire to negotiate an end to the civil war and in 1989 Renamo responsed by allowing the railway line from Malawi to the Mozambican port of Nacala to stay open, but the civil war continued into 1990.

Reforms in the army led to improved security in central Mozambique and some progress against Renamo, but there was a setback in 1987 when conservative United States groups dissuaded President Reagan from helping the government of Mozambique in the civil war. As the 1980s ended the country's situation was desperate. In 1989 the Population Crisis Committee in Washington concluded that Mozambique was the unhappiest nation on earth. This conclusion was supported by figures on infant mortality, life expectancy, medical care, drinkable water, diet and public safety.

Late in 1990, Frelimo and parliament announced that a multi-party democracy would be introduced and that there would be presidential and parliamentary elections in 1991. Renamo was invited to register as a political party, provided that it laid down its arms. Renamo's initial reaction was to refuse a cease-fire.

MPC (Multi-Party Conference), Namibian group of seven ethnic political parties established in 1983 with South African backing. The largest party was the *DTA, a coalition of ten ethnic groups. Six smaller parties represented the mixed race *COLOUREDS, the *BASTERS, the Hereros, the Ovambos in *SWAPO-D, the Afrikaners of the *NATIONAL PARTY and the Damaras who withdrew in 1984. The MPC drew up proposals for an interim government. When South Africa established the *TRANSITIONAL GOVERNMENT of national unity the MPC took office (Jun. 1985). The MPC government had little popular support and was plagued by divisions. It came into conflict with South Africa over its proposals to abolish the remnants of *APARTHEID and was already a spent force when the transition to independence under UN supervision began in 1989.

Mphahlele, Es'kia (Ezekiel) (b. 1919), South African writer of novels, short stories, essays and memoirs. He was a teacher until the *BANTU EDUCATION ACT was passed and then worked as a journalist before going into exile for twenty years (1957–77) in Nigeria, France, Kenya, the United States and Zambia. On returning to South Africa he worked as a schools inspector in the Lebowa *HOMELAND before joining the faculty of Witwatersrand University (1979), where he researches oral tradition. He has written novels about the frustration of the urban African unable to enjoy his fair share of the rewards of western industrial society. His other work includes *Chirundu*, a novel about independent Zambia, and several autobiographical pieces.

MPLA (Movimento Popular de Libertaçao de Angola), Angola's only legal party, it is a Marxist-Leninist party which played a leading part in the struggle for independence. The MPLA was founded in secret in Luanda (Dec. 1956) when Agostinho *NETO, its first recognized leader, was in prison. Mário *PINTO DE ANDRADE became leader (1960–2). The MPLA inspired the Luanda rising (1961) which was ruthlessly suppressed by the Portuguese authorities. Some leaders escaped into exile and regrouped in Kinshasa where the first national conference (1962) elected Neto to replace Pinto de Andrade as President. Neto organized and led *FAPLA (the military wing of the MPLA) in its struggle for the independence of Angola. At the same time the MPLA was campaigning for support abroad and for recognition as the legitimate representative of the Angolan people; it was particularly successful in the Soviet bloc.

Unlike its rival nationalist movements (*FNLA and *UNITA) the MPLA aimed to represent all Angolans whatever their ethnic background. It looked for support from both rural and urban areas and welcomed white and

*MESTIÇO supporters. It sought to unite members in the armed struggle for a democratic non-racial state, but Neto had to face radical challenges and factionalism in the movement. The *ACTIVE REVOLT and the *ALVES coup were serious threats to the MPLA leadership. In 1975 the MPLA was one of the participants in the short-lived transitional government (1975); it proclaimed the independence of Angola (Nov. 1975) and declared itself the sole legitimate representative of the Angolan people. Neto, the MPLA president, became President of the People's Republic of Angola.

Since independence the MPLA has defeated the FNLA and has fought a long civil war against UNITA and its South African backers. It has succeeded in gaining diplomatic recognition from most of the world's major powers – with the notable exception of the USA. Within Angola President Neto and his successor President *DOS SANTOS have worked to transform what had been a successful but rather undisciplined liberation movement into an effective and efficient Marxist-Leninist party of government. Both men purged the party of radical dissidents and attacked corruption and inefficiency in the party. At the first party congress (Dec. 1977) President Neto tried to make the party more effective and more representative of the Angolan people. He reorganized it as the MPLA–PT (Movimento Popular de Libertaçao de Angola – Partido de Trabalho), the People's Movement for the Liberation of

Angola – Workers' Party. President Neto became chairman of the reconstituted party. President Dos Santos, who succeeded President Neto as chairman of the party and head of state (1979), has continued the policies of his predecessor but since the middle of the 1980s there have been signs that President Dos Santos is modifying the rigid Marxism of the MPLA in the 1970s in favour of a more pragmatic approach.

MPR (Mouvement Populaire de la Révolution), founded and led since April 1966 by President *MOBUTU, it has been Zaire's only legal political party since 1967 and has been used by Mobutu to strengthen his authority over the country. Late in 1970 constitutional changes gave its Political Bureau supremacy over central and local government, the legislature and the judiciary. The MPR is the official guardian of the state doctrine of Mobutism. From birth all Zaireans are members. The head of the MPR is the sole presidential candidate and all the single list candidates for election to the National Legislative Council are approved by the MPR. Under the proposed reforms, which are scheduled for 1991, the MPR will lose its special constitutional role and there will be three legal political parties in Zaire.

MRND (Mouvement révolutionnaire national pour le développement), founded and led by President *HABYARIMANA of Rwanda since 1975. Its avowed purpose is to mobilize the Rwandan people for the economic, social, cultural and political development of their country. Under the constitution approved by referendum (1978), it is the country's only legal political party. From birth every Rwandan is a member of the party. The President of the MRND is the sole candidate in presidential elections and in legislative elections voters choose between two candidates selected by the party.

Mswati III (b.1968), King of Swaziland since 1986 with the traditional title of Ngwenyama (Lion). The second youngest of King *SOBHUZA's seventy or more sons, Prince Makhosetive was chosen by traditional leaders to succeed after his father's death (1982). During his minority there were two Queen Regents – *DZELIWE (1982–3) and his mother *NTOMBI (1983–6).

He returned from school in Britain in 1984 to choose his first bride from ten thousand bare-breasted maidens. Because of royal feuding his coronation was brought forward from 1989 to 1986. At his coronation he was crowned as King Mswati III in traditional splendour. The young king soon acted decisively against the traditionalist faction; he dissolved the *LIQOQO which he saw as an obstacle to progress (May 1986) and sacked the traditionalist prime minister, Prince Bhekimpi *DLAMINI (Oct. 1986). He has shown sympathy for the *AFRICAN NATIONAL CONGRESS exiles in Swaziland, but is not seen in a strong enough position to defy South Africa openly.

Mudge, Dirk, white South African millionaire active in Namibian politics. He was chairman of the *NATIONAL PARTY in South West Africa and a member of the South West Africa Executive Council. In 1977 he chaired the *TURNHALLE CONSTITUTIONAL CONFERENCE, founded the Republican Party and became chairman of the *DTA. Mudge was effectively prime minister of the South African-sponsored DTA government (1978–83) but resigned partly because of disputes with the South African authorities. He served as a minister in the *MPC government (1985–9). He led the DTA in the pre-independence elections (Nov. 1989), winning twenty-one of the seventy-two constituent assembly seats.

Mugabe, Robert Gabriel (b.1924), political leader who became independent Zimbabwe's first prime minister (1980–7) and first executive president. After a mission school education he graduated from *FORT HARE (1951) and qualified as a teacher. He taught in Zambia and Ghana before returning home in 1960 with a Ghanaian wife to become active in nationalist movements, as Publicity Secretary for the *NDP (National Democratic Party) (1961–2) and for *ZAPU (Zimbabwe African People's Union) (1962–3). He was arrested, but escaped to Tanzania and became Secretary-General of *ZANU (Zimbabwe African National Union) in 1963.

He returned to Zimbabwe where he was detained for ten years (1964–74); during his detention he took correspondence courses to gain four more degrees. After his release late in 1974 Mugabe escaped to Mozambique in 1975

233

to continue to war against the white minority regime in Zimbabwe (then Rhodesia). As President of ZANU and Commander-in-Chief of *ZANLA (its military wing) from 1977, he launched increasingly effective attacks on Rhodesia from Mozambique.

As joint leader of the *PF (Patriotic Front) he attended the talks which led to the *LANCASTER HOUSE AGREEMENT on independence. As leader of *ZANU (PF) he won a convincing majority in the pre-independence elections and became Zimbabwe's first prime minister (Apr. 1980) and executive president at the end of 1987.

As leader of Zimbabwe for a decade Mugabe has stressed the importance of national reconciliation and he has modified his socialism with a pragmatic and realistic approach to government. He is an intelligent and moderate statesman who lives simply and unostentatiously, but also plays a major role in regional and international affairs. He is a prominent campaigner against South Africa's system of *APARTHEID and a leading Commonwealth and Third World spokesman. He has been criticized for condoning atrocities by the *FIFTH BRIGADE in Matabeleland (1983–4) and for the corruption of his associates which was so clearly revealed in 1989. During the campaign for the March 1990 election his determination to crush the *ZIMBABWE UNITY MOVEMENT and his wish to make Zimbabwe a one-party state caused concern. President Mugabe had apparently

heeded the Politburo of ZANU (PF) and the Central Committee which have both rejected his proposals for a one-party state (Aug.–Sept. 1990). Mugabe is seen as one of Africa's most successful leaders who has transformed himself from a guerrilla leader into a statesman. Under his government Zimbabwe is stable and prosperous, and he is respected in his own country and abroad.

Muhammed, General Murtala Ramat (1938–76), Nigerian military ruler who was assassinated after less than a year as head of the Federal Military Government. Born in Kano in the north, he was a devout Muslim who enlisted in the Nigerian Army (1957) and served in the United Nations Congo peace-keeping force. In July 1966 he took part in the coup against *AGUIYI-IRONSI who made him a Lieutenant-Colonel after the January 1966 coup. During the *BIAFRAN civil war he served with distinction as a divisional commander, taking Benin (Sep. 1967) and Onitsha (Mar. 1968). In 1971 he was promoted Brigadier and in 1974 became Federal Commissioner for Communications.

Alarmed by Nigeria's economic problems, corruption and inefficiency and concerned at the postponement of civilian rule, he ousted General *GOWON in a bloodless coup (Jul. 1975). After taking power Murtala Muhammed acted swiftly and decisively. He outlined a new timetable for the return to civilian rules, decided to move the capital from Lagos to *ABUJA, increased the number of states from twelve to nineteen, imposed austerity, and began a drive against corrupt and inefficient public servants. Over ten thousand public officials were purged. The assassination of Murtala Muhammed in February 1976 was a great blow to the Nigerians who had expected him to bring stability, efficiency and prosperity to Nigeria. His successor, General *OBASANJO, pledged to continue Murtala Muhammed's policies.

Mulder, Cornelius Petrus (Connie) (1925–88), controversial white South African politician whose career was ruined by the 'Muldergate Scandal'. He taught and worked in local politics before his election as a *NATIONAL PARTY MP (1958). In 1968 he became Minister of Immigration, Information, Social Welfare and Pensions and in 1974 was chosen to lead the National Party in the Transvaal. In 1978 he became Minister of Plural Relations, while retaining control of the Ministry of Information. As a dedicated and doctrinaire supporter of *APARTHEID Mulder was the leading right-wing contender in the leadership contest which followed *VORSTER's resignation in 1978; he came within six votes of victory.

The 'Muldergate Scandal' then broke with revelations that Mulder had been organizing unauthorized fund-raising both in South Africa and abroad. These funds were used surreptitiously for pro-government propaganda; sometimes 'dirty tricks' were used. In 1979 he was disgraced and expelled from the National Party. He resigned his seat in parliament and formed the National Conservative Party (1979); this later merged with the *CONSERVATIVE PARTY (1982). Mulder won a seat for the Conservative Party in the 1987 election.

Muller, Hilgard (1914–85), South African Minister of Foreign Affairs (1964–77). He was a lawyer before his election as a *NATIONAL PARTY MP (1958). He was then High Commissioner in London (1961–4), an exceptionally difficult post at the time of South Africa's reluctant withdrawal from the Commonwealth. He was recalled to take over foreign affairs at a time of increasing international pressure on his country. One of the more moderate members of the National Party, he persuaded Prime Minister *VORSTER to try to establish links with African states. He did his best to minimize South Africa's isolation and had to try to justify South African support for Rhodesia following *UDI (1965).

Mungai, Dr Njoroge (b.1926), Kenyan politician who had considerable influence when he was President *KENYATTA's personal physician. A Kikuyu, he studied at *FORT HARE University College before qualifying as a doctor in the United States. He was in parliament (1963–5), Defence (1965–9) and Foreign Affairs (1969–74) before losing his seat in the 1974 elections.

Museveni, Yoweri Kagera (b.1944), President of Uganda since early 1986, he studied politics and economics at Dar es Salaam University where he developed his radical political beliefs. He served briefly in President *OBOTE's government before *AMIN seized power. In exile Museveni fought for *FRELIMO in the early 1970s before building up an effective and disciplined guerrilla organization – the Front for National Salvation. By 1979 he was a seasoned and charismatic guerrilla leader, and was a leading member of the *UGANDA NATIONAL LIBERATION FRONT when Amin was overthrown.

Museveni served as Minister of Defence under Presidents *LULE and *BINAISA in 1979 until the latter demoted him to the Ministry of Regional Co-operation (Nov. 1979). From May 1980 he was Vice-Chairman of the Military Commission which ousted President Binaisa. Museveni campaigned in the December 1980 election but his Uganda People's Movement won only one seat in the much-disputed election.

Early in 1981 Museveni sent his family abroad and went underground to fight President Obote. With twenty-seven men he launched the National Resistance Army, a well disciplined force which grew rapidly; its high standards of behaviour made it popular and it soon commanded the loyalty of villagers in south-west Uganda. After failing to reach agreement with the military leaders who overthrew Obote (Jul. 1985) Museveni fought on until he entered Kampala and was sworn in as President of Uganda early in 1986.

Once in power Museveni worked for national reconciliation, overcoming much of the opposition from supporters of the ousted military leaders and persuading different political groups to join in the broadly based National Resistance Council. He was faced with an appalling situation after twenty years of bitter conflict. It took two years for Obote's supporters to agree to a ceasefire. There have been plots against him and the army has fought since 1987 to crush the fanatical rebels in the *HOLY SPIRIT MOVEMENT. The tide of terror has receded; the present army is better disciplined than its predecessors. In 1989 a report by the Minority Rights Group praised Museveni's respect for human rights and pointed out that elections earlier that year had given the government legitimacy. Despite progress in restoring law and order, many Ugandans have little respect for any government after their experiences since independence.

There has been some economic recovery despite the border disputes with Kenya which have hindered both the flow of imports and the export of coffee, Uganda's main foreign currency earner. Late in the 1980s he ordered a survey on *AIDS and courageously ordered the publication of the results in 1990; these show that a million Ugandans, or 6 per cent of the population, are affected. President Museveni has the courage and the vision to win the support and trust of his people and he is seeking practical help from the international community. He seems the best hope of redeeming Uganda's fortunes.

Muslim Brotherhood (Ikhwan), the most influential of the reform movements in Arab lands during the inter-war years. Founded by an Egyptian schoolteacher, Hasan al-Banna, in 1928, the Brotherhood's original aims were strongly moral rather than political. It was intent on eradicating Western influences as well as what it considered 'decadent medieval anomalies' from Islamic life. Members met for prayer and were assiduous in observing their religious duties. They abstained from the 'evils' of alcohol, gambling, usury and fornication. During and after the Second World War, the Brotherhood became radicalized as a result of the mounting crisis over Palestine. Many of its members turned to terrorism, including the murder of Egypt's Prime Minister, Muqrashi Pasha, in 1948. The following year Hasan al-Banna was killed by the security forces. The Brotherhood played a leading part in the overthrow of the monarchy in 1952 and then confronted President *NASSER's secular nationalism. Nasser abolished the old political parties and the Muslim Brotherhood was outlawed. When a member tried to murder Nasser in 1954, the movement was violently suppressed. Many of its members were imprisoned or exiled. However, affiliated movements sprang up in Jordan, Syria, Sudan, Pakistan, Indonesia and Malaysia. Saudi Arabia, an enemy of Nasser's Egypt, offered the Brotherhood great support. During President *MUBARAK's administration the Brotherhood has been given legal status and has members in parliament, even though it is still tacitly committed to the overthrow of secular regimes and to the restoration of Iranian-style theocratic rule. See *REPUBLICAN BROTHERS.

Mutesa II, His Highness Sir Edward Frederick (1924–69), 36th Kabaka (King) of *BUGANDA (1939–66) and first President of Uganda (1963–6). After succeeding his father he studied at *MAKERERE COLLEGE and Cambridge University. He was exiled by the British colonial authorities (1953–5) for opposing proposals which he considered a threat to Buganda's special status in Uganda. Restored as a constitutional monarch he had considerable popular support and exercised the traditional powers of the Kabaka.

Mutesa II expressed his worries about Buganda's status after independence at the London constitutional conference (1961–2). He made an electoral pact with Dr *OBOTE, Uganda's foremost nationalist political leader, and obtained a semi-federal status for Buganda after independence. He became President but soon clashed with Prime Minister Obote over Obote's radical socialist policies. When Buganda lost disputed territory to Bunyoro, relations between President and Prime Minister broke down. In 1966 Obote staged a coup; he sent troops into Buganda and deposed Mutesa II from his throne and the presidency. The ex-Kabaka died in exile in Britain.

Muwanga, Paulo (b.1925), Ugandan politician who supported *OBOTE for many years. He was an early member of the *UGANDA PEOPLE'S CONGRESS and held diplomatic posts under the Obote and *AMIN governments until forced into exile by Amin (1975). He returned to Uganda and served the caretaker governments of Presidents *LULE and *BINAISA as Minister of the Interior (1979–80). Shortly after Binaisa demoted him to the Ministry of Labour, Muwanga played a prominent part in the coup of May 1980 and became head of government and played a key role in organizing the elections which brought Obote back to power (Dec. 1980). There were many allegations of intimidation, corruption and ballot-rigging during these elections.

He served during Obote's second presidency as vice-president and Minister of Defence (1980–5). He became prime minister after the military coup which ousted Obote (Jul. 1985). When *MUSEVENI seized power (Jan. 1986) Muwanga was stripped of office. He was arrested (Oct. 1986) and accused of plotting to overthrow the government. This charge was dropped. In May 1988 he was acquitted of an abduction charge, but immediately rearrested on a similar charge.

Muzorewa, Bishop Abel Tendekayi (b.1925), Zimbabwean churchman and political leader, a Methodist minister and a Bishop from 1968. He became politically prominent in 1971 when he founded the *AFRICAN NATIONAL COUNCIL, the first African political organization allowed to operate openly in Zimbabwe (then Rhodesia) since nationalist parties were finally banned in 1964. He mobilized African opinion against the proposed Anglo-Rhodesian settlement of 1971 and convinced the *PEARCE COMMISSION that it was unacceptable to the African majority. Some small African groups joined him to form the United African National Council in 1974, but he had no support from the two main nationalist bodies resisting white minority rule.

In March 1978 he agreed an 'internal settlement' with the white minority government and joined a transitional government preparing the country for independence. He won the dubious 1979 elections and became Prime Minister of Zimbabwe-Rhodesia (Jun. 1979). Unable to stop the war or to win the approval of the international community his government handed back power to Britain by the *LANCASTER HOUSE AGREEMENT (Dec. 1979). In the 1980 elections during the transition to independence his party won only three seats. It won no seats in the 1985 elections. Bishop Muzorewa retired from politics in 1986 and resumed his work for the Methodist Church.

Mwakenya, shadowy Kenyan underground movement, probably formed in 1981. It has campaigned for the overthrow of President *MOI's government, which it regards as corrupt and dictatorial. It has distributed leaflets calling for a guerrilla war to establish a radical socialist state. Some academics support Mwakenya, but its popular support is difficult to assess. President Moi has taken the movement seriously and has imprisoned a number of supporters or alleged supporters. People have allegedly been tortured to make them confess their membership of Mwakenya. In July 1990 riots broke out in at least six Kenyan towns after Mwakenya issued leaflets calling for an armed insurrection.

Mwalimu, Swahili title of respect meaning teacher, often used to refer to President *NYERERE.

Mwambutsa IV, Mwami (King) of Burundi from 1915 to 1966. He was a Tutsi prince who succeeded to the throne of Burundi when Belgium was replacing Germany as the colonial power. Most of his reign fell under the Belgian system of indirect rule. At independence (1962) observers thought that only the monarchy had any hope of reconciling the majority Hutu with the minority Tutsi. The King tried to give each group equal authority, but tension mounted as five unstable governments rapidly succeeded each other (1962–5). After an abortive Hutu coup (Oct. 1965) the king fled to Switzerland and was supplanted by his son (Jul. 1966).

Mwinyi, Ali Hassan (b. 1925), President of Tanzania since 1985, born on the mainland, he was brought up in *ZANZIBAR. He taught at and was Principal of Zanzibar's teacher training college until 1963. After a short spell as Permanent Secretary in Zanzibar's Ministry of Education (1963–4), Mwinyi worked for the Zanzibar State Trading Corporation (1964–70). Impressed by his abilities President *NYERERE appointed Mwinyi to various ministerial posts in the Tanzanian government (1970–84). When Aboud *JUMBE was forced out of office, Mwinyi succeeded him as President of Zanzibar and Vice-President of Tanzania (1984–5). Mwinyi made economic reforms in Zanzibar and improved relations with the mainland.

In 1985 he succeeded Nyerere as President of the United Republic of Tanzania, but with less power than his predecessor; a new constitution (1984) makes him more accountable to the legislature and he is limited to two five-year terms in office. Moreover, Nyerere has stayed on as chairman of *CHAMA CHA MAPINDUZI (Tanzania's only legal political party). There are serious economic problems, notably a large balance of payments deficit, inflation and low prices for Tanzanian exports.

Although he shares Nyerere's socialist ideals Mwinyi has demonstrated a measure of pragmatism and realism in office by liberalizing the economy, ending some state monopolies and allowing private enterprise more freedom. Since the agreement with the International Monetary Fund (Aug. 1986) the pace of economic reforms has accelerated, despite the reservations of orthodox socialists, including ex-President Nyerere. Mwinyi overcame many of these reservations and won Nyerere's tacit support for the economic recovery programme. By 1989 there were indications that he was making progress. Incentives are encouraging the growers of export crops, exports rose by eight per cent in 1987–8, foreign donors are providing foreign exchange for machinery and spare parts, and a massive road repair programme has started.

N

Naguib, General Muhammad (1901–79), Egyptian soldier and head of state. Born into a well-to-do family, Naguib was trained as a soldier from an early age. He fought as a brigadier in the Arab war against Israel in 1948–9, although he never showed any strong political views and was not drawn to the revolutionary Free Officers Movement led by Gamal Abdel *NASSER. The coup launched by these officers in July 1952 was outstandingly successful but a respected figurehead became a necessity. Nasser and his colleagues chose Naguib, now a general. He was appointed commander-in-chief of the armed forces and chairman of the Revolutionary Command Council (RCC). In accordance with his own plan, in 1954 Nasser ousted Naguib and placed him under house arrest. This constraint was lifted in 1960 but Naguib never again entered public life.

Namibia, a member of the Commonwealth, known as *SOUTH WEST AFRICA when ruled by Germany and South Africa, and the last African colony to win independence (Mar. 1990). It is a vast, dry and sparsely populated country in southern Africa, bordered on the west by an Atlantic coastline of over 1000 km., on the north by Angola, on the east by Botswana and on the south by South Africa. To the north-east the long and narrow *CAPRIVI STRIP extends to the borders of Zambia and Zimbabwe. On the Atlantic shore the Namib Desert froms a coastal plain from sixty-five to one hundred and sixty kilometres wide. East of the Namib an escarpment rises to a plateau with an average height of 1100 metres and a maximum of over 2000 metres. Further east and to the north is the Kalahari Desert.

In the Namib only the ports and mining centres are inhabited and there are only a few thousand *SAN (or Bushmen) in the Kalahari. Most Namibians live on the central plateau; the Ovambo, about half the country's population, live in the northern third of the plateau where most of the country's food is produced. Namibia's other racial groups include six *BANTU peoples, two of mixed ancestry, the San and the whites.

Namibia has rich mineral resources, including uranium, diamonds, copper, iron, lead and zinc. There is also an Atlantic fishing industry. The minerals and the fish have been exploited and seriously depleted by South African and other foreign companies. White settlers did make fortunes from ranching, especially cattle, sheep and *KARAKUL, but during the 1980s droughts and political uncertainty have damaged both ranching and subsistence farming.

The Republic of Namibia

THE COUNTRY
824,269 sq. km.

Major Cities
Windhoek (capital)
Walvis Bay (in dispute
with South Africa)
Ondangwa
Tsumeb
Luderitz

Economy
Mining
Ranching & Farming
Fishing

Principal Exports
Diamonds
Uranium
Base metals
Livestock products
Fish

Currency
South African Rand (R)
of 100 cents

THE PEOPLE
1,218,000

Ethnic Groups
Ovambo
Kavango
Herero
Damara
Nama
Rehoboth
Coloureds

Language
English (official)

Religion
Christian (80%)
Traditional beliefs

THE STATE
Multi-party republic

Head of State
President Nujoma

Ruling Bodies
Presidential Cabinet
National Assembly

Party in Power
SWAPO

Political Opposition
DTA

From prehistoric times Namibia was inhabited by the *KHOISAN, later joined by the Damara. The *BANTU speaking Herero and Ovambo peoples arrived in the sixteenth and seventeenth centuries. In the north the Ovambo led fairly settled lives, raising livestock, cultivating land and developing monarchical states. Elsewhere people were less settled living as hunters and gatherers and in some cases owning cattle, sheep and goats.

By the second half of the nineteenth century European powers were taking an interest in Namibia. In 1878 Britain annexed *WALVIS BAY to the Cape Colony and in 1884 Germany established the protectorate of South-western Africa; its borders were agreed by European powers in 1890. The German authorities savagely suppressed any opposition and gave the best farmland to white settlers. In 1915, during the First World War, South African forces defeated the Germans and occupied the country; in 1920 the League of Nations confirmed South Africa as the mandatory power. The

South African authorities continued to seize land and to enforce political, economic and social discrimination against the Namibian people. After the Second World War the United Nations called on South Africa to accept that it was a trustee for the territory. South Africa insisted that it was the sovereign power and began a long dispute with the United Nations.

During the 1950s South Africa began its attempt to impose *APART-HEID and to incorporate Namibia into South Africa. Namibian students, intellectuals and trade unionists, notably *TOIVO JA TOIVA and *NUJOMA, began to organize protests and to appeal to the international community. During the 1960s the Namibian people organized their first effective liberation movement. *SWAPO (formed 1960) began the armed struggle for independence in August 1966, and formally inaugurated *PLAN (People's Liberation Army of Namibia) in 1969. There was also continuing external pressure on South Africa to withdraw. The United Nations declared the South African occupation of Namibia illegal (1966), established a council to administer it (1967) and formally adopted the name of Namibia for the territory (1968). Nevertheless South Africa went ahead with the implementation of apartheid as recommended by the *ODENDAAL COMMISSION (1962) and proclaimed Ovamboland as Namibia's first *HOMELAND (1967). In 1969 the South West Africa Affairs Act made Namibia

virtually a province of South Africa, leaving the South West Africa Legislative Assembly (elected by whites) with very limited powers.

During the 1970s South Africa continued its attempts to implement apartheid in Namibia, but other developments made these plans increasingly irrelevant. When Angola became independent of Portugal (1975) SWAPO was greatly strengthened by the acquisition of bases in southern Angola and South Africa found it increasingly difficult to maintain its military campaigns. In 1971 the International Court of Justice declared the South African occupation of Namibia illegal. Subsequently, in 1974 South Africa announced it was planning self-determination for Namibia. The outcome was the *TURNHALLE CONSTITUTIONAL CONFERENCE (1975–7); both were boycotted by SWAPO and won limited support from the Namibian people.

The five Western powers of the *CONTACT GROUP then persuaded South Africa to agree in general to the United Nations plan for Namibian independence (*UN SECURITY COUNCIL RESOLUTION 435 of 1978), but South Africa resorted to various delaying tactics and refused to negotiate directly with SWAPO until 1984. In 1982, with United States support, South Africa linked the Namibian issue to the presence of Cuban troops in Angola, refusing to withdraw from Namibia until the Cuban troops left Angola. In 1983 the DTA government collapsed.

243

After a period of direct rule South Africa established another government (June 1985). This was the ★TRANSITIONAL GOVERNMENT OF NATIONAL UNITY run by the ★MPC (Multi-Party Conference); SWAPO was excluded and it was soon clear that this government was not supported by the Namibian people.

South Africa was persuaded to discuss regional problems with Cuba and Angola under United States mediation (May 1988). By the end of 1988 they reached an agreement which started to come into effect in April 1989. Cuban troops began to leave Angola and South African troops began to leave Namibia while ★UNTAG (United Nations Transition Assistance Group) began supervising Namibia's progress to independence. In November 1989 there were elections for a Constituent Assembly which must agree, with a two-thirds majority, on a constitution for Namibia. SWAPO won forty-four of the seventy-two seats and with the co-operation of other parties drew up a constitution. In March 1990 Namibia celebrated its independence.

After decades of colonial exploitation and twenty-three years of war Namibia now has to adjust to peace. It still has to live with the economic and military power of South Africa, which intends to keep ★WALVIS BAY. It cannot afford to alienate the small white minority which owns sixty per cent of the land and has skills vital to the future of the country. Despite its radical socialist beliefs the SWAPO government is prepared to be pragmatic. SWAPO no longer adheres to a rigidly Marxist ideology and it accepts both a mixed economy and a multi-party democracy. It wants reconciliation to assure all Namibians that SWAPO will not operate only in the interests of the Ovambo. Certainly the SWAPO government has started well and there are considerable grounds for optimism about Namibia's future.

Nasser, Gamal Abdel (1918–69), first leader of the modern Egyptian republic. Born in Alexandria, the son of a postal clerk, Gamal Nasser had his only education in Cairo and Alexandria. After training at Cairo Military Academy he was commissioned in 1937. He served in the Sudan, was an instructor at the military academy and took part in the Arab-Israeli war of 1948. The defeat of the Arabs crystallized his thoughts about the need to remedy corruption in the Egyptian Government and to restore Egypt's pride and self-confidence. His revolutionary activity, which began after 1948, brought him into contact with the Muslim Brotherhood and other groups likely to support the overthrow of King Farouk's regime. As a colonel, he formed the Free Officers' Movement, out of which grew the Council of Revolutionary Command, which overthrew Farouk in July, 1952. In 1954 Nasser emerged as the leader of the revolution after deposing General Muhammad ★NAGUIB, its nominal leader. He was elected president of Egypt in 1956 and was re-elected twice in uncontested elections.

Friendly to the West and uncertain of his policies in the beginning, Nasser gradually adopted a radical foreign policy, which was soon reflected in his internal rule. A series of events made Nasser a world personality and a champion of nationalism, non-alignment and anti-colonialism. Those events were the Egyptian arms deal with Czechoslovakia; the final departure of the British from Egypt in 1954; the Bandung Conference in 1955, at which he was a leading speaker; the seizure and nationalization of the Suez Canal in 1955; the abortive British-French Israeli attack on Egypt in 1956.

Nasser banned political parties and strove to create an organization that would embrace the whole nation. The Liberation Rally (1953–6), the National Union (1958–62) and the Socialist Union (1962) all derived from his efforts to create a mass party. The union of Egypt and Syria as the United Arab Republic in 1958 was a great victory for him. The collapse of the union when Syria withdrew, in 1962, was a severe political reverse.

Nasser's political thought was determined by the nature of Egyptian society, which he described as 'not yet crystallized', and by the role he foresaw for Egypt in international affairs. This he described in three circles or zones – Arab, African and Islamic. The Islamic and African circles were to coalesce and shrink considerably

while Arabism, comprising nationalism and Islam, became the core of Nasser's thought, and so developed into 'Nasserism'. Nasserism amounted to the view that pan-Arabism would lead eventually to the unification and integration of the Arab nations in one Arab state. Nasserism opposed colonialism, neocolonialism, 'spheres of interest', foreign military bases and alignment with the Great Powers. However, Nasser's own policy in Yemen, which he tried to subjugate, 1962–7, contradicted his own principles.

In 1961 he adopted a series of laws to nationalize large enterprises. This was part of his attack on feudalism, monopolies, imperialism and the 'domination of capitalism'. It aimed also at establishing social justice, a democratic system and a powerful army. Nasser's nationalist and socialist views acquired their final form in the National Charter of 1962. It describes revolution as 'the only way that enables the Arab struggle to abandon the past and orient itself towards the future'.

Nasser wanted a showdown with Israel and believed that he would win a war. In May 1967 he asked the United Nations to remove the Emergency Force from the Egyptian-Israeli frontier in Sinai and he closed the Tiran Straits to Israeli shipping. Israel struck first and in six days defeated the armies of Egypt, Syria and Jordan. After this devastating blow, Nasser resigned the presidency but, on wild popular demand, reassumed office the following day. He died of a heart attack on 28 September 1969. Most Egyptians believed that the shame of the 1967 defeat had weakened his health. His influence on the Arab world remains awesome. Colonel *GADDAFI of Libya claims to be his spiritual successor. Even in the 1990s, Nasser's name is revered in Egypt.

National Consultative Council, interim legislative body in Uganda between the overthrow of President *AMIN (Apr. 1979) and the elections in December 1980.

National Democratic Party of Liberia (NDPL), formed in 1984 by Samuel *DOE as a vehicle for his presidential campaign, and used also to fight the parliamentary elections as Liberia returned to civilian rule. In October 1985 it won fifty-one of sixty-four seats in the House of Representatives and twenty-two of the twenty-six seats in the Senate. Doe won the presidency.

National Forum, grouping of between one and two hundred black organizations in South Africa which came together in June 1983, largely due to the efforts of the *AZANIAN PEOPLE'S ORGANIZATION. Its membership of about half a million subscribes to *BLACK CONSCIOUSNESS and rejects the African National Congress for its communist links and for opening up its membership to all races. The National Forum sees the struggle against *APARTHEID as a racial conflict and insists that the forces of liberation must be led by black people. Its organizations have been banned and its leaders have

been arrested by the South African government.

National Party, since its election victory in 1948 the ruling party in South Africa. The party was founded in 1940 as an aggressive Afrikaner nationalist party. It was anti-English, and during the Second World War some of its members supported Germany. When it came to power it secured the dominance of the Afrikaner in all walks of life and implemented its policy of *APARTHEID to separate the races in South Africa and to keep the Afrikaner race pure. Since the 1970s the party has had some success in its efforts to win support from English-speaking South Africans.

The tentative and limited adoption of reforms by the leadership has led to defections from the National Party to more extreme right-wing parties like the *HERSTIGTE NASIONALE PARTY (1969) and the *CONSERVATIVE PARTY (1982); the defectors felt that the party was betraying the interests of the Afrikaners. Since 1958 the party has been led by *VERWOERD, *VORSTER, P.W. *BOTHA and *DE KLERK. President de Klerk has shown his willingness to end apartheid and to share power with all racial groups. In May 1990 a National Party government delegation held talks with the *AFRICAN NATIONAL CONGRESS to prepare for negotiations which may lead to a new constitutional settlement in South Africa. In October 1990 it was confirmed that the party's official policy is to throw open its membership to all races.

National Patriotic Front of Liberia (NPFL), rebel army led by Charles *TAYLOR and backed by Libya. It invaded Liberia late in 1989 in an attempt to overthrow President *DOE. It suffered from the defection of Prince *JOHNSON and his supporters. By late 1990 it was one of the three forces fighting in the Liberian civil war, the other forces being Prince Johnson's rebel group, and those troops still loyal to the memory of President Doe, who was killed in September 1990. The NPFL was further weakened by more defections late in 1990 and by the apparent loss of Libyan support.

Naude, Christiaan Frederick Beyers (b. 1915), Afrikaner clergyman whose rejection of *APARTHEID has been widely acclaimed in South Africa and other countries. As a member of the *AFRIKANER BROEDERBOND for over twenty years and as a *NEDERDUITSE GEREFORMEERDE KERK (Dutch Reformed Church) minister he supported the *NATIONAL PARTY until the early 1960s when he became convinced that apartheid could not be reconciled with Christianity. He was Director of the multi-racial and ecumenical Christian Institute (1963–84) and Secretary-General of the South African Council of Churches (1984–7). In 1980 he left his church to join a black church. Despite being arrested, intimidated and banned he has spoken out against the government's disregard for human rights and against its racial policies. He opposes violence, but supports sanctions against South Africa. His courage has brought him honours from universities, churches and other bodies all over the world. In May 1990, Nelson *MANDELA invited him to join an *AFRICAN NATIONAL CONGRESS delegation which had preliminary talks with a South African government delegation, led by President *DE KLERK.

NCNC, Nigerian political party (1944–66). In 1961 when the people of the Southern Cameroons decided not to join Nigeria the NCNC changed its name from National Council of Nigeria and the Cameroons to National Convention of Nigerian Citizens. The party had a strong base in the Eastern Region and was mainly supported by Ibo. Led by Herbert Macaulay and Nnamdi *AZIKIWE the party campaigned for independence and after the 1952 elections it formed the Eastern Regional government (1954–66). Azikiwe was premier until 1959 when he went into federal politics. Following the 1959 pre-independence elections the NCNC became a junior partner to the *NPC in the federal government coalition from 1959 to 1964. After the breakdown of the coalition in 1964 the NCNC retained control of both the Eastern Region and the newly created Mid-Western Region until its dissolution after the military coup of January 1966.

N'Dour, Youssou (b. 1959), a singer and composer from Senegal. An exponent of *MBALAX music, he uses traditional Wolof rhythms and sings in Wolof. For many years he was the star turn at the Miami Night Club in

Dakar, but has established himself and his band (Super Etiole) in Paris and has made a number of international tours. He returns regularly to his loyal fans in Dakar.

NDP, National Democratic Party, militant Zimbabwean nationalist party which campaigned against white rule in Southern Rhodesia (now Zimbabwe). It was formed in 1960 after the banning of the *AFRICAN NATIONAL CONGRESS and led by *JOSHUA NKOMO until it was banned in 1961.

Nederduitse Gereformeerde Kerk (Dutch Reformed Church), South African Calvinist church with about two million members; it has affiliated African and *COLOURED churches with a combined membership of another two million. The church is closely associated with the political and social beliefs of Afrikaner nationalists. From 1857 to 1986 it rigidly segregated whites from other races. At the synod in 1986 it decided to open its membership to people of all races; some right-wing members left the church in 1987 in protest against its 'liberalism'.

négritude, a cultural movement which rejects Western cultural domination and asserts pride in Africa, the African identity and its civilization. The movement was launched in Paris in the 1930s by Leopold *SENGHOR of Senegal, Aimé Césaire of Martinique and Léon Damas of Guyana. The early exponents of *négritude* wrote mainly poetry – in French.

Neto, Agostinho (1922–79), leading Angolan statesman and poet. The

son of a Protestant pastor and a teacher, Neto worked in the colonial health service before being awarded a grant to study medicine at the University of Lisbon. As a student in the 1950s Neto was active in nationalist politics, joining protests against the wretched conditions in the colonies, calling for Angolan independence and suffering imprisonment (1952; 1955–7). He was also publishing his poetry. *NÉGRITUDE and his grief at the destruction of African self-respect by foreign political and cultural oppression are major themes in *Poemas* (collected poems published in 1961) and *Sagrada Esperança* (Sacred Hope, 1974). When he returned to Angola (1959) to devote himself to the campaign for independence, Neto stopped writing poetry. Neto's political activities led to his imprisonment (1960–2), but the Portuguese authorities released him after an international outcry. Neto then ousted Mário *PINTO DE ANDRADE to become president of the exiled *MPLA (Movement for the Liberation of Angola) in 1962 and to lead the fight for an independent, multi-racial, socialist and democratic Angola.

After the defeat of the Portuguese, Neto became the first President of independent Angola (1975) under very difficult circumstances. His authority was challenged by the *FNLA and *UNITA, while South Africa and the USA tried to thwart his plans to build a Marxist state. He had to defeat challenges to his authority from factions in the MPLA while trying to rebuild a country shattered by colonial exploitation and the long war for liberation. With help from the Soviet bloc, notably Cuban troops, he drove South African forces out of Angola and had won the civil war by 1976; but he failed to crush UNITA. Neto also looked for friends outside the Soviet bloc and gained international recognition, with the notable exception of the United States.

Under Neto's leadership Angola suffered a number of economic setbacks. These were due partly to the long years of fighting UNITA and its South African backers; but the over hasty application of Marxist remedies also did much damage. Towards the end of his life Neto relaxed some of his Marxist economic strategies, much to the fury of hardline Marxists in the MPLA. By the time of his death from cancer in September 1979 Neto had made little progress in rebuilding Angola's shattered economy, but he had successfully led his people to independence and transformed the MPLA from an armed liberation movement into a party of government. His chosen successor, President *DOS SANTOS, has continued the pragmatic and moderate policies of President Neto with some success.

Ngouabi, Marien (c.1939–77), President of the People's Republic of the Congo (1969–77). After military training in France, Ngouabi returned to the Congo (1962) as a paratroop officer. During Massamba-Débat's presidency (1963–8) Ngouabi emerged as a leading personality in the armed forces, which he represented in the Mouvement national de la révolution (MNR). During 1967 and 1968 Massamba-Débat was in open conflict with both the MNR and the army. As the various parties failed to resolve their differences, Ngouabi took control of Brazzaville (Aug. 1968) and had talks with Massamba-Débat; these talks led to the appointment of Major Raoul (Ngouabi's associate) as Prime Minister. This agreement ended the next month when Massamba-Débat was sacked and the country was put under military rule. At the beginning of 1969 Ngouabi became President.

Although he had come to power with the support of both Right and Left, President Ngouabi committed himself openly to the Left by establishing the *PARTI CONGOLAIS DU TRAVAIL (PCT) as the supreme party (Dec. 1969). This was a vanguard Marxist-Leninist party for the implementation of Ngouabi's socialist policies. The army's authority was challenged by the creation of a people's militia, ideologically trained to secure the fruits of the revolution. Those who were not fully committed to Ngouabi's policies were driven out of the army, the police and the government. The government was hostile to the United States and established close links with communist states. After several earlier coup attempts, President Ngouabi was assassinated in March 1977.

Ngugi wa Thiong'o, formerly James Ngugi, (b.1938), Kenya's leading novelist who is now in exile. He is a prolific and powerful writer of novels, short stories, plays, literary criticism and political comment. After studying at *MAKERERE UNIVERSITY COLLEGE and in Britain, Ngugi began a successful academic career in Kenya. He chaired the Department of Literature at Nairobi University until his outspoken radicalism led to conflict with the authorities and his imprisonment (1977–8). Since going into exile in Europe (1982) he has continued to campaign for greater democracy in Kenya.

The exploitation of the Kenyan people by the British Empire and by post-independence governments is a major theme in his works. His first big international success was *Weep Not, Child* (1964), a novel about how the *MAU MAU emergency affected a Kenyan family. *A Grain of Wheat* (1967) focuses on Kenyan independence and the disillusion which followed. *Petals of Blood* (1977) starts with the murder of three corrupt politicians and in a series of flashbacks pays tribute to the peasants and workers who built modern Kenya. *Detained: A Writer's Prison Diary* (1981) is an account of his year in prison. Like Okot *P'BITEK Ngugi believes in a truly African literature and culture. In *Decolonizing the Mind* (1986) he deplored the fact that most Africans were writing in European languages or Arabic. He decided to write only in Gikuyu, his mother tongue. *Matigari* (1989) is a novel about an African Che Guevara who leads a rebellion against a system of capitalism that is worse than colonialism. It has been banned in Kenya. In July 1990 *MWAKENYA, a radical dissident movement, named Ngugi as one of its leaders.

Ngwane National Liberatory Congress (NNLC), political party in Swaziland founded and led by Dr Ambrose *ZWANE. After the Swaziland Progressive Party split (1961), radicals, trade unionists and intellectuals formed the NNLC in 1963 with strong support in urban areas. Despite winning 12 per cent of the vote in the 1964 election and 20 per cent in 1967 it did not win any seats in the legislature and was not represented in the negotiations (1967), which gave the monarchy substantial powers at independence (1968).

Although the electoral system was weighted against it, the NNLC won three seats in the 1972 election. This angered King *SOBHUZA II who suspended the constitution and banned the NNLC and other political parties (1973). During the 1970s the NNLC organized strikes and demonstrations by transport workers, schoolchildren, students and teachers. Dr Zwane was detained, but escaped to Mozambique and announced the formation of the Swaziland Liberation Movement (1978).

NIBMAR, acronym standing for No Independence Before Majority Rule, the phrase used by the British Prime Minister (Harold Wilson) when negotiating over the independence of Zimbabwe (then Rhodesia) in the 1960s. Britain's refusal to grant independence without majority rule meant that there could be no agreement with the *SMITH regime in Rhodesia and led to *UDI in November 1965.

Niger, the Republic of Niger is situated in West Africa in the arid, *SAHEL region. This remote land-locked state is surrounded by Libya on the north, Chad on the east, Nigeria on the south, Mali on the west and Algeria on the northwest. Two thirds of the country is desert. In the north the mountain range of the Aïr region has low rainfall, but sufficient to support the cattle-owning Tuaregs. Further south the country changes from semi-desert to savannah. Near the border with Nigeria, Hausa farmers are able to cultivate groundnuts and millet. Much of the population is concentrated in the south-west corner where rice and other crops can be grown. Niger is sparsely populated; it has a number of Fulani and Tuareg nomads as well as the more settled Hausa, Zarma and Kanuri peoples.

With limited natural resources and so little cultivable land, Niger is a poor country. When the rains are good and when there are no natural disasters like plagues of locusts Niger can just manage to produce enough to feed its people. Groundnuts used to be the main foreign currency earner, but falling world prices and the switch to food production have cut groundnut production. Much of the remaining groundnut harvest is unofficially taken across the border to Nigeria. Mining now accounts for most foreign earnings. Uranium ore exports are the most important, accounting for over 80 per cent of exports. There are also deposits of tin and iron ores, phosphates and salt.

Archaeological evidence shows that parts of Niger which are now desert were inhabited over four thousand years ago. People were forced south by the spread of the *SAHARA desert. Niger, or parts of Niger were included in the Songhai and Borno empires or ruled by the Hausa prior to the European colonial period. Niger was the southern base of the trans-Saharan slave trade. During the nineteenth century France took an interest in the territory and overcame resistance to establish it as a colony in French West Africa by 1906. After the Second World War Niger began its transition to self-government. Under the leadership of Hamani *DIORI it gained autonomy in the French Community in 1958.

With the achievement of full independence in 1960 Diori became Niger's first president (1960–74). His government was seen as cautious and moderate and pro-Western, but corruption and his authoritarianism caused great discontent. By 1973 the collapse in groundnut prices and severe drought meant considerable hardship for the people of Niger. Diori was deposed by a military coup (1974) and Niger was ruled by a military government under President Kountché (1974–87). Kountché died in 1987 and was succeeded by another military officer, President Saïbou. Saïbou has attempted

The Republic of Niger

THE COUNTRY
1,267,000 sq. km.

Major Cities
Niamey (capital)
Zinder

Economy
Agriculture
Mining

Principal Exports
Uranium ore
Livestock & hides

Currency
CFA franc of 100
centimes

THE PEOPLE
7 million

Ethnic Groups
Hausa
Zarma
Kanuri
Fulani
Tuareg

Languages
French (official)
Hausa
Zarma
Fulani
Tamachek
Kanuri

Religion
Islam

THE STATE
Military rule

Head of State
President Ali Saïbou

Ruling Bodies
Supreme Military Council
Council of Ministers
National Development
Council

Official Party
Mouvement national
pour une société de
développement

---

to reconcile differing factions in Niger. In 1988 he ordererd the drafting of a new constitution and formed a new ruling political party – the Mouvement national pour une société de développement. It is not yet clear whether some form of civilian government will eventually be restored.

Nigeria, a member of the Commonwealth, the Federal Republic of Nigeria is Africa's most populous country, with an estimated 100 million people late in the 1980s. Situated in West Africa on the Gulf of Guinea, it lies between the Equator and the Tropic of Cancer. It is bordered on the east by Cameroon, on the south by the Atlantic Ocean, on the west by Benin, on the north by Niger and on the north-east the border with Chad runs through Lake Chad. The landscape varies from swamps, lagoons, and tropical rain forests in the south to woodland and savannah in the north; it rises to the central plateau 2000 metres above sea level. The extreme north borders on the Sahara Desert.

The coastal areas are hot and humid; in the north the climate is more extreme and temperatures range from 4 to 43 degrees Centigrade. During the winter the harmattan wind from the Sahara keeps humidity low, especially in the north. Nigeria has many rivers. The country is named after the Niger, one of the world's great rivers, which rises in Guinea and flows north-east through Mali before flowing southeast through Niger and Nigeria to its

The Federal Republic of Nigeria

THE COUNTRY	THE PEOPLE	THE STATE
923,777 sq. km.	106,736,000	Military rule
Major Cities	*Ethnic Groups*	*Head of State*
Abuja (capital)	Hausa	President Babangida
Lagos	Yoruba	
Ibadan	Ibo	*Ruling Bodies*
Kano	Fulani	Armed Forces Ruling
Abeokuta	250+ others	Council
Ogbomosho		National Council of
Port Harcourt	*Languages*	Ministers
Enugu	English (official)	
	Hausa	*Political Parties*
Economy	Yoruba	All banned
Mixed	Ibo	
Principal Exports	*Religion*	
Crude petroleum	Islam	
Cocoa	Christian	
	Traditional beliefs	
Currency		
Naira (N) of 100 kobo		

delta on the Gulf of Guinea. Nigeria's second river is the Benue which rises in the Cameroon highlands and flows west to join the Niger.

The people of Nigeria are divided into over 250 ethnic groups. The most numerous are the Hausa-Fulani who are concentrated in the north, the Yoruba in the south-west and the Ibo in the south-east. The heaviest concentrations of population are near Kano in the north and near the great cities of the south.

Nigeria's greatest problem is the construction of an economy strong enough to support its rapidly increasing population, which is expected to reach 400 million by AD 2050. Agricultural development is crucial, but there is little accurate information available. Most agricultural production is simply subsistence: peasant farmers feeding themselves and their families. The main crops are sorghum, maize, taro, yams, cassava, rice and millet; it is not known how much is produced and how much is sold. Nor is it known whether the peasant farmers' nutritional habits are better or worse than in the past. What is known and recognized is that the peasant farmers who produce at least two thirds of Nigeria's food are no longer able to keep up with the rapidly rising demand for food and that for the last twenty years there has been a crisis in agriculture.

NIGERIA

Before independence in 1960 agriculture was Nigeria's most important industry; the country produced enough to feed its people and to export agricultural surplus. As the oil boom peaked in the 1970s, agriculture declined as the young men left the rural areas for the money and excitement of urban life. Nigeria was forced to rely more on food imports. At the same time its cash crop exports declined dramatically. Exports of groundnuts and palm oil collapsed and cocoa exports fell; cocoa, palm kernels and rubber are still exported, but only account for about 3 per cent of Nigeria's foreign currency earnings. Different governments have tried to increase agricultural production with such initiatives as *OPERATION FEED THE NATION (1976–9) and the Green Revolution (1979–83). Money was spent on plantations, vast irrigation projects and rural development programmes; marketing boards for different commodities were set up. Lacking the necessary administrative expertise and infrastructure the authorities had little success in these schemes, which merely wasted money.

Since independence Nigeria's non-agricultural economy has been dominated and distorted by the oil boom. Oil production near the Niger Delta began in 1958 and rapidly expanded during the 1960s and 1970s to reach a peak of nearly two and a half million barrels a day in 1979. Oil accounted for nearly all export earnings and led to substantial real economic growth during the 1970s. It provided the

money for investment in ambitious public and industrial projects, for the massive expansion of imports (often of unnecessary luxuries) and for the servicing of debts. When the oil boom collapsed in 1981 Nigeria was in serious trouble, unable to pay for its imports, unable to service its debts and unable to finance its major development projects. The 1980s has seen repeated devaluations of Nigeria's currency (the naira), high inflation, balance of payments deficits, a mounting international debt and a real fall in the standard of living of many Nigerians – problems which have had serious political repercussions.

Nigeria also has large deposits of natural gas associated with petroleum; schemes to utilize the gas more effectively are planned although problems in funding and an inefficient infrastructure have caused delays. There are also substantial coal deposits and plans to improve coal production for the benefit of important customers like the railways and the electricity industry. Finally Nigeria was a leading exporter of tin, but declining reserves, high production costs and low world prices have led to a sharp drop in production.

For such a big country Nigeria has a relatively small and low technology manufacturing sector which concentrates on providing substitutes for imports, in particular textiles, beverages, cigarettes, soaps and detergents. During the 1980s manufacturing suffered from a shortage of foreign currency to buy raw materials, a lack of capital investment, transport

254

problems and the inadequacies of the electricity supply.

An international debt of nearly $30 billion is but one of the serious financial and economic problems which have led the present military government to impose the austerity measures of the structural adjustment programme and to apply to the World Bank and the IMF for aid. In December 1988 the IMF supported Nigeria's economic reform programme and cleared the way for debt rescheduling and a $500 million loan from the World Bank. During 1989 there were riots against austerity measures and it is not at all clear that the government will be able to continue administering this bitter economic medicine.

The early history of Nigeria is complex. About seven thousand years ago farming people were settled in the Plateau in the centre of the country, where the *BANTU people may have originated. In this area the Nok culture with its fine terracotta sculpture and its ironmaking skills flourished over two thousand years ago. The earliest state systems were developed in the north and deeply influenced by the cultures of North Africa and Islam. The climate favoured the domestication of cattle and horses and the growth of cereals and cotton. By the eleventh century two well established state systems, Kanem-Bornu and Hausa-Bokwoi, dominated the north and enjoyed the benefits of the rich trans-Saharan trade in leather, salt, slaves and gold. Despite civil wars and external aggression these

states expanded to put pressure on the people of the southern forest belt. Early in the nineteenth century Shehu Usman dan Fodio, a Fulani leader, decreed a *JIHAD which led to the installation of Fulani Emirs in most of the Hausa states. Islamic administrative systems were set up in the Fulani-Hausa states and beyond Hausaland.

In the south-east the Ibo had not developed major states before the arrival of the Europeans, but they had beaten off invaders from the north and the west and developed their agriculture to feed their ever-increasing numbers. In the southwest the Yoruba had established an empire at Ife by the tenth century and later empires at Oyo and Benin. The famous Benin bronzes are amongst the world's greatest artistic masterpieces.

The Portuguese arrived on the coast in the fifteenth century and were soon followed by other Europeans. Portugal began the transatlantic slave trade, but by the eighteenth century the British were the leading slave traders. Before Britain abolished the slave trade early in the nineteenth century an estimated thirty million West Africans were shipped across the Atlantic as slaves and the economic, social and political systems of southern Nigeria were shattered.

During the nineteenth century missionaries and British traders in the south put pressure on Britain to intervene more actively in the area. Lagos became a British colony in 1861 and was expanded to include

Yoruba states. Having won the recognition of the European powers at the Congress of Berlin (1884) for their claims to Nigeria, Britain overcame strong resistance to conquer the south by the end of the century. It then subdued northern Nigeria (1901–6). In 1906 the Lagos Protectorate and the Niger Coast Protectorate were united to form the Southern Protectorate; in 1914 the Northern and Southern Protectorates were united to form Nigeria. Once its authority was established Britain favoured the system of indirect rule which was cheaper and less likely to provoke opposition than direct colonial rule. The existing Ibo and Yoruba structures were not suitable, but in the north Britain used the Fulani Emirs to apply indirect rule.

As the Second World War ended Nigerians began campaigning for independence. There were three major political parties with strong regional bases. In the Eastern Region there was Dr ⋆AZIKIWE's National Council for Nigeria and the Cameroons (⋆NCNC) founded in 1944; in the Western Region Chief ⋆AWOLOWO's ⋆ACTION GROUP was founded in 1950; in the Northern Region the ⋆NPC (Northern People's Congress) was founded in 1951 and led by Ahmadu ⋆BELLO. Britain agreed to independence and under the Macpherson constitution the first national elections were held in 1952. The successes of the NPC in the north, the Action Group in the west and the NCNC in the east were followed by serious

256

disagreements over the constitutional arrangements for independent Nigeria.

The Muslim north feared that the educated Christians of the south would dominate Nigeria. The south feared that the populous north would have a natural majority in national elections. The prosperous west was unwilling to share its wealth with the other two regions. The east wanted a centralized system which would give its people opportunities in all parts of the country. The Macpherson constitution was abandoned in favour of a federal constitution with considerable powers for regional governments. In the pre-independence federal elections (Dec. 1959) regional differences ensured that no party won an overall majority. The NPC won most seats and under the leadership of ⋆BALEWA formed a coalition government with the NCNC and led Nigeria to independence in the Commonwealth (Oct. 1960), as a constitutional monarchy until it became a republic (Oct. 1963).

As a powerful and independent African state Nigeria played a leading part in Third World and Commonwealth affairs, but suffered from severe constitutional and political problems. The interests of Nigeria's many smaller ethnic groups were ignored and the federal system based on three regions meant the exclusion of one major political party and one region from power at the national level. The Action Group in the west was in this unenviable position as Nigeria became independent. The attempts of the other two major political parties to exploit the split in the Action Group (1962), the arrest and imprisonment of Awolowo (1962) and the creation of a new Mid-Western region (1963) destabilized the west as well as seriously weakening the credibility of the federal government.

While opportunist factions schemed for political power and feathered their own nests the interests of the people were neglected. Increasing rents, rising food prices, blatant corruption and the growing gap between rich and poor fermented popular discontent and led to general strikes in 1963 and 1964. The breakdown of the government coalition and the exclusion of the NCNC from power after the openly corrupt and violent federal elections in December 1984 was followed by the even more corrupt and violent regional elections in the west (Oct. 1965). By late 1965 various groups took to the streets in the west and other parts of the country. Law and order was clearly breaking down.

Against this background the military seized power for the first time (Jan. 1966), assassinating the federal prime minister, the federal minister of finance and the regional premiers of the north and the west. Ibo officers organized the coup and one of them, Maj.-Gen. *AGUIYI-IRONSI, took power. Northerners feared Ibo domination of Nigeria. After a series of anti-Ibo riots northerners took control in a counter coup (Jul. 1966); General Aguiyi-Ironsi was assassinated and replaced by Lt.-Col. *GOWON, a northerner.

In the east Lt.-Col. *OJUKWU and most Ibo refused to accept the new military government. In May 1967, after months of rising tension, the east seceded from Nigeria and proclaimed itself the independent Republic of *BIAFRA. Despite initial successes in the Mid-Western Region the 'Biafrans' were gradually worn down by the manpower and resources of the federal government. In a bitter war of attrition federal forces tightened their stranglehold on the east and starved it of supplies. Some estimates say that two million easterners died – mainly from starvation. As the war ended (Jan. 1970) General Gowon embarked on a reasonably successful campaign of national reconciliation. His economic policies were less successful. Corruption, inflation and shortages rose as the government failed to develop the country's infrastructure and its economic base. Nigerianization of the economy caused disruption and benefited only the rich, the corrupt and the acquisitive.

Gowon made no progress in returning Nigeria to civilian rule. In 1970 he surprised the country by announcing that the military would stay in power until 1976. Hopes of national reconciliation were undermined by the 1973 census results which were to be the basis for political representation in future elections. These reported a remarkable increase in the population of the northern states. Arguing that Nigeria was not yet ready, Gowon shocked the

257

country in 1974 when he indefinitely postponed the return to civilian rule.

In July 1975 Gowon was overthrown in a bloodless coup by another military officer from the north, General Murtala *MUHAMMED. He instituted a ruthless and popular drive against corruption and inefficiency in the public services. Over ten thousand civil servants were sacked or retired; university lecturers, diplomats, senior police officers and army officers were also purged. Official investigations led to the confiscation of property and the trial and conviction of the corrupt. Murtala Muhammed also announced (Oct. 1975) the timetable for a return to civilian rule by 1979.

Nigeria was stunned and dismayed by the assassination of Muhammed in an abortive coup (Feb. 1976), but his deputy, Lt.-Gen. *OBASANJO, took over and continued with Muhammed's plans. While Nigeria was facing increasingly serious economic problems, a complex federal constitution was drawn up. Steps were taken to ensure that no single region could dominate the country. Despite various problems the elections were held in 1979. After thirteen years the military stepped down and Alhaji Shehu *SHAGARI was sworn in as President of the Second Republic (Oct. 1979). His party, the National Party of Nigeria (*NPN), did well in the federal and state elections, but did not win a majority in the federal parliament.

Nigeria had high hopes of President Shagari, but the country was soon disillusioned by blatant corruption, fiscal malpractice and economic mismanagement. Certain unsavoury characters speedily acquired large fortunes. After a short boom which was partly fuelled by the government's extravagance, the slump in world oil prices early in the 1980s brought Nigeria to the bring of complete financial collapse. To borrow money abroad the government had to impose austerity measures which caused great hardship to the Nigerian people. Disgust at 'western' corruption and social injustice encouraged the rise of Islamic fundamentalism. There were riots and heavy loss of life in the north (1980–2); the government blamed Muslim extremists, ignoring the social and economic causes of unrest.

Despite all these problems Shagari and the NPN were successful in the 1983 elections. They took advantage of the efficient party machine and of divisions among their opponents. As the economy continued to collapse and as Shagari refused to acknowledge the situation, the military intervened again. On the last day of 1983 Shagari was deposed in a bloodless coup and Nigeria had a new military government led by Maj.-Gen. *BUHARI. Buhari was welcomed as a national saviour and acted sternly against corruption. Although he imposed harsh austerity measures Buhari failed to find any remedies for Nigeria's economic problems. He became increasingly authoritarian, resorting to secret trials without the right of appeal and arbitrarily imprisoning political critics.

In August 1985 General *BABANGIDA seized power from Buhari in a bloodless coup. As a military ruler he has been able to adopt economic policies which would lead to the downfall of any elected government. The Structural Adjustment Programme is hated; it has brought hunger and destitution to many. Despite riots in 1989 and yet another attempted coup by junior officers (Apr. 1990), Babangida is determined that Nigeria has to take its economic medicine to secure a better future. He has promised that the military will step down in 1992 and has established a Constituent Assembly. The military government plans that Nigeria will have two political parties – one slightly to the left and the other slightly to the right.

The 1990s are going to be difficult for Nigeria. If there is a smooth transition to civilian rule and if the new civilian government continues to exercise economic discipline there is some hope that by the beginning of the next century Nigeria will be over the worst of its problems and that it will be able to look forward to the future with confidence.

Nile The justification for including an ageless river in a dictionary covering events 'since 1960' is that Egypt is facing a catastrophe as successive African droughts reduce the river's flow to its lowest levels this century. The main White Nile stream begins in the lake country of east Africa; the Blue Nile originates in the Ethiopian Plateau. After the rivers meet at Khartoum the united Nile runs 1875 miles north to the Mediterranean. Egypt and Sudan share the Nile's waters, with Egypt using 5.5 billion cubic metres annually and Sudan 18 cubic metres. Of Egypt's share, 48 billion cubic metres are allocated for agricultural purposes and most of the rest for municipal and industrial uses. Egypt's Aswan High Dam complex was built in the 1960s to provide irrigation and hydroelectric power for the Nile Valley. While the dam has successfully regulated the river, many fields must now be artificially fertilized since the silt left behind by Nile floodings is now deposited in reservoirs and canals. Many times during the 1980s, droughts over the Nile's African watersheds caused the planned level of Lake Nasser, the strategic water reserve, to drop over seventy feet. Hydroelectric capacity at the Aswan High Dam has also been adversely affected. Lack of irrigation-water means an alarming reduction in food supply. With the help of US water supply grants, the Egyptian water authorities are building a multi-million dollar monitoring system. This will enable monitors to take data from 250 telemetry stations and make minute-by-minute water-saving adjustments to the flows that pass through the 30,000 miles of canals in the irrigation network.

Nimeiri, Jaffar Muhammad (b. 1930), army officer and Sudan's head of state 1971–85. Born in Omdurman, Nimeiri received his main education at the Sudan Military College. The peak of his military career was his command, as a colonel, of the Shandi district, 1966–9. In 1969 Sudan's economy was in ruins, foreign aid had dwindled and the civil war had reached stalemate. In these conditions, Nimeiri plotted with fourteen other relatively junior officers to take over the state. Their coup, on 25 May 1969, was practically bloodless. Much influenced by the earlier Egyptian Free Officers Movement, Nimeiri became Chairman of the Revolutionary Command Council as well as prime minister. His rule was for a time progressive and benevolent and he leaned towards the Right. A group of pro-Communist army officers attempted a coup against Nimeiri in 1971 and failed. To strengthen his position, Nimeiri, now a general, declared himself president. Falling out with President *SADAT over Egypt's peace treaty with Israel, Nimeiri turned to *GADDAFI of Libya for economic and military help. He became more authoritarian and when labour strikes turned into riots he blamed 'Communists and atheists' and purged many opponents. In 1980, in deference to Saudi Arabia and Sudan's own powerful Islamic fundamentalists, Nimeiri brought in the *SHARIA, or Islamic law. His administration became oppressive and cruel, with barbaric punishments being inflicted on alleged offenders against the sharia. The elderly pacifist leader of the Republican Brothers, Muhammad *TAHA was hanged for protesting against the sharia. In March 1985 Nimeiri flew to Washington to seek $194 million in US aid. In his absence, General Abdul Rahman Swaredahab

seized power and declared martial law. President *MUBARAK gave Nimeiri sanctuary in Egypt, from where he tried to destabilize the Sudanese government in order to make a comeback as president.

Njonjo, Charles (b. 1920), Kenyan lawyer and politician of Kikuyu origins who studied at *FORT HARE UNIVERSITY COLLEGE and London University before being called to the Bar in London (1954). He held various legal posts in Kenya before becoming the first Attorney-General of independent Kenya (1963–80). When *MOI succeeded to the presidency (1978) Njonjo was his trusted adviser. In 1980 Njonjo resigned as Attorney-General, won election to parliament and became Minister for Home and Constitutional Affairs.

In the 1982 cabinet reshuffle he lost the portfolio of Home Affairs to *KIBAKI, the Vice-President. In 1983 President Moi accused him of plotting. He was sacked from the cabinet and forced out of parliament while a lengthy judicial inquiry was held (1983–4). Moi announced that Njonjo was guilty of plotting to overthrow the government, but pardoned him to mark the twenty-first anniversary of independence (Dec. 1984).

Nkomati Accord (Mar. 1984) non-aggression pact signed by President *MACHEL of Mozambique and President P. W. *BOTHA of South Africa, at a town on the border between the two countries. By late 1982 military and economic pressures had persuaded Mozambique to start negotiations with South Africa on security, economic relations, tourism, guerrilla activities and the use of power from *CABORA BASSA. At Nkomati South Africa agreed to stop supporting the Mozambican rebel movement, *RENAMO; Mozambique promised to stop the *AFRICAN NATIONAL CONGRESS (ANC) from using it as a base for raids on South Africa. The agreement was not successful. Documents captured from Renamo showed that South Africa continued to support it and Mozambique was reluctant to act against the ANC. President *CHISSANO resumed negotiations and by the late 1980s there was evidence of more co-operation; South Africa has distanced itself from Renamo. The Nkomati Accord showed that a radical socialist African neighbour could be persuaded to negotiate with South Africa.

Nkomo, Joshua Mqabukonyongolo (b.1917), veteran Zimbabwean political leader, currently a senior cabinet minister. A member of the minority Matabele, he studied in South Africa before returning to his homeland and becoming a leading trade unionist. In 1952 he became leader of the *AFRICAN NATIONAL CONGRESS, which he reorganized in 1957 to become a powerful advocate of the African cause until it was banned in 1959. Nkomo then led the more militant *NDP (National Democratic Party) from 1960 until it was banned in 1961. He founded *ZAPU (Zimbabwe African People's Union) in December 1961 and organized mass rallies against

the government until ZAPU was banned in September 1962.

In 1963 Nkomo and other ZAPU leaders went to Tanzania where they formed a government in exile. The party split in 1963 when some of its members left to form *ZANU (Zimbabwe African National Union). Nkomo returned to Zimbabwe where he was imprisoned or detained for eleven years (1963–74). Meanwhile his lieutenants who were based in Zambia built up the strength of *ZIPRA (ZAPU's military wing) for the struggle against white minority rule. After the failure of negotiations with Ian *SMITH (1975–6), Nkomo's ZAPU joined *MUGABE's ZANU to form the *PF (Patriotic Front) in 1976 – thus unifying the two main nationalist forces in the struggle for independence.

As joint leader of the PF, Nkomo attended the talks which led to the *LANCASTER HOUSE AGREEMENT (Dec. 1979). Nkomo's ZAPU (under the label of PF) and Mugabe's ZANU (under the label of ZANU (PF)) fought the pre-independence elections separately. Although Nkomo may have banked on his reputation as father of Zimbabwean nationalism giving him victory, his party won only a quarter of the common roll seats and he became a junior partner in Mugabe's coalition government (1980–2), serving in various cabinet offices including Home Affairs. Relations between Nkomo and Mugabe were strained and in 1982 Nkomo and other members of his party were sacked from the cabinet. Nkomo returned to Matabeleland and accused Mugabe of trying to overthrow the constitution. The two men were reconciled and agreed a unity pact in 1987, in which ZAPU agreed to merge with ZANU (PF). Early in 1988 Nkomo rejoined the cabinet as a senior minister without any specific departmental responsibility. After the March 1990 elections it was announced that Nkomo would become a vice-president.

Nkrumah, Dr Kwame (1909–72), African statesman who led Ghana to independence. Born Francis Nwia Kofi, he was involved in African and West African associations in Britain and the United States. In the Gold Coast in 1947 he became a full-time politician as General Secretary of the United Gold Coast Convention (UGCC), the colony's most powerful nationalist body. In this post Nkrumah made a name for himself not only as an effective organizer but also as an opponent of colonialism and an advocate of a federation of African socialist states.

After disturbances in 1948 Nkrumah and other UGCC leaders were arrested and deported from Accra. In 1949 Nkrumah broke with the UGCC and formed the more radical *CONVENTION PEOPLE'S PARTY (CPP) which campaigned for positive action and immediate independence. For inciting illegal strikes Nkrumah was imprisoned for a year (1950–1), but while he was in prison the CPP won the 1951 general election and the colonial

authorities released him to become Leader of Government Business (1951) and Prime Minister (1952). In 1957 he led the Gold Coast and British Togoland to independence as Ghana, the first African colony to win independence.

Nkrumah had triumphantly led Ghana to independence, but he had little success in securing his other great ambition – the union of African states. This was partly because his Pan-Africanism was distorted by being made part of his personal political creed – 'Nkrumahism'. In 1960 he led Ghana into the unsuccessful 'Union of African States' with Guinea and Mali; he had hoped this would be a pioneer scheme for African unity.

Initially, Nkrumah was popular in Ghana and much admired by African nationalist leaders and the political Left all over the world. He disillusioned many supporters when he fostered his own personality cult, assuming the honorific title of Osagyefo ('he who is successful in war') and publishing volumes of his speeches and thoughts. In Ghana he adopted draconian measures to concentrate power in his hands and to crush any opposition. Isolated from his people he listened only to self-seeking sycophants and allowed the CPP to become enmeshed in a web of corruption and intrigue. In 1958 he removed the obligation to consult regional assemblies on constitutional changes and in 1960 made Ghana a republic, and himself President. In 1964 he finally eliminated any legal opposition by making Ghana a single-party socialist state.

Internationally he moved closer to the communist world, while maintaining his own version of socialism and seeking western financial aid. In his attempts to break Ghana's dependence on cocoa, Nkrumah spent heavily on development, mainly on massive and prestigious projects like the Akosombo Dam, which created Lake Volta in 1966. The economy was overstretched and Ghana accumulated heavy debts. Nkrumah was toppled by a military coup while he was abroad (Feb. 1966). He went into exile in Guinea, where he died.

Nkumbula, Harry (1916–83), Zambian nationalist leader who first entered politics in the 1930s, founder and president of the *AFRICAN NATIONAL CONGRESS II (1951). He unsuccessfully opposed the *CENTRAL AFRICAN FEDERATION in the early 1950s and was imprisoned in 1955. In 1958 his decision to co-operate in the federal election split the party. More radical elements left to form *UNIP which seized the political initiative and won the 1962 election. Nkumbula served as Minister of African Education in the coalition government (1962–4). After independence he led the opposition until Zambia became a one-party state (Dec. 1972). Reluctantly he joined UNIP in 1973.

NNDP (Nigerian National Democratic Party), a political party in Western Nigeria formed by Chief *AKINTOLA in 1964, following his bitter disputes with Chief *AWOLOWO (leader of the *ACTION GROUP) in 1962/63. In 1964 the NNDP joined the *NPC as a junior partner in the federal coalition government. In October 1965 after blatant corruption and fraud, the NNDP announced its victory in the Western Region elections. The election and the disorder that followed was largely responsible for the decision of the military to seize power in January 1966 and to ban all political parties.

Northern Rhodesia, named after Cecil Rhodes and under British rule from the late nineteenth century until it became the independent Republic of *ZAMBIA in 1964.

NPC (Northern People's Congress), Nigerian political party which began as a cultural organization of northern Nigerians (1949) and was organized as a political party under the leadership of Sir Ahmadu *BELLO (1951). The NPC had strong support in the Muslim north. It feared domination of Nigeria by southerners after independence and campaigned for regional autonomy and respect for traditional forms of government. After the 1952 elections it formed the Northern Regional government with Bello as premier (1954–66).

Its deputy leader, Sir Abubakar Tafawa *BALEWA, became federal prime minister in 1957 and led Nigeria to independence in 1960. The NPC was the largest party after the 1959 pre-independence election, but did not have a majority in the legislature. It governed in coalition with the *NCNC until 1964. After the coalition broke down the

263

NPC joined Chief *AKINTOLA's *NNDP (Nigerian National Democratic Party) in a coalition which presided over an increasingly chaotic situation until it was overthrown in the military coup of January 1966.

NPN (National Party of Nigeria), political party founded in 1978 during the run up to civilian rule. Based at Kaduna, it included businessmen, traditional rulers and veterans from the *NPC, but it worked hard to make itself a national party and chose Lagos not Kaduna for its national convention in 1978. Its policies were right of centre – the need for law and order, a free-market economy, the protection of individual rights and respect for tradition.

The NPN was probably the best organized of the five parties contesting the 1979 elections. Shagari won the presidential election; the NPN won seven of the nineteen state governorships and 35 per cent to 40 per cent of the seats in the senate, the House of Representatives and the state assemblies. It governed with the support of the *NPP (Nigerian People's Party) until the alliance was dissolved in July 1981. By this time the NPN was under attack as a Kaduna clique milking the system for the benefit of its cronies, and Shagari was at odds with the federal legislature.

The NPN spent heavily in the run up to the 1983 election and took advantage of the divisions among its opponents. After much corruption and malpractice the party gained a clear majority in both houses of the legislature and Shagari was re-elected with over twelve million votes. It may well have won in a fair fight, but was now discredited by its election tactics and its corruption. As fears of an economic collapse grew the military seized power at the end of 1983 and banned all political parties.

NPP (Nigerian People's Party), political party founded by Waziri Ibrahim (1978) as Nigeria prepared to return to civilian government. It was one of the five parties contesting the 1979 elections. Its conservative policies were supported by small business. The party split at the convention late in 1978; Ibrahim lost control and formed another party. The NPP persuaded *AZIKIWE to be its presidential candidate. In the 1979 elections Azikiwe came third and the party won three state governorships and majorities in three state assemblies. It made an alliance with the ruling federal party, the *NPN (National Party of Nigeria). After this alliance broke down (1981) the NPP allied itself to the main opposition party – the *UPN (Unity Party of Nigeria). This alliance could have ousted President *SHAGARI in the 1983 election, but the two parties quarrelled and each put up their own presidential candidate. After the military coup at the end of 1983 the NPP and all other political parties were banned.

Nqumayo, Albert Muwalo (d. 1977), Malawian politician who supported the nationalist campaign and joined the government after independence.

He was Minister of State from 1966 until 1977 when he and the head of the Special Branch were tried in secret and executed on charges of plotting to assassinate President *BANDA. The two men may have been scapegoats for the harshness of government policies; their execution was followed by the release of about two thousand political detainees and some minor liberalization. From 1978 voters could choose from three *MALAWI CONGRESS PARTY candidates instead of having just one candidate.

Ntare V (d. 1972), last Mwami (King) of Burundi, a Tutsi prince who in July 1966 supplanted his father, *Mwambutsa IV. At his accession *MICOMBERO, who had helped him take the throne, was made Prime Minister and promoted to the rank of colonel. The two men soon quarrelled and Micombero overthrew the monarchy (Nov. 1966). Following the failure of the Hutu rising in 1972 Ntare, who had recently returned to Burundi, was executed on the orders of Micombero.

Ntombi Latfwala, Queen Regent of Swaziland (1983–6) with the title of Indlovukazi (The Great She Elephant), one of King *SOBHUZA II's fifty widows and King *MSWATI III's mother. She replaced Queen Regent *DZELIWE who had angered the powerful traditionalists in the *LIQOQO. Ntombi was expected to continue as regent until her son turned twenty-one in 1989. She clashed with the Liqoqo, sacking two of its powerful members and reducing its powers (Oct. 1985). As feuding in the royal family threatened the stability of Swaziland, Mswati III's coronation was brought forward to 1986.

Nujoma, Sam (b. 1929), Namibian political leader, co-founder of *SWAPO (1960), and President of SWAPO since its formation, and from 1990 the first President of Namibia. With little formal education Nujoma worked on the railways before working as a clerk. During the 1950s he was a member of the Ovamboland People's Congress and an active trade unionist. After playing a leading role in protests against the contract labour system in the late 1950s he escaped into exile and was at the United Nations as SWAPO's representative (1960). He set up SWAPO's provisional headquarters in Dar es Salaam (1961). When Nujoma returned to Namibia he was detained and ordered out of the country (1966), and was not able to return until 1979.

He then devoted himself to the armed struggle and led an effective campaign to win international recognition for the claims of the Namibian people to self-determination. After SWAPO won forty-four of the seventy-two seats in the November 1989 elections Nujoma became president-elect, but without a two-thirds majority he had to seek the co-operation of other parties in drafting a constitution. Nujoma has modified his socialism and accepted a constitution which commits Namibia to multi-party democracy and a mixed economy. There is a declaration of rights and the constitution can only be changed by a two-thirds majority. Nujoma has sought reconciliation among all Namibians. There are some hopes that under Nujoma's leadership Namibia will at last enjoy peace, prosperity, liberty and democracy.

Nwapa, Flora (Florence Nwanzuruaha) (b.1931), Nigerian writer of novels, short stories, children's books and non-fiction. Educated in Scotland, Flora Nwapa worked as a teacher, an educational administrator and as a civil servant in Nigeria – where she launched her own publishing company. She is particularly concerned about the role and status of Nigerian women. Her first novel, *Efuru* (1966) is about a dignified woman suffering in silence. The heroine of *Idu* (1970) lives in a small Nigerian town and wants more from life than just raising a family. *Never Again* (1976) is an indictment of the evils of war, based on Nwapa's experiences in *BIAFRA during the civil war.

Nxumalo, Simon Sishayi (b.1936), Swaziland politician who taught before entering politics and founding the Swaziland Democratic Party (1962). After his defeat in the 1964 election he joined *IMBOKODVO and served in the legislature (1967–73). He won the confidence of King *SOBHUZA II and held various ministerial posts (1967–84). He was the first chairman of *TIBIYO TAKA NGWANE (Swaziland National Development Fund) from 1968 to 1983 when he was appointed Minister of Finance. In 1982 he negotiated with South Africa over the

proposed cession of territory to Swaziland. After Nxumalo was sacked from the *LIQOQO and the Ministry of Finance (1984) he claimed that members of the Liqoqo were involved in massive customs frauds. He was then accused of high treason and detained until his release in the amnesty declared by Queen Regent *NTOMBI at the end of 1985.

Nyagumbo, Maurice (1924–89), a prominent Zimbabwean nationalist and political leader who committed suicide after revelations of corruption. He was an early member of the *AFRICAN NATIONAL CONGRESS, *ZAPU and *ZAMU and was imprisoned for nearly twenty years during the struggle for African majority rule. He was released in 1979 to attend the talks which led to the *LANCASTER HOUSE AGREEMENT. After winning a seat in parliament in the pre-independence elections he joined the cabinet (1980), serving as Minister of Mines and Energy Resources. Later he concentrated his efforts on party organization, becoming a senior minister and the third ranking member of the *ZANU *(PF) Politburo. In 1989 after revelations of his involvement in a corruption scandal involving the illegal sale of government cars Nyagumbo resigned from the cabinet and killed himself. He was declared a National Hero and buried in *HEROES' ACRE.

Nyasaland, former name of the Republic of Malawi, used while Britain exercised a protectorate over the country (1891–1964). Lake Malawi was then called Lake Nyasa.

Nyasaland African Congress, Malawian nationalist movement (1944–59). During the 1950s it became more radical and effective under the leadership of *CHIPEMBERE and *CHIUME who persuaded Hastings *BANDA to return home in 1958 to lead the campaign against the *CENTRAL AFRICAN FEDERATION. During the state of emergency it was banned and replaced by the *MALAWI CONGRESS PARTY.

Nyerere, Julius Kambarage (b.1922), influential African statesman, ex-President of Tanzania, Third World spokesman and campaigner against colonialism and *APARTHEID. In many ways Nyerere has not been a typical African leader. He has lived austerely, paying himself a modest salary and ignoring the trappings of high office. An intellectual socialist and an idealist, he has earned respect at home and abroad. In Tanzania he is revered as *MWALIMU (teacher).

He taught in *TANGANYIKA before founding and becoming the President of *TANU (Tanganyika African National Union) in 1954. He led an energetic and peaceful campaign for independence from British rule. After TANU won seventy out of seventy-one seats in the 1960 election Nyerere was Chief Minister until late 1961 when he became independent Tanganyika's first Prime Minister. He resigned early in 1962 to devote himself to strengthening the organization of TANU and to developing its political ideology. His pamphlet *UJAMAA, *the Basis of African Socialism* emphasized the values of African communities and greatly influenced TANU's programme. Later (1967) Nyerere amplified his ideas with the *ARUSHA DECLARATION which was adopted by the party and incorporated into the constitution; the declaration emphasized egalitarianism and self-reliance and made rural development a priority.

By the end of 1962 the country's republican constitution was complete and Nyerere became President. He had to face pressure from trade unionist activists for speedier Africanization (1963–4) and an army mutiny (Jan. 1964) which was close to success until the arrival of British troops. After these events he moved to establish his authority more firmly and made TANU the country's only legal political party. After that there were few challenges to his authority; the country became a model of political stability in Africa. Also in 1964 Nyerere negotiated with *ZANZIBAR to merge Tanganyika with Zanzibar to create the state of Tanzania; he was the new state's first President (1964–85). In 1977 he negotiated the merger of TANU with the *AFRO-SHIRAZI PARTY (Zanzibar's only legal political party) to form *CHAMA CHA MAPINDUZI (CCM), Tanzania's only legal political party. Nyerere has been its chairman since 1977.

Nyerere's social policies had only limited success, mainly in the provision of health care and education in the rural areas. The country was spared the horrors of coups and civil wars, but there were considerable economic problems. State-run industries proved to be corrupt and inefficient and under state direction the production of cash export crops declined. Tanzania suffered high inflation, shortages of essential goods, and still has a large balance of payments deficit. In the early 1980s, partly because of drought, Tanzania was unable to feed itself. Critics attributed the problems to the failings of Nyerere's African socialism, but he blamed droughts, floods, falling world prices for Tanzanian exports and sharply increased prices for petroleum and other essential imports. Nyerere had to look for aid from international bodies, but was reluctant to modify his socialist policies and embark on the economic restructuring favoured by the International Monetary Fund and the World Bank.

Nyerere is well known for his work at Third World summits, in African organizations and in the campaign against apartheid – activities which may have distracted him from problems nearer home. Certainly there were many problems with his neighbours. Ethnic massacres in Burundi and the flood of refugees into Tanzania (1973) strained relations between the two countries. The *EAST AFRICAN COMMUNITY collapsed after bitter disputes among its members. The Kenyan border was closed for six years (1977–83). Nyerere clashed with President *AMIN of Uganda during the 1970s and refused to sit at the same table with him. Finally the Tanzanian army and Ugandan dissidents invaded and overthrew Amin (1979).

In 1985 Nyerere resigned the presidency, one of the few African leaders to retire voluntarily, to make way for *MWINYI, his chosen successor. He planned to resign the chairmanship of the CCM in 1987, but changed his mind and retained the post. He may be holding on to the party chairmanship to safeguard his ideals and to support his followers in the party. He is worried by Mwinyi's relaxations of socialist policies, but he has admitted to making mistakes in the pursuit of African socialism and he gave at least tacit support to the country's economic recovery programme late in the 1980s.

Obasanjo, General Olusegun (b. 1937), former military ruler of Nigeria (1976–9). A military engineer, he enlisted in 1958 and served in the United Nations Congo peace-keeping force (1960). He was promoted Lieutenant-Colonel (1967) and Colonel (1969). He saw action in the civil war (1967–70) and was the officer who accepted the *BIAFRAN surrender (Jan. 1970). He became a Brigadier (1972) and served *GOWON's government as Federal Commissioner for Works and Housing (1975). Under Murtala *MUHAMMED's military government he was Chief of Staff (1975–6) and after Muhammed was assassinated Obasanjo took over as Head of State and Commander-in-Chief of the Armed Forces (Feb. 1976)

He kept the promise of his predecessor to return Nigeria to civilian rule by 1979, after devoting much time and effort to complicated constitutional matters. He seemed to lack any coherent or clearly defined policies to tackle Nigeria's social and economic problems, although he introduced universal primary education and launched *OPERATION FEED THE NATION in a vain attempt to make Nigeria self-sufficient in food. After handing over to President *SHANGARI (1979) he retired to his farm. Since then he has taken part in international initiatives and has been a Co-Chairman of the Commonwealth *EMINENT PERSONS GROUP which visited and reported on South Africa (1985–6).

Obote, (Apollo) Milton (b.1924), ex-President of Uganda. One of a large peasant family, he was expelled for political activism at *MAKERERE COLLEGE (1949) and not allowed by the colonial authorities to take a scholarship to study abroad. He worked in Kenya as a labourer and a clerk (1950–7) and joined the Kenya African Union. Back in Uganda he was a radical member of the *UGANDA NATIONAL CONGRESS and won election to the Legislative Council (1958). In 1961 he founded the *UGANDA PEOPLE'S CONGRESS which won more seats than any other party in the pre-independence elections (1962).

In coalition with the royalist *BUGANDAN party, Kabaka Yekka, he became independent Uganda's first prime minister (Oct. 1962). A year later Uganda became a republic with Obote as prime minister and *MUTESA II as president. For much of his first spell in power (1962–71) Obote enjoyed considerable international esteem. He was a respected Third World leader, an outspoken critic of *APARTHEID and colonialism, a supporter of regional co-operation in the *EAST AFRICAN COMMUNITY and a close friend of President *NYERERE of Tanzania and President *KAUNDA of Zambia.

Within Uganda he was less successful. Refugees from neighbouring countries put a burden on Uganda's resources. There were bitter tribal divisions and the traditionalists were alarmed at Obote's socialist vision of Uganda in the future. He was strongly opposed by traditionalists from Buganda. Obote made no concessions to the mounting opposition to his authority. To overcome tribal and social divisions and to weaken the traditionalists he planned an egalitarian society under one-party rule. He dropped Kabaka Yekka from the coalition, abrogated the 1962 constitution and made himself President of Uganda (1966). He sent the army into Buganda and drove Mutesa II into exile. The following year (1967) his new constitution abolished traditional kingdoms and divided Buganda into four administrative districts.

In 1969 he announced his programme for moving to the left; the state would take majority control of leading commercial, financial and industrial concerns and would implement social and economic changes to wipe out feudalism. Further policy documents followed, but little was done as tension mounted between the government and the army. In December 1969 Obote was wounded in an assassination attempt; in January 1970 a prominent critic of *AMIN, then Chief of Staff, was murdered. Obote ordered the investigation of Amin; he sacked him as Chief of Staff late in 1970 and was planning further action when Amin seized power (Jan. 1971). Obote fled
270

to exile in Tanzania – as President Nyerere's honoured guest.

In exile Obote plotted to return to Uganda and master-minded the disastrous invasion attempt of 1972. By 1978 Nyerere had decided that Amin had to be overthrown and called on Ugandan exiles to join him in an invasion. Obote's supporters joined other dissidents to form the *UGANDA NATIONAL LIBERATION FRONT at the *MOSHI CONFERENCE (Mar. 1979), but Obote was disappointed not to be chosen as leader of the front. After Amin was ousted Obote's supporters gained power in the interim government while Obote delayed his return until May 1980.

Obote won the December 1980 election and became President of Uganda again (1980–5), but many felt the election results had been rigged. He had little success in his professed aim of national reconciliation. The army was out of control and there were brutal massacres in the *LUWERO TRIANGLE. As law and order collapsed various groups fought the government. Economic problems included the lack of transport, soaring inflation, mounting international debts and shortages of vital goods. Obote was deposed by the military (Jul. 1985) and fled into exile in Zambia; some of his supporters continued operations in Uganda until agreeing to end hostilities with the *MUSEVENI government in 1988.

Odendaal Commission (1962), South African appointed commission of inquiry which drew up a blueprint for *APARTHEID in Namibia in its report (1964). Namibians were to be divided into twelve racial groups and given ten *HOMELANDS, eight of them for Africans. The proposals would have given the small white minority (about seven per cent) more territory than the rest of the population. The Ovambo homeland was proclaimed in 1967 and others followed in the 1970s, but Namibian opposition defeated South Africa's attempts to maintain its power by dividing the Namibian people.

Odinga, Ajuma Oginga (b.1911), radical Kenyan politician of Luo origins. After graduating from *MAKERERE COLLEGE he taught for many years and was active in nationalist politics, recruiting many Luo into the Kenya African Union which he joined in 1946. He was elected to the Legislative Council (1957) and to parliament (1961). He was Vice-President of the *KENYA AFRICAN NATIONAL UNION (KANU) (1960–6), Minister for Home Affairs (1963–6) and Vice-President of the Republic of Kenya (1964–6).

As a radical socialist he felt that *KENYATTA favoured capitalism and was angry at the government's termination of land reform. He left the government (1966) and with the support of twenty-nine MPs formed an opposition party – the Kenya People's Union (KPU). In the by-elections which followed the KPU retained only seven seats.

In 1969 the KPU was banned; Odinga was barred from standing for parliament and detained until 1971. He was ultimately reconciled with Kenyatta and rejoined KANU (1971–7). Then in 1977 he was arrested and expelled from KANU. After pledging support for President *MOI (1978), Odinga was readmitted to KANU and made head of the Cotton Marketing Board. Odinga attacked Moi's government for tolerating corruption, neglecting human rights and supporting the United States; he was expelled from KANU again for advocating the formation of a new party (1982). After the abortive coup in 1982 he was restricted to his house until October 1983, but he has continued his campaign against Moi's government.

Ogaden, an immense desert region, straddling the central borders of Ethiopia and Somalia, and the source of a bitter dispute between the two countries beginning in the mid-1970s. Somalia claimed the region since the majority of the Ogaden's population are ethnic Somalis. However, Ogaden comprises about one third of the area of Ethiopia and the government was unlikely to surrender it. In 1977, war broke out between the Ethiopian and Somali armies, the latter being aided by the Western Somali Liberation Front (WSLF).

At first, WSLF captured much territory but huge shipments of Soviet arms and the aid of ten thousand Cuban troops enabled Ethiopia to launch a counteroffensive in Feb.–Mar. 1977. On 12 February, Somalia threw most of its army into the war to support the guerrillas. The major action was the battle of Jigjigs, which Russian generalship won for Ethiopia. In

March 1978, Somalia withdrew from Ogaden.

in 1980 fighting flared up again when the WSLF attacked Ethiopian positions. The Ethiopian air force bombed Somali cities. Ethiopia's leader, Colonel *MENGISTU, began a campaign to depopulate the southern Ogaden and by May 1980 at least 1.4 million refugees had fled into Somalia. The Soviet Union increased the pressure by sending Mengistu helicopter gunships for use against the WSLF. Somalia responded by sending its regular troops to help the guerrillas. Within the year, however, the WSLF was fighting the war alone. Intermittent conflict still takes place.

Ojukwu, Chief Chuckwuemeka Odumegwu (b.1933), former president of the *BIAFRAN Republic. An Ibo who was born in Northern Nigeria, he completed his education in England before working in the Nigerian Public Service (1955–7) and joining the army (1957). After serving in the United Nations peace-keeping force (1960) Ojukwu quickly gained promotion to the rank of Lieutenant-Colonel (1963) and was in command of the 5th Battalion in Kano (1964–6). Although he did not take part in the January 1966 military coup, Ojukwu was chosen by *AGUIYI-IRONSI as Military Governor of the Eastern Region. After the second military coup (Jul. 1966) Ojukwu continued as Military Governor, but there were soon serious problems between the Eastern Region and *GOWON's new military government.

Following the massacres of Ibo people in the north (Sep.–Oct. 1966), Ojukwu asked Gowon to remove northern troops from the Eastern Region. Fearing domination of Nigeria by the Muslim north, he began building up his own army. Negotiations with the federal military government failed and in May 1967 the Ibo consultative assembly gave Ojukwu the authority to declare the secession of the Eastern Region from Nigeria – as the Republic of Biafra.

The secession led to a bitter civil war (1967–70). The Biafrans mounted a sophisticated campaign to win international support and they fought bravely, but they were starved into submission by the beginning of 1970. Shortly before Biafra surrendered Ojukwu went into exile in the Ivory Coast. He returned to Nigeria after President *SHAGARI declared a political amnesty (1982). He joined Shagari's party, the *NPN, and unsuccessfully stood for the Senate in the 1983 elections. He was detained after the military coup at the end of 1983 and released in October 1984.

Okara, Gabriel Imomotimi Gbaingbain (b.1921), Nigerian novelist and poet, the son of an Ijo chief. He has worked as a teacher, a journalist, a publisher and an information officer in the civil service. During the civil war (1967–70) he travelled in the United States and spoke on behalf of *BIAFRA. His best known novel, *The Voice* (1964) is a moral fable. His poetry has strong links with oral tradition and Ijo idiom; some of it was collected in *The Fisherman's Invocation* (1978).

Okotie-Eboh, Chief Festus Samuel (1912–66), Nigerian politician and businessman from Western Nigeria. Before entering politics he went into business on his own and made a fortune from timber, rubber and a chain of schools. As a supporter of *AZIKIWE and the *NCNC (National Council of Nigeria and the Cameroons) he was elected to the Western Region House of Assembly (1951) and to the Federal House of Representatives (1954). He was Federal Minister of Labour (1955–7) and Federal Minister of Finance (1957–66). Okotie-Eboh's opponents accused him of corruption, and he was one of the leading Nigerians assassinated in the January 1966 military coup.

Okpara, Dr Michael Ibeonukara (1920–84), a doctor who became a political leader in Nigeria. A member of the *NCNC (National Council of Nigeria and the Cameroons), Okpara was elected to the Eastern Region House of Assembly (1953) and was Premier of the Eastern Region after *AZIKIWE went into federal politics (1959–66). He supported the federal coalition government of the *NPC (Northern People's Congress) and the NCNC from 1959 until it broke down in 1964. He then led an opposition coalition and asked Azikiwe, the Nigerian president, to postpone the December 1964 federal elections. When Azikiwe refused a postponement Okpara called for a boycott of the elections, which was

effective in the Eastern Region. He supported the *BIAFRAN cause during the civil war (1967–70) and joined the *NPN (National Party of Nigeria) as Nigeria returned to civilian rule (1979).

Olympio, Sylvanus (1902–63), Togolese politician and first head of state. Born in Lomé, to a wealthy trading family, Olympio was first educated in France and then studied at the London School of Economics. In 1946 he was prominent as a director for Togo of the United Africa Company. Fiercely nationalistic, he was active in the Comité de l'Unité Togolaise (CUT) which won the territorial elections of 1946. Olympio was chosen as president of the territorial assembly. In UN-supervised elections in 1958, CUT won and Olympio became prime minister. When independence was proclaimed in 1960 he was installed as first president of the new republic. He made the mistake of ruthlessly repressing his political opponents and in 1963 he was killed during the coup which brought Nicolas *GRUNITZKY to power.

Operation Feed the Nation, General *OBASANJO launched this ambitious programme in a vain attempt to end Nigeria's dependence on imported food (1976). The government hoped that propaganda, education and the subsidization of such agricultural aids as fertilizers and insecticides would encourage farmers to produce more and make the country self-sufficient in essential foodstuffs. There were many problems. There were too few agricultural officers and distribution was inefficient. In 1980 President *SHAGARI scrapped the scheme and replaced it with the Green Revolution which had similar aims.

Organisation de l'armée sécrète (OAS), the 'secret army' organized by some dissident French soldiers and *pieds-noirs*, which prolonged the Algerian War of Independence. The OAS fought its campaign of terror to provide an excuse for the French army to remain in Algeria. The murder in Algiers of a distinguished lawyer by two former French soldiers brought about the formation of the OAS. It assassinated the mayor of Evian, France, on the eve of the first peace talks there, and President de Gaulle himself was on several occasions the target for murder attempts. The OAS attracted regular officers, including, in April 1961, France's most decorated soldier and former commander-in-chief in Algeria, General Raoul Salan. Other famous officers joined the OAS, to serve under Salan and his deputy, General Edmond Jouhaud. All were determined that Algeria would remain French, whatever the cost. The OAS set off explosions in Algiers and carried out many bloody murders, including that of Comissaire Gavoury, the senior police officer who had been ordered to track down the OAS. During the month of September 1961 the organization killed 15 and wounded 144. Gradually, the security forces overcame the OAS, which finally collapsed with the coming of peace in 1962. Some of

its members were tried and executed but its senior leaders, though found guilty, had their lives spared.

Organization of African Unity (OAU), founded in 1963 to promote unity and solidarity among African states and based in Addis Ababa. The OAU aims to coordinate efforts to improve living standards in Africa, to defend the sovereignty and integrity of African states, to eradicate colonialism and to promote international cooperation. It includes nearly all African states, two notable exceptions being Morocco and South Africa. The heads of state meet annually, foreign and other ministers meet twice a year, it has a permanent secretariat and a number of specialized agencies for economic and social matters, for transport, communications, education, science, health, defence, human rights and labour.

Organization of the Islamic Conference (OIC), umbrella organization dedicated to dealing with problems and issues concerning the forty-six nation Islamic world. The OIC came into being in 1970 in Jedda, Saudi Arabia, with Tunku Abdul Rahman of Malaysia as its secretary-general. He was followed by Hassan al Tuhami of Egypt (1974–5), Ahmad Karim Gai of Senegal (1975–9), Habib Chatti of Tunisia (1980–4), Sharifuddin Pirzada of Pakistan (1985–8), and Hamid al Gabid of Niger, who took up his duties in January 1989. There was much criticism of the choice of al Gabid because of his country's lack of political weight.

It was feared that this would cause OIC to descend into obscurity at a time when many Muslim issues such as Palestine, Lebanon, Muslim minorities and intra-Islamic trade and co-operation need vigorous lobbying in international and regional forums.

Apart from political problems which the OIC has never been able to resolve, the major issues facing its members are development, organization, trade, and economic, social and financial co-operation. The OIC has three basic blocs – Asian, Arab and Black African. The secretary-general is elected under a rotation scheme. Many leading Muslims argue that because of the diverse nature of the OIC it needs prominent secretary-generals to bind together the disparate member-states and to lobby governments, which really have the final say in the policies of the organization. In the case of Africa, the most prominent nation, Nigeria, with a very large Muslim population, has considered joining the pan-Islamic body but there is strong opposition from the country's Christian groups who fear that the country might be swamped by Islamically oriented policies as a result. OIC is accused of holding too many conferences and disseminating too much rhetoric while achieving little of substance. For instance, the OIC could not resolve the Iran–Iraq War. Also, the OIC is many years from setting up an Islamic common market because the political will is lacking. Many OIC organs, such as its statistical research bureau in Ankara, were, in 1988, faced with closure because staff had not been paid for months. Similarly, the OIC's cultural branch, in Istanbul, survives more on well-wishers' donations than OIC member-country subscriptions.

P

Palestine Liberation Organization (PLO) The PLO did not directly enter African political affairs until 1982. In that year, following Israel's attack on PLO positions in Lebanon, the PLO leader, Yasser Arafat, was forced to move his principal headquarters from Beirut to Tunis. Many groups, some of them avowedly terrorist, are part of the PLO and most have links with the Arab countries of Africa: since 1969 Libya has been one of its main financial, logistical and ideological backers. The PLO, which in 1989 declared itself the 'government in exile' for Palestine, is a full member of the *ARAB LEAGUE, whose headquarters are in Tunis. The PLO has secretariats in the Arab capitals of Cairo, Algiers, Casablanca, Khartoum, Mogadishu and Tripoli, as well as in many black African countries.

Pan-Africanist Congress (PAC), radical socialist black South African organization founded by Robert *SOBUKWE (1959), who broke away from the *AFRICAN NATIONAL CONGRESS (ANC). Supporters of the PAC believe that other racial groups cannot be associated with the black South Africans in their struggle. Unlike the ANC, it does not welcome whites into its ranks. It believes that Africans should be masters of their own struggle. In 1960 it joined the campaign against the *PASS LAWS and was banned after the events in *SHARPEVILLE.

The PAC went underground and set up its military wing, called Poqo (ourselves). By 1963 Poqo was smashed by the authorities. Since 1985 Johnson Mlambo has been the effective leader of the PAC and its military wing, the Azanian People's Liberation Army. In 1986 the PAC chose Zephaniah Mothopeng, then a political prisoner, as its President; he died in October 1990. The PAC opposed the talks between the ANC and the South African government in May 1990.

Parmehutu (Parti de l'émancipation du peuple Hutu), Rwandan political party which began as the Hutu Democratic Republican Movement in 1959. It was founded and led by Grégoire *KAYIBANDA who became the first President of Rwanda in 1962. In 1965 it became the country's only legal party. In the elections of 1965 and 1969 Parmehutu candidates were elected unopposed to the legislature; as leader of the party Kayibanda was the sole presidential candidate. Kayibanda used Parmehutu in support of his increasingly authoritarian regime and appointed people from central Rwanda, his district, to senior posts in the party. Parmehutu was suspended during the 1973 coup. Since 1978 *MRND has been Rwanda's only legal political party.

Parti congolais du travail (PCT), the sole legal political party in the People's Republic of the Congo. The PCT was founded in December 1969 by President *NGOUABI as a Marxist-Leninist party to implement scientific socialism. Every five years the party congress meets to elect the chairman of its Central Committee, who is also President of the Congo. Since 1979 Colonel Denis *SASSOU-NGUESSO has held both these posts, and the ten members of the Political Bureau occupy leading positions in the government. The Central Committee appoints judges to the Revolutionary Court of Justice and can initiate revisions to the constitution. At the 1989 congress it was clear that the hardliners were losing ground to the moderates in the PCT. Despite its socialist rhetoric, the government of President Sassou-Nguesso has been prepared to drop some of its doctrinaire ideas in favour of more pragmatic and liberal policies.

Partido Africano da Independência da Guiné e Cabo Verde (PAIGC), formed in 1956 and based in Conakry, Guinea. PAIGC campaigned for the liberation of Guinea-Bissau and the Cape Verde Islands from Portuguese rule. Finding peaceful demonstrations and political appeals fruitless, PAIGC began a guerrilla struggle under the dynamic leadership of Amilcar *CABRAL. Following independence in 1975, PAIGC became the Cape Verde Islands' only legal party. Following a coup in Guinea-Bissau in November 1980, Cape Verde broke from PAIGC and set up its own party, the Partido Africano da Independência da Cabo Verde (PAICV). It meant a total split between the two parties and governments.

Pass Laws, to prove they had the right to be in 'white' areas black South Africans had to carry passes or permits; they were liable to be stopped frequently by police checking their passes and every week thousands were arrested for not carrying them. The Pass Laws were introduced for men in 1958 and women in 1963, and caused great resentment. The *SHARPEVILLE killings (1960) began with a peaceful protest against the Pass Laws. The Pass Laws were abolished in 1986. Now South Africans of all races have to carry identity cards, which include their racial classification.

Paton, Alan Stewart (1903–88), white South African writer who campaigned against *APARTHEID. He taught, and as principal of a large reformatory for black youths (1935–48) made a number of humane reforms. A deeply religious man, he was a founder of the South African Institute of Race Relations (1929) and of the multi-racial Liberal Party (1958). He was President of the Liberal Party until 1968 when it had to be dissolved following government legislation banning multi-racial political organizations.

Alan Paton wrote short stories, biographies and South African history books, but is best known for three novels. *Cry, the Beloved Country* (1948) brought him international fame; it tells of an innocent country youth corrupted in the black townships near Johannesburg and is a powerful protest against the degradation of blacks in South Africa. *Too Late the Phalarope* (1953) is a study of

Afrikaner morality and sexual fear across the race barrier. *Ah, But Your Land is Beautiful* (1981) has passive resistance in South Africa during the 1950s as its theme.

p'Bitek, Okot (1931–82), Ugandan poet, novelist and academic who argued that African literature should be written in African languages. After training as a teacher (1952–4) he studied law and anthropology in Britain and presented a thesis on Acholi oral literature. He returned to Uganda and directed the cultural centre for less than two years before going to Nairobi University as a lecturer in literature. Shortly before his death he returned to Uganda to become Professor of Creative Writing at *MAKERERE UNIVERSITY (1982).

p'Bitek's writing demonstrates his commitment to African tradition and culture. His novel, *Lak Tar* (1953) was written in his native Acholi. His poetry, notably *Song of Lawino* (1966) and *Song of Ocal* (1970), follows traditional Acholi verse forms. In *Africa's Cultural Revolution* (1973) he voiced his concern at the threats to African arts. In his last years he collected and published traditional animal tales.

PDG (Parti démocratique gabonais), until 1990 Gabon's only legal political party, founded in 1968 by President *BONGO. Its motto is 'Dialogue-Tolerance-Peace' and it is supposed to end ethnic discrimination and bring national unity to Gabon. It approves the candidates for election to the national assembly and its political bureau can issue decrees without reference to the government. Its chairman is President Bongo. The PDG won the 1990 elections which many observers described as chaotic.

Pearce Commission, a British commission headed by Lord Pearce. It was sent to Zimbabwe (then Rhodesia) in 1972 to determine whether the 1971 Anglo-Rhodesian agreement for independence was acceptable to the population. It travelled widely and found that the whites were in favour but that the Africans were strongly opposed to the agreement, which was not put into effect.

People's Redemption Party (PRP), radical Nigerian political party, founded by Alhaji Aminu *KANO in 1978 as Nigeria prepared to return to civilian rule. Based in the north, it was a populist party which wanted to give power to the people and to redistribute income. It was one of the five parties contesting the 1979 elections. It won two state governorships and Kano came fourth in the presidential contest. Its position was weakened by factional disputes, although it did win the Governorship of Kano State in 1983. After the military coup at the end of 1983 it was banned with all the other political parties.

Pereira, Aristides Maria (b.1924), politician and first President of Republic of Cape Verde. Educated in Senegal, Pereira was trained as a radio telegraphist. In 1956, with Amilcar *CABRAL, he founded the liberationist political party, *PARTIDO AFRICANO DA INDEPENDÊNÇIA DA GUINÉ E CABO VERDE (PAIGC). His activities caused the Portuguese administration to exile him to Guinea in 1960. Here he was leader of the controlling council of PAIGC in its guerrilla war against Portugal between 1965 and 1974. With such revolutionary credentials it was not surprising that, when Cape Verde won its independence on 5 July 1975, Pereira was chosen as president. In January 1986 he was elected for a third five-year term. President Pereira has steered a cautious course through the complexities of African and world politics and has kept Cape Verde stable and relatively prosperous.

PF (Patriotic Front), alliance of the two main Zimbabwean nationalist parties fighting white minority rule in Zimbabwe (then Rhodesia). Partly because of pressure from the *ORGANIZATION OF AFRICAN UNITY and the *FRONT LINE STATES, *ZANU combined with *ZAPU to form the Patriotic Front in October 1976. The PF spoke for the nationalist forces at the talks leading to the *LANCASTER HOUSE AGREEMENT (Dec. 1979), but the two parties in it fought the pre-independence elections separately. ZAPU fought as the PF; ZANU fought as *ZANU (PF).

Phatudi, Cedric Nameni (1912–87), a teacher and a writer who became Chief Minister of Lebowa, one of the South African *HOMELANDS. He entered politics in Lebowa in 1969 and became Minister of Education and Culture when Lebowa was given 'self-government' in 1972. He was Chief Minister from 1973 until his death. Like other Homeland leaders he was criticized for selling out

to the South African government, although he refused 'independence' and rejected P. W. *BOTHA's new constitution in 1984. During the 1980s there was considerable unrest in Lebowa; the attempts to quell the unrest and evidence of police brutality led to violent protests against Phatudi.

PIDE (Polícia Internacional de Defesa do Estado), Portuguese security police who were used to stifle dissent in Portugal's African colonies. They were renowned for their brutality. PIDE's crackdown on nationalist leaders in the late 1950s provoked the launch of the armed struggle in Angola.

Pinto de Andrade, Mário (1928–90), Angolan poet and intellectual, a founding member of the *MPLA, and its president (1960–2). He grew dissatisfied with the leadership of Agostinho *NETO who had ousted him in 1962. He and his brother Joaquim broke with the *MPLA (1974) and formed *ACTIVE REVOLT which was suppressed by 1976. Andrade was imprisoned by the Angolan government in 1976; he was later released.

PLAN (People's Liberation Army of Namibia), military wing of *SWAPO which launched the armed struggle for the independence of Namibia in 1966 with an attack on a South African military base. PLAN was formally inaugurated in 1969 and reorganized in 1973. Few observers expected the small force of about eight thousand men and women to defeat the military might of South Africa, even after its position was strengthened by the establishment of bases in southern Angola (1975). Despite heavy casualties PLAN succeeded in wearing down South African resolve in a long and expensive war of attrition which ended in April 1989 with a formal cease-fire and the beginning of Namibia's transition to independence under the supervision of the United Nations.

Polisario, the resistance front movement of *WESTERN SAHARA, more formally known as Popular Front for the Liberation of Saguia el-Hamra and Río de Oro. Its mission in the 1930s was to liberate the Sahrawi people of Western Sahara from Spanish colonialism. In effect, Polisario is the army of the state-in-exile, the *SAHRAWI ARAB DEMOCRATIC REPUBLIC (SADR). The Spanish government and army suppressed the Sahrawi movement and in 1958 it seemed to be dormant. In fact, it was reorganizing for the founding, in 1968, of the 'Avante-Guarde Organización' for the liberation of the territory. It opposed the Spanish policy of integrating and controlling the various population groups by settling them in towns. This tactic enabled Spanish companies to exploit the recently discovered phosphate deposits at Bou Cras, the largest in the world. On 17 June 1970 a large demonstration by Sahrawis in the capital, Al-Aioun, was bloodily put down.

The founders of the Polisario Front were mainly young people who had studied in the universities of neighbouring countries. In the next two years, skilfully linking political and armed action, the liberation movement was strong enough to mobilize the great majority of Sahrawis. On Spain's withdrawal, Morocco occupied Western Sahara in 1975, and Polisario found itself with a new enemy, King *HASSAN II. Despite the use of enormous force and the building of the *HASSAN WALL, the Moroccans have been unable to subdue the hit-and-run Polisario guerrilla groups, which are supported by Libya and Algeria. Polisario has no more than twelve thousand fighting men but at times it has taken the offensive. Its most notable feat was the capture of Tan-Tan, the base for the *GREEN MARCH and a large military base, in southern Morocco, in 1979 – an embarrassing reverse for Hassan. Polisario has managed to survive largely because of its Algerian backing and the resilience of the Sahrawis themselves. Algeria also provides camps for the Sahrawi refugees. In August 1988 the Moroccan government and the Sahrawi leadership agreed to a form of cease-fire, under UN auspices, pending peace talks. However, in September 1989 the peace talks broke down, and although, in 1990, a referendum on the future of the country was decided on, no progress was made. In the meantime, Polisario thrice breached the Hassan Wall in daring large-scale raids. Foreign diplomats in Morocco and Algeria credit Polisario with a genuine desire for peace and democracy through a referendum and say that the organization's attacks in 1990 were the result of intense frustration over lack of progress. Polisario continues to see itself as a broad front whose purpose is to gain independence rather than to achieve total control, and to wait for implementation of the UN resolution on the referendum.

Political prisoners: both before and after independence many men and women have been imprisoned in Africa for their political beliefs. Some like Kwame *NKRUMAH and Robert *MUGABE were leaders in the struggle for independence and later became leaders of their countries. Nkrumah went from prison to being prime minister in a remarkably short time. In South Africa, late in 1990, there were still an estimated three thousand prisoners, despite the release of many prisoners and the comparative 'liberalism' of President *DE KLERK. There are still thousands of political prisoners in Africa; most of them are unknown. The fate of the *CHIRWAS, in prison in Malawi since they were kidnapped from Zambian territory late in 1981, did arouse concern for a while; now the Chirwas are nearly forgotten. Others, like Nelson *MANDELA in South Africa were not forgotten; he was released in 1990 after twenty-six years in prison.

Population in Africa, estimated in 1988 at 552 million, according to the United Nations Population Division, while the World Bank estimated 570 million. The number is large but its true significance can only be seen in comparison to earlier figures. For instance, in 1940 the total population was estimated at 158 million; in 1960, 260 million; and in 1975, 410 million. The projection for the year 2000 is 800 million. Lack of accurate data for the continent make any figures speculative. Many African states have never taken a census and in other countries the population figure is arrived at by sample surveys. Also, many census returns are known to be inaccurate. Exceptions include Mauritius and Ghana. Figures given in this entry are likely to be conservative. One statistic that is known with accuracy is the annual growth rate for the various communities in South Africa. The increase for the Black and Coloured population is 3 per cent while that for the White population is only 1 per cent.

Overall, Africa's population is growing at 2.8 per cent per annum. Half the people are below the age of twenty. While 80 per cent of all people live in rural areas, urban growth is rapid, not only by natural growth but because of a steady drift to the cities. According to UN estimates made in 1985, one in five of the continent's people lived in towns of twenty thousand or more. The largest city is Cairo with an estimated twelve million inhabitants. Other cities with one million or more people are: Algiers, 2 million; Addis Ababa, 1 million; Abidjan, 1 million; Maputo, 1 million; Lagos, 3 million; Johannesburg, 1.5 million; Soweto (near Johannesburg), 1 million; Tunis, 1 million; Casablanca, 1.5 million; Alexandria, 1 million.

Areas with the greatest density are the *NILE valley, Rwanda, Burundi, and the regions of southern Nigeria. Some of the African islands, such as Mauritius and Zanzibar, also have high densities. Low population density exists in the arid regions. For instance, Libya, Mauritania and Somalia, on the rim of the *SAHARA and *SAHEL, have a low density. This applies also to Namibia, much of whose area is taken up by the *KALAHARI Desert.

Despite the general increase, some countries have suffered drastic reductions in population because of drought-caused famine, emigration and genocide. Between 1960 and 1962, nearly one million European settlers left Algeria. Between 1970 and 1978 about one third of the population of Equatorial Guinea fled to neighbouring countries during political unrest. Ethiopia lost 400,000 people because of drought and famine in the early 1970s and another 500,000 in 1985–6. From the same cause, about 600,000 Sudanese died in the period 1984–7.

Progressive Alliance of Liberia, unofficial opposition group in Liberia. The group became prominent when it co-ordinated massive protests against President *TOLBERT's decision to raise the price of rice (1979). At the end of 1979 it was allowed to register officially as the Progressive People's Party; but its leaders were arrested soon afterwards when they called for a national strike. Their arrests precipitated the military coup of April 1990.

Progressive Federal Party (PFP), a leftist political party in South Africa (1977–89). It was formed by the merger of the Progressive Reform Party and more liberal elements of the *UNITED PARTY. It opposed *APARTHEID and after the repeal of legislation banning multi-racial political parties welcomed members of all races. The PFP did not accept majority rule based on the principle of 'one man, one vote', but proposed the division of South Africa into a number of states with federal links. Colin Eglin led the party (1977–9) until he was ousted by Frederick van Zyl *SLABBERT (1979–86), who despaired of the parliamentary process and resigned. Eglin became leader again (1986–8) until he was replaced by the more dynamic Dr Zacharias de Beer (1988–9).

The party has had limited electoral success. There was some truth in the *NATIONAL PARTY's portrayal of the PFP as ineffectual, except for Helen *SUZMAN who is still widely respected for her outspoken attacks on the government. Some of the more liberal elements were dismayed at the unwillingness of the party to commit itself to radical reforms. In the 1977 elections it won seventeen seats to become the official opposition; in 1981 it won twenty-six seats. In 1987 it was down to twenty seats and lost its place as the official opposition to the *CONSERVATIVE PARTY. In 1989 the PFP emerged with other liberal groups to form the *DEMOCRATIC PARTY.

Qoboza, Percy (1938–88), a fearless black South African journalist who had close links with *SOWETO. After some years at a Catholic seminary he started as a journalist on *The World* (1963) and became its editor (1974–7). He made his paper the most widely read by black South Africans. He attacked corruption and violence in the townships, but it was his attacks on the government over events in Soweto (1976–7) and the death of Steve *BIKO in custody that attracted attention. In 1977 the government closed the paper and imprisoned Qoboza. After his release he worked for the *Post* and the *Sunday Post* and in the United States. Back in South Africa he edited the *City Press* (1985–8) and soon had the largest black readership in South Africa once more.

Rand Daily Mail, liberal English language newspaper in South Africa (1902–85), first edited by Edgar Wallace. From the late 1950s the newspaper's courageous opposition to *APARTHEID and its investigative journalism gained worldwide attention. The government repeatedly tried and failed to silence the paper. In 1985 the paper was closed because it was losing money, but also for political reasons. In June 1990 the paper was reopened as *The Daily Mail*, but folded in August 1990.

Rand Monetary Union (Dec. 1974), agreement by South Africa, Namibia, Botswana, Lesotho, Swaziland. The South African Rand became the common currency of the union, which gave South Africa considerable financial power in the region. Botswana withdrew, but Lesotho's Loti and Swaziland's Lilangeni remained at par with the Rand.

Rassemblement Démocratique Africain (RDA), the first political organization founded in black Africa after the Second World War. The RDA's founder (1946) was Felix *HOUPHOUËT-BOIGNY, later to be President of *IVORY COAST. Houphouët-Boigny intended RDA to be the umbrella international organization for all the national political parties which he expected to see come into being. He was encouraged and assisted in the formation of the RDA by France, which intended to use the organization as a form of indirect political and economic control over its former colonies. The RDA's first affiliate, naturally, was Houphouët-Boigny's own Parti Démocratique de la Côte Ivoire, in 1946. RDA soon had branches in all of France's colonies and former colonies. Its useful life ended in the 1970s but it still maintains a head office in Abidjan.

Rawlings, Fl.-Lt. Jerry (b.1947), Ghanaian head of state. The son of a Scotsman and a Ghanaian, he was commissioned as a Pilot Officer in the Ghanaian Air Force (1969). He led NCOs and dissatisfied junior officers in the coup against General *AKUFFO's military government (Jun. 1979). As Chairman of the Armed Forces Revolutionary Council and head of state for three months Rawlings acted speedily and decisively in his drive to cleanse Ghana. The execution of eight military leaders, including *ACHEAMPONG and Akuffo, was condemned abroad but was popular in Ghana. Before relinquishing power to President *LIMANN's civilian government (Sep. 1979) he set up People's Courts, confiscated the assets of corrupt officials and organized the collection of taxes.

He retired from the armed forces (Nov. 1979) but retained his popularity with the Ghanaian people. His relations with President Limann grew more and more tense as the civilian government disintegrated.

Rawlings seized power again on the last day of 1981, but this time did not promise to step down from his position as head of state and Chairman of the Provisional National Defence Council.

Rawlings has had to face many challenges and problems, including numerous attempted coups. Ghana's economic problems forced him to appeal for international aid; to secure this aid he has had to impose a very strict austerity programme which has caused much suffering, although by the end of the 1980s there were signs that the harsh economic medicine was beginning to work.

Rawlings has included civilians in the Provisional National Defence Council and he has held elections for local authorities, but apparently intends to stay in power for some time yet. He has had some successes and is respected for his personal integrity; he may prove to be the person who will bring stability and prosperity to Ghana.

Renamo, Mozambique National Resistance Movement (MNR), rebels who have brought devastation and civil war to Mozambique since 1975. Renamo originated in the late 1960s when Rhodesian intelligence recruited Mozambicans to spy on its nationalist opponents based in Mozambique. When Mozambique became an independent socialist state in 1975 Renamo became a guerrilla movement fighting to overthrow the government. It was funded and trained by Rhodesia until the collapse of white minority rule there (1980). South

Africa then became the movement's sponsor. Renamo has gained support from the *FLECHAS (Mozambicans who fought *FRELIMO), disgruntled Frelimo soldiers and Portuguese who had lost their homes and wealth in Mozambique. There are factional disputes and little is known about the leadership, but Alfonso Dhlakama is generally regarded as the leader of Renamo's twenty thousand men.

Renamo presents itself as a democratic free-market movement struggling to overthrow a Marxist dictatorship, but others see it as a band of brutal misfits being used by South Africa and other enemies to destabilize Mozambique. Renamo has extended its operations throughout the country. It has disrupted social services, agriculture and industry, destroying schools, health centres, farms, shops, roads, railways, oil pipelines, dams and power stations. It has kidnapped foreign workers and tortured and massacred villagers. By the late 1980s Renamo activities had threatened about three and a half million Mozambicans (a quarter of the population) with famine and forced up to a million people to seek refuge in neighbouring countries. The destruction of agriculture during the civil war caused a catastrophic decline in foreign currency earnings.

In the *NKOMATI ACCORD (1984) South Africa promised to withdraw its support from Renamo, but it was soon clear that South Africa was not honouring the agreement. In the same year Zimbabwe agreed to send troops to guard the oil pipeline and the railway from Beira to Zimbabwe. In 1985 Zimbabwean troops captured the Renamo base at Casa Banana and found documents confirming South African support for Renamo. In 1986 Renamo recaptured Casa Banana and seemed to be gaining in strength; since then President *CHISSANO has claimed some success in the civil war. In 1989 there were signs that South Africa was withdrawing support and there were hopes of negotiations to end the fighting. The railway from Malawi to the Mozambican port of Nacala was able to reopen in 1989 when Renamo stopped attacking it. The war has continued into 1990 and Renamo is still a grave threat to the state of Mozambique and its people. Late in 1990 it rejected the government's offer to allow it to operate as a political party – after laying down its arms. The civil war has caused an estimated 600,000 deaths and left half the population dependent on food aid.

René, France Albert (b. 1935), radical socialist politician, an austere and dedicated leader who has been President of the Seychelles since 1977. Called to the Bar in London (1957) he returned to the Seychelles and entered politics as founder (1964) and leader of the *SEYCHELLES PEOPLE'S UNITED PARTY (SPUP) which campaigned for independence from Britain. He was elected to the legislature in 1965. The SPUP lost the 1970 and 1974 elections, but in 1975 formed a coalition government with the victorious *SEYCHELLES DEMOCRATIC PARTY. René served as Minister of Works and Land Development in *MANCHAM's government (1975–7) and as Prime Minister (1976–7). Unhappy at the conservative and pro-Western policies of President Mancham, Rene seized power in a coup in June 1977 and became President.

René consolidated his power by reorganizing the SPUP as the *SEYCHELLES PEOPLE'S PROGRESSIVE FRONT (SPFF) in 1978 and in 1979 by proclaiming the Seychelles as socialist republic with the SPFF as the only political party. He set up a regular army, the Seychelles People's Liberation Army, and a People's Militia. President René has attempted to achieve socialism in two five-year plans. His measures have included land redistribution, the expansion of public housing, the abolition of private medicine, doubling the minimum wage, guaranteed work for all and social security for those in need. He has acted firmly against corruption. In foreign affairs René has established close links with Tanzania and Algeria and alarmed the West by forging links with the Soviet bloc, but he maintains relations with the United States and insists that the Seychelles is a non-aligned country. In the late 1980s he received aid from both the United States and the Soviet Union.

Unhappy at the country's heavy dependence on tourism, he has worked with some success to diversify the economy by developing fishing and agriculture. Nevertheless, in the late 1980s the Seychelles still depended heavily on tourism and suffered from high inflation and a trade deficit.

René's radical socialist policies and the authoritarian nature of his regime have made him many enemies. There have been various attempts to overthrow him, including the South African-backed attempt (Nov. 1981) which came close to success. Political problems have discouraged tourism and damaged the economy, but by the late 1980s René had modified his socialism and adopted more pragmatic policies. The position of his government has begun to seem more assured.

Republican Brothers, a group of Muslims of the Sudan whose unorthodox interpretation of *ISLAM is contested by mainstream Sunni Muslims. They consider sunna – the traditions and ways of Muhammad – to be the source of the Islamic religion, rather than the Koran, though this remains their holy book. The Brothers argue that the *SHARIA or holy law is a mere branch of Islam, not the thread binding it. It was this line of thought which brought the Brothers into dispute not only with more fundamentalist Sudanese sects but with President Nimeiri. Nimeiri ordered the execution by hanging of one of the most respected Brothers, Muhammad *TAHA. The Republican Brothers, who oppose violence, argue that an Islam-oriented socialism would be the best model of economic organization for Sudan and other Arab countries.

Republican Party, Namibian political party representing the interests of the white community, founded in 1977 and led by Dirk *MUDGE. More *VERLIGTE (or enlightened) than *SWANP (South West Africa National Party), the Republican Party was prepared to co-operate with other racial groups and played a leading role in the *DTA government from 1978 until its collapse in 1983. The party joined the *MPC which formed the *TRANSITIONAL GOVERNMENT OF NATIONAL UNITY in 1985. In the 1980 elections for the white legislative body the Republican Party lost to the SWANP. The party opposed *SWAPO and the implementation of the United Nations plan for Namibian independence.

Rhodesian Front Party, political party founded in 1962 in Southern Rhodesia (now Zimbabwe) by Winston Field, Ian *SMITH and Clifford Dupont who were determined to maintain white supremacy. After winning thirty-five of the fifty white seats in the 1962 elections the Rhodesian Front took office with Field as Prime Minister until he was ousted by Smith (1964). As the *CENTRAL AFRICAN FEDERATION collapsed Field and then Smith negotiated in vain with Britain for independence. In the May 1965 elections the party won all the white seats, a sweeping victory which it took as a mandate for *UDI (Unilateral Declaration of Independence) in November 1965. In 1969 the Rhodesian Front government implemented a new constitution which offered no prospect of majority rule. Weakened by guerrilla warfare and economic pressures the party made an 'internal settlement' which meant sharing power with some black leaders (1978) and it supported the government of Bishop *MUZOREWA (1979). After independence it was renamed the Republican Front (1981) and the *CONSERVATIVE ALLIANCE OF ZIMBABWE (1985).

Rivonia Trial, in July 1963 South African security policy raided the *UMKONTO WE SIZWE headquarters in Rivonia and captured a number of its leaders. In the so-called Rivonia Trial (1963–4) eight of these leaders and Nelson *MANDELA (who had been captured earlier) were tried on charges of sabotage and conspiracy to overthrow the government. At the end of the trial eight of the nine (including Mandela, Govan *MBEKI and Walter *SISULU) were sentenced to life imprisonment.

Robben Island, notorious South African maximum security prison. Situated on a rocky island near Cape Town, the prison has been home to many leading black nationalists, including Nelson *MANDELA, Govan *MBEKI, Walter *SISULU, Robert *SOBUKWE and Andimba *TOIVO JA TOIVA. The prison is a harsh, bleak and unhealthy place. Its inmates have been subjected to hard labour. Although well known prisoners were moved from Robben Island during the 1980s, it is still a political prison.

Roberto, Holden (b.1925), dissident Angolan, *FNLA leader who has spent most of his life in exile. A member of the Kongo people, he was born in northern Angola

288

and educated in the Belgian Congo (now Zaire), where he worked in the civil service. During the 1950s Roberto travelled widely in Africa and Europe and joined the opposition to Portuguese colonial rule in Angola. From the late 1950s he led *UPA which organized the 1961 rising in northern Angola. With Zairean backing Roberto merged the UPA with another northern group to form the *FNLA (1962). As FNLA president Roberto claimed to speak for the Angolan people even though he had limited support outside the north, especially after the southerners in the FNLA broke away and formed *UNITA (1966).

In Zaire he proclaimed a revolutionary government in exile and engaged in limited guerrilla action against the Portuguese in northern Angola during the war of independence (1961–74). During this period he was criticized as the tool of Zaire and of certain western powers who wanted to avoid Marxist rule in Angola. Roberto participated in the short-lived transitional government (1975), but was already in conflict with the *MPLA. He declared himself leader of Angola (Nov. 1975), although he controlled only a small part of the country. By early 1976 the FNLA had lost the war against the MPLA government and Roberto was in exile in Zaire (1975–6), ruled by his brother-in-law, General *MOBUTU. Roberto moved to Senegal (1976–9) and was in Paris by 1980.

Ruanda-Urundi, name given to Rwanda and Burundi under colonial

The Republic of Rwanda

THE COUNTRY
26,338 sq. km.

Major City
Kigali (capital)

Economy
Farming
Mining

Principal Exports
Coffee
Tea
Tin
Pyrethrum

Currency
Rwanda franc of 100
centimes

THE PEOPLE
6,454,000

Ethnic Groups
Hutu (85%)
Tutsi (14%)

Languages
Kinyarwanda
French

Religion
Catholicism
Traditional beliefs

THE STATE
Military rule

Head of State
President Habyarimana

Ruling Bodies
Council of Ministers
National Development
Council

Official Party
MRND

---

rule. Populated by the Hutu and the Tutsi, this part of east central Africa was annexed to German East Africa (1899) and taken by Belgium (1916). Ruanda-Urundi was administered by Belgium as a mandate of the League of Nations and the United Nations until the two territories gained their independence in 1962. See *BURUNDI and RWANDA.

Rwanda, the Republic of, in east central Africa is the most densely populated state on the continent. This small and land-locked country is bordered by Uganda on the north, Tanzania on the east, Burundi on the south and by Zaire on the west. Much of it is covered by steep hills and deep valleys with a powerful chain of volcanoes (the Virunga) in the north. With an average altitude of about 1500m.,

Rwanda enjoys a cool and temperate climate.

The Twa pigmies, now only about 1 per cent of the population, were early inhabitants; they were hunters and gatherers. A thousand years ago *BANTU peasant farmers, the Hutu settled in the area and now make up about 84 per cent of the population. The cattle-owning Tutsi, who began to arrive from the north in the fifteenth century, established the feudal system which they used to dominate the Hutu; now about 15 per cent of the population is Tutsi.

Rwanda's economy depends heavily on agriculture, with most of the working population growing sweet potatoes, bananas, beans, sorghum, rice and maize. Low rainfall, poor soil and the damage done by traditional methods

289

of agriculture have made Rwanda unable to feed its population, which increased rapidly during the 1980s at an annual rate of 3.7 per cent. The most important cash crop is coffee which accounts for 85 per cent of export earnings; tea accounts for 14 per cent. Some tin and wolframite are exported and efforts have been made to expand tea production and to develop forestry, tobacco and cotton resources. There are food processing and textile firms, but otherwise there is little industrial activity.

Rwanda's development has been seriously hindered by transport difficulties. It has no railway lines and Mombasa, the nearest port, is 1655km. away from Kigali, the capital. Violence and warfare in Uganda have frequently closed or disrupted communications with the coast. With a per capita GNP of only $250 in 1983 Rwanda is one of the poorest countries in the world. Rwanda has borrowed and sought aid to finance its heavy trade deficits; in 1986 its international debt was $412 million. Overspending by government, budget deficits, the high price of imports, transport difficulties through Uganda, poor weather and the lack of incentives to subsistence farmers impelled President *HABYARIMANA to introduce a programme of austerity in 1984. Since then money has been set aside to service the national debt, some expensive publicly owned enterprises have been privatized and rises in public expenditure have been kept down. With international help the

government has invested in major development projects in agriculture, water and power. A new international airport was opened in Kigali in 1986 and the telecommunications system has been modernized.

Little is known of Rwanda's early history. By the time Europeans arrived in the nineteenth century the Tutsi minority had established a highly effective feudal state which kept the majority Hutu in political, social and economic subjection. Late in the nineteenth century Rwanda and Burundi, then called *RUANDA-URUNDI, were annexed to German East Africa. The country was taken by Belgium (1916), and remained a Belgian mandate under the League of Nations and the United Nations until independence in 1962. For most of the colonial period the Germans and then the Belgians governed by the system of indirect rule which strengthened the power of the Tutsi minority. Tutsi domination was increasingly challenged by the Hutu majority in the run up to independence.

After the death of Mwami (King) Mutara III (Jul. 1959) and the controversial accession of Kigeri V the Tutsi tried to eliminate the Hutu leadership. The Hutu rebelled and there was much bloodshed until Kigeri V fled. The Belgian authorities restored order and made democratic reforms which ensured the power of the Hutu majority. In 1960 *PARMEHUTU, the Hutu's principal party, won massive majorities in communal elections. In 1961 the monarchy was abolished after a referendum; Parmehutu won the national elections and Grégoire *KAYIBANDA became independent Rwanda's first President (1962).

President Kayibanda was unable to contain ethnic tensions, particularly in 1963-4 when Tutsi attacks were followed by Hutu reprisals and the death of thousands of Tutsi. In 1965 Rwanda became a one-party state and its authoritarian government was increasingly dominated by Hutu from central Rwanda. By 1973 the country was in a critical state with renewed tension between the Hutu and the Tutsi and northern Hutu angry at the domination of the government by central Hutu. In July 1973 northern Hutu army officers staged a bloodless coup and General Juvénal *HABYARIMANA was made President.

President Habyarimana has made political changes to strengthen his authority. In 1975 he announced the formation of a new party, the *MRND, to mobilize the Rwandan people for the development of their country. In 1978 he proclaimed a constitution which would return the country to civilian rule, but the first legislative assembly was not elected until the end of 1981. As the sole candidate the President was returned at elections in 1978, 1983 and 1988. The second republic has brought a measure of stability, although the attempted coup of April 1980 was a serious threat to the government. In October 1990 Rwanda was threatened by the invasion of the Rwandan Patriotic Front, mainly consisting of Tutsi exiles, from Uganda. By November 1990 the invaders had lost their three commanders. Some retreated to Uganda; others took to the hills, presumably to organize a guerrilla campaign.

Rwanda has many serious economic and political problems. To date, little progress has been made in strengthening the economy, despite President Habyarimana's avowed commitment to austerity and discipline. Many of the country's problems derive from its neighbours. It has had to cope with a massive influx of refugees from the troubles in Uganda (1982) and Hutu refugees from Burundi (1988). Until regional stability is achieved and the tension between the ruling Hutu and the minority Tutsi is resolved Rwanda has little chance of achieving stability and prosperity.

S

Saadawi, Nawal (b. 1930), probably the most controversial Egyptian feminist, author and playwright. Her *The Diary of a Female Physician* was the first modern feminist book to be written in Arabic; it appeared in English in 1957. Her best known book *The Hidden Face of Arab Eve* (1967), explains the plight of women in the Arab world. Dr Saadawi refused to accept the religious and colonial limitations she was born to; she qualified as a doctor and rose to become Egypt's Director of Public Health, a position from which she was dismissed for writing *Women and Sex* in 1972. Undeterred by the banning of her books, and a period of detention under President *SADAT, she continued to write about Arab women's problems and their struggles for liberation. *Women at Point Zero*, about a woman condemned to death for killing a pimp, is a novel drawn from Saadawi's experience as a psychiatrist at the notorious Qanatir Women's prison. *Two Women in One* tells the story of eighteen-year-old Bahiah Shaheen's quest for emancipation and fulfilment, while *God Dies by the Nile* illustrates the class dimension of the oppression of women through the study of Zabeya, a peasant woman victimized by a landlord. *The Fall of the Imam*, published in English in 1988, could not find an Arabic publisher because of its controversial nature. Dr Saadawi said, 'I tried to deploy the unreal as well as the absurd creation of the unconscious to draw a picture of everyday reality in the Arab world, especially the negative aspects of it.' The book contains much political satire and fantasy. The technique of using fantasy to put across a political or theological idea is one which many Egyptians have used to escape the censor, but nobody has been so innovative as Saadawi.

Sadat, Muhammad Anwar El- (1918–81), Egyptian head of state and the first Arab leader to negotiate peace with Israel. Sadat was educated at the Christian-run St. George's School, Cairo, before going to the Egyptian Military College. He joined the army, after being commissioned, in 1938. Opposed to the British presence in Egypt and to the corrupt regime of King Farouk, Sadat joined the Free Officers Movement in 1948 and after its coup in 1952 became a member of the Revolutionary Command Council under Colonel *NASSER, to whom he was very close. He then held a succession of offices: Minister of State, 1952–6; Vice-Chairman, National Assembly, 1957–61; Speaker, United Arab Republic National Assembly, 1961–9; Vice-President, 1964–6, 1969–70; 'Interim President' 1969–70.

On Nasser's death in 1970 Sadat became President of Eygpt. Having consolidated his position, Sadat dealt with the great economic and political problems he had inherited. In May

1971 he arrested a group of political rivals, led by Ali Sabri, who were plotting, with Soviet backing, to seize power. Nevertheless, in the same month Sadat signed a friendship treaty with the Soviet Union. More than 15,000 Soviet military experts went to Egypt, but relations between Cairo and Moscow became strained. In July 1972 Sadat ordered all Soviet personnel out of the country. On 6 October 1973 he launched an attack on Israel. His armies poured across the Suez Canal and broke through the Israeli defences. The war, which was over by 22 October, was not a victory for Egypt but it boosted the morale of Egypt and the Arab world. With US mediation, Sadat signed two disengagement agreements with Israel, in January 1974 and September 1975. As a result Israel handed back the Sinai oilfields. On 20 November 1977 Sadat flew to Israel in one of the most dramatic political missions of the century. The consequent negotiations resulted, on 17 September 1978, in the Camp David Accord, a peace treaty signed by Prime Minister Begin of Israel and President Carter of the USA. *ISLAMIC FUNDAMENTALISTS regarded Sadat's action as a betrayal of the Islamic principle that Muslims should not make peace with 'infidels'. On 6 October 1981 President Sadat was shot to death by a group of fundamentalist soldiers passing before him in review during a parade to mark the anniversary of the 1973 war. Apart from his courageous peace initiative, Sadat is remembered in Egypt for stern action in arresting 'agitators'. In 1981 he imprisoned about 1500 people, including prominent journalists and authors. Nevertheless, he left a stable country for his successor, Husni *MUBARAK.

Sahara, a vast desert area about the size of the United States – over three million square miles. In the main it is lowland but it contains two large volcanic mountain masses, the Ahaggar and the Tibesti mountains. From these uplands minor amounts of water flow down into the surrounding basins and create oases. Larger oases are created by the streams flowing southward out of the much better watered Atlas mountains. Such streams, even when they sink into the sand, often flow immense distances. Water also enters the Sahara in substantial quantities by the *NILE, which flows to the sea, the Niger which enters the desert but turns back near Timbuktu, and the Shari, which flows into Lake Chad. While the Sahara itself is unchanging, the uses to which it is put have changed since 1950. For example, in many parts of the Saharan sand seas belonging to Libya, Algeria and, to a lesser extent, Tunisia and Morocco, oil has been discovered and exploited. During the search for oil, water was also found in vast amounts under the sand. This water enlarged the oasis of Kufra in Libya a thousandfold, turning it into farmland which annually supports several crops of tomatoes, fruits and lucerne. The fodder crop is used to feed sheep, reared in large numbers for their meat. With the example of Kufra, several governments are surveying for subterranean Saharan water. In Morocco and Algeria the frontiers of the desert are being pushed back by the planting of tree barriers, the first step towards land reclamation. Egypt has ambitious plans to turn the Qattara Depression into an enormous lake by digging a canal from the Mediterranean. Such an area of water in the Sahara could conceivably 'change the climate' to some extent. It would certainly open up badly needed new areas for irrigation.

Sahel, a region covering about one million square miles, stretching from Senegal in West Africa to the *HORN OF AFRICA in the east, and containing some of the world's least developed countries. The countries concerned are Burkina Faso, Chad, Mali, Mauritania, Niger and Senegal. Poorly endowed with natural resources, much of the area is handicapped by semi-desert conditions and an arid climate. More seriously, the region is prone to periodic droughts, the worst recent ones occurring in 1969–71, 1982–4 and 1987–8. The economic situation in the Sahelian belt has been marked by a declining gross domestic product (GDP) and even sharper falls in per capita income. The increasing incidence of malnutrition and famine, particularly in Chad, captured international concern in 1984. This resulted in concentrated efforts by donor countries and international organizations to provide emergency food aid and balance of payments assistance. The threat

of drought-induced food crises hangs over the Sahel. Food production must be increased, livestock herds replenished and food reserves built up. No matter what is done, agricultural development will remain severely limited by a combination of desertification, land erosion, deforestation and the lack of water resources. In some Sahel countries income per head is steadily falling as increases in the population more than offset any GDP rises. This is compounded by the size of the Sahel debt burden, currently totalling $5 billion. The sharp fall in oil prices, 1985–8, helped to bring considerable foreign exchange savings, but this favourable state of affairs has, unfortunately, not persisted.

Salam, Shadi Abdul (1930–86), Egyptian architect and scriptwriter. His film *The Mummy* won sixteen international awards. His documentaries included *The Armies of the Sun, King Tutankhamen's Gold Chair, Horizons* and *Ramses II*. Salam's special talent was in designing the scenes and costumes of historical films. His great ambition, to induce Egyptians to recognize their pre-Islamic heritage, remained unfulfilled at the time of his death.

Salim, Salim Ahmed (b.1942), Tanzanian politician born on Pemba Island (in the state of *ZANZIBAR). He began his career as a diplomat and was Tanzania's permanent representative at the United Nations (1970–80). He was a leading candidate for the post of United Nations Secretary-General (1981). Back in Tanzania, Salim served as Minister of Foreign Affairs (1980–4) and Prime Minister (1984–5) and was a leading contender to succeed President *NYERERE in 1985. He lost the contest, perhaps because President *NYERERE and the party thought he was not committed strongly enough to the cause of African socialism. He was then Deputy Prime Minister and Minister of Defence (1986–9). In 1989 Salim became Secretary-General of the *ORGANIZATION OF AFRICAN UNITY.

San (or Bushmen), nomadic people who are now confined to the arid northern areas of Botswana and Namibia. The San and *KHOI (or Hottentots) were the early inhabitants of Southern Africa. They were driven out of their fertile lands by the *BANTU and the whites. The Khoi are extinct and the numbers of the San are dwindling. There are now less than twelve thousand San and they are finding it increasingly difficult to survive by hunting in the small areas of near-desert they inhabit.

Sankara, Captain Thomas (1949–87), army officer and president of Burkina Faso. Born at Yago and educated at mission schools, Sankara impressed the administrators of what was then Upper Volta and they sent him to France for a military education. Back in independent Burkina Faso as an army captain, he served as Secretary for Information in the Saye Zerbo government. When Zerbo was overthrown in 1982 Sankara was nominated as prime minister. The new president, Jean-Baptiste Ouedraogo, distrusted Sankara's left-wing ambitions and arrested him. He was a popular army officer and soldiers freed him from detention. On 4 August 1963 Sankara himself seized power from Ouedraogo.

For four years Sankara, who called himself a revolutionary, captured the imagination of much of black Africa. His policies mirrored those the World Bank continually advocates African states adopt. He helped small farmers and cut back privileges for urban workers. Sankara urged the nation's small farmers to organize themselves. He built hundreds of new primary schools and health units in rural areas. School enrolment soared but many health units remained unstaffed and unequipped. He ended some taxes that burdened rural concerns, but as the energetic and dedicated Sankara kindled the dreams of the rural poor he 'destroyed the dream' – the phrase of a European aid official – of urban workers. He curbed the power of trade unions and trimmed civil servants' salaries.

Sankara was an unconventional ruler. He decreed that on one designated Saturday no women would be allowed to shop in the markets. Instead, men would have to bargain and buy. Sankara said, 'You men will see just how hard your women have to work.' He appointed several women to his cabinet, though he remained an authoritarian ruler, with a great sense of presidential style. As giant Nigeria was expelling hundreds of thousands of Ghanaians in May 1985 Sankara ordered every

Nigerian in Burkina Faso to report to a camp one Saturday. The Nigerian government angrily announced that the government would send aircraft to evacuate its people. When the day came the Nigerians were politely told that provided their passports were in order they were welcome in Burkina Faso. It was Sankara's way of showing Nigeria how he believed Africans should treat other Africans.

He was assassinated by his 'best friend', Captain Blaise Compaore, on 15 October 1987. Indirectly, he lost his life for ignoring one of the hard realities of Black Africa – that real political power lies in its cities. His death serves as a warning to other African leaders of the difficulty of balancing the demands of rural and urban dwellers.

Sassou-Nguesso, Col. Denis (b.1943), army officer and politician who has been President of the People's Republic of the Congo since March 1979. A supporter of President *NGOUABI's socialist ideals, he served on the Council of State (1976–7). After Ngouabi's assassination, Yhombi-Opango became president and Sassou-Nguesso was Vice-President of the Military Committee of the *PARTI CONGOLAIS DU TRAVAIL (PCT); he was charged with the co-ordination of PCT activities. He led the more militant group in the PCT which opposed Yhombi-Opango. In March 1979 he assumed power.

President Sassou-Nguesso indulges in revolutionary rhetoric and declares his loyalty to Ngouabi's socialism, but in practice his policies have been pragmatic and liberal. He has improved relations with the West and with his conservative neighbours, Cameroon, Gabon and Zaire, and has liberalized economic policy. He has survived attempted coups and other challenges to his authority, and after more than a decade in power his position is not secure. Yet, the president has served the Congo well by giving it over a decade of comparative stability.

Savimbi, Jonas (b.1934), Angolan dissident who has led *UNITA since its formation (1966). The son of a station master on the *BENGUELA RAILWAY, Savimbi is one of the Ovimbundu people. After qualifying as a lawyer in Switzerland he joined the struggle against Portugal and became General Secretary of *UPA (1961). After co-operating with *ROBERTO in forming the *FNLA Savimbi served as Foreign Minister in Roberto's Angolan government in exile (1962–4). He broke with Roberto in protest against the domination of the FNLA by northern tribesmen (1964). He refused to join the *MPLA and in 1966 formed his own nationalist movement, UNITA, to fight the Portuguese.

By 1972 Savimbi was apparently collaborating with the Portuguese. In the short-lived transitional government (1975) Savimbi was already fighting the MPLA. Savimbi proclaimed himself head of independent Angola (Nov. 1975), but by early 1976 was driven into the bush, from where he continued to fight

The Republic of Senegal

THE COUNTRY	THE PEOPLE	THE STATE
196,192 sq. km.	7.9 million	Democratic republic
Major Cities	*Ethnic Groups*	*Head of State*
Dakar (capital)	Wolof (40%)	President
Thiès, Kaolack, Saint	Serer	Abdou Diouf
Louis, Ziguinchor	Tukulor	
	Fulani	*Ruling Body*
Economy	Diola	National Assembly
Groundnuts	Malinke	
Much French		*Official Party*
development	*Languages*	Parti Socialiste
	French (official)	
Principal Exports	Wolof	
Groundnuts		
Machinery & metal	*Religion*	
products, sugar, rice,	Islam (85%)	
petroleum products	Christian (10%)	
	Traditional beliefs	
Currency		
CFA franc of 100		
centimes		

the MPLA government. With help from South Africa and the United States Savimbi controlled large areas of southern and central Angola and caused much destruction, but he was never strong enough to overthrow the MPLA government. His men have been accused of torture and brutality, but they also have strong support from the Ovimbundu – about one third of the population of Angola. Savimbi is seen as a pragmatic pro-Western nationalist willing to accept support from anybody in his battle against Marxism. Savimbi agreed to a cease-fire in June 1989, but this broke down. In April 1990, after a number of setbacks, he called for a fresh cease-fire.

Selous Scouts, irregular military force named after a famous British nineteenth-century hunter and explorer, it fought the nationalist forces during the struggle for Zimbabwean independence (1966–79). There were many reports of atrocities committed by the Selous Scouts against innocent civilians.

Senegal, a country of plains, covering an area of 196,192 sq. km. in West Africa, with a population of eight million. Its neighbours are Mauritania, Mali, Guinea and Guinea-Bissau, and it almost totally surrounds Gambia. Settled for at least fifteen thousand years, Senegal was 'discovered' in 1455 by a Portuguese navigator and for more than a century Portugal held the monopoly of trade with the Senegalese coastal tribes. The French conquered the area in the second half of the seventeenth century but lost it to the British during the Napoleonic wars. Senegal was restored to France in 1814 and remained under French domination for 130 years.

Nevertheless, Senegalese society was highly politicized with the first political party formed in 1914. In 1935 the Parti Socialiste Sénégalais (PSS) was formed and, backed by the trade unions, it became the most potent political force in the country. It demanded and won French citizenship for all Senegalese, a privilege which conferred the right to vote. As a consequence, Léopold *SENGHOR and Lamine Guèye were elected as deputies to represent Senegal in Paris. In 1948 Senghor broke from PSS and with Mamadou *DIA formed the Bloc Démocratique Sénégalais (BDS). It quickly became powerful and in 1957 grouped with other parties to form the Bloc Populaire Sénégalais (BPS). Political complexities and differences abounded but there was a consensus for continued association with France.

Senegal linked with the French Sudan to form the Federation of Mali in April 1959, and on 20 June 1960 the federation became independent. The ill-conceived union came to an end two months later when Senegal seceded and proclaimed itself the independent Republic of Senegal.

The president was Léopold Senghor, with Mamadou Dia as prime minister. Senghor at once moved to give himself sweeping constitutional powers and banned most opposition parties. In the riots in Dakar which followed, police shot dead more than a hundred people. Senghor tightened his authority still further and in 1966 incorporated the last remaining legal opposition party, the Parti du Regroupement Africain-Sénégal, into his own Union Progressiste Sénégalaise (UPS).

With the economy in disarray, the government imposed wage freezes. They caused serious unrest among trade unions and students at Dakar University in 1968 and only the presence of French troops prevented revolution and the president's overthrow. Resentment simmered and in January 1973 the university became a battleground as Marxists and government supporters fought each other. In March, Senghor banned trade unions and teachers' unions and imprisoned the more militant leaders.

The government continued to be high-handed and in 1969 attempted to seize the land of peasants in Casamance province and give it to a tourist firm. The peasants resisted and managed to keep their land. Other disputes occurred over high taxation, the high cost of fertilizer and farm equipment and the low prices the government paid for crops. Even the previous supportive business community opposed many government edicts. Senghor retaliated, as always, by banning some organizations and forming others, which he could control.

The insistent opposition to his measures led Senghor, during the elections of 1978, to legalize a three-party system. Even this was manipulated to government advantage, since each of the three groupings was given an official label which had to be used in all publicity. Senghor's UPS was described as 'liberal and democratic.' The Parti Africain de l'Indépendence (PAI) had to call itself 'Marxist-Leninist', a label which damned it in the eyes of the Muslim voters, who hated atheistic communism. In later elections, a fourth party, Mouvement Republicain Sénégalaise, was permitted to campaign but, as Senghor had foreseen, it attracted little support.

Senghor retired at the end of 1980 and, by prior arrangement, was succeeded as president, without elections, by the prime minister, Abdou Diouf. While retaining most of Senghor's cabinet and continuing the Senghor austerity policies, Diouf nevertheless made some changes which he claimed were democratic and many opposition parties were permitted to develop.

Under Diouf, Senegal united with Gambia on 1 February 1982, a sensible step in principle considering the two states' geopolitical and tribal links. As *SENEGAMBIA, each country retained its own sovereignty but planned to develop joint policies for defence, foreign affairs, finance and customs; but Senegambia was dissolved in 1989. Meanwhile, the Diola tribe of Casamance province demanded independence on the grounds that their region was being neglected by the government. Diouf's response to the demonstrations was typically Senghorian: he imprisoned the secessionist leaders, subdivided Senegal's two southern regions into four and by a process of decentralization weakened opposition to his central government.

In February 1983, Diouf submitted himself for election and won overwhelmingly while his PS was similarly successful in the general elections. Diouf had been consistently bypassing his prime minister, Habib Thiam, and when Thiam resigned in protest in April 1984, Diouf abolished the office of prime minister. Later, he castigated the Senegalese press for 'abusing its liberties' in criticizing his government. That government became ever stronger as Diouf cleverly continued his policy of fragmenting the opposition; in May 1985 he legalized the sixteenth political party.

The one effective opposition leader, Abdoulay Wade of PDS, began an aggressive campaign in April 1985, calling for elections and a 'government of transitional unity'. Even more controversially, he asked PDS supporters to assemble in the mosques to pray for changes in Senegal's internal policies. The alarmed government tried to prevent certain people from entering the mosques and government-controlled newspapers attacked Wade for 'exploiting religious feeling'. Diouf warned Wade 'not to go beyond a certain threshold', and when the PDS leader continued with his activities he was arrested and briefly detained. Wade tried to create an alliance of five parties but it was promptly banned under a law that precludes the grouping of political parties. The struggle for greater democratization has never ceased.

In foreign affairs, Senegal has managed to remain reasonably independent. Libya has made several attempts to restore diplomatic relations, previously broken off by Senegal in 1980, following Libyan interference in its affairs. President *GADDAFI's visit to Senegal in December 1985 brought about better relations but no resumption of diplomatic activity. French influence on Senegalese foreign affairs is great, though much less obtrusive than in Central African Republic and Chad.

Senegal's economic policy since independence has promoted the diversification of agriculture and broadening of the manufacturing base. Sugar, rice, cotton and market-garden produce are the main farming activities and when no drought intervenes the country is self-sufficient in grains other than wheat. Even so, Senegal imports over half its staple foodstuffs, a great drain on its funds. Cattle farming suffers from the periodic droughts but in partial counterbalance the fishing industry became prosperous in the mid-1970s. Fish exports account for 10 per cent of export earnings. Another important export is refined petroleum. Phosphate mining, carried out on

terms of equal partnership with the French, is successful and profitable. In 1989 production of iron ore commenced and much is expected of the industry.

Before 1960 Senegal had the most advanced manufacturing sector in Francophone Africa, but in the 1970s it was overtaken by Ivory Coast and Cameroon. Nevertheless, the textile industry remains the largest in Francophone Africa and is responsible for more than a tenth of total turnover. The largest single industrial project is the ICS chemical project which produces phosphates, fertilizers, chemicals, plastics, paints and soap. In general terms, food processing is the most widely based industry. It involves groundnut-crushing, fish-processing, sugar-refining and the production of soft drinks.

Periodically, President Diouf is forced by drought to introduce austere budgets. Despite his political inflexibility, he has encouraged privatization and has withdrawn many subsidies. While many observers might see this as economic liberalization, others are severely critical. One authority calls it 'brutal state disengagement'. 'Disengagement' has certainly been sweeping. For instance, in 1986, Diouf announced that the state would no longer be responsible for the distribution of seeds. This decision backfired because it disrupted an established system and led to smaller yields.

In 1989 Senegal reached agreement with the EEC on fishing rights. In return for these rights, the

EC countries involved supply large quantities of fresh and frozen tuna to Senegalese canning factories. In the long term, Senegal should gain from Diouf's policy of attracting foreign investors. The government, backed by outside capital, has built a major shipyard at Dakar. As Dakar is West Africa's most important port, it has been promoted as a giant free-trade zone so that foreign manufacturing companies can exploit Senegal's cheap labour without being subject to punitive taxes and duties.

Senegambia, a confederation of Senegal and The Gambia which was formed in 1982, the year after President *JAWARA of The Gambia had to call in Senegalese troops to suppress an attempted military coup. There was a council of ministers of five Senegalese and four Gambians and a Confederal Assembly of forty Senegalese and twenty Gambians. The Senegambia was supposed to work towards economic and military union, the strengthening of cultural and technical links and the harmonization of foreign policy. Senegal saw it as the first step towards a much closer union, but The Gambia saw it merely as a strengthening of the special relationship between the two countries. The Gambia's fear of losing its sovereignty and its reluctance to move speedily to strengthen the confederation led to deteriorating relations between the two states and the dissolution of Senegambia in September 1989.

Senghor, Léopold Sédar (b.1906), first president of Senegal and regarded as founder of the modern state. Educated in Roman Catholic mission schools in Dakar and then at the University of Paris, Senghor was a teacher in France from 1935 to 1939, when he joined the French army. Captured by the invading Germans in 1940, he was held prisoner until he escaped to become a member of the Resistance, (1942–4). In 1945 he helped to found the Bloc Africain, a political union of French African countries. As Senegal's most senior politician, he was deputy for his country in the French National Assembly between 1946 and 1958. Throughout this period Senghor earned his living as a university professor. He also formed, in 1948, the Bloc Démocratique Sénégalais. Ten years later he linked with another party to form the Union Progressiste Sénégalais.

When Mali and Senegal came together, in April 1959, as the Mali Federation, Senghor was appointed president of the federal assembly. The union was short-lived and when Senegal seceded, Senghor became president of the independent republic of Senegal on 20 August 1960. His early rule was authoritarian and he revised the constitution to strengthen his powers, enabling him to ban some political parties, and to imprison strikers and demonstrating students. In the late 1970s he introduced limited democracy but only by manipulating the constitution to his own ends. His supreme tactic was to ascribe damaging labels to his opponents, such as 'Marxist-Leninist'. He also gained Muslim

The Republic of Seychelles

THE COUNTRY
376 sq. km.

Major City
Victoria (capital)

Principal Islands
Mahé
Praslin
La Digue

Economy
Fishing
Tourism

Principal Exports
Copra
Cinnamon
Fish

Currency
Seychelles rupee of 100
cents

THE PEOPLE
75,000

Ethnic Groups
Creole
Indians
Chinese
Europeans

Languages
English (official)
French (official)
Creole

Religion
Catholicism

THE STATE
Single-party republic

Head of State
President René

Ruling Bodies
Council of Ministers
National Assembly

Official Party
Seychelles People's
Progressive Front

peasant support by currying favour with Muslim leaders. At the end of 1980 Senghor retired after twenty years in office, to be succeeded by his own nominee, the Muslim prime minister Abdou Diouf. Senghor is a celebrated poet in French.

Senussi, a major Arab nomadic clan, living in the Cyrenaica region of Libya. In 1911, the Senussi fiercely resisted the invading Italians and continued to fight until 1932 when the Italians completed their conquest. At the end of the Second World War, the Senussi, under British influence, sought control of Cyrenaica for Sayyed ★IDRIS, the leader of the clan, who had found sanctuary in Egypt during the Italian period. At the end of 1951 Libya became a separate kingdom, with Idris as its first king, and its last; Colonel Muammar ★GADDAFI overthrew the monarchy in 1969.

Seychelles, the Republic of the Seychelles is a member of the Commonwealth, situated in the tropics a thousand miles east of Kenya. It consists of 115 islands in two groups scattered over more than a million square kilometres of the Indian Ocean. There are forty-one granitic islands in the central Mahé group. The largest island is Mahé where over 90 per cent of the country's population lives and where Victoria, the capital, is situated. Mahé is seventeen miles wide and rises to nearly three thousand feet above sea level; the second largest island is Praslin. The outer island group is coral; its small and low-lying islands lack water and are very sparsely populated. The climate is tropical but not oppressive; the average rainfall is over 2200 mm. a year.

The Seychellois are of mixed racial origins, descended from African, Chinese, British, French, Indian and Malayan people who came to the islands as settlers, labourers or slaves. They speak a Creole patois, but the official languages are English and French. Most are Roman Catholic. The country is known for its natural beauty and its exotic wildlife and great efforts have been made to promote tourism. There is little cultivable land and food has to be imported to feed the population. The main export crops are coconut products (mainly copra) and cinnamon; vanilla and patchouli are also exported. The fishing industry is being developed and the licensing of foreign fishing vessels brings in revenue. There are prospects of developing forestry and achieving self-sufficiency in meat, fruit and vegetables.

British explorers found no indigenous inhabitants when they first landed on the Seychelles (1609). It was only after France annexed the islands (1756) that people settled there. After the cession of the islands to Britain (1814) African, British, Chinese, Indian and Malayan arrivals joined the French. Under British rule the country was an economic and political backwater.

Political change began when the first members were elected to the Legislative Council (1948). Two political parties were formed in 1964 – the *SEYCHELLES DEMOCRATIC PARTY (SDP) led by *MANCHAM and the *SEYCHELLES PEOPLE'S UNITED PARTY (SPUP) led by *RENÉ. In 1970 a constitution was agreed, giving the legislature a majority of members elected by universal adult suffrage. Mancham won the 1970 election to become Chief Minister. A constitutional conference (1975) was followed by self-government with Mancham as Prime Minister of an SDP/SPUP coalition (1975–6). This coalition led the Seychelles to independence as a republic in the Commonwealth (Jun. 1976), with Mancham as President and René as Prime Minister. There were sharp differences between the two men. René favoured socialism and links with the communist world. Mancham was a pro-western capitalist who wanted the islands to be a tax haven for international financiers and a playground for tourists.

When René seized power and became President (Jun. 1977), he moved the Seychelles sharply to the left, establishing friendly relations with the Soviet bloc and adopting socialist policies to bring the economy under state control and to lessen the gap between rich and poor. A new constitution in 1979 created a one–party state with a People's Assembly and strengthened the powers of the president.

René's authoritarianism and his radicalism, particularly his espousal of the redistribution of land and nationalization of services and businesses, provoked opposition. The government has also banned private medicine, expanded public housing, doubled the minimum income and guaranteed work for all. The government's socialism and its friendly relations with the Soviet bloc angered many and led to several plots against the government. There were two coup plots in 1978. The coup backed by South African mercenaries (Nov. 1981) came close to success. There were further abortive coups in 1982, 1983 and 1986.

The political uncertainty and the inefficiency of those state bodies controlling the economy contributed to the economic difficulties of the 1980s, including high inflation and a heavy balance of trade deficit. Late in the 1980s the economy began to improve, partly because President René has modified his socialist policies and allowed more private economic enterprise. He has improved relations with the United States and other Western powers. He has had some success in developing agriculture and fishing and in increasing revenues from tourism. President René has earned respect for fighting corruption and for his honesty and dedication. The country's prospects for political stability and greater prosperity in the 1990s have improved.

Seychelles Democratic Party (SDP), a pro-western and capitalist political party in the Seychelles, founded and led by James *MANCHAM (1964). Initially it opposed independence and favoured association with Britain – policies which the electorate supported in 1970. After Britain rejected association (1973) the SDP campaigned for independence. It won the 1974 elections, taking thirteen seats in the legislature with 21,902 votes; the *SEYCHELLES PEOPLE'S UNITED PARTY (SPUP) won only two seats with 19,920 votes. The SDP formed a coalition with the SPUP; this coalition led the country to independence and continued to govern until the coup (Jun. 1977). The new government immediately disbanded the SDP.

Seychelles People's Progressive Front (SPPF), the ruling party in the Seychelles since its formation by President *RENÉ (Jun. 1978). Since the promulgation of the 1979 constitution it has been the only legal party. René founded the SPPF to replace the *SEYCHELLES PEOPLE'S UNITED PARTY (SPUP) and to mobilize support for the socialist policies of his government. The party is led by a central committee and a secretary-general, currently President René. It is committed to socialism and the demilitarization of the Indian Ocean. The SPPF selects the three candidates for each single-member constituency in the elections to the People's Assembly.

Seychelles People's United Party (SPUP), radical and socialist political party in the Seychelles, founded and led by President *RENÉ (1964–78). It campaigned for independence and socialist policies, but lost both the 1970 and 1974 elections. It was the junior partner in the coalition with the *SEYCHELLES DEMOCRATIC PARTY which led the country to independence (1976). After President René seized power (Jun. 1977) the SPUP was the only party allowed to operate in the Seychelles. In May 1978 the SPUP was replaced by the *SEYCHELLES PEOPLE'S PROGRESS-IVE PARTY.

Shaba, mineral-rich province in the south of Zaire, called Katanga in the years of colonial rule and the early years of independence. Its resources account for the bulk of Zaire's export earnings, including 90 per cent of the country's copper and all its cobalt. Under colonial rule its riches were exploited by Belgian mining companies. In July 1960, a few days after independence, *TSHOMBE announced the secession of Katanga from the Congo (now Zaire); there are strong suspicions that he was supported by min-ing companies and other Belgian interests. The secession was finally crushed with the help of United Nations forces early in 1963. The people of the province, now renamed Shaba, resented the way in which the rest of the country exploited its wealth. This and the weakness of the army explain why the invasions of Shaba in 1977 and in 1978 by the rem-nants of Tshombe's forces and other dissidents based in Angola came close to success. The first invasion

across the Angolan border was only crushed with the help of Moroccan troops and the French air force. The second invading force which entered the province via Zambia captured the major mining centre of Kolwezi and seized the railway to the Angolan border; it was defeated with the help of France, Belgium and sympathetic African states.

Shagari, Alhaji Shehu Aliyu Usman (b.1924), ex-President of Nigeria (1979–83). A devout Muslim and a gifted poet in the Hausa language, Shagari was born in Northern Nigeria and trained as a teacher. A founder member of the *NPC (Northern People's Congress) in 1949, he was elected to the federal legislature in 1954. He held various posts in *BALEWA's government (1959–66) and then in provincial government. Shagari returned to federal politics as Commissioner for Economic Development, Rehabili-tation and Reconstruction (1970–1) and for Finance (1971–5). After Gowon was ousted Shagari retired to his farm.

As Nigeria returned to civilian rule, Shagari was elected to the Constituent Assembly (1977) and was a founding member of the *NPN (National Party of Nigeria) in 1978. Shagari had modest politi-cal ambitions, but his reputation for integrity and his considerable politi-cal experience led to his nomination as the NPN's presidential candidate. He and the NPN were ahead in the 1979 elections and won substantial support from many states, but they did not win absolute majorities in the presidential race nor in the federal legislature.

Nevertheless, his presidency began with high hopes. Nigerians enjoyed greater personal and political freedom than ever before; there were no political prisoners. Shagari began a drive against corruption and instituted a Green Revolution to make Nigeria self-sufficient in basic food. Yet in less than two years the government was in serious trouble.

President Shagari managed to do very little. He shelved tough decisions, partly because of tribal and factional rivalries. With an indecisive leader the country drifted. Corruption flourished as never before; much of the plunder went to presidential associates in the so-called Kaduna clique. Nearly three billion dollars were embezzled in the oil scandal, and men like *DIKKO became obscenely rich. Smuggling and armed robbery were rife while production of commodities declined. The federal legislature was unwilling to pass government bills. In federal and state governments politicians ignored mounting deficits while they squabbled with each other. The economy, dependent on oil exports for 90 per cent of its foreign earnings, was devastated by the collapse in world oil prices.

The government used all its resources and all its influence to ensure success for Shagari and NPN in the 1983 elections. Because there was no other credible candidate Shagari would probably have won in a fair fight, but the party machine

resorted to widespread intimidation, corruption and other electoral malpractices to give it a sweeping victory. Disgust at the behaviour of politicians and the corruption of the elections, and alarm at the economic situation prompted the military to seize power yet again at the end of 1983 – just three months after the beginning of Shagari's second term. Shagari was detained, but was cleared of corruption by the military government in 1986. He is banned from holding political office or engaging in political activity for the rest of his life.

Sharia, the system of Islamic law based on the Koran, the teachings of Mohammed and Muslim jurists; it is mainly concerned with family law and other civil matters. There are sharia courts in northern Nigeria. During the preparations for the return to civilian rule in Nigeria in 1992 the constituent assembly has been split between the Muslims who want sharia included in the new constitution and the Christians who oppose it. During 1989 and 1990 this contentious issue disrupted the timetable for civilian rule.

Sharpeville, South African black township where police shot sixtynine unarmed protesters on 21 March 1960. The police shot at a crowd demonstrating against the *PASS LAWS and continued firing as people fled. The world was horrified and international action forced South Africa to withdraw from a number of international bodies. The government declared a state of emergency and banned the two leading

The Republic of Sierra Leone

THE COUNTRY	THE PEOPLE	THE STATE
71,740 sq. km.	3,845,000	Single-party republic
Major Cities	*Ethnic Groups*	*Head of State*
Freetown (capital)	Temne	President Momoh
Koidu	Mende	
Bo	Lokko	*Ruling Bodies*
Kenema	Sherbro	Presidential Cabinet
Makeni	Limba	House of
	Creole	Representatives
Economy		
Farming	*Languages*	*Official Party*
Mining	English (official)	All-People's Congress
	Temne	
Principal Exports	Mende	
Diamonds	Krio	
Iron ore		
Bauxite	*Religion*	
Rutile	Traditional beliefs	
Cocoa	Islam	
	Christian	
Currency		
Leone (Le) of 100 cents		

black nationalist organizations, the *AFRICAN NATIONAL CONGRESS and the *PAN-AFRICANIST CONGRESS. Robert *SOBUKWE was arrested for organizing the protest. The Sharpeville killings are remembered annually; on the twenty-fifth anniversary (1985) the police killed twenty protesters in the township of Langa in the Cape.

In the late 1980s the case of the Sharpeville Six again focused international attention on Sharpeville. In December 1985 five men and one woman were sentenced to death for sharing 'the common purpose' of a mob which had killed a Deputy Mayor in Sharpeville (Sep. 1984).

After many protests, including an appeal from Mrs Thatcher, President P. W. *BOTHA reprieved them (Nov. 1988).

Sierra Leone, the Republic of Sierra Leone is a member of the Commonwealth. Situated on the West African coast, it is bordered by Liberia to the east and south, by the Atlantic Ocean to the south and west and by Guinea to the north-west, north and north-east. Lying just north of the Equator it has a warm and humid tropical climate with heavy rainfall on the coast. The coastal region has mangrove swamps, a plain up to 120 km. wide and the hilly Freetown peninsula. Inland an escarpment rises to the central forest region about 500 m. above sea level; much of the land has been cleared for agriculture and the region is drained by a number of rivers. The land rises to mountainous plateaux in the north-east.

Sierra Leone's economy is primarily agricultural; over two thirds of the population are farmers and the great majority of these grow rice for domestic consumption. Sierra Leone does not produce enough rice to feed itself and imports about a quarter of its needs. Agriculture accounts for over a third of exports. Cocoa is the most important – followed by coffee, palm kernels, ginger, piassava (a fibre) and kola nuts.

The economy has become heavily dependent on mining as the principal source of export earnings. Sierra Leone has rich diamond deposits, but officially recorded production has fallen dramatically. In 1980 diamonds accounted for over half of the country's exports; in 1986 they were down to 20 per cent. The most easily accessible deposits are being exhausted and miners and dealers smuggle diamonds across the border to avoid government taxes and to get a better price in hard currency. Iron ore has also been a valuable export, but deposits were becoming exhausted by the second half of the 1970s and most mines have been closed. During the 1980s Sierra Leone exported increasing amounts of rutile (titanium oxide) and bauxite – valuable foreign currency earners.

The manufacturing industry is small and accounts for only about

6 per cent of economic activity. It attempts to provide import substitutes, but is hindered by shortages of foreign exchange for the purchase of equipment and semi-processed goods. Much of the wholesale trade is under Lebanese control.

Like many other Third World states Sierra Leone has been suffering from an economic and financial crisis since the mid-1970s. The rising price of oil imports coupled with declining exports have put the balance of trade heavily into the red. The problems have been aggravated by heavy government spending, inefficiency, corruption and smuggling. Sierra Leone applied for international financial aid, but had difficulties in servicing its loans. The standby arrangement made with the IMF in 1980 was suspended by the IMF in 1984. After agreeing to further austerity which it has found very harsh, Sierra Leone made a new credit arrangement with the IMF in 1986. In return for financial support Sierra Leone's currency, the leone, was allowed to float – in effect a steep devaluation. The government cut rice and petrol subsidies and adopted strict monetary and fiscal policies. These measures led to higher rice prices and caused unrest. Although President *MOMOH introduced emergency economic regulations to deal with smugglers and hoarders in 1987, the IMF felt Sierra Leone was not meeting its conditions and withdrew its support in 1988.

The largest groups in Sierra Leone are the Mende of the south and the Temne of the north; each comprise about 30 per cent of the country's population. About 2 per cent are *CREOLE, based mostly near Freetown and descended from the slaves settled by Britain. The rest of the population is divided into six ethnic groups.

The name Sierra Leone was given to the coastal region by Portuguese navigators in the fifteenth century. They named the coastal mountains as Serra Lyoa (Lion Mountain Range). The name was later applied to the whole country. Late in the eighteenth century British philanthropists founded Freetown as a colony for the resettlement of destitute freed black slaves. In 1808 Britain made Sierra Leone a colony and used it for the resettlement of slaves freed from slave ships by the Royal Navy. These people and their descendants who became known as Creoles were better treated than most colonial subjects. Missionaries gave them good educational opportunities; some Creoles qualified as lawyers and doctors and others held important posts in the administration during the nineteenth century. In contrast Britain did little to develop Sierra Leone's hinterland; after declaring it a British protectorate (1896) they left its administration to the traditional rulers.

After the Second World War Britain began preparing Sierra Leone for independence. The *SIERRA LEONE PEOPLE'S PARTY (SLPP) emerged as the dominant political party; its leader, Dr Milton *MARGAI (later Sir Milton) became Chief Minister (1954), Prime Minister (1956) and led Sierra Leone to independence in

the Commonwealth (1961). Sierra Leone was prosperous and stable under Sir Milton. When he died (1964) Albert (later Sir Albert) *MARGAI succeeded him as prime minister. There were economic problems and Albert alienated the Creoles. He was suspected of planning to make Sierra Leone a one-party state.

The SLPP narrowly lost the March 1967 elections to the opposition *ALL PEOPLE'S CONGRESS (APC), led by Siaka *STEVENS. Albert Margai refused to step down and Brigadier Lansana staged a coup to prevent the APC from taking office. Two days later Lansana was deposed in another military coup. The new military rulers formed the National Reformation Council and pledged to end corruption and return Sierra Leone to civilian rule. They made little progress and were overthrown by the lower ranks of the army in 1968. Siaka Stevens returned to Sierra Leone and formed a government.

Stevens took various steps to strengthen his power. He made Sierra Leone a republic in 1971 and became executive president. After winning the 1977 elections which were marred by irregularities and violence, he imposed a new constitution making Sierra Leone a socialist one-party state in 1978. His increased power did not bring political stability. There were various attempts to assassinate him and overthrow the APC government. The most dangerous attempt was made by Brigadier Bangura, the

309

army commander, in March 1971. Stevens sought the aid of Guinea and kept Guinean troops in Sierra Leone for two years to protect himself and his government. Bangura and three others were executed. Stevens also drew closer to Liberia in 1973 by joining the *MANO RIVER CONVENTION which provided for economic co-operation between the two countries.

Throughout his presidency Stevens had to contend with mounting economic problems and unrest. There were student riots in 1977 and 1984, strikes, factional fighting and general unrest – often provoked by rising prices and shortages of food. On several occasions a state of emergency was declared. There were scandals involving top politicians and administrators.

In November 1985 Stevens retired and was succeeded as President by Maj.-Gen. Joseph *MOMOH. Momoh was well received at first; there were hopes that he would be able to improve the economy and to stamp out mismanagement and corruption. After over four years in power he has achieved little. There have been attempted coups; in October 1987 sixteen defendants were sentenced to death for plotting to overthrow the government in March 1987. There have been more student riots and more general violence. The economy has yet to improve and Momoh has been either unwilling or unable to impose the financial discipline demanded by the IMF. Sierra Leone's economic and political future remain uncertain.

Sierra Leone People's Party (SLPP), party founded and led by Sir Milton *MARGAI after the Second World War. It dominated Sierra Leone politics from the 1951 elections until 1967, forming the government before and after independence in 1961. When Sir Milton died (1964), Sir Albert *MARGAI became leader of the party and Prime Minister of Sierra Leone. After losing the 1967 elections the SLPP government refused to resign; this provoked a series of military coups which ended with the restoration of civilian government in 1968. The SLPP formed the opposition. In the 1977 elections (the last before Sierra Leone became a one-party state) the SLPP won fifteen of the seventy-seven seats in the House of Representatives. The SLPP was dissolved when the one-party state was proclaimed in 1978; some of its leading members joined the *ALL PEOPLE'S CONGRESS and President *STEVENS' government.

Simango, Revd. Uria, Mozambican nationalist who led one of the groups which combined to form *FRELIMO (1962). He was Vice-President of Frelimo (1962–9) and hoped to succeed *MONDLANE as President in 1969, but the Central Committee entrusted the leadership to a triumvirate (Simango, *MACHEL, *DOS SANTOS). In November 1969 Simango denounced Frelimo and joined *COREMO, leaving the way clear for Machel to become the leader.

Sisulu, Nontsikelelo Albertina (b.1918), wife of Walter *SISULU whom she married in 1944, and mother of Zwelakhe *SISULU. She is a leading black South African opponent of *APARTHEID and campaigner for women's rights. Although her husband, a leading member of the *AFRICAN NATIONAL CONGRESS (ANC), has been in prison for much of their married life, she has not only raised five children but has also actively campaigned for a non-racial democratic South African state. She joined the ANC Women's League in 1948; her protests have led to detention and *BANNING ORDERS, including ten years house arrest. In 1983 she became one of the three Presidents of the *UNITED DEMOCRATIC FRONT (UDF), an organization which she hopes will unite South Africans of all races. With other UDF leaders she was charged with treason in 1985, but the trial collapsed.

Sisulu, Walter Max (b.1912), veteran black South African nationalist, husband of Albertina *SISULU and father of Zwelakhe *SISULU. He joined the *AFRICAN NATIONAL CONGRESS (ANC) in 1940 and became Treasurer of the ANC Youth League. He became Secretary-General of the ANC in 1949. During the 1950s when he was effectively running ANC operations in the Transvaal he moderated his racially exclusive views and became willing to work with other racial groups. He was often arrested and detained, and subjected to a *BANNING ORDER under the *SUPPRESSION OF COMMUNISM ACT.

He was among the 156 charged with high treason and acquitted in a long treason trial (1956–61). After the events of *SHARPEVILLE he was detained, tried and put under house arrest. In April 1963 he went underground to join *UMKONTO WE SIZWE but was captured less than three months later. At the *RIVONIA TRIAL he was sentenced to life imprisonment in 1964 for planning political sabotage and revolution. With Nelson *MANDELA and other convicted ANC members he was sent to *ROBBEN ISLAND. He was released in October 1989 after twenty-six years in prison. Despite the long years in prison, Sisulu still supports the idea of negotiations with the South African government and looks forward to the establishment of a non-racial democracy in South Africa.

Sisulu, Zwelakhe (b.1950), son of Walter and Albertina *SISULU. He trained as a journalist in 1975 and began work on the *RAND DAILY MAIL, a newspaper known for its opposition to *APARTHEID. He worked as news editor on the *Sunday Post* until a *BANNING ORDER was imposed on him (Dec. 1980). From 1980 to 1984 he was President of the Media Workers' Association of South Africa and played a crucial role in organizing the strike that persuaded newspaper employers to recognize the union (Dec. 1980). After a spell in detention (1981–2) he joined the *Sowetan* in July 1983. Early in 1986 Sisulu became editor of *New Nation*, a radical anti-apartheid weekly, but was then detained without trial for nearly two years (1986–8). During his detention he

311

won numerous awards and international pressure may have accounted for his release, although under severe restrictions.

Sithole, the Revd. Ndabaningi (b.1920), Zimbabwean nationalist leader and politician who was ordained as a Methodist minister (1958). The founder and first leader of *ZANU (1963), he was imprisoned and restricted for many years until his release in 1974. After losing the leadership of ZANU to Robert *MUGABE (1977), he formed his own ZANU party and served in the transitional government (1978–9). Sithole contested the 1980 pre-independence elections without success and during the 1980s went to live in the United States. Although he is still in exile in the United States, one of his supporters won a seat in the 1990 elections.

Six Day War On 5 June 1967, the Israeli air force attacked airfields in Egypt, Jordan and Syria in order to pre-empt an Arab invasion of Israel. The Israeli warplanes destroyed 374 aircraft, mostly on the ground. Israeli armour made a three-pronged advance towards the Suez Canal and routed the Egyptian army. On 7 June, Israeli forces occupied the Old City of Jerusalem and attacked the Jordanian army. The war ended on 10 June, with 679 Israelis and 3000 Arabs killed. The rapid defeat demoralized the Arabs and drastically reduced Egypt's prestige. See *NASSER; *SUEZ CRISIS.

Slabbert, Frederik Van Zyl (b. 1940), liberal white South African political leader, who began his career as a sociologist and a university lecturer (1964–74). His rejection of *APARTHEID stemmed from his sociological work and his contact with other races at university and in the church. He joined the *PROGRESSIVE FEDERAL PARTY (PFP) in 1974 and won election to parliament the same year.

Late in the 1970s Van Zyl Slabbert chaired the PFP's constitutional committee which formulated franchise proposals more generous to non-whites than the party's previous policy. As PFP leader and Leader of the Opposition (1979–86) he argued for a national convention in which South Africans of all races could work out a just constitutional settlement. He believed the PFP had an important part to play in persuading people to negotiate rather than resort to violence. In February 1986 he suddenly resigned as party leader and from parliament, declaring that party politics no longer had any relevance in South Africa. Since then he has devoted himself to extra-parliamentary activities, notably the promotion of the Institute for a Democratic Alternative for South Africa (IDASA).

Slavery, offensive and barbarous practice rife in many parts of East, West and North Africa for much of the eighteenth and nineteenth centuries and persisting, especially in North Africa, until well into the twentieth century. Slave markets were regularly operating in Djibouti in the 1950s. The slaves were rounded up mostly in Chad and other parts of north-central

Africa, the slave-dealers were mostly African themselves and the buyers were predominantly from the Arabian peninsula.

*ISLAM did not prohibit slavery and according to legal theory, those who were captured in war could be enslaved; so could those who were imported from the 'area of war', or *dar-al-Islam*. Free-born Muslims could not be enslaved, but the children of slave parents were themselves slaves. Islam traditionally encouraged the freeing of slaves, for religious reasons, and the law provided means by which a slave could regain his freedom. During the 1950s and 1960s various Arab governments banned slavery.

Since 1960, slavery has been noted in two parts of Africa – Mauritania and Sudan. In Mauritania, it has been in the form of chattel slavery or bondage. Wealthy families have either bought the children of poor families as household servants or have acquired them as collateral when debts have not been paid. The problem of modern slavery in Sudan came to light when two professors from Khartoum University were investigating the massacre in March 1988 of more than a thousand Dinka men, women and children by Rizeigat Arabs in western Sudan. The professors found that about 1100 Dinka people were being worked as slaves on Arab farms. Others had been sold to buyers in Central African Republic and Chad. Dr Ahmed Ushari, co-author of the report *The Diein Massacre and Slavery in Sudan*, estimated that 1500 Dinkas were being held in slavery by Rizeigat and Messariya Arab tribesmen. Many of them were rounded up from the villages of Achoro and Mabyur Nyang. The Khartoum professors claimed that the government policy of arming the Rizeigat people against the Sudan People's Liberation Army had contributed to slavery and banditry. Some parents, desperate to escape the civil war, handed over their children as slaves to pay for their own transport by truck to the relatively peaceful north. Dr Ushari was arrested after publication of his revelations, imprisoned and tortured.

There is no doubt that the tyrant Emperor *BOKASSA of Central African Republic had slaves and that he butchered some of them. Reports persist of types of slavery or bondage in certain parts of northern Nigeria, Rwanda and Niger but proof is lacking.

Slovo, Joe (b.1926), as the only South African white in the top ranks of the *AFRICAN NATIONAL CONGRESS (ANC) he is feared and detested by many white South Africans and admired by many black South Africans. Born in Lithuania, he arrived in South Africa at the age of nine and joined the South African Communist Party (SACP) at the age of sixteen. After qualifying as a lawyer, he married Ruth *FIRST (1949). In 1950 he and his wife were among the first people to be named under the *SUPPRESSION OF COMMUNISM ACT. Slovo contributed to the drafting of the *FREEDOM CHARTER in 1955, but could not attend the meeting that adopted it because of his restriction order.

With other ANC activists he was charged with treason in 1956, but the charges were dropped in 1958. He was detained during the 1960 state of emergency which followed the *SHARPEVILLE killings. Slovo was a leader of *UMKHONTO WE SIZWE, but escaped arrest because he was abroad when the leadership was arrested at its Rivonia headquarters (1963). He then worked for the ANC and the SACP abroad, moving to Mozambique where he established an ANC operational centre. It was in Mozambique that Ruth First was assassinated by a parcel bomb (1982). Slovo held the post of Umkhonto we Sizwe Chief of Staff until he retired from the job (1987). He returned to South Africa after twenty-seven years in exile to be a member of the ANC delegation which had preliminary talks with the South African government (May 1990). Slovo still argues passionately for working class solidarity and the redistribution of wealth.

Smith, Ian Douglas (b. 1919), political leader who sought to retain white control of Zimbabwe (then Southern Rhodesia). After distinguished service in the Second World War he entered politics and was elected to the Legislative Assembly in 1948. Smith was a founder of the *RHODESIAN FRONT PARTY (1962), Deputy Prime Minister in Winston Field's government (1962–4) and Prime Minister (1964–79). He led the Rhodesian Front and its successors (the Republican Front and the *CONSERVATIVE ALLIANCE OF ZIMBABWE) from 1964 until 1987.

After the *CENTRAL AFRICAN FEDERATION collapsed at the end of 1963, Smith failed to persuade Britain to grant independence to Southern Rhodesia without majority rule. Declaring that there would never be African majority rule, he proclaimed *UDI (Unilateral Declaration of Independence) in November 1965. The international community refused to recognize the Smith regime and the nationalists began the long war of independence. Under military and economic pressure Smith negotiated an 'internal settlement' with some African leaders and formed a transitional government (1978–9). He stepped down as Prime Minister in 1979 after Bishop *MUZOREWA's rather dubious electoral success. The deteriorating situation forced Smith to accept the *LANCASTER HOUSE AGREEMENT (Dec. 1979) which led to independence in April 1980. After independence Smith led the Rhodesian Front and its successors until he was forced to resign (1987) after making remarks detrimental to Zimbabwe. He lost his parliamentary seat when the reserved white seats were abolished (1987), and now lives in retirement on his farm.

Sobhuza II (1899–1982), head of the *DLAMINI clan and King of Swaziland (1921–82) with the title of Ngwenyama (Lion). His father, Ngwane V, died when he was an infant and there was a long regency before he ascended to the throne. In many ways he was a figure from the past. A patriarch who imposed his authority on a numerous and quarrelsome royal clan, he favoured traditional dress and had at least a hundred wives and hundreds of children.

At the same time Sobhuza II was shrewdly aware of the realities of twentieth century politics. He was an able ruler who led Swaziland to independence (1968) with a constitution that gave him considerable power. He protected his country's interests against Mozambique and South Africa, but did not complete the land deal with South Africa which would have increased Swaziland's territory by about 40 per cent and given it a corridor to the Indian Ocean. He bought land back from expatriates and settlers and founded *TIBIYO TAKA NGWANE (Swaziland National Development Fund) to invest in the country.

In 1964 Sobhuza II instigated the formation of the royalist *IMBOKODVO NATIONAL MOVEMENT which held all the seats in the legislature until the opposition *NGWANE NATIONAL LIBERATORY CONGRESS won three seats in 1972. Unable to tolerate opposition he suspended the constitution (1973) and ruled by decree. During his last years he was increasingly repressive and showed little concern for human rights. When he died the monarchy was strong and Swaziland was one of Africa's most stable states.

Sobukwe, Robert Mangaliso (1924–78), radical black South African leader who inspired the *BLACK CONSCIOUSNESS movement with his message that blacks must rely only on themselves. While studying at *FORT HARE UNIVERSITY he was politically involved as Secretary-General of the *AFRICAN NATIONAL CONGRESS (ANC) Youth League. After being forced out of teaching because of his political activism, Sobukwe lectured and edited *The Africanist* for two years. In 1958 he broke with the ANC because it included sympathetic white members and formed the exclusively black *PAN-AFRICANIST CONGRESS (PAC), which mounted a series of demonstrations against the *PASS LAWS. He was arrested on 21 March 1960, the day of the *SHARPEVILLE killings, and sentenced to three years in prison followed by six years in detention. After he was released (1969) he was the subject of a *BANNING ORDER for life, but managed to qualify as a lawyer (1975) and practised law until his death.

Sokoine, Edward Moringe (1938–84), Tanzanian politician of Masai origins. He entered parliament in 1965 and held various ministerial posts before his first term as Prime Minister (1977–80). He resigned because of ill health (Nov. 1980), but was recalled for a second term by President *NYERERE (Feb. 1983) and entrusted with the task of dealing with Tanzania's grave economic problems. His first notable successes (1983) were agreements with Kenya and Uganda restoring diplomatic relations and reopening trade. Sokoine was greatly respected for his abilities and was expected to succeed *NYERERE as President in 1985, but he died in a road accident (Apr. 1984).

Somalia, forming the Horn of Africa, with a coastline of over three thousand kilometres, the Gulf of Aden to the north and the Indian Ocean to the east and south. A country of rolling bushland, it rises from the coastal plains to mountains over two thousand metres high in the north. Somalia's neighbours are Djibouti to the north, Ethiopia to the west and Kenya to the south-west.

Muslim traders established trading posts along the Somali coast between the seventh and twelfth centuries. The small centres became Muslim sultanates and from Mogadishu, Berbera, Hobyo and Kismayu exports included slaves, valuable gums and adornments such as ostrich feathers. The nomads of the interior were converted to *ISLAM and became colonizing soldiers for the holy cause.

The modern history of Somalia began in 1899 when a famous Islamic religious leader, Muhammad Abdilla Hassan – 'the Mad Mullah of Somaliland' to the British – inaugurated a major rebellion against colonial rule. The resistance campaign continued until the Mullah's death in 1921. He is venerated by Somali nationalists to this day. Italy overran Ethiopia in 1935, and in 1940, during the Second World War, occupied the British Somaliland Protectorate. All Somalis were placed under one administration. Having defeated the Italians in 1941–2, the British continued this system. In 1943, with the war still in progress, the Somali Youth League (SYL) was founded and soon became the country's most important political party.

In 1949 the United Nations granted the Italians their former colony as a ten-year trusteeship. On 26 June 1960 British Somaliland became independent. Five days later, on 1 July, as the Italian trusteeship ended, the two parts of the country became the Somalia Democratic Republic. At that time there was no *de jure* border separating Somalia from the *OGADEN region of Ethiopia, inhabited almost entirely by Somali-speaking nomads. The 'provisional administrative line' decided on by Britain, Italy and Ethiopia at the time of the establishment of the Italian trust in 1949 was all that existed. Repeated United Nations attempts to secure a demarcation line between Ethiopia and Somalia between 1950 and 1960 show that the UN did not believe that the provisional administrative line was a legal border.

The SYL joined with the two main parties of the north to form the new Republic. The principal tribes or rers united under the new prime minister, Dr Abdirashi Ali Shirmarke of the Darod rer. In 1964, in the first elections since independence, the SYL won most of the seats in the new national assembly. In the following elections, in 1969, the SYL again had an overwhelming victory. In October that year the president,

The Somali Democratic Republic

THE COUNTRY	THE PEOPLE	THE STATE
637,657 sq. km.	5.2 million	Multi-party presidential republic
Major Cities	*Ethnic Groups*	*Head of State*
Mogadishu (capital)	Somalis only	Ali Mahdi Mohamed
Kismayu		
Marka	*Languages*	*Ruling Body*
Burao	Somali (unwritten until 1972)	President
	Italian	
Economy	English	
Livestock – camels, sheep, goats, cattle		
Fruit, especially bananas	*Religion*	
Sugar	Islam	
Principal Exports		
Livestock		
Bananas		
Currency		
Somali shilling		

Muhammad Haji Ibrahim Egel, was assassinated and on 21 October 1969 the army, under Major-General Siad *BARRÉ, seized power in a bloodless coup. The country became a socialist state – the Somali Democratic Republic – with Barré as president and leader of the only party now permitted, the Somali Revolutionary Socialist Party. Barré decreed that Somali language would replace English, French and Italian as the official language, though it would be written in Roman rather than Arabic script.

From 1970 Somalia, from having been largely Western-oriented, turned to the Soviet bloc for aid and advice. In 1974 Somalia joined the *ARAB LEAGUE and came under increasing pressure to undertake political realignment. When the Soviet leaders armed the Ethiopian forces during the Ogaden crisis, Somalia withdrew all military facilities given to the Soviets and expelled all Soviet military and civil advisers. In January 1979 a new draft constitution was passed for public referendum and was approved in August that year. This constitution was the basis for a People's Assembly, which holds office for five years and which elects a president for a six-year term. In January 1980 Barré was unanimously elected and in November 1984 the Assembly passed constitutional amendments which transferred all effective power to the president. Barré was re-elected in 1986, survived an army coup in 1987, only to fall to concerted opposition in 1991.

In the latter half of 1990, Barré and his Marehan clan came under pressure from many rebelling groups, and the government's power was steadily eroded. As fighting between government and rebel forces intensified (Dec. 1990–Jan. 1991), most foreign nationals were evacuated from Mogadishu and thousands of locals were killed, more fleeing. The United Somali Congress (USC) emerged victorious, Barré fled the capital, a transitional government was established, and free elections promised. The USC, dominated by the Hawiye clan of central Somalia, promised that it would not exclude any clan from consultations about democracy, even its rivals the Issaq-dominated Somali National Movement from the north and the Somali Patriotic Movement of the south.

Somalia's centrally planned economy is based on livestock rearing, which provides a subsistence livelihood for three-quarters of the population and the major share of export earnings. Bananas, the second largest export earner, are grown on riverside plantations. Output has fallen steadily for many years but the government's decision to sell most of its shares in the National Banana Board to the private sector aroused hopes of revival. Other products are cotton, fruit, frankincense, of which Somalia is the world's largest producer, and subsistence maize and sorghum. Development of fishing is a priority, with finance coming from Japan, Italy, the EC and China. Somalia has a number of minerals, including uranium, iron ore and coal. Drought and a ban in 1983 on the import of livestock into Saudi Arabia, Somalia's largest market, caused severe economic difficulties. In addition, the country harbours 1.7 million refugees, mostly ethnic Somalis from Ethiopia. More than half of Somalia's imports, which total $500 million a year, are aid-dependent. Despite the advantage of a long coastline Somalia's fishing industry is undeveloped; the potential is vast, especially in the fish-processing sector.

South Africa, the Republic of, covers the southern end of the continent of Africa. Excluding ★WALVIS BAY and including the 'independent ★HOMELANDS' it has an area of 1,221,037 sq. km. Most of the country lies south of the Tropic of Capricorn and enjoys a temperate climate. It is bordered by Namibia on the north-west, Botswana on the north, and Zimbabwe, Mozambique and Swaziland on the north-east. Lesotho is entirely surrounded by South African territory.

Most of the country consists of a large plateau ranging from 600 to 2000 metres above sea-level. The plateau is divided into three regions. The High Veld covers most of the Orange Free State and parts of the Transvaal; it is

The Republic of South Africa

THE COUNTRY
1,211,037 sq. km.

Major Cities
Pretoria (capital)
Cape Town
Bloemfontein
Johannesburg
Durban
Port Elizabeth

Economy
Mixed

Principal Exports
Gold
Diamonds
Base metals
Wool
Fruit
Maize
Sugar

Currency
Rand of 100 cents

THE PEOPLE
33,285,000

Ethnic Groups
Bantu (74%)
European (14%)
Coloured (9%)
Indian (3%)

Languages
Afrikaans (official)
English (official)
Bantu languages

Religion
Christian

THE STATE
Multi-party republic

Head of State
President de Klerk

Ruling Bodies
Presidential Cabinet
Tricameral Parliament

Party in Power
National Party

Official Opposition
Conservative Party

---

from 1200 to 1800 metres high. The Witwatersrand is a ridge over 1500 metres high and includes rich goldfields around Johannesburg. The Middle Veld is from 600 to 1200 metres high. Around the central plateau there are various features. These include the mountainous eastern escarpment down to the eastern coastal belt, the less dramatic slope down to the western coastal belt, the mountainous ranges of the Cape to the south of the plateau and the Low Veld in the northern Transvaal from 150 to 600 metres above sea-level.

South Africa is well endowed with natural resources. Despite scanty rainfall in parts of the country a wide variety of crops is produced and wool and fruit are major exports. South Africa does not have important oil reserves, but is otherwise richly endowed with minerals. These include 89 per cent of the world's chromium reserves, 80 per cent of its platinum and 53 per cent of its gold. In addition to mining and agriculture, South Africa has a well developed manufacturing sector which produces a wide variety of goods. There are

319

highly developed industrial areas near Johannesburg, Cape Town, Port Elizabeth and Durban.

The earliest known inhabitants were the *KHOISAN (*BUSHMEN and *HOTTENTOTS) of whom few survive; about 1500 years ago they were displaced by waves of *BANTU immigrants. About three-quarters of South Africa's population are Bantu. The white minority is divided between the Afrikaners who are descended from Dutch and Huguenot arrivals in the seventeenth and eighteenth century and the English-speaking South Africans who are mostly descended from the British arrivals of the nineteenth and twentieth centuries. The *COLOURED or mixed-race South Africans are of Bantu, white, Malay, and Khoisan descent. Most *INDIANS are descended from labourers brought in by Britain in the nineteenth and early twentieth centuries.

Since 1948 the party of Afrikaner nationalism, the *NATIONAL PARTY, has been in power. Successive National Party governments have offered *APARTHEID as the solution to the problems of the country's multi-racial society, but their policies have only intensified the difficulties. The fruits of apartheid have included the violation of human rights, hardship for non-whites, bitter black nationalist opposition, conflict with neighbouring states, worldwide criticism and economic problems.

The year 1960 saw three developments crucial to South Africa's future. Britain's Conservative Prime Minister, Harold Macmillan, made it clear in his 'winds of change' speech that if a choice had to be made Britain and the West would support African states under black majority rule rather than South Africa under white minority rule. The *SHARPEVILLE killings and their aftermath led to international protests and to greater black militancy in the campaign against apartheid. The white electorate voted to make the Union of South Africa into a republic. When the extent of Commonwealth opposition to South Africa was made clear, Dr *VERWOERD withdrew from the Commonwealth Prime Ministers' Conference and took South Africa out of the Commonwealth. The Republic of South Africa came into being on 31 May 1961.

By the 1960s the foundations of apartheid were firmly established. Legislation such as the *GROUP AREAS, Bantu Education, Separate Universities, *IMMORALITY, and *MIXED MARRIAGES ACTS had done much to separate the races. The *PASS LAWS and influx control enabled the authorities to decide where people could or could not live. The *SUPPRESSION OF COMMUNISM ACT, detention without trial, *BANNING, treason trials and the secret police were part of the formidable state machinery deployed to suppress dissent.

Eager to demonstrate what he considered the more positive side of apartheid Dr Verwoerd pressed ahead with the formation of Homelands for different Bantu peoples. In theory these are supposed to become independent of white South Africa, but they are too small and too limited in resources to accommodate South Africa's Bantu population – 15 per cent of the land is expected to accommodate about 75 per cent of the population of South Africa. By the late 1980s four of the ten homelands had accepted 'independence' – a status not recognized outside South Africa.

After Verwoerd's assassination (1966) his successor John *VORSTER announced he would continue along the road to apartheid and then modified some of the more unpleasant aspects of racial discrimination. Vorster wanted better relations with South Africa's black neighbours and discussed co-operation over the Rhodesian and Namibian problems. Any diplomatic advantages South Africa might have gained with neighbours were lost when it invaded Angola (1978). Subsequent raids on *AFRICAN NATIONAL CONGRESS (ANC) bases and sanctuaries in neighbouring countries and the assassination of anti-apartheid activists further damaged South Africa's international standing. On one day in May 1986 South Africa raided alleged ANC bases in Botswana, Zambia and Zimbabwe, killing three and injuring many. South Africa has destabilized its neighbours, notably by supporting *UNITA and *RENAMO, rebel movements active in Angola and Mozambique respectively. Since 1980 her neighbours

have met regularly in the *SOUTHERN AFRICAN DEVELOPMENT CO-ORDINATION CONFERENCE to work out ways in which they can lessen their economic dependency on South Africa, even though severing links with South Africa could cost them a great deal.

P. W. *BOTHA became Prime Minister in 1978; as the Minister of Defence he had master-minded the invasion of Angola earlier that year. As he had been regarded as a hardline white supremacist, there was considerable surprise at his apparent willingness to modify apartheid. In 1979 he accepted the recommendation of the Wiehahn Commission that black workers should have the right to form trade unions and to go on strike. He encouraged some desegregation in sport, hotels, and restaurants. In 1985 his government repealed the Mixed Marriages Act, Section 16 of the Immorality Act, and laws banning multi-racial political parties.

A referendum of the white electorate (1983) supported Botha's new constitutional arrangements which came into effect in 1984. These created an executive presidency and gave Coloured and Indian people a share of political power. Three chambers of parliament now represent three different racial groups – Whites, Coloureds, and Indians. Non-whites can be in the cabinet; there is an Indian cabinet minister but the Coloured leader left the cabinet after a dispute with President Botha. An electoral college which includes representatives of the three races chooses the President. There is a President's Council to resolve any differences between the three chambers. The whole system is heavily weighted in favour of the whites who control both the electoral college and the President's Council. More seriously the new constitution excludes the Bantu from any share of political power, because they are supposed to be able to exercise power in their Homelands. In 1986 Botha proposed a National Council in which Bantu could serve and discuss constitutional arrangements, but this plan did not get off the ground.

South Africa faced many difficulties in the 1980s. Racial discrimination and aggression towards her neighbours have caused increasingly grave political and economic problems at home and abroad. The United Nations has repeatedly condemned South Africa and has imposed mandatory sanctions against the sale of military equipment to South Africa; the exercise of vetoes by Britain and the United States on the Security Council has saved South Africa from further United Nations measures. Various international organizations, including the Olympic movement, have expelled South Africa. The Commonwealth has condemned South African attacks on her neighbours and set up the *EMINENT PERSONS GROUP to assist in the transition to majority rule in South Africa and to make recommendations on sanctions. The European Community has imposed sanctions. Oil producing countries have banned the sale of oil to South Africa. Sanctions and South Africa's economic problems have led many international firms to withdraw wholly or partly from South Africa. In three years (1985 to 1987) 59 British and 144 American firms disposed of investments in South Africa; they included General Motors, Ford, IBM, Barclays Bank and Kodak.

South Africa's currency, the rand, has slumped in value. Inflation is high, and blacks in particular suffer from the high rate of unemployment. At the end of 1985 her foreign debt was twenty-four billion dollars. A longer-term worry is South Africa's rapid population growth; at the current rate of expansion this is estimated to reach eighty million by 2020 and one hundred and thirty-eight million by 2040. The rural Bantu population is growing faster than other groups.

The recent spate of unrest which began in Sharpeville (Sep. 1984) and spread rapidly has exacerbated the problems. The toll of casualties in the first year was over 700. A state of emergency was imposed in July 1985; after 7996 arrests and 757 more deaths (according to official reports) it was suspended in March 1986 and reimposed in June 1986. Anti-government protests and violence have continued. Fighting between the Bantu supporters of the rival *UNITED DEMOCRATIC FRONT and *INKATHA movements caused an estimated 280 deaths in the townships in 1987.

In February 1988 the South African authorities banned the activities of seventeen major opposition groups, including the United Democratic Front, student and youth organizations, those supporting detainees and their families and any organizations linked to *BLACK CONSCIOUSNESS. The most politically active trade union group, *COSATU, has been limited to activity related to pay and working conditions. Albertina *SISULU, Archie Gumede and other leading dissidents had their activities restricted. This crackdown led to fresh international calls for mandatory economic sanctions.

By late 1988 the situation began to change. South African negotiations with Angola led to agreement. South Africa agreed to withdraw from Namibia, a process completed by March 1990, and Angola agreed to send the Cuban troops home. In January 1990 President Botha had a stroke. F. W. *DE KLERK succeeded him as leader of the National Party, but President Botha expressed his determination to carry on as president until his term expired. After increasing tension between Botha and de Klerk, Botha resigned (Aug. 1989), less than a month before the election. In the election both the right-wing *CONSERVATIVE PARTY and the more liberal *DEMOCRATIC PARTY made gains, but the National Party still won an absolute majority of seats.

Within six months, President de Klerk made a series of dramatic movements which raised hopes that the government and the nationalists would be able to negotiate a peaceful settlement of South Africa's future. He started releasing political prisoners, including Mr Walter *SISULU. In February 1990 he lifted the ban on the ANC and about thirty other organizations. He toned down the state of emergency, relaxed press controls and announced there would be more reforms. A few days later he released Nelson *MANDELA who had been in prison for twenty-seven years. In October 1990 de Klerk repealed the Separate Amenities Act.

Many problems still remain. When negotiations are held, it is difficult to see how the views of the two sides can be reconciled. The nationalists want 'one man, one vote' and majority rule. President de Klerk is not prepared to have the interests of the white minority subordinated to those of the black majority and favours some sort of power-sharing agreement. Despite their differences a government delegation had successful preliminary talks with the ANC (May 1990); there are hopes that full constitutional negotiations will follow. Too great a diminution of white power could well provoke a white backlash. The Conservative Party and more extreme right-wing groups feel that de Klerk has betrayed the whites, and they are bitterly opposed to power sharing – let alone black majority rule; the right wing could gain majority support from a white electorate which feels threatened by events. Another problem is the mounting violence between the ANC and Inkatha –

323

hundreds were killed in 1990–1. The situation in the Homelands is fluid; there have been coups and attempted coups in the last year. Some of the Homeland leaders want reintegration with South Africa; others do not.

South Africa urgently needs to find solutions to its political, social, and economic problems. It will have to move quickly to settle the future of a multi-racial society now dominated by the white minority. President de Klerk's pragmatism offers a ray of hope for the future, but it is still difficult to see how a settlement will be achieved peacefully.

Southern African Development Co-ordination Conference (SADCC), formed in 1980 with headquarters in Botswana. The nine members (Angola, Botswana, Lesotho, Malawi, Mozambique, Swaziland, Tanzania, Zambia, Zimbabwe) are neighbours or near neighbours of South Africa. They meet regularly to work out ways in which they can reduce their dependence on South Africa. The former ★HIGH COMMISSION TERRITORIES (Botswana, Lesotho, Swaziland) are the most dependent on South Africa for trade, transport, customs revenues, investment, and employment for their migrant workers. Malawi, Zambia and Zimbabwe rely heavily on South Africa for trade and transport links. In principle the members want sanctions against a regime they detest, but in practice sanctions and South Africa's probable retaliation would mean great hardship for members of the SADCC. South

Africa sees the SADCC as a threat and has put pressure on its members by supporting dissident groups in SADCC countries and by direct military action against them. In the long term Southern African states would benefit from the end of the political and military disruption caused by South Africa; this can only be achieved by the overthrow of the present social, economic and political system in South Africa.

Southern Rhodesia, name given to Zimbabwe during the period of colonial rule from the late nineteenth century until ★UDI (1965) when the ★SMITH government renamed it Rhodesia. Northern and Southern Rhodesia were named after Cecil Rhodes whose British South Africa Company was granted a royal charter in 1889 to develop the territories.

South West Africa, ★NAMIBIA's former name. Germany referred to the country as German Southwestern Africa. South Africa called it South West Africa even after the United Nations formally adopted the name Namibia in 1968.

Soweto (South West Township), a South African town for about one and a quarter million black South Africans who commute to work in Johannesburg. It was developed in the 1950s to house those evicted from townships and squatter camps nearer Johannesburg and is still short of amenities for its inhabitants. The rich middle class has smart and spacious houses, but most Sowetans live in small two-bedroom houses – with an average occupancy of twelve. Since 1983 some tenants have been allowed to buy ninety-nine year leases on the properties they occupy and there have been promises of freehold possession in the future.

Soweto has been a centre of violence and unrest – typically it had about 1700 murders in 1985. Hundreds of Sowetans died and thousands were arrested in the rising which started in June 1976 in protest against the government's plan to make Afrikaans a compulsory school subject. Soweto has been prominent in the disturbances which began in 1984. In 1986 the government sealed it off and declared a state of emergency shortly before the tenth anniversary of the 1976 rising.

Soweto has been, and still is, the home of many leading campaigners against *APARTHEID. When Nelson *MANDELA was released from prison (Feb. 1990), the people of Soweto turned out in their thousand to welcome him home.

Soyinka, Wole (b. 1934), internationally known Nigerian author. Soyinka studied at the University College of Ibadan before continuing his studies at Leeds University. He worked at the Royal Court Theatre in London, where his play, *The Invention*, was produced. Since 1960 he has followed an academic career – with some unhappy interruptions. In 1965 he was tried and acquitted of armed robbery and was detained in Nigeria (1967–9) for allegedly supporting the *BIAFRAN secession. *The Man Died* (1972) is a fearless account of his prison experiences. After years of self-imposed exile he returned to Nigeria to become Professor of Comparative Literature and Head of Dramatic Arts at Ife University (1975).

Soyinka has published novels, poetry, collections of lectures and memoirs, but is best known as a prolific and successful playwright. He deals with cultural confrontation and combines traditional Yoruba themes with the more contemporary themes of corruption, the lust for power and loss of faith. In *A Dance of the Forests* performed in celebration of Nigerian independence (1960) he attacked myths about the glories of Africa's past and the claims of *NÉGRITUDE that Africa's cultural heritage should be the sole inspiration of the continent's revival. *Kongi's Harvest* which opened the World Festival of African Arts (1966) satirised African dictatorships. In 1986 he became the first African to be honoured with the Nobel Prize for Literature.

Ssemogerere, Paul (b. 1932), Ugandan politician from *BUGANDA. He was a schoolteacher before becoming a prominent member of the *DEMOCRATIC PARTY in the 1960s. In 1980 he was the leader of the party and its presidential candidate. He claimed victory in the December 1980 elections, but the rather dubious official results gave the presidency to *OBOTE, and Ssemogerere became leader of the official opposition. His strong attacks on the government's poor human rights record won him respect. He became Minister of Internal Affairs in the military government which ousted Obote (1985–6). Since 1986 he and his party have co-operated

STEVENS

with President *MUSEVENI's government. Mr Ssemogerere became one of Uganda's three Deputy Prime Ministers in February 1988.

Stevens, Siaka (c.1905–88), Prime Minister (1968–71) and President of Sierra Leone (1971–85). Before entering politics he served in the police, worked for the Sierra Leone Development Company in the 1930s and spent fifteen years as the general secretary of the United Mineworkers Union. After quarrelling with the leadership of the *SIERRA LEONE PEOPLE's PARTY (SLPP) he formed his own political party – the *ALL PEOPLE'S CONGRESS (APC) in 1957. He was Leader of the Opposition at independence (1961), but won control of Freetown in the 1964 municipal elections. In 1967 he narrowly won the general elections, but the SLPP government refused to step down. The military seized power and Stevens went into exile in Guinea until 1968 when the restoration of civilian rule enabled him to take office as Prime Minister of Sierra Leone.

In 1971 he made Sierra Leone a republic and became Executive President. In 1978 he introduced a Socialist one-party state. As Secretary-General of the APC he was the sole presidential candidate. These measures to consolidate his power did little to help Stevens solve the political and economic problems of Sierra Leone. He had to contend with attempted coups and army plots, factional violence, economic mismanagement and corruption. There was much controversy

after the March 1971 attempted coup because Stevens called in troops from Guinea to protect himself and his government, arguing that he could no longer trust his own army. When he stepped down in favour of his chosen successor, Maj.-Gen. *MOMOH, President Stevens left Sierra Leone in dire economic straits.

Sudan, the largest country in Africa and the ninth largest in the world, covering more than 1.35 million square miles. It stretches 1200 miles from its northern border with Egypt to the equatorial forests it shares with Zaire and Uganda. Its neighbours, clockwise, are Egypt, Ethiopia, Kenya, Uganda, Zaire, Central African Republic, Chad and Libya. Within its vastness Sudan has virtually every kind of terrain and vegetation. Its people are miliarly diverse, with 19 major ethnic groups and another 597 sub-groups.

During the nineteenth century, Sudan was a largely pagan country and a prime source of slaves until it came under the influence of British missionaries and administrators. Until 1956 an Anglo-Egyptian 'Condominium Administration' ruled Sudan, with the British always dominant. Following the July 1952 revolution in Egypt, the British agreed to demands for Sudanese independence. The Christians of the south had wanted either separation from the north or federal association with it. They got neither and tensions increased. From 1954 Britain and Egypt argued about Sudan's future. Egypt claimed that

The Republic of Sudan

THE COUNTRY
2,505,813 sq. km.

Major Cities
Khartoum-Omdurman
(capital)
Port Sudan (only port)
Wadi Halfa
El-Obeid
Nyala
Juba
Dongola
Kassala
Wau

Economy
Cotton
Groundnuts
Sorgham
Livestock

Principal Exports
As above

Currency
Sudanese pound of 100
piastres

THE PEOPLE
25.2 million

Ethnic Groups
Arabs in north
Mostly African
Negro in south

Languages
Arabic (official)
English (language of
government in south)
More than 100 other
languages, including
Sudanic and Darfurian

Religion
Sunni Muslim
Christianity (large
minority)
Traditional beliefs
(south)

THE STATE
Presidential democracy

Head of State
Gen. Hassan al-Bashir

Ruling Body
Cabinet
Prime Minister
Five-man Council of
State

Dominant Party
Hizb al-Umma

Sudan should be united with it under the Egyptian monarchy but Britain wanted to guide Sudan towards independence. In August 1955, just before independence, the garrison of Torit in southern Sudan mutinied when ordered to Khartoum, without their arms. They saw this as a ruse to lead them to capture and slaughter. This incident began the civil war, which was to last seventeen years. The southerners, a mixture of Christians and animists, were afraid of Muslim domination. This war was in progress when Britain withdrew from Sudan in 1956, confident that a parliamentary system of government was in place. The latter lasted only until 1958 when it was overthrown by a military coup led by General Ibrahim Abboud.

From 1958 until the end of 1964 Sudan remained under army rule. Students protested against the military government and other groups followed them into the 'October Revolution' of 1964. This resulted in a genuine coalition and government of national unity. The politicians tried to find a political end to the civil war but the elections of May 1965 ended the coalition and the compromise it had embodied. Sadiq al-Mahdi came to power on a promise of reform in 1966 but the civil war continued and the economy collapsed. This crisis brought another military takeover in a coup led by Major-General Jafar *NIMEIRI, who was elected president in 1971. His major achievement, in March 1972, was to reach agreement with the southern rebels and end the war which had cost perhaps one million lives. The south was given regional autonomy and the seventeen-year war ended. However, apart from exploiting the south's oil reserves the government did not develop the region. Nimeiri nationalized foreign banks and companies as he pursued his goals of 'democracy, socialism and non-alignment'. Saudi Arabia gave him massive aid on the understanding that the *SHARIA Law would be applied to Sudan. Petrol and bread shortages, rampant inflation and heavy taxes on tobacco and alcohol – both forbidden under the sharia – caused prolonged riots in August 1979. Nimeiri called for fresh elections and in January 1980 was elected president for another six years. His plans for the economy were strained by the presence of 500,000 Ugandan, Somali and Eritrean refugees.

Unrest simmered in the south. The regional government in Juba was corrupt and inefficient, Khartoum was exploiting southern Sudan's oil and water and Islamic domination was again feared. Nimeiri announced that the south would be divided into three provinces. Southern leaders recognized this as a way of weakening them and they incited mutinies. In 1983 Colonel John Garang, a southern Christian, founded the Sudan People's Liberation Army, which quickly showed that it was a formidable guerrilla force. True to his promise to Saudi Arabia, Nimeiri imposed SHARIA law in all its vigour in September 1983 and martial law in March 1984. Floggings became commonplace, more than a hundred offenders had limbs amputated and others were executed. Meanwhile, in the south the rebel SPLA grew stronger. Even in the north the increasingly autocratic Nimeiri became unpopular and basic shortages and removal of food-price subsidies led to strikes. Nimeiri could have weathered these but when professional men banded together in a campaign of civil disobedience the army acted against him. On 6 April 1985, when Nimeiri was out of the country on a mission to seek American aid, a military government under Lt.-Gen. Swar el-Dhahab took control. Following elections a year later, Sadiq al-Mahdi became Prime Minister of a new civilian coalition government while Swar el-Dhahab remained as President.

Al-Mahdi faced many problems. Khartoum-Omdurman became the home of a million refugees who had fled from the ravages of war and famine in the south. Muslim fundamentalists were increasingly militant and demanded that Sudan remain true to the Sharia. When Saudi money was not sufficient to restore the economy, other Arab donors, the International Monetary Fund and foreign banks made a series of rescue attempts.

Cotton generates fifty per cent of Sudan's foreign exchange while groundnuts, sorghum and livestock produce some revenue. Most Sudanese are involved in agricultural or pastoral farming but in large areas their methods remain primitive. Prosperity depends on efficient irrigation. While the Gezira irrigated cotton-farming project is the world's largest farm under single management, the country needs many more such projects. The Jonglei Canal scheme is designed to help irrigation but in 1984 the civil war blocked all progress. Oil exploitation ceased in the same year for the same reason. Sudan has much to offer foreign tourists and tourism could be lucrative but the civil war prevents any development.

Fundamentalists object to the presence of foreigners and have attacked and killed European aid-agency workers in Khartoum. In the south, other aid workers have been held hostage. When the SPLA shot down a Sudan Airways plane the agencies stopped their air-supply of food to the starving south. In April 1987 the International Red Cross suspended its food distribution because of difficulties created by the government.

On 30 June 1988, a paratroop brigadier, Oman Hassan al-Bashir, overthrew the al-Mahdi government and installed a fifteen-man military junta. All these officers were trained at the Nasser Academy in Cairo and have strong links with Egypt. Within hours, Egypt recognized the new government and flew in much-needed humanitarian aid as well as military supplies. The US, however, disapproved of the coup and cut aid.

While Bashir is a devout Muslim he was believed to be a political moderate. His junta faced an enormous task in lifting the country from near bankruptcy. Sudan had foreign debts of $12 billion and inflation was then running at ninety per cent.

As a supposed concession to Colonel Garang and the SPLA, President al-Bashir announced that he would hold a referendum on whether or not to introduce the sharia law in Sudan. This was an error of judgment. Since Sudan is overwhelmingly Muslim, it would be difficult to administer a referendum in the war-torn south, and the result would be a foregone conclusion – the sharia would be voted in. An Amnesty International report published in December 1989 further damaged al-Bashir's credibility. It claimed that Sudanese government forces and their supporters had executed tens of thousands of unarmed civilians and tortured rebel prisoners. The report, one of the most disturbing ever produced by Amnesty, stated that the lands of the Dinka people in northern Bahr el-Ghazal province had been deliberately devastated during the army's years of oppression. The UN put Sudan's death toll between 1983 and

1989, as a result of war, at 500,000.

All foreign studies indicate that Sudan will never have peace without partition. Its huge area provides space for two separate countries, one Muslim, the other Christian and animist. However, as the Muslims, who are in the majority, control the economy, the army and the communications system they are unlikely to meet the demands of the Christians. During 1990 Bashir showed himself to be an Islamic extremist.

Suez Crisis, the international event which marked the end of European involvement in Middle East affairs. In 1955, relations between Egypt and combined Anglo-American interests were already poor and they grew worse when President *NASSER of Egypt broke the Western monopoly of arms supply to the Middle East by buying arms from Czechoslovakia. In 1956, the US and Britain cancelled their offer of financial backing for the vast High Dam project. Nasser retaliated by nationalizing the Suez Canal, which had always been controlled by Anglo-French financiers. An international crisis erupted. Britain, France and Israel conspired to end Nasser's rule. In October, Israel invaded Egypt's Sinai peninsula. By pre-arrangement with Israel, Britain and France issued an ultimatum to both countries to cease hostilities. Their real aim was to send in an army not to separate the belligerents but to overthrow Nasser. On Egypt's refusal to obey the ultimatum, British and French forces landed in the Canal Zone. Opposition to the British-French act was universal and

it was particularly strong from the United States and the Soviet Union. Neither of the superpowers could permit Britain and France to act as if they were still the dominant powers in the Middle East. After some fighting the invasion force withdrew and Nasser's prestige became immense.

Suppression of Communism Act (1950), South African law, now superseded by the Internal Security Act (1982). Under the Act opponents of the government could be listed as communists and subjected to various penalties which included *BANNING ORDERS and detention without trial. In 1966 *VORSTER, then Minister of Justice, said 'You don't have to be a communist to be banned under the Suppression of Communism Act.'

Suzman, Helen (b.1917), white South African MP (1953–89), for many years the only voice in parliament resolutely opposing *APARTHEID and attacking the government's poor record on human rights. Her courage and determination earned her considerable respect in South Africa and abroad. She was a lecturer in economic history before taking her seat in parliament as a member of the official opposition, the *UNITED PARTY. When the United Party split in 1959 she and her more liberal colleagues formed the Progressive Party (later the *PROGRESSIVE FEDERAL PARTY), and from 1961 to 1974 she was its only MP. Suzman opposes economic sanctions against South Africa because she feels that economic pressures should come from within, through black trade union activity and consumer boycotts. When she retired from parliament (1989) she was appointed an honorary Dame Commander of the British Empire in recognition of 'her record of persistent opposition to discriminatory legislation', and the Foreign Office announced that twenty black South Africans would be brought to Britain every year under a scholarship scheme to be called 'the Helen Suzman Awards'.

Swahili or Kiswahili, the word Swahili is derived from the Arabic and means of the coast. It is a *BANTU language which is widely spoken in the coastal regions and offshore islands of East Africa, either as a mother tongue or as a second language. It serves as a lingua franca in Kenya, Tanzania, Uganda and much of Zaire; it is Tanzania's official language and is recognized as Kenya's national language. Many words are derived from the Arabic and the oldest surviving written Swahili – from the early eighteenth century – is in Arabic script. The twentieth century has seen the development of a substantial Swahili literature.

SWANP (South West Africa National Party), political party for Namibian whites, affiliated to the *NATIONAL PARTY in South Africa until 1977. It controlled the local legislature and held all the territory's seats in the South African House of Assembly (1950–77). It was unhappy at South Africa's attempts to make an internal settlement in Namibia first through the *DTA government and then the

*TRANSITIONAL GOVERNMENT OF NATIONAL UNITY. Many of its members felt that South Africa was ignoring the interests of the Namibian whites by bringing other racial groups into the political process.

SWANU (South West African National Union), Namibian nationalist political party formed in 1959 by students and intellectuals and supported by the Herero. SWANU co-operated with *SWAPO in the National Convention of Namibia (1971–5), but refused to merge with SWAPO (1976) and joined smaller parties in the Namibian National Front. SWANU opposed the *DTA government, but was persuaded to join the *MPC. In 1984 SWANU split. The minority stayed in the MPC and headed by Moses Katjiuongwa joined the *TRANSITIONAL GOVERNMENT OF NATIONAL UNITY in 1985. The majority joined SWAPO.

SWAPO (South West Africa People's Organization), Namibia's leading political movement formed in 1960, led by Sam *NUJOMA, President since its foundation. It originated from the Ovamboland People's Congress founded in 1957 by *TOIVO JA TOIVA (now SWAPO's General Secretary) to campaign against the contract labour system. SWAPO has campaigned successfully for international recognition and fought a long war of attrition against South Africa. It established provisional headquarters in Dar es Salaam (1961) and began the armed struggle for independence

(1966). After a major reorganization (1969–70), which included the formation of its army, *PLAN, SWAPO became increasingly effective despite the efforts of South African-led counter-insurgency forces combined with emergency regulations and the detention of SWAPO leaders.

SWAPO opposed South African attempts to make an internal political settlement and called for boycotts of South African-controlled elections. SWAPO has had a long commitment to a non-racial and democratic government and a pragmatic form of socialism by which the major means of production – land, minerals, fishing rights, utilities – will be in the hands of the people. During the transition to independence under United Nations supervision (1989–90) Nujoma and other SWAPO exiles returned to Namibia. SWAPO won the November 1989 elections for a constituent assembly, with forty-four of the seventy-two seats. Lacking a two-thirds majority it relied on the co-operation of other political parties in drawing up a constitution for independent Namibia. SWAPO has abandoned its rigid Marxism and accepted both a multi-party democracy and a mixed economy. It is determined to respect the rights and interests of all racial groups, including the white minority. Its new pragmatism is also attested to by its willingness to stay in a customs union with South Africa and to use the South African currency.

SWAPO-D (South West Africa People's Organization – Democrats), a Namibian political party formed by *SWAPO dissidents led by Andreas Shipanga (1978). SWAPO-D joined the *TRANSITIONAL GOVERNMENT OF NATIONAL UNITY (1985–9).

Swart, Charles Robberts (1894–1982), South African politician, last Governor-General of the Union of South Africa (1959–61), and first State President of the Republic of South Africa (1961–7). He was a *NATIONAL PARTY MP (1923–38; 1941–59) and a cabinet minister (1948–59). As Minister of Justice in the 1950s he was responsible for legislative programmes which limited personal freedoms and put *APARTHEID into effect. He piloted laws like the *SUPPRESSION OF COMMUNISM ACT and the *IMMORALITY ACT through parliament.

Swaziland (Kangwane in the Swazi language), the Kingdom of Swaziland in the Commonwealth; formerly the Swaziland Protectorate and a *HIGH COMMISSION TERRITORY. It is a small and land-locked mountainous state in southern Africa. To the east it is separated from the Indian Ocean by the Mozambique coastal plain and it is bordered by South Africa to the north, west and south. Swaziland has a comprehensive road system and rail links to two ports – Maputo in Mozambique and Richards Bay in South Africa.

There are four main regions. In the west is the well watered High Veld (1050 to 1200 metres above sea-level) which irrigates the lower and drier regions and is a potential source of hydroelectric power. Wood pulp

The Kingdom of Swaziland

THE COUNTRY	THE PEOPLE	THE STATE
17,363 sq. km.	713,000	Constitutional monarchy
		Single-party state
Major Cities	*Ethnic Groups*	*Head of State*
Mbabane	Swazi	King Mswati III
Manzini	Zulu	
		Head of Government
Economy	*Languages*	Prime Minister Sotsha
Farming	Siswati (official)	Dlamini
Mining	English (official)	
		Ruling Bodies
Principal Exports	*Religion*	Cabinet
Sugar	Christian	Senate
Timber	Traditional beliefs	House of Assembly
Asbestos		
Coal		*Official Party*
Citrus fruit		Imbokodvo National
		Movement
Currency		
Lilangeni (E) of 100 cents		

from the High Veld accounts for about 20 per cent of export earnings. The Middle Veld is blessed with moderate rainfall and good soil suitable for the cultivation of maize for domestic consumption and citrus and sugar for export. Sugar accounts for about 40 per cent of export earnings. In the east is the hot and dry Low Veld (150 to 300 metres above sea-level) where cotton is cultivated for export. On the eastern edge is the Lebombo Range, an impressive mountain escarpment.

Swaziland also exports asbestos, coal and iron ore. Its tourist attractions include spectacular scenery and casinos where South Africans can gamble. During the 1970s Swaziland's prosperous industry and agriculture gave its people one of the highest per capita incomes in Africa, but the 1980s have been less prosperous. The kingdom's geographical position and its economic difficulties have made it vulnerable to South African domination. As a member of the ★SOUTHERN AFRICAN DEVELOPMENT CO-ORDINATION CONFERENCE, Swaziland wants to lessen its dependence on South Africa.

The country's recent history dates back to the reigns of Sobhuza I (died 1839) and Mswati I (ruled 1839–68), members of the powerful ★DLAMINI clan. They welded the Ngwane, a ★BANTU people, into the Swazi nation. Swaziland was ruled jointly by Britain and the ★BOERS

(1894–1902) before becoming a British Protectorate and a High Commission Territory. It joined South Africa in a customs union (1910) and was expected to become part of South Africa, but Swazi opposition and the election of a South African government committed to *APARTHEID (1948) ruled this plan out. As a protectorate (1902–68) the country made little economic and political progress. Britain left it to be dominated by a small number of white settlers who owned great tracts of land. In 1907 the Swazi people owned less than 40 per cent of their country. Since then they have bought back land although much of the best land still belongs to settlers and non-residents.

Progress towards independence began with the formation of the Swaziland Progressive Party (1960). It split in 1961 and the radicals formed the *NGWANE NATIONAL LIBERATION CONGRESS (NNLC) in 1963. As Britain granted a constitution (1963) preparations were made for an election in 1964. The electoral system was so heavily weighted in favour of the royalist *IMBOKODVO NATIONAL MOVEMENT (founded in 1964) that it won all the seats. Despite substantial support in the urban areas the NNLC were not represented in the Legislative Council. Similarly, in the 1967 election the NNLC had 20 per cent of the votes without winning a single seat and the right to attend the independence conference in London in 1967.

At independence (1968) Swaziland became a constitutional monarchy under *SOBHUZA II; his considerable powers included the right to block certain constitutional changes, direct control over minerals and communal land and the appointment of one fifth of the Assembly and half the Senate. The electoral system neutralized support for the NNLC by creating eight constituencies in which the winning party took all three seats. Despite the obstacles the NNLC won a three-member constituency in the 1972 election. The king would not tolerate even limited opposition and a constitutional crisis followed. In 1973 he abrogated the constitution, dismissed parliament, banned political parties, ruled by royal decree and began to create an army which would be trained and armed by South Africa.

The royal government became increasingly repressive. The army and the police were expanded; political dissidents were harassed and imprisoned without trial. By 1977 any pretence of moving towards a democratic system was abandoned. The new parliament which met in 1979 had two chambers. The House of Assembly had forty members indirectly elected by tribal assemblies and ten chosen by the king. The Senate had ten members chosen by the House of Assembly and ten chosen by the king. Parliament's powers were restricted to discussing government proposals and advising the king. There was limited opposition to the government. The police broke up strikes and demonstrations. After escaping from detention in Swaziland Dr *ZWANE founded the Swaziland Liberation Movement (1978) to fight for democracy.

When King Sobhuza II died (1982) one of his fifty widows, Princess *DZELIWE, became Queen Regent and ruled with the support of the *LIQOQO – the Supreme State Council. The Liqoqo chose Prince Makhosetive to succeed his father. Before the coronation of the new king there was a power struggle between the traditionalists of the Liqoqo and Prince Mabandla *DLAMINI, the prime minister who was supported by the Queen Regent in his campaign for reforms. Prince Mabandla strongly objected to the proposed land deal with South Africa favoured by the traditionalists – and the late king. South Africa offered to cede the *KANGWANE *HOMELAND (which had been Swazi territory in the nineteenth century) and a strip of *KWAZULU to Swaziland; this would have added about 40 per cent to Swaziland and given it a corridor to the Indian Ocean. In return Swaziland would have to give citizenship to the 800,000 Swazis and Zulus in the ceded territories and to end sanctuary for *AFRICAN NATIONAL CONGRESS (ANC) guerrillas. Strong opposition which included protests from Chief *BUTHELEZI of KwaZulu persuaded South Africa to suspend this deal in 1984.

Under pressure from the Liqoqo the Queen Regent sacked Prince Mabandla and replaced him with Prince Bhekimpi *DLAMINI (Mar. 1983). A few months later Queen Regent Dzeliwe was dismissed and Princess *NTOMBI (mother of Prince Makhosetive) became Queen Regent (Aug. 1983). As the struggle for power continued Swaziland drew closer to South Africa. After negotiating a secret pact (1982) Swaziland started expelling ANC refugees. In 1985 a South African trade mission was given diplomatic status in Swaziland.

After Prince Makhosetive was crowned King *MSWATI III (Apr. 1986), he acted firmly to end the feuding and impose his power. The Liqoqo was dissolved, and Prince Mfanasibili *DLAMINI, a leading traditionalist, was imprisoned for seven years for attempting to undermine the monarchy. Later in 1986 the king dismissed his prime minister, Prince Bhekimpi. He has apparently tamed his opponents, but feuds in the Dlamini clan may well start again.

Swaziland's problems at the start of the 1990s include the strength of South Africa which shows little respect for its borders and its weak economy. The Swazi economy is not expanding fast enough to provide for its rapidly growing population and depends heavily on South Africa. If *détente* does work in southern Africa Swaziland's political and economic prospects may well be much brighter by the end of the century.

T

Taha, Mahmoud (1909–85), leader of the *REPUBLICAN BROTHERS of the Sudan, Taha was a non-violent man with equally non-violent followers in the Republican Brothers but the *NIMEIRI regime accused him of apostasy and of 'elevating himself to the position of God'. When he refused to recant, Nimeiri had him hanged in January 1985. Taha's death was the catalyst of the popular upheaval which brought down Nimeiri's regime. In November 1986 a committee chaired by Sudan's Attorney-General declared that the death sentence had been corrupt and illegal. His family sued Nimeiri and his advisers for murder and they demanded that Taha be declared a martyr, a request not yet granted.

Tambo, Oliver Reginald (b. 1917), veteran black South African campaigner against *APARTHEID, President of the *AFRICAN NATIONAL CONGRESS (ANC) since 1977. A devout Christian, he was educated at church schools (1924–38) before studying at *FORT HARE UNIVERSITY (1938–41) and graduating with a science degree. He planned to teach, but was sent down for organizing a student protest while studying for a diploma in education. Soon after joining the ANC (1944) he became friendly with Nelson *MANDELA and the two men helped to establish the ANC Youth League. Tambo rose through the ranks of the ANC to become a member of the executive (1949), Secretary-General (1955), Deputy President (1958), Acting President (1967) and President (1977).

Tambo was subject to a *BANNING ORDER (1954). Shortly after being accepted as a candidate for ordination in the Anglican Church he was held on treason charges (1956); these were dropped in 1957. Tambo received his second banning order in 1959. On the instructions of the ANC National Executive he left South Africa after the *SHARPEVILLE killings (1960) to set up the external wing of the ANC, and has been in exile since then. Tambo spent many years travelling the world and had some success in winning international recognition and support for his people's cause from the Soviet bloc and radical African and Arab states. Western leaders had reservations about supporting the ANC because it was prepared to use violence, but official brutality in South Africa from the middle 1980s made many more sympathetic to the ANC cause.

Tambo is a moderate in black nationalist ranks; he rejects the racial exclusiveness of *BLACK CONSCIOUSNESS in favour of a non-racial democratic state. He has supported limited violence since 1960, but has controlled the extremists who advocate indiscriminate violence. In 1989 he became seriously ill after a stroke.

He has remained as President, but since early 1990 Nelson Mandela as Deputy-President has been in effective command of the ANC.

Tanganyika, now mainland Tanzania. From the first century AD Tanganyika's coastline was dominated by Arabian traders, notably those of the Sultanate of Kilwa from the eleventh to the fifteenth centuries. The arrival of Vasco da Gama (1498) was followed by a century of Portuguese influence, and rivalry between the Portuguese and Arabs in the seventeenth and eighteenth centuries. The second period of Arab domination began in 1832 when the Sultan of Muscat moved his capital to Zanzibar and established slave-trading centres on the coast and at inland centres like Tabora. The interior of pre-colonial Tanganyika was inhabited by over a hundred different peoples, mainly *BANTU. Some were hunters and gatherers and some were farmers, but others were living in states organized on feudal lines when Germany proclaimed the Protectorate of German East Africa over Tanganyika, Burundi and Rwanda (1885).

During the First World War British and Belgian forces took the territory (1916–7). It became a League of Nations mandate (1919); Tanganyika went to Britain, and Ruanda and Urundi (now Rwanda and Burundi) went to Belgium. In 1926 Britain set up a Legislative Council of Official and Unofficial Members. The first two African members were appointed by the Governor in 1945, when Britain began preparing the territory for independence as required by the United Nations Trusteeship Council. The first general election was held in two stages (1958–9) and three of the twelve ministerial posts went to Africans. The general election of 1960, a triumph for *TANU under the leadership of Julius *NYERERE, was followed by a constitutional conference; Tanganyika became self-governing under Prime Minister Nyerere (May 1961) and gained independence in the Commonwealth (Dec. 1961). The Republic of Tanganyika was inaugurated in 1962 with Nyerere as president. In 1964 it merged with *ZANZIBAR to form the United Republic of Tanzania. See entry on Tanzania for events since 1964 and general information on climate, economy, geography and the peoples of Tanganyika.

TANU (Tanganyika African National Union), leading nationalist movement in Tanganyika, reshaped from the Tanganyika African Association by *NYERERE (1954), its founder and only President (1954–77). In an energetic, peaceful and successful campaign, TANU demonstrated its popular support in elections (1958–60) and became independent Tanganyika's first government (Dec. 1961). In the early days of independence Nyerere resigned as prime minister and spent 1962 strengthening TANU's organization and developing its African socialist ideals. After the unsuccessful army mutiny of 1964 President Nyerere strengthened the role of the party in the state, making it the only legal political party. Increasingly TANU was entrusted with developing policies for the government to carry out. It adopted the *ARUSHA DECLARATION (1967) which stressed egalitarianism and self-reliance and the more radical socialist programme of the 'Dar Declaration' (1971). In 1977 TANU joined the *AFRO-SHIRAZI PARTY (Zanzibar's only legal party) to form *CHAMA CHA MAPINDUZI which is now Tanzania's only party.

TANZAM (or TAZARA), Africa's most spectacular post-colonial railway, completed by China in 1975. The 1680 km. line links Zambia to the Tanzanian port of Dar es Salaam. The transport links include roads which have greatly improved communications within Tanzania. TANZAM is important to the *SOUTHERN AFRICAN DEVELOPMENT CO-ORDINATION CONFERENCE, because it provides an alternative route to the sea which lessens the dependence of southern and central African states on South Africa. TANZAM carries Zambian minerals to the coast, but the line has suffered from inefficient administration, poor facilities at the port of Dar es Salaam and poorly maintained engines and rolling stock.

Tanzania, United Republic of, formed in April 1964 by the union of the states of *TANGANYIKA on the East African mainland and *ZANZIBAR (the Indian Ocean islands of Zanzibar, Pemba and Latham). See entries on Tanganyika and Zanzibar for their history and political development until 1964.

The low lying islands of Zanzibar have a hot and humid tropical climate, suitable for the production of spices for export, including the bulk of the world's cloves from the Pemba Island plantations. There are three groups of people on the islands. The descendants of Arab immigrants over the last two millenia claim that their ancestors came from Shiraz in Persia. The 'mainlanders' are descended from slaves and more recent immigrants from the mainland. The islands also have a significant population of Asian descent.

To the east of mainland Tanzania (Tanganyika) is the Indian Ocean, to the north is Lake Victoria, Kenya and Uganda. To the west are Rwanda and Burundi – and Zaire across Lake Tanganyika. Zambia, Malawi, Lake Malawi and Mozambique lie to the south. Volcanic activity and faults associated with the rift valleys have given mainland Tanzania considerable topographical variety, including the highest and lowest points in Africa. Mount *KILIMANJARO with a permanent ice-cap is 5950 metres above, and the floor of Lake Tanganyika 358 metres below, sealevel. The climate varies from the humid tropical coastal region to the dry central plateau, semi-temperate mountains, grasslands, bush and semi-desert.

Tanzania's largest river, the Rufiji, has considerable potential for irrigation and hydroelectric power. It is one of the major rivers draining into the Indian Ocean; others drain into the interior basin or Lakes Tanganyika, Victoria and Malawi. Dar es

The United Republic of Tanzania

THE COUNTRY 945,087 sq. km.	THE PEOPLE 23,884,000	THE STATE Single-party republic
Major Cities Dar es Salaam (capital) Dodoma (proposed capital) Zanzibar Mwanza Tanga	*Ethnic Groups* 120 Bantu groups Shirazi Arab	*Head of State* President Mwinyi
	Languages English (official) Swahili (official)	*Ruling Bodies* Presidential Cabinet National Assembly
Economy Farming	*Religion* Islam Christian	*Zanzibar Ruling Bodies* Supreme Revolutionary Council of Zanzibar House of Representatives
Principal Exports Coffee Cotton Tobacco Tea Cloves Diamonds Cashew nuts		*Official Party* Chama Cha Mapinduzi
Currency Tanzanian shilling of 100 cents		

Salaam is the country's busiest port and the terminus of three main railway lines; the *TANZAM line to Zambia, the western line with branches to the shores of Lakes Victoria and Tanganyika and the northern line to Kenya.

Tanzania is populated by over one hundred and twenty different peoples, mainly of *BANTU origin. There are also small Arab, Asian and European communities. No single group is large enough to attempt to dominate the others and the use of *SWAHILI as a common first or second language bridges the differences among the Tanzanians. Tanzania is one of the few African states not to be plagued by tribal rivalries; its people are aware of tribal distinctions but tend to put the nation first.

Since 1964 there has been a marked contrast between Tanzania's economic problems and its political achievements, although some of the economic problems can be ascribed to President *NYERERE's political decisions. He committed

339

the country to African socialism and rural development and gave massive economic power to the state. The consequences have included corruption and inefficiency. Rigid state marketing policies and low prices discouraged producers, and production of many cash crops declined.

The economy of Tanzania depends heavily on agriculture. Most Tanzanians are peasant farmers in rural villages. There they cultivate crops to feed the country and cash crops for export. At independence the country was self-sufficient in food, and during the First Five-Year Plan (1964–9) agricultural production grew faster than the population. Since then ill considered political decisions, drought and economic mismanagement by state-run bodies have transformed the situation. Tanzania has to import cereals to meet the needs of its rising population. There have been similar problems in the production of crops for export, compounded by falling world prices. The main cash crops are cloves from Zanzibar, coffee, cotton, tea, sisal, pyrethrum and cashew nuts; the decline in cash crops has led to a shortage of foreign currency earnings.

The mining and industrial sectors are comparatively small. Diamonds, mostly from the Williamson Mine, are an important export and gold and coal are mined. Recent prospecting may lead to the discovery of oil and mineral deposits worth developing. The industrial sector has been working far below capacity, hampered by the lack of foreign capital to buy necessary equipment and by the inefficiency and dogmatism of officials in state-run industries.

By the late 1970s economic problems and the cost of the war with Uganda led to a crisis in Tanzania. The economy had not grown to meet the needs of the people and Tanzania was unable to solve its problems without outside help. These problems included mounting trade deficits, a shortage of foreign currency, a high level of international debt, inflation and sluggish economic growth. The government devalued the Tanzanian shilling, imposed austerity measures and began negotiating with the International Monetary Fund. Tanzania was at first unwilling to meet IMF conditions (austerity measures and a liberalization of the economy) and agreement was only reached in 1986. Tanzania then devalued its currency again, made deeper cuts in official expenditure, gave incentives to private producers of export crops and strengthened the private sector at the expense of the public sector. It was rewarded by easier terms for the servicing and repayment of its international debt and by substantial foreign aid. By the late 1980s the economic recovery programme was apparently working; mining and agriculture were picking up and exports were rising.

Despite economic problems Tanzania has been in many ways a model of political and social stability with little tension and little effective opposition to Presidents Nyerere

(1962–85) and *MWINYI (since 1985). Only in Zanzibar, which has its own history and culture, have there been serious political problems. Some feel they have done badly out of the union with Tanganyika and argue for more autonomy or even secession from Tanzania, even though Zanzibar has retained its own government under a Revolutionary Council and a President, who is also Vice-President of Tanzania.

Tension between Zanzibar and the mainland was particularly severe during *KARUME's despotic regime (1964–72), but relations improved during Aboud *JUMBE's presidency (1972–84) and the union was strengthened when the *AFRO-SHIRAZI PARTY merged with *TANU to form *CHAMA CHA MAPINDUZI (CCM) in 1977. There was another crisis when the CCM dismissed Jumbe from the presidency (1984) – alleging separatist sympathies. Jumbe's successor, Ali Hassan Mwinyi (1984–5) made reforms and improved relations with the mainland. He was succeeded in Zanzibar by Idris Abdul Wakil (1985), who sacked his ministers (Jan. 1988) for plotting against him and entrusted the government to officials pending the appointment of a new Revolutionary Council. More recently (1989) Zanzibaris have complained at their inadequate share of development aid.

During the 1960s and 1970s the history of Tanzania was dominated by President Nyerere's commitment to African socialism. TANU became the only legal political party on the mainland (1965). The *ARUSHA DECLARATION (1967) declared the principles of egalitarianism and self-reliance and was followed by the nationalization of banks and major industries and the creation of community or co-operative farms (*UJAMAA). More radical was the Dar Declaration (1971) calling for political education and a people's militia. President Nyerere favoured decentralization and announced that the capital would be moved from Dar es Salaam to *DODOMA.

In 1975 the National Assembly passed a bill giving TANU legal supremacy as the national political party. Following the formation of CCM (1977) President Nyerere reshuffled his cabinet and made Edward *SOKOINE Prime Minister (1977–80). In 1980 President Nyerere was re-elected with massive support, but the anger of voters at corruption, inefficiency and shortages was shown when many members of the National Assembly lost their seats. Following the discovery of a plot to kill Nyerere and overthrow the government early in 1983, Sokoine became Prime Minister again and began a series of purges against corruption, smuggling and the black market. In 1985 President Nyerere resigned the presidency but retained the chairmanship of the CCM. Under his successor, President Mwinyi, Tanzania has followed a more liberal path and there are some signs that ex-President Nyerere and the party ideologists are concerned at the move away from socialism, although they realize that economic problems have forced the country to modify its socialist stance.

In foreign affairs Tanzania has played a prominent role. President Nyerere has been a leading spokesman for Third World and African causes. As a *FRONT LINE state and a member of the *SOUTHERN AFRICAN DEVELOPMENT CO-ORDINATION CONFERENCE Tanzania has been a leading campaigner against *APARTHEID. Yet, internal economic problems and problems with its neighbours may well have lessened Tanzania's influence in the world.

When Nyerere led Tanganyika to independence he was strongly committed to closer co-operation with Kenya and Uganda and joined them in the formation of the *EAST AFRICAN COMMUNITY (1967), but quarrels with Kenya led to the closure of the border in 1976 and there was even greater tension between Tanzania and Uganda. Nyerere had given refuge and support to President *OBOTE after he was ousted by *AMIN in 1971, and Nyerere refused to sit at the same table with Amin. The community collapsed in 1977 and it took some years to sort out the division of its assets and liabilities. In 1978–9 Tanzania was at war with Uganda and the Tanzanian army helped Ugandan dissidents to overthrow Amin (1979) and to reinstate Obote. The borders with Kenya were reopened in 1983 and relations have improved with Uganda, ruled by President *MUSEVENI since January 1986. In early 1973 relations with Burundi were severely strained after tribal massacres led to an influx of refugees into Tanzania and to battles on the border between Tanzanian and Burundi troops.

Tanzania and its leaders have made mistakes, especially in the hasty implementation of doctrinaire policies by socialist idealists. The people have suffered as national growth has failed to keep up with population growth. But Tanzania has given its people political stability and saved it from the horrors of military coups and civil war. Ex-President Nyerere has earned the respect and gratitude of his people, despite his mistakes. Under his successor, President Mwinyi, more pragmatic policies may lead to a higher standard of living for Tanzanians in the 1990s.

Taylor, Charles, leader of one of the two Liberian rebel armies fighting in Liberia in 1990. Charles Taylor claims to have played an important part in the overthrow of President *TOLBERT in 1980. He then served the *DOE government as a departmental head (1980–3) until he fled to the United States, accused of embezzling close to a million dollars. He avoided extradition by escaping from a prison in the United States and from a base in Burkina Faso began preparing to overthrow President Doe's regime. With Libyan support he led the *NATIONAL PATRIOTIC FRONT OF LIBERIA in the invasion of Liberia late in 1989. His force was weakened by the defection of Prince *JOHNSON and his supporters (Mar. 1990). By late 1990 the position in the Liberian civil war was still confused as Taylor's men,

Johnson's men and those still loyal to the memory of the late President Doe fought for control of Monrovia.

Tekere, Edgar (b. 1937), controversial Zimbabwean politician, he joined the *AFRICAN NATIONAL CONGRESS and was a founder member of the *NDP (1960), *ZAPU (1961) and *ZANU (1963). His nationalist activities led to his arrest and detention for ten years (1964–74). He escaped with Robert *MUGABE to Mozambique (1975) and campaigned for Mugabe to become leader of ZANU (1977). As Secretary-General of ZANU Tekere played a leading part in the second *CHIMURENGA (independence war) and attended the talks which ended with the *LANCASTER HOUSE AGREEMENT (Dec. 1979). He won a seat in the 1980 pre-independence elections and served in the cabinet until he was charged with murdering a white farmer in 1981 and acquitted on a technicality.

Since then his eloquent attacks on the party leadership have cost him his party posts. He was sacked from his post as *ZANU (PF) chairman in Manicaland Province in 1987. In 1988 he was threatened with an action for defamation by Maurice *NYAGUMBO and thrown out of the party after making allegations of governmental corruption. After corruption scandals showed there was some truth in his allegations he formed a new political party in 1989, the *ZIMBABWE UNITY MOVEMENT; he pledged to fight mismanagement and corruption. When his party failed to win a by-election in July 1989 he accused the government of vote-rigging. During the campaign for the March 1990 elections he alleged governmental intimidation and harassment. He won about a fifth of the votes in the presidential contest against President Mugabe and his party won only two parliamentary seats.

Tembo, John Zenas Ungapake (b. 1932), experienced Malawian politician, except for President *BANDA the last survivor of the independence cabinet of 1964. He was a teacher before his election to the Legislative Council (1961) and to the legislature (1963). Tembo held various ministerial posts in Finance and Trade (1964–70) before serving as Governor of the Reserve Bank of Malawi (1970–84). After the death of Dick *MATENJE (May 1983) Tembo was thought to be President *BANDA's likely successor. His claims to be Banda's heir were diminished when Banda sacked him from the Reserve Bank and failed to promote him to the vacant secretaryship of the *MALAWI CONGRESS PARTY, the post which Matenje had held. He is still on the Malawi Congress Party Central Committee and has acted as its Treasurer General since 1987.

Terreblanche, Eugene Ney (b. 1941), white South African extremist who leads the neo-Nazi *AFRIKANER WEERSTANDSBEWEGING (AWB), which he founded in 1973. He served as a policeman and worked as a farmer before entering politics. He believes that there should be a white people's state in South Africa and that foreign investors should not be allowed access to South Africa's mineral resources. He wants to keep blacks away from white areas. After the discovery of a comprising arms cache late in 1982, Terreblanche was arrested, tried, and given a suspended prison sentence. He remains the head of the AWB despite another scandal over an extra-marital affair.

Tibiyo Taka Ngwane (Swaziland National Development Fund), founded by King *SOBHUZA II in 1968 to handle mineral royalties. Under its first chairman, Simon *NXUMALO (1968–83) the fund invested in economic development and took large shares in major Swazi enterprises, but during the 1980s its reputation was tarnished by allegations of corruption.

Tigre, a northern province of Ethiopia. Tigre was affected in the 1960s by demands for independence from Ethiopia by the neighbouring province of Eritrea. Through the guerrillas of the Tigre People's Liberation Front (TPLF), Tigre engaged in irregular warfare against the large Ethiopian garrison army from 1966. The TPLF tried several times to capture some of the fortified towns but succeeded only in isolating a few of them. At the end of February 1988 the TPLF embarked on more ambitious and carefully planned offensives and in March captured four towns, Wukro, Abi Adi, Senkata and Debub. Wukro and Abi Adi are food distribution centres and their loss threatened to cut off supplies for 400,000 people. The Ethiopian government did not permit international relief agencies to operate in rebel-held territory. Tigre has an area of about 30,000 sq. km. and by 1989 the TPLF controlled large parts of it and had the complete support of the population of two and a half million. Its future as an independent entity is inextricably bound up with that of Eritrea.

Todd, (Reginald Stephen) Garfield (b. 1908), white political leader who became Prime Minister of Southern Rhodesia (now Zimbabwe) in 1953. His liberal policies cost him the support of his party and he fell from power in 1958. An outspoken critic of the *RHODESIAN FRONT government, Todd was restricted and imprisoned for a number of years in the 1960s and 1970s. At independence he was appointed to Zimbabwe's Senate (1980).

Togo, situated in West Africa on the northern coast of the Gulf of Benin, with a coastline of only fifty kilometres, but stretching five hundred kilometres into the interior. A mountain range divides the country into two areas of savannah. The country readily supports the population of four million, who come from thirty different ethnic groups. The largest single group, the Ewes (44 per cent) are growers of coffee and cocoa while the Kabre, the second largest group, (28 per cent) combine hunting with terrace farming.

The slave trade drew Europeans to Togo in the eighteenth century and palm oil kept them there in the nineteenth. The French predominated at first, but in 1884 Germany made the country a protectorate. On the defeat of Germany in the First World War,

The Togolese Republic

THE COUNTRY
56,000 sq. km.

Major Cities
Lomé (capital)
Atakpame
Palime
Sokode

Economy
Subsistence farming
Cocoa, coffee, palm oil, cotton
Phosphates

Principal Exports
Phosphates
Cocoa
Coffee

Currency
CFA franc of 100 centimes

THE PEOPLE
4 million

Ethnic Groups
The Ewe and Kabre tribes are the largest of many

Languages
French (official)
Ewe, Kabre, English, French

Religion
Christian 30%
Muslim 30%
Voodoo 30%
Traditional beliefs 10%

THE STATE
Presidential autocracy

Head of State
President Major-General Etienne Eyadèma

Ruling Body
Military–civil cabinet under the president

Official Party
Rassemblement du Peuple Togolais

---

the British and French divided up the territory. In 1957 the western strip, British Togoland, was ceded to Ghana. The remainder became independent from France in 1960. Sylvanus *OLYMPIO and his party were elected to rule the new nation but since he was unpopular with the French he had little chance of success. He was assassinated in 1963 and the army overthrew the government. Nicolas *GRUNITZKY then headed a civilian government but lasted only four years before Colonel Kléber Dadjo seized power in January 1967. Four months later on 14 April, Dadjo's government was dissolved and Lt.-Col. Étienne

*EYEDÈMA became President.

Soon after Eyedèma began his rule Togolese leaders adapted African first names to replace their French ones. Eyedèma became Gnassingbe instead of Étienne. Eyedèma modelled himself on General *MOBUTU and his regime on that of Zaire. President Eyedèma managed to reconcile the warring tribal factions, largely by absorbing them into the government-sponsored single party, the Rassemblement du Peuple Togolais (RPT). Farsightedly, Eyedèma made a special effort to develop the northern regions, which had been ignored by his predecessors.

345

During the rule of President *NKRUMAH in Ghana, Togo's relationship with its more powerful neighbour was strained. Large numbers of Ewes of Ghana demanded that their part of Ghana should secede to Togo. Eyedèma campaigned incessantly, but not aggressively, for a reunified Togo. He also steadily introduced constitutional reforms. In 1979, following a special National Congress meeting, a parliament of deputies was created with its sixty-seven members to be elected under a regional list system. While these reforms brought much-needed political stability, political power is still largely exercised by the President through his party's network.

Just before Pope John Paul II visited Togo in August 1985 and immediately after his departure at least thirty large bombs were detonated in Lomé. This first experience of terrorism was a shock to the Togolese but the events of 24 September 1986 were even more traumatic. On that date, fifty Ghanaian soldiers 'invaded' Lomé in an attempt to mount an uprising against President Eyedèma. Shooting went on for several hours and the attackers lost seven men killed and nineteen captured. The raid had been organized by Ghana's President, Flt. Lt. Jerry *RAWLINGS, who was said to have imperial ambitions, and who supported the family of the deposed President Olympio. At the request of the Togolese Government, the French rushed two hundred and fifty paratroopers and three Jaguar

aircraft to Togo while Zaire sent fifty paratroopers. The French–Togolese agreement of 1963 pledges France to help its former colony against any external threat. The 'small war', as the French called the Ghanaian raid, indicates the brittle nature of African politics.

Trade unions are a feature of Togolese political life. There were local branches of French unions and of the autonomous West African unions in the 1950s and 1960s and the Union Générale des Travailleurs de l'Afrique Noire (EGTAN) branch became the Union Nationale des Travailleurs du Togo (UNTT). The rival trade-union centres were replaced in 1973 by the Confederation Nationale des Travailleurs du Togo (CNTT) which is close to the ruling RPT party. The African-American Labour Centre (AALC) has its headquarters in Lomé.

The country has extraordinary cultural and religious diversity, having been penetrated by missionaries from various Christian denominations as well as by *ISLAMIC FUNDAMENTALISTS. Despite the massive religious influence from outside, the native voodoo religion is strong. Many young girls, having fulfilled their novitiate, devote their lives to voodoo and to the village priest.

The country is predominantly agricultural and 80 per cent of the population lives in rural areas. Each harvesting season many Togolese cross the border to work in Ghana. Togo grows its staple foods, cassava, yams, millet, maize and sorghum in abundance but has to import rice, wheat and much sugar. Cocoa is the main export crop. The government has plans to increase cash crops so that the nation will become self-sufficient in most foods. Livestock production was virtually non-existent in 1960 but is now important. Phosphate mining, begun by French companies in 1961, is Togo's main export earner. The industry was nationalized in 1974 and generally does well. When world prices drop the Togolese economy suffers badly. The Nangbato dam, completed in 1987, supplies all the national energy requirements. This is particularly important for the one steel mill, which makes profits for its American owners, who pay lease fees to the Togo government.

Since 1978 Togo has tried to make tourism into a major industry by encouraging tourists from Europe, the Americas and other parts of Africa. One device was to turn the capital, Lomé, into a free port, where many goods can be bought at cheaper prices than anywhere on the West coast. Most of this trade is controlled by women, known in Togo as *revendeuses*.

Toivo ja Toiva, Andimba (Herman), (b. 1924), Namibian trade union organizer and political leader. In Cape Town he founded the Ovamboland People's Congress (1957), but the South African authorities sent him back to Namibia where he continued his political activities and was a co-founder of *SWAPO (1960). In 1968 he was convicted of terrorism and sent to *ROBBEN ISLAND, where Nelson *MANDELA, Walter *SISULU and other black nationalists were imprisoned. In 1984 he was released unconditionally with four years of his twenty-year sentence to run. He continued his fierce criticism of South Africa and was elected Secretary General of SWAPO (1984) shortly after his release. He is second to *NUJOMA in the party hierarchy.

Tolbert, William (1913–80), President of Liberia (1971–80), he spent his whole career in administration and government. The grandson of an Afro-American, he was an ordained Baptist Minister and the President of the Baptist World Alliance for Africa (1965–70). He was a member of the Liberian House of Representatives (1943–51) and Vice-President (1953–71). When he succeeded President *TUBMAN in 1971 Tolbert had good intentions. He stressed equal opportunities and the need to stamp out corruption and economic mismanagement, but made little progress. Rising petroleum prices and falling world demand for iron ore and rubber, important Liberian exports, caused economic problems. Tolbert wanted to make Liberia self-sufficient in basic food and in 1979–80 he raised rice prices. This sparked off protest and violence, made worse by Tolbert's determination to crush the main opposition, the *PROGRESSIVE ALLIANCE OF LIBERIA. Tolbert was killed in the military coup of April 1980.

Tombalbaye, François, later N'Garta (1918–75), Chad teacher who became first president of his country. Born in Chad and educated at mission schools, Tombalbaye was simultaneously a trade union organizer and a teacher. In 1947 he was prominent in the establishment of the Chad branch of the Rassemblement Démocratique Africain. He became a member of the territorial assembly in 1952 and in 1957 a member of the General Council of West Africa. Tombalbaye now made his move towards supreme power. He overthrew the regime of Gabriel Lisette in 1959 and after the declaration of independence on 11 August 1960 he was promoted head of state. Tombalbaye's dictatorial rule began at once. He purged the Parti Progressiste Tchadien (PPT) of Lisette's supporters and then made PPT the sole political party. By conspiracy and harsh suppression he strengthened his grip on Chad. In reaction, his opponents formed the Chad National Liberation Front (FROLINAT). The French army intervened to save Tombalbaye from his downfall. He then agreed, in December 1972, a secret deal with Colonel ★GADDAFI of Libya, 'giving' Gaddafi the ★AOUZOU STRIP in return for Gaddafi withdrawing support from Frolinat and paying Tombalbaye 23,000 million CFA francs. As part of a new nationalist policy he banned Christian names, introduced initiation rites and replaced French placenames with Chadian names. Discontent increased and in April 1975 General ★ODINGAR had Tombalbaye assassinated and seized power.

Touré, Ahmad Sekou (1922–84), President of Guinea, one of modern Africa's strongest if least-loved leaders. Touré was first educated in a Koranic school and then attended a college in Conakry. A commercial worker and trade union organizer, from 1945, Touré helped form the Union Cégètiste des Syndicats de Guinée in 1947 and was imprisoned by the French for 'subversive activity'. When released in 1952 he became secretary of the Guinea branch of ★RASSEMBLEMENT DÉMOCRATIQUE AFRICAIN and organized a general strike against French administration in 1953. His political ascent became impressive. In 1953, he was a member of the territorial assembly; 1955, Mayor of Conakry; 1956, a deputy in the French national assembly; 1957, founder of Union Générale des Travailleurs d'Afrique Noir; 1957, Vice-President of the Governor's Council.

In 1958 it was Touré's organizational skill which resulted in the overwhelming defeat of General de Gaulle's referendum on joining a French-African Community. As Guinea was the first country to break away from the French empire, Touré gained great status in Africa and his foreign policy of 'positive neutralism' also won admirers. Touré systematically stifled opposition by picking off and purging one group after another. In all cases, he announced that a 'conspiracy' had been uncovered and that it had foreign involvement – usually French, American, Russian or South African – at its root. In this way he dealt with 'reactionaries and feudalists' in 1960; intellectuals, 1961; 'antinational' business leaders, 1967; heads of national enterprises, 1969;

civil service chiefs and army leaders, 1970. In 1976 he found an excuse for the imprisonment and execution of Diallo Telli, a former secretary-general of the OAU. That year Touré felt secure enough to travel abroad and in 1978 he induced the French president Giscard d'Estaing to visit Guinea. As a result, France gave massive amounts of money for development projects. From time to time Touré visited Arab and Islamic countries in search of funds. Having been elected unopposed, on May 1982, for a further seven-year term as president, Touré urged the French government to invite him to Paris. His human rights record was appalling but as he supported French policy in Africa he was duly invited to France. Back home, Touré continued to uncover 'conspiracies' and arrest more enemies. In March 1984 he collapsed with heart trouble and died as he was being operated upon. He had ruled Guinea as a despot for twenty-seven years and on his death more than one thousand political prisoners were set free.

Trade Unions, those which exist in Africa's fifty-two states represent only about 5–15 per cent of the population, some indication of the weak state of development of trade unionism. Trade unions are a minor element in African states' institutional structures. This is because industrial sectors are small in terms of labour demand in most African countries. Agriculture employs the largest number of people but as it is based on primitive or near-primitive land-use systems it is not susceptible to labour organization. Trade sectors are overwhelmingly dominated by the self-employed, while governments only rarely tolerate trade unions within state organizations.

In most North African and black African states the concept of trade-unionism is regarded as irrelevant. When unions exist, it is not for the sole purpose of protecting and improving workers' right. Many national leaders see them at best as a factor in integrating the working class in the state structure. Nevertheless, in one way the labour movement is an important force. The trade unions have, in many countries, secured a role in the machinery of government alongside the ruling political parties and other organizations. Sometimes they are an integral part of a ruling party. As a general statement, trade unions are more respected in black African countries than in Arab states. British and French rulers permitted their colonies to develop a degree of trade unionism but the Portuguese banned it. In South Africa, the growth of African unions was restricted and in many places the system of migrant labour prevented any lasting relationship between wage-earners and employers.

Large-scale urbanization and industrialization, which might be expected to lead to the formation of unions, has been confined to a few regions, notably South Africa and the mining areas of Zaire and Zambia. Organized work-forces are found only in some large cities, such as Cairo, Lagos, Algiers and

Dakar. Industrialized agriculture, as on plantations where large numbers of people are employed, has resisted trade unionism.

Before 1960 unions were small and ineffective, especially in West Africa. The various British administrations refused to permit unions to be formed in essential industries and there was an almost standard insistence that they must remain 'non-political'. Strikes could take place legitimately only if they had no 'political overtones'.

French administrations used all these restrictive devices and also made membership of a union legal only for those relatively few people with French civil status. Following independence, most Africans in the formerly French colonies wanting to be part of a union joined branches of the communist-oriented Confédération Générale du Travail (CGT) and to a much lesser extent the Confédération Christian Française des Travailleurs Croyants (CCFTC) and the social democratic Confédération Générale du Travail–Force Ouvrière (CGT–FO). The strongest unions represented railwaymen. Gradually, these African unions broke away from the French labour organizations.

In the British-ruled areas, trade unions tied themselves to political parties in the approach to independence. This meant that in the significant year of 1960, when so many nations achieved independence, some trade union leaders had great power – as they had planned. They included President Sekou *TOURÉ of Guinea, President Siaka *STEVENS of Sierra Leone and Tom *MBOYA of Kenya. Nevertheless, relationships between unions and new governments were anything but harmonious. Many union leaders were imprisoned and their unions dissolved. New national political leaders saw unions as a threat to social stability and to economic growth. In Ghana, the number of 'industrial federations' – that is, unions – was restricted to twenty-four, all of which had to use a single trade union centre. One motive for this action was to prevent power struggles between unions. Governments, even when at their most benevolent, have controlled the unions. For instance, trade unionists were permitted to sit on many government planning and consultative committees. It was believed that this would greatly reduce their taste for 'disruption', and so it proved.

By the 1980s, most African countries had trade union organizations which were linked to and, more important, sympathetic towards government. Almost every military coup brings in its wake new rules for trade unions, and presidents and prime ministers insist on appointing their own nominees to trade union committees. Affiliations with international unionist federations, even when tolerated, are viewed with disfavour. Nevertheless, some agencies have established themselves in Africa to promote trade unions. The most important is the African-American Labour Centre (AALC), based in Lomé, Togo. Financed by

US trade unions and other sources, AALC publishes various African labour journals.

In 1973 the Organization of African Trade Union Unity (OATUU) was formed to end the deep divisions in the African labour movement. By 1976, sixty-seven trade union centres from fifty-two countries were affiliated with OATUU. Only white unions in South Africa remained outside it, while only seven African states had trade unions which were still affiliated to some other organization. The *ORGANIZATION OF AFRICAN UNITY recognizes OATUU as the only labour movement in Africa. Its headquarters are in Accra, Ghana, and it has consultative status at the UN with the OAU and the International Labour Organization.

The principle of trade unionism was widely accepted in Africa in the late 1980s but neither in numbers nor in political strength do unions compare with those in the Western world. At any time most are vulnerable to proscription or serious government interference. In 1986 President *BOURGUIBA of Tunisia virtually crushed trade unionism after accusing union leaders of 'sabotaging' the national economy.

To a large extent, governments directly control unions. For instance, on *ZANZIBAR, the Workers Department of the *AFRO-SHIRAZI PARTY, the ruling group, is responsible for trade union work. The Egyptian Federation of Labour, with about three million members in sixteen national unions, was the creation of President *NASSER. He harnessed trade union activity to the government interest and the Federation was nothing more than an extension of the Arab Socialist Union party. However, this no longer applies. Several trade unions in Egypt are actively concerned with the welfare of their members. The greatest threat to unions since 1982 has been from *ISLAMIC FUNDAMENTALISTS who have captured most of the more professional union organizations and are intent on taking over the workers' unions.

In Algeria, the Union Générale des Travailleurs Algériens is virtually an extension of the ruling FLN party, as are the Union Nationale des Paysans Algériens, the Union Nationale de la Jeunesse Algérienne and the Union Nationale des Femmes Algériennes. Before 1956 Tunisia had a progressive and effective union organization, the Union Générale des Travailleurs Tunisiens (UGTT). It was in equal partnership with the nationalist Destourien Socialist Party (DSP) while struggling for independence. Since 1956 the government and the DSP have prevented UGTT from expressing itself independently. In 1978 and again in 1985–6, UGTT's Secretary-General and leading officials were imprisoned after being held responsible for riots. Now UGTT is entirely under government control.

In Libya, trade unions are not permitted to exist. They functioned before Colonel *GADDAFI came to power in 1969 but his system of government prevents the

351

establishment of any organizations that represent segments of Libyan society. In 1978 he permitted the formation of the General Federation of Trade Unions but it is a fiction and its few employees are paid by the government.

Trade unions in Sudan were repressed during the *NIMEIRI regime, which they helped to destroy. Sudanese trade unions benefited from British influence, in that they have a tradition of independence from government and of alliance to political parties. Since Nimeiri's departure they have been more prominent. In 1978 the Ethiopian Government dismissed the leaders of the All-Ethiopian Trade Union. Several union leaders have been in prison since 1974 and unions are impotent. In Morocco, the situation is more liberal. The three trade union confederations are extensions of specific political parties and partly because of this are independent of the government.

In general, if a democracy is judged by the right of workers to join trade unions, which then have the rights enjoyed by organized labour in the West, trade-unionism has a long way to go in Africa; the only exception being among white workers in South Africa, where trade-unionism began in 1881. From 1956 all unions were organized in accordance with *APARTHEID. White Africans' interests have been represented, since 1957, by the South African Confederation of Labour (SACL). The Trade Union Council of South Africa (TUCSA) covers unions which have white, racially mixed and black African membership; about sixty-five unions are involved. The law has prevented the growth of black African unions, nevertheless about twenty-four unions with sixty thousand members exist. A series of strikes in 1973 resulted in government repression but there is still much union activity in the African townships. Representatives of various international trade unions aid the black South African unionists, who are in the forefront of the struggle for a non-racial democratic South Africa.

Transitional Government of National Unity (1985–9), one of South Africa's unsuccessful attempts to procure an internal settlement in Namibia. South Africa wanted to establish it before independence to obviate United Nations involvement and to avoid a *SWAPO government in the future. The complicated constitution was based on proposals by the *MPC which assumed power at formal inauguration of the constitution (Jun. 1985). It was seen as a South African puppet government, and had little popular support. It also suffered from serious disagreements among the six parties participating in the government. By 1987 it was in conflict with South Africa which had refused to approve its plans to abolish the remnants of *APARTHEID in Namibia. Even before the United Nations began to supervise Namibia's transition to independence (Apr. 1989) the Transitional Government of National Unity had little credibility.

Transkei, a South African *HOME-LAND, the first to be set aside for the Xhosa people, it was declared 'independent' in October 1976, a status not recognized outside South Africa. It covers 41,002 sq. km. in the south-east of South Africa. In 1983 its population was estimated at 2.5 million. Transkei is over-crowded and lacks major natural resources. Its economy depends on agriculture and remittances from migrant labourers in South Africa.

For the first eleven years after 'independence' Transkei was con-trolled by the Matanzima family, whose grip on power was weak-ened by a family feud. The regime's leaders have been accused of corrup-tion and violence against opponents. Relations between Transkei and the South African government were tense because Transkei objected to the *CISKEI being established as a sec-ond Xhosa Homeland and because the South African government would not recognize Transkei's claim to additional territory. Rela-tions with Ciskei were strained when Transkei was involved in a family dispute in the Sebe family which con-trolled Ciskei. Maj.-Gen. Holomisa seized power in a military coup (Dec. 1987); he favours co-operation with the *AFRICAN NATIONAL CONGRESS and reintegration into a reformed South Africa.

Traoré, Moussa (b. 1936), soldier and Mali's head of state. Born in Kayes, Traoré was educated at the army cadet college in Kati, and in France. He was first a non-commissioned officer in the French army, but on Mali's independence in September 1960 he transferred to the small national army as a lieu-tenant. On 19 November 1968 he was one of a small group of officers which overthrew President Modibo *KEITA. Traoré became head of state and quickly promoted himself to the rank of general. He also became, in 1974, Secretary-General of the Democratic Union of the Malian People (UDMP). Having survived a coup, Traoré dealt harshly with the conspirators. In 1979 he was elected president. Following another attempted coup at the end of 1981, Traoré extended his power. He could now appoint and dismiss the prime minister and other ministers. When he came to the end of his six-year presidential term in 1985 he induced the UDPM to alter the constitution so that he could hold the presidency for another term. Only the UDPM could nominate candidates and, not surprisingly, Traoré was the only candidate. It was announced that he had received 99.94 per cent of the vote. Traoré has a poor human rights record. Amnesty International reported that during student unrest in 1980, thir-teen students were shot, bayoneted or tortured to death. Some of Traoré's leading opponents have been executed. In 1986 Traoré for the first time appointed a prime min-ister and at the same time divested himself of the defence portfolio, two steps which indicated that he was less intent on being a dictator. That year he also visited the Soviet Union for the first time and secured a rescheduling of Mali's debt to the Soviets. Between 1986 and 1990 he ruled more benignly and announced that he would step down from the presidency in 1991, though his enemies doubted that he would keep his word.

Treurnicht, Andries Petrus (b. 1921), extreme right-wing South African politician who has led the *CONSERVATIVE PARTY since its foundation in 1982. He was a minister of religion and a journalist before becoming a *NATIONAL PARTY MP (1971). In the 1970s he had great influence as Chairman of the *AFRIKANER BROEDERBOND. He served the governments of *VORSTER (1966–78) and P.W. *BOTHA (1978–82) as Deputy Minister for Bantu Administration and Education (1976–9), Minister of Public Works and Tourism (1979–80) and Minister of State Administration (1980–2). As party leader in the Transvaal (1978–82), he was a prominent spokesman for the right wing and strongly criticized what he perceived as the government's failure to protect the interests of the whites in South Africa.

Early in 1982 he opposed P.W. Botha's plan for sharing political power with *COLOUREDS and *INDIANS. He left the Cabinet and the National Party and formed the Conservative Party, retaining his seat in a by-election. In the 1987 and 1989 elections the Conservative Party was the second largest in parliament and Treurnicht has been leader of the official opposition since 1987. His party has links with the extremist *AFRIKANER WEERSTANDSBEWEGING. To preserve the identity of the white man in South Africa, Treurnicht advocates the political separation of the races into thirteen states; in addition to a state for whites he plans one Coloured, one Indian and ten black *HOMELANDS.

True Whig Party, political party founded in Liberia in 1868. Representing the interests of the coastal elite, it governed Liberia continuously from 1878 until 1980, when President *TOLBERT's government was overthrown in a military coup.

Tshombe, Moise (1919–69), controversial political leader born in *SHABA (then Katanga) in Zaire (formerly the Congo). He was regarded by many Africans as a stooge of the whites who had commercial interests in Katanga. Tshombe entered politics in the 1950s during the last decade of Belgian rule and founded CONAKAT, a Katangan-based party supported by his own Lunda tribe and encouraged by some Belgian mining interests. At the Brussels Round Table Conference on independence (1959–60) he argued unsuccessfully for a loosely federated Congo state with close links to Belgium. A few days after independence, in July 1960 Tshombe announced the secession of Katanga from the Congo and declared himself President of Katanga. During the bitter civil war that followed Tshombe's reputation was tarnished by the murder of *LUMUMBA in Katanga (1961) and by his use of

TUNISIA

white mercenaries against fellow Africans.

With United Nations assistance the central government defeated Tshombe and he fled into exile (1963). When the Congo was threatened by further conflicts, President *KASAVUBU appointed Tshombe Prime Minister (1964). Tshombe won over 70 per cent of the parliamentary seats in the elections of May 1965, but President Kasavubu refused to call on him to form a government. A period of constitutional deadlock was followed by *MOBUTU's seizure of power (Nov. 1965). Tshombe went into exile again. He was kidnapped in mysterious circumstances and died in captivity in Algeria.

Tubman, William Vacanararat Shadrach (1895–1971), President of Liberia (1944–71). A member of the coastal elite, he practised law and was popularly known as 'the poor man's lawyer'. He became a senator (1922) and a judge (1937). During his long presidency the exploitation of iron ore and United States aid made Liberia prosperous. President Tubman advocated closer unity to lessen the gap between the coastal elites and the people of the hinterland. He also pursued an open-door policy to break the economic power of the Firestone Company in Liberia and to encourage foreign investment other than from the United States. A firm friend of the United States and the West, he played an important part in the formation of the *MONROVIA BLOC – an attempt by the more moderate African states to counteract the influence of the radical and socialist *CASABLANCA BLOC.

Tunisia, located on the southern Mediterranean coast and sandwiched between Algeria and Libya. Tunisia is a bigger country than it looks on a map of Africa.

The south is an extension of the Sahara, then successively northwards there are arid plains, a range of the Atlas mountains and then two small coastal plains surrounded by hilly country. The desirable Mediterranean climate has attracted about 70 per cent of the population of 7.25 million to live on the coast.

Tunisia's recorded history goes back to the thirteenth century BC. Phoenicians, Romans, Byzantines, Muslim Arabs, Spaniards and Turks have all played a major part in its history. In 1881 the French invaded the country, threw out the Ottomans and set up a protectorate. Protected by the Foreign Legion, French settlers seized a fifth of the cultivable land. During the Second World War, Tunisia was part of the North African battlefield and in its hills, in 1943, the Allies finally defeated the Germans and Italians. Many Tunisians, including Habib *BOURGUIBA, aided the Free French forces, who opposed occupation by the pro-German Vichy government.

After the war, Bourguiba campaigned for independence but the French crushed his movement politically and militarily and he was exiled. In 1955, as armed resistance to imperialism spread throughout

355

The Republic of Tunisia

THE COUNTRY	THE PEOPLE	THE STATE
163,610 sq. km.	7.2 million	Single-party republic
Major Cities	*Ethnic Groups*	*Head of State*
Tunis (capital)	Arab	President Ben Ali
Sfax	Bedouin	
Bizerta		*Ruling Body*
Dougga	*Languages*	136-seat National
Gabes	Arabic (official)	Assembly elected from a
	French	limited list
Economy		
Tourism	*Religion*	*Official Party*
Olive Oil	Sunni Islam (official)	Parti socialiste
Phosphates		destourien
Principal Exports		
Oil, olive oil		
Currency		
Dinar of 1,000 millimes		

North Africa, the French reluctantly decided that autonomy for Tunisia might dampen demands for independence. The autonomy was generous, with Tunisians managing everything except defence and foreign affairs. But it was still not enough for the Neo-Destour Party and on 20 March 1956 France granted independence. Bourguiba returned to become the new nation's first president. The nationalists deposed the Bey of Tunis, declared a republic and made Neo-Destour the single official party. The French retained Bizerta as a military base but, after clashes with Tunisian nationalists that verged on war, in October 1961 they evacuated Bizerta as well.

Bourguiba was determined to reconstruct Tunisia, with an equal mixture of European-Christian and Arab-Muslim values. To this end, he gave women many freedoms which other Arab countries did not grant. He also tried to eliminate Islam's Ramadan fast on the grounds that it was damaging to the national economy. Bourguiba and the DSP became more authoritarian in the 1970s, occasioning vociferous demands from many quarters for great democracy.

The Neo-Destour Party renamed itself the Destourian Socialist Party (DSP) in 1963 and adopted a mixed economy. While private enterprise was tolerated, the public sector was reconstructed along co-operative lines. In 1969 Bourguiba wanted all private land to be brought into a co-operative net but the protests were so great that he moved back to a mixed economy. The tensions reached crisis level in 1978 with a general strike and widespread demonstrations. Bourguiba's neighbour, Colonel *GADDAFI of Libya, saw his opportunity to exploit unrest in Tunisia and in 1980 sent a commando force to raid the desert town of Gafsa.

During the national assembly elections of 1981, Bourguiba faced hostility from the Islamic Trend Movement, the Tunisian Communist Party, the Movement for Popular Unity and the trade union movement. Serious riots in 1984 so shook the government that it moved towards the social democrats and permitted the communists to operate legally. In 1987, ninety members of the illegal Islamic Trend Movement (STI) were tried for alleged terrorism and subversion. In October, seven were condemned to death while the rest received sentences ranging from two years to life imprisonment. Had it not been for pressure by Western governments the verdict would have been much harder and, in fact, only two men were hanged. Among the MTI terrorist activities was the bombing of four Tunisian hotels in August 1986.

In February 1988, in a 'quiet coup', General Ben Ali deposed President Bourguiba and assumed the presidency. Tunisia readily accepted the change since Ben Ali was known as a liberal and progressive but strong man. President Ben Ali's reforms were instant and radical. He instituted sweeping changes in senior management, notably in the oil, mining, ports, archaeology, civil aviation, publishing and television industries. He also patched up Tunisia's differences with France, which had been aggravated by claims on the remainder of French colonial assets. The French, whose political influence remains important, accepted Ben Ali. One of his major early tasks was to stabilize and expand agricultural output. He announced that sixteen new dams would be built by 2006, to increase the national dam storage from 1.5 billion cubic metres to 2.6 billion.

While one of the richest countries in Africa in terms of GDP per capita, Tunisia suffers from acute unemployment; about 200,000 Tunisians work abroad. The two basic exports – olive oil and phosphates – have suffered from a decline in demand, and oil exports are limited. More than half the country's work-force is engaged in agriculture. Since 1980 the government has encouraged industry, with incentives for foreign and domestic export-oriented industries. The economy has been increasingly dominated by the private sector since the collapse of the co-operative schemes. Even so, the government retains control of heavy industry and communications. The greatest source of foreign currency is the annual arrival of one million foreign tourists. Many small islands, such as Jerba, are popular with visitors, as are the desert oases of the south. Among Tunisia's attractions is the great mosque of the holy city of Kairouan, the oldest mosque in

Africa. The International Film Festival of Carthage – the Punic city founded in 812 BC – is held every two years and was the first of its kind.

Unless *ISLAMIC FUNDAMENTALISM or Colonel Gaddafi's imperial ambitions prevent it, Tunisia is likely to remain one of the most peaceful of African countries. In 1982 Bourguiba allowed the *PALESTINE LIBERATION ORGANIZATION (PLO) to set up its headquarters in Tunisia, and it has not attempted to interfere in Tunisian politics.

Turnhalle Constitutional Conference, delegates from Namibia's eleven ethnic groups met in the Turnhalle hall in Windhoek (1975–7) to draft a constitution to protect minority rights. It was organized by South Africa and strongly influenced by the white leader, Dirk *MUDGE. *SWAPO and other nationalists denounced it as a South African ruse to delay independence under United Nations supervision. After working out a complicated constitution the conference dissolved and became a political party, the *DTA, which took office late in 1978.

Tutu, The Most Reverend Desmond Mpilo (b. 1931), Anglican Archbishop of Cape Town since September 1986, the first non-white to hold the post and a leading opponent of *APARTHEID. Until the *BANTU EDUCATION ACT made it impossible for him to continue he was a teacher (1955–8). After ordination (1961) he studied in London (1962–6). He then taught at a South African seminary and lectured at Roma University in

Lesotho, before returning to London to work for the World Council of Churches (1972–5). While Dean of Johannesburg (1975–6) he led a column of *SOWETO protesters and became known as a political activist.

Tutu then served as Bishop of Lesotho (1976–8) before becoming Secretary-General of the South African Council of Churches (1978–84), a body which rejected apartheid and was under considerable pressure from the South Africa government, which used smear tactics against Tutu, accusing him of financial irregularities. Tutu's refusal to submit to official pressure gained international attention, especially after his address to the United Nations Special Committee against apartheid. He so incurred the wrath of the South African authorities that they arrested him (1980) and more than once took his passport away. From the beginning of 1985 until his elevation to the see of Cape Town he was Bishop of Johannesburg.

Tutu's courage in speaking out against the government has been recognized abroad. He has received many awards and honours, including the Athinai Prize (1980), the Nobel Peace Prize (1984), numerous honorary doctorates and fellowships and a standing ovation from the United States Congress.

In South Africa Tutu has been a patron of the *UNITED DEMOCRATIC FRONT and for years was the only credible black South African leader neither in prison nor in exile. He has consistently advocated international sanctions against South Africa, in the hope that international pressure could bring victory without bloodshed for black South Africans. He continues to denounce violence on both sides and to condemn official restrictions on individual freedoms. He was overjoyed at the release of Nelson *MANDELA (Feb. 1990) and strongly supports negotiations between the *AFRICAN NATIONAL CONGRESS and the government, negotiations which began with preliminary talks in May 1990.

Tutuola, Amos (b. 1920), one of Nigeria's most unconventional and original authors. Since his family could not afford secondary school fees Tutuola went to work after leaving primary school and was employed as a blacksmith, a messenger and a stores officer for the Nigerian Broadcasting Corporation. His first novel, *The Palm Wine Drinkard* (1952), was an international success despite – or perhaps because of – its imperfect and unusual English. In his novels and short stories Tutuola has imaginatively reworked Yoruba oral tradition and added elements of fantasy and magic.

U

UDEAC (Union douanière et économique de l'Afrique centrale), regional customs and free trade association in West and Central Africa, created by the Brazzaville Treaty (1964). Its members are Cameroon, Central African Republic, Chad, Congo, Equatorial Guinea and Gabon. Congo has benefited most from the association and has favourable balances of trade with the other members. In 1977 UDEAC had ambitious plans for a petrochemical complex in Gabon, the manufacture of chemicals in Congo, pharmaceutical and watchmaking industries in the Central African Republic, and an aluminium plant in Cameroon, but no progress has been made in carrying out these plans.

UDI (Unilateral Declaration of Independence), was made on 11 November 1965 by Ian *SMITH's government of Southern Rhodesia, following long negotiations with Britain on the issue of independence. Britain was not prepared to grant independence without majority rule while Smith's *RHODESIAN FRONT government was determined to maintain white supremacy. Negotiations broke down and the Southern Rhodesian government declared its independence. After years of war and international sanctions UDI was renounced in the *LANCASTER HOUSE AGREEMENT (Dec. 1979). Under British supervision Southern Rhodesia became the independent Republic of Zimbabwe (Apr. 1980).

Uganda, a member of the Commonwealth, the Republic of Uganda lies across the Equator. It is a landlocked state at least eight hundred kilometres from the Indian Ocean. It is bordered on the north by Sudan, on the east by Kenya, on the south by Tanzania and Rwanda and on the west by Zaire. A fifth of its area consists of large freshwater lakes or swamps, including parts of Lakes Victoria, Mobutu Sese Seko (Albert) and Edward and all of Lakes George and Kyoga. From Lake Victoria at Jinja the Nile begins its six thousand kilometre journey to the Mediterranean. Over 80 per cent of the land is on the East African plateau between 900 and 1500 metres above sea-level. There are mountainous regions of over 2100 metres altitude near both the eastern and the western borders. In the west the Ruwenzori Mountains include Mount Stanley, at 5109 metres Africa's third highest peak. The western arm of the *EAST AFRICAN RIFT VALLEY includes lowlands flanking the rift lakes (Mobutu Sese Seko and Edward). Parts of the north-east (Karamoja) are dry savannah and semi-desert.

Uganda's climate is moderated by its altitude. Most of the country has ample rainfall, short dry seasons and fertile soil. Before it was desolated by political and social turmoil Uganda's mainly agricultural economy was rich and productive. Agriculture is

The Republic of Uganda

THE COUNTRY	THE PEOPLE	THE STATE
241,139 sq. km.	15,655,000	Military rule
Major Cities	*Ethnic Groups*	*Head of State*
Kampala (capital)	Baganda	President Museveni
Jinja	Basoga	
Masaka	Banyankole	*Ruling Bodies*
Mbala		Presidential Cabinet
Mbarara	*Languages*	National Resistance
Entebbe	English (official)	Council
Gulu	Swahili	
	Luganda	*Ruling Party*
Economy		National Resistance
Farming	*Religion*	Movement
	Christian	(Other parties are
Principal Exports	Islam	represented in the
Coffee	Traditional beliefs	cabinet)
Cotton		
Currency		
Uganda shilling of 100		
cents		

the most important sector of the Ugandan economy, accounting for about 95 per cent of export earnings and employing about 90 per cent of the labour force. During the troubles of the last twenty years many farmers switched to subsistence crops like plantains, cassava, sweet potatoes, millet, sorghum, maize and beans. Coffee is the main cash crop, grown by about a million smallholders. In 1979 coffee production fell to 103,000 tonnes, less than half the 225,200 tonnes produced in 1973. By the late 1980s coffee exports had recovered nearly to the 1973 level and accounted for close to 90 per cent of Uganda's foreign earnings. At the same time the fall in world coffee prices has partly offset the gains from increased production. Tea, cotton and tobacco are also significant cash crops; like coffee their production peaked around 1970, fell dramatically and recovered during the 1980s. Sugar and cocoa production are also beginning to recover.

Production of copper, Uganda's main mineral, fell sharply from 1970 as the Kilembe mines stopped working and the Jinja smelter fell into disrepair. Late in the 1980s there were plans to rehabilitate the Kilembe mines, despite doubts about profitability. Superphosphates and other minerals are mined on a small scale.

UGANDA

Before the turmoil of the 1970s there was a small but efficient industrial sector processing agricultural produce and substituting for imports. The lack of money for spare parts and raw materials, shortage of fuel, the absence of managers and technicians and the general disorder caused a dramatic drop of production in the 1970s. By the late 1980s President *MUSEVENI's government was gradually renovating and upgrading tourist facilities. Industry is being rehabilitated, but still operates far below capacity. During the late 1980s the government negotiated for aid to improve the provision of hydroelectric power at Owen Falls and to expand production.

Museveni has also had some success in obtaining aid to rehabilitate roads and the railway system which had collapsed completely. Uganda has to depend on Kenya and Tanzania for access to the sea and is particularly vulnerable to pressure from either country. Both have cut and/or restricted Ugandan traffic through their territories when relations with Uganda have been bad. There is a scheme to link Uganda with Tanzanian ports, by shorter routes than the 1160 kilometres by rail to Mombasa.

When *AMIN was in power during the 1970s many states cut their aid to Uganda both because of his economic incompetence and his flagrant disregard for human rights. In the early 1980s there was greater willingness to give aid to President *OBOTE, but he had exhausted his credit by 1985 and was unable to control

raging inflation. At first international donors were wary of President Museveni's government, but he has cut expenditure and devalued the Uganda shilling. Satisfied with Uganda's progress, in May 1987 the International Monetary Fund agreed to give financial help for three years.

The people of Uganda have complex origins. There are a few pygmies, the earliest inhabitants, in the forests of the south-west. The *BANTU in the south and the centre form about two thirds of the population. In the north are the Nilotic and Hamitic peoples, each accounting for about one sixth of the population.

For centuries the fertile country attracted waves of migrations by the Bantu from the west and the Hamitic and Nilotic peoples from the north. By the fifteenth century the Bantu were being organized in strongly centralized kingdoms. Initially Bunyoro dominated, but when Europeans arrived in the nineteenth century *BUGANDA was the most powerful kingdom. It was Speke's arrival at the source of the Nile (1862) that persuaded missionaries and traders from Europe to go to the country, where they found Islamic missionaries and slave traders were already active.

In 1890 British influence was recognized by its European rivals and in 1893 Buganda became a British protectorate; from Buganda Britain extended its protectorate over Uganda. Britain encouraged the development of cotton plantations, but because land freeholds remained in African hands Uganda did not have the problems that Kenya had over white-settler land ownership. The main difficulties came from the relations of the royal kingdoms with their people and with Britain.

By the early 1950s Uganda was preparing for independence. The Uganda National Congress, the first national party, was founded in 1952; radicals led by Milton Obote left it and in 1960 formed the *UGANDA PEOPLE'S CONGRESS (UPC). In 1956 the more moderate *DEMOCRATIC PARTY was established with the help of Catholic priests. There was a crisis in 1953 when the Kabaka of Buganda, *MUTESA II, was exiled until 1955 for opposing British plans for a unitary state after independence.

As independence approached over 95 per cent of the Bugandans boycotted the 1961 election. This gave the Democratic Party, whose supporters had registered, twenty of the twenty-one Bugandan seats. With twenty-three seats from the rest of the country the Democratic Party was able to form the government. It was then agreed that Buganda would have a semi-federal status after independence and the UPC made an electoral alliance with the Kabaka Yekka (KY) – the Bugandan royalist party. The UPC-KY alliance won the 1962 election and formed the government which led Uganda to independence (Oct. 1962). Obote was prime minister and after the proclamation of the republic (Oct. 1963) Mutesa II was president.

There was a struggle for power between the Bugandans and the UPC, which ended when Obote sent Colonel Amin to storm the Bugandan palace (1966) and abolished the kingdom (1967). The violent suppression of Buganda and other repressive acts made Obote unpopular. Late in the 1960s he sought to swing public opinion behind him in a move to the left which was to include breaking the power of traditional rulers and the redistribution of wealth from the rich to the poor. These plans were stalled by a number of problems, including the deteriorating relations between the government and Amin's faction in the army.

In January 1971 Amin seized power and Obote fled to Tanzania. As President, Amin proved a disaster for Uganda. He overthrew the political system; he abolished the constitution, made himself Life-President, ignored civil rights, purged the armed forces of ethnic groups whose loyalty he suspected and presided over the massacres of hundreds of thousands of Ugandans. Uganda moved rapidly towards anarchy. His economic policies were equally disastrous; by the end of his eight years in power industry was working at 15 per cent of capacity and transport and communications had collapsed. The expulsion of Asians (1972) dealt the wholesale and retail trades, services and industry a mortal blow. Further problems followed after the nationalization of British companies (Dec. 1972).

363

Amin's reign of terror and economic hardship generated considerable discontent and hatred in Uganda. Factional fighting broke out in the army and in 1974 led to an attempted coup which was only suppressed after fierce fighting. For economic and military support Amin turned to the Soviet Union and the Arab world. His commitment to Islam and his denunciation of Israel earned him rich rewards.

In 1976 and 1977 Amin dealt with unrest and protests by wholesale murder. An estimated 300,000 were killed between 1971 and 1979; victims included students at *MAKERERE UNIVERSITY, the Chief Justice and the Anglican Archbishop. In 1976 he supported the Palestinian hijack of an aeroplane to Entebbe, but was humiliated by the successful Israeli commando raid to rescue the passengers who were taken as hostages.

In 1978 Amin responded to pressure on his regime by launching an invasion of Tanzania. This was repelled by the Tanzanian army which then invaded Uganda with the support of dissidents who had combined to form the *UGANDA NATIONAL LIBERATION FRONT (UNLF). Once Amin was ousted (Apr. 1979) the UNLF became the caretaker government. Under Presidents *BINAISA and LULE it tried to restore law and order while preparing for elections at the end of 1980, but its work was undermined by the growing influence and power of Obote's supporters. In December 1980 Obote won the

presidential election under dubious circumstances and became President of Uganda for the second time (1980–5).

Obote and the UPC failed to bring stability to Uganda. Law and order had broken down. Ethnic hatred was strong. Various factions in the UPC were struggling for power. Several guerrilla groups were fighting the government. The army was out of control and responsible for brutal massacres in the *LUWERO TRIANGLE. An estimated 300,000 were killed during Obote's second presidency, the same number as during Amin's presidency. When fighting broke out in the army, the military seized power (Jul. 1985) and Obote fled into exile again.

The new military government was soon in difficulties; it was unable to defeat Museveni's National Resistance Army which controlled much of the west and the south. After negotiations with the government failed Museveni entered Kampala and was sworn in as President of Uganda (Jan. 1986). In pursuit of national reconciliation President Museveni has brought members of different ethnic and political groups into government. He has had some success in restoring law and order. The national army is more disciplined than its predecessors. In 1989 the Minority Rights Group praised Museveni's record on human rights and pointed out that elections earlier that year had conferred legitimacy on the government. The government has had to continue to fight to extend its authority over the country. In 1989 it persuaded Obote's supporters to agree to a cease-fire and other rebellions have been crushed. The government still faces opposition from rebel groups. Fighting has continued in the north and the east; the strangest rebels are the religious fanatics of the *HOLY SPIRIT MOVEMENT.

President Museveni has tried to improve relations with neighbouring countries. There were problems with Kenya over the transportation of coffee (1987–8), but relations improved after he met President *MOI of Kenya. He has also negotiated with Sudan and Zaire for the return of refugees to Uganda. President Museveni has had some success in obtaining international aid and support. The general feeling is that he is beginning to put Uganda on the way to recovery and that he compares favourably to his predecessors.

Uganda National Liberation Front (UNLF), a wide-ranging coalition of President *AMIN's exiled opponents which was formed at the *MOSHI CONFERENCE (Mar. 1979) – at the urging of President *NYERERE of Tanzania. After objections were made to ex-President *OBOTE the delegates chose Professor *LULE to lead them; he was a compromise candidate acceptable to both the supporters and the opponents of Obote. UNLF forces fought alongside the Tanzanian army to overthrow Amin (Apr. 1979). The front then became Uganda's caretaker government charged with the daunting tasks of restoring law and

order, organizing democratic elections and starting the reconstruction of the shattered economy.

In Uganda the work of the front was undermined by the growing power and influence of Obote's supporters. After about two months in office Lule was ousted by the *NATIONAL CONSULTATIVE COUNCIL (Jun. 1979). His successor, President *BINAISA, was ousted by the military in May 1980. Uganda was then governed by the Military Commission headed by Mr Muwanga. The front collapsed in September 1980 when the ministers who refused to support Obote were sacked.

Uganda People's Congress (UPC), radical political party founded in Uganda by Milton *OBOTE (1960). It lacked support in the Catholic south but was strongly supported by the Protestants in the north of Uganda. It won more seats than any other party in the pre-independence elections (1962), and led Uganda to independence (Oct. 1962) in coalition with Kabaka Yekka, the *BUGANDAN royalist party. After by-election successes gave the UPC a clear majority in parliament Obote dropped his coalition partners. By 1969 all other political parties were banned and in a series of documents Obote proclaimed that the UPC was moving to the left. As a socialist party, UPC was set to become Uganda's only legal party.

In January 1971 *AMIN seized power and the UPC operated from exile in Tanzania. With the support of President *NYERERE the UPC joined the Uganda National Liberation Front (Mar. 1979), which fought alongside the Tanzanian army to overthrow Amin (Apr. 1979). Despite its many enemies the UPC won the December 1980 elections under rather dubious circumstances and Obote became President of Uganda again (1980–5). After Obote was deposed and went into exile, some of the UPC participated in the military government (1985–6). Since then some have supported President *MUSEVENI's government.

Ujamaa, *SWAHILI word meaning familyhood, first used by President *NYERERE of Tanzania in 1962 to describe his ideal of African socialism and applied to communal farms and villages. Basing his ideas on an idealized model of pre-colonial Africa, Nyerere emphasized rural development and began to establish ujamaa. Up to nine million farmers were forced to move into these hastily planned villages, causing great resentment. Farmers were unwilling to share resources and help each other and agricultural production declined. By the late 1980s the leadership of Tanzania had recognized the failure of the ujamaa and gave more encouragement to individual farmers.

Umkonto we Sizwe (Spear of the Nation), the military wing of the *AFRICAN NATIONAL CONGRESS (ANC) which has operated in South Africa and in exile since it was founded by Nelson *MANDELA and his associates (1961). After the South African government banned the ANC (1960), the leadership abandoned its policy of non-violent

resistance and adopted a policy of limited violence against the government. Mandela organized a campaign of sabotage and limited guerrilla warfare until he and other leaders (including Walter *SISULU and Govan *MBEKI) were arrested (1963) and sentenced to life imprisonment at the *RIVONIA TRIAL.

Umma (1963–4), radical political party in Zanzibar founded and led by Abdul Rahman *BABU. Shortly after the 1964 revolution Umma merged with the ruling *AFRO-SHIRAZI PARTY.

Union Monetaire Ouest Africaine (UMOA), the West African Monetary Union is the umbrella organization which preserves the franc zone system and the common currency of the Communauté Financière Africaine (CFA) franc. UMOA was formed by a treaty of November 1973 but the CFA franc had been established in West Africa by the French colonial authorities in 1962. Members of UMOA are Benin, Burkina Faso, Ivory Coast, Niger, Senegal, Togo and Mali. UMOA has no secretariat and functions through the Central Bank of West African States.

Union Nationale Camerounais (UNC) of Cameroon. The one-party system of Western Cameroon was extended to Eastern Cameroon in 1966, when all six parties merged to form the UNC. Its policy was based on pan-Africanism, together with a mixture of state dominance and encouragement of private initiative. President *AHIDJO was not only the national leader but also president of the UNC as well. He resigned on 27 August 1983, after he had given up the state presidency and gone to France to live. The new president, Paul *BIYA, declared himself UNC president while, ironically, announcing 'a more authentic democracy' and an open society. The UNC met only four times between 1966 and 1985, always to 'approve' decisions already made by the President. In 1985, at the fourth UNC meeting, it was widely hoped that genuine democracy would be announced. However, Biya insisted that the one-party system would continue. The only change was that the UNC's name was changed to Rassemblement Démocratique du Peuple Camerounais (RDPC) under a new motto 'Union, Truth and Democracy'. In fact, all three qualities were singularly lacking in Cameroonian political life.

UNIP (United National Independence Party), Zambia's only legal political party. Founded in 1958 as the Zambian African National Congress, it organized a massive and successful campaign of civil disobedience against the *CENTRAL AFRICAN FEDERATION. When Zambia (then Northern Rhodesia) gained internal self-government in 1962 UNIP was the leading coalition partner; after winning the election of January 1964 it led Zambia to independence (Oct. 1964). After economic problems (1970–1) and after *KAPEPWE left UNIP to form his own political party the constitution was amended to make UNIP Zambia's only legal political party (Dec. 1972).

The 1975 constitutional amendments established the power of the party more strongly. The Central Committee of UNIP formulates policy; in case of a disagreement with the cabinet it overrides cabinet decisions. The President of UNIP is the sole candidate in presidential elections.

UNITA (União Nacional para a Independência Total de Angola), National Union for the Total Independence of Angola. It was founded by Jonas *SAVIMBI (Mar. 1966) after he broke with the *FNLA. Savimbi has led and dominated UNITA from the beginning. UNITA has proclaimed its belief in a democratic socialist state, but is primarily a movement for the Ovimbundu of southern and central Angola and apparently does not welcome all Angolans. It is anti-Marxist and pro-capitalist. It was initially formed to fight Portuguese rule in Angola, but by 1972 made some sort of accommodation with the Portuguese who saw UNITA as a lesser evil than the *MPLA.

In 1975 UNITA joined the short-lived transitional government. It proclaimed its rule over Angola (Nov. 1975) and joined the FNLA against the MPLA. In the war that followed (1975–6) UNITA was driven out of its capital, Jamba; its forces were scattered and driven into the bush. UNITA then regrouped and waged a devastating war against the MPLA government, which it believed was dominated by city men and northerners intent on destroying traditional values and handing Angola over to the Russians and the Cubans. UNITA has been much criticized for accepting substantial military and financial support from South Africa, which has itself repeatedly sent forces into Angola. The United States has given military aid to UNITA; the delivery of Stinger missiles (1986) was an important contribution to UNITA's campaigns. In June 1989 it agreed to a cease-fire, which was soon broken. In April 1990, after suffering some setbacks, UNITA proposed a fresh cease-fire.

United Democratic Front (UDF), an alliance of over six hundred political, social and trade union bodies in South Africa, formed in 1983 to resist *APARTHEID. Most of the estimated one and a half million members are non-white, but sympathetic whites are welcomed. Following a call by Allan *BOESAK for unity, the UDF was formed to continue the campaign of the banned *AFRICAN NATIONAL CONGRESS for a democratic non-racial South African state; more specifically it was formed to fight P.W. *BOTHA's constitutional changes which continued to exclude blacks from political power.

The South African government tried to suppress the UDF. UDF leaders were arrested and accused of treason, but the trial collapsed at the end of 1985. Under the state of emergency declared in July 1985 hundreds of UDF supporters were arrested and detained. In February 1988 the UDF and other opposition bodies were banned; the Mass Democratic Movement then emerged to assume the role of the UDF. After the government lifted bans on the UDF and the ANC early in 1990 the UDF supported negotiations with the government.

United Party, South African political party which formed the government of South Africa from 1934 to 1948. After it lost the 1948 election to the *NATIONAL PARTY it was the official opposition until it split into three parts (1977). The right wing joined the National Party, the centre was reconstituted as the New Republic Party and the left wing joined other groups to form the *PROGRESSIVE FEDERAL PARTY. The United Party was more acceptable to English-speaking white South Africans than the National Party, but in many ways its policies were nearly as conservative as those of the government. The United Party generally opposed any reforms that would have given non-whites a real say in South Africa.

United States Raid on Libya, one of the most dramatic events in modern African history. President Reagan's administration was angry with Colonel *GADDAFI over his support for international terrorism and his attempts to organize a coup against President *MUBARAK of Egypt. Following terrorist bombings at Rome and Vienna airports on 27 December 1985 the US considered a military strike against Libya. A major US naval exercise, Operation Prairie Fire, took place in the Gulf of Sidra, off Libya. Gaddafi had always insisted that the entire gulf is Libyan territorial water. On 24 March 1986,

Libyan forces fired missiles at US warplanes. The Americans retaliated by sinking two Libyan patrol boats and blowing up a missile site.

On that day US intelligence agencies intercepted messages from Tripoli to Libyan missions in eight countries ordering them to attack American targets. On 5 April a West German discotheque, crowded with American service personnel was bombed. There were 232 casualties. President Reagan ordered F1-11 bombers to attack selected targets in Libya on 15 April 1986. Two waves of aircraft hit the three main targets in Tripoli, killing or wounding sixty-six people and Navy planes bombed Benghazi barracks and airfield. One American warplane failed to return. The attack lasted only eleven minutes but it generated intense political protest and controversy. The American action embarrassed Egypt, even though President Mubarak wanted to see Gaddafi overthrown. The entire Arab world declared itself shocked. The American legal justification was based on the argument that the US was exercising its 'inherent right of self-defence' after attacks on its citizens organized by the Libyan government. Even if the raid had not been entirely legal it nevertheless achieved some of its objectives. The incidence of terrorism lessened and Gaddafi was less frequently implicated.

The British Government actively supported the American military action by allowing US land-based aircraft to take off from airfields in Britain for the strike on Libyan targets. The British used the same justification as the US: that it had suffered for twenty years from Gaddafi's support for terrorist groups.

UN Security Council Resolution 385 (30 Jan. 1976), the United Nations threatened South Africa with appropriate measures unless it withdrew from Namibia and allowed free elections under UN supervision.

UN Security Council Resolution 435 (29 Sep. 1978), blueprint for the implementation of Namibian independence under the supervision of the United Nations. The *CONTACT GROUP had mediated and persuaded both *SWAPO and South Africa to accept the blueprint in principle, although South Africa then rejected it a few days before its adoption by the Security Council. The proposals included the formation of *UNTAG (United Nations Transition Assistance Group) to oversee the transition to independence, a cease-fire, partial demobilization, the release of political prisoners, the return of exiles and refugees, the end of discriminatory legislation, the election of a Constituent Assembly and independence. In 1982 South Africa agreed to the resolution provided that the Cubans left Angola, but final agreement on Namibia and on the Cubans in Angola was only reached late in 1988. The transition to independence began in April 1989 and was completed by April 1990, very much in accordance with this resolution.

UNTAG (United Nations Transition Assistance Group), political and military force drawn from fifty nations to supervise Namibia's transition to independence (1989–90). Originally a force of 7500 was planned but this was reduced to save money. As the transition began (Apr. 1989) *SWAPO guerrillas suddenly returned to Namibia from their Angolan bases and there was fighting between them and South African forces. UNTAG managed to restore order and succeeded in guiding Namibia peacefully to independence by March 1990; some members have stayed on in Namibia after independence.

UPA (União das Populações de Angola), Union of the Peoples of Angola, a nationalist organization founded in 1958 and dominated by the Kongo people of northern Angola. The UPA opposed Portuguese rule and under the leadership of Holden *ROBERTO (1960–2) it inspired the northern Angolan rebellion in 1961. In 1962 Roberto merged the UPA with a smaller northern nationalist organization to form the *FNLA.

UPN (Unity Party of Nigeria), Nigerian political party founded by Chief *AWOLOWO in 1978, as Nigeria returned to civilian rule. Mainly a Yoruba party with strong support in the western states, it had enough national support to be one of the five parties allowed to contest the 1979 elections. Its populist programme included free health care and free education for all, full employment and rural development. In 1979

the UPN came second to the *NPN (National Party of Nigeria) in the federal legislature and became the federal opposition party. In the nineteen states it took five governorships and won control of five state assemblies. In the presidential race Awolowo had 4.9 million votes compared to President *SHAGARI's 5.7 million. Before the 1983 elections it made an alliance with other parties, including the third strongest party – the *NPP (Nigerian People's Party). This broke down and the UPN fared badly in the 1983 elections. After the military coup at the end of 1983 the UPN and other political parties were banned.

UPRONA (Union pour le progrès national), nationalist party in Burundi, founded in 1958 to campaign against Belgian rule. Led by Prince Louis Rwagasore (son of Mwami *MWAMBUTSA IV), UPRONA had remarkable success in winning support from both the Hutu and the Tutsi peoples. After the assassination of Prince Louis (1961) ethnic rivalries dominated and the Tutsi drove the Hutu out of the party. President *MICOMBERO, who seized power in 1966, made UPRONA the sole legal party and became its Secretary-General in 1974. Under the leadership of President *BAGAZA, who seized power in 1976, UPRONA's Central Committee took over the powers of the revolutionary committee in 1980; under the constitution of 1981 only members of UPRONA could be candidates for election to the National Assembly. When

Major *BUYOYA seized power in 1987 he suspended UPRONA, the 1981 constitution and the National Assembly.

V

Venda, a South African *HOME-LAND, set aside for the Venda people, it was declared 'independent' in September 1979, a status not recognized outside South Africa. It is a small and overcrowded territory of 6667 sq. km. in the north-east Transvaal. At 'independence' it had a population of about half a million, a third of whom were non-resident. In 1986 it was agreed with South Africa that those living and working permanently in South Africa would regain South African citizenship. Venda is a poor agricultural community, which depends on the earnings of its workers in South Africa.

At 'independence' it was ruled by president Patrick Mphephu, who died in 1988. He was succeeded by President Frank Ravele, who was deposed in a military coup (Apr. 1990). The new leader, Col. Ramushwana, wants reintegration into a reformed South Africa.

verkrampte, an Afrikaans word meaning narrow, restricted or cramped. It is used in South Africa to describe the more uncompromising supporters of *APARTHEID and white supremacy. Generally the verkrampte have rejected the *NATIONAL PARTY in favour of more right-wing parties like the official opposition, the *CONSERVATIVE PARTY.

verligte, an Afrikaans word meaning enlightened. It is used in South Africa to describe the more progressively minded members of the *NATIONAL PARTY who are prepared to accept at least some limits on white supremacy. They favour cautious reforms to give non-whites some say in the political process.

Verwoerd, Dr Hendrik (1901–66), South African Prime Minister (1958–66) and the architect of *APARTHEID. He was born in the Netherlands and arrived in South Africa as a baby. A member of the *NATIONAL PARTY and the *AFRIKANER BROEDERBOND, Verwoerd held the Chairs of Applied Psychology (1927–33) and Sociology and Social Work (1933–7) at Stellenbosch University. To further his political ambitions he edited *Die Transvaaler* (1937–48), an extremist newspaper known for its pro-Nazi sympathies during the Second World War.

Having failed to win a seat in the 1948 election, he was rewarded with a seat in the Senate. As Minister of Native Affairs (1950–8) and as Prime Minister he was responsible for much apartheid legislation and was a keen advocate of the *HOMELANDS which were legalized by the Promotion of Bantu Self-Government Act (1959). Verwoerd campaigned successfully to make South Africa a republic and led it out of the Commonwealth (1961). His policies provoked resistance within South

Africa and strong international condemnation, which led to South Africa's isolation from the world. He was assassinated by a right-wing fanatic in 1966.

Viljoen, Gerrit van Niekerk (b. 1926), leading South African political figure, *VERLIGTE member of the *NATIONAL PARTY and an ally of President P.W. *BOTHA. He defeated the *VERKRAMPTE Andries *TREURNICHT to lead the *AFRIKANER BROEDERBOND (1974–80) and served as *ADMIN-ISTRATOR-GENERAL of Namibia (1978–80) until he joined the South African cabinet in 1980. He was Minister of Education and Development Aid (1985–9). In 1989 President *DE KLERK appointed him Minister of Constitutional Development with the crucial task of trying to negotiate with black leaders on power-sharing.

Vorster, Balthazar Johannes (1915–83), South African Prime Minister (1966–78) and State President (1978–9). Shortly after taking his law degree Vorster joined the Ossewabrandwag, an extremist pro-Nazi group, and was interned in 1942 for his support of Germany during the Second World War. As a *NATIONAL PARTY MP from 1953 and as Minister of Justice (1961–6) he was a harsh and uncompromising advocate of white supremacy.

As prime minister he surprisingly adopted a more pragmatic approach. He relaxed some *APARTHEID laws, talked of real independence for the *HOMELANDS, negotiated with black African states and in principle accepted the idea of Namibian independence. In practice the cause of the Afrikaners was of paramount importance to him throughout his career. Vorster's modest concessions failed to appease either domestic or international opinion. In South Africa the mounting tide of protest against apartheid led to protests, strikes, riots and general unrest – notably in *SOWETO (1976). The government's suppression of opposition and its disregard for human rights prompted the international community to show its revulsion by increasing sanctions and further isolating South Africa. Vorster resigned to become State President, but had to leave this post when it became apparent that he had condoned *MULDER's irregularities. In retirement he was a more outspoken advocate of white supremacy and fiercely criticized P.W. *BOTHA 's modest attempts to modify apartheid.

Wakil, Idris Abdul, President of
*ZANZIBAR since 1985 in succes-
sion to Ali Hassan *MWINYI (now
President of Tanzania). Early in 1988
he sacked his ministers and put the
government in the hands of officials
pending the appointment of a new
Revolutionary Council.

Walvis Bay, South African-
controlled enclave four hundred
miles north of South Africa, a deep-
water Atlantic port on the edge of the
Namib Desert and in the centre of
Namibia's Atlantic coastline. It was
annexed by Britain (1878) in a vain
attempt to keep the Germans out
of the area, then transferred to the
Cape Colony (1884), to South Africa
(1911) and to *SOUTH WEST AFRICA
(1922). In 1977 South Africa resumed
the administration of the enclave.
Walvis Bay is vital to Namibia for
economic and strategic reasons as
a rich fishing centre and the area's
only deep-water port through which
ninety per cent of Namibia's exports
and imports pass. Its future is still a
matter of dispute: Namibia claims it,
but South Africa is determined not to
surrender control of such a powerful
weapon which could be used to put
pressure on Namibia in the future.

Welensky, Sir Roy (b. 1907), former Prime Minister of the *CEN-
TRAL AFRICAN FEDERATION, he was
born in Southern Rhodesia (now
Zimbabwe). Welensky worked for
the railways in Northern Rhodesia
(now Zambia) where he was an
active trade-unionist and a campaigner for the federation of both
the Rhodesias and Nyasaland (now
Malawi). He was a member of
the federal government from the
beginning (1953), serving as Prime
Minister from 1956 until its dissolution at the end of 1963. He then
settled in Rhodesia before moving to
England.

Western Sahara, located on the
north-west Atlantic coast of Africa,
at the extreme western edge of the
Sahara desert, Western Sahara covers
an area of 160,000 square miles.
Arid, barren and inhospitable, the
territory lies between Morocco to
the north and Mauritania to the
south and has a short border with
Algeria to the west. The estimated
population of 250,000 is mostly tribal
and nomadic.

At the Berlin Conference of 1884,
when the European powers shared
out Africa among themselves, the
Western Sahara was allocated to
Spain. However, Spanish activity
was restricted to the few urban settlements, such as Layyoune, Smara
and Dakhla. After the Second
World War nationalism expressed
itself throughout North Africa and
most violently in Algeria, where the
fight for independence from France,
gained in 1962, profoundly affected
the nature of nationalism in Africa.

In the Sahara, as elsewhere,
the colonizers reacted violently to
nationalism. In June 1970 Spanish

troops opened fire on peaceful Sahrawi demonstrators at Zemla, near the capital, El Aioun. The result was a massacre and the peaceful struggle for independence to which the Sahrawis had committed themselves came to an end. In 1973 some Sahrawi intellectuals formed the Popular Front for the Liberation of Saguia el-Hamra and Río de Oro, the names by which they knew the Western Sahara. The long title was shortened to Polisario Front or just *POLISARIO. When it was clear that Polisario meant to wage war, the Spanish government assured its Sahrawi leaders that their right to self-determination would be respected.

Meanwhile in 1956, Morocco had gained its independence from the French and was pressing a claim to take over Western Sahara. In 1974 the International Court of Justice in the Hague rejected Morocco's claim and ruled that neither Morocco nor Mauritania, which was also laying claim to the territory, had any title to it. The Sahrawis were free to determine their own destiny. King *HASSAN II of Morocco persisted in his demands and organized the *GREEN MARCH. In November 1975, General Franco, the Spanish dictator, who was near death, signed the Madrid Accord, which handed over the larger part of the Western Sahara to Morocco and a small section to Mauritania. This was in direct contradiction of Spain's earlier promise of self-determination. Most important, Franco gave the Moroccans a sixty-five per cent share

in the exploitation of the Western Sahara's valuable phosphate deposits. The phosphate, together with the rich fishing banks off the Western Sahara's coast, were the key to the battle for the barren land.

By arrangement, when Spanish troops withdrew from Western Sahara in February 1976 the Moroccan and Mauritanian armies replaced them. During the fighting which followed, the Moroccan army used napalm bombing against the Sahrawis and more than 100,000 fled into neighbouring Algeria, an enemy of Morocco. From its refuge in Tindouf, Algeria, the Polisario Front announced the birth of the Sahrawi Arab Democratic Republic (SADR). The Moroccans and Mauritania found, to their surprise, that they could not defeat Polisario in the field. The war caused Mauritania such severe economic and social problems that the Ould *DADDAH regime fell in a *coup d'état*. The new leaders signed a peace treaty with SADR in 1979, leaving Morocco alone to fight Polisario's marauding guerrillas.

The Moroccans held a large part of the Western Sahara, including El Aioun and Dakhla. Moroccan officials repeatedly claimed that they had the 'free allegiance' of the Sahrawis who stayed in Moroccan-held territory. Not so well publicized are the allegations of human rights abuses against Sahrawis. Amnesty International and the organization Western Sahara Campaign in the United States issued reports that some Sahrawis had 'disappeared' or had been imprisoned for political reasons.

From living as nomads, the Sahrawis became a nationalistic people with yearnings for a settled democratic way of life. By 1988, seventy-one countries had recognized the SADR. When it was admitted to the *ORGANIZATION OF AFRICAN UNITY at a meeting in 1984 Morocco's delegates walked out. However, the *ARAB LEAGUE and the Gulf states supported Morocco in the name of 'Arab unity'. The leader of the SADR is Muhammad Abdelaziz, whom King Hassan describes as 'chief of a gang of mercenaries'. The number of people living in the refugee camps reached 165,000 in 1988. SADR has a literacy rate of 80 per cent, the highest in Africa. This is largely because of the influence of Sahrawi women; Suelma Emhamed is director of the schools where all Sahrawi women receive their professional training. Creches, kindergartens, and primary and secondary schools take care of their children during the day while the women themselves are busy on training courses. Western educationalists, economists and other experts who have visited the SADR region say that, given peace with Morocco, the new state could be a success in every way.

It may not be given the opportunity, since Morocco has made major investments in Western Sahara. By 1986, $650 million had been spent on development in housing, roads, ports, airports, education, health and commerce. The economy is increasingly integrated with that of Morocco and the region is administered from the southern Moroccan town of Gwilimin. The war against Polisario costs Morocco up to $700 million annually, though much of this expense is covered by aid from the US, Saudi Arabia and France. It seemed unlikely, in 1990, that Morocco, having spent so much, would withdraw and leave Western Sahara to the Sahrawis, despite the UN and *OAU resolution for a referendum in the territory.

Wit Kommando (White Commando), extremist group of white terrorists who became active in South Africa in 1980–1. It has been responsible for the intimidation and murder of blacks and of whites opposed to rigid *APARTHEID. There are fears that groups like the Wit Kommando will lead to a white backlash against the proposed reforms of President *DE KLERK.

Y

Yacine, (Kateb) (1929–89), leading Algerian author, playwright and theatrical presenter. Born in Constantine, Algeria, Yacine went to school until the age of fifteen when he took part in the first colonial demonstration at Setif in 1945. Expelled from school, he was sent to prison where he narrowly escaped being shot by a French firing squad. On leaving prison, he chose a wandering life and devoted himself to literature. His first published work was a collection of poetry entitled *Soliloques*, published in 1946. He joined the Algerian Communist Party and became a reporter on the party newspaper. His first novel, *Nedjma*, published in 1956, is considered to be a landmark in Algerian Francophone fiction. It concerns social injustice and the evils of colonialism. His only other novel is *Le polygone étoile*, 1966. He wrote several plays, of which the best known are *L'homme aux sandales*, which deals with the war in Vietnam, and *Muhammad prend sa valise*, which concerns the plight of migrant workers in European cities. In 1975 Yacine brought together a company of players, as a collective enterprise. In songs and readings, the company spoke of Algeria and the dire plight of various groups, especially women. In effect, Yacine presented a new language or oral poetry. In 1977 the fundamentalist Muslim Brothers prevented him from staging *Muhammad prend sa valise* in Algiers but by the mid-1980s Yacine was the most influential voice in Algeria for liberalism and equality.

Yameogo, Maurice (b. 1921), first president of Upper Volta, later Burkina Faso. A member of the Mossi tribe, Yameogo was educated at Koranic schools, then at a commercial college. Becoming a civil servant in Ouagadougou, he was elected to the territorial assembly in 1946 and to the Grand Council of French West Africa in 1948. In opposition to the French, in 1957 he founded the Mouvement Démocratique Voltaique. His first ministerial post was as minister of agriculture in 1957 and a year later he was minister of the interior. When independence was proclaimed on 5 August 1960, Yameogo became president of the new republic and in October 1965 he was re-elected with ninety-nine per cent of the votes. He had become increasingly autocratic and was responsible for the country's disastrous economic maladministration. His final mistake was to ban the more progressive parties. This led to a popular uprising, on 3 January 1966, which brought to power Lt.-Col. Sangoule *LAMIZANA. Yameogo was imprisoned for embezzling £1.2 million of public money. Released by amnesty in 1970, he went into exile in the Ivory Coast.

Yapwantha, Edward, leading Malawian dissident who has led the

*MALAWI FREEDOM MOVEMENT since 1983.

Youlou, Abbe Fulbert (1917–72), a controversial politician who led the Congo to independence in 1960. He was a Roman Catholic priest who entered politics as an independent. He was suspended by the church in 1956, the year in which he founded a political party (Union Démocratique pour la Défense des Intérêts Africains). The party won exactly half the seats in the 1957 Territorial Assembly elections and Youlou became Prime Minister of the Congo Republic in November 1958.

As president in the first years of independence (1960–3), he was a controversial figure who greatly increased his presidential powers by amending the constitution (1961) and infuriated the radicals with pro-Western policies; they accused him of neo-colonialism. In 1963 angry crowds surrounded the presidential palace and forced him to resign. After two years in a military camp he escaped to take refuge with *TSHOMBE (1965). After Tshombe's death Youlou went into exile in Spain, and died there.

Z

Zaire, the Republic of Zaire straddles the Equator in central Africa. This vast country of 2.3 million square kilometres is bordered by Sudan on the north-east, Uganda, Rwanda, Burundi and Tanzania on the east, Zambia on the south-east and south, Angola on the south and south-west, the Congo on the west and the Central African Republic on the north. On the west Zaire has limited access to the Atlantic Ocean through a narrow corridor north of the River Zaire estuary. The Zaire River is navigable for 240 km. from the Atlantic to the port of Matadi. Much of the west and centre of Zaire is drained by the Zaire River. In the east lie mountains and lakes and much of Zaire's fertile land; in the southern province of *SHABA there are plateaux and savannahs. The climate is generally hot and humid, but cooler in the higher areas of the east and south-east than in the Zaire River basin.

The people of Zaire are divided into about two hundred different ethnic groups, many of them crossing the political boundaries into neighbouring states. Most are *BANTU speaking, but others are linked to the Sudanese, Nilotic, Pygmy and Hamitic peoples.

Zaire has rich natural resources. Heavy rain has leached nutrients out of the soil in some parts, but in other parts there is a good climate for agriculture. About eighty per cent of the population works in agriculture, mostly as subsistence farmers growing cassava, rice, maize and plantains. The country was self-sufficient in food, but has been unable to feed itself since independence. A rapidly rising population, political and economic upheavals, poor transport and marketing facilities have made Zaire partly dependent on food aid and costly imports. Since President *MOBUTU made agriculture a priority in the 1977 financial reforms and the 1986–90 development plan, agricultural production has grown even though self-sufficiency cannot be achieved for many years.

The production of coffee, by far the most lucrative cash crop, increased during the 1980s, but efforts to increase exports of palm products, rubber, cotton and other cash crops have been less successful. The government realized the great commercial potential of the forests and during the 1980s began encouraging logging for domestic consumption and export.

Zaire's rich mineral resources account for over eighty per cent of export earnings. Except for the diamond mines in Kasai Oriental, the country's most lucrative mines are in Shaba province. The state-owned La Générale des Carrières et des Mines (GÉCAMINES) controls all the cobalt and ninety per cent of the copper mining, but there are many difficulties in Shaba. Political upheavals and rebel activities make it

The Republic of Zaire

THE COUNTRY	THE PEOPLE	THE STATE
2,344,885 sq. km.	32,655,000	Single-party republic
Major Cities	*Ethnic Groups*	*Head of State*
Kinshasa (capital)	200 Bantu groups	President Mobutu Sese
Kananga		Seko
Lubumbashi	*Languages*	
Mbuji-Mayi	French (official)	*Ruling Bodies*
Kisangani	Swahili	National Executive
	Tshiluba	Council
		National Security Council
Economy		National Legislative
Mining	*Religion*	Council
Farming	Christian	
	Islam	
Principal Exports	Traditional beliefs	*Official Party*
Copper		Mouvement populaire de
Crude oil		la révolution
Cobalt		
Coffee		
Diamonds		
Zinc		
Currency		
Zaire of 100 makuta		

hard and expensive to recruit expert staff. Transport problems have hindered both the import of machinery and spare parts and the export of minerals, but the situation could improve if and when the Angolan conflict is finally resolved and the *BENGUELA railway becomes fully operational again.

Copper accounts for 38 per cent of export earnings and cobalt for 12 per cent. Zaire is the world's largest producer of industrial diamonds and it also produces gem diamonds – both substantial export earners. More gems have been produced since private syndicates were

allowed to mine. During the 1980s crude petroleum from near the Zaire estuary became an important export. Zaire has various industries producing for local consumption; most work below capacity because of transport difficulties, the lack of foreign exchange and slack domestic demand.

For long-term economic development Zaire needs to develop and improve both its resources of transport and the provision of energy. The Zaire and Kasai rivers and their tributaries are vital links connecting with an extensive system of low-quality roads and about

4750 km. of railway lines. Transport in such a vast country with limited access to the sea is difficult and forty per cent of its mineral exports still go on the expensive route through South Africa; the rest goes through Matadi or Dar es Salaam. If the government's transport rehabilitation scheme (begun in 1989) succeeds and if the Benguela railway to the port of Lobito becomes fully operational Zaire's transport problems will be eased; it will be less dependent on South Africa for links with the outside world. With major petroleum reserves, vast deposits of coal and the great potential of the Zaire River for hydroelectric power Zaire has the potential to become a major producer of energy.

Little is known of the early history of Zaire. From time immemorial pygmies and other hunter–gatherers lived in the heavily forested areas while farming and fishing communities settled by the rivers and the edges of the forest. From the tenth to the fourteenth century waves of Bantu immigrants arrived from the north and west and built up states. When they reached the mouth of the Congo River (1482) Portuguese explorers found the well established kingdom of Kongo. Later explorers encountered a number of semi-feudal kingdoms in the interior. From 1876 to 1885 King Léopold II of Belgium acquired the country, then known as the Congo Free State. His ruthless exploitation of the resources of the country and the atrocities committed in the collection of rubber led to widespread international condemnation. Léopold was persuaded to hand the colony over to the Belgian government (1908).

Belgium governed the *BELGIAN CONGO through customary authorities, by indirect rule. Education was left to Roman Catholic missionaries who concentrated on primary education and the education of those who might become priests. Yet, a small group of educated people known as the évolués emerged. Refused the same status as Belgians, these évolués became the first leaders of those cultural and nationalist movements pressing for independence in the 1950s. The *MNC (Mouvement national congolais), founded by Patrice *LUMUMBA, had substantial support in four of the six provinces and could claim to be a national movement; others were mainly ethnic or regional.

After riots in Léopoldville (now Kinshasa) in January 1959 the country moved to independence with surprising speed. Elections were followed by a Round Table Conference in Brussels and the Republic of the Congo was proclaimed (30 Jun. 1960) with Lumumba prime minister and Joseph *KASAVUBU president. Within a few days the army mutinied, most of the remaining Belgians fled the country and with the support of Belgian mining interests Moise *TSHOMBE declared the secession of Katanga (now Shaba). Belgian troops intervened and Lumumba asked the United Nations for help. The crisis was intensified by a dispute between

381

Prime Minister Lumumba and President Kasavubu. Colonel Mobutu and the army staged their first coup (Sep. 1960) and suspended the constitution.

After the murder of Lumumba (Jan. 1961) his followers proclaimed a provisional government in the east; this gave way to a government of national unity formed under Cyrille *ADOULA (Aug. 1961). With United Nations assistance the Katanga secession was defeated (Jan. 1963) and the country reunited. During 1964 a new federal constitution was drafted. Challenged by renewed rebellions and secessionist movements, President Kasavubu turned to Tshombe for help and appointed him prime minister. With help from mercenaries and Belgian paratroopers the rebellions were crushed early in 1965. Elections in 1965 gave the coalition led by Tshombe over seventy per cent of the seats in the new parliament, but President Kasavubu dismissed Tshombe and called on Evariste *KIMBA to form a government. When Kimba failed to secure a parliamentary majority there was a constitutional deadlock which was only resolved by Mobutu's second military coup (Nov. 1965). All executive powers were transferred to Mobutu as head of state of the Second Republic.

From 1965 to 1970 Mobutu strengthened his authority. Political opponents were exiled or imprisoned or executed. In April 1966 Mobutu founded his own political organization, the *MPR (Mouvement

Populaire de la Révolution); this became increasingly powerful as Zaire's only legal party from May 1967. Mobutu assumed legislative, executive and administrative powers. The 1967 presidential constitution was approved by 98 per cent of the voters, but the presidential election was delayed until 1970 when Mobutu, the only candidate, reached the age of forty – the minimum age for the presidency. In 1970 the MPR became the supreme political body. In 1971 Mobutu proclaimed his policy of authenticity, changing the country's name from Congo to Zaire and encouraging the adoption of Zairean style names and apparel. From 1973–4 he intensified the Zaireanization of the economy, but only disrupted industry and agriculture without transferring it to efficient Zairean control.

Zaire's economy deteriorated even more in the 1980s with large annual balance of payments deficits and an international debt which reached an estimated $6900 million in 1988. Inflation has been high and the zaire has been heavily devalued. The 1986–90 development plan, supported by the International Monetary Fund, is intended to give Zaire steady growth, an improved infrastructure and a greater productive capacity. The targets of the 1987–90 adjustment programme, supported by the World Bank, are lower balance of payments deficits, lower inflation and increased investment. By 1988 these programmes were encountering great difficulties.

Zaire's relations with its neighbours have been tense. There were particular problems with Angola when Zaire was sheltering the *FNLA, one of the movements challenging the *MPLA government of Angola. During the Shaba crisis (1977–9) rebels supported by Angola invaded and seriously threatened the Mobutu regime. Only with help from Morocco, France and Belgium was the Zairean army able to beat off this challenge. Zaire has also accused Tanzania of supporting Zairean rebels (1984). Zambian allegations that Zaire was helping the United States to supply weapons to *UNITA rebels in Angola (1986) caused tension with Zambia. Islamic countries have objected to Zaire's recognition of Israel (1982). Zaire also suspended its membership of the *ORGANIZATION OF AFRICAN UNITY (1984–6) over the issue of Western Sahara.

The regime has come under mounting international criticism for its authoritarianism and its ruthless suppression of opposition. Amnesty International has drawn attention to its abuses of human rights. Attention has also been focused on corruption and President Mobutu's vast personal fortune. Late in 1988 criticisms of Mobutu's government in the Belgian Press led to a bitter dispute between the two countries. Nevertheless Western countries like France and the United States see Zaire as a useful strategic ally in central Africa and a potentially valuable trading partner. In 1989 Zaire's efforts to mediate in the Angolan conflict seemed close to success, which further enhanced its status as a valuable ally of the West in the heart of Africa – even though the cease-fire was shortlived. There was great indignation at the murder of about fifty university students in 1990; there have been riots and protests and pressure for reform from the United States. In May 1990 President Mobutu promised reforms and appointed a cabinet to preside over a one-year transition to multi-party democracy.

Zambia, the Republic of, formerly the British colony of Northern Rhodesia, is a member of the Commonwealth. It is a land-locked country situated in south central Africa between the Tropic of Capricorn and the Equator. Much of the country is a high plateau of tropical grassland from 1000 to 1400 metres above sea level, which moderates the climate. In the north-east the Muchinga Mountains rise to over 2000 metres. Zambia is bordered by Tanzania on the north and north-east, Malawi and Mozambique on the east, Zimbabwe, Botswana and the *CAPRIVI STRIP (Namibia) on the south, Angola on the west and Zaire on the north. Since independence Zambia has been troubled by the problems of neigh- bouring countries, problems which have eased since the independence of Mozambique (1975), Angola (1975) and Zimbabwe (1980). More recently the independence of Namibia (1990), progress towards settling the Angolan civil war and signs of a more liberal policy in South

The Republic of Zambia

THE COUNTRY	THE PEOPLE	THE STATE
752,614 sq. km.	7,196,000	Single-party republic
Major Cities	*Ethnic Groups*	*Head of State*
Lusaka (capital)	Bemba	President Kaunda
Kitwe	Nyanja	
Ndola	Tonga	*Ruling Bodies*
Mufulira	Lozi	Cabinet
Kabwe		National Assembly
Chingola	*Languages*	House of Chiefs
	English (official)	
Economy	Bemba	*Official Party*
Farming	Nyanja	United National
Mining	Tonga	Independence Party
	Lozi	
Principal Exports		
Copper	*Religion*	
Cobalt	Christian	
	Islam	
Currency	Traditional beliefs	
Kwacha (K) of 100		
ngwee		

Africa (1989–90) have made the outlook for Zambia a little brighter.

Most of the population is descended from *BANTU herdsmen and farmers who came in waves from the ninth to the nineteenth centuries and soon dominated the original Stone Age peoples. Some, like the Lozi, the Lunda and the Bemba established highly organized states; others, like the Tonga, remained stateless. There are seventy-three ethnic groups in Zambia; the Bemba (with a third of the population) is the most numerous group. Other large groups are the Nyanja, the Tonga and the Lozi.

Over two thirds of the economically active population is engaged in agriculture. Most are traditional subsistence farmers growing maize, cassava, millet, sorghum, beans and tobacco for local consumption. Although the government has helped small and medium scale farmers to produce more and to diversify, half the output still comes from about five hundred large farms run by expatriates. Zambia is not self-sufficient in food, but since Operation Food Production was launched (1980) there has been progress – interrupted only by drought in 1982; there is reason to hope Zambia will become self-sufficient in food in the 1990s.

Copper is the mainstay of the Zambian economy, accounting for about ninety-five per cent of export earnings in 1986. Cobalt, zinc, lead, emeralds, amethysts and coal are also mined. For the last two decades copper mining has had its problems, including a shortage of foreign currency for spare parts and new machinery, a shortage of skilled staff and depressed world copper prices, which have made some mines unprofitable. Most of the copper will be exhausted early in the twenty-first century; it is therefore vital for the government to succeed in its efforts to diversify the economy. The government plays a commanding role in industry through state-owned companies which have majority interests in mining and other commercial and industrial concerns. During the prosperous decade after independence the government took advantage of high copper prices and invested in industry. Despite the dislocation caused by *UDI in Rhodesia (1965) new industries were established and manufacturing expanded until copper prices fell sharply in 1975. Foreign exchange was in short supply and the boom ended. Zambia had to turn to the International Monetary Fund (IMF) for credit. As the crisis continued new plans were announced (1977) to lessen dependence on copper, to increase agricultural production, to reorganize state-owned companies, to encourage investment and to cut government spending savagely.

Economic problems persisted in the 1980s as growth fell and inflation and international debt rose. The Zambian kwacha was devalued and nearly collapsed after the introduction of the auction system (Oct. 1985); those who needed foreign currency had to bid for it in weekly auctions. The scheme had to be suspended and reorganized. Zambia imposed austerity to get financial help from the IMF while restructuring the economy, but austerity is very unpopular. In particular the removal of the subsidy on maize meal (Dec. 1986) led to violent riots in the *COPPERBELT which only stopped when the subsidy was restored. In May 1987 the government discarded the IMF economic recovery plan and instituted its own plan. There is no evidence that this has worked well and during 1989 it was clear that Zambia still needed international help for its economic restructuring.

Transport difficulties still hinder economic development, although progress has been made since the colonial period when Zambia was linked to the South African transport network. Despite its strong support for the efforts of the *SOUTHERN AFRICAN DEVELOPMENT CO-ORDINATION CONFERENCE to reduce dependence on South Africa, Zambia still relies on South Africa for some of its links with the outside world. The closure of the border with Zimbabwe (then Rhodesia) in the 1970s caused serious problems which were alleviated by the opening of the *TANZAM railway in 1975 to the Tanzanian port of Dar es Salaam (1840 km. away), but the limited capacity of the railway and the port is limited.

ZAMBIA

The *BENGUELA railway connecting the Copperbelt to the Atlantic port of Lobito has been disrupted by the Angolan conflict, but it may soon function regularly again. In the 1980s the reopening of the border with Zimbabwe and improvements in the Great North Road to Tanzania and the Great East Road to Malawi eased transport problems.

In its plans for economic recovery Zambia has the benefit of abundant energy supplies. The *KARIBA DAM and the Kafue Gorge hydroelectric scheme provide Zambia with surplus electricity for export; since Zimbabwe stopped importing Zambian electricity (1987) Zaire has been the main customer. Zambia has good supplies of coal which it began mining in 1965. In the early 1980s coal production declined but there are hopes that the economic recovery programme will boost output.

The success of the copper mines and other industries under the British protectorate gave the whites of Northern Rhodesia a high standard of living, but the African workers gained little. In 1949 mineworkers formed the African Mineworkers' Union and won large wage increases after striking in 1952. At the same time, Africans organized politically in the Northern Rhodesian African Congress (1948), led by Harry *NKUMBULA and renamed the *AFRICAN NATIONAL CONGRESS (ANC) in 1951. The ANC campaigned in vain against the *CENTRAL AFRICAN FEDERATION (CAF) which was mainly for the benefit of the whites in the federation and did little to improve the lives of the Africans of Northern Rhodesia despite the continuing copper boom. The ANC split when Nkumbula was prepared to co-operate in the 1958 federal elections. Young radicals under the leadership of Kenneth *KAUNDA founded *UNIP (United Nations Independence Party) to campaign for the end of the federation and independence.

UNIP's massive civil disobedience campaign (1962) was partly responsible for the dissolution of the federation at the end of 1963. UNIP won the pre-independence elections early in 1964, but it had to overcome various problems before independence (Oct. 1964). The traditional rulers of Barotseland were reluctant to accept the new government and there was a rebellion by the followers of the *LUMPA CHURCH (1964).

After independence Zambia's support for nationalist movements in Rhodesia (now Zimbabwe) and the Portuguese ruled colonies of Angola and Mozambique made it an obvious target for attacks by forces from the white-ruled states of southern Africa. The closure of the border with Rhodesia (1973) put a severe economic strain on Zambia.

By the end of the 1960s UNIP had lost support in much of the south and west of Zambia; in 1971 Simon *KAPEPWE left UNIP to found his own party which gained popular support as economic problems grew worse. Late in 1972 Kaunda strengthened his authority by making Zambia a one-party state. At the end of 1975 UNIP was given the power to formulate policy.

During the 1980s there were a number of challenges to the government's authority. There was an attempted coup in October 1980 and there were riots in early 1981 after Kaunda suspended prominent trade-unionists from UNIP. Measures of austerity provoked riots at Lusaka University early in 1984 and strikes early in 1985. There have been further riots and strikes in protests against austerity measures. In 1987 arrests were made after allegations that a coup was being prepared.

Despite economic difficulties and social and political unrest Zambia has been influential internationally as a leading member of the Commonwealth and a Third World spokesman. It is an important regional power; as a *FRONT LINE STATE and a member of the SADCC it has been in the forefront of the battles against white minority rule in southern Africa. Zambia supported Joshua *NKOMO and *ZAPU in the struggle against the white minority Rhodesian regime. It helped persuade the *CONTACT GROUP to accept the United Nations plan for Namibian independence. It incurred the wrath of South Africa for supporting the *AFRICAN NATIONAL CONGRESS in the struggle against *APARTHEID and for its success in campaigning for international sanctions against South Africa. Consequently South Africa has launched a number of attacks on Zambia and has tried to destabilize the Zambian government; more recently, however, South Africa

has been willing to negotiate with Zambia.

There have been manifestations of discontent in Zambia, most recently the riots in June 1990 which were prompted by rises in food prices and demands to end one-party rule. In the same month an attempted coup was speedily crushed. During 1990 it was announced that there would be a referendum to consult the voters on whether they wanted to have a multi-party system or not; the referendum was postponed until 1991. Zambia has been stable since independence and has overcome the problems posed by its neighbours, notably the white minority Rhodesian regime and a hostile South Africa. It has also been hit hard by the sharp decline in world copper prices. Nevertheless, there is good reason to predict that Zambia will overcome many of its difficulties and build a better life for its people.

ZANLA (Zimbabwe African National Liberation Army), *ZANU's military wing which eventually defeated the white minority government of Zimbabwe (then Rhodesia). Its first guerrillas were trained in China (1963). Operating from Zambia, it launched the second *CHIMURENGA (war of liberation) at the Battle of Chinhoyi (Sinoia) in April 1966. From 1972 ZANLA shifted its activities to Mozambique and forged close links with the *FRELIMO guerrillas. After Mozambique became independent (Jun. 1975) ZANLA received valuable help from the FRELIMO government. ZANLA guerrilla incursions from its bases in Mozambique were the major factor in the achievement of Zimbabwean independence. At independence ZANLA merged with *ZIPRA and the Rhodesian Army to form the Zimbabwean Army.

ZANU (Zimbabwe African National Union), leading Zimbabwean political party which was formed on 8 August 1963 under the leadership of Ndabaningi *SITHOLE and joined by Robert *MUGABE and other *ZAPU dissidents. Soon banned by the government of Southern Rhodesia, it set up *ZANLA (its military wing) which began the war of independence in 1966 and bore the brunt of the fighting. In 1976 it combined with ZAPU to form the *PF (Patriotic Front). In 1977 Mugabe replaced Sithole as leader. The PF attended the talks which led to the *LANCASTER HOUSE agreement (Dec. 1979), but its two parties contested the 1980 pre-independence elections separately. ZANU campaigned as *ZANU (PF).

ZANU (PF), originally *ZANU which was founded in 1963. ZANU (PF) has dominated the government of Zimbabwe since its convincing victory in the 1980 pre-independence elections and its greater success in the 1985 elections. President *MUGABE, its First Secretary, heads both the Politburo which is responsible for policy and the Central Committee which is elected by the party congress. The party is committed to socialist policies and aims to make Zimbabwe a one-party state. In the 1987 unity pact it was agreed that ZANU (PF) would absorb *ZAPU. After an overwhelming victory in the March 1990 elections, it is expected that ZANU (PF) will become Zimbabwe's only legal political party.

Zanzibar, the islands of Zanzibar, Pemba and Latham which merged with Tanganyika to form Tanzania in 1964. At the beginning of the Christian era Zanzibar was controlled by the rulers of south-west Arabia. During the sixteenth century Portuguese influence was strong, but by the seventeenth century power in the region was passing to the Turks and the Arabs from Oman. The Sultan of Muscat and Oman moved his capital to Zanzibar (1832) and by 1860 Zanzibar, now independent of Muscat and Oman, was a thriving centre for trade in slaves and ivory. Britain declared a protectorate over the Sultanate of Zanzibar (1890). In 1960 there was responsible government, followed by internal self-government and full independence under the Sultan as head of state (Dec. 1963). After a month the government which represented the interests of the Arab ruling classes was overthrown. A period of confusion followed before Abeid *KARUME and the *AFRO-SHIRAZI PARTY formed a Revolutionary Council and took control. Shortly afterwards Zanzibar merged with Tanganyika to form the union of Tanzania (Apr. 1964), a union which left Zanzibar with a considerable degree of autonomy. See *TANZANIA.

ZAPU (Zimbabwe African People's Union), Zimbabwean nationalist party founded by Joshua *NKOMO (1962) following the banning of the NDP. ZAPU was banned a few months after its foundation. In 1963 dissidents left ZAPU to form *ZANU. After *UDI (Nov. 1965) ZAPU established its military wing – *ZIPRA – to fight white minority rule in Rhodesia, basing its forces mostly in Zambia where it had the support of President *KAUNDA. It negotiated and failed to reach agreement with Ian *SMITH's Rhodesian government (1975–6).

In 1976 under pressure from the *FRONT LINE STATES and the *ORGANIZATION OF AFRICAN UNITY ZAPU combined with ZANU to form the *PF (Patriotic Front) to fight for the freedom of Zimbabwe. After the *LANCASTER HOUSE AGREEMENT ended white minority rule, the two parties contested the 1980 pre-independence elections separately; ZAPU fought as the PF and won only twenty seats. It was the junior partner in coalition with ZANU (PF) until 1982 when *MUGABE sacked Nkomo and other members of ZAPU from the government. In 1987 in a pact of unity ZAPU agreed to merge with ZANU (PF).

Zimbabwe, a member of the Commonwealth, the Republic of Zimbabwe is a land-locked state in south central Africa, between the Tropic of Capricorn and the Equator. To the north and the east it is bounded by Mozambique, across the Limpopo River to the south by the Republic of South Africa, to the south and the west by Botswana and across the Zambezi River to the north and the north-west by Zambia. Much of the country consists of high plateaux over 1200 metres above sea level; the land gradually slopes down to below 900 metres in the Zambezi basin in the north and north-west and in the Limpopo and Sabi-Lundi basins in the south and the south-east. The eastern highlands near the Mozambican border include Zimbabwe's highest mountain – the Inganyani at 2594 metres. In much of the country the high altitude moderates the climate.

Most Zimbabweans belong to two major *BANTU groups, the Shona (Mashona) with 80 per cent and the Ndebele (or Matabele) with 20 per cent of the population; 1–2 per cent of the population is of European or Asian descent and there are various small ethnic groups.

Excluding South Africa, Zimbabwe has the most developed and diversified economy of any African country south of the Sahara. There is a rough balance between the three major sectors of the economy – agriculture, mining and manufacturing.

Agriculture has recovered well from the damage done during the 1970s at the height of the struggle for independence. Most Zimbabweans are still subsistence farmers, producing maize, wheat, millet, sorghum and barley for domestic consumption, but agriculture is also a vital export industry. The principal cash crops are tobacco, cotton and sugar; despite fluctuating world prices these are important earners of foreign currency. In 1987 tobacco accounted for 17.9 per cent and cotton for 5.1 per cent of all export earnings. When the rains are good

The Republic of Zimbabwe

THE COUNTRY	THE PEOPLE	THE STATE
390,759 sq. km.	9,001,000	Multi-party republic

THE COUNTRY
390,759 sq. km.

Major Cities
Harare (capital)
Bulawayo
Chitungwiza
Gweru
Mutare

Economy
Farming
Mining
Manufacturing

Principal Exports
Tobacco
Manufactures
Cotton
Sugar
Livestock products

Currency
Zimbabwe dollar (Z$) of
100 cents

THE PEOPLE
9,001,000

Ethnic Groups
Shona
Ndebele
Europeans

Languages
English (official)
Shona & Ndebele

Religion
Christian
Traditional

THE STATE
Multi-party republic

Head of State
President Mugabe

Ruling Bodies
Presidential Cabinet
House of Assembly
Senate

Ruling Party
ZANU-PF

Opposition Parties
Zimbabwe Unity
Movement
Conservative Alliance of
Zimbabwe

there is surplus maize for export. Ranching is an important part of the agricultural economy and produces beef for export.

Zimbabwe has rich and varied deposits of over forty different minerals. In 1987 gold accounted for 18.6 per cent of foreign earnings; altogether gold and other important minerals (asbestos, nickel, coal, copper, iron ore and chromite) accounted for about 40 per cent. Both the public and the private sectors are developing the country's mineral resources. The major government bodies are the Zimbabwe Mining Development Corporation and the Minerals Marketing Board; major private companies include such international concerns as the *ANGLO AMERICAN CORPORATION, Rio–Tinto–Zinc and Lonrho.

During the sanctions imposed during the years of *UDI (Unilateral Declaration of Independence) from 1965 to 1980, Zimbabwe built up a strong manufacturing sector which meets local needs and now exports to neighbouring countries. Yet, sometimes there are shortages of commodities and goods. Currency controls have restricted expansion by keeping industry short of the money for new machinery, spare parts and raw materials. Generally Zimbabwe's balance of trade has been healthy since the middle of the 1980s – with small surpluses in 1986 and 1987.

There are transport difficulties. Despite the serious political differences between the two countries, Zimbabwe still has to rely heavily on transport links to the sea through South Africa. Her other major access to the sea through Mozambique to the port of Beira has been seriously disrupted by *RENAMO which has often closed rail and road links as well as the oil pipeline from Beira to Zimbabwe. Zimbabwe has also had to import electricity from Zambia, but as the Hwange power station is improved and as the power station on its side of the *KARIBA DAM is expanded Zimbabwe should be able to meet its electricity needs. Zimbabwe has ample coal reserves, but there have been recent problems in its coalmines.

The early inhabitants of Zimbabwe were *SAN (or Bushmen), hunters and gatherers who were displaced by Bantu farmers who began arriving in the country about 1500 years ago. Over a thousand years ago the Shona began moving into the country. They established the powerful Mwene Mutapa Empire which from its capital at *GREAT ZIMBABWE dominated the area from the thirteenth to the sixteenth centuries and controlled the lucrative trade with the east coast of Africa. By the seventeenth and eighteenth

centuries a second Shona empire, the Rozwi, had risen. In turn the Rozwi empire fell in the first half of the nineteenth century to the Ndebele who had come from the south and who dominated Zimbabwe until the arrival of the first European settlers late in the nineteenth century.

In 1888 Lobengula, the Ndebele ruler, signed the Rudd Concession giving mineral rights to representatives of Cecil Rhodes who formed the British South Africa Company and secured a royal charter (1889). In 1890 the company sent the Pioneer Column of 200 settlers and 500 paramilitary to establish a settlement in Salisbury (now Harare). In 1894 the country was named Rhodesia in honour of Cecil Rhodes. The Ndebele in 1893 and 1896 and the Shona in 1896–7 resisted the settlers in the first *CHIMURENGA (war of liberation), but white supremacy was firmly established by 1897. The British South Africa Company encouraged white settlement and ran Southern Rhodesia until 1923 when it became a self-governing colony after the 1922 referendum. The dominant white settlers further strengthened their position with the Land Apportionment Act (1930) which gave the small European minority the best farming land, and with the Industrial Conciliation Act (1934) which barred Africans from skilled employment.

By the 1940s and the 1950s some moderate white leaders were prepared to make limited concessions to encourage economic growth and to gain the support of a small middle

391

class African elite. They argued for a limited multi-racial partnership in a federation of Southern Rhodesia with Northern Rhodesia (now Zambia) and Nyasaland (now Malawi). The outcome was the *CENTRAL AFRICAN FEDERATION (1953–63), which was opposed both by outright white supremacists and also by African leaders who rejected this partnership as a sham and campaigned for a non-racial democracy based on the principle of 'one man, one vote'.

Leading the nationalist campaign against white rule was the *AFRICAN NATIONAL CONGRESS (ANC) which was reorganized by Joshua *NKOMO (1957). Banned in 1959, it became the *NDP (National Democratic Party) in 1960. When the NDP was banned (1961) it was succeeded by *ZAPU (Zimbabwe African People's Union) in 1962. ZAPU and *ZANU (a group that had broken with ZAPU in 1963) were both banned in 1963. While the nationalist campaign gathered strength in the early 1960s white attitudes were hardening; the *RHODESIAN FRONT PARTY which opposed concessions to the blacks won the 1962 elections and took power. After the dissolution of the Central African Federation at the end of 1963, Malawi and Zambia prepared for majority rule; but Britain would not grant independence to Southern Rhodesia until its white government accepted the principle of majority rule (no independence before majority rule – *NIBMAR).

Negotiations broke down and Ian *SMITH, the Rhodesian Prime Minister, proclaimed UDI (Nov. 1965).

Britain and most of the international community regarded the Smith government as illegal and imposed sanctions, but the greatest pressure on the regime came from the second chimurenga (war of liberation) which began when *ZANLA fought the Rhodesian forces at the Battle of Chinhoyi (Sinoia) in April 1966; by the mid-1970s the guerrilla forces based in Mozambique were seriously weakening the Smith regime. In 1978 the Rhodesian government made the so-called internal settlement with some African groups; this led to the formation of Bishop *MUZOREWA's government in 1979.

By late 1979 the regime admitted defeat; it renounced UDI and accepted the *LANCASTER HOUSE AGREEMENT (Dec. 1979), which provided for a cease-fire and for Britain to supervise a rapid transition to independence under African majority rule. The constitution reserved twenty of the hundred parliamentary seats for the white voters for seven years and included a number of clauses entrenched for ten years from the date of independence. Robert *MUGABE, leader of ZANU since 1977, won a convincing majority in the pre-independence elections and became the first prime minister of Zimbabwe (Apr. 1980).

After the bitterness of the fight for independence, Zimbabwe's first decade of independence has been generally successful. It has one of the most successful African economies, even though the poorer people have been disappointed in their hopes for a high standard of living. The government has worked hard to achieve national reconciliation, with success in the case of the white minority which has been treated with respect. Many whites have stayed on to make an important contribution to Zimbabwe.

There have been serious problems with the minority Ndebele who are based in Matabeleland. At independence Nkomo and some of his supporters joined the cabinet, but early in 1982 he was sacked by Mugabe. Nkomo returned to Matabeleland and accused Mugabe of trying to overthrow the constitution; during 1982 and 1983 there was violence and terror in Matabeleland, made worse by drought and hunger. Mugabe sent in the *FIFTH BRIGADE, which was blamed for killing innocent civilians as it restored order. Late in 1987 the unity agreement came as an important step towards reconciliation and the creation of a one-party state; it announced that ZAPU was merging with ZANU (PF). Early in 1988 Nkomo rejoined the cabinet and in May 1988 an amnesty was granted to Matabeleland dissidents. After the 1990 elections it was announced that Nkomo would become a vice-president.

Other political changes have included the abolition of the reserved seats for white voters (Sep. 1987), which had been protected for seven years by the Lancaster House Agreement. Then the constitution was amended to give Zimbabwe an executive presidency and Mugabe was sworn in as the first executive president at the end of 1987. During 1989 the government's reputation was tarnished for a number of reasons. There were revelations of widespread corruption and a number of cabinet ministers were disgraced. There were doubts about the government's commitment to human rights following allegations of torture by Africa Watch and criticisms of the repeated extensions of the state of emergency first imposed by the Smith government. Little respect for political freedom was shown as Zimbabwe prepared for the March 1990 general election. Attempts were made to intimidate and crush Edgar *TEKERE's new political party, the *ZIMBABWE UNITY MOVEMENT. President Mugabe and ZANU (PF) won an overwhelming victory in the election. It was believed that Mugabe would regard this victory as a mandate for the creation of a one-party state, but this has been rejected by both the Politburo and the Central Committee of ZANU (PF).

In external affairs during the 1980s Zimbabwe established itself as an important and respected member of the Commonwealth and the Third World grouping of states. Despite its avowed state socialism the government has tackled economic and social problems with pragmatism. Many of the country's problems have stemmed from its neighbours. Zimbabwe has been directly affected by the civil war in Mozambique where Renamo has disrupted Zimbabwe's communication with the coast and caused turbulence in border areas; Zimbabwe has joined the Mozambican government in its efforts to defeat Renamo.

South Africa has been the most difficult neighbour, strongly resenting Zimbabwe's campaign against *APARTHEID and its support for the efforts of the *SOUTHERN AFRICAN DEVELOPMENT CO-ORDINATION CONFERENCE to reduce the region's dependence on South Africa. Zimbabwe has found it impossible to sever its transport and economic links with South Africa, which until the late 1980s did its best to destabilize both the Zimbabwean economy and its government. There are signs that the more liberal government of President *DE KLERK is prepared to co-operate with Zimbabwe and its other neighbours. If regional peace can be secured and there is a peaceful transition to a non-racial South African democracy, the 1990s could be a decade of success and prosperity for Zimbabwe.

Zimbabwe Unity Movement (ZUM), political party founded in Zimbabwe by Edgar *TEKERE in 1989. It has challenged the domination of the country by *ZANU (PF) and the ideas of African socialism. It favours a market economy and a drive against corruption and mismanagement by the government. ZUM did badly in its first by-election. During the campaign for the March 1990 elections it was endorsed by the *CONSERVATIVE ALLIANCE OF ZIMBABWE. ZUM

blamed government intimidation for its poor showing in the election. Tekere won about a fifth of the votes in the presidential contest and the party won two seats in parliament.

ZIPRA (Zimbabwe People's Revolutionary Army), military wing of *ZAPU which began preparing for the war of independence in 1965. Based in Zambia, it had considerable support from the Soviet bloc. It was not noticeably successful in the armed struggle and there were accusations that it was deliberately allowing *ZANLA to bear the brunt of the fighting. After independence in 1980 it became part of the Zimbabwean Army, although some of its members took to the bush and opposed the government in the early 1980s.

Zulu, The Rt. Revd Alphaeus (*c.* 1905–88), the first black diocesan bishop in Southern Africa, much admired for his integrity and efficiency. He served the Anglican Church as curate, vicar and assistant bishop before his elevation to the see of Zululand (1966). After retiring from the diocese (1976) he served as Speaker of the KwaZulu Legislative Council until he retired in 1987.

Zwane, Dr Ambrose Phesheya (b. 1924), Swazi politician exiled in Mozambique. He practised medicine before entering politics as a founding member of the Swaziland Progressive Party (1960) – which split in 1961. Zwane founded and led the radical *NGWANE NATIONAL LIBERATORY CONGRESS (NNLC) in 1963. The NNLC had substantial urban support but did not win any seats in the 1964 and 1967 elections.

When the NNLC won three seats in the 1972 elections, Zwane became a member of the legislature, but in 1973 King *SOBHUZA II abrogated the constitution and banned political parties. After some spells in deten-tion, Zwane escaped to Mozambique (1978) and formed the Swaziland Liberation Movement which aims to establish a socialist democracy in Swaziland.